THE PRICE OF AID

THE PRICE OF AID

The Economic Cold War in India

DAVID C. ENGERMAN

Harvard University Press

Cambridge, Massachusetts · London, England

2018

Library of Congress Cataloging-in-Publication Data
Names: Engerman, David C., 1966– author.
Title: The price of aid : the economic cold war in India / David C. Engerman.
Description: Cambridge, Massachusetts : Harvard University Press, 2018. |
Includes bibliographical references and index.
Identifiers: LCCN 2017036333 | ISBN 9780674659599 (alk. paper)
Subjects: LCSH: Economic assistance—Political aspects—India—History—20th century. |
Economic assistance, American—Political aspects—India—History—20th century. |
Economic assistance, Soviet—Political aspects—India—History—20th century. |
Cold War—Influence. | Cold War—Economic aspects. |
Geopolitics—India—History—20th century. |
India—Economic conditions—1947–
Classification: LCC HC433 .E54 2018 | DDC 338.910954 / 09045—dc23
LC record available at https://lccn.loc.gov/2017036333

For Stephanie

Contents

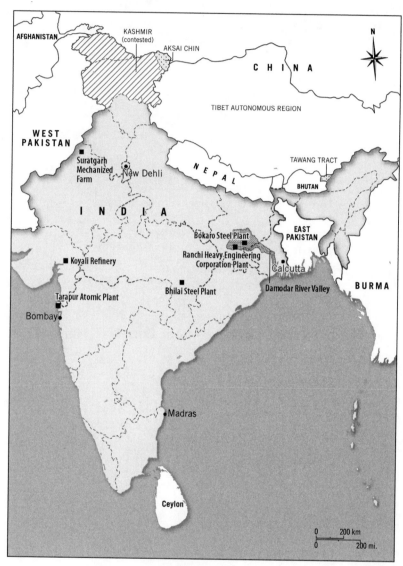

India, circa 1960. Map created by Isabelle Lewis.

THE PRICE OF AID

FOREIGN AID AND DEVELOPMENT POLITICS IN INDIA

In February 1960 a delegation of American atomic scientists headed to India to discuss American technical and financial aid for Indian atomic energy. Upon landing in New Delhi, they were immediately and inexplicably dispatched on an impromptu excursion to the Taj Mahal—a remarkable site, to be sure, but not part of their original schedule. Only when they returned to New Delhi did they learn why their plans had changed. Newspapers reported that they were only one of two "high-powered official delegations"—no pun intended—invited to discuss atomic matters; a Soviet delegation was also in town. Both groups were hosted by Homi J. Bhabha, the entrepreneurial head of the Indian atomic establishment. Each superpower hoped to win an exclusive deal to provide technology, materials, and financing for India's civilian atomic programs, and Bhabha hoped the dueling visits would stoke competition and help him extract better terms for India. He did not mind if the delegations knew of each other's presence, but did not want them to cross paths. The Americans' hastily arranged sightseeing trip prevented a minor scheduling glitch from becoming an international incident.[1]

Bhabha's nimble diplomacy, at first glance, suggests the leverage that recipient states could use to vie for superpower aid during the Cold War. Nations like India, Bhabha believed, should invoke the Cold War "battle for hearts and minds" to obtain more aid on better terms—meaning lower prices, cheaper financing, and fewer restrictions on use. He was hardly alone; the great Polish economist Michał Kalecki (who went on an extended advising mission to India) viewed nonaligned nations as "the proverbial clever calves that could suckle two cows." The competition, Kalecki predicted, would spur each bloc to provide more assistance.[2]

But Bhabha also had a second, less obvious motive in bringing the superpower delegations to India. He pursued external assistance not simply to get a better deal but also to advance his position in internal battles over how to power the Indian future. Ranking economic agencies did not share his vision of a nuclear-powered India, so Bhabha spurred international competition in the hopes that foreign aid could help him convince—or, alternatively, outmaneuver—skeptics in Indian officialdom. American diplomats quickly grew wise to this effort. Even before the Taj Mahal episode, they worried that the Indian scientist was trying to turn the U.S. embassy into a "middleman between Bhabha and his own Government."[3]

Bhabha's efforts to play donor nations against each other ultimately bore limited and even bitter fruit. The American offer of atomic aid came years after he began his campaign, and was so tightly tied to American technology and materials that it outraged some of Bhabha's colleagues. The superpowers' competitive spirits ran high, but so did their mutual interest in preventing the spread of nuclear weapons. When Bhabha pressed the nuclear powers to relax the safeguards that restricted use to civilian purposes, they collaborated to stymie Bhabha's plans. Ironically, the pursuit of aid to establish energy independence undermined the self-sufficiency that Bhabha and many of his compatriots had sought. Economic aid promised opportunities for transformation but came at a steep price.[4]

Meanwhile, Bhabha's use of external assistance to fight domestic battles had unsettling internal consequences. The interpenetration of the international and the domestic politics of aid affected much more than the sightseeing diversion of a group of American scientists; it changed all countries involved, and especially India. International aid often rendered new nations' pursuit of autonomy quixotic or even counterproductive. It also weakened Indian political institutions and ultimately constrained the nation's exercise of sovereignty. Though competing donors celebrated their aid programs—in identical language—as a way to help new nations get "on their own two feet," their assistance often had the opposite effect. Development aid came with constraints that increased dependence and limited the prospects of national autonomy. More than 90 percent of such aid, for starters, came in the form of loans, often denominated in foreign currencies. The first generation of aid in the 1950s, furthermore, focused on support for individual projects; donors chose which nations and which projects to fund.[5]

The availability of external aid also intensified existing internal disputes and reinforced institutional rivalries within recipient nations. Bhabha was one of many trying to leverage external aid to promote his own agenda. He and many others sought donors' resources—symbolic, technical, and not least financial—to fight domestic battles. Such resources fueled and even intensified existing divisions over economic policies. The aid relationships that grew over the 1950s and 1960s first built and then relied upon tight connections between superpower aid agencies and individual ministries in the recipient countries. As these relations deepened, individual ministries gained power and operated more and more independently of central decision-making bodies. External assistance, in the end, came about through the efforts of one or another group of policy makers—not necessarily the Government of India writ large—to utilize their connections to advance their own economic visions and interests. I call this dynamic—the competition for external aid and its entanglement with domestic politics—*development politics.*

Development politics exerted a major if unquantifiable influence on the trajectories of Indian policy and politics. All of the major economic debates in India—about broad strategies and specific investments, about broad priorities and narrow bureaucratic configurations—took the shape they did in relation to external agents and agencies. To be clear, economic decision making in independent India was not the property of foreign powers, stray accusations to the contrary. But there was no purely domestic economic policy in independent India; the opportunities and constraints that came with external assistance shaped every major economic decision and many minor ones as well.

Development politics turned the quintessential nationalist pursuit, building a national economy, into an international enterprise. External assistance influenced the scale, scope, and shape of Indian economic development in the decades after Independence in 1947. Over many decades, foreign aid provided recipients with crucial—if constantly renegotiated and highly unpredictable—sources of food, machinery, investment capital, industrial materials, and military equipment. Those resources paid for new facilities and programs all across India, constituting as much as 3 percent of gross domestic product. The road to economic independence, officials in India and across the Third World dis-covered, ran through foreign aid agencies.[6]

Events in India had worldwide impact. The country stood at the center of a global contest over the economic future of the Third World by virtue of its early independence, its size, and the outsize presence of founding prime minister Jawaharlal Nehru. The case of India drove the practices, and later the theories, of both American and Soviet economic assistance; both superpowers learned development assistance by reckoning with Indian conditions. Shift-ing American approaches to economic relations with the Third World, which changed so quickly as to appear faddish, emerged from efforts to address spe-cific problems of Indian development. Likewise, Soviet approaches to what they called "economic cooperation" in the Third World were driven by Indian conditions and in fact began with India.

The Price of Aid opens by showing how the superpowers learned about eco-nomic aid in the years between Indian independence in 1947 and the emergence of full-fledged aid competition in 1954–1955. The book ends in 1975, after the formation of Indian joint economic commissions with each superpower and the expulsion of the large American aid mission. In the intervening decades, the superpowers financed dozens of large factories, village-level community improvement projects, transportation links, and the import of food, equipment, and raw materials. This global contest over development added dams, power plants, experimental farms, "miracle seeds," and economic expertise to donors' national security toolboxes as diplomats and aid officials worked closely with their Indian counterparts to advance mutually held visions.

From Development to Development Politics

Economic development predated the emergence of development politics in the 1950s. It was a global enterprise to effect linked economic and social change based on three prerequisites: concept, capacity, and commitment.[7] First, to con-template development entailed a way of conceiving of the "national economy" and "population" as objects of development. This conceptual apparatus took shape in the first decades of the twentieth century, as Western colonial officials and social scientists used their newfound analytical tools to stake claims to humanitarian responsibility as well as a corresponding role in governance. Calculations of national income figures like gross national product in the 1930s provided a misleadingly simple metric for economic activity in a given region, a metric that tracked growth across an entire national economy and encouraged easy comparisons between nations.[8] Such comparisons heightened the sense of economic "backwardness" that drove campaigns for economic change.[9]

Second, development required a level of state capacity sufficient to undertake the tasks of conjoined economic and social transformation. Early efforts in the middle of the nineteenth century focused primarily on economic transformation, but within a few decades, states and empires began to accumulate the resources and to build administrative structures that brought the instruments of government more directly into the economic and social spheres of metropoles and colonies alike. Contrary to historical accounts of development insisting that it was a foreign imposition, developers and the objects of their efforts often lived within the same national borders. Some developers took as their object distant others, while others took compatriots close at hand.[10]

Finally, economic development required the commitment to deploy state capacity in order to achieve linked economic and social transformation, a tendency visible by the early twentieth century. The reasons behind the commitments varied widely: pursuing national greatness, overcoming self-defined backwardness, or calming increasingly restive colonies. Tsarist officials in Russia organized efforts at industrialization and agricultural reform, tasks taken on with deadly ambition after the Bolshevik Revolution of 1917. The Young Turks emerging after the collapse of the Ottoman Empire similarly used the power of their state to promote rapid change, unswayed by the high human and financial costs incurred. In Europe's colonies, too, development became an increasingly important enterprise by the 1930s. British and French officials in West Africa, for instance, undertook colonial development plans—developing people and economies, not just natural resources—in order to quell growing labor unrest and in the hopes of strengthening (or at least prolonging) imperial rule.[11] In India, anticolonial activists saw state-sponsored development as essential to their future. This, in turn, spurred a handful of British officials to propose deploying the power of the government of India for development purposes. Colonial officials and anticolonial nationalists alike spoke of development even as they pursued not just divergent but antithetical visions of what that meant. The term *development* could encompass the pursuit of independence or the strengthening of imperial rule.[12]

Development, then, existed in the era of empires. With such multifarious meanings, it could generate its share of controversy. Colonial officials and nationalist leaders argued fiercely over the broad frameworks as well as the details of specific schemes. The intensity of policy disputes in British India prompted one beleaguered colonial official to complain that "economics in India tend to be treated politically."[13] Yet this dispute amounted to a competition for the favor of a single sponsor. Empires had monopolies over access to external resources, so only one sovereign power had the power to allocate resources for development in any given place. When external support could come from multiple sources, however, the dynamics of economic policy changed dramatically, allowing for the emergence of development politics. If development required concept, capacity, and commitment, development politics added a fourth element: competition.

The Economic Cold War

Development politics emerged after World War II out of the convergence of two distinct shocks to the international system. First, the slow collapse of Europe's colonial empires in Asia and Africa created new demands for economic assistance. The dissolution of British India in August 1947 inaugurated a decades-long era of decolonization that eventually created dozens of newly independent states out of European empires that had once spanned the globe. These former colonies faced inauspicious circumstances for independence. External and internal boundaries had been drawn with the express purpose of hindering collective action. Colonial economies were organized to extract resources for the benefit of the colonizer. Regime change alone did not remake the colonial infrastructure and organizations built for such purposes, so patterns of extraction were hard to overcome. Decolonization left in its wake new governments that were ill equipped for the rapid transformation of their economies that they keenly sought. Given the sharp limits on domestic resources, these aims soon led officials in India (and throughout the Third World) to pursue external assistance.

If decolonization prompted demand for development, then the Cold War—the second international shock of the 1940s—provided the supply. The globalization of American and Soviet ideological competition after World War II created the dynamic for offering economic aid.[14] Both the United

States and the Soviet Union were universalistic, holding that their conceptions of society applied to all nations and peoples. Both sides, furthermore, portrayed history as an irreversible march to improvement, which (they believed) would lead inevitably to the victory of their ideas. Both antagonists equated the growth of their own power and influence with historical progress, and yet neither was willing to stand aside and let history take its course. For each side, economic aid became a means of accelerating the march to its eventual victory. The path to that victory could be mapped in terms of the spread of economic systems; each superpower sought to replicate a stylized version of its own economic system around the world, and to construct a world economy in which it played the central role.

These arguments for aid won out in the mid-1950s. Both superpowers created apparatuses to disburse development aid to Third World nations, and in the process built up the institutions of an economic cold war. Scholars and experts in both countries highlighted potential political and economic benefits of aid—interpretations that aid proponents seized upon in policy battles. The administration of President Dwight D. Eisenhower (1953–1961) used development aid, in various forms, to attract loyalty and wield influence. Under the leadership of Nikita Khrushchev (1953–1964), meanwhile, Soviet officials turned to economic cooperation, extending it beyond the politically reliable socialist world into India and other nonaligned states.

The International Politics of Development Aid

The emergence and expansion of development aid in the decade after 1945 were part of a paradoxical reconfiguration of international politics in the aftermath of the Second World War. On the one hand, the institutions that emerged in the 1940s—the World Bank and the International Monetary Fund, not to mention the many agencies under the United Nations umbrella—enshrined the nation-state as the fundamental unit of world politics. And on the other, the practice of development assistance threatened the stability of actually existing nation-states.

The postwar international landscape was constituted through intergovernmental organizations whose members were all states. They were so effective at building up the state that many of the insurgencies that emerged in the postwar decades—for instance the Afro-Asian and Non-Aligned movements and the Group of 77—spoke the language of state sovereignty as they defended the interests of member states.[15] The national form quickly came to dominate, overwhelming or overriding any alternative postimperial world orders. Scholars of midcentury India have been particularly astute in identifying the range of alternatives to the nation as well as the dynamics that led to their exclusion. They have also shown how British India—a patchwork of colonies and principalities—yielded not one but two (and eventually three) sovereign states.[16]

Similarly, the global project of development was conceived in terms of economic activity within a bounded territory. It relied upon state capacity to intervene in the economy and depended on state commitment to use that capacity. If, as Mark Mazower points out, the global development project was "world-making," it was simultaneously state-making. The instruments of development, in India and around the newly named Third World, enhanced state power: central governments and planning organs aspired to strong central rule over a territory and came to instantiate that rule.[17] Bilateral aid agreements took place between two states. Multilateral organs, whether founded at the Bretton Woods Conference or as part of the United Nations family, took the state as the basic unit of development (and were themselves, of course, composed of states). Even nongovernmental agencies rarely undercut the state as object of development in the 1950s; globe-spanning private philanthropies based in the United States collaborated closely if not always formally with U.S. government officials—and worked with recipient governments as counterparties.[18]

Development was state-making in other ways, as anthropologists, armed with Foucauldian tools, have demonstrated. James Ferguson, Tania Li, and others have charted how the discourse and practice of development empowered states, smoothing their penetration into the social lives of their citizens and colonial subjects. This vein of scholarship has shown how the development impulse reshaped the nature of rule, affecting everything from mass politics to intimate interactions. As insightful as such scholarship has been, it generally focuses on governmentality to the exclusion of geopolitics. *The Price of Aid* adds international context to such accounts, allowing for a deeper and broader understanding of development, one of the core global projects over the twentieth century.[19]

And yet. Just as development assistance helped create a world of sovereign states, it also helped erode that very sovereignty. The international politics of development aid—the mounting debts (especially in foreign currencies), the donors' relentless pursuit of policy leverage, and the corrosive effects on recipient governments—impinged on the ability of recipient nations to shape their own economic futures. The domestic dynamics of development politics ultimately added new impediments to postcolonial governance.

The Domestic Politics of Foreign Aid in India and Beyond

Development assistance altered domestic politics in both donor and recipient nations, and especially the latter, by providing groups with resources to advance their own economic visions and interests. Indian officials used the aid to promote their own agendas amid intense domestic competition. Those in favor of heavy industry in the public sector under central planning used the logic of Cold War competition to court Soviet aid. And those favoring integration into the capitalist world economy, freer markets, the private sector, and a focus on agriculture generally looked to the West. But such divisions over policy did not exist only in recipient nations. Officials in Moscow and Washington, D.C., each used the "case" of India to add new tools to the diplomatic repertoire and to make international economic inequality into an arena to further their notions of geopolitical interests. In short, officials in the superpowers used development aid as a Cold War weapon while constituencies in recipient nations used the Cold War as a development weapon.[20]

Debates in India, as in donor nations, did not revolve solely around interests, national or otherwise. Economic visions, and not just economic interests, were at stake: different parties in India, as in the superpowers, held divergent visions of the Indian future and thus charted different paths from the present to those futures. Pecuniary interest was present, but not dispositive. As sociologist Peter Evans noted in an analogous context, state actions take place because "some group of individuals within the state apparatus has a project"; such projects are not simply a result of "personal biographies or individual maximizing strategies," but are consonant with broader visions. The questions, then, were not narrowly focused on economic benefit or bureaucratic self-interest but expanded to include the core issues facing the postcolonial world: how to build a modern, prosperous, independent nation out of an impoverished, exploited, and divided colony.[21]

Institutional patterns did not emerge randomly; different ministries attracted leaders with different economic visions, and these leaders sought different foreign sponsors. Those in the Indian Planning Commission and industrial ministries generally favored a more muscular government role in the economy, and looked to the Cold War East. Oil minister K. D. Malaviya, for instance, used Soviet and Romanian assistance to wage war on the western oil firms that dominated India. He sought Soviet technology, advice, and financing to create a vertically integrated oil enterprise in the public sector. Similarly, statistician Prasanta Chandra Mahalanobis, the éminence grise of Indian planning in the 1950s, worked tirelessly to cultivate close relationships with experts and officials in the USSR and other socialist states. Mahalanobis, Malaviya, and others with similar inclinations used Soviet expertise and financing as resources to promote their economic visions.

The same logic brought other Indian officials, especially in the ministries of Trade and Finance, into close conversation with the West. Morarji Desai, who served twice as finance minister and once each as deputy prime minister and prime minister, was inclined toward Western economic ideas; he was joined by most of his predecessors and successors holding the cabinet's finance portfolio. Similarly, B. K. Nehru, a longtime Finance Ministry official whose cousin served as prime minister, devoted his long career to expanding India's economic ties with the West.

The Price of Aid analyzes development politics in India, but the phenomenon it describes applies more widely. In Afghanistan, for instance, Soviet economists took up residence at the Ministry of Planning while their American counterparts camped out in the ministries of Commerce and Finance. In postcolonial Kenya, antagonisms between the vice president and the minister of economic planning invoked similar superpower polarities. Even in the western hemisphere, where American power dominated, Soviet aid offers played to differences within Bolivian revolutionary parties. Officials and business interests in Colombia similarly used the resources of Western aid to advance their ideas and enhance their positions. Finally, in India's rival Pakistan, warring factions of the central government turned to opposite superpowers to support their battles against each other. Though broadly applicable in different settings, development politics did not take precisely the same shape, or have precisely the same impacts, across the Third World; the specifics varied in each national context. Still, because few independence movements or postcolonial governments were monolithic on economic questions, few could avoid development politics.[22]

Development politics played out in donor countries as well. The rise of foreign aid emerged out of domestic political struggles and at the same time gave new authority and resources to groups within respective governments.[23] New institutions came into being in states and multilateral organizations alike. In the United States, the Technical Cooperation Administration inaugurated aid to the Third World; after a handful of short-lived successors, the U.S. Agency for International Development (USAID) took over its functions. In the Soviet Union, the State Committee for Foreign Economic Connections (Gosudarstvennyi Komitet po Vneshnim Ekonomicheskim Sviaziam—GKES) took over from a predecessor oriented toward socialist states. And the World Bank, founded in 1945, established the International Development Association. Some of these new institutions emerged directly out of superpower encounters with India, while others reflected the increasing focus on economic aid prompted by conditions in India and other Third World nations. New approaches to the Third World called for new ways to organize knowledge, so both superpowers saw reconfigurations of academic knowledge in the 1950s.[24]

These new organizations and institutes jostled against the apparatus of traditional diplomacy as well as against the many other bodies that shaped foreign economic policy. Geopolitical arguments for development assistance played well in both superpowers. Economics, in the words of Cold Warrior John Foster Dulles, constituted "far and away the most important single aspect of our foreign policy ... designed to meet the threat ... from Russian rulers."[25] Soviet proponents of aid like Presidium member Anastas Mikoian made a similar case against those who doubted the wisdom of going up against the deep-pocketed United States, arguing that "state interests" required entering the "competition between two systems."[26] Aid could be a new front in the Cold War, a chance to use new tools to advance geopolitical interests and their vision of the world economy. In superpowers as well as in recipient nations like India, development aid was wrapped up in core debates about the shape of both international and domestic politics.

Scholarly Context

The Price of Aid builds on existing scholarship to reframe historical understandings of the Cold War in four ways. First, it investigates, rather than assumes, the boundaries of state power, examining disputes within governments as well as transnational networks crossing between them. The emphasis on Third

World agency—a salutary trend in recent international history scholarship—
must not stop at the entrance to Cabinet rooms; it must examine the contests
behind policy decisions.[27] Thus this book analyzes international relations by
looking *within* governments as well as *between* them. In spite of the American
adage that partisan politics should stop "at the water's edge," domestic politics
profoundly shaped foreign policy in general, and foreign economic policy in
particular; this is true in India as in the United States—and also, with different mechanisms, in the USSR.[28] In pointing out visions shared across national
boundaries, the present volume also contributes to a growing vein of scholarship that traces the power of transnational networks to shape domestic politics
and international affairs.[29]

To map out the dimensions and effectiveness of these networks requires
analyzing not just development talk but development practice. These networks
were held together not by identities of interest but by overlapping viewpoints;
the contours of agreement and disagreement comes into stark relief by observing practices of development aid. Thus *The Price of Aid* looks beyond donors'
sweeping claims of altruism and recipients' grandiose declarations of imminent
prosperity and equality. Behind such broad public declarations stood an arena
for debating a nation's economic future as well as a field for personal and professional ambition. This focus on practice uses the quotidian struggles of building
and operating projects to reveal tensions that are occluded in official celebrations.
Moving beyond development talk also reveals how theory typically followed practice; new approaches emerged in the pursuit of solutions to particular problems.[30]

Second, the present study demonstrates the importance of economics in the
evolving global Cold War, an ideological conflict expressed in terms of different
economic systems. The quest for prosperity and economic independence in
the late twentieth century drove popular aspirations and official policies across
the Third World. Questions of economic organization, economic priorities,
and economic inequality (within and between nations) shaped all manner of
interactions between nations in all three Cold War worlds—especially after 1955.
Prior to that date soldiers and spies contested the division of Europe and the
shape of military alliances. From the mid-1970s onward, militaries returned to
the fore in the farthest corners of the globe. For the two decades in between,
however, economic competition, especially in the Third World, was the core
dynamic of the global Cold War. From the Afro-Asian Conference in Bandung
in the 1950s, to multilateral and bilateral economic aid programs in the 1960s,

to debates over a New International Economic Order in the 1970s, economic issues between the three worlds were central to the international relations of the Cold War.[31] Yet many studies of the "global Cold War" remain focused on diplomatic and military affairs with less attention to economic concerns. *The Price of Aid* seeks to apply the analytical sophistication and empirical depth of scholarship on the global Cold War to the conflict's economic aspects.[32]

Third, *The Price of Aid* expands the frame of reference for histories of development by more fully incorporating Soviet aid programs.[33] A handful of studies on the activities of the USSR and its allies in the Third World have explored economic and political relations between the Second and Third Worlds.[34] These works shed light on international history as well as on the domestic histories of donors and recipients alike. At the same time, in recognizing that Soviet aid took place in the context of "competition between two systems," this book keeps both competitors in its frame of reference.[35]

The Price of Aid seeks, finally, to contribute to the economic and political history of independent India by showing how those histories were profoundly shaped by international events. In doing so it carries forward recent studies of transnational connections during the last decades of British India.[36] The pursuit of external assistance shaped political alignments and realignments that are familiar territory for scholars writing about India after 1947. Their works have produced an extraordinarily complex picture of Indian politics, a picture inspired by (and inspiring) broad theories while attending to the kaleidoscopic permutations of disagreement at every level of Indian politics.[37] The episodes recounted here show how the availability of external resources shaped these disputes, in ways too often neglected even in the most insightful and influential accounts. Exploring these international elements is not to reduce Indian politics to Cold War politics, or to search out fifth columns in Indian ministries; it is to chart the complex interplay of domestic and international forces. The Indian pursuit of economic development aid from abroad, in other words, shaped domestic political developments.

Calculating the Price of Aid

The arguments in this volume are sustained through the analysis of actors in three nations over a quarter century. Though other donors were active in India, especially by the 1960s, *The Price of Aid* focuses upon American and

Soviet aid because these donors provided the largest as well as the politically most significant portion of assistance. American loans amounted to about one quarter of total foreign development assistance to India in this period, with the U.S.-dominated World Bank providing another quarter. And the Soviet Union accounted for one-third of the remainder.[38] British aid to India— which through the 1950s really amounted to loan repayments dressed up as aid—ran a distant third among Western donors.[39] The present study relies on extensive archival and published materials from India as well as each of these donors—the United States, the USSR, and the World Bank—and more targeted research elsewhere. (For more details on the source base, see the "Note on Sources.") While archives can occlude as well as reveal, they offer an expansive and richly detailed chronicle of key disputes taking place within and between national governments. Each chapter of this book brings together materials from multiple archives to trace the origins and impact of development politics.

The preconditions for the economic cold war are the focus of Part I, "Learning Development, 1947–1955." Chapter 1, "Debating Development and Discovering India," offers crucial national contexts for economic debates in the United States, the Soviet Union, and India before their most intense interactions began. It provides a genealogy of the economic debates of independent India, demonstrating how they emerged out of decades-old conversations among Indian nationalists. The chapter also shows how the would-be Cold War antagonists came to "discover" independent India's economic problems and made plans to address them. Of marginal concern to both powers before independence, India quickly assumed a more substantial role in superpower calculations even amid the eventful years of the early Cold War.

Chapter 2, "Inventing Development Aid," shows how reckoning with India drove intellectual and policy changes in the superpowers in the early 1950s. Those in each superpower who emphasized the significance of India and the possibility of economic aid began to win more arguments in their respective governments. In the Soviet Union, officials began to shake off late Stalinism's seeming disdain for former colonies, promoting the possibility of trade and even "economic cooperation" for India. Heterodox Soviet scholars bolstered the case for expanding economic relations, arguing that the decline of European empires offered new opportunities for the spread of socialism. In the United States, too, the notion of aiding newly independent nations received public expression when President Harry S. Truman called for technical assistance in the fourth point of his 1949 inaugural address. An India lobby in Washington grew in power and influence as it responded to famine conditions in India in 1950–1951. Its members—including future two-time ambassador to New Delhi Chester Bowles—made the case for American technical assistance for the world's largest democracy. The case of India proved central to these trends in both superpowers.

Part II, "The Heyday of the Economic Cold War, 1955–1966," shows how direct superpower competition emerged in India. The first stage of this competition took the form of dueling groups of visiting economic experts. Chapter 3, "The Geopolitics of Economic Expertise," shows how Prasanta Chandra Mahalanobis organized these visits in order to fight—and ultimately win—domestic battles over the shape of India's Second Five-Year Plan (1956–1961). While the range of visitors gave the enterprise the trappings of ecumenicalism, Mahalanobis scheduled the visits to further his sectarian economic ideas. What seemed like an open competition over economic ideas operated to the distinct advantage of Mahalanobis's faction of Indian public life, which favored rapid industrialization under central planning.

Chapter 4, "The Aid Project and Cold War Competition," moves from intangible to tangible forms of foreign assistance. It documents superpower competition over aid projects, showing how groups within India sought financing for their own aims and how diplomats in the superpowers eventually maneuvered their governments into supporting such projects. The Soviet Union jumped out to a quick advantage in the competition; its large-scale industrial projects in the public sector garnered worldwide attention. By comparing the fates of a number of American and Soviet projects in India, the chapter demonstrates that development projects had the best prospects for success when they reflected international networks of support.

As Chapter 5, "'Free Money' and the Tilt toward the West," demonstrates, the Soviet advantage was fleeting. An informal group of senior officials in India, led by B. K. Nehru, worked assiduously to expand the horizons of aid to include what he called, appealingly, "free money" not attached to any project. This emergent America lobby in India used the foreign-exchange shortages of the late 1950s to make the case for approaches to the West—the United States and the World Bank—and for shifting away from Soviet aid. As a result, the West quickly came to dominate nonproject aid (B. K. Nehru's "free money") while the Soviet Union reigned supreme in the battle over projects.

While the bulk of *The Price of Aid* examines economic aid, Chapter 6, "Military Supply and the Vicissitudes of Aid Politics," reveals how the dynamics of development politics operated in the military sphere. Facing a crisis after their humiliation at the hands of China's People's Liberation Army in the fall of 1962, the Indian armed services overhauled military procurement, working closely with both the American and Soviet defense establishments as well as with the British firms that had traditionally supplied the Indian military. As the United Kingdom lost its role as India's principal supplier of weapons and materiel, groups within the uniformed military and the Indian Ministry of Defence used superpower aid to contend over national and international politics.

The crystallization of these networks of support within and beyond India complicated Indian policy making in the 1960s, as Part III, "The Bitter Fruits of Development Politics, 1960–1974," shows. No sooner had Indian factions come to rely on superpower sponsors then those relations began to fray. By the late 1960s the groups that had cultivated external support in pursuit of their domestic agendas faced new tribulations at home and abroad. Chapter 7, "Bets, Bargains, and the Price of American Aid," tallies the high costs of Western aid, especially the nonproject aid that B. K. Nehru had sought. Indian officials at the highest levels pushed for acceptance of the stringent conditions worked out by the U.S. Department of State and the World Bank. Those sympathetic to the economic vision proffered by the United States used external pressure to promote major policy changes, hoping that the promised American aid would quiet opponents and buy time. When Western aid officials did not live up to their end of bargain, though, their Indian allies felt betrayed by the West as their own political power declined.

Chapter 8, "Soviet Aid from Inspiration to Armory," tracks the fate of those supporting heavy industry in the public sector supported by Soviet technology and financing. The Soviet Union had inspired many in the Third World (including India) with its vision of an integrated public sector under central planning; as that vision faltered, so too did the Soviet reputation in the Third World. In place of its earlier role as an exemplar of central planning and heavy industry, the Soviet Union became an armory better known for military aid than for economic practices or development aid.

By the early 1970s development politics had become even more disruptive to Indian politics, as Chapter 9, "India's Double Crisis and the Price of Aid," argues. Indian ministries' relations with both superpower aid agencies deteriorated in the late 1960s, leaving them poorly equipped to respond to what one astute observer called India's "dual crisis of economic stagnation and political stability."[40] As the Soviet-supported public sector dragged down the Indian economy, Soviet aid officials and their Indian interlocutors looked to mechanisms like trade to solve economic problems—and continued their deeper military relationship. The America lobby, already feeling betrayed by Western officials in the late 1960s, promoted a relationship with the United States that relied on trade and financial flows over development projects. As these efforts took shape, they only weakened the Indian government further.

A brief conclusion traces the legacies of development politics through the 1970s and after. The patterns of superpower aid to the Third World in the last decades of the Cold War reflected (with, of course, local variation) the trends visible in India by 1975. American aid embarked on so-called New Directions in 1973, moving away from direct aid work in recipient nations. The Soviet Union, meanwhile, remained an armory long after its moment as an economic inspiration had passed. American financial flows and Soviet weapons deliveries grew increasingly important in the aid landscape in India and beyond.

Taken individually, these chapters explore the politics of development aid in India: how different groups within India advanced their visions by using the superpowers as resources in their struggles, and how superpowers' theories and practices of development evolved through their engagements with India. Taken together, the chapters demonstrate the extent to which development politics reflected—indeed, initiated—many transformations in the purposes and practices of development as a global project. Indian officials pursued the potential opportunities from foreign donors, but in the process incurred the price of aid.

I
LEARNING DEVELOPMENT,
1947–1955

CHAPTER 1

DEBATING DEVELOPMENT
AND DISCOVERING INDIA

On August 14, 1947, when Jawaharlal Nehru stepped up to the podium to address India's Constituent Assembly—and all of India—on the eve of its independence from Britain, he celebrated: "At the stroke of the midnight hour, when the world sleeps, India will awake to life and freedom." In literal terms, Nehru was mistaken; Delhi's midnight was early evening in Moscow, suppertime in London, and midday in Washington, D.C. In a larger sense, however, Nehru was right. The pressing issues of recent Indian history—how India would achieve independence, how it could accommodate the extraordinary diversity of British India, and what its economic basis would be once it left the British empire— were all but ignored in the two powers whose antagonism would define international politics for the coming decades. Soviet and American positions on India were not so much in conflict as indiscernible.[1]

In the capitals of the emerging Cold War world, the independence of the largest empire's largest colony received scant attention. Most American newspapers discussed Indian independence below the fold, beneath articles on the Greek Civil War and Italian debts to the United States, not to mention local concerns like census returns and East Coast summer weather. Soviet newspapers printed little about Indian independence, as their pages were already overflowing with news about harvesters, a preview of the upcoming Latvian theater season, and grateful letters to Joseph Stalin from Soviet citizens far and wide. The official government newspaper *Izvestiia* did acknowledge the Delhi ceremony briefly on its last page—in a dispatch, tellingly, from London.

Indian newspapers, of course, covered independence exhaustively. The front page of the *Times of India* devoted its entire front page to independence; only an advertisement for the latest Frank Sinatra film diverted attention from this momentous event. Articles described "frenzied enthusiasm" and "wild scenes of jubilation." Beyond the front page, though, other articles—on communal violence and food shortages, for instance—augured future difficulties. And even in this euphoric moment politics came into play, as disputes at the local, state, and national levels undercut hopes for national unity.[2]

This simple snapshot indicates a pattern that dominated the years before 1950. The promise and perils of independent India, including long-running disagreements not forgotten even in the exhilaration of August 1947, shaped India's future. And, at least at the start, these debates garnered little attention from the newly ascendant superpowers. Disagreements within India ranged widely, covering official policies toward religion and language, mechanisms of state power in the aftermath of British rule, and—most important for these purposes—the shape of India's economic future. Yet these debates took place, in large part, before the would-be superpowers had discovered India.

Debating Development in India

When an exasperated British official complained in 1930 that "economics in India tend to be treated politically," he had in mind the nationalists' tendency to rally anti-imperial sentiment around economic programs. Yet the politics of economic ideas had many fronts other than just the battle between British rule and those who opposed it. Anticolonial agitators, within and beyond the dominant Indian National Congress, offered sharply contrasting visions of India's economic future. In doing so they set the stage for debates about the economic meanings of independence and the mechanisms to instantiate them. The Indian National Congress organized by far the most influential and effective opposition to British rule, even as its elected officials helped administer some colonies. Congress declarations in the economic sphere insisted upon the core goals of improving living standards and reducing economic inequality. Such goals could be achieved, Congress leaders argued, only with *swadeshi*, or self-sufficiency. Swadeshi began as a rallying cry for a movement that convulsed Bengal, and eventually large swaths of British India, in the early decades of twentieth century; it gave expression to the belief that India's poverty resulted directly from the British presence. Yet the term *swadeshi* held many possible meanings. Its modern history began as a weapon against British rule, so it certainly encompassed the boycott of British goods as well as the expansion of indigenous production. But what self-sufficiency meant beyond its anti-British aspects was not entirely clear.[3]

The power of swadeshi as a slogan inhered in its ability to draw together divergent groups within the Indian National Congress. Gandhians, Nehruvian socialists, and business leaders battled within Congress over any number of issues, including economic ones. Each group reached important constituencies within India, varying by region, by economic condition, and by political persuasion. Followers of Mohandas K. Gandhi took swadeshi to be an anti-industrial position; self-sufficiency would be at the village level, with homespun khadi and few manufactured products from any country; Gandhianism also imparted spiritual meanings to the term. The Gandhian perspective remained especially strong among those who celebrated the Indian villages and their inhabitants as repositories of essential Indianness and sites of India's particular virtues—and saw the debilities of British rule in the way it brought not just foreign rule but foreign economic ideas to India.[4]

Socialists like Jawaharlal Nehru, on the other hand, viewed swadeshi at the national level, interpreting economic self-sufficiency to mean building up domestic industry so India would not need to import industrial products. The Nehruvians took the opposite tack from Gandhians, criticizing British rule not for bringing in foreign ideas and industries but for preventing the industrialization of India. Nehruvians, much like their namesake, drew inspiration from the Soviet Union. While acknowledging manifold problems with the Soviet political system, Nehru and his followers sought lessons for India in the economic transformation of the USSR from a nation of peasants into an industrial power. Reflecting on his visit to the USSR as news about Soviet planning and the Great Depression grabbed the headlines, Nehru sought to adapt the Soviet model—a "bright and heartening phenomenon in a dark and dismal world"—to Indian conditions.[5]

For their part, business magnates in Bombay and Calcutta saw in swadeshi the chance to expel foreign business and to grow along with India's domestic market.[6] They joined Congress in the hopes of advancing the national cause, and stayed there in the hopes of containing the group's growing tendencies toward socialism in the 1930s—even as they differed among themselves about the major threats and opportunities of independence. To propound swadeshi was to frame a debate, not resolve one.[7]

The first Soviet five-year plan (1928–1932) helped spark discussion of planning around the world, and India proved no exception. Nehru expressed special enthusiasm for planning, which he hoped could provide a means to resolve scientifically the heated disagreements over India's economic future. One well-known engineer (and onetime royal adviser) tied planning to industrialization. Industry connoted "production, wealth power and modernity," he argued, and was crucial to making a "self-sufficient" nation; the "advance of industry" required a "planned economy." The business world sung planning's praises. G. D. Birla offered a "plea for planning" that could put an end to the long period of policy "drifting." Calcutta's Chamber of Commerce considered economic planning a "supreme necessity" in order to achieve self-sufficiency and to allow India to "rank amongst the industrial nations." And Bombay's powerful Federation of Indian Chambers of Commerce and Industry (FICCI) excoriated Soviet planning but endorsed other variants. Even officials in the British administration adapted to the spirit of the times by calling for some form of central economic planning.[8]

The political landscape in which Congress operated shifted with the Government of India Act, passed at Westminster in 1935. The act created a separate entity called, helpfully enough, the Government of India; it remained part of the British Empire, but moved (as one scholar put it) "the apex of British rule from London to Delhi." The law also established a number of new venues for Indian representation and even limited forms of Indian rule, including provincial ministries. As one historian aptly concluded, the act "extend[ed] representation" and "promote[d] economic growth" without altering "any of the basic relations of power and wealth" established by decades of British rule. Though passed in an effort to thwart the Indian National Congress's claims, it ultimately gave the movement new opportunities; only Congress could draw adherents from across India's various provinces and variegated principalities to become an "all-India" force.[9]

With the expansion of its ranks and the deepening worldwide depression by the early 1930s, the Indian National Congress took up economic concerns with increasing regularity, and in forms that slighted the Gandhians. Official programs, to be sure, nodded to Gandhi's venerated cottage industry, but increasingly emphasized heavy industry as the vehicle to attaining swadeshi.

A 1931 Congress resolution, for instance, called for economic expansion by asserting state control of "key industries," including also mineral resources and transportation. Nehru, on ascending to the presidency of the Indian National Congress in 1936, began to tie together these various elements of an economic vision. Swadeshi remained at the center, continuing to unify the party. In a similar gesture to his divided party, Nehru placed independence at the center of his call for planning, which "require[d] the air and soil of political and social freedom." But Nehru also proposed policies less universally popular among Gandhians on the one hand and business on the other. Nehru cited the Soviet example's reliance on heavy industry and central economic planning— both of which had allowed "backward Russia, with one mighty jump" to make "tremendous progress."[10]

This set of interconnected desiderata—self-sufficiency, industrialization, planning, and independence—remained central to Congress's economic discussions through the 1930s. Paradoxically, plans for self-sufficiency soon enough provided footholds for external intervention. The divergent ambitions that Indians nurtured in the colonial era became rival visions pursued after 1947. A group of Congress ministers of industry convened in fall 1938 to discuss these themes, insisting that none of India's pressing social problems could be solved without industrialization, emphasizing what one Congress leader called "mother industries" that produced capital goods. It is no wonder that one editorial observed that this group seemed to treat industrialization as "almost a panacea for all the country's economic ills." Even while Gandhi remained the head of the nationalist movement, his economic vision did not hold sway.[11]

The National Planning Committee (NPC), formed as a result of the 1938 ministerial confabulation, institutionalized this new Congress focus on planning and heavy industry. The committee contained four business representatives, with Gandhians and the despised British government each receiving a single seat. Nehru served as committee chair, with London School of Economics–trained socialist economist K. T. Shah as secretary. Leaving no doubt about his interests, the new chair insisted that the NPC would be "failing in its duties" if it neglected "large-scale industries." Gandhians, no enthusiasts of central planning to begin with, faced a distinct disadvantage, while socialists and business leaders argued over the shape of India's industrial future.[12]

While recent scholars have drawn attention to Nehru's hopes that planning would be a rational scientific process that could resolve political disputes through dispassionate calculation, the experience of the National Planning Committee demonstrates that those hopes were in vain. At its very first meeting, "pandemonium" broke out (according to one historian) over the group's purpose. The sole Gandhian challenged the committee's focus on heavy industry. The business contingent was so effective, Nehru complained to Shah, that he was prevented from "tackling [economic] questions on a socialist basis." Nehru finessed the issue by asserting that the committee could focus on large-scale industry so long as it would not compete with Gandhi's preferred cottage industries; no doubt Gandhians hoping to expand home-forged steel were greatly relieved by this clarification. Gandhi himself seemed perplexed by the committee, considering it a "waste of effort." If the NPC functioned as Congress's "state-in-waiting" (in historian Sunil Amrith's pithy phrase), then it sketched out the dimensions of conflict in independent India.[13]

Nehru defused disagreement by diffusing it in a strategy of subdivide and conquer. He appointed a raft of NPC subcommittees, each of which consisted of enthusiasts for its topic. Not surprisingly, those assigned to discuss mining and metallurgy saw steel as the key to economic self-sufficiency. Ditto for subcommittees on power and fuel, and on engineering industries. Bombay industrialists and bankers were especially prominent on the Subcommittee on Industrial Finance. Meanwhile, the Subcommittee on Rural and Cottage Industries became a Gandhian redoubt; Gandhi himself served on it. In its initial work, then, the NPC and its subsidiary bodies could keep the peace simply by keeping everyone in separate groups; at that stage, at least, the committee did not need to balance one set of interests against another but could endorse moving forward on all fronts. This structure allowed the NPC to defer any moments of direct zero-sum conflict.[14]

World War II quickly halted the National Planning Committee's momentum and opened the field for the articulation of contending visions of India's economic future. Growing nationalist ferment culminated in the massive Quit India campaign, which led to the arrest of much of Congress leadership, including Nehru and other planning stalwarts, in 1942; they remained in jail until just before the end of the war. The temporary absence of the NPC hardly spelled the end of planning talk in India; indeed, G. D. Birla observed that the colony became "seized by the fever of planning" during the war.[15]

Nationalist business leaders quickly stepped into this breach, devising a plan that illustrated their hopes for the economy of independent India while simultaneously trying to head off more radical planning efforts. The group of business leaders, including G. D. Birla, John Mathai, and J. R. D. Tata, established key goals that matched prior Congress aims imperfectly; they shared the hopes for a "more equitable distribution of resources" while focusing on "aggregate national income" rather than the NPC's focus on standards of living. Anticipating a leftward drift, the business group sought to "examine how far socialist demands [could] be accommodated without capitalism surrendering any of its essential features." It would not "vindicate capitalism as an institution" but would instead outline modifications to capitalism that served their understanding of Indian national interests. While Congress planners had ignored foreign trade, the business group exhorted that India could not "act in isolation from the rest of the world." Thus its economic ideas, broadly construed, overlapped incompletely with those of the Indian National Congress: it took self-sufficiency and independence for granted, and (like Congress) favored industrialization. But the business version of swadeshi included a wide range of international connections and government support for, rather than regulation or ownership of, private enterprise.[16]

Under Purshotamdas Thakurdas's leadership, the group published its modestly titled *Plan of Economic Development for India* in 1944; it quickly became known as the Bombay Plan, in reference to the group's offices in India's economic capital. Thanks to the NPC's enforced hiatus, not to mention the stature of the business leaders, this plan quickly took off. With two editions and two reprintings in the first three months alone, the Bombay Plan quickly dominated discussions of postwar India. Crediting the conceptual and practical work of Congress's NPC, the business plan called for rapid growth, celebrating industrialization as essential for rapid change. It stressed basic industries, especially capital goods, and proposed government expenditures where private capital was insufficient. It differed sharply from Congress's NPC in its hopes for expanded international trade. The Bombay Plan had such power and reach in Indian economic discussions that the British viceroy of India tried to co-opt its authors, ordering his officials to "take a 'friendly' attitude" toward the plan; he even sent a delegation to meet with the plan's authors and sponsors.[17]

In spite of this prominent support, the Bombay Plan did not put an end to economic debate in India; it only led to competing plans. The People's Plan circulated by the Indian Federation of Labour offered an especially broad challenge to the business effort. Labor's plan emphasized agricultural improvement where the Bombay Plan favored industry, called for expansion of internal markets while the business plan looked overseas, and preferred state-owned industry to private enterprise. The Gandhian Plan issued an even more fundamental attack on the principles of the Bombay Plan. In spite of the Gandhians' heritage, not to mention their optimistic prediction that decentralization and "cottage communism" represented the future, their plan endorsed the creation of a Central National Planning Committee, with not just one but two adjectives establishing its scope. Differing sharply from the business and labor plans, the Gandhian effort nevertheless shared hopes for planning, and for state involvement in the economy. By the end of the war, though, Gandhian voices had little impact on Congress economic policy. Both the business and the Nehruvian groups promoted industrialization; as G. D. Birla noted with satisfaction, "India has adopted the slogan 'industrialize or die.'" The Congress Working Committee, recently released from jail, demanded not just government support for industry but government ownership—a position secretary Shah asserted with particular vehemence.[18]

The release of Congress leadership allowed its NPC to leave what Shah called "cold storage" and retake the initiative in planning. The proliferation of wartime plans fed the expansion of the Congress committee, with Bombay Plan author (and longtime Tata aide) Mathai joining the group at its first meeting in five years. Mathai succeeded in getting the NPC to rethink its skeptical view of international trade. By authoritative accounts, trade became "the most considerable" of postwar revisions to the planning effort; citing the new international environment, the NPC celebrated the "growing demand for international cooperation" that included "the removal of trade barriers." By the end of World War II, then, the most influential groups engaged in planning, including the NPC and the business leaders behind the Bombay Plan, had embraced or at least reconciled themselves to increased openness to foreign economic relations—even as they remained wary of untrammeled American access to Indian investment and markets. In doing so they did not renounce self-sufficiency but now hoped that trade could be a means to it. Industrialization was the key to ultimate self-sufficiency, the argument went, but could not take place without foreign technology and capital. Swadeshi was intact, of course, but the precise meaning of the term became even less clear.[19]

When the British announced in 1946 the establishment of an interim government with Nehru at the head, all sides prepared for impending independence.

At Nehru's behest, the government formed the Advisory Planning Board to consider the direction and mechanisms for Indian economy after independence. The board included both the most conservative member of the National Planning Committee (Mathai) and one of the most radical (Shah). It clearly took Mathai's arguments seriously, rejecting the goal of "national self-sufficiency" and insisting that no country could remain isolated in the postwar world. "We are necessarily dependent," the board's report concluded, on other nations for capital goods. Foreign goods and technology, then, composed an essential part of Indian strategy—but not necessarily foreign capital; the report demanded measures to prevent the "intrusion of foreign firms" into Indian markets. The board furthermore endorsed government ownership of industry while rejecting nationalization. The report's emphasis on industrialization reflected the meager influence of Gandhian views on the planning board. And judging by the tone and scope of Shah's dissent (which was longer than the majority report), the Advisory Planning Board did not live up to socialist hopes either. Shah called for extensive (even "total") nationalization, a strong central government, and a resolute focus on domestic industry to the exclusion of agriculture and foreign trade.[20]

Frustrated by the board, Shah nevertheless had the chance to advocate socialist ideas through his role as the secretary of Congress's long-dormant NPC. As reports from the NPC's varied and dispersed entities rolled in, he put his stamp on its final report. He reached well beyond the group's deliberations, contradicting the conclusions of some subcommittees. Calling heavy industry "synonymous" with planning, Shah mapped a large swath of industry that would be "*reserved exclusively*" for the public sector. Shortages of labor, he hoped, could be met by "*industrial conscription.*" He also sought a strong planning effort, warning against "excessive restriction of central authority." Yet his National Planning Committee was limping toward its impending demise, issuing a flurry of inconclusive subcommittee reports before eventually dissolving in March 1949. The committee's poignant final act, in a poorly attended meeting, was to split its remaining debts between industrial magnate J. R. D. Tata and socialist Shah.[21]

Shah's discussion of India's future took seriously the challenges of independence, but gave short shrift (as did many economic works of era) to the other momentous event of 1940s South Asia: the Partition of British India into two states, the Muslim Pakistan (excised from Punjab in the west and Bengal in the east, its two sections separated from each other by a thousand miles of India) and secular India. Partition, the maps of which were announced only weeks before August 1947, convulsed the region in violence, with population movements numbering fifteen million or more as Hindus left areas slated to become Pakistan and Muslims fled Hindu-dominated areas that would become independent India. As many as two million people died in pogroms that shook cities and towns across northern India, or in attacks on the migrant convoys in both directions. Partition also affected the economies of India and Pakistan in less immediate ways. In Bengal, for instance, the new national boundaries separated the jute fields (which ended up predominantly in Pakistan) from the jute mills and the port of Calcutta (which went to India). National planning, in other words, at last had a nation, but not the one anticipated by Congress.[22]

The furling of the Union Jack in front of the viceroy's residence in August 1947 signified the end of British rule in India but set in motion new conflicts. Both the mechanisms and the direction of economic policy became crucial indicators of India's functioning as an independent state. When Nehru took the helm as India's founding prime minister, he ironically wielded more power over the machinery of government than over his own party. In Congress he faced leading figures (including Gandhi) who differed sharply from him on a variety of political and economic issues. In some ways, Congress functioned less as a conventional political party united around a core ideology and more as a parliament that contained divergent interests and even formal groupings. Nehru's own ideas may have centered around a liberal "amalgam" (as a leading historian argues), but the range of views in that amalgam included the farthest ideological reaches of a party that was vast, varied, diffuse, and highly contentious.[23]

In that context, what an independent Indian economy would look like remained an important question, if one that seemed less urgent than partition. Planners in Congress wasted no time in promoting their ideas; "Free India," one advocate declared, "must . . . be followed by Planned India, for without the latter the former can never survive." The first resolutions of the All-India Congress Committee continued in this vein; "real democracy" required economic advances, including self-sufficiency (especially in "the essentials of life"), and required "large-scale industry" that "belong[ed] to the community." Planning took on a similar role in Indian politics; "democracy in the modern age necessitates planned central direction." The Industrial Policy Resolution of 1948 enshrined these views; it had been drafted by two junior civil servants,

S. Bhoothalingam and L. K. Jha, who would become prominent and generally pro-Western economic officials in the 1960s. It insisted that increased production provided the best means to increase standards of living, and called for the state's "progressively active role in the development of industries" to see that take effect. It proposed the nationalization of only a handful of directly defense-related industries but reserved a wider range of fields that could expand only via public-sector enterprises. In the keen phrase of one observer, the general thrust was not nationalization per se but "nationalization of the vacuum" in a number of key areas where India had little or no existing capacity. In a nod to the Gandhians, the resolution acknowledged the place of cottage industries, noting that they would remain under state rather than central control. And it carried forward the views of Congress's planning committee vis-à-vis foreign economic engagements: foreign investments might be "of value to . . . rapid industrialization" but the resolution insisted that they be "carefully regulated in the national interest," with controlling stakes held in Indian hands.[24]

Independence imparted new import to debates that had, for many decades, remained purely hypothetical. Nehru and his followers hoped that increased production could improve living standards and reduce inequality—without resorting to zero-sum decisions like land reform and nationalization, which could prove divisive and strain Congress's broad and divergent electoral coalition. But as with planning itself, which Nehru wanted to keep apart from politics, economic policy proved to be a profoundly contested process. Nehru's exhortations to increase production tracked closely with industrial problems; he aimed such calls at business owners wavering amid the uncertainties of the day and at labor leaders calling strikes across India.[25]

The tasks that Nehru and his fellow ministers faced were formidable and required both steadfastness and compromise. Their priorities in independent India's first months included ending the communal violence that both invoked and resulted from partition; building a new and independent government apparatus out of the British inheritances; determining Indian foreign policy and creating the mechanisms to enact it; creating a nation out of a dozen provinces and hundreds of small principalities; and rebuilding an Indian economy shaped by empire, distorted by war, and then divided by partition.

While the clamor of daily domestic crises occupied much of his attention, Nehru nevertheless managed to articulate a foreign policy of nonalignment, which introduced both opportunities and complexities into its international economic relations. Though the posture grew out of a desire to create distance between India and its former colonizer, it also contained strident criticisms of "the miserable failure in the foreign policy of every great Power" in the post-war period. India, Nehru proclaimed, would pursue its own interests in the international arena, and would resist any attempts to be pulled or pushed into any permanent bloc. He noted further that nonalignment was "the outcome of economic policy" in the sense that India should not become politically or economically dependent on any one country.[26]

Nehru's insistence that India stay within the British Commonwealth did not threaten his calls for nonalignment, and indeed maintaining good relations with Britain ensured access to one particularly valuable (if vexed) legacy of colonial rule: a "sterling balance" that the British owed to the government of India for its efforts in defense of the British Empire during World War II. Even after dividing the full amount with Pakistan, the new Government of India was suddenly flush in pounds sterling. And yet the balance came with its own limits and problems. Fears that rapid draws from the balance could set off inflation soon gave way to the unhappy acknowledgement that the United Kingdom had no intention of allowing free use of that balance. More important, the sterling balance arrived precisely as the U.S. dollar supplanted the British pound in international markets. Indian business groups that had spent the war lobbying for free access to the balance, including its conversion to dollars, were disappointed by the results.[27] India's situation became, in the words of one prominent Indian business leader, like that of a "man with a million dollar balance in the bank but not sufficient cash to pay his taxi fare."[28]

Political differences within Congress (let alone in a wider political sphere that ranged from an active communist movement to Hindu parties), combined with the posture of nonalignment, gave free play to policy entrepreneurs seeking to influence the direction of Indian foreign policy. A number of diplomats favoring ties with the West, for instance, sought to build Indo-American ties. Vijayalakshmi Pandit, India's first ambassador in Moscow and then its third ambassador in Washington, tried to win over American diplomats by intimating that Prime Minister Nehru was inclined toward the West but could not publicly say so. Another distinguished diplomat tried to woo the American secretary of state by insisting that only the United States, and definitely not the Soviet Union, could help India economically. From outside the Ministry of External Affairs offices in Delhi's South Block came other voices seeking to bolster ties to the United States. The *Eastern Economist*—owned by Birla enterprises—dismissed the risk of "foreign domination," instead highlighting the massive resources that the U.S. government could bring to bear in India. And an important new magazine, *Economic Weekly,* editorialized that India was "desperate" for dollars. Nehru accepted this line of reasoning, at least in principle; Indian diplomats should "be friendly to America" but should not enmesh themselves "too much with their world or their economic policy." This was not just a statement of nonalignment but also a negotiating stance: by maintaining a "free hand," Nehru concluded, India would "ultimately get more" from the United States.[29]

Pro-Western Indians, whether inside or outside government, looked to the World Bank to help make the case for closer ties to the capitalist world. The Ministry of Finance, led by John Mathai, requested a World Bank mission to India—a call consistent with his general orientation toward Western economic ideas, including the expansion of international trade. Meanwhile B. K. Nehru, a cousin of the prime minister and a former Indian Civil Service official who became India's first representative at the World Bank, approached the bank with a list of some fifteen projects for potential loans. He sought in addition a $500 million balance-of-payments loan, an instrument well outside the bank's practices in that era. The World Bank Mission, which toured India in winter 1949, amplified Mathai's policy prescriptions, exhorting Prime Minster Nehru to focus on agriculture and to seek foreign investors by improving conditions for private capital from abroad.[30]

In the wake of the World Bank Mission, Prime Minster Nehru reexamined Indian policy toward foreign investment. In an important speech to the Lok Sabha (the Parliament's lower house) in April 1949, he announced an official policy that echoed earlier conversations with bankers; it promised more guarantees for foreign capital than restrictions upon it. Well aware that large swaths of Congress leadership remained wary of foreign investment, Nehru acknowledged past British domination but insisted that "circumstances today are quite different." Jolted by the notion that foreign firms could soon be competing in India, FICCI immediately protested what it termed the government's abandonment of swadeshi. Nehru's statement on foreign investment—which became a reference point for many years—was a coup for B. K. Nehru and his colleagues, who were hoping to use the World Bank to advance their own ideas about Indian openness to capital.[31]

If the Congress left lost out on foreign investment policy, they quickly learned the new technique of using foreign expertise. A handful of left-wing Indian diplomats made the case that engineer Solomon Trone should serve as a planning consultant for the government of India. He became an impresario—or perhaps a charlatan—of planning in India and elsewhere in the late 1940s. Indian proponents emphasized Trone's American citizenship without noting that he was born in Latvia and had joined the Russian Communist Party, working at a Soviet power station in the 1920s. Disillusioned by the show trials against noncommunist engineers, Trone moved to the United States in 1931, soon thereafter becoming a naturalized citizen. His Russian background received little attention, and his prior political affiliations none at all; his dubious claims to be an expert on industrialization and planning, in contrast, found wide circulation. Traveling across India on his consulting mission, Trone barraged Nehru with exhortations about central planning. He warned the prime minister that "powerful, influential industrial groups" were scheming to "deepen the existing economic crisis" in order to pave the way for "their laissez-faire policy." He praised heavy industry as the only path toward rapid growth, and insisted that only a strong planning apparatus could manage industrialization. The prime minister cited Trone's reports prominently as he advanced his proposal for a powerful planning commission.[32]

Prime Minister Nehru needed all the support he could get for a strong planning apparatus when he took the matter to the Congress Working Committee. The Congress right tried at every turn to dilute the planning authority's powers, proposing advisory bodies that included industrialists. The left, meanwhile, insisted that only central planning could (in the words of labor leader G. L. Nanda) "give economic content to the word 'freedom.'" Deadlocked, the Congress leadership approved a Planning Commission (PC), but continued in the fine tradition of punting controversy forward by concluding that only the government could decide its ultimate form and function.[33]

Even after Trone's reports had long since been forgotten, controversy about the place of planning (or at least the power of the PC) rocked the top ranks of the Government of India. The founding resolution of the PC was heavy on sweeping statements and pleasant platitudes. But its verbs tended toward formulating, indicating, and appraising—not executing, building, funding, organizing, or even coordinating. The *Times of India* soon enough offered its condolences to those hoping for a stronger commission. The PC's initial membership strayed greatly from 1930s conceptions of planning as an apolitical, expert-led process; most of the members were politicians, only two had specific economic expertise, and Nehru in the chair, by his own admission, "knew little of economics."[34]

Such a modest organization, however, did not quell the ongoing debate, which focused on how planning would shape the Indian state. Officials in the ministries continued to worry that they would become subservient to a PC "super-cabinet." Pro-American food minister K. M. Munshi declared that planned economies were "inseparably associated with totalitarian regimes." Finance Minister John Mathai expressed a similar concern, threatening to resign because the PC would reduce the cabinet "practically into a registering body" rather than a policy-making one. Mathai ignored Nehru's pleading to remain in office, resigning his post in summer 1950. This was the first, but hardly the last, turf war between the Ministry of Finance and the PC; V. K. Krishna Menon, a left-wing Congress leader close to the prime minister, wondered later whether finance ministers were collectively "allergic" to planning.

Such fears hardly seemed merited by the actual activities of the Planning Commission. In the first year, the commission delayed releasing its initial report as it awaited approval from the Cabinet. A more poignant sense of the PC's powers and purposes appeared in the handwritten notes of Vice Chairman Nanda, a Congress figure long active in both Indian and international labor movements. After carefully recording various reports, and enumerating many pages of "questions for consideration," Nanda titled one page of his notes "aspirations"; the rest of the page was blank.[35]

The initial product of the Planning Commission—the First Five-Year Plan—revealed its limited powers. Released on the eve of the plan's April 1951 start, it called for modest spending, much of which was devoted to infrastructure (about 51 percent) and agriculture (about 17 percent); only 8 percent went to industry. Even Nehru later conceded that the plan was "not planning in the real sense of the word."[36]

The First Plan hardly resolved, indeed barely addressed, the meaning of swadeshi; it did not even invoke the word. It seemed vaguely open to expanding India's economic ties, but with uncertainty, a distinct lack of enthusiasm, and perhaps even a little innocence. Following the precedent of the National Planning Committee, the new Planning Commission devoted only nine pages (out of 659) to "foreign trade and commercial policy"; most of those pages focused more on the past, not the present or future, of Indian trade. The plan did call, somewhat nebulously, for expanding trade to the dollar area, but offered no details about specific commodities or mechanisms for expanding trade. Foreign trade did occasionally come up in PC deliberations, but usually in generic calls to assemble foreign experts or to expand the production of cash crops (like jute, tea, and indigo) for export. Economist Jagdish Bhagwati later accused Indian planners of "export pessimism," against which he argued with increasing strenuousness over the 1960s. Yet his colleague I. G. Patel aptly noted that Bhagwati's term was "too charitable" since it implied that an export-oriented policy came up for discussion but was rejected. Indeed, though the prospects for export-led growth using those commodities faced many limits, discussions on the future of the Indian economy did not dwell on the constraints. Patel, recalling no such debates or analyses in the halls of power, thus preferred the term "export amnesia."[37]

Foreign investment received only slightly more attention than foreign trade. The "draft outline" of the First Plan, completed in summer 1951 (four months after the plan had official begun), concluded that foreign capital should "naturally be welcome" and cited Nehru's April 1949 statement in support. But it quickly undercut that warm welcome by limiting foreign investment to a few high-priority fields that were beyond the capabilities of domestic Indian enterprise. The final plan document contained even more restrictive language; it admitted that foreign resources might provide "much assistance," but insisted that no such resources should be accepted if they "might affect even remotely" Indian nonalignment. "It goes without saying," one didactic version of the plan had it, that "there will have to be close regulation" of any foreign economic activities in India.[38]

The First Plan addressed only a few elements of the long-running debate about India's economic future and resolved even fewer. The initial fruits of Indian planning instead suggested that compromise and modesty were the order of the day. Ultimately the plan did a better job of framing future debates than resolving past ones. While hardly a call for rapid industrialization, it did not allocate major resources to Gandhian efforts like village industry. In the First Plan document, as in Congress politics more broadly, Gandhian influence had quickly waned. Debates raged instead over favored sectors and speed of progress. One of the major successes of the PC, in short, was that it has established itself as a key organ of economic policy, a venue for arguing over policy and an object with a symbolic importance that lasted some six decades—up until Bharatiya Janata Party prime minister Narendra Modi in 2014 replaced the PC with the National Institute for Transforming India (Niti Aayog, which means "policy commission" in Hindi). The core questions of India's economic future—ownership (public versus private), priorities (agriculture versus industry), and exposure to the larger economic world—remained very much up for grabs. And as the superpowers discovered India in its first years of independence, foreign powers became part of the debate over India's future plans.

The Soviet Discovery of India

These Indian events, however dramatic, received scant attention in Moscow. Soviet ideology, as it stood in the 1940s, did not have space to reckon with the existence of independent India, let alone the vagaries of its planning process. When, for instance, chief ideologue Andrei Zhdanov met with Communist Party of India (CPI) leaders on August 16, 1947—independent India's second day of existence—the minutes did not include any mention of the week's momentous events in India. India had come up occasionally in Soviet discussions in past decades, but more as a concept than an actual place. Such dismissive views of India lasted well into World War II, and indeed survived in some Soviet quarters past Indian independence in 1947.[39]

A distinguished Marxist tradition considered India (and other colonies of Europe) primarily in relation to Britain and Europe. Karl Marx cheered British imperialism in the 1850s, arguing that it alone could bring the subcontinent out of primitive timelessness and into the stream of history. England, Marx wrote, was "causing a social revolution" in India, which was all to the good; "mankind [could not] fulfill its destiny" without a "fundamental revolution in the social state of Asia." Decades later, as Russia's wartime chaos gave way to revolution, radicals updated Marx's views for their own era. In his pamphlet *Imperialism, the Highest Stage of Capitalism* (1916), Vladimir Lenin mentioned British India only in passing, engaging neither with its politics nor its economics. In the aftermath of the Great October Socialist Revolution in 1917, a call to arms meant for Muslims in and beyond the now defunct Russian Empire mentioned India, only to shame other regions for their lack of revolutionary spirit. "Even far-off India," the appeal read, was showing signs of rebellion; Central Asians in the Russian empire, surely, could follow suit.[40]

In the decade after World War I, as the Indian National Congress grew into a mass organization with members across the expanse of the region, revolutionaries in and beyond Moscow began to take note—not for India itself but for its potential impact on the British Empire. A report for the Communist International (Comintern) proclaimed India a "citadel of revolution in the East"—but this mattered only because turmoil there would "resound most strongly in the West." From India and other places in the East, it continued, communism could launch an attack on "the bastions of imperialism—England, America, and Japan." Stalin, then a midlevel Bolshevik functionary, agreed that India mattered primarily as a mechanism for bringing revolution to Europe: "The task of Communism is to do away with the century-old slumber of the oppressed peoples of the East"; this would deprive "world imperialism of its 'most reliable' and 'inexhaustible' reserve." Stalin's future nemesis Leon Trotsky agreed; the road to European revolution, he argued with a dialectical geography, might run through India rather than through central and eastern Europe. India had a place on revolutionaries' world maps—but only as a transmission belt, causing trouble for the European nations at the center of revolutionary thought.[41]

M. N. Roy, one of only two Indians in the early Comintern, spent the 1920s trying to spread the word about India's revolutionary potential. By mid-decade he began to find success, helped not just by his powers of persuasion but also by the formation of the CPI on Boxing Day 1925. So India garnered increasing attention in the circles of global revolution—a good deal of which was devoted to criticizing the Indian National Congress for being insufficiently revolutionary. Stalin had little room for "bourgeois nationalist" movements in India or elsewhere; he dismissed the Indian National Congress leaders as worried more about "their moneybags than about the interests of their own motherland," and "fearing revolution more than imperialism." Only a communist party, he concluded, could bring about revolution, so only such a party merited Comintern support. Another Stalin foe, Nikolai Bukharin, agreed, calling the bourgeois nationalists in India "already an actively hostile force." Hungarian economist Eugen Varga, a devoted socialist not overly deferential to the party line, agreed; he dismissed Indian nationalists as seeking nothing more than "an improvement of their [own] position within the Empire." In this spirit, the Comintern slammed Congress for using "nefarious play with slogans of 'independence'" to sow "confusion and twaddle" among Indians. "Bourgeois nationalism," not British repression, was the "greatest danger" to Indian revolution.[42]

This general hostility toward noncommunist social movements, and toward nationalism in particular, became a common Soviet refrain in later decades—all the more so as India drew increasing attention from the Comintern. Such attention, however, still focused less on India itself and more on the impacts in England. In the wake of accelerating nationalist agitation in India in the early 1930s, for instance, one Soviet official lectured his colleagues: "This is not a simple revolt in a little colony. The struggle in India is of tremendous importance." But he quickly shifted the locale away from India, noting, "it is the ground upon which the fortunes of British imperialism are going to be settled" and adding for good measure, "He who fails to see this is generally a hopeless case." A Comintern official agreed, exhorting his colleagues to devote fully half of their attention to India. The demise of the Comintern in 1943 put an end to that particular debate, but interest in India did not vanish.[43]

Those revolutionaries interested in India divided, generally, into two groups, some seeing India's relevance solely in terms of Europe and others valuing revolution in India for its own sake. Traditionalists like V. M. Molotov, at the helm of the Soviet Foreign Ministry through the 1940s, argued that Europe's colonies offered little to the USSR except the chance to foment revolution in Europe itself. But a growing number of internationalist officials in the state or party bureaucracy in Moscow challenged this view: the emerging postwar international order would turn India into "a most important political and economic factor in world development." The USSR should, therefore, extend diplomatic recognition and expand cultural ties with India. This view found only a few Soviet adherents during the war but garnered increasing numbers over the late 1940s.[44]

The conflicted place of India in Soviet thought is well illustrated by debates over the postwar world economy, a debate centered around Varga's book, *Changes in the Economics of Capitalism as a Result of the Second World War* (1946). Varga highlighted the new, indeed unprecedented, relationship between England and India. Leninist theories of imperialism claimed that a metropole would keep its colonies impoverished and indebted—and yet after the war England owed well over one billion British pounds sterling to the government of India. The fact that Varga made so little of this debt indexes the position of India in postwar Soviet thought: even as he argued about an emerging world order, Varga kept his focus resolutely on European capitalism.[45]

In terms of formal diplomacy, the Stalinist Molotov was prepared to extend official recognition to independent India but seemed distinctly unenthusiastic. His notes on a conversation with emissary V. K. Krishna Menon mentioned that closer bilateral ties would "meet the interests of both countries and would advance world peace and progress"; he then struck the latter phrase from the record. The Soviet foreign minister had thus envisioned pursuing mutual interests with a nascent Indian government—but did not see India within the Soviet framework of progress toward world revolution. When diplomatic relations began in spring 1947, *Pravda* contained only a brief factual announcement; Soviet officials still considered Indian independence as purely notional.[46]

This question of "true independence" loomed large in Soviet discussions about India in the late 1940s. If India had really found meaningful independence, it merited full engagement; if not, it deserved attention only in relation to its impact on Britain and on world capitalism. The nature of Indian independence could also affect Soviet theoretical (or eschatological) debates about the path to communism and the future of imperialism. In a multiday *diskussiia* on his book at the Institute of Economics, Varga argued that India challenged key elements of Soviet theory. Such discussions were a ritual of Soviet academic life in those years, allowing (as one historian put it) "temporary, public disagreements over important political questions." They could be sharply critical, but were as often about revisiting (or revising) an orthodoxy as they were about enforcing one. At this particular diskussiia Varga quickly dismissed the standard Stalinist view of decolonization, which he ridiculed accurately: "The empires have remained empires, the colonies have remained colonies, everything has remained as it was before." Returning once again to the sterling debt, Varga noted that it demonstrated not just India's growing strength but the rapid decline of British power, which was on its way to becoming "a 49th, overseas state of America." Meanwhile, the sterling balance provided a material basis for Indian independence.[47]

Orthodoxy won the day at the diskussiia, rendering India again an afterthought in the Soviet worldview. A number of scholars, including the chair of the proceedings, rejected Varga's claim about the sterling debt, arguing that it marked merely a "change in the forms of the colonies' dependence"; sterling debt did "not change the general situation . . . in its fundamental aspects." Peaceful decolonization, as had taken place in South Asia, was a dead end; true independence could be achieved, the argument went, "only in one way—the revolutionary way." Neither Indian independence nor the sterling debt, in this view, altered European dominance or Indian dependence.[48]

Other Soviet scholars, with fewer institutional resources and lower profiles, engaged Indian matters more directly, though they echoed the early debates between traditionalists and internationalists about the relative importance of India in the postwar world. Also at stake was the question of Indian independence: would its new situation (as Varga hinted) constitute a meaningful independence, or would it remain for all intents and purposes a colony of Britain? At the Pacific Ocean Institute, the orthodox historian A. M. D'iakov opted for the latter, arguing that Nehru and his colleagues in the interim government remained "loyal vassal[s] of British imperialism." Another India expert emphasized England's "commanding position" in its former colony, with the result that India remained a tool of the "Anglo-Saxon bloc." The gap between the Indian situation and "true" (*podlinnaia*) or "full" (*polnaia*) independence was wide indeed—never mind the minimal U.S. presence in India and the growing problems of British investment there. D'iakov's skepticism predominated at the Pacific Ocean Institute, where most doubted that India had achieved true independence. They blamed not just England but also the Indian bourgeoisie, which had conspired with "English imperialism" to imperil "true independence." Thus the prevailing sentiment considered the Indian National Congress as "full[y] in the camp of reaction and imperialism." Gandhi came in for special criticism as "an apostle of backwardness" and "an inveterate enemy of the people." Congress was an obstacle to, not the instrument for, true independence.[49]

Without true independence, of course, there was no place for an independent foreign policy—or so Soviet observers argued. Some Indian efforts to assert the state's independence internationally did little to please Soviet diplomats; India's pursuit of a seat on the Security Council of the newly formed United Nations incurred the wrath of Soviet leaders, who called India a slave of Anglo-Americans and a tool in the powers' anti-Soviet crusade. Indian claims of independence in international affairs found little sympathy in the USSR, especially after Zhdanov's September 1947 speech that divided the world into two antithetical groups: an "imperialist and anti-democratic camp" under American control and an "anti-imperialist and democratic camp" led by the Soviet Union. The process of ideological purification known as the *zhdanovshchina* divided the world into two camps; there was no position between imperialism and communism. Indian nonalignment thus was at best a delusion and at worst a deception; Soviet writers usually assumed the worst. E. M. Zhukov, a Stalinist at the Pacific Ocean Institute, denounced nonalignment as "a false theory" that ultimately "slander[ed] the USSR and Communism" and revealed its proponents as "agents of imperialism."[50]

As crises mounted in India in 1948, including strike waves organized or promoted by the CPI, Soviet observers paid closer attention to domestic Indian conditions. In March of that year, the Indian Cabinet approved an active campaign against the CPI, banning its participation in elections and arresting party leaders. Such actions only confirmed Soviet antipathy toward Congress. D'iakov even argued for Soviet support of ethnoreligious separatist movements in order to weaken Congress rule (and India itself). Elsewhere D'iakov doubted that India was even ruled by Nehru; he published an article about the "crisis of English rule in India" in 1949, two years after Nehru's speech at the Red Fort. Zhukov, a convenient barometer of Stalinist orthodoxy, combined criticisms of domestic and foreign policy, equally harsh about both. India had become a "cunning servant" of England and the United States abroad and a "bloody suppressor of progressive forces" at home.[51]

A handful of heterodox scholars took a more expansive view of world affairs and a more sympathetic approach to India in particular. One member of the Pacific Ocean Institute, for instance, considered the sterling debt as evidence of the waning of British power in its former colony. Varga himself, even as he faced public criticism and bureaucratic opposition, took on a broader claim that would eventually resound in debates over India. In a 1947 recap of three decades of communism, Varga tempered his fulsome praise of the Russian path ("without doubt the best and fastest" route to socialism) with a dogged insistence on alternatives. He focused on Eastern Europe, especially his native Hungary, but also noted the circumstances of the poorest parts of the world where capitalist development had barely begun. In describing a variety of paths to socialism, Varga sought to limit the role of the Soviet Union in imposing a single model on other countries—not least his own.[52]

This debate, while not originally focused on India, soon bled into discussions of India and the decolonizing world. Zhukov, for instance, blasted Varga's focus on "specific laws and features" (which Zhukov put in scare quotes) and called for renewed emphasis on the "general laws of social development." Lest this be considered only a question about Hungary and the people's republics in Europe, Zhukov slammed Varga's approach as an effort to "poison the people with [nationalist] chauvinism"; even worse, this would "tear away the colonial and dependent countries" from the Soviet camp. For the most part, tactics for India emerged out of broader discussions, like Varga's; India was far from the center of Soviet debates.[53]

India's marginal position in scholarship echoed its place in Soviet diplomacy. While Nehru sent Vijayalakshmi Pandit, a well-known Congress figure (and his own sister) to Moscow months before independence, the Soviet Ministry of Foreign Affairs moved slowly; indeed, the ministry was under orders to "hold for a while" its ambassadorial appointment to New Delhi. And the appointment, when finally made, hardly matched Pandit's high profile; Ambassador K. V. Novikov was a stolid, square-jawed party apparatchik with more experience in textile factories than embassies. As Soviet grievances about Indian policy mounted, Pandit and her brother met with him to clear the air; the meeting itself only repeated (and escalated) ill feeling between the diplomats. The only progress in formal relations was a bilateral trade deal that amounted to barter: Indian jute and tea in exchange for Soviet grain. Neither the exchange of ambassadors in 1947 nor small quantities of goods two years later warmed Soviet attitudes toward India.[54]

The first real thaw in Soviet views of India came in 1950. Pandit's successor in Moscow, Sarvepalli Radhakrishnan, scored a meeting with Stalin at the start of 1950, fielding scattered questions on everything from Hindi script to—surprisingly enough—the implications of joining the British Commonwealth. With the outbreak of the Korean War that June, Soviet diplomats appreciated the Indian delegation's efforts to make peace in the corridors of the United Nations. Such policies indicated that India might not be part and parcel of Anglo-American imperialism after all. By early 1951, strife within the CPI led to a Moscow summit during which Soviet leaders were, at last, ready to consider actual Indian conditions. Stalin sharply criticized those Indian communists who believed that revolution was nigh; India, he noted bluntly, did not "stand on the threshold of (*stoit pered*) socialist revolution." The CPI should not carry out revolution, but should instead join a "national front" with progressive elements—even those within the ruling Congress Party. There was no universal path to revolution, and under the circumstances the CPI needed to work within the system.[55]

By early 1951, then, two key Soviet assumptions over the preceding years had become the subject of intense dispute. Stalin had sided with the less orthodox scholars and theorists who accepted the possibility that revolution might arrive in different places at different times and through different mechanisms. Communism, of course, was inevitable, but paths to it might vary with local conditions. At the same time, the notion that imperialism could be defeated only by violent revolution came under attack. The Soviet experience, therefore, no longer defined the path and the pace of revolution elsewhere in the world. The frame for these policy changes reached well beyond India, though India became increasingly prominent in the discussions. But the new framework, whatever its origins, contained space for new relations with India, and by extension with the decolonizing world writ large.

The American Discovery of India

American officialdom underwent a similar process of discovery in the years following Indian independence. As late as 1951 President Harry S. Truman admitted to future ambassador Chester Bowles that he "thought India was pretty jammed with poor people and cows wandering around the streets, witch doctors and people sitting on hot coals and bathing in the Ganges"; he did not "realize that anyone thought it was important." Bowles, a liberal Democratic Party politician, differed; he saw India as the key to creating a more egalitarian world under American leadership. Until 1950, the U.S. State Department stored all of its correspondence about India under a heading for the British Empire; it took three years for its filing system to recognize India's independence. Reviews of the world situation and U.S. foreign policy throughout Truman's presidency (1945–1953) confirmed this view of India's marginality to the United States.[56]

In broad strategy documents as well as narrower regional assessments, American diplomats, military officers, and intelligence analysts agreed that India mattered only in terms of its potential loss to the Soviet Union—and even then mattered little. Take, for instance, a CIA tour d'horizon circulated weeks after Indian independence. It acknowledged the events of August 1947 in India and Pakistan only parenthetically, putting the two new nations in a "belt of colonial (or former colonial) territories" in the region. Acknowledging "insurgent native nationalism," the report ranked this region fourth of four in importance for U.S. national security. Calling the area "remote from the USSR" (never mind that Pakistan's northern border came within ten miles of Soviet Tajikstan) and "not subject to direct Soviet aggression," the CIA report gave license to American policy makers to focus their attentions elsewhere.[57]

Strategist George Kennan, then at the peak of his power and influence as head of the State Department's Policy Planning Staff, stated the matter even more categorically in early 1948. He consigned the whole "Far East" (including

China and India) to a future of poverty and despotism, warning against any American efforts to get involved. Until India solved its "basic demographic problem," he wrote, it would face only "hunger, distress, and violence"; adaptation to the modern world, if it ever took place, would similarly be "violent." Kennan, with characteristic pessimism, considered it "probable" that large swaths of Asia would "fall, for varying periods, under the influence of Moscow"; he warned that any attempt to challenge this fate would entail untenable effort and expense. His vision of American global interests contemplated only an attenuated globe, one in which areas beyond Europe mattered little if at all.[58]

If India did not fare well in U.S. analyses of global politics, studies of the region did identify a few reasons that the emerging superpower should care about Indian events. A massive interagency analysis of South Asia in 1949, for instance, evaluated potential Indian contributions to the defense of the free world and outlined some simple (and inexpensive) measures to keep India out of the communist camp. CIA reports of the era reached similar conclusions, noting the advantages of keeping India out of the Soviet bloc, but rejecting the notion that India was worthy of substantial investment.[59]

To the extent that American observers considered Indo-American economic relations at all, they placed them into a framework that assumed that all nations would benefit first and foremost from the free flow of goods and capital around the world. Decolonization, in this view, marked an unusual opportunity; the demise of European empires could expand the field of play for American enterprise to the ostensible benefit of all concerned. American diplomats proceeded accordingly. The first American ambassador in New Delhi, Henry Grady, fresh from his work as a shipping agent, got right down to the business of shilling for American firms. Within weeks of his arrival, he arranged for his friend Stephen Bechtel, head of a family business well known for major engineering projects around the world, to come pitch infrastructure projects to the prime minister. Grady also hoped to open India to international trade, which he considered the only means to allow India to "enjoy a future as rich and glorious as its past." Grady's successor Loy Henderson, a stiff career diplomat with no business experience, continued agitating on behalf of free trade and American trading partners. In conversations with Prime Minister Nehru, oilman-turned-diplomat George McGhee, then assistant secretary of state, enumerated the regulatory changes necessary to attract American capital; McGhee's lower-ranking colleagues did the same at other meetings. Meanwhile, desultory discussions over a bilateral treaty of trade and navigation unfolded sporadically over the late 1940s (and indeed well into the 1950s); American diplomats seemed more energetic than Indian diplomats, who were happy to continue negotiations indefinitely without concluding a treaty.[60]

These early views echoed across Washington. A blue-ribbon government commission called for overseas investment of American capital to expand not just American prosperity but also to ensure American security. The U.S. National Security Council agreed, though remained wary of anything beyond trade relations with India; it cautioned that the U.S. government must avoid "responsibility for [India's] economic welfare." Promoting private American trade and investment in India, then, could advance American economically while maintaining an appropriate distance from Indian affairs.[61]

Most of the early analyses of India focused on the political affiliations of Congress leaders like Prime Minister Nehru. (Future U.S. secretary of state John Foster Dulles, for instance, created a brief scandal when he told one lecture audience in 1947 that Nehru's "Hindu government" was a vehicle for Soviet influence in the region.) But as American assessments of actual Indian conditions grew more detailed, they drew increasing attention to economic issues, concerned primarily that continuing poverty or economic turmoil would breed communism. So while the National Security Council advocated keeping its distance from the Indian economy, Ambassador Henderson warned of the regional or even global implications of its economic troubles. Without American involvement, he worried, India "might degenerate into a vast political and economic swamp, the unclean exhalations of which would pollute the international atmosphere" for years to come.[62]

Such economic concerns garnered more attention after Truman's 1949 inaugural address. Hoping to "relieve the suffering" of the poor through the "improvement and growth of underdeveloped areas," the president called for a "bold new program for making [available] the benefits of our scientific advances and industrial progress." In his famous fourth point, Truman proposed going bold but not too bold; he declared at the outset that American "Point Four" efforts would spread "inexhaustible" American technical knowledge—but would not share American "material resources."[63]

As Point Four took shape as an actual government program, different elements of the U.S. government sought to use it to advance their own visions of America's role in the postwar world economy. Though India was not central in the minds of Point Four planners, it soon became a leading site for technical assistance. Only the State Department demurred here, remaining skeptical of the whole enterprise; the secretary of state recalled that he and other top officials were "neither enthusiastic nor impressed with [the] utility" of technical assistance. The U.S. Congress followed this lead, declining to fund the program until the president underscored its anticommunist goals and emphasized the opportunities for overseas private investment.[64]

Other bureaucrats, however, sought advantage from Point Four, hoping to bend it to their own purposes. For some, Point Four was little more than a tool to promote American trade and investment in the newly emerging Third World. White House economists thus eyed gratefully the "new international markets" that Point Four would open up, thus ending the "self-defeating struggle for present limited markets." Americans in New Delhi seemed to concur; one of the very first experts sent to India under the auspices of the Technical Cooperation Administration (TCA) was a banker tasked with "stimulat[ing] foreign investment." This line of thinking about U.S. engagement overseas remained dominant after World War II, though it soon enough faced major challenges.[65]

Meanwhile, those focused on India saw Point Four as an opportunity to use American assistance to improve Indian agriculture, building on small-scale private efforts dating back some decades. Successive ambassadors Loy Henderson and Chester Bowles, whatever their differences in politics and temperament, shared this agriculture-first approach. The rural focus reflected their serious doubts about the possibility of an industrial India as well as their assessment of economic benefits of increased agricultural production.[66]

Technical assistance found enthusiasts among officials in Washington and New Delhi. State Department leaders, once persuaded that Point Four would not threaten the programs for Europe that mattered so much to them, acceded to the program. The promise of promoting private investment overseas brought others on board. The program also flattered American feelings of technical superiority and humanitarianism. Different groups found different reasons to support technical assistance. A parallel process unfolded in India. Those enthusiastic about Indo-American relations saw Point Four as a first step toward closer ties. And those afraid of American "dollar imperialism" (as Ambassador Grady huffily put it) could take solace in the fact that few actual dollars would circulate in India.[67]

Even from the start, American diplomats ran up against the severe limits of technical assistance. In 1949, Ambassador Henderson requested a $500 million program over the next five years to ensure that India could "serve as one of the bulwarks against the expansion of Communism." This proposal—which amounted to spending three times the total Point Four appropriations on a single country—faced stiff resistance in Washington. Assistant Secretary of State George McGhee held steadfast that official U.S. "grants or credits" served little purpose. White House aides cited congressional disapproval as they rejected any aid beyond technical assistance. Early efforts to use India to expand the scope of American aid thus met a quick and quiet death. Indian diplomats aptly summed up the early history of Point Four: "what appeared at one point as a program of vast expenditures on the economic development of the underdeveloped areas of the world" quickly devolved into "a limited program of technical service personnel only."[68]

Though Henderson's efforts came to naught, the notion of economic (and not just technical) assistance did not disappear. The creation of the People's Republic of China in late 1949 gave new impetus to the Cold War in Asia generally, not least vis-à-vis India and Pakistan. Proponents of economic aid used these changed circumstances to make their case. One report commissioned by the Truman White House acknowledged technical assistance but considered it inadequate for economic progress, which required "capital of some sort." India, in this analysis, was "the most difficult problem, both short-term and long-term," and private capital was insufficient for the task. The report thus proposed a major program of official economic aid for the Third World. Another body, this one headed by a liberal Republican, reached a similar conclusion, endorsing a major aid program as "a vital part of our defense mobilization." A bipartisan American lobby for aid took shape, making the case to push beyond technical assistance toward economic aid.[69]

In the middling reaches of the State Department, far from the skeptical secretary, similar sentiments emerged. A conference of American ambassadors in winter 1951 agreed that economic aid could produce great political benefits, especially since American investors had not exactly flocked to South Asia. They called for expanding technical assistance packages to include economic aid, which they called "the best means presently available for achieving or strengthening their orientation to the West." Other diplomats made tentative probes, suggesting specific programs that would expand the definition of technical assistance. As economic aid became a topic of conversation in 1951, American policy debates established a geopolitical logic for economic aid to the Third World; it could bring the uncommitted nations to the West and could prevent the sorts of economic catastrophe that might invite communist insurgency—a logic all the more important after the creation of the People's Republic of China and the outbreak of the Korean War the following summer. Impeccable though the logic was in the early 1950s, though, it had not yet yielded an actual aid program on any scale.[70]

Until 1950 India maintained only distant and proper relations with the two emerging superpowers. Its diplomats, to be sure, operated in Moscow and Washington while the two superpowers opened their first embassies in New Delhi. But the existence of these new embassies did not create meaningful or even frequent intergovernmental contacts. When Indian officials sought international help for their domestic battles, they turned to individual impresarios like Solomon Trone, or to new multilateral institutions like the World Bank.

Nehru's determination to maintain a nonaligned stance did not win him friends in superpowers that divided the world into two blocs locked in existential struggle. But it was not just nonalignment that rendered India invisible in the superpowers; both American and Soviet security calculations and ideological predispositions had little place for an impoverished ex-colony, however large. American officials did not at first use India to establish a new category of postcolonial nations. They instead prescribed for India the same approach they favored elsewhere: integrating it into international flows of goods and capital; only globalization could lead to shared prosperity. One astute economist later termed this assumption "monoeconomics": there was only one set of economic rules, no exceptions permitted. Soviet experts and apparatchiks took an analogous view of India for decades; rejecting the notion of national particularities, they understood India only in terms of Marxian precepts for global revolution. Thus, when they considered India at all, they contemplated only its potential impact on England. Soviet ideologues and scholars downplayed the events of August 1947 so much that they seemed to doubt that anything had changed at all.[71]

In India, of course, 1947 was the occasion for elation, even amid the tragedies of partition. But decades of discussion among Indian nationalists had not yielded a unified vision for independent India. While swadeshi became a powerful rallying cry for the Indian National Congress, the meaning of self-sufficiency was not self-evident. Even a quarter century later, one leading Congress aide felt the need to specify that he favored "self-reliance . . . [but] not in a narrow autarchic manner." Within Congress itself, socialists, Gandhians, and business leaders all celebrated swadeshi even as they differed about whether it meant autarky or international openness, agriculture or industry, private enterprise or government ownership, and so on. These debates necessarily held less significance before independence, when critique of British rule occluded internal differences within Congress, or at least deferred the need to resolve them. Thus Congress's National Planning Committee did not identify a single set of priorities, but could establish enough subcommittees to defer any budget-based (and therefore zero-sum) discussion of what mattered most.[72]

The arrival of independence in 1947 invested these old debates with new meaning—and Indian politics grew that much more contentious as a result. At first these debates continued, as they had before independence, in relative isolation from the superpowers. For the preceding decades, Indian nationalists debated their economic future with both oblique and direct references to broader economic systems that the two superpowers came to represent—but with few direct engagements from anyone from the United States or the Soviet Union, let alone any meaningful government contacts. And in the American and Soviet governments, officials evinced little knowledge of and even less interest in the first, largest, and most populous European colony to attain independence after World War II.

The 1950s changed the nature of Indian economic debates, which came to encompass the superpowers more frequently and more directly. As American and Soviet officials seeking deeper economic engagements in India gained influence in their respective governments, official policy moved slowly but definitively toward increased awareness of India and the postcolonial predicament. In the process, all three nations changed in significant ways. The American and Soviet governments invented development aid, which emerged out of both trial and error and internal argument. And within the Indian government, officials found new ways to advance their own claims and their own ideas for economic policy. Following the examples of Trone and the World Bank in 1949, they began to use superpower aid and attention as weapons in their own internal disputes. With these new endeavors, development politics was born.

CHAPTER 2

INVENTING
DEVELOPMENT AID

On the eve of his autumn 1949 trip to the United States, Prime Minister Jawaharlal Nehru met with his advisers about the visit's agenda, including the pursuit of development assistance. Coming months after President Harry S. Truman's inaugural address announcing Point Four, and about two years after Secretary of State George Marshall made the case for the eponymous aid program for war-ravaged Europe, the notion of American aid was no longer far-fetched. Yet the prime minister recoiled at the thought. He lashed out at advisers like Minister of Finance C. D. Deshmukh whom, he thought, put economic assistance too high on the agenda: "Am I going to America," he asked querulously, "with a begging bowl in my hand?" The reply that aid "just happens to be one of the pending matters between two independent countries" offered little consolation. And such sensitivity was hardly out of order; American officials, expecting requests for aid, saw the "begging bowl" as perhaps the most important item in Nehru's baggage for that visit. Over the next five years, however, the prospects of superpower aid became an increasingly frequent topic of debate within India.[1]

By 1954, American Technical Assistance programs and early inklings of Soviet aid shifted the focus of official Indian conversations with the superpowers. These conversations required a new official Indian openness to aid as well as changes in superpower attitudes. Each superpower, in its own way, began on a path that led to the inauguration of aid competition in India by the mid-1950s. In the United States, technical assistance programs devoted American technical know-how (though not American capital) to address Indian economic problems. A fierce debate in 1950–1951 over emergency food aid revealed the different views of Indo-American economic relations in Washington, D.C., and also energized an "India lobby" in the United States that sought to promote a more generous policy toward India. In the Soviet Union, new ideas abounded after Joseph Stalin's death in March 1953; these underwrote a new approach to India and the decolonizing world. At the same time, small-scale improvements in Indo-Soviet relations, both diplomatic and economic, provided opportunities to put this new ideological acceptance of India's path into practice. Both superpowers, then, used Indian circumstances to advance the case for new foreign policy instruments, what would ultimately become American development assistance or Soviet economic cooperation. Within India, these new instruments provided opportunities for policy entrepreneurs to use external resources for their internal purposes, whether promoting dam projects, village reform, or steel plants. With the emergence of development aid, then, came development politics. As Nehru's exchange with his advisers suggests, economic development might solidify independence, but development aid could undermine it.

Debating Food Relief, 1950–1951

Dwindling food supplies in northern India in summer 1950 provided an occasion to reshape India's bilateral relationships with the superpowers. The Indian Planning Commission (PC), hard at work formulating the First Five-Year Plan, could promise prosperity five years hence but could do little to feed the population in the coming months. The Indian government continued to buy grain overseas, rapidly depleting the sterling balance it inherited and spending down its limited dollar reserves. The shortage of food was not just a humanitarian crisis, though it was of course that; given the centrality of shortages to the nationalist critique of British rule and the importance of basic provisioning to the legitimacy of the new state, food quickly sparked a political crisis. Indian officials, following the lead of Prime Minister Nehru, were profoundly reluctant to seek aid directly. The urgency of the food situation, however, provided a crucial opportunity to Indian officials hoping to expand aid relations to one of the superpowers.[2]

The pursuit of significant aid would, however, have to take into account India's growing role on the world stage. The creation of the People's Republic of China in fall 1949—days before Nehru's visit to Washington—quickly altered

American calculations about India. With China "lost" to communism, the logic went, India could be a vital Western counterweight in Asia. The rapidly shifting geopolitics in Asia invested Indian diplomatic initiatives with new importance. Indian diplomacy at the United Nations quickly won American favor for endorsing the U.S.-sponsored resolution to send troops to South Korea in response to the incursion from the north in June 1950. Yet Indian diplomats angered their American counterparts only days later, when they abstained from other Western initiatives in Korea. As Assistant Secretary of State George McGhee put it, "Americans like to be liked"—and treated anything less than devotion as opposition. That decision, in turn, quickly garnered the praise of Soviet officials, who seemed ready at last to conceive of India as a truly independent nation. American calculations of the place of India also changed dramatically.[3]

Jawaharlal Nehru's determination to avoid asking for aid shaped many aspects of his foreign policy, and especially his relations with the United States. Reports of shortages in India's populous and poor northeast did not reduce Nehru's reluctance to seek aid. Some of his ministers and advisers, however, wanted to use the looming crisis to sway him. Minister of Food and Agriculture K. M. Munshi came perilously close to asking directly for aid, discreetly informing Ambassador Loy Henderson that if the United States intended to provide any food aid, this would be the "psychological moment" to do so. Munshi found a kindred spirit in Deshmukh, whose long and successful career in the civil service gave him the chance to promote a vision of a modern India deeply connected to Western economies. Munshi and Deshmukh lobbied cabinet colleagues as well as American diplomats; they sought food supplies, of course, but also wanted to use the occasion to expand Indo-American economic ties more generally. After receiving positive feedback from American diplomats, Vijayalakshmi Pandit, the ambassador to Washington, submitted an official request for two million tons of food grains. B. K. Nehru, then a civil servant in the Ministry of Finance, led the negotiating team. Deshmukh optimistically called this a "turning point" in India's U.S. policy. The turning point, however, was hard-fought: when the nascent American lobby in New Delhi (Munshi and Deshmukh) presented the arrangements to Nehru, the prime minister again upbraided his interlocutors: "I had never realized that this was going to be *aid*."[4]

American officials hoping to expand their country's aid to India saw the crisis in similar terms to those of Munshi and Deshmukh: they seized on this request as a means to build U.S. support for aid to India. But it did not come easily. Midlevel bureaucrats in Washington outlined a program of "constructive and practical assistance" for countries in the region (not just India), tethering their proposal to Cold War imperatives. Such a program should focus on "arrest[ing] a process of economic deterioration" that might lead them to "defect to Communism." Increasing local food supplies, the proposal concluded, offered a means to "directly and immediately strengthen the will and patience of the people." Senior American diplomats endorsed Ambassador Pandit's request for emergency grain shipments (at below-market prices), citing a similar logic: grain would serve "broad political" as well as "humanitarian" purposes. They worried that famine "promise[d] to create conditions ideally suited to the subversive activities of the Communist Party of India." Following the logic of Food and Agriculture Minister Munshi, the American diplomats concluded that providing food would produce "psychological"—meaning political—benefits for the United States and its Indian allies. From New Delhi, Ambassador Henderson noted the stakes in Indian domestic policy, and most importantly the need to support the emerging America lobby in New Delhi; delays would "almost automatically destroy the position of [American] friends in Indian government." Secretary of State Dean Acheson noted that the food sale would come at minimal cost to the United States, which had surpluses of most of the commodities desired, and thus agreed to ship U.S. food to ensure India's "internal stability." The domestic political and geopolitical logics swayed the secretary of state and president to favor emergency food aid—but the logics did not extend to enthusiasm for any broader economic assistance; Acheson peremptorily declared that food was "the only practicable way we can be of help."[5]

Congressional critics, however, remained unconvinced by the administration's arguments. The chairman of the Senate Foreign Relations Committee noted Nehru's criticisms of the United States, which he blamed on the prime minister's dislike for "every white man." The Truman administration, therefore, was "going to have one hell of a time getting this thing [Indian food aid] through Congress or through this committee." Liberal Democrats could not overturn this self-fulfilling prophecy. Other congressional leaders complained about India's votes in the United Nations, which, they argued, disqualified it from U.S. support.[6]

Congressional recalcitrance prompted a response among American liberals enthusiastic about India, who rallied to its cause. Building on liberal networks responding to the wartime famine in Bengal, journalist Dorothy Norman enlisted a who's who of liberals to lend their names to an American Emergency Food Committee for India; the letterhead sported the name of Eleanor Roosevelt and those of the heads of organizations like the NAACP, the National Council of Churches, and the YMCA. The group worked closely with Indian diplomats, a relationship visible in the fact that Ambassador Pandit announced the committee's founding. A flurry of letters to the editor and editorials soon appeared in liberal magazines and newspapers. Congressional committees, however, did not work like editorial boards, and Norman's group found less traction on Capitol Hill.[7]

President Truman reframed the food as a "wheat loan"—no longer a grant— while doubling down on Cold War logic; a major address on the topic was titled "Indian Food Crisis: Opportunity to Combat Communist Imperialism." But many critics in Congress seemed more than willing to pass on this particular opportunity. Some argued about fiscal discipline while others railed on Indian nonalignment. A Republican minority in the House demanded a quid pro quo: American wheat for Indian atomic materials. Nehru bristled that such arrangements disregarded India's "self-respect" and impinged upon its "freedom of action." American diplomats had little room to maneuver between congressional opposition and Indian urgency. They relied more and more heavily on the logic that the wheat loan was a weapon against the USSR, with Secretary Acheson concluding that delays in sending the grain "will hurt us in India and help the Communists."[8]

This turn of events in Washington empowered Indian officials favoring Soviet and possibly even Chinese aid.[9] Ambassador Sarvepalli Radhakrishnan in Moscow, for instance, sought Soviet aid for the very same reasons as his antagonist Munshi favored American aid: not just to obtain food relief, but to expand ties with the donor. The ambassador used what one observer called a "merciless exchange of telegrams" to maneuver around Munshi's opposition.[10] The arrival of Soviet grain shipments in May 1951 garnered great fanfare. The fact that the Indian government agreed to pay for the wheat with jute, silk, tobacco, and tea did not appear in the news reports, which instead emphasized Soviet beneficence.[11]

The Soviet offer eventually spurred the U.S. Congress to action; it sent an aid bill to President Truman's desk in mid-June. Indian newspapers spent the subsequent weeks tracking the shipment of American and Soviet grain as well as smaller contributions from other countries. By the time the American food arrived, Munshi was already busy seeking more. While Munshi and Deshmukh hoped that American wheat could not just feed the hungry but also nourish closer Indo-American relations, the ultimate result was the opposite. The six-month delay in fulfilling the Indian emergency request revealed the power of conservative opponents in Congress as well as their low estimation of Indian leadership.[12]

At the same time, though, the controversy galvanized important domestic and international networks. The Emergency Food Committee united American supporters of India, creating relationships that long outlasted the emergency itself. This emergent India lobby straddled government, politics, and journalism and sought to increase American assistance to (and more broadly, enthusiasm for) India. The group that Dorothy Norman had founded soon added members; liberal activists in and out of the U.S. Congress joined the cause. One senator boasted that he wanted to make the India lobby as powerful as the better-known China lobby. And a New York representative was so committed to India that he enlisted his brother, an international lawyer, as well. The lobby extended into the State Department even before Chester Bowles became ambassador in 1951. Bowles relied on the emergency group as well as his own connections to promote the cause of India in Washington, and did so for decades.[13]

Famine relief in 1950–1951 also revealed the state of the Indian debate about foreign assistance. The America lobby in India made the case for Western aid even as events in Washington hindered their efforts. Minister of Finance Deshmukh led the charge within the cabinet, insisting that the need for aid went beyond emergency food supplies: "Finance from abroad, and that on a substantial scale, has to be forthcoming" to make the First Plan succeed; he cited in particular the "more fortunately placed countries of the West." A few officials inclined toward the USSR acted similarly, using the pursuit of food to expand ties.[14]

But even in this emergency, reluctance to accept foreign aid remained strong in the top circles of the Indian government. Such concerns appear in documents related to the First Five-Year Plan, which began in April 1951. Early drafts of the First Plan duly noted the possibility of external assistance, focusing especially on the West. They discussed foreign loans and grants through the British Colombo Plan, identifying specific projects that would benefit directly from such aid. (The United Kingdom advertised the Colombo Plan for Asian economic cooperation as British relief for former colonies though the program's resources came from the release of India's own sterling balances—that is, debts that the UK already owed to India. Ultimately, then, British aid under the Colombo Plan amounted to gift wrapping loan repayments.) While the PC expressed concern about the inflationary effects of aid, nonalignment was a more important worry; plan documents demanded that any aid arrangements "avoid" granting "undue leverage" for donors. India should seek multilateral programs or perhaps bilateral ones with "guarantees in place" to ensure that aid did not come with political strings attached.[15]

Deshmukh and his allies thus faced an uphill battle but did manage to prevail on the prime minister to sign the Indo-American Technical Cooperation Agreement with the United States in 1952. Nehru seemed more worried than pleased with the agreement; in writing to Indian state leaders about it he bemoaned the fact that aid came with "a certain involuntary dependence." The following year he told assembled Indian diplomats that "Foreign assistance, even without strings, breeds moral obligations and induces a sense of dependence." Or, as he told the chief ministers of India's states, "We are convinced that foreign aid does not strengthen a nation but rather weakens it in the long run." Nehru expressed particular qualms about American aid, telling one colleague that "we are not anxious that it should come to us"; he would accept it only to avoid provoking American feelings of "ill-will." Nehru, in short, refused to ask for aid, and would accept American aid only to avoid insulting donors. While multilateral agencies like the World Bank might avoid some of the concerns of bilateral aid programs, Nehru had few kind words for the World Bank. He considered its representatives increasingly "troublesome" negotiators who threatened to "interfere with our basic policies." He exhorted, in vain, that India should "keep away from it as far as possible."[16]

Nehru's reluctance to seek foreign did not halt the day-to-day activities of various ministries seeking to realize the vision of a modern, industrial India by looking to donors—at this stage, primarily from the West. In spite of general exhortations against relying upon foreign aid and foreign powers, many Indian officials looked to aid. Broad statements of policy, even from the undisputed leader of the government and the dominant party, garnered attention but not necessarily obedience. Yet as a slow-motion debate over aid from the West unfolded, the Soviet Union creaked toward a more open perspective on the Third World.

Rethinking the Third World in the USSR

Soviet views of India changed dramatically in the early 1950s, thanks to new ideological impulses, a shifting terrain of academic institutes, geopolitical events
(especially around the Korean War) and, above all, changes in the Politburo. A
new institute for Asian Studies focused on contemporary affairs; based in Moscow,
it incorporated the staff of the recently dissolved Pacific Ocean Institute. The
new institute also raided Eugen Varga's group at the Institute of Economics,
obtaining wholesale the entire sector on the economics of the colonial areas.
The appointment of E. M. Zhukov as one of three deputy directors of the new
Institut Vostokovedeniia symbolized its commitment to ideological orthodoxy.
The Moscow branch became the institute headquarters, downgrading the original branch in Leningrad, heir to a centuries-old legacy in Orientalism, to satellite
status. These appointments, as well as the new location, announced the new
role for academic institutes in serving politics and diplomacy.[17]

The newly reconstituted Oriental Institute confirmed these tendencies in a
November 1951 symposium about Zhukov's paper, "The Attributes of People's
Democracy in the Orient." Participants at the workshop debated the state and
the fate of revolution in Asia in light of the creation of the People's Republic
of China two years prior. What lessons should communists draw from China's
revolution? Did it provide a template for Asian revolutions, or was it sui generis?
Though the conversation centered on China, India cropped up frequently;
questions about the next Asian revolution inevitably centered upon the new
republic. In his keynote address, Zhukov argued that the victory of the Chinese Communist Party in 1949, despite its "immense significance," would not
become a model for Asia: "it would be risky to regard the Chinese revolution
as some kind of 'stereotype' for people's democratic revolutions in other Asian
countries." When one participant challenged Zhukov's argument and called
for a Chinese strategy of armed revolution in India and across Asia, another
responded by citing the "total error of applying the experience of the Chinese
revolution to Indian circumstances without consideration of India's specific
features." Zhukov agreed with the latter point: the Chinese experience "must
not be fetishized by viewing it as universally applicable to all situations." India's
particular situation, Zhukov and A. M. D'iakov (now head of the India sector
at Zhukov's institute) agreed, favored a "broad anti-imperialist . . . front" that
could harness antipathy to the West without making the final preparations

for communist revolution. In taking this perspective, the assembled scholars tended toward a strategy of accommodation to the Indian government, biding time until a revolutionary situation appeared.[18]

The scholars' tilt to the right also shaped a related debate about the *noncapitalist path,* a term with a long and controversial pedigree in Marxist thought. Karl Marx's historical determinism led to his insistence that capitalism was an essential stopover on the path toward socialism. For that reason, he applauded British rule in India in the 1850s and rooted for the spread of capitalism in Russia a few decades later. The question of the noncapitalist path reemerged at the Second Congress of the Comintern in 1920—this time specifically revolving around India. While debating Indian communist M. N. Roy at the Second Congress, Vladimir Lenin called it a "mistake to assume that the backward peoples must inevitably go through the capitalist stage of development." Communist parties could, with the aid of the proletariat from advanced countries, proceed to communism "without having to pass through the capitalist stage." Debates about the necessity of capitalism recurred through the peregrinations of the Comintern line in the 1920s and 1930s. Until his expulsion from the Comintern in 1929, Roy had insisted that revolution in the colonies (citing British India in particular) would play a crucial role in advancing global revolution. Even after his expulsion, others took up his banner: "*The slogan of 'complete State independence for India' is the most important strategic slogan not only for England, but for the whole world proletariat in its struggle to overthrow the capitalist system,*" a Comintern member wrote in prose italicized for emphasis. One lengthy exposition on the noncapitalist path noted that the mere existence of the Soviet Union, and therefore its ability to aid revolutions elsewhere, opened up new possibilities for other nations; these paths might detour through national independence, but avoid capitalism, on their way to communism. Through these doctrinal debates in the early 1930s, the noncapitalist path took on a broad meaning, tied to big questions of historical determinism.[19]

When the term *noncapitalist path* reemerged at the November 1951 conference at the Oriental Institute, its meaning and scope were very much up for debate. Some of the participants invoked the earlier sense, tied to Marxist eschatology. Others, however, offered a narrower and more concrete definition, suggesting that pursuing a noncapitalist path was merely accepting that there would be some kind of capitalist sector even as nations began the path toward socialism. The noncapitalist path, in this framework, amounted to an admission that that a plurality of economic structures could coexist in a single country at a single moment. Employing that definition, Zhukov argued that the path "was now inherent [*prisusushch*]" all across Asia. This abstract conversation about paths—Chinese, noncapitalist, and so on—revealed a newly emerging perspective on India's future while at the same time undergirding a new approach to India. It could also be more patient with governments in the former colonies that had not (yet) accepted Soviet-style socialism.[20]

Similar results came out of a *diskussiia* among economists held at the same time as the Oriental Institute's. The economists met in the offices of the Central Committee of the Soviet Communist Party, suggesting the high priority placed on their work. Their topic was a prospective textbook on political economy, a project with a tortured history dating back a dozen years or more. Among the many controversies surrounding the book was its geographic scope; the project had begun in the late 1930s, when the USSR stood as the sole communist state in a capitalist world. But by the early 1950s, it had been joined by the people's democracies of Eastern Europe as well as by the People's Republic of China. How would the existence of these new states shape Soviet economic theory? How would they alter the development of socialism on a global scale? At the November 1951 meeting, the current form of the book came under attack for its Russocentrism; the textbook draft under review failed to portray the USSR as a model for other nations and ignored the brewing "crisis of colonialism." For his part, Eugen Varga offered a series of fundamental challenges to Soviet orthodoxy, calling into question even Lenin's claims about the inevitability of war between the capitalist states. Stalin declared that the critics were right about the need for coverage of the postcolonial world, but that Varga's heterodox stance on the resilience of capitalist economies was unjustified.[21]

Varga came to heel, retracting or revising his most unorthodox claims in his book *The Fundamental Questions of the Economics and Politics of Imperialism after the Second World War* (1953). Whereas he had earlier proclaimed the significance of Indian independence in August 1947, the economist now conceded that the country remained "in economic terms . . . , as before, subject to the colonial exploitation of the English bourgeoisie." Indeed, even the English sterling debt to India, which he had earlier lauded as an omen of imperialism's demise, merely "tied" India to England and limited its autonomy. While heeding such economic orthodoxies, Varga also took a harder line on contemporary Indian politics. He sought a strategy to bring about the "final liberation of the country from the imperialists"; only then could "radical agrarian reform" and "the improvement of the situation of the working class" take place. India's Congress Party government, Varga asserted, was standing in the way of such measures; Nehru's talk of socialism was simply an effort to draw the masses into the independence struggle without revealing his party's true, "reactionary," nature.[22]

In spite of Varga's growing obeisance to Stalinist orthodoxies, he nevertheless found opportunities to promote alternatives. Even if academic economics required more and more obedience to Comrade Stalin, other venues allowed more leeway. At the International Economic Conference in Moscow in April 1952, for instance, Varga promoted trade as the best path to advance all nations' economic, not its political and revolutionary, interests. The divergence between imposed orthodoxies in economic debates and wider possibilities in diplomacy suggested that changes in Indo-Soviet relations would come first in practice—and only later in theory.[23]

Expanding Indo-Soviet Trade and Diplomatic Ties

While the dialectics of communist revolution occupied the Soviet party apparatus as well as the Communist Party of India, officials in both governments handled more mundane matters. Indian diplomats hoping to expand ties with the USSR saw an opportunity in the shipment of Soviet grain in spring 1951. No sooner was the barter deal signed than a handful of Indian diplomats fished around for an invitation for Prime Minister Nehru to visit the Soviet Union, one of many such requests that were duly cataloged but otherwise ignored by Soviet diplomats.[24]

Soviet trade officials were less reticent, inviting Indian delegations to economic conferences; they teamed up with the sympathetic statistician Prasanta Chandra Mahalanobis to recruit Indian government officials and business executives. The chief Soviet representative to the UN's Economic Commission for Asia and the Far East (ECAFE) declared his country's interest in expanded trade with ECAFE members, sending manufactured goods and agricultural equipment in exchange for raw materials; the Soviet pattern for trade with India had thus become a model for all of Asia. The Soviet trade offensive, similarly, came onto Indian territory. At the International Industries Fair in Bombay, the

Soviet ambassador, with the enthusiasm of a carnival hawker, made a blanket offer that his nation "would accept gold, soft or hard currency as payment" and was also open to barter arrangements; Western representatives rarely offered such flexibility.[25]

Indian trade officials responded in kind, sending one of the largest national delegations to the International Economic Conference in Moscow in April 1952. Mahalanobis joined the delegates interested in expanding trade and diplomatic relations with the USSR. Soviet officials reiterated their interest in expanding trade with India, anticipating the exchange of Soviet industrial goods for Indian raw materials. Though the talk of trade excited participants in both countries, the excitement had to focus on future prospects since current trade was negligible.[26]

With trade an increasingly frequent topic of bilateral discussions, diplomatic ties also began to improve—though, to be sure, from a level wavering between nonexistent and moribund. For instance, Ambassador Radhakrishnan met Stalin in April 1952—for the first time since his arrival seven months earlier—for a farewell audience. The session hardly overflowed with serious topics: Stalin gave an enthusiastic if vague endorsement of land reform by parliamentary means, while the ambassador expressed gratitude for the Soviet wheat shipments—which, he pandered to the Soviet leader, arrived in India before any American grain. This meandering and desultory conversation might serve as a synecdoche for Indo-Soviet relations writ large. The contacts remained distant even as they shed some of the unpleasantness that had plagued the first years of Indo-Soviet relations.[27]

Such sporadic contacts continued on the diplomatic front, with Soviet officials barely acknowledging the arrival of Ambassador Radhakrishnan's successor, K. P. S. Menon, in October 1952. Menon, a senior Foreign Ministry official who had risen through the ranks of the Indian Civil Service under British rule, arrived during the Soviet Party's Nineteenth Congress, an affair of pomp and circumstance that would be Stalin's last. India hardly appeared in the Congress's transcripts, though Stalin's heir apparent Georgii Malenkov went out of his way to praise India and the other nonaligned nations for their distance from British foreign policy. This vague endorsement of nonalignment was soon followed by more fulsome praise; the well-connected writer Il'ia Ehrenburg admitted that Soviets might "differ with the neutralists in our understanding of the overall tasks of the struggle for peace," but went on to emphasize that "as soon as the neutralists oppose the aggressive forces, we greet them, support them, and go with them." Soviet assessments of Indian nonalignment were rebounding; there seemed to be room, in principle, for common ground in foreign relations—even as Soviet officials continued their harsh criticisms of Indian domestic policy.[28]

That changed by the first months of 1953, as a few glimmers of changing Soviet views of Indian domestic politics appeared. After one leader of the Communist Party of India (CPI) returned from a trip for to Moscow for medical treatment, his prescriptions for India changed dramatically; CPI leadership now officially warned that "the nationality of the worker must not be allowed to destroy his internationalism as a class." Continuing the CPI's tactics of fomenting ethnoreligious tensions, in other words, would be "disastrous." None of these issues came up when Stalin met Ambassador Menon in February 1953, his final event with a foreign diplomat; the generalissimo contented himself with idle chitchat.[29]

Small steps, taken at lower levels, yielded small fruit; major initiatives got under way only after the death of Stalin in March 1953. Soviet officials pulled out all the stops for a two-month tour of the USSR by Nehru's daughter Indira Gandhi. Malenkov, a would-be successor to Stalin, offered high praise for India in August 1953 in a widely distributed speech only days before India's sixth Independence Day. While the references amounted to little more than a paragraph in a twenty-two-page address, the change in tone, coming from on high, was unmistakable. Malenkov praised the increasing traffic in cultural delegations between the two countries, acknowledged India's "peace-loving" foreign policy, and expressed his hopes for expanding trade relations with India.[30]

Indo-Soviet trade was very much on the mind of Soviet leaders that autumn, not least as they announced the arrival of a new Soviet ambassador, M. A. Men'shikov. Men'shikov came to the New Delhi after a long career in the Soviet foreign-trade apparatus; he organized the recent Moscow International Economic Conference and had earlier served as minister for foreign trade. He was, furthermore, fluent in English, a relatively rarity in the postpurge Soviet diplomatic corps. By his own report Men'shikov got right down to business, taking control of negotiations over an Indo-Soviet trade agreement that had already been languishing at the lower levels of respective bureaucracies for over a year. Within two months of his arrival, the ambassador proudly signed the agreement.[31]

The Indo-Soviet Trade Agreement of December 1953 revealed both Soviet and Indian intentions. From the Indian side, it indicated a determination to expand relations with both superpowers without choosing sides. Indian officials enthusiastic about the USSR flexed their muscles by having the Indo-Soviet agreement signed while American vice president Richard Nixon was on a brief visit to New Delhi. From the Soviet side, too, the agreement was revealing; it sought to expand trade with India, to be sure. But the list of goods to be exchanged established an economic relationship that differed little from India's trade relations with England. The USSR would export industrial and technologically sophisticated goods to India, and would import in return agricultural commodities and raw materials. These goods, furthermore, constituted a miniscule share of each nation's trade, less than one quarter of 1 percent in each case. Yet hope sprang eternal; Soviet officials enthusiastically called for trade to be expanded rapidly in the wake of the agreement.[32]

U.S. Technical Assistance

As Soviet officials moved haltingly toward expanded trade relations, American attention to the Indian economy also increased, especially in the sphere of technical assistance. The impetus for strengthening a new diplomatic instrument emerged out of the confluence of broad humanitarianism and narrow national interest. The "loss" of China and the Korean War drew American attentions to Asia, and especially to strengthening the nonaligned nations before they "went communist."

Some new American engagements with India took place through the formal technical assistance program, while others emerged from networks of foundation officers and individual entrepreneurs. Though technically nongovernmental, these networks operated in close concert with American and / or Indian officialdom. Their efforts benefited from the new ambassador to India appointed in 1951: Chester Bowles, a liberal Democrat who became the highest-ranking and most energetic member of the India lobby. He was joined in New Delhi by a young and ambitious agricultural sociologist, Douglas Ensminger, who led the Ford Foundation's India office. The efforts of Bowles and Ensminger, as well as other diplomats and experts, demonstrated the promises as well as the problems of technical assistance. Since Point Four, such aid had proven its potential in public relations; its economic and political effects had yet to be measured.

The first projects of the U.S. Technical Cooperation Administration (TCA) in India varied greatly; many were scattered and small-scale, a far cry from Bowles's ambitious aims. Yet even these efforts worried Nehru; in spring 1954, he issued a steady stream of complaints about the behavior of "so-called experts" from the United States, prompting him to call for a "cautious" approach to American aid—to the point of "trying to do without."[33] At that point, roughly one hundred American experts were engaged in official technical assistance efforts in India.[34]

Technical assistance projects typically emerged out of a common assumption: that American expertise could unlock India's latent economic potential without significant public investment. Some projects, like the Damodar River valley project, constantly invoked the American example but received only small grants and loans from official American sources. Others, like the Community Development Program, operated at the village level but aspired to national transformation. While Bowles considered community development (CD) the signal achievement of his 1950s stint in Delhi, its rhetorical profile massively overshadowed the modest financial investments. Indeed, this was the point; technical assistance was predicated on the notion that India need organization and expertise, not capital. Eventually the challenges these projects faced suggested the importance of resources to the question of development—a conclusion resisted by fiscal conservatives but eventually acknowledged by the administration of President Dwight D. Eisenhower.

Within India these particular projects found wide support, in large part because they could serve multiple purposes. Those impresarios who promoted initiatives like the Community Development Program and the Damodar Valley Corporation (DVC) were often inclined to Western economic ideas, but even those with other inclinations found things to appreciate. CD, for instance, was not just a political strategy, but also promised rapid increases in agricultural production at relatively low cost—thus winning over officials in the PC who wanted to stint agricultural investments in favor of heavy industry. Similarly, the aspirations of the DVC—a multipurpose river valley development corporation—had something for everyone; the large dam projects promised irrigation water for agriculture and hydroelectric power for industry, not to mention flood control for all.

Damming Damodar

One version of the technical assistance mythology emphasized the reproduction of American institutions in India. Thus the Damodar Valley Corporation, under discussion for decades, earned the moniker "Indian TVA" for applying the experience of the Tennessee Valley Authority to an (ostensibly) similar complex of problems in northeastern India. David Lilienthal, who left his post as chairman of the TVA, promoted multipurpose river valley development as a cure-all for social, economic, and political problems. Indian enthusiasts like economist Sudhir Sen happily celebrated this connection. "Unimpressed" by Gandhi's economics, he endorsed a vision of modern industrial India, and saw the DVC as a means to achieve this while also expanding ties to the West, where he had studied economics with Joseph Schumpeter. Claiming inspiration from the TVA helped Sen advance his economic vision and political agenda. Physicist Meghnad Saha shared a similar vision of a modern industrial India, but was more inclined to state-centered economics, so he celebrated the prospects of DVC even as he complained that Sen's narrative ignored the pioneering role of Soviet dam projects like Dnieprostroi. As an indication that the politics of the dam project were still in play, Saha, Sen and other DVC staff made pilgrimages to the TVA headquarters in Knoxville, Tennessee, as well as to the USSR. The notion of building a system of dams in the Damodar River valley predated these pilgrimages; British engineers had long identified the region as ripe for building dams for irrigation and flood control. Early government films promoting the DVC, like *River of Hope* (1953), stressed this element of taming a dangerous river.[35]

The devastating Bengal floods of 1943, and the major food shortages left in their wake, provided further impetus for a Damodar River project. An official committee of enquiry into the famine suggested the construction of dams to prevent future flooding of the river; the committee furthermore proposed that hydroelectric stations could finance the flood-control schemes. The British viceroy in New Delhi followed up on this report by inviting a TVA engineer, William Voorduin, to undertake "sustained" planning of river valley development in Bengal. Unsurprisingly, Voorduin called for the creation of a Damodar Valley Authority that could become a "watershed for India" much like the TVA had been for the United States. A technical mission stocked with TVA veterans soon followed up on Voorduin's initial efforts.[36]

Those concerned with politics did not share the technical experts' enthusiasm for the Damodar valley project. In fact, some turned to a large integrated plan only because piecemeal efforts (which had an especially disproportionate division of costs and benefits) had failed to win the approval of the relevant state governments. One American intelligence officer publicly doubted that the project could work because it would raise fraught questions about sharing power in a federal system. Under the Government of India Act (1935), irrigation remained a responsibility of Indian states, not the New Delhi government. Since the Damodar crossed state boundaries (between Bihar and Bengal), creating a "DVA" would be an imposing if not an impossible political task. Early British efforts confirmed these concerns; an initial agreement brokered by the viceroy fell apart after only a month.[37]

Proponents like Saha and Sen believed that river valley development, whether in Appalachia or Bengal, could be a nonpolitical, expert-led affair despite abundant evidence to the contrary. Perhaps not surprisingly, Saha invoked not just American but also Soviet examples, projecting onto Roosevelt as well as Stalin his idealized vision of "perfectly apolitical but determined backers of pure, rationalized, utilitarian development." Both Sen and Saha maintained their faith in apolitical science even as they reckoned with the political forces at work.[38]

Sen was slated to start working on the DVC in summer 1946 when he was unexpectedly dispatched on expeditions to both the Dnieprostroi and TVA projects. While in the United States, Sen enlisted former TVA chief Arthur Morgan to pitch the idea of U.S. support for the DVC to the State Department; such clever efforts to seek American allies did not pay off, as U.S. officials evinced polite skepticism. Sen then became secretary to the Damodar valley project, responsible for everything except constructing the facilities themselves. He lobbied Nehru directly and organized a campaign of American supporters to do the same. He continued to call on Morgan for help navigating the internal politics of the DVC. Sen, therefore, made effective use of American TVA experts to promote his own vision for the Damodar project.[39]

In spite of his declarations that the DVC was nonpolitical, Sen needed all the help he could get to navigate domestic political battles. He found himself shuttling between New Delhi, Calcutta, and Patna, trying to implement Voorduin's plan and explaining the benefits that would accrue to each state. Much as British administrators had predicted, Bihar officials worried that they would receive little benefit from the Damodar project even as they paid a high portion of the total bill. Sen's difficulties led to feuds with his boss, the DVC's chairman; what the latter saw as the everyday give-and-take of political compromise Sen took as an affront to technocracy. Sen's perspective resonated with the editors of the glossy *Indian Journal of Power and River Valley Development,* which applauded him for bringing the engineer's tool kit, rather than the politician's corrupting interest, to the DVC. Sen used the pages of the journal to insist that the DVC allowed "no politics," slamming the Bihar government for intransigence—which was solely due, in his assessment, to its lack of an "objective approach" and a failure to engage in "factual analysis." Sen's belief in scientific objectivity, in other words, became a tool for domestic politics. Even the routine appointment of a chief engineer dragged on for months as it became embroiled in the politics of American expertise.[40]

Sen approached the World Bank for funding of the whole project. The bank offered only a much smaller commitment, agreeing to cover the foreign-exchange costs of a thermal / hydroelectric plant at Bokaro in Bihar. (The thermal plant was essential to provide a year-round electrical supply; the hydroelectric stations would generate power seasonally.) U.S. aid organs provided $632,000 to cover the costs of DVC engineering services hired in the United States. The negotiations revealed an advantage of supporting a multipurpose project: each side could find (and fund) its own benefits: Indian engineers had their eyes on building infrastructure for industry, while American aid officials—along with Lilienthal—emphasized the gains to agriculture. The World Bank, willing to countenance loans for publicly owned utilities, drew attention to the possibility of providing power to rapidly growing Calcutta. Though receiving grants from American technical assistance agencies and inspired by the Tennessee Valley Authority—too much so, World Bank economists worried—the DVC project was only tangentially an American one. It incorporated equipment from Britain, Germany, and even the Soviet Union, as well as from the United States. What was more, the first major industrial beneficiary of the power supply was a British-sponsored steel plant at Durgapur.[41]

The project reflected American visions for Indian development. The DVC sought to leverage American technical superiority to solve Indian problems without major expenditures of (American) funds. It emerged out of a transnational network, with Indian members drawing heavily on the authority of prominent Americans to promote their own visions for India's future economic development. The multiple purposes of the project, finally, offered all sides a chance to take what they wanted from the effort.

Within India, however, the projects were more controversial, though not so much along Cold War lines—witness the support from both Meghnad Saha and Sudhir Sen—as along regional axes. Indian supporters could focus on the DVC as a barometer of (indeed a spur for) Indian modernity and celebrated the industrial and power-generating aspects of the DVC. Yet Bihar state government officials complicated the project's construction because they saw the project as profiting nearby West Bengal at their state's expense. And similarly there were wide disparities between urban populations (who benefited from the power generation, among other things) and rural populations whose lives were disrupted through relocation or changing water patterns—a tendency that shapes dam projects in India to this day. Development politics, in other words, could intensify regional as well as political conflicts.[42]

Developing Communities

If the DVC claimed inspiration from the values of riverine America, another high-profile U.S.-supported enterprise—the Community Development Program—claimed its origins in the values of American rural democracy. But that program, even more than the DVC, demonstrated the limits of technical assistance as a form of aid. It also illustrated the efforts of the nascent Indian lobby. Ambassador Chester Bowles took up the cause of community development upon his arrival in New Delhi in autumn 1951, just as the famine crisis began to recede. The India lobby had its first taste of power, and Bowles was determined not to waste it.

Within weeks of his arrival in India, Bowles latched onto community development as the key to India's transformation. According to its boosters, CD would build democracy one village at a time. Trained extension experts would work with villagers to empower them politically while offering basic technical assistance. CD would "awaken the villagers' desire for improvement," thus "helping the villagers to help themselves." Or, in the words of a United Nations primer, village workers would start by trying to meet the "felt needs" of rural dwellers, but would ultimately expand their work to "identify needs not yet perceived and make the people conscious of them." The program emerged out of a small but dedicated transnational network of rural sociologists who insisted upon the importance of social transformation both as an end in itself and as a means to increased production.[43]

Community development grew out of an international network, but also built on generations of Indian reformers promoting rural reform. Its postwar history began with an American urban planner's experiment in Etawah District, then overflowing with refugees from the Partition of India. Enthusiasts looked to Etawah for answers to their own concerns. Rural sociologists appreciated the chance to apply their expertise to development; one called community development "one of the great social inventions of this era." Gandhians who saw villages as the antidotes to the ills of modern life were similarly enthralled—as was Prime Minister Nehru. Newspapers in and beyond the United States offered high praise; Eleanor Roosevelt celebrated the program in her *Ladies Home Journal* column and elsewhere.[44]

Bowles lauded the political as well as the productive possibilities of the Etawah experiment. On Thanksgiving Day 1951, he pitched his idea for a national Community Development Authority to Prime Minister Nehru; such a body, the ambassador argued, could deploy "modern scientific knowledge" to solve Indian poverty. The ambassador hoped to devote a large portion of the $54 million U.S. technical assistance budget for India to this "village campaign." Douglas Ensminger at the Ford Foundation's New Delhi office also shared these enthusiasms; he promised additional funds from his foundation's substantial coffers.[45] With Bowles and Ensminger at the forefront, the international CD network used U.S. government and Ford funds to provide Indian proponents with both moral and financial support. In these efforts, the Ford Foundation was a full partner with the government of India and a close coworker with the American embassy and aid mission. Technically nongovernmental, the foundation and its representatives were deeply enmeshed in intergovernmental affairs.

Community development was hardly an American imposition. S. K. Dey, a U.S.-trained engineer and veteran of General Electric, led the cheerleading on the Indian side. Dey had long been critical of Indian agricultural policy for focusing too narrowly on production and failing to consider the "psychological elements of the whole village community." Nehru appointed Dey as chief of the Community Projects Administration, which opened for business on the anniversary of Mahatma Gandhi's birth in October 1952. Nehru extolled community development at the inaugural, calling it "this sacred work" of bringing about a "revolution of cooperation." The project opened with an ambitious program serving 16.7 million people in 27,000 villages—but aimed to increase to 88.8 million people in 157,000 villages by 1956. Competitors in the Ministry of Food and Agriculture, who sought to redirect CD to focus on production, made an unsuccessful bid to take over the Community Projects Administration, which by 1956 became its own cabinet ministry.[46]

Bowles celebrated the social improvement aspects of Community Development, but remained attuned also to production; his initial attraction to Etawah, after all, had as much to do with increased productivity as with democratic participation. The inaugural announcement of the Indo-American Technical Cooperation Fund highlighted CD and promised it would deliver "more food for India's people." A senior U.S. aid official agreed, calculating that every dollar invested would yield ten dollars in additional crops. Ford Foundation support for CD was likewise premised on the expectation that such programs would "increase food production." The goal of expanding production on the cheap clearly weighed heavily on the American technical expert who tried to cut costs by soliciting voluntary donations of labor and materials from villagers. The same impulse for production drove Indian enthusiasm. S. K. Dey's rhapsodies about improving rural life and "building a people's movement" went alongside his claims that these were ways to increase agricultural output. And one senior Indian agriculture official appreciated CD's "integrated effort" because he believed that it could "double or even triple" yields.[47]

Top American officials often cast CD as a tool for fighting communism—for instance, responding to one of Bowles's lengthy and breathless missives about CD's democratic potential with approval of its ability to build anticommunist communities. Bowles wrote excitedly that Indian communists "feared the community projects concept far more than any tools in the hands of the Government." Americans in particular saw CD's promise of "democratic development" as a way to draw a sharp and positive contrast with Soviet or Chinese models of collective farms.[48]

Community development, in sum, exemplified American technical assistance in action. It sought to effect change not through an infusion of capital, but through the presence of a handful of Western experts. These experts trained Indian students in the knowledge and techniques they needed to become village-level workers. For all the celebration of CD in the glossy black-and-white brochures produced by the Ford Foundation, or in the dittoed handouts of the U.S. Technical Cooperation Mission, resource commitments were limited.

Ambassador Chester Bowles, sleeves duly rolled up, helping Indian villagers with their tasks during one of his many excursions through the Indian countryside. *Source:* Chester Bowles Papers, box 373A, Sterling Memorial Library, Yale University Library.

In its early years, U.S. assistance for community development averaged less than $4 million per year, about six cents per villager per year, and a mere 7.5 percent of the technical assistance budget for India. Only thirteen of the Technical Cooperation Administration's one hundred experts focused on CD. For its part, the Ford Foundation never devoted more than one-third of its support in India to rural programs. The same was true on the Indian side; the First Five-Year

Plan allocated less than one-sixth of its expenditures to the rural sector, which included a wide range of programs beyond Community Development. State Department analysts argued that community development provided more production (and political) bang for the rural development buck. These low commitments emerged from the diagnosis, aptly summarized by S. K. Dey, that India's agricultural problems were "much less financial or technical" than organizational.[49]

Community development, then, offered many things to its sponsors—an authentic celebration of rural life, a means of democratic development, a spur to agricultural production, and an inoculation against communism in the villages—at a low cost. The program furthermore reflected the stereotypes of rural dwellers held by wide swaths of American and Indian urban elites. For Americans as well as those Indians employed in the new state, CD fit neatly in what one political scientist called "infantile citizenship," which insisted upon the "need for state tutelage and protection in order to realize the potentials of citizenship." Or in the sharp phrase of historian Nick Cullather, villagers were "the target" of CD operations.[50]

Community development serves as a paradigm of American aid in India in the 1950s but not necessarily for the reasons that its proponents suggested. Bowles, Dey, Ensminger, and other enthusiasts celebrated CD for promoting democracy and social transformation. Yet the American aid paradigm operated at a high ratio of rhetoric to resources: small sums of money and the efforts of a handful of American technical advisers were expected to yield extraordinary results in both production and social change. Americans favoring community development found plenty of sympathy among Indian government officials, up to and including Prime Minister Nehru; the program was hardly foisted upon an unwilling Government of India. Dey and his colleagues in India made excellent use of American public and private resources to advance their vision of rural transformation.

Looking Beyond Technical Assistance

The indefatigable Bowles did not rest his case on community development, though; he used it to lobby for new and different forms of aid, including direct grants. While he celebrated the DVC and especially community development, he also worked to expand the concept and practice of aid to cover larger infusions of funds. Running up against the small scale and limited repertoire of technical assistance, Bowles wanted to incorporate a broader and more ambitious vision for development aid. Such lobbying, however, did not sway his correspondents in Washington; TCA headquarters sharply corrected the ambassador's requests, asking him to revise such expanded proposals to "make sure *technical cooperation* [was] the core" of the requests. Other executive branch officials, even those who endorsed Bowles's efforts to expand beyond technical assistance, reminded the energetic ambassador that a commodity grant "simply does not fit within the structure of the present TCA plans." Bowles persisted, renaming the commodity grants "balance of payments support" that could free up foreign currency currently devoted to food imports. Bowles worked his Washington contacts to try to convince his friends in Congress to support this "crucially important" commodity grant, citing what it could allow India to buy from the United States: "fertilizer, DDT, Tube Wells, [and] bulldozers"—not to mention more American community development experts. The Bureau of the Budget used Bowles's requests to test Congress; top budget officials suggested including a token grant beyond technical assistance to see how it would fare on the Hill.[51]

Congressional opposition quickly shot down this trial balloon, showing how difficult a task Bowles and the India lobby faced in expanding the scale, let alone the scope, of aid. A handful of liberal Democrats aside, the notion of economic aid beyond technical assistance was beyond the pale. One southern congressman considered it a threat to the republic: "If this thing is not brought to a halt, there is no telling how many billions of dollars do-gooders and world spenders are going to take from the pockets of American taxpayers." With attitudes like that, it was no surprise that the State Department's request for aid to India was slashed to $45 million, or 18 percent of Bowles's original $250 million request. Deeply dissatisfied with this process, Bowles then tried to convince the State Department to pursue separate aid legislation solely for India, quickly winning the ire of Secretary of State Acheson. In the end, Bowles's significant efforts yielded an aid budget 11 percent smaller than the one he inherited—leading Bowles, counterintuitively, to ask for even more aid. In the meantime, the American technical assistance portfolio in India relied more on rhetorical than on financial resources.[52]

While President Truman struck humanitarian chords in making the case for Point Four, by the early 1950s the logic of anticommunism quickly came to dominate domestic justifications for American aid in Congress. A CIA report completed on the eve of Bowles's departure for India, for instance, situated aid in Cold War geopolitics. It worried that India had exhibited a "tendency to appease World Communism" and—in any case—was in such poor economic shape that Indian communists might soon be able to "seize control of the government." The report thus favored development aid as an anticommunist tool. "External economic assistance," the report concluded, "appears the only possible means of checking an economic decline which would otherwise create greater difficulties for the West." Bowles struck similar chords in his steady stream of letters to President Truman. Yet Bowles faced a Congress that had placed severe restrictions on the forms and amounts of aid. Moving beyond technical assistance, it turned out, required more than the breathless twenty-page missives that Bowles sent into the maw of the State Department's massive files.[53]

The final days of the Truman administration in January 1953 set in motion a tension that defined Indo-American relations for decades. On the one hand, lame duck secretary of state Dean Acheson endorsed Bowles's efforts to increase dramatically the economic assistance program for India. He specifically endorsed major infusions of capital to complement technical assistance. The secretary also showed how much he had internalized Bowles's claims that economic development was a security issue: "technical and developmental aid," Acheson exhorted, would be an important step to "avert India's being lost to the free world." Bowles's arguments about India were slowly turning the ship of state toward economic assistance.[54]

That same month, however, also saw the crystallization of a competing policy that would loom just as large, if not larger, in Indo-American relations: the American military commitments to India's rival Pakistan. Vice President Richard Nixon, who favored Pakistan over India because its leaders had "fewer complexes" than India's, pushed the case for strengthening ties to Pakistan. A week before he left office, Acheson was accosted by the Indian ambassador in Washington, who threatened that recent efforts toward recent improvements in the bilateral relationship "would be, to a large measure, destroyed" by American military aid to and alliance with Pakistan. Acheson's mealymouthed reply did little to allay Indian concerns. These two issues—economic aid for India and military aid for Pakistan—still vex Indo-American relations well into the twenty-first century.[55]

The major shift in Pakistan-American relations in 1954 reverberated through Indian politics for decades. The Eisenhower administration approached the

Third World in the early 1950s like the game of Risk, trying to build military alliances that surrounded the USSR and could thus contain it. Officials in Pakistan proved susceptible to the blandishments of an alliance with the United States. Though outside most maps of the Middle East and Southeast Asia, Pakistan joined military alliances in both regions; it soon enough opened an air base for U.S. intelligence. Its reward came in the form of a large package of military aid, followed by significant economic aid.

Disparate Indian politicians, from Nehru on down, lashed out against not just the two parties but also against aid more generally. At a speech before Indian business leaders, the prime minister insisted that India would "not need to go about on crutches supplied by others. He soon expressed to the American ambassador his qualms about the "moral problem" of accepting aid from the United States at the same time it was also providing military aid to Pakistan. Aid might be attractive in principle, but American aid, to say the least, had little appeal.[56]

Nor did Soviet aid—under the banner of "economic cooperation"—necessarily provide the answer. Even as the Indian ambassador to Moscow, for instance, sought to expand economic relations, he rejected "any kind of assistance which would place us in the debt of the Soviet Government." To take this caveat literally would rule out concessional financing, and to take it figuratively would likely exclude any grants. As Finance Minister Deshmukh aptly concluded, foreign aid "on an extensive scale" would not be "likely" in the near future. Indian economic policy was not oriented internationally, whether in terms of aid, direct investment, or trade. *Swadeshi* (self-sufficiency) would be not just an ultimate aim of Indian policy, but also a means toward that end—at least as the most influential Indian politicians imagined the situation in the early 1950s.[57]

The inauguration of Republican Dwight D. Eisenhower in early 1953 did not augur well for Bowles and others trying to expand American aid; the new president campaigned on an economic agenda of free trade and budget cutting. Yet early in his term Eisenhower hinted at the need to take action against "the brute forces of poverty and need" in the Third World. Secretary of State John Foster Dulles, whose black-and-white worldview hardly endeared him to Indian nonalignment, also indicated that India in particular would be a prime case to start a broader aid program. But he preempted any large-scale aid effort by indicating that the United States would not magically become "Father Bountiful"—not that this was a major risk.[58]

These tentative Republican efforts, however, met with continued opposition in Congress and around Washington. A commission to study foreign economic policy, headed by steel executive Clarence Randall, for instance, insisted that foreign assistance "should not become a 'big money' program and should not involve capital investment." Arguing that aid would distort the global economy, Randall called for the rejection of "economic aid other than that devoted to the immediate considerations of security," carving out only a small exception for "technical assistance" narrowly defined. The answer to America's—and the world's—urgent needs, he insisted, was trade liberalization.[59]

The State Department opposed the Randall Commission, arguing that official American aid should move beyond its cramped constraints. One route here was to expand "security considerations" beyond the Randall Commission's stricture of "immediate" military concerns. A stronger case, or at least a more enthusiastic one, came from aid agitator in chief C. D. Jackson, a Time-Life executive seconded to the White House. Blithely ignoring both legislative wariness about economic aid and the bureaucratic challenges posed by the Randall Commission, Jackson entered the fray with typical abandon in late March 1954, when he "uncorked"—his word—a "World Economic Policy" in a luncheon with Secretary of State Dulles. Billing the program as a "peaceful weapon in the Cold War," Jackson proposed spending $10 billion over five years on economic development. But this was too much, too late; Eisenhower's address to Congress on foreign economic policy a few days later resolutely endorsed technical assistance—and specifically proscribed "capital for investment" and aid to countries not directly tied to American security interests.[60]

Skirting normal channels for making policy, Jackson gathered a group of like-minded aid enthusiasts at Princeton University to storm the barricades of executive wariness and legislative antipathy. He was, of course, preaching to the converted; figures like MIT economists Max Millikan and Walt Rostow, both proud alumni of U.S. government service, already supported economic aid programs and had long been attracted to the problems of Indian development. Jackson's enthusiasms, however, did little to sway his many opponents. In the agencies charged with actually administering aid, skepticism shaded into cynicism: one senior aid official bluntly rejected direct U.S. loans to India, whose officials were "hoping that the United States will be 'sucker' enough" to underwrite large loans. "The Lord protect us," he incanted in conclusion, "from soft and fuzzy loans."[61]

The pro-aid contingents and the India lobby, even taken together, could not overcome opposition, though they kept up their efforts. Rosy-eyed optimists like Millikan and Rostow circulated a detailed report calling for economic aid as a major tool in foreign policy. Jackson used the report to press for a "partnership for economic growth" that would focus primarily on Asia; he emphasized his program's "special hooker" for nonaligned nations in Asia, citing India in particular. Jackson was joined by a liberal Republican then serving as the first (and only) director of the Foreign Operations Administration. Long attentive to Asia in general, and to India in particular, he sought to establish an Asian Development Fund that would provide capital, not just technical assistance, to "uncommitted" nations of Asia. Yet President Eisenhower would have none of it. While acknowledging the potential benefits of expanding beyond technical assistance, he admitted that "trying to sell it to Congress scares me." Secretary Dulles told Jackson that he stood behind him—though he must have stood very far behind, given the difficulties of "fighting [it] out" with those who opposed the program. Dulles's staff echoed these concerns, vaguely endorsing the overall aims of the program while despairing of the possibility of enacting it.[62]

The aid director took a page from Jackson's playbook, publicly announcing the U.S. intention to create a $1 billion Asian Development Fund. His proposal provoked fierce attacks from aid opponents and tongue-lashings from Eisenhower and Dulles for going rogue. Eisenhower tried to defuse the controversy by appointing a group of senior officials to study external aid. Opponents of large-scale aid quickly a vocal skeptic of aid into the chair of the study group. Even proponents of technical assistance like Clarence Randall argued that any development aid should be limited to " 'know-how' and not capital." Efforts to contain the pressure for development aid thus came from highly placed officials.[63]

Jackson, more comfortable writing columns than sitting on committees, mounted a publicity campaign. Rostow similarly pressed the case to his friends, using India as his leading example in arguments about the need for economic development in Asia. India needed not just "industrial advice and technical assistance," Rostow wrote, but also "additional capital." Glossy articles and sermons to the converted, however, did little to slow the mechanisms seeking to limit aid. When the working group chaired by Undersecretary of State Herbert Hoover Jr. finished its work in spring 1955, it proposed a capitalization of $205 million—one-fifth of the initial request and one-fiftieth of Jackson's earlier proposal.[64]

India lobbyists (like Bowles), even when joined with those pressing for a more generous aid program (like C. D. Jackson), did not win early battles. Bowles saw India's aid budget decline in his first year in New Delhi; it rebounded only in 1954, after Bowles's departure. Perhaps the only cause for optimism about aid was that the once-sharp budget-cutting knives of Congress seemed to be growing dull with use. But economic aid levels amounted to rounding errors in the rapidly expanding "mutual security" budget for military aid. State Department proposals for aid to India hovered around $100 million in the mid-1950s, the same period during which military commitments to Indochina jumped annually in increments of $400 million.[65]

By early 1955, the American position toward foreign aid in general, and toward aid for India in particular, was deeply divided. This split represented, in itself, a substantial change; only six years earlier, American officials did not seriously contemplate any form of direct economic assistance. Indeed, even full-throated endorsements for modest efforts at technical assistance like CD and the DVC came few and far between. The case of India had played an important role in this shift of American policies to encompass what came to be called development aid.

Toward Soviet Aid

While Indian enthusiasts for community development and the TVA sought out technical assistance from the United States, others sought out closer economic ties with the Soviet Union. The year after Stalin's death, 1954, would prove crucial to many of these efforts, as Indian government officials, scholars, and policy freelancers experimented with a variety of different approaches to different Soviet organizations. Most energetic and effective was physicist-turned-statistician Prasanta Chandra Mahalanobis, the founding director of the Indian Statistical Institute (ISI) in Calcutta. Mahalanobis sought the assistance of Soviet experts as he set up an ISI unit devoted to Indian planning, and beyond that sought Soviet computing technology, export of which was banned beyond the reliable people's republics of Eastern Europe. Mahalanobis was an especially persistent presence in Moscow; his contacts at the Academy of Sciences generated well over three hundred pages of correspondence to, from, or about him in the 1950s.[66]

Mahalanobis did not stand alone. One Indian winner of the Stalin Peace Prize proposed (without success) a broad spectrum of technical aid efforts.

Indian embassy officials in Moscow also bruited a handful of projects—a tractor factory, for instance—that they hoped might attract Soviet assistance. Here
low-level Indian and Soviet diplomats found common cause, as when a Soviet
Foreign Ministry desk officer told a junior Indian diplomat in Moscow that the
USSR had helped build a steel plant in China—and there was "no reason why
a similar plant could not be put up in India." Such aid, he continued, could be
channeled through the United Nations, or could be part of a bilateral agreement. But such low-level and low-key discussions were inconclusive—at least
at first.[67]

Soviet officials responded positively to these overtures, and made some proposals for closer Indo-Soviet ties of their own. At a meeting of ECAFE in February
1954, for instance, Ambassador Men'shikov announced his nation's intention
to provide technical assistance to ECAFE countries through the Special United
Nations Fund for Economic Development. He also invited delegations from
among the ECAFE members on all-expense-paid tours of the USSR. Men'shikov
had not by any stretch abandoned his hopes for Indo-Soviet trade, but expanded
his repertoire to include discussions of technical aid. He strategized with
Radhakrishnan, the former Moscow ambassador then serving as Indian vice
president, about how to dislodge requests for Soviet technical assistance that
seemed to be stuck on the desks of unsympathetic Indian bureaucrats. Indian
politicians, even those in high places, worked with and through Soviet diplomats to promote closer economic ties to the USSR. Various forms of economic
cooperation moved forward in 1954, promoted within government circles by
Ambassador Men'shikov. He circulated a twenty-step program to strengthen
Indo-Soviet ties, with items ranging from diplomatic initiatives to cultural delegations but focused especially on trade and technical assistance. Men'shikov's
program won approval from top apparatchiks.[68]

These advances also gained support in the highest reaches of Indian government and from business leaders. Two groups took up Men'shikov's invitation
and dispatched delegations to the Soviet Union. Nehru was especially optimistic, as he contrasted American and British firms' obsessions with secrecy with
the relative openness of Soviet aid. The Soviets expected the Indian visitors to
be wowed by industrial prowess, but quickly found themselves disappointed.
Members of an Indian business delegation enjoyed their travels but were distinctly unimpressed by Soviet factories and the goods they produced. They
noted in particular problems of reliability and quality, and concluded that the

future of Indian industry—at least in the private sector—did not point toward the Soviet Union. The early 1950s, in sum, saw both superpowers ready to calculate the potential political dividends of larger aid / cooperation projects—but not yet ready to realize that potential.[69]

The Domestic Politics of Steel

While neither superpower had fully committed to economic assistance for Third World countries, discussions in India soon raised the prospects of such aid—and did so in concrete and specific terms that paved the way for future programs. Indian officials' pursuit of foreign financing and technology for a steel mill thus helped precipitate aid competition in the early 1950s. Even as the notion of a steel mill won wide support in Indian policy circles, factions within the Indian government pursued external resources in the hopes of pursuing their own vision of that mill in terms of ownership (public versus private) and location. As the Indian pursuit of an expanded steel industry became the first site for Cold War economic competition, therefore, it also became an ideal site for observing development politics in action.

Interest in steel was hardly new to the 1950s, and was reflected, among other places, in the National Planning Committee deliberations in the late 1930s and early 1940s. True to its divide-not-debate strategy, this Congress committee had created a Subcommittee on Mining and Metallurgy that wholeheartedly endorsed "basic industries" like steel as essential to "all-round economic development." A few years later, an official body with the bland title of the Iron and Steel (Major) Panel agreed: "For a rapid industrialization of India, no industry at present is comparable in importance with iron and steel. . . . If private capital shows any unnecessary shyness in coming forward promptly, Government should not hesitate to undertake the task." The panel evaluated a number of potential plant sites, primarily in central India. Bhilai in Madhya Pradesh, with its proximity to large veins of iron ore, was one of the leading contenders in spite of its great distance from major population centers. In the unkind words of one journalist, the town of Bhilai had been "little more than scrub, duck ponds, and paddy fields with few links to the outside world besides the occasional visit from a revenue collector or health inspector"—hardly an auspicious launching pad for the dreams of industrial India. American and British industrial consultants came to India and continued the momentum for going big in steel. The

Industrial Policy Resolution of 1948 enshrined the notion that the expansion of basic industries should take place in the public sector. It did not contemplate the dispossession (or, really, even the disposition) of India's two private steel firms; it simply declared expansion in metallurgy a monopoly of the public sector.[70]

The discussions of the late 1940s determined where the steel mill would go, but not where it would come from. Having excluded from any expansion plans the privately owned plants in Jamshedpur and Burnpur, officials began looking for technology and capital from abroad. The cabinet authorized a steel mission to the United States in late 1952 that included senior civil servants oriented toward the West—most notably S. Bhoothalingam from the Ministry of Commerce and Industry. Its members spent four weeks in the United States, meeting with executives of American steel firms in Pittsburgh as well as with U.S.-based representatives of Japanese firms; they also met with U.S. government officials and with World Bank executives in Washington.[71]

Domestic disputes quickly engulfed the steel mission. T. T. Krishnamachari (popularly known as TTK), then minister of commerce and industry, demanded that the steel mission be under his authority, beating back an effort from Minister of Finance Deshmukh to take control of the expansion of steel production. The issue revolved in no small measure around bureaucratic turf, but also reflected a debate about how to conceive of development loans: were they primarily related to the terms of the loan agreement (i.e., a Ministry of Finance topic), or were they part of the larger strategy of industrialization (and therefore within the ambit of the Ministry of Commerce and Industry)? TTK made the latter claim, calling the question of finances "merely secondary" to the question of where, when, and how to build the steel plant—questions, of course, best handled by his own ministry. TTK then launched a preemptive attack on the PC and reiterated his position that the planners should not be involved in administration; he considered the issue sufficiently important that he submitted a letter of resignation to Prime Minister Nehru over the role of the PC. Nehru tried to allay TTK's concerns by agreeing that "the Planning Commission is only an advisory body"—while at the same time calling on the ministries to take advantage of the commission's advice. Ultimately, Nehru refused to accept the resignation, so TTK kept up his assault on the Planning Commission, echoing earlier complaints that it had become a "super-cabinet" and that it became a new resource for firms seeking to evade the decisions of his ministry. These skirmishes continued to shape the steel mission, which in the short run had a greater effect in precipitating a new round of political infighting than in increasing steel production.[72]

Reflecting the inclinations of the Ministry of Commerce and Industry at that time, the steel mission focused on Western sources to provide technology and financing. Its members met with Japanese firms but ultimately rejected their proposal since it offered little opportunity to expand production for domestic use. Conversations with the World Bank about the Indian steel sector proved more fruitful, but proceeded from the assumption that the bank would finance private-sector steel capacity—not, per the Industrial Policy Resolution, in the public sector. Without resolving this core contradiction, the mission invited World Bank experts to study the future needs of the Indian steel industry. Bank experts called for far more ambitious expansion than had the Indian commission a few years earlier: India, it concluded, needed an increase in capacity of as much as four million tons per year—a fourfold increase over earlier Indian estimates. The World Bank's representative in New Delhi, erstwhile investment banker George Woods, favored expansion of Indian steel with the tenuous logic—meant to play well among bankers skeptical of publicly owned industry—that more Indian steel was essential for the "modernization of agricultural methods."[73]

Even before receiving word from World Bank executives, Indian officials began negotiations with the West German firms Demag and Krupp to build a large steel plant in India. On the sixth anniversary of Indian independence in August 1953, Indian and German officials signed an agreement to build a 500,000-ton steel plant at Rourkela, in Orissa. This project quickly stalled; the World Bank rejected financing for the West German proposal since the resulting facilities would end up under government ownership. So a Ministry of Production official, S. S. Khera, went to Moscow at the invitation of the Soviet ambassador to explore a joint Soviet project.[74]

Representatives from the family of business leader G. D. Birla made the next effort to expand Indian steel capacity, trying to convince TTK to support a private-sector plant. When those efforts came to naught, they aligned with British industrialists still hoping to arrange something in the private sector. Birla rejected the possibility of World Bank financing, citing the need to steer clear of government agencies that such a loan would entail. While not rejecting Birla's efforts out of hand, Prime Minister Nehru favored public-sector projects; he also wanted to diversify the sources of Indian steel technology beyond the "narrow circle" of Anglo-American firms. British companies strained against this impulse. Though they were not consulted when Indian government officials spoke with Japanese, Soviet, and West German enterprises, British steel executives later landed one plant in India.[75]

Nehru's interest in diversifying sources of industrial technology stood Soviet officials in good stead. Even as the ill-fated delegation of Indian industrialists embarked upon their tour in fall 1954, Soviet hosts fastened onto the notion that the USSR might deliver equipment for a steel mill, quickly raising the stakes to propose building a whole steel mill in India with concessional financing. They began to mobilize the state organs that administered economic cooperation, even though those had been limited to projects in communist countries. The negotiations with India ultimately led to an administrative shake-up that culminated in the creation of the State Committee for Foreign Economic Connections (Gosudarstvennyi Komitet po Vneshnim Ekonomicheskim Sviaziam—GKES), the successor to the State Administration for Economic Connections with Socialist Countries. Experienced industrial manager S. A. Skachkov took the helm of GKES within months of its establishment; he remained director, at the ministerial level, until the 1980s—a period in which counterpart American aid agencies ran through multiple reorganizations and a dozen directors. The case of India had expanded—in title if not yet in fact—the concept of Soviet "economic cooperation" efforts.[76]

The Indian cabinet decided in September 1954 to pursue a Soviet agreement, though the reliably pro-Soviet Mahalanobis still worried that a cabal of Indian bureaucrats would sabotage Indo-Soviet cooperation. The process moved slowly as the Soviet Union had to invent procedures and channels for providing aid. Thus, by the time that the private-sector Indian delegation published their skeptical views of Indo-Soviet trade in December 1954, midlevel officials had already settled on seeking a Soviet-financed steel plant. Commonwealth officials closely followed the Indo-Soviet negotiations in early 1955, hoping somehow to garner insights that would help them win a steel plant for British firms. Observers, in short, were seeking their own advantage from the possibility of an Indo-Soviet agreement.[77]

Even before the heyday of aid competition, development politics began to take shape in the early 1950s. Soviet diplomats and trade officials joined with their

Indian interlocutors to promote increased bilateral trade. Like-minded Indian and American officials, meanwhile, used large-scale (but inexpensive) technical assistance programs to further improve bilateral relations. The economic aid lobby in Washington and Cambridge, Massachusetts, meanwhile, fastened on to India to make its case. These efforts produced plenty of enthusiastic memoranda and optimistic pamphlets, but little noticeable policy change—at least through the end of 1954.

By that point both superpowers had expanded the horizons of possibility—if not the actuality—of their engagements with India and, by extension, with the Third World in general. American officials, in particular, had been talking a big game—reengineering a river valley, remaking rural India—even if they were not ready to commit sums commensurate with their aspirations. Dissatisfaction with the constraints of technical assistance prompted policy debates over development aid, with larger amounts and an expanded scope (beyond technical assistance) under discussion. New forms of aid were discussed but not delivered: opponents of expanded economic aid in the Third World retained the upper hand and sharply limited funds available for development. With the death of their namesake in March 1953, Stalinist orthodoxies about the Third World—already under challenge in Stalin's last years—quickly faded. Though few concrete results emerged right away, discussions of Indo-Soviet trade accelerated (even if the trade itself did not). The more immediate impact came from expanded cultural and scientific relations, which resulted in the departure of a Soviet delegation of economists and planners for Calcutta and Delhi in late 1954. This delegation was the culmination of these first efforts—and the start of the next phase of aid competition.

II

THE HEYDAY OF THE
ECONOMIC COLD WAR,
1955–1966

CHAPTER 3

THE GEOPOLITICS OF ECONOMIC EXPERTISE

When Soviet economist M. I. Rubinshtein arrived at the campus of the Indian Statistical Institute (ISI) in fall 1954, he came armed with a lengthy set of "directive instructions" issued by the Soviet Party apparat. None of those directions, though, mentioned Rubinshtein's first task upon arrival in Calcutta: planting a mango seedling in the backyard of the director's house on the ISI campus. Before talk of economic planning, apparently, came mango planting. Rubinshtein was not the first important visitor to plant a tree in what soon enough became an overgrown mango grove that still sits at the center of the ISI's main campus.

This scene, with institute director Prasanta Chandra Mahalanobis presiding over a mango planting, occurred dozens of times in the years after Rubinshtein's shovel work. Though the ISI campus, located in the northern reaches of Calcutta, sat some eight hundred miles from New Delhi, it soon became the site of a rich intellectual interchange and an important node in an international network of economists and planners. Mahalanobis organized a busy program of visitors, inviting dozens (indeed, in many years hundreds) to take up residence at his institute. He arranged many of those visits while on his own travels, spending ten or more weeks each year abroad. This constant flow of visitors led Swedish economist Gunnar Myrdal to conclude that "every second-rate economist from Europe or America" came to India in the 1950s. True enough, though he might have noted that dozens of first-rate economists, including three of the first four Nobel Prize laureates in economics, also made the trip.[1]

M. I. Rubinshtein planting a mango seedling at the Indian Statistical Institute as ISI director Prasanta Chandra Mahalanobis (standing on left) and other colleagues observe. As the
number of foreign economic advisers increased in the mid-1950s, such ceremonies became
increasingly common. *Source:* Indian travels of M. I. Rubinshtein photo album, in author's
collection.

Recruiting economists, statisticians, and planners from the Cold War East
and West, Mahalanobis appeared at first glance to be open-minded in his pursuit
of economic expertise. In the rosy recollections of John Kenneth Galbraith,
the liberal American economist (and future ambassador), the ISI was special:
"In no other place in the world at the time was there such easy and intense
exchange between peoples of the socialist and the nonsocialist worlds and of
the rich countries and the poor." If reports like this are to be believed, the topic
of the conversations was the Indian future, and the language was technical
economics. Indeed, a strong endorsement of the ostensibly apolitical character

of the foreign experts' work at the ISI came from an East German economist who noted that he and his comrades could only work on "the solution of practical questions" and could not appear "propagandistic" in offering their advice; this explanation came by way of apology that they could not complete the agitational tasks assigned to them.[2]

These characterizations aside, though, the flow of experts through the Indian Statistical Institute hardly constituted the pursuit of apolitical technical analysis. After all, the official and unofficial organizations sending experts from the superpowers to India had politics very much in mind; simply put, they hoped that their experts might convince Indian policy makers of the wisdom of their respective ideas for India's economic future. American experts promoted an export-oriented policy that called for openness to the international economy, favored agriculture over industry, and relied on market forces rather than central planning. Soviet experts favored the exact opposite: a focus on self-sufficiency, industry, and central planning.

The flows of expertise marked a new kind of international conflict. In this economic cold war the superpowers deployed a number of economic weapons—including expertise, goods, and financing—to win friends and influence people in the newly emergent Third World. Economists and planners tried to spread their respective visions of the world economy by shaping the policies of recipients like India. This effort was not simply an effort to shill for one or another enterprise (though this certainly happened, too) but an attempt to build a world economic system—capitalist or socialist—that fit with each superpower's vision and not coincidentally served its interests. The results of the flows of intangible expertise ultimately foreshadowed the outcome of the larger economic cold war: the Soviet Union won a number of short-term victories but ultimately lost the war.

The economic cold war itself may have been fought between the superpowers, but recipient nations like India participated actively; they were not just the terrain for or the prize of great-power conflict. The contests over expertise underscore this conclusion; Mahalanobis did not simply invite foreign scholars to visit in order to enjoy their company or to expand his backyard mango grove. He deployed their expertise strategically. Foreign economic advisers in India made crucial, if often unintended, contributions to development politics as Mahalanobis drew on international resources to fight domestic battles. The flow of experts helped him advance his vision of a centrally planned Indian economy with a strong heavy industrial sector under public ownership. Mahalanobis, to be sure, was not the only Indian scholar with good overseas connections, nor was his ISI the only destination for foreign experts. The Delhi School of Economics, founded in 1947 by a distinguished rival of Mahalanobis to provide policy-relevant economic knowledge, also served as a node for visitors. Yet few foreign economists, first-rate or otherwise, came to India without stopping at the ISI; even ideological antagonists like Milton Friedman paid Mahalanobis a visit. Such operations marked the escalation of development politics, as international resources (in this case mostly intangible ones like ideas, techniques, and prestige) shaped domestic Indian discussions.[3]

The Battle over the Second Plan

The domestic debate over India's Second Five-Year Plan had grown fierce even before international resources entered the picture. The plan, set to start in April 1956, marked the first extensive and intensive effort of the planning apparatus, most notably the Planning Commission (PC) and the larger National Development Council (NDC), which included not just the PC members but also leaders of the Indian states. Most observers, irrespective of their hopes for the Second Plan, considered the First Plan unworthy of the name. Prime Minister Jawaharlal Nehru, who chaired both the PC and the NDC, admitted that the First Plan was "not planning in the real sense of the word." Though Minister of Finance John Mathai resigned in 1949 over the powers of the Planning Commission, even those who shared his predilections for a Western-oriented economic policy considered the First Plan barely a plan at all; Mathai's successor C. D. Deshmukh admitted, with understatement, that it was "not completely integrated." Mahalanobis, much more devoted to planning than ministers of finance, told one protégé that the First Plan had been merely an "anthology"; the Second should be a "drama." Genre was only one of many aspects of the Second Plan up for debate in the mid-1950s. Continuing along the lines of prior disputes, the conflict over the Second Plan focused as much on who made key decisions as on the actual decisions themselves. The weapons ranged from economic argumentation to scandal-mongering to red-baiting.[4]

Such red-baiting ignored the global debates about planning in the middle decades of the twentieth century. While the young Soviet Union instituted economic planning with its famous State Planning Commission (Gosplan) in the 1920s, the Great Depression in the capitalist world brought planning to the forefront of debates among politicians and economists alike in the subsequent decades. A scholarly debate raged over the economics of planning: a Viennese right wing argued that planning was inherently inferior to markets since a planned economy abolished market prices, which they considered essential to economic calculations. Others defended the theoretical possibility that planners could make better economic decisions because they could reduce waste and duplication. Politicians in the United Kingdom and other Western nations promoted planning as a means to increase economic efficiency and to reduce waste and overproduction. Even one British Tory concluded in 1934 that "we are all planners now." In India, the Depression decade also brought enthusiasm across the political spectrum, as nationalists planned for a self-sufficient new nation, British officials planned for continued rule, and socialists and business leaders alike saw planning as a means to creating a modern, industrial India. World War II saw the spread of emergency economic planning, as authoritarian regimes like Nazi Germany and the USSR bolstered their already existing planning organs while other combatants—even the United States—imposed new government controls over production and consumption. The postwar years saw, in the words of one distinguished historian, a "vogue" for planning in Western Europe. While the powers of such planning enterprises diverged from the Soviet planned economy (and from each other), the language of economic planning was very much alive in the early 1950s and was not necessarily a sign of commitment to building a Soviet-style economy. What one British colonial official argued in 1931—that planning was "a tendency that is very general throughout the world"—was still true as India inaugurated its Planning Commission. That said, Mahalanobis's enthusiasm for planning drew more closely and explicitly on the Soviet vision than most in India or beyond.[5]

In order to bring his vision to fruition, Mahalanobis, a Cambridge-trained physicist with no formal training in economics, required support from abroad. Without it he stood little chance of getting his plan through the gauntlet of the PC, the NDC, and eventually the Cabinet. His effective orchestration of visits, from Rubinshtein and many others, bolstered his efforts; they improved the odds that Mahalanobis could get his way—even if they did not necessarily improve the plan itself. Seemingly cosmopolitan in consulting with experts ranging from Tokyo to Cambridge, Massachusetts, to Cambridge, England, and to Moscow, Mahalanobis used these varied experts to advance his own parochial goals.

Mahalanobis's pursuit of foreign resources, both tangible and intangible, began even before Indian independence. In 1946 he visited the United States and the United Kingdom to study the organization of statistical work. Toward that end, he spent weeks consulting with experts in universities, government agencies, and private businesses. He met a number of mathematicians at AT&T to discuss the application of statistics to planning within the corporate behemoth. He also toured the Soviet Union, which he found an exhilarating experience in spite of the dreariness of postwar Moscow. "My first visit to the USSR in 1951," Mahalanobis wrote his friend and colleague Pitamber Pant, "was of crucial importance because I got a vivid impression of planning." Though travels in the West had piqued his interest in the role that statistics could play in planning, it was the Soviet Union, he recalled, that inspired him to bring planning to India. In a remarkable letter to the Polish economist Oskar Lange, Mahalanobis indicated the depth of his enthusiasm for the Soviet system. Writing a fortnight after Joseph Stalin's death in winter 1953, Mahalanobis seemed distraught: "I heard of the passing away of the great Stalin. One epoch is now closed. The Soviet Union and the socialized [i.e., socialist] countries will constantly miss his guiding hand." Mahalanobis's trips to Moscow, and his commitment to the Cold War East, eventually gave new meaning to his travels and investigations in the West.[6]

Mahalanobis faced a fairly elementary challenge as he entered the world of economic policy: he was no economist. He had earned his academic degrees in physics before turning to statistics. He was a great success in his adopted field, best memorialized by the institute he created, by the fact that India's National Statistics Day takes place on his birthday, and also by the Mahalanobis Distance, a measure of the representativeness of a statistical sample. He acutely felt his own distance from the economics profession as he sought to put his imprint on Indian economic policy. Indeed, in a confessional letter to Pant (who had similarly parlayed his physics training into a career in economic policy), Mahalanobis confessed that his travels abroad were designed to overcome an "inferiority complex" about his lack of economics training. Western visitors to the ISI taught him a "common language" for conversations with Indian economists, but they did not lead him to rethink his policy aims.[7]

Through his travels, Mahalanobis engaged in a dual-track recruiting effort. On the one hand, he told Pant, he sought out economists who were "wholeheartedly in sympathy with our outlook"; here he had in mind Western Marxists like the French communist Charles Bettelheim—not to mention, of course, planners and economists from the centrally planned economies of Eastern Europe. On the other hand, he wanted to bring to India scholars who could "help us at the technical level," naming as examples econometricians Ragnar Frisch of Norway and Jan Tinbergen of the Netherlands.[8] Technically adept economists and econometricians, almost exclusively from the West, arrived to explore optimization problems within the framework already established. Western experts, in other words, were consulted only about the means, not the ends, of Indian planning. Mahalanobis's energetic efforts to bring foreign scholars to India by and large followed this two-track system: he conducted ongoing conversations about planning with scholars, from the Cold War East and West, who were believers in central planning, and he sought to learn specific techniques from statistically inclined Western economists. Thus Mahalanobis established a division of labor for the experts, and sequenced their visits so that the planners came before the econometricians.

Plan Formulation in Calcutta

Mahalanobis led off the visits with a delegation of Soviet economists and planners. He told Soviet officials of the two competing tendencies in Indian planning, and sought their help in making sure his side—and theirs—won out. Mahalanobis described his own camp as favoring a planning process that would encompass all aspects of the economy, including not just government spending but also the private sector. It would focus on levels of production and consumption rather on cost—"physical" as opposed to "financial" planning. This vision shared much with the Soviet planning system, and thus Mahalanobis wanted to take advantage of the Soviet Union's "vast experience with planning." He portrayed his antagonists, centered at the Ministry of Finance, as those hoping to plan in financial terms, primarily focused upon government resources and investments. He insisted that his efforts were purely scholarly in nature, proposing that any programs be organized between scholarly institutions rather than governments; there was "no need," he told his Soviet interlocutors, to "excite [*draznit'*] those unfriendly to India and the USSR."[9]

Mahalanobis hoped that a Soviet delegation could enhance Indian planning as well as his own role in it. He told Pant that Soviet advisers and assistance would be instrumental to building a planned economy—and, not coincidentally, to building a planning apparatus in which he would himself play a leading role. While in Moscow, he queried Rubinshtein and others about specific policies and practices. He was reassured by their insistence that Chinese-style agricultural cooperatives could be organized without compulsion. He responded with similar enthusiasm (and credulity) to Soviet talk of physical planning, which he saw as "the heart" of any planning effort. He linked planning to the nationalization of industry, a step that he strongly supported. In a breathless letter to Pant, Mahalanobis insisted that he sought not aid but information: "it is not money, *not money, NOT MONEY* I am worrying about" but "*technical knowledge.*" With such technical knowledge acquired through his Soviet connections, Mahalanobis might be able to win bureaucratic battles against trained economists; otherwise, he worried, he and the PC would find themselves relegated to merely "writ[ing] background papers" for the Ministry of Finance. He saw the budding connections with Soviet scholars and officials as a chance to advance his own agenda and his own career in India. For many reasons, then, Mahalanobis was, in his own words, "greatly stimulated and excited by the possibilities of planning on the lines indicated by Soviet experts."[10]

For their part, Soviet scholars were optimistic that a visiting delegation could enhance their scholarly profile in India. They faced a number of disadvantages in competing for influence with Anglo-American scholars. The colonial legacy meant that Oxford, Cambridge, and London School of Economics (LSE) graduates could be found in major Indian universities. And the predominance of English in Indian academic life gave the American and British scholars a strong edge over their Soviet counterparts in getting their work read in India. Soviet leaders thus hoped that a visiting delegation could establish a Soviet beachhead in India. If followed by an effort to translate Soviet publications into English, and with exchange programs bringing Indian scholars and students to the USSR, Soviet scholars hoped to increase their influence in Indian intellectual life. Closer Indo-Soviet scholarly ties, in sum, would serve Soviet interests through the "long-term strengthening the authority of the USSR and its science" in India. The relatively warm welcome Mahalanobis received from Soviet officials may well have been related to their confusion about his status; they treated him as a government official, a misunderstanding that Mahalanobis actively encouraged.[11]

Some Soviet officials, however, expressed dissenting notes. They cataloged the ways in which Indian economic policy fell short of the Soviet ideal. One memorandum regarding that 1954 delegation, for instance, referred to Indian "planning" in scare quotes, demonstrating a profound skepticism about Indian economic policy: "The task of our Soviet economists should be limited to consultations, communicating our experience. We should not take responsibility for the formulation of a perspective 'plan' or become official advisers and experts working out this 'plan.'" Mahalanobis had no such reticence; within a few years, he proposed precisely this arrangement. He envisioned flows of economic expertise in the context of a larger effort to "strengthen the bonds of friendship" between the two nations.[12]

The delegation nominated by the president of the Soviet Academy of Sciences reflected Mahalanobis's interests as well as Soviet concerns. Mahalanobis was particularly interested in hosting M. I. Rubinshtein, a veteran of Gosplan by then serving as a senior member of Eugen Varga's sector at the Institute of Economics. A leading heterodox Soviet economist of late Stalinism, Rubinshtein's presence (and his ties to Varga) suggested a new openness to rethinking Soviet connections to the postcolonial world. Rubinshtein's involvement also responded to Indian economists' interest in the experience of Gosplan, which one venerated as "the mother of all planning commissions." Tellingly, Indian interest lay especially in the Gosplan of the 1920s, before the Stalinization of the Soviet economy. Rubinshtein, who had worked during those years, was thus an ideal expert.[13]

At the same time, the delegation also contained the usual party stalwarts, and in any case did not have much chance to exercise intellectual independence: its members received "directive instructions" (*direktivnye ukazaniia*) that they should "familiarize Indian scholars with the history of the creation of the Soviet planned economy" in order to help India build its own planning apparatus, and should promote expanded industry in the public sector. In a paragraph that memorialized the short-lived friendship between the USSR and the People's Republic of China, the orders also required the delegation to highlight the value of Chinese peasant cooperatives as a model for India. While Soviet officials hoped that the delegation would deepen Indo-Soviet relations, both the tenor and the content of the delegation's charge suggest that the relationship was not one between equals. Soviet scholars had much to teach their Indian counterparts, but the lessons were drafted well before departure; they were derived from Soviet ideology, not rooted in Indian circumstances or ideas.[14]

The arrival of the Soviet delegation on November 7, 1954, marked a celebration of Soviet prowess on the thirty-seventh anniversary of the Russian Revolution and, more important, came precisely while ISI officials were outlining
the goals of the plan and working out the procedures for planning. Rubinshtein
and his colleagues set themselves up at Mahalanobis's ISI in Calcutta, where
they devoted themselves to explicating the experience of the Soviet planned
economy to fellow scholars at the ISI as well as to leading Indian officials. They
contributed to debates over the fundamentals of the Second Five-Year Plan,
including the emphasis on heavy industry, the best approach to formulating
the plan, the best means to increase employment, and the size of the public
sector. They were not content simply to advise Mahalanobis but sought to
deploy all available Soviet assets in India, including the Communist Party, to
influence policy.[15]

The Soviet delegation hardly limited its interaction to scholars in Calcutta;
they also operated in the corridors of official power. They met with Minister
of Finance C. D. Deshmukh, PC secretary Tarlok Singh, and Nehru himself,
who visited the ISI on Christmas Day 1954. Citing their country's experience,
Soviet visitors exhorted Indian policy makers to think boldly, and not to limit
aspirations because of a shortage of funds. Rubinshtein, for instance, imagined
that some of the financing might come from the Soviet Union.[16]

The Soviet delegation shared the ISI campus with Frisch, the Norwegian
econometrician who would later become a cowinner of the first Nobel Prize in
economics. Well acquainted with Mahalanobis from their service on a United
Nations commission, Frisch told his Indian colleague about his "special sympathy for the Indian people and Indian philosophy"—but also his excitement in
tackling "the particular technical problems now in question" there. With great
confidence, Frisch called for a "streamlined rational methodology for planning
work, a methodology that utilizes deep-ploughing scientific procedures . . . for
selecting the optimum way" to advance economically. Shortly after arriving in
India in November 1954, Frisch articulated a vision of Indian development
that operated very much along the lines of Mahalanobis's own instincts. Frisch
boasted that his ideas would save the lives of "millions and millions" while
avoiding "unnecessary political friction" through the calculation of an "ideal
optimal solution" for India's economic woes. Such a solution, he insisted, could
be derived only through physical planning: "the first condition for getting a
firm grasp on the problem of economic planning is to begin by ridding one's

mind of the monetary way of thinking." He also shared the predisposition for self-sufficiency that dominated economic thought in newly independent India: "India would follow a safer and more economical course by developing her own resources." Finally, Frisch called for expanding the public sector and for heavily regulating private industry. For a scholar renowned for his technical abilities, and for his vocal insistence on promoting economic science, Frisch made an extraordinary series of a priori claims about the form and methods of economic development—in a country he had seen for only a few weeks, during much of which he was bedridden.[17]

Mahalanobis hoped to enlist Frisch in his ongoing effort to shape economic policy through the Planning Commission. He confided in Frisch much as he had in the Soviet delegation. There were two schools of thought about Indian planning, Mahalanobis said: he favored what he called "integrated planning" over what he dismissed as the "'anthology' approach" that had defined the First Plan. Mahalanobis recruited Frisch to help with integrated planning, which required both technical and political proficiency. Frisch had already sold Mahalanobis on input-output (i-o) analysis—which would entail planning in physical rather than financing terms—and also promoted linear programming. First formulated in the 1930s, i-o matrixes mapped the interrelationships between different sectors of the economy: how much coal it took produce steel, for instance, but also how much steel was necessary to build railroads. The introduction of computers to economic analysis made the moment all the more exciting, as even small matrixes were difficult to resolve without them. It is no wonder that Mahalanobis devoted some of his energy to obtaining computers from the Soviet Union and the United States.[18]

Frisch made an unmistakable contribution to the argot and process of Indian planning. He introduced the term *plan-frame* into the vocabulary of economic policy and established the basic procedures for working out the Second Five-Year Plan and many of its successors. In two essays in winter 1954–1955, he outlined a method of planning that would start with the formulation of goals, for which "political organs" would take primary responsibility. Next came the plan-frame, produced by "technical and economic experts" who would convert those broad goals into specific aims and then apply "scientific analysis" to determine appropriate policies and investments. Frisch set out a detailed schedule for when the plan-frame should be circulated, how long the elaboration of that plan-frame would take, and so on. His focus on such mundane details hardly seemed the best use of his considerable talents—not least because visitors like Rubinshtein had far more experience in the practicalities of planning than did Frisch, who never worked in a planning agency.[19]

Frisch made the case for physical planning directly to Prime Minister Jawaharlal Nehru, and in dramatic circumstances. Since he adjusted so poorly to Indian climate and food, Frisch was confined to quarters when the prime minister came to the ISI in December 1954. Sitting at Frisch's bedside, Nehru endorsed physical planning. The prime minister celebrated the work being done at the ISI, enthusing that "techniques were now available for solving almost all the problems that arose in planning." Science, Nehru continued, would allow the "whole subject" of planning to "be considered anew." Toward that end, the PC delegated the work of providing a "framework" for the Second Plan to the ISI. Soon, in Nehru's words, the PC and the ISI were operating as "one joint whole," with Mahalanobis at the joint; he ordered the deputy chairman of the PC to consider Mahalanobis "a de facto member of the Planning Commission." Nehru's request catapulted Mahalanobis from his obscure official post (honorary statistical adviser to the Cabinet) into the forefront of economic policy.[20]

By New Year's Day 1955 Mahalanobis had organized a new planning process with the help of the Soviet delegation and the ailing Frisch. Their advice became a recurring theme in the subsequent years, with other visitors soon adding to the stock of Mahalanobis's advice—and to the list of names he could drop. The great Polish economist Oskar Lange came to India in 1955, finally succumbing to years of Mahalanobis's cajoling. Lange had remarkable theoretical and practical credentials; he defended socialist planning in fierce interwar debates with Viennese critics. After the war, he returned to Communist Poland to serve on the State Economic Council. Lange was thus ideally situated to carry on an ostensibly apolitical (and highly mathematical) discussion of economic policies—while at the same time endorsing the economic vision that Mahalanobis had in mind.[21]

Lange spent almost six months at the ISI in 1955, during which time ISI staff developed the draft plan-frame for the Second Plan. Lange saw that plan as a chance to bring true socialism to India, and laid out a remarkable, even revolutionary, set of policy recommendations. He focused especially on land reform, which in his case meant the creation of cooperative farms—voluntarily if possible, involuntarily if necessary. He also called for a program that would (in the words of one later analyst) "transfer ownership of all basic means of production to the state." All of this came under the rubric of what Lange called "a military economic tactic"—evoking the language of Soviet "War Communism" from the years following the Bolshevik Revolution. Contrasting this bold vision to ideas under discussion in India, Lange worried that the Indian Planning Commission ran the "danger [of] being too cautious in the formulation of plans." His activities in India thus worked along both of the tracks that Mahalanobis had established. Like the Western-oriented economists, Lange engaged in technical economic analysis, circulating an extended report on the use of I-O analysis—an approach, he argued, that "achieves its full justification only if applied as a tool of economic planning." At the same time, he also wrote a number of nontechnical papers extolling the benefits of central planning and drawing on the Polish planning experience. He was thus the ideal visitor for Mahalanobis, one with impeccable technical credentials but who also favored planning—even a stronger version than Mahalanobis was promoting at that point.[22]

Few economists could match Lange's combination of theoretical and practical experience, or his mathematical and political skills, but Mahalanobis invited many economists who shared Lange's enthusiasm for planning. Cambridge economist Joan Robinson, who had spent the 1920s in India, told Mahalanobis that she wanted to "knock some sense into the heads of the economists" there. Mahalanobis apparently welcomed Robinson's attitude, telling his friend Pant that she "might be of very great help to us" and that she might be able to convince others that "our approach to development planning is not foolish." Like Mahalanobis, Robinson favored a quantum leap over gradual change, and dismissed the static nature of I-O analysis: "the task for Indian planners, to adapt Marx's famous slogan, is not to calculate [interindustry] coefficients but to change them." This move, she argued, required increasing the rate of capital accumulation through labor policies on the one hand and the pricing of consumer goods on the other. Such funds would then be available for public-sector investment, which she considered the key to economic growth. She endorsed large-scale industry under public ownership along the lines that Mahalanobis favored.[23]

Others picked up where Robinson left off. Her Cambridge colleague Nicholas Kaldor proposed a tax system that could accumulate the resources necessary for public investment. The French communist Bettelheim, a devotee of Soviet planning, favored a broad program of nationalization. Though foreign experts advising Mahalanobis in winter 1954–1955 did not toe a party line, their general views coincided: all favored (to varying degrees) public-sector industry and central planning.[24]

The visits provided Mahalanobis reassurance as well as support. The winter's conversations did not alter his views but his tone grew more declarative. He concluded that a massive investment in industrialization offered the only route to long-term growth. The foreign experts spending that winter in Calcutta either agreed with this priority (Bettelheim, Lange, and Rubinshtein) or accepted it as a goal and sought to optimize investment around the goal of building heavy industry (Frisch). Whether or not he could match economists' techniques equation for equation, Mahalanobis proved an adept orchestrator of economic talent.[25]

Toward a Socialistic Pattern of Society

Mahalanobis's machinations in Calcutta fit well with the public discussion about the Indian economic future in that winter of 1954–1955. In December 1954 the Lok Sabha passed a resolution declaring a "socialistic pattern of society" as the ultimate aim of the Indian government. The Congress Party echoed this in the platform approved at its January 1955 meeting in Avadi, calling for the "equitable distribution of the national wealth" by ensuring that "the principal means of production are under social ownership and control." The Avadi Resolution confirmed the major policies of planning, public ownership, industrialization, and limited exposure to the world economy. Though it did not use the term *swadeshi* (self-sufficiency), it did specify that the "physical needs of the people" should be "mainly provided for within the country." Domestic production could reach this goal, the resolution continued, only by building up heavy industry, a process that would take place primarily in the public sector. While the private sector would not be eliminated, the Avadi Resolution called for government to "prevent [the] evils of anarchic industrial development" through regulation and control. Congress also endorsed physical planning at the Avadi session.[26]

The phrase "socialistic pattern of society" revealed the dilution of a doctrine into a platitude—and an ambiguous one at that. Indian policy did not aim to create *socialism*—itself a capacious term. Nehru's own definition was, to say the least, undogmatic. Insisting that he did not use the word *socialism* "in the historical sense which it has evolved in Europe," Nehru declared that his socialism would be modern and it would be Indian. Beyond that, however, he did "not propose to go into in detail." Adding the phrase "pattern of society" broadened the vision still further, leaving up for grabs exactly what kind of economic policy India would pursue. As open-ended as it was, though, the Avadi Resolution of Congress suggested that some elements of Mahalanobis's vision would hold a place in India's future.[27]

Mahalanobis skipped the Avadi meeting, instead preparing for important meeting of his own: the inaugural session of the PC's advisory Panel of Economists, to take place at the end of that month. The panel itself came into being in order to provide an impartial technical evaluation of Mahalanobis's plan-frame— but also to provide it with the imprimatur of India's leading economists. Thus the panel's first meeting was a crucial moment for evaluating the plan's broad outlines as well as rallying support among a normally disputatious group. The panel included (in the words of observer I. G. Patel) "all of the good and great—and some not so bright and beautiful—in the Indian economic firmament." Its stated purpose was to bring together a wide range of economic experts to pass judgment upon—or, as it turned out, simply to pass—the Second Plan. Finance Minister Deshmukh, generally pro-Western but also an old friend of Mahalanobis's from their student days in Cambridge, chaired the panel.[28]

Mahalanobis's speech at the first meeting of the Panel of Economists was the culmination of years of work, and marked his official entry into the policy process. He came duly armed with his own analysis as well as the support of his foreign visitors. Mahalanobis made the case for investments in heavy industry, arguing that it was not a "political question" but emerged from the application of linear programming to optimize the impact of planned investments. In extolling the virtues of such techniques, he drew upon the authority of Frisch and other foreign experts who had passed through the ISI; their participation provided a level of technical sophistication unmatched elsewhere in India—and mobilized in support of Mahalanobis's concept of planning.[29]

Winning over the Panel of Economists was but a way station for Mahalanobis's larger goals. As the panel met in Delhi, Mahalanobis worked with Frisch and with his ISI colleagues to determine the parameters of the Second Plan. Frisch was ultimately engaged in both political battles (winning over the PC and its Panel of Economists) and analytical work on the technical front. Similarly, Lange and the Soviet delegation addressed successive meetings of the PC in early

February, making their case for boldness in aims and for physical planning: it was not to "allow financial resources to impede economic development," one of Rubinshtein's colleagues urged the commission. After these meetings, the PC, at Mahalanobis's behest, organized a series of rapid-fire discussions with the various economic ministries to review technical details of the plan, from the prospects for natural resource exploitation to the regulation of trade to the expansion of education and of transportation. Given that as many as four such meetings took place on a single day, they must have been cursory at best. Mahalanobis brought foreign experts to Delhi to support his cause; Frisch, once restored to health, attended a meeting of the PC, where he touted linear programming as a tool for formulating the plan-frame. The whirlwind of meetings continued into March 1955. That same month, the Panel of Economists set out its agenda for analyzing the Draft Plan-Frame—which, at that point, had not been circulated.[30]

Throughout this flurry of meetings and consultations, Mahalanobis formulated what would become the crucial document of the Second Plan, the plan-frame—again, deploying the authority and ideas of foreign experts to win his case. This work took place in isolation from the PC and its Panel of Economists. It had little connection with the economic ministries themselves beyond the economic-policy speed-dating sessions that winter. The plan-frame that Mahalanobis circulated in March derived directly from the initial ideas that he had set out some six months earlier; months of economic discussion and weeks of ministerial meetings had little discernable effect on the plan-frame. The foreign visitors, in contrast, had offered their techniques for optimization and even given the plan-frame its name. Just as important, their presence had shone some luster on the planning process and its results. Mahalanobis's efforts with foreign scholars had played a crucial role in the formulation of the plan: he brought in both fellow planners—primarily Eastern Europeans—as well as technical experts from Western Europe. At that crucial stage, in 1954–1955, there were few Americans present; they would only arrive in late 1955 and early 1956, after the plan-frame had become the reference point for both official calculation and public debate.[31]

With uncharacteristic modesty, Mahalanobis called his first version of the plan-frame a "draft of a draft," but it was really a slightly touched-up version of his initial estimates from fall 1954. In its first substantive paragraph, the plan-frame endorsed physical planning as the core organizing principle. By the third page it had accepted the call of Lange and Robinson for the plan to be a "bold" one. The largest share of government investments went to expansion of public-sector industry, with iron / steel and heavy machinery plants accounting for most of the investments. For all of the advice from abroad, Mahalanobis's vision for the Second Plan had barely budged from his 1954 draft.[32]

The circulation of the Draft Plan-Frame was only the first step in the process, but it quickly "monopolized the public discussion," as one analyst aptly noted. Even though Mahalanobis's initial version of the plan-frame remained unpublished that spring, it quickly sparked controversy on a number of counts—some predictable, others perhaps less so. Among the biggest surprises was the vehemence on both sides of the argument about the use of physical planning, which may have seemed narrowly technical but in fact indexed the plan's scope and ambitions. Starting in late 1954 Nehru frequently mentioned the debate between physical and financial planning; following his Christmas Day bedside conversation with Frisch, he offered a firm endorsement of the physical approach, a position affirmed at Congress's Avadi session. This position favored the PC, as one British economist noted approvingly; the commission could undertake "expansive planning," while the Ministry of Finance could only take on "budgeting." Those wary of planning offered sharp criticism of the turn to physical planning. One magazine published an article calling physical planning a "program for rendering private savings and investment impossible." Drawing attention to Mahalanobis's "well-known pro-Soviet leanings," the article went on to identify physical planning as a crucial instrument in his "blue-print for forced industrialization." An economist writing in the journal of the U.S.-funded Indian Committee for Cultural Freedom lambasted the "totalitarian tendencies of physical planning," portraying the decisions as an existential political concern, not a narrowly technical one. Such criticism aside, physical planning remained in force, at least in principle.[33]

The major tests for Mahalanobis's Draft Plan-Frame arrived in spring 1955. First came the Panel of Economists, and here he relied especially on the reflected prestige of foreign experts. Mahalanobis had more rivals than friends in the Indian economics profession, so the panel might well have challenged, if not outright opposed, the plan-frame. But it had little time to prepare its commentary; members discussed a set of draft recommendations only three weeks after Mahalanobis first circulated his Draft Plan-Frame. Panel members had been assigned specialized papers on various technical aspects of the Draft

Plan-Frame—assignments made even before they read it. The result was an unusual final report, one that offered an unequivocal collective (and all-but-unanimous) endorsement of Mahalanobis's ideas in its overall recommendation but then contained hundreds of pages of technical solo-authored appendixes that subjected almost every single element of the plan-frame to withering criticism. The main report praised the nature of the Draft Plan-Frame; the only criticism leveled therein was that the plan was insufficiently bold to achieve its professed aims. The appendixes, meanwhile, served as a compendium of criticisms about the plan at every level; these papers considered the plan-frame too oriented toward heavy industry at the expense of agriculture, insufficiently attuned to the need for land reform, too reliant on the public sector, stingy in the provision of consumer goods, and too likely to generate inflation. Yet these reports, full of equations and equivocations, stood apart from the official recommendations.[34]

Only one economist dissented from the panel's recommendations: University of Allahabad economist B. R. Shenoy, a member of the free market Mont Pelerin Society and a vocal critic of government involvement in any aspect of economic life. Shenoy's views, however, were easily marginalized by his own vehemence and by panel members' desire to present a unified front. However laudable this desire for unity, the end result was an insincere endorsement of a document that ultimately defined Indian economic policy in its era. In the words of one journalist, "sheer intellectual honesty" demanded a stronger and more critical report—except that "the economists had already decided to surrender even before the battle was properly joined." They surrendered willingly, if not happily, approving the recommendations and then complaining at length that Mahalanobis had excluded them from the policy process.[35]

Panelists' criticisms came to light not long after the final report appeared. One prominent economist published a book that criticized the plan-frame and proposed an alternative basis for the Second Five-Year Plan. And at the annual gathering of Indian economists, some of the panel's leaders rejected core aspects of its recommendations. The highly regarded D. R. Gadgil, a specialist on rural economy, offered a major criticism of both the parameters of the plan and the procedures used to win its approval. Yet such protests had not appeared in the panel's published recommendations.[36]

At least two observers saw the panel's strong endorsement as a missed opportunity. I. G. Patel, then a young civil servant, noted that the panel gave "neither alternatives nor implementability . . . much thought"; well aware of the infeasibility of the Mahalanobis plan, panelists nevertheless "gave [it] the benefit of doubt." Planner Tarlok Singh, who spent decades in various roles within the PC, agreed, recalling that the panel "did not . . . pierce into the flaws of logic and substance in the draft plan-frame . . . and limited itself unduly to the conditions to be met in the specific context of a 'bolder' Second Plan." Yet these observations came only decades later.[37]

The Draft Plan-Frame quickly sailed over the remaining hurdles. The PC held a tumultuous discussion about the document in early May, in a meeting featuring direct attacks on Mahalanobis's plan-frame; one critic went so far as to suggest that the economic proposals would require a dramatic shift away from "India's democratic and federal political system." Mahalanobis defended his approach, insisting that he had incorporated the ideas and the data from the ministries—presumably referring to his whirlwind February meetings. He professed indifference to political questions; "he believed," the minutes recorded laconically, "that he had quite correctly pointed out that administrative or even constitutional changes might be necessary. Whether or not such changes would be made was not his responsibility."[38]

The National Development Council, a body that brought chief ministers and economic policy makers from the Indian states together with the PC and other top economic officials in New Delhi, quickly fell into line. In his remarks to the NDC, Nehru papered over the controversies raised in the Planning Commission discussion, remarking somewhat dubiously that the PC had reached "broad agreement about the targets proposed in the draft plan frame." With this generous description, the Draft Plan-Frame quickly gained NDC approval. Mahalanobis's ideas for the Second Plan may have gotten an inadvertent boost from the absence of his friend and opponent Deshmukh, the minister of finance, who had fallen ill.[39]

Public criticisms of the plan-frame had little effect. Business leaders attacked it for raising taxes and focusing on employment rather than efficiency. Communists blasted it for being insufficiently bold—"other nations," they chided vaguely, were growing faster; they also attacked what they saw as an undue burden on the poor. The socialists were much less critical, approving the general thrust of the plan-frame but expressing frustration that it did not work out all of the "political, organizational and institutional problems" involved in implementing such an ambitious effort. And from the right, the organ of the Congress for Cultural Freedom compared the plan-frame to Soviet-style planning, bemoaning Mahalanobis's nefarious involvement and hoping that Nehru's "democratic instincts" would be powerful enough to save the day. Despite such strong criticisms from so many quarters, the Second Plan marched forward. Mahalanobis had won his battle by using his wits, and his guests, to overwhelm the opposition.[40]

American Invasion

Throughout the crucial winter of 1954–1955, when the Second Plan's parameters were established, the ranks of foreign experts included no Americans. Most Western economists—and all of the Americans—arrived in India only after the plan-frame had made it through the gauntlet of planning bodies in spring 1955—and thus could have little impact on the shape of the plan. The first key American visitor, Milton Friedman, quickly wised up to this predicament. His India excursion in late summer 1955 came midway through his transition from technical economist into political figure—though he would no doubt have rejected such a distinction. In the early 1950s Friedman was best known for his contributions to "positive economics," heavily empirical work that he considered superior to reigning approaches of "normative economics." In India, however, Friedman operated in a strictly normative vein. His trip came about after the head of America's aid agency agreed with pro-Western Indian finance minister Deshmukh about the need to send a conservative economist associated with the administration of President Dwight D. Eisenhower.[41]

Friedman recalled that the Eisenhower administration sent him to India to "counter the influence of the left-wing advice" that Mahalanobis was receiving from others. He was especially critical of American foundations, which were, in Friedman's words, "highly sympathetic to the central planning propensities of Indian authorities." Though such philanthropies were independent of government, that Friedman defined his government-sponsored trip this way suggests the fine line between official and unofficial.[42]

Friedman's purposes, in short, were unabashedly political. Just as Rubinshtein's delegation had done, Friedman wrote his economic prescriptions before observing India firsthand. Visiting Washington, D.C., for predeparture briefings, Friedman left U.S. State Department officials with the impression that he saw no middle ground between "an entirely free enterprise course" and a society "mostly if not entirely regimented." In a conversation with Tarlok Singh, Friedman realized the futility of his effort to effect changes to the Second Plan. "Apparently," he wrote in his notes, "*major* policy issues have [already] been decided." Friedman's visit had as little impact on his own views as it did upon Indian policy; after returning, he reported to his sponsors that he was "struck" by "the disparity . . . between what [the Indian] government thinks it is doing and the facts of economic life." In later reflections Friedman pointed to the dual economic and political threats of Indian planning, which he called "adverse to Indian development and to political and civil freedom." Friedman and his hosts—including but not limited to Mahalanobis—participated in a dialogue of the deaf.[43]

If Friedman justified his trip on political grounds, other American visitors claimed to be pursuing technical economic science. A major project led by economists at the Massachusetts Institute of Technology (MIT) sought to theorize development while simultaneously influencing Indian economic policy and American diplomacy; the project's leaders, economists Max Millikan and Walt Rostow, both had plenty of recent government experience and saw their work as closely linked to American foreign policy aims. They applied to the Ford Foundation to study (as their grant proposal had it) "economic development and political stability." Ford staff enthusiastically supported this program, not least because they saw it as a way to catch up with recent Soviet efforts to harness scholarship to policy. They also appreciated the efforts to inform American policy. Though the project was originally a comparative one, India soon received the most attention from MIT and the most funding from Ford. Shedding its original interdisciplinary aims, the project widened its economic interests to cover many of the cutting-edge techniques of the day, including explorations of capital formation, unemployment and underemployment, and national income. The project devoted substantial resources to the creation of an I-O table of the Indian economy to identify bottlenecks as well as potential areas for growth. The project also aimed to win Indian hearts and minds by bringing junior scholars for advanced training in the United States.[44]

While the project won approval in the United States, including commitments from the Ford Foundation, it had a tougher time in India. When project director Max Millikan embarked on a grand tour of project sites in 1953, few in India welcomed him with open arms. The Ford Foundation's imperious representative in New Delhi, former U.S. Department of Agriculture sociologist

Douglas Ensminger, considered himself the most important American in that city—in his own mind outranking the ambassador, with whom he worked closely. Ensminger argued strenuously against the MIT project in his correspondence with his superiors in New York—and, most likely, in conversations with his friends in the Indian government as well. His motives were primarily bureaucratic; he stood against any project that remained beyond his control. Indian officialdom proved little more hospitable. One Planning Commission economist politely rebuffed Millikan's efforts to establish any collaborative research projects. The cabinet ultimately channeled Millikan's requests for research into a subgroup of the PC, which in turn endorsed collaborative research in principle but rejected every project that Millikan proposed. Millikan persisted, and soon worked out an arrangement for his MIT economists to work with counterparts in various Indian institutions, including Mahalanobis's ISI and the new Delhi School of Economics. Soon afterward, MIT began to send Western personnel on yearlong stays to India. In principle, any of the participating Indian institutions could host a visitor, but ultimately the PC's new Perspective Planning Division would host all but one visiting expert. While MIT economists remained critical of the Indian economists they encountered, they appreciated the chance to work with the PC since it stood close to the center of economic policy making. Determined to shape India's Second Plan, the MIT scholars wanted to get as close to Delhi as possible.[45]

The first MIT visitor, however, soon found out that the key battleground was Calcutta, not Delhi, and that the key battles had already been fought. Arriving in late 1955, economist Wilfred Malenbaum, fresh from a string of State Department jobs, set up shop in an office of the PC. His mission was to help solve economic questions technically, free from political and ideological disputes. Yet he never limited his work to calculating ratios and multipliers; he offered declarative statements, right from the start, that Mahalanobis's enthusiasm for heavy industry was mistaken. Most American officials shared his view. Though he spoke in a technocratic language in India, when writing for American audiences he described Indian events in bluntly political terms, offering a sharp contrast between Indian and Chinese approaches to development. Malenbaum's criticisms of Indian policy buttressed his reputation for prickliness and won him few friends in India. Then again, even the smoothest operator could not have meaningfully influenced the Second Plan by winter 1955. Millikan's instinct to focus on Delhi as the center of power, ironically left

Malenbaum far removed from the most important efforts to formulate the Second Plan, which were taking place—indeed, had already taken place—at the main ISI campus in Calcutta. Malenbaum arrived almost a year after the process began, by which point Mahalanobis's Draft Plan-Frame had already become the touchstone for all subsequent discussions of the Second Five-Year Plan.[46]

The MIT project, though sending a steady stream of economists to India for the next decade, had no monopoly on the provision of Western economic expertise to India. Other experts differed, too, in their commitment to making political claims as opposed to ostensibly technical ones. Dutch economist Jan Tinbergen, for instance, offered similar scientific rhetoric, but without Malenbaum's cantankerousness. Like Mahalanobis, Tinbergen had earned his PhD in physics before turning to statistics and then economics; rising to international prominence in the 1930s for his timely writings on business cycles, Tinbergen worked for the Dutch Central Bureau of Statistics, interrupted by secondments to the League of Nations. After World War II he became the founding director of the Dutch Central Planning Bureau and thus shared with Lange a combination of scholarly and practical experience. He first visited India, under United Nations auspices, in 1951; that experience inspired him to focus on improving the economic circumstances in the newly independent nations—what he called, in the first article of the inaugural issue of the *Indian Economic Journal*, "world economic problem number one." The Indian sojourn led Tinbergen to shift his scholarship toward development economics, which remained a core interest for the remainder of his career. Seeking to build on his experience as a planner, he then wrote a primer on development planning for the World Bank: it made the case for using "development programming," mathematical techniques he had pioneered, to shape economic policies in the developing world.[47]

By the time he arrived in India in winter 1955, however, Tinbergen was too late to shape the broad outlines of Indian policy. He embraced the goal of optimizing those plans, writing papers on a range of technical topics, including an endorsement of financing planning that had little sway. Like other Western European economists not explicitly identified with the left, Tinbergen helped work out some of the technical details of India's Second Five-Year Plan but was not involved in the setting out the plan's central goals.[48]

Visitor John Kenneth Galbraith from Harvard lacked the quantitative skills to take on the optimization questions that Tinbergen did. And thanks to a broken leg that delayed his trip from January until December 1955, he also missed the any chance of shaping the plan-frame. Galbraith was primarily an economic essayist, offering scattershot evaluations of the Second Plan as it had taken shape shortly before its April 1956 inauguration. Though Galbraith's trip had little impact on Indian policy, it shaped his own ideas, sparking his well-known 1958 book on the United States, *The Affluent Society*. The initial Western efforts to shape the Second Five-Year Plan, then, were too late and (at least in the case of Friedman) too distant from Indian assumptions about its economy to have much effect on the plan. The most technically proficient, like Tinbergen, solved optimization problems within the parameters of Mahalanobis's plan-frame. And the others, like Friedman and Galbraith, left with their views of the Indian economy more or less intact—and without making a discernable difference in Indian debates.[49]

Indian Economics as a Front in the Cold War

Ultimately, the travels of so many foreign experts to India in the mid-1950s had little effect on the Second Plan's content; they did, however, help enormously in getting Mahalanobis's plan-frame approved. Many experts, feted and flattered by their Indian hosts, graciously accepted praise for their role in the planning process. Other observers, however, remained skeptical, intuiting that Mahala-nobis used foreign expertise primarily for ulterior purposes. As one economist later connected with the MIT project wrote, he saw "no sign" of Western experts' influence on Indian planning. An American observer asserted astutely that the ISI leader used Western experts in particular for "prestige purposes rather than for actual advice." In spite of the generally hospitable reception of foreign visitors, they raised suspicions from many quarters of the Indian government. Even before the influx of experts to the ISI, for instance, Nehru complained that too often "some kind of halo attaches to a foreign expert" whose advice was taken much too seriously within India.[50]

Mahalanobis, for his part, was more interested in connections with the USSR. Soviet visitors helped bolster Mahalanobis's prestige. He later compared Soviet experts to "air force cover for the army"; their advice did not change the direction of attack but provided support for the campaign already under way. He boasted of his connections in Moscow, thus providing ammunition to critics who used those connections against him. Accounts in the English-language press portrayed the ISI as a den of communists and sympathizers, where Eastern bloc communists mingled with their Indian comrades. Public accusations likely drew upon separate investigations undertaken by the ministries of Home Affairs and Finance. Nehru, for his part, defended "theoretical Communists" who could "turn their minds to constructive work" but nevertheless worried that they were responsible for leaking official information to outsiders. So the experts became enmeshed in internal Indian debates over economic policy, their names invoked to score points on economic policy. The Draft Plan-Frame, in particular, relied on the authority—but not necessarily the ideas—of foreign experts.[51]

Though foreign economists had little influence over the content of Indian economic policy, they did affect the Indian economics profession in concrete ways. In the process, they revealed an important dynamic of the economic cold war: the Soviet Union had an immediate and tangible impact, while the West had the advantage over the long term and in less tangible ways. While Indian economic policy, thanks to Mahalanobis, swung in the direction of Soviet visions in the early 1950s, the well-trod path of foreign experts ultimately worked to the advantage of the West, which came to dominate the economics profession in India.

In spite of Nehru's concerns, visitors from both east and west found a warm and generous welcome in academic circles. Especially at the ISI and the Delhi School of Economics, they were an important part of intellectual life; they taught specific techniques but also enhanced a general mood of excitement about the study of economics at these institutions. Recollections from faculty and especially students of the 1950s rarely fail to mention the succession (if not always the success) of foreign visitors in their seminar rooms. India in the 1950s was, in the words of one Delhi student, a "Mecca of planners and economists from all over the world," hosting (in the words of another) a "galaxy of world-renowned economists." Whether expressed in spiritual or in celestial metaphors, Indian enthusiasm for the foreign visitors was palpable.[52]

Such enthusiasms, however, were not equally distributed among the visitors. By virtue of a common language—English—and a common intellectual framework, Western economists had a distinct advantage. Young economists in Calcutta, Delhi, and elsewhere were informed and inspired not just by the visiting experts but also by the tasks they faced: applying the latest Western economic techniques to build up the Indian economy. Through both their own studies abroad and their discussions with illustrious visitors, these students also immersed themselves in the worldview and the techniques of the Western economics profession of the postwar years. They were able to combine the universalistic aspirations of the economics profession with the particular—and particularly compelling—circumstances of their home country. The faculty and students of those days participated in the debates of the late 1950s through their scholarship: Nobel laureate Amartya Sen wrote about capital intensity in industry; Jagdish Bhagwati on deficit financing, Manmohan Singh on monetary policy, and so on. One student recalled the intellectual atmosphere of the Delhi School of Economics as "a unique mix of advanced economic thinking—as taught in Oxford and Cambridge—with . . . a strong commitment to the cause of building a democratic and socially equitable Indian nationhood." Or as Amartya Sen recalled, "The teaching of Indian economics was . . . never quite divorced from other things happening" in the capital and around the country. The opportunity to simultaneously advance economic analysis and the Indian economy was an exciting prospect.[53]

This combination of academic interest and real-world relevance energized the cohort of Indian economists entering the profession in the era of the Second Plan, many of whom joined a "glittering array" that shone nationally and internationally. Indian economists getting their start in the 1950s would eventually hold chairs at the most important American universities, including Harvard (Amartya Sen, who also held appointments at the University of Cambridge), Columbia (Jagdish Bhagwati), and Berkeley (Pranab Bardhan), not to mention the LSE, the University of Pennsylvania, and Yale. Others of that cohort reached the highest rungs of government service—most notably Manmohan Singh, who compiled an impressive résumé that covered every major economic organ in India and a good number overseas. Singh applied his decades of scholarship on international trade to devise a major liberalization of trade that took place in 1991, while he served as finance minister. He later served as Congress prime minister for a decade starting in 2004.[54]

The haughty Mahalanobis expressed smug satisfaction in this achievement. He proudly called the process of using foreign scholars to teach young Indians "brain irrigation," the opposite of brain drain. The Indian economics profession used imports in the form of foreign visitors to build up the profession at home—a form of import substitution that paralleled the economic policies of the Second Five-Year Plan itself. This approach was hardly unique to India; Indonesian officials opened their planning machinery to foreigners in the hopes of "ultimately reduc[ing] dependence on foreign experts."

Visiting economists also sought to impart sufficient technical knowledge that India might become self-sufficient in expertise. Ragnar Frisch, for instance, devoted much of his stay at the ISI to training his successors with that purpose explicitly in mind. So too did Mahalanobis hope that foreign experts would eventually render themselves obsolete.[55]

The process of brain irrigation, however, ultimately worked against Mahalanobis's cause. In the short term, he was able to use the experts to push through his plan-frame focused on heavy industry. But brain irrigation in the long term built up connections with the Western economics profession, not the Soviet one. These young economists like Bhagwati and Singh began their careers as believers in planning but later turned into very public critics of the Mahalanobis model. Singh, in fact, later oversaw the dismantling of the Nehruvian economic system. The MIT program, for instance, included the training of Indian economists as an important element of its India programs; under that program's auspices, Jagdish Bhagwati, Sukhamoy Chakravarty, I. G. Patel, and Amartya Sen, among others, visited Massachusetts. Similarly, the Ford Foundation offered direct grants running into the millions of dollars to Indian institutions—the Delhi School, the Gokhale Institute, the ISI, and the universities of Bombay and Madras—to "strengthen India's institutional competence in economics." The Rockefeller Foundation, whose Indian presence had been primarily related to medical and public health projects, embarked on a smaller-scale program—funding, for instance, the ISI's programs for foreign visitors. These programs added faculty lines, graduate fellowships, journals, computers, and travel funds to expand and improve the economics profession in India.[56]

While American foundations displaced British universities as key movers in Indian economics, neither group needed to worry about the Soviet Union. Increasing numbers of Indian scholars studied in the United Kingdom and the United States; Indian students, for instance, composed the third-largest contingent of foreign students at the London School of Economics, trailing only the United States and Canada. But none of the many Indian economists who rose to prominence abroad trained in Eastern Europe or the USSR. While Mahalanobis was hardly a popular figure in American policy and social science circles, he found common cause with Americans in the desire to build up Indian economic expertise. By comparison, the first Soviet delegation in 1954 had much less success in raising the profile of the USSR in Indian intellectual life. Soviet economists were rarely if ever mentioned in the exaltations about foreign expertise—and appeared in economists' recollections primarily for the purpose of railing on Mahalanobis's leftward leanings. Nor was there much flow from South to Cold War East; Soviet records indicate that only a handful of Indians were studying in Soviet universities in the mid-1950s. Mahalanobis's success in the policy sphere relied heavily on Soviet planners, but brain irrigation was a Western project.[57]

Import substitution in the realm of economic expertise worked to the advantage of the West. The policy of brain irrigation prepared generations of exceptional economists and ultimately provided Indian self-sufficiency in economic expertise. Indeed, India's brain irrigation project ultimately overfulfilled the plan; as Sunil Khilnani aptly put it, economists quickly became, "next to mystics and godmen," India's top export.[58]

Foreign experts' place in the worldly realm, as compared to the divine one, went in the other direction. Though not all of the visiting experts shared Mahalanobis's views, he managed to orchestrate the visits so that they ultimately sang his tune. The internationalization of domestic Indian policy disputes expanded dramatically, moving from one-off attempts to use foreign visitors as weapons in these disputes to a bold and systematic plan to shape what became the most important economic document of Nehru's seventeen-year premiership: the Second Five-Year Plan. This effort inaugurated the economic cold war, a dynamic that soon expanded as foreign resources in India moved from intangible expertise to dollars and cents—and rubles and kopecks. And as it did, the dynamics of development politics—the use of external resources to fight domestic battles—multiplied and intensified.

CHAPTER 4

THE AID PROJECT AND COLD WAR COMPETITION

Speaking before the Indian Parliament in February 1960, Soviet leader Nikita Khrushchev celebrated progress at the Soviet-aided steel mill in Bhilai: "Let the friendship between our nations," he announced with his best effort at poetry, "be as strong as metal from the Bhilai Metallurgical Factory." Indian officials eventually installed an obelisk sporting that exhortation at the plant entrance. Though his comments garnered "loud applause" (at least according to a Soviet transcript), the days that followed Khrushchev's speech did little to promote friendly feelings. While he was still in India, workers at the steel mill went on strike. Soviet engineers on-site complained about harassment from the strikers and demanded police protection, leading Minister of Steel Swaran Singh to promise that any future trouble would be met by the Indian Army. The Bhilai Steel Plant, the hallmark Soviet aid project in India during the 1950s and 1960s, demonstrated both the power and the limits of Indo-Soviet activities in the economic sphere.[1]

The Bhilai plant exemplified foreign-aided development projects in India during the Second (1956–1961) and Third (1961–1966) Five-Year Plans. While politicians celebrated such projects in public addresses and in slurred after-dinner toasts to the friendship of nations, the projects themselves rose or fell on the basis of support networks within their own country and abroad. The Bhilai project, for instance, brought Indian officials enthusiastic about closer Indo-Soviet ties together with colleagues who were not necessarily enamored of the USSR but saw Soviet aid as essential to achieving their goal of heavy industry in the public sector. The relationships that mattered were thus not only those between national leaders but also between midlevel executives who worked with their foreign counterparts to pursue their respective visions of India's economic future.

Different groups of Indian officials quickly found themselves working closely with one superpower or the other. Those interested in central planning, industrialization, and government ownership of economic enterprises not surprisingly found their way to the Soviet aid agency, the State Committee for Foreign Economic Connections (Gosudarstvennyi Komitet po Vneshnim Ekonomicheskim Sviaziam—GKES). And those favoring agriculture, private enterprise, and international trade typically worked closely with Western agencies, both the World Bank and the succession of U.S. agencies that eventually became the U.S. Agency for International Development (USAID).

As such projects proliferated in India after the announcement about the Bhilai plant in February 1955, the economic cold war accelerated and intensified. For the next decade, American and Soviet officials, along with their counterparts across Eastern and Western Europe, fought over Indian projects large and small, and sought to win over Indian officials by offering loans on favorable terms and by sending technologies and technical experts to India. Soviet observers called this phenomenon "competition between two systems," while Americans preferred "competitive coexistence." Whatever its name, this new kind of Cold War competition had India at its center.[2]

Development politics expanded noticeably in this period, as India's economic relationships with the superpowers expanded beyond intangible forms of expertise, small-scale technical assistance efforts, and low levels of trade. As the density of interactions that Indian officials had with superpower diplomats and aid officers increased, so too did the opportunities to use international resources to fight domestic battles. These opportunities helped Indian officials build centers of power that sat uncomfortably with—and eventually could be arrayed against—overarching political authority. These relationships became clear when looking beneath public platitudes like Khrushchev's into the quotidian back-and-forth between Soviet and Indian plant managers, executives, and engineers.

The Bhilai Steel Plant initiated the economic cold war, but the conflict entailed more than a single project. It may have been the largest Soviet project in India in this period, but it was hardly the only one; many clustered in heavy industry, but others ranged from pharmaceutical plants to mechanized farms.

Envious of the public relations success of Bhilai, American officials scrambled to strengthen their portfolio of aid projects, which remained oriented especially toward agriculture; grains shipped under the Food for Peace program (known by its founding legislation, Public Law 480) or of course the community development programs that began in the early 1950s. At the same time American agencies also contributed to the industrial sector by financing imports by private firms. And of course aid came from other countries on both sides of the Cold War divide, though these sit for the most part beyond the boundaries of this study.

Even as the superpowers' aid programs in India soon fell into an informal division of labor, areas of direct competition remained, most notably in the power sector. Here, too, a rough division of labor took place, with thermal (usually coal-burning) plants sponsored by the USSR and hydroelectric plants by the United States. The two superpowers competed most directly in atomic power. Indian scientists hoped to use Cold War competition to improve the terms of atomic assistance, but ultimately could not evade the unequal structures that defined the economic cold war.

The economic cold war put donors in the position of trying to outdo each other in generosity. Leaders in the superpowers expressed reservations about this competitive dynamic even as they participated in it. The American ambassador in Delhi, for instance, worried that "Indians may be playing us off against the Russians, and vice versa, to get as much as they can from both." An influential member of the Soviet Politburo, meanwhile, worried that his nation's inferior resources would make it difficult to win any such competition.[3] Such reservations were thrown aside in the heat of competition. Proponents of aid in the superpowers' respective foreign policy apparatuses may have viewed development as a Cold War weapon, seeking to nonaligned nations like India with promises of funds and technical assistance. But from the perspective of Indian economic officials, superpower sponsors were a weapon for fighting internal battles to advance their own economic interests and visions.

Understanding aid competition requires disaggregation. Foreign-funded development projects in India had important domestic proponents who saw superpower assistance as a chance to advance their own vision of a modern, economically independent India. Indian officials in the economic ministries, in private enterprise, or in the Foreign Service worked their own international networks, some recently created and others decades old, in order to promote and instantiate their visions. Donor-recipient relationships were plural and complex, just as hotly contested *within* each nation as *between* nations. Indian officials competed intensely for the attentions and resources of officials within the donor nations—while those officials themselves were using contacts with Indian officials to promote the policies they sought.

The Second Five-Year Plan

As the Second Plan began on April 1956, the geopolitical advantage lay squarely with the Soviet Union. The plan itself bore the marks of Prasanta Chandra Mahalanobis's desire for rapid industrialization under central planning; his effective maneuvers through the Planning Commission (PC), its Panel of Economists, and the National Development Council delivered a plan that promoted industry over agriculture, and public-sector industry above all. The Indian National Congress's declared aim (at its Avadi session in 1955) of creating a "socialistic pattern of society"—whatever that meant—fit more neatly in Soviet visions than American ones. And the announcement of an Indo-Soviet agreement to build the Bhilai Steel Plant symbolized the resonance of the Second Plan with Soviet inclinations.

The Second Plan demonstrated Mahalanobis's ability to convince the planning authorities of the need for a bold plan that focused on industry. In comparison with the First Plan, the Second reduced spending on the rural sector by one-third and reallocated that amount directly to industry. Yet Mahalanobis's calculations on the resource side were much sketchier. Almost one quarter of the Second Plan would be financed from deficits, and even that figure counted on unprecedented—and unconfirmed—amounts of foreign assistance. Mahalanobis did not interest himself much in foreign assistance; he focused on the allocation, not the accumulation, of resources. Finance Minister C. D. Deshmukh discussed the prospect of foreign aid only vaguely in late 1955, admitting to reporters that that foreign loans had been mooted only in a "distant way." He conceded that "a time might come when [we] have to look around" for additional foreign financing but could not indicate exactly when or how much.[4] Minister of Commerce and Industry T. T. Krishnamachari (commonly known as TTK) was more categorical in his own speech to business leaders that winter: he was "personally very much against asking for foreign aid" for the Second Plan. Like his prime minister, TTK made a distinction between receiving

Early Indian Five-Year Plans: Projected Allocations and Resources

	ALLOCATIONS (CRORES RUPEES, CURRENT) →				Shares of Total Allocation			
	FYP I	FYP II	FYP III	FYP IV	I	II	III	IV
EXPENDITURES								
Agriculture / community development	361	568	1,068	4,323	17%	12%	14%	17%
Irrigation / power	561	913	1,662	3,610	27%	19%	22%	15%
Village industry	27	200	264	853	1%	4%	4%	3%
Industry / mining	146	690	1,520	5,338	7%	14%	20%	21%
Transport / communications	497	1,385	1,486	4,157	24%	29%	20%	17%
Social services / miscellaneous	477	1,044	1,500	6,601	23%	22%	20%	27%
TOTAL	2,069	4,800	7,500	24,882				
RESOURCES								
Domestic resources	1,258	2,400	4,750	21,418	61%	50%	63%	86%
External assistance	521	800	2,200	2,614	25%	17%	29%	11%
Deficit	290	1,200	550	850	14%	25%	7%	3%
Gap		400				8%		

Plan Dates	I: 1951–1956	III: 1961–1966
(starting April 1):	II: 1956–1961	IV: 1969–1974

Sources: GOI PC, *The First Five Year Plan* (New Delhi: Manager of Publications, 1952), 3, 82; GOI PC, *Review of the First Five Year Plan* (New Delhi: Manager of Publications, 1957), 23; GOI PC, *The Second Five Year Plan* (New Delhi: Manager of Publications, 1956), 51–52, 77–78; GOI PC, *The Third Five Year Plan* (New Delhi: Manager of Publications, 1961), 58, 95; GOI PC, *Fourth Five Year Plan* (New Delhi: Manager of Publications, 1969), 52, 76–78.

aid and asking for it; he worried especially that Indian officials would become supplicants and accepting political conditions—"strings"—attached to the aid.[5]

Whatever reluctance Prime Minister Jawaharlal Nehru and other Indians evinced about external aid in the mid-1950s was quickly overcome by the start of the Second Plan. Aid receipts for the Second and Third Plans actually exceeded projections, though these cash infusions proved insufficient to avoid perennial foreign-exchange crises. Given the publicity bonanza that the Bhilai plant prompted, it is worth noting that only in the Second Plan did Soviet aid even approach American levels—though aid from Western allies (predominantly the United Kingdom and West Germany) put the West well in the lead in terms of aid provision. American aid to India's Second and Third Plans (1956–1966), for instance, almost tripled that of Soviet levels; the Cold War West outspent the East in that period by a factor of six. As one British-trained scholar put it, with some consternation, "nowhere has such small substance cast such a great shadow." If aid competition is measured by money spent, then, the race tilts to the West. But in terms of publicity, the USSR punched well above its weight in the competition over Indian economic aid, in large part because its smaller donations were tied to identifiable and popular projects.[6]

Bhilai and the "Noncapitalist Path"

The Indo-Soviet agreement on the Bhilai Steel Plant, signed in early February 1955, marked a major change in the economic cold war but at the same time built on prerequisites in both nations. The Indian path to Bhilai was a meandering one, full of the backroom politics and failed approaches detailed in Chapter 2. The Soviet path toward aid, meanwhile, was halting and uneven. Though official announcements trumpeted friendship between nations, the path to the project was littered with false starts and bureaucratic battles—even before construction began. Despite the initial fears of Western observers, the steel plant was hardly the result of Soviet efforts to lead India along its own costly path of rapid industrialization. The Bhilai deal demonstrated the appeal of the Soviet vision among many Indian officials, including those on the left but also those favoring centrally planned heavy industry in the public sector. Soviet projects like the steel mill found warm welcome in India, especially among Indians who saw steel as both a symbol of and an instrument for India's modernization. Yet the agreement hardly constituted proof that Indian officials sought to create a Soviet Socialist Republic in South Asia. Indeed, sharp opposition to the Soviet agreement brewed in the highest ranks of the Indian government.[7]

The exchange of top-level visits marked the earliest and highest-profile of efforts to convert paeans to bilateral friendship into concrete cultural, economic, and political ties. Nehru's tour of the Soviet Union in June 1955 revealed good feelings and promoted high expectations. He was warmly received at every stop, perhaps even dangerously so; one Soviet official accompanying the prime minister recalled that the numerous roses thrown toward his official car drew blood. While no concrete agreements came out of the trip, Nehru and his entourage left firmly impressed by Soviet economic achievements. The visit of Khrushchev and his entourage in November of that year garnered similar enthusiasms but produced no new agreements.[8]

This new era did not necessarily rest easy with the Soviet *nomenklatura,* which faced grave difficulties in defending the decision to support the Bhilai plant from the perspective of Soviet ideology. But elements within the Soviet bureaucracy began to invoke the pluralist views under debate at least since Eugen Varga's *diskussiia* in 1947 and which eventually reached the highest levels of the Party. In one of his shorter speeches at the Twentieth Party Congress in February 1956, Nikita Khrushchev offered such a pluralist view: "It is quite possible that the forms of transition to socialism will become all the more varied." Some such paths, he continued, may not even be "connected with civil war"; a "parliamentary path for the transition to socialism" seemed increasingly possible. Anastas Mikoian, a rising figure in the Soviet leadership and one especially attuned to foreign trade (and to India), dispensed with such qualifiers in his speech at that event. In promoting "peaceful paths of development of socialist revolution," Mikoian opted for the plural. He elaborated elsewhere that "the method of capturing power cannot be identical in different countries, in different times, and in various international circumstances," calling in particular for the consideration of "the institutions, customs, and traditions of individual countries."[9] The pendulum of Soviet thinking about revolution—and about the nonaligned countries of the Third World—had swung back toward the specific and contingent rather than the general and universal. This broader move against Stalinist orthodoxy meant, also, imagining a variety of paths toward communism. The ultimate goal remained constant, of course, but Khrushchev's openness to a plurality of paths to that destination underwrote the new approach to India and other noncommunist nations.

In the months after the Twentieth Party Congress, economist M. I. Rubinshtein built on his earlier and more tentative probings about multiple paths in print. A two-part article titled "The Non-Capitalist Path for the Developing Countries" appeared in *New Times,* an English-language Soviet journal aimed at foreign audiences. Those essays stated clearly that the path to communism need not run through capitalism. India's experience suggested an alternative route, one that might not even entail violent revolution. He described the Avadi

Resolution's language about the "socialistic pattern of society," and noted in particular the Industrial Policy Resolutions of 1948 and 1956, which promoted the expansion of public-sector heavy industry. Indian strategy, he claimed, was tantamount to "state capitalism," which was progressive in that it struck a blow against global capitalism.[10]

Rubinshtein's six-month trip to India in 1954–1955 prompted the views that appeared in the "Non-Capitalist Path." It led him to a significant rethinking of his position on India's recent past, not to mention its economic future. Upon returning from the trip in April 1955, Rubinshtein noted the distance between the Indians' "socialistic pattern of society" and true (i.e., Soviet-style) socialism. The failure of India to live up to true socialism, however, hardly dimmed Rubinshtein's hopes for the country's future. Intellectually he saw India as a remarkable case study, one that revealed the complexity of modern economies. Following the lead of his mentor Varga, Rubinshtein emphasized that these complexities meant that the stages in the standard Marxist teleology from primitive economies to communism could coexist: "Like a geologist at a huge section [razrez] sees strata of different geological eras, so too can the economist see firsthand in modern India the elements and the remnants of various socioeconomic systems. The remnants of the distant past, the complex and often contradictory present, and the first seeds of the future are interwoven in a bizarre combination." Neatly inverting Karl Marx's claim that the industrialized nations showed a less developed one "the image of its own future," Rubinshtein sought to use the Indian present to shed light on the past development of other societies.[11]

Rubinshtein's brief pamphlet on Indian economic policy also departed from familiar Marxist teleology. He continued to highlight the substantial differences between Indian and Soviet approaches to economic issues. Rather than score these differences as Indian demerits, Rubinshtein stressed the effectiveness of the Indian approach for Indian economic conditions. He noted that it was not the task of the USSR (or, for that matter, of the Communist Party of India) to remake India in the Soviet image.[12] He was, in other words, already open to discussing various paths (plural) toward communism. As Varga had long insisted, there was still only one ultimate destination for history—communism—but there was, theoretically, more than one way to get there. These issues had been at the core of diskussiia within the Soviet Academy of Sciences and, in a different argot, in the Comintern and communist parties around the world. Indeed, the debate dated back to Vladimir Lenin's arguments with M. N. Roy in the Comintern in the 1920s or even to Karl Marx and Friedrich Engels's nineteenth-century disputes with Russian radicals. How did local conditions shape possible avenues of progress toward communism?

Soviet encounters with India in the 1950s contributed to a rethinking of this question, part of an ideological sea change that had clear and direct effects on Soviet policies toward India and the rest of the Third World. The ideological transformation had begun prior to Rubinshtein's arrival on the anniversary of the Great October Socialist Revolution in 1954; indeed, his delegation's trip resulted from growing awareness of India's importance to Soviet policies and ideas. When describing the noncapitalist path, Rubinshtein drew most of his evidence from India, though he considered his ideas relevant to the whole Third World. Chastising "dogmatists" determined to "squeeze realities into their own artificial schemes," he celebrated the noncapitalist path as proof of the "multiplicity of forms of socialist development."[13] The notion of the noncapitalist path underwrote Soviet approaches to India and other Third World nations. Without it, the only available yardstick was similarity to the USSR; measured in such terms, India was hopelessly bourgeois in rule and too deeply implicated in global capitalism to be worthy of anything other than vitriolic attack. So this abstraction of the noncapitalist path had real consequences in Soviet dealings with the growing ranks of ex-colonies. It was the antithesis of Andrei Zhdanov's Manichean "two camps" approach, which insisted that all noncommunist countries were enemies of peace, justice, and the Soviet way.

Armed with new ideological support, Soviet leaders opened up to the possibility of economic cooperation beyond the socialist bloc. Soviet leaders and officials insisted that their government's aid, unlike that from the greedy Americans, was an act of pure selflessness. The chief engineer at Bhilai, for instance, announced that Soviet aid was solely to "help the Indians stand on their own two feet" economically, with no desire to convert anyone to any political doctrine. The Soviet embassy in Delhi hoped to build on this spirit of generosity, drafting a long list of new possibilities for closer economic ties, including many avenues that would soon be realized: oil, steel, atomic power, and military materiel. They contrasted their generosity with Western aid—for which Khrushchev, in turn, took the credit: "The aid which the capitalist countries are planning to provide to the states which have recently won their independence should also be viewed as a kind of Soviet aid to those countries. If the Soviet Union did not exist, would it be possible for monopolistic circles and imperialist governments to provide aid to underdeveloped countries? Of course not. This has never happened before." Privately, he even calculated that the USSR was "a catalytic agent" for 70 percent of the aid India received from the West. Khrushchev had a point: the announcement of the Bhilai plant altered American debates about dealing with India, and by extension the Third World, dramatically.[14]

A Bhilai Bombshell in the West

As American observers scrambled after the Bhilai agreement in February 1955, they went through a form of the five stages of grief before ultimately revising their approach toward foreign aid. First came depression; one American keenly recalled the "tones of palpable sadness" in American radio reports on the Bhilai deal. By April the mood had shifted to anger as diplomats convinced themselves (though not their Indian interlocutors) that the agreement worked against Indian economic interests. Next came denial, as the U.S. National Security Council discussed the possibility of using highly placed supporters in the Indian Cabinet to steal the Bhilai project away from the Soviet Union. By June 1955, as Nehru toured the USSR, resignation reigned. One American diplomat conceded that Bhilai was "an unfavorable political development" but hoped nevertheless that "it could contribute to our overall economic objective of strengthening India's basic economy."[15] This relaxed view, however, did not predominate. By the time Khrushchev visited India in November 1955, the final stage emerged: competition, which prompted a broader initiative to rethink the role of economic assistance in the Third World. Bhilai announced what American Russia-watchers called the "Soviet economic offensive" and eventually provoked strong political and economic responses from the United States.

The fears of a Soviet takeover of the Indian economy seem in retrospect grossly exaggerated. In the months following the Bhilai agreement, the Indian Cabinet authorized the construction of two other public-sector steel mills. The West German plant at Rourkela (Orissa) got back on track, even without World Bank funding; it still involved the Demag and Krupp companies, but was ultimately funded by private capital with the support of the West German economic ministry. And the British diplomats who worried that the German and Soviet efforts might "oust us in the steel manufacturing department" in India were relieved when a consortium of thirteen firms assembled by the British government won a contract to build a steel plant in Durgapur, West Bengal; in that location it would draw on the power infrastructure created by the Damodar Valley Corporation. These plants provided a sop for the pro-Western circles in India that opposed Soviet aid though still did little to console those hoping to expand the private-sector steel industry. Business leader G. D. Birla continued to press for foreign support, hoping to leverage the Soviet offer into an American deal with his firm; this proposal quickly failed. Thus the Bhilai steel agreement firmly established the notion of building industrial facilities with aid from the Cold War East and West—but at the same time confirmed that any such facilities in India went to the public sector.[16]

With the bombshell announcement about Bhilai, the Soviet Union quickly overtook the American efforts at development aid. And Khrushchev made a real point beneath the bluster: Soviet aid to India eventually led to expanded American aid programs. White House aide C. D. Jackson, long interested in expanding American development assistance to the Third World, seized on the Bhilai deal and Indo-Soviet arrangements (plus a little humor) to make his case: "The moment of decision is upon us in a great big way on world economic policy. So long as the Soviets had a monopoly on covert subversion and threats of military aggression, and we had a monopoly on Santa Claus, some kind of seesaw game could be played. But now the Soviets are muscling in on [our] Santa Claus as well, which puts us in a terribly dangerous position."[17] Few elements of this statement withstand scrutiny. The United States hardly served as Santa Claus in much of the Third World, and least of all in India; almost all American economic aid prior to 1955 had gone to Japan and Western Europe. And most aid to the Third World was in the form of military assistance to allies like Pakistan. By the same token, the Soviet Union did not have a "monopoly" on covert subversion; it faced serious competition from the CIA and other Western intelligence agencies.

American responses to the idea of a Soviet Santa Claus were constrained by the widely held notion that the poor countries of the newly named Third World should focus on improving agriculture rather than on developing industry and should operate primarily in the private sector. This economic vision impeded the search for a showcase project to compete with Bhilai. When American officials devoted their attention to the private sector, they all but foreclosed the possibility of aiding major industrial projects—which, according to the Industrial Policy Resolutions of 1948 and 1956, would take

place within the public sector. Western experts, furthermore, were generally contemptuous of the industrial aspirations of Third World nations like
India. One, for instance, wryly dismissed a query about steel mills for India
by indicating that this was a subject for experts in "comparative religion," not
for economists like him. Another scholar mocked Third World leaders who
were "hypnotized by modern industry." American officials instead stressed
agriculture as the path to economic modernity; India lobby economist Walt
Rostow, for instance, praised India for its focus on agriculture—though he
did so, ironically enough, at the precise moment that its planners turned to
heavy industry.[18]

These inclinations toward the private sector and agriculture profoundly
shaped the American aid profile in India. What support American aid agencies
offered to industry went to the private sector, and in the form of small packages
of capital goods imports rather than complete facilities in front of which a
Made in the USA billboard—let alone a stone obelisk—might be erected.
About half of American aid to India in the Second and Third Plans covered
the import of such capital goods. But publicity for aid programs became a
priority in the Second Plan period, not just among American diplomats but
among Indian industrial magnates and pro-Western officials who were part of
the loose America lobby.[19]

Because the economic cold war in India incorporated competition over
projects (Bhilai, community development, and the like), as well as related competition over overall resources, keeping score was no simple matter. The Soviet
Union had a distinct advantage in the realm of projects while the United States
held an advantage in the realm of resources. This distinction was one many
of complexities in the economic cold war as it took shape in India—a conflict
that began with the dream of high modernity on the sandy plains of Madhya
Pradesh.

Building Bhilai

Though American and Soviet diplomats alike considered the Bhilai agreement
a down payment on closer Indo-Soviet ties, the actual construction of the
plant prompted a steady stream of minor scuffles. An expanded Indo-Soviet
relationship was not necessarily a happier one, public proclamations to the
contrary. Overcoming the physical and organizational challenges of building a

greenfield steel mill in an isolated territory revealed the two sides' different aims in embarking on the project in the first place. Soviet leaders saw Bhilai as a symbol of Soviet beneficence and of Indo-Soviet friendship. Khrushchev, for instance, celebrated Bhilai with levels of self-satisfaction notable even by the standards of political memoirs: "Some people might ask, 'But what could the Indians give us in return?' Of course, there wasn't anything they could do for us except express their gratitude. We're not like the Americans, who spend billions of dollars in foreign aid but—capitalists that they are— always look for some way of getting concessions on raw materials or setting up joint ventures so that they can squeeze a profit out of the 'presents' they've given other countries. We simply wanted to create the basis of friendship and mutual confidence on which to build our relations with India." The Soviet definition of *economic cooperation*—the common term for aid projects like the Bhilai Steel Plant—incorporated building up economic capacity as well as friendship with the USSR; the obelisk in front of the Bhilai facility said as much.[20]

From an official Indian perspective, however, the Bhilai project was one part of a long-planned expansion of public-sector steel capacity, not necessarily a symbol of better bilateral relations. Nehru called the plant a "portent of the India of the future"—a future that was industrial and self-sufficient but not Soviet. To the extent that Soviet authorities could aid those goals, so much the better. But if others could help more, Indian officials did not feel obliged to stick with the USSR. These divergent aims shaped responses to the inevitable hiccups that dominated the plant's construction.[21]

Problems with equipment plagued the early years of joint Indo-Soviet work at Bhilai. In the first year, for instance, only about one-third of the promised construction equipment had actually arrived on time. When a Soviet official denied Indian managers' requests for expedited delivery, they turned to American and British suppliers. Similarly, when the Soviet installation of the electrical system was postponed, again because of supply-chain delays, Indian officials quickly went shopping on the international market. And after Indian frustration with the operation of Soviet construction cranes, the Indian officials opted to spend scarce foreign exchange on West German ones. Ultimately, the Soviet-aided steel plant used Western equipment ranging from Otis elevators to Fedders air conditioners, and installed with Krupp cranes. If Soviet authorities expected the Bhilai plant to be an advertisement for Indian reliance on the USSR, Indian executives had other plans; they hired the American firm J. Walter Thompson to handle marketing and publicity.[22]

While some supply problems pushed Indian managers to purchase from the West, others led to mutual recriminations, further undermining hopes for "friendship between nations." Soviet factories produced equipment that may (or may not) have worked at home but was ill suited to Indian ore and/or Indian climate. Miscommunication about lading capacities at the ports created bottlenecks. Soviet engineers scrambled to find alternatives, but their Indian counterparts had a simple solution: purchase American cranes. Bureaucrats on the two sides traded accusations and insults over missing shipments and storage arrangements; spats between senior officials like K. D. Malaviya and Anastas Mikoian did little to improve the tone. Faced with looming deadlines and missing or broken equipment, Indian managers ultimately arranged for a good deal of construction work at Bhilai—the symbol of Soviet technology and India modernity—to be done by hand.[23]

Labor recruitment also became a flashpoint in Indo-Soviet conflicts—a problem directly tied to the decision to locate the plant far from population centers. While delays due to shabby equipment or insufficient supplies could be solved on the international market, labor was a different matter entirely. And here the shortages were more dramatic and more damaging. One Soviet executive, for instance, complained to S. Bhoothalingam (then serving as secretary in the Ministry of Steel) that construction plans called for forty thousand Indian laborers—a sign of both the scale of the project and the heavy reliance on labor-intensive methods—but only ten thousand were working on-site. Though recruiting efforts intensified in 1957, the number of construction laborers never approached the targets. Such problems would persist for years, with labor shortages frequently cited as the "greatest problem" in keeping Bhilai's expansion on track. Labor productivity also became a topic for discussion by Soviet and Indian negotiators. Finance Minister Morarji Desai blamed continuing delays in construction on the fact that Indians were "not very industrious." Soviet officials agreed.[24]

These conflicts between the two governments also played out on the ground in Bhilai, in tensions between Indian and Soviet employees as well as labor unrest. American diplomats were keenly interested in the extent of communist "penetration" of the Bhilai labor force, in part because they reveled in the irony of communist agitation against a management team advised by Soviet experts.

Soviet leaders, in turn, blamed Western embassies for inciting the unrest, hoping to tarnish the major Soviet effort in India. According to one American report, almost two hundred Indian workers were fired for suspected communist leanings in late 1959. This crackdown did not have the desired effect; a handful of workers went on strike in February 1960, just as Khrushchev made his triumphant visit to the plant site. Strikers demanded more chances for promotion, more comfortable living conditions, and improvements to worker safety. Efforts to end the strike led to violence, as police used tear gas, a lathi charge, and revolver shots to control the crowd. Soviet officials claimed to be above the fray, blaming the strike on tensions between Indian workers and Indian supervisors.[25]

Skilled labor presented Bhilai managers with even greater challenges than did unskilled labor. Early disagreements about how to apportion expenses for training in the USSR—including haggles over who paid for laundering trainees' linens—led Indian managers to explore other training alternatives. One proposed using the Tata Iron and Steel Company plant, India's oldest, at Jamshedpur. Mere mention of this plan brought Soviet counterparts to paroxysms of anger and threats of retribution. After scotching plans for training at the Tata facility, Soviet diplomats had the temerity to complain that the lack of trained personnel led to missed deadlines. While Indian officials sought expertise from all available sources, their Soviet counterparts insisted upon the superiority of the Soviet system.[26]

Soviet engineers at the Bhilai plant played important symbolic as well as practical roles. As part of the Soviet message of friendship and equality between nations, the agreement designated that Soviet experts be officially employed by the Government of India, and not by the USSR. Thus could Soviet propagandists celebrate that no Soviet expert was giving orders to any Indian (with the exception, they noted with precision, of chauffeurs). Soviet officials used such arrangements to present Bhilai publicly as a project undertaken by equals, which required an adjustment in Soviet working styles; senior leaders exhorted privately that they need to instill in their Soviet comrades "a taste for Indian orders [vkus k indiiskim zakazam]." Soviet engineers also had to survive central Indian summer temperatures upwards of 40°C (104°F) without air-conditioning. An American diplomat later reported, with evident pity, about those "Slavs in the Sun" doomed to the hard work and discomfort of Soviet expatriate life.[27]

Soviet and Indian engineers high atop the Bhilai Steel Plant, celebrating social equality and industrial modernity, in 1962. *Source:* RIA Novosti/Sputnik Images, Federal State Unitary Enterprise, International Information Agency Rossiya Segodnya, Moscow.

Despite that discomfort, Bhilai became a powerful political statement about Soviet aid and Indian control. As an American journalist famous for his reporting from a Soviet steel plant in the 1930s concluded, "the Russians are not building the Bhilai plant. The Indians are." An American diplomat, after touring the British, Soviet, and West German steel plants, agreed; locally, at least Bhilai, was not considered a "Soviet steel mill" but "an Indian steel mill on which some Soviet technical consultants are employed." Another American diplomat saw the Indian leadership of Bhilai less charitably, as a sign that "Russians have refused to take administrative and executive responsibility" for the plant's construction. Whatever the spin, though, such details took on political significance.[28]

Because the British- and West German–aided plants at Durgapur and Rourkela, respectively, got under way around the same time as the Soviet plant at Bhilai, observers from all sides saw the steel contest as a battle for the Indian future, a front in the economic cold war. Each donor sought to prove its superiority and win the Indians over to its side. But observers found more or less what they were looking for in the contest. Pitamber Pant, Mahalanobis's man in Delhi for the Planning Commission, favored Soviet experts over their haughty

British and West German counterparts. West German managers, for their part, sneered that Bhilai was poorly organized and unsystematic in comparison to their own work at Rourkela. Soviet and Western diplomats and executives visited competing sites to assess the relative conditions. Senior Soviet officials kept close tabs on monthly production figures at all three plants, hoping to use the competition to give a boost to "progressive forces" in India. Indians also kept close score, as when Nehru brought visiting dignitaries to Bhilai so they could celebrate the fact that construction there was well ahead of Rourkela.[29]

In the eyes of Indian bureaucrats, another Soviet advantage was the Soviet willingness to share trade secrets, unlike the private-sector contractors working at Durgapur and Rourkela. As one Indian "old steel hand" told a British journalist, "Give me a deal with the Commies every time! . . . To begin with there is no hankey-pankey [*sic*] about trade secrets, patents, etc. They may violate the secrets of others, but *you* get the benefits. . . . They do not use their working here to indoctrinate; not a bit of it; they are far too busy working." As a result, Soviet technology undergirded much of the Indian steel industry by the 1970s. All of the senior executives in India's public-sector steel plants had experience at Bhilai, and most had gone to the USSR for training. If the West had a major advantage in the competition over economic expertise, the Soviets made the most of their opportunities in steel and heavy industry. In the envious words of one American consul, "there is nothing in India that has so caught the imagination of Government officials, the press, and the public as has the Bhilai steel mill." Based on such impressions, American industrialists and officials, together with Indian bureaucrats and business leaders, devoted much of the decade after 1955 to winning a steel plant to build under American sponsorship.[30]

The trio of public-sector steel plants under construction during India's Second Five-Year symbolizes the economic cold war in action: competition between the Cold War East and West brought more attention—and aid—to India. The negotiations that led to the plants, however, show how these decisions were contested within donor and recipient countries alike. The breakthrough for the Soviet plant at Bhilai required the ascendance of a group of interested personnel within the Indian Ministry of Steel, as well as a group of Soviet scholars and apparatchiks who hoped to expand the range of Indo-Soviet economic contacts. And the subsequent Indian agreements with the United Kingdom and West Germany suggested that different groups within the Indian bureaucracy would all have their chance. The strong Soviet ideological commitment to the public sector helped the USSR increase its influence in India's industrial ministries.

The Bhilai plant also reveals that successful projects required common cause, not common vision (let alone common political affiliation). While the Soviets pursued steel as a path to friendship, those Indians who supported the project pursued Soviet friendship, in large part, as a path to steel. Yet not all Soviet projects would find so many adherents in India.

Blooming Deserts at Suratgarh

Successful development projects required robust networks within and between donor and recipient nations—an injunction that goes a long way toward explaining the failure of the Soviet efforts to promoted mechanized farming in India. While interest in agricultural mechanization did not automatically imply an orientation toward Soviet-style agriculture, its adherents in India typically leaned that way; without larger-scale farms (for which Soviet officials recommended a version of their own experience with collectivization) farm plots would be too small to benefit from the increased capital intensity.

In the debates over Indian agricultural reform prior to the 1950s, a few scattered adherents of large-scale mechanized farms appeared in India. A 1949 meeting of agricultural economists, for instance, included a number of references to mechanization in the Soviet Union and the United States. Even these proponents of mechanization acknowledged the irony of promoting capital-intensive agriculture in rural India, which had little capital but plenty of underutilized labor.[31] But most Indian economists, even those on the left, had much more enthusiasm for steel and central planning than for large-scale farms. It was thus hardly a surprise that a Soviet-aided mechanized farm found few Indian supporters, and that it therefore quickly faltered.

That said, there was some casting around for radical changes in agricultural organization in the 1950s. Not one but two Indian study tours followed the advice of Rubinshtein's delegation and traveled to rural China in the mid-1950s. China's recent agricultural program appealed to some observers, even as they acknowledged the "sacrifice of individual freedom"; other members of the delegation were aghast. Pitamber Pant worried that Chinese methods of compulsion would be insufficient for the task, promoting instead the army as an "organizing agent" for labor.[32] Even extreme measures of economic reorganization found at least a few adherents in 1950s India—though this enthusiasm did not necessarily extend to Suratgarh.

The farm opened for business on the eighth anniversary of Indian independence (August 15, 1955), in the period between Nehru's visit to the USSR and Khrushchev's reciprocal trip a few months later. The location, in Rajasthan, was a curious choice: the land was arid, though a major dam project promised irrigation in the future. Soviet gifts provided the farm's equipment, about one hundred pieces of agricultural machinery. The initial gift also included some spare parts and a repair workshop, both of which would loom disturbingly large in Suratgarh's future. The original plan was to devote the bulk of the thirty-thousand-acre farm to grain cultivation; this would provide, Soviet organizers hoped, the best demonstration of a "fully mechanized basis for agriculture"—which might, in turn, lead to growing Indian interest in purchasing agricultural machinery from the USSR. Khrushchev, after visiting Suratgarh, compared it to Soviet collective farms, conveniently omitting any discussion of just how much harm collectivization had inflicted on the Soviet economy.[33]

Every Soviet report from the 1950s, whether from local staff or party officials in Moscow, tracked the success of the Suratgarh Central Mechanized Farm at increasing agricultural production. Early praise came from Khrushchev, who on his 1960 visit to India proclaimed that "mechanized large-scale farming is the answer for the shortage of food." The Soviet ambassador in New Delhi crowed that the Suratgarh farm was a "major supplier of agricultural produce." Harvests grew over the late 1950s, though mostly because the area under cultivation expanded; this was a case of extensive rather than intensive growth, much like the Soviet Virgin Lands campaign of the same era. Beyond production, publicity seemed to be the other key performance measure; reports counted the many delegations visiting the farm, especially after a film and three-color companion pamphlet appeared in 1962.[34]

The problems at Suratgarh, though it was much smaller-scale than Bhilai, far outnumbered its successes. Delays in the dam project meant a constant shortage of water. More important, the machinery that justified the mechanized farm's mission was highly problematic. Every Soviet report enumerated numerous equipment problems. In spring 1959, for instance, at least half of the machines were broken; many working machines, furthermore, stood idle because they could not work Rajasthan's dry and sandy soil.[35]

The two sides pointed fingers at each other until all hands were in use. Indian officials and journalists blamed Soviet equipment as ill-suited for Indian conditions or just plain defective. Soviet agronomists tried to shift the blame onto Indian workers, arguing that they needed "decisive measures" to force farm employees to work harder. The labor mobilization techniques used in Soviet enterprise—"voluntary" Saturday workdays and urban workers coming to the collective farms during harvest season—were unavailable in India, and production suffered in their absence. The end result was that workers at the showcase mechanized farm in India harvested many crops, including cotton, sorghum, and corn, by hand. Such techniques were familiar in the Soviet Union, but abroad they were, as one Soviet specialist warned, "a major shock to the prestige of Soviet technology."[36]

The Bhilai Steel Plant managed to weather a similar range of problems because it had so many proponents in the Ministry of Steel, as well as in the cabinet and indeed the prime minister's office. Suratgarh, in contrast, attracted little enthusiasm. K. D. Malaviya, a chemical engineer who stood firmly on the leftmost ramparts of the Congress Party, cheered on the farm—but could do little more than that from his post at the Ministry of Fuel and Mines. The Ministry of Food and Agriculture, never enthusiastic about mechanization, issued half-hearted complaints about a shortage of funds. Soviet diplomats continued to celebrate the farm's potential, with Ambassador I. A. Benediktov, an agricultural specialist, calling for "100 Suratgarhs" to help reduce Indian food imports from the West. In spite of the farm's slow start, Soviet officials nevertheless lauded it as the future of Indian agriculture.[37]

By 1960, however, Indian skeptics shifted the tenor of public discussion. The *Times of India* grew especially critical, condemning any attempt to expand farm mechanization as "foolhardy." Even the few proponents of mechanization shifted their defense; they no longer wanted to measure Suratgarh's productivity but instead praised its ability to serve as an experimental station. Suratgarh could become a facility for developing and maintaining new lines of hybrid seeds; it could also serve as a model for soil conservation in arid areas like the remote corner of Rajasthan where the farm was located. For such purposes, India needed not one hundred or even a dozen Suratgarhs—just a small handful. The Third Five-Year Plan, for instance, called tepidly for "one or possibly two" new mechanized farms, though earmarked no funds for such purposes. And even Nehru, usually prone to grandiose declarations about the future, announced his uncharacteristically modest aspiration to have "a few more Suratgarhs." The Ministry of Food and Agriculture eventually did create a second mechanized farm nearby; it functioned essentially as an adjunct to Suratgarh. An official ministerial report on the farm offered a discouraging analysis: it concluded that any gains to production came through increased acreage under cultivation, not increased yields per acre. A parliamentary committee, meanwhile, concluded that Suratgarh's production targets were "not capable of achievement." Then came a government committee to study mechanized farming; its 1961 report praised Suratgarh for meeting its aims—but defined such aims very narrowly as "the production and multiplication of improved seeds."[38]

Without a domestic constituency and facing growing opposition, Soviet agronomists—and perhaps more important, Soviet tractor mechanics—withdrew from Suratgarh by November 1962. One official described the turn of events optimistically: the Suratgarh Central Mechanized Farm, having completed its first stage, no longer required the same Soviet presence. Yet as that same official observed, the absence of Soviet personnel would "have a significant impact on all branches of work at the farm." By early 1962 the hopes for mechanized farming, at least in the Soviet style, had already proven as unsuccessful as collective farms had in the USSR itself. This turn of events did not prevent Soviet economic officials from declaring Suratgarh "not just a gift to India, but to the whole world." Meanwhile the farm limped along, subject to ever sharper domestic criticisms. The Indian Administrative Reforms Commission, for instance, blasted Suratgarh for not only failing to be profitable but for being unable even to calculate the extent of its losses. Soviet officials, making accusations familiar in other settings, blamed "right-wing circles" for causing trouble. Finding few proponents in India politics or administration, Suratgarh never came close to fulfilling its own goals, even as those goals shrank.[39]

The Problems of Developing Communities

American assistance in rural India met with more success, thanks in part to the strength of the network of proponents in and beyond India. Community Development (CD), a signature project of American technical assistance, generated great enthusiasm and photo shoots of clean-cut Americans and young Indians rolling up their sleeves to help Indian villagers. Yet even this initial support could not sustain the program, as skeptics seized on increasing pressure on food supplies in the mid-1950s in order to marginalize CD.

The debates over the purpose of CD—was it to increase democratic participation or food production?—grew more intense in the mid-1950s as overall crop levels stagnated and shortages loomed. With engineer-turned-impresario S. K. Dey serving as India's first minster of community development, the program's extraordinarily ambitious expansion continued, pushed along by outside enthusiasm more than evidence of success. The Planning Commission opposed expanding CD, proposing instead that simple measures like naming good farmers to serve as "non-official agricultural leaders" and undertaking an "all-out effort" on the use of manure would be sufficient to meet higher production targets. The Planning Commission deployed the claims of CD proponents—that Indian agriculture needed better organization, not more money—to argue against funding community development. The Ministry of Community Development responded by creating a National Extension Service, a cut-rate version of CD, leading Planning Commission economists to conclude that the proponents were spreading too few resources too thinly.[40]

A food crisis in 1957 soon brought new scrutiny to the CD program. The shortages emerged from a confluence of factors, including population growth and volatile Indian monsoons and harvests. But political factors also mattered; a small run of good harvests just as the Second Five-Year Plan was being formulated in 1954–1955 led to complacent assumptions about food production that quickly became embedded in the plan.[41] Yet as weaker harvests followed these better years, shortages were endemic. They rippled throughout the Indian economy in the mid-1950s, not least because the demand for imported food ran up against foreign constraints.

Community development programs were quickly swept up into this controversy. A blue-ribbon commission concluded that in spite of its rapid expansion, CD had not succeeded in India. The crucial village-level worker had, in the words of the report, had not been "as effective as we would like him to be." While fully one-third of India had been incorporated into community development or National Extension districts, the actual results were limited: the number of villagers in the CD regions who had "begun to take a live interest in the development activities," the report stated, was "far from assuming significant proportions." Similarly, Planning Commission evaluators grew increasingly skeptical that CD offered any kind of benefits, whether intangible changes of villagers' outlook or measurable increases in agriculture production. The *Economic Weekly* offered a simple gloss on the report: "community projects . . . cannot succeed." Economist D. R. Gadgil was even harsher; those who considered the program a success, he seethed, merely revealed their total ignorance of actual conditions in the countryside.[42]

The Ministry of Community Development and National Extension managed to withstand these challenges in large part because it still had some outside support, albeit waning. Its leaders adapted to the growing clamor by conceding that production needed to be a higher priority. By 1960 Dey belatedly began to emphasize production, offering a mea culpa that he had given inadequate attention "to production, particularly of food." But more damaging—and ultimately fatal to the ministry—were criticisms from foreign groups that had originally sponsored CD in India. A group of United Nations consultants hired by the Indian government dismissed the notion that production and democratization went hand in hand; it concluded that most improvements came through the directives issued by village-level workers, not through the expression of villagers' preferences. Sponsors soon began to back away. The U.S. Department of Agriculture concluded that meaningful work to improve agricultural production—which it saw as the goal of CD—required quantum increases in both American and Indian staff, which it did not ultimately endorse. Most damningly, the program's greatest benefactor, the Ford Foundation, put a two-year moratorium on CD funding; it zeroed out a budget line that had run as high as $1 million annually. In a major defeat for Douglas Ensminger, CD's greatest supporter in the Ford Foundation, a Ford-sponsored mission of American agronomists to India concluded that the Ministry of Community Development had done little for food production. The Ford Foundation offered one last (and relatively small) grant for CD in 1959, but then eliminated funding entirely. When a new ambassador came to New Delhi in 1961—agricultural economist John Kenneth Galbraith—CD faced yet another foreign challenge. Rural India, in his assessment, needed pest control specialists and soil scientists, not "home economists or communications specialists, whatever in hell communications specialists are."[43]

The Community Development project was ultimately doomed by the chasm between promises and results—especially in the realm of production: the inability to transform Indian village politics also played a role. As grandiose promises of social transformation gave way to Potemkin programs to boost output in the mid-1950s, one keen observer noted that CD's vaunted "revolution of ris-ing expectations" had given way to a "revolution of mounting frustration." The Ministry of Community Development and National Extension limped along for another seven years before being folded into the Ministry of Food and Agriculture. Its proponents had ever shrinking bases of external support (whether official or, like the Ford Foundation, semiofficial), and even they acknowledged CD's troubles. A sense of defeat and defensiveness loomed over a 1966 workshop sponsored by the National Institute for Community Devel-opment, which insisted that it was "fallacious" to evaluate CD only in terms of production. The participants ultimately blamed "political policies" for the project's demise—an awkward but accurate phrase to describe the way that CD's opponents first established production as the measure of success—and then found it wanting.[44]

The dozen years or so years of community development in India illustrated the contradictions of the enterprise. It was a paradigmatic technical assistance program, and CD proponents called for agricultural change without any politi-cally perilous discussions of rural inequality (which might suggest the need for land reform) and without calling for the investment of significant resources from domestic or foreign sources. Community development was indeed threat-ened by "political policies" domestically but managed to survive, at least until the foreign support disappeared.[45]

Unloading Grain with PL480

In contrast to community development, the American Food for Peace program found natural constituencies in both India and the United States that assured the program's long life in India. Though the sale of food grains at conces-sional prices transferred far more resources from the United States to India than technical assistance programs like community development, it transferred only resources available in surplus in the United States. The priorities of Food for Peace appear in the full name of the original legislation: the Agricultural Trade Development and Assistance Act (PL480) of 1954, which was adminis-tered, tellingly, by the Interagency Committee on Agricultural Surplus Dis-posal. Firmly supported by the farm bloc in the U.S. Congress, the program sold agricultural surpluses owned by the U.S. government to needy nations overseas, and donated smaller amounts of food on an emergency basis. As

George McGovern—a successful PL480 administrator before he was an epically unsuccessful presidential candidate—aptly summed up, the program was a "near perfect blend of American self-interest and international humanitarianism." That blend, to be sure, was ultimately much heavier on self-interest than humanitarianism.[46]

The domestic American politics of PL480 were both arcane and fierce. Congress's powerful farm bloc made the dubious but ultimately successful case that PL480 was a meaningful aid program, which meant that the program's costs were charged to international aid budgets rather than to the U.S. Department of Agriculture, much to the dismay of the State Department and the Council of Economic Advisers. Even as diplomats opposed PL480, then, they had to pay the bills; to make matters worse, they had to field the frequent complaints of grain-exporting allies that PL480 commodities were cutting them out of traditional or prospective markets. U.S. foreign aid officials doubted that providing cheap food served the cause of economic development in recipient nations; one senior official complained that any positive effects in recipient nations were purely accidental—and were in any case unrelated to the "original purpose" of the law. The bureaucratic battles got so heated, one White House aide joked, that Secretary of State John Foster Dulles got "a nervous tremor" any time the law was mentioned.[47]

That said, the White House found the practical benefits of the program worth all of the infighting. The program earned the support of farm-state representatives in Congress, who were otherwise among the staunchest critics of foreign aid. Its funds came from the Commodity Credit Corporation, an independent entity beyond everyday congressional oversight. The program got its name—Food for Peace—in 1958 to make it more palatable to foreign audiences. But this was simply a new name for an old program; the basic purposes had not changed.[48]

Many within recipient governments found PL480 irresistible. The financial terms were especially advantageous; purchases were arranged at concessional rates and could be repaid in local currencies (e.g., rupees, not dollars), thus conserving scarce foreign exchange. Recipient governments, furthermore, served as wholesalers, obtaining the grain from the U.S. government and then selling it directly to their citizens while pocketing most of the proceeds; the U.S. government claimed a small portion of those funds for its own use, though even some of these could be used for development purposes. Roughly 80 percent of the proceeds went to the Indian government, and another 7 percent for development loans (to the private sector); the remaining 13 percent went for U.S. government use. In the Second and Third Plan periods, most of the counterpart funds were used for multipurpose river valley development (including hydroelectric power) and education. On these grounds, one Indian bureaucrat lauded PL480 counterpart funds as a "unique and effective way" to mobilize "internal financial resources" for development.[49]

PL480 grain agreements did not, however, receive universal approbation within India. Critics lashed out from the left and the right, and from rural areas where livelihoods were threatened by low grain prices that imports left in their wake. But the issues at stake in PL480 were about economic visions as much as economic interests: was self-sufficiency in food essential? Or should American surpluses be put to use attaining Indian self-sufficiency in steel or other industries? Debates about food production and self-sufficiency, then, could not be separated from conflicts over the specific terms of PL480 aid— and vice versa. India's heavy reliance on PL480 in the 1950s and 1960s gave plenty of opportunity to map the internal conflicts. Over that period India received more grain than the second, third, and fourth largest PL480 recipients combined. PL480 aid, furthermore, accounted for over half of the total U.S. aid to India in the 1950s and 1960s.[50]

From the start, Indian PL480 agreements emerged out of domestic disputes over how best to handle threats to the food supply. The inaugural agreement in 1956, for instance, rescued Indian food supplies from the unrealistic enthusiasm over food production after relatively good harvests of 1954–1955. When harvests declined in 1956, Prime Minister Nehru dispatched the minister of food and agriculture to Washington, D.C., to negotiate a PL480 grain purchase. Nehru had come to this decision reluctantly, reporting to one official that he did "not like the idea of our obtaining rice from the U.S. unless we are forced to do so." The minister shared this ambivalence, pursuing the agreement even as he felt "disgust" that such requests were necessary.[51]

The August 1956 agreement provided some $360 million in American commodities to India. The food minister was most interested in obtaining rice, but limited U.S. stocks and a hard-line U.S. negotiating position resulted in an agreement dominated by wheat; while U.S. officials worried only about farm supplies, Indian officials had to account for highly politicized regional differences in grain preferences. A small quantity of rice was added at the last minute—but at the request of the Arkansas congressional delegation, not the Indian government. Similarly, Indian objections to including tobacco were overruled by PL480 officials eager to please tobacco-growing constituents. As with all PL480 agreements, Indian officials promised to purchase a small amount of grain on international markets—a sop to Australia and Canada, whose diplomats complained that PL480 undercut their own exports. Factoring in these required purchases, World Bank economists argued that the agreement was too large, importing wheat well in excess of Indian needs. Nehru apparently disagreed, asking the Soviet ambassador whether his nation could provide rice for India; the diplomat demurred, saying that the USSR imported rice and thus could not help.[52]

Yet even these quantities of grain did not stabilize prices, prompting the appointment of the Foodgrains Enquiry Committee in 1957. The committee favored keeping low prices for consumers, calling for increased regulation of food markets and moving toward the "progressive and planned socialization of the wholesale trade." The Foodgrains Committee ultimately encouraged an increased reliance on PL480, which would allow India to solve its food problems without further depleting its foreign exchange. Yet the PL480 foods did not hold out; the 1956 agreement was designed to last three years, but its supplies were exhausted in only twenty-one months.[53]

Acknowledging the mixed results of PL480, the Foodgrains Committee nevertheless insisted that the program could contribute to Indian development efforts. The report called for purchasing grain at below-market rates, selling it in Fair Price Shops, and then using proceeds for development purposes that would serve India's long-term economic interests. This conclusion built on the research of the Food and Agriculture Organization (FAO), which had studied the effect of surplus food programs on economic development in general, and on Indian development in particular. The FAO report trumpeted the ways in which surplus foods could play an important role in Third World development—a position echoing the arguments of the largest exporters, especially the United States.[54]

For donors and recipients alike, the political benefits of PL480 overshadowed development aims. The Indian Planning Commission, and others promoting rapid industrialization, saw that PL480 could help keep grain prices low for the growing ranks of urban workers. Yet low grain prices provided little incentive for farmers to maintain levels of agricultural production, let alone invest in improvements. The result was the emergence, even by the conclusion of the first Indian PL480 deal, of a vicious circle. Though initiated in response to food shortages, PL480 actually exacerbated the problems it purported to solve; it relieved shortages, one well-placed observer noted, only at the cost of "discourag[ing the] production of food."[55]

Counterpart funds, furthermore, did not remotely live up to hopes that they would advance development. Indian economic officials, fearing the inflationary effects of releasing significant new funds into the economy, preferred to hoard the proceeds from PL480 rather than spending them on development projects; indeed India spent less than half of the counterpart funds generated in the first seven years of PL480. As B. K. Nehru, by this point commissioner general for economic affairs, told American diplomats, "we had been anxious to sterilize rather than mobilize" the PL480 counterpart funds. Thus PL480 solved short-term problems in India (as in the United States) but did little for Indian development. Indian negotiators, furthermore, resented the Americans' imperious negotiating posture. An economist who served on the Foodgrains Committee recalled that American negotiators rarely missed an opportunity to impose conditions on the PL480 contracts—a surprising tendency given the large and growing agricultural surpluses and the drumbeat of demands from the New Delhi embassy to expand and expedite shipments.[56]

Though Indian editorialists criticized PL480 as "economically unnecessary," policy makers in New Delhi disagreed. As the 1956 agreement ran its course, a group of Indian officials, led by Food and Agriculture Minister S. K. Patil, sought a new and larger deal. Patil wanted PL480 food to build a buffer sufficient to withstand the deregulation of food; his main goal was to "remove all controls, rationing and other obstructions" in food markets. American diplomats rushed to help Patil, whom they considered a "friend to the U.S. and U.S. ideals, and a staunch advocate of private enterprise." A blockbuster PL480 deal with India, then, would bolster Patil's position and promote "U.S. political and psychological aims" in India. At the same time, PL480 food provided Patil with breathing room to initiate his liberalization program.[57]

By early 1960, however, Indian criticisms of PL480 grew louder, not least from rural landowners and tenants whose incomes depended on high food prices. Left-wing contingents in Parliament assailed a new PL480 agreement as the start of a "dangerous process of American infiltration into our economy." K. D. Malaviya complained to the prime minister that PL480 betrayed the ideals of self-sufficiency upon which Indian independence was established. And the *Times of India* published criticisms from the right, as economist B. R. Shenoy attacked the program for its inflationary consequences.[58]

Patil was undaunted, maximizing his visibility in Washington while negotiating the final details—and signing the agreement in May 1960 in a ceremony with President Dwight D. Eisenhower. This agreement, worth $1.276 billion over four years, was almost four times the size of the 1956 one, and once again broke the record for the largest PL480 deal. In India the news prompted more criticism than celebration. Economist D. R. Gadgil concluded that PL480 food provided "immediate advantages" but warned that such advantages would "prove temporary and illusory" unless agricultural production increased dramatically and permanently. Meanwhile firebrand V. K. Krishna Menon railed against PL480 from the left, calling it "economically, financially and militarily wrong." He mocked the American need to offload grain by demanding that Americans should pay Indians for disposing of surplus American grains. And Shenoy kept up pressure from the right, with a three-part series on the deleterious financial effects of American grain.[59]

Public debates echoed those raging in the highest councils of Indian government. By May 1963 Patil's latest proposal to request additional rice from the United States came to the Cabinet. The Planning Commission as a whole was not enthusiastic about a new PL480 agreement, insisting that internal procurements would be sufficient for the food supply; editorialists agreed, chastising Patil for his "premature" actions and his "mistaken zeal" for PL480 grain. Ultimately the Cabinet took a middle position, authorizing Patil to negotiate only a brief extension of the current deal. While in Washington, Patil exceeded this mandate, laying the groundwork for a major new PL480 agreement. He expected kudos for his work but instead got a pink slip. PL480 had become a dangerous but necessary program for Indian planners and politicians.[60]

The fight over PL480 contained within it many big questions in Indian politics—about the direction of the rural economy, economic priorities more generally, the importance of food self-sufficiency, and the desirability of strengthening ties with the United States. These are the very issues that defined Indian development debates over the 1950s and early 1960s. And while these debates of course had domestic dimensions to them, they frequently implicated Cold War superpowers. PL480 became a resource deployed by Indian officials in favor of unregulated trade domestically and free trade internationally, and for that reason it prompted a great deal of enthusiasm—and plenty of opposition.

Importing Capital Goods via the ICICI

While Soviet projects like the Bhilai Steel Plant established a prominent beachhead for the USSR in public-sector heavy industry, American aid agencies ultimately found a small base of their own from which they could support private-sector industry. Creating the Industrial Credit and Investment Corporation of India (ICICI) gave U.S. and World Bank officials a channel for American funds and American influence—as well as a site from which to agitate for the private sector and against the general inclination toward public-sector industry. The ICICI supplemented small-scale loans for industrial raw materials and equipment and gave a firmer institutional base for Western support to the Indian private sector.[61]

Large-scale projects like steel mills remained off-limits for U.S. aid agencies; the Industrial Policy Resolutions of 1948 and 1956 decreed that any expansion in heavy industry would be in the public sector while U.S. agencies were, with few exceptions, committed to aiding private enterprise. The private sector was a long-standing concern, even obsession, of American officials. One U.S. aid agency defined its aspirations for India, for instance, as building an economy "based upon a Profit Motive Free Enterprise system."[62]

Building up the private sector included financing Indian purchases of American raw materials and small-scale equipment; aid accounting from both countries enumerated "capital equipment loans," repayable in rupees, that facilitated the export of American capital goods to India. Such aid accounted for about one-third of American aid to India after 1955, exceeded only by agriculture at 45 percent. They clustered in the sorts of projects that had been present from the very start of Western aid to India in the late 1940s: infrastructure development (especially of railways); multipurpose river valley development (including hydroelectric power, flood control, and irrigation); natural resource exploitation (especially of mineral ores); and thermal power plants. American grants and loans were not to build full power plants but to equip them—and hence the facilities were harder to publicize as symbols of American beneficence.[63]

The ICICI, created in 1955, became a major vehicle for financing these imports. It emerged from a network of private-sector proponents in Washington,

New York, New Delhi, and Bombay who sought to evade the Government of India's own industrial financing mechanisms. As early as 1953 the Foreign Operations Administration (as the U.S. aid organ was then called) agreed to allocate $20 million for "the promotion of industry," but at the same time sought to steer clear of the Indian government's Industrial Finance Corporation. American staff concluded that Western organizations, together with Indian industrialists and financiers, could easily set up a freestanding organization. U.S. government officials, worried about the restrictions upon and reverberations of operating directly in India, set up the organization under World Bank auspices, appointing American investment banker George Woods as its initial director. Eventually resources would flow into the ICICI from a variety of sources, including World Bank loans, PL480 counterpart proceeds, and future U.S. aid allocations. It won praise from American officials, many of whom promoted it as a model to be emulated elsewhere. Ironically, even though the ICICI was originally set up to avoid the Indian government, Prime Minister Nehru eventually approved interest-free government loans to increase the corporation's capacity.[64]

Though initially foreign managed, the ICICI found its first Indian director through the transnational network that had supported the organization in the first place. When Woods returned stateside and joined the World Bank, G. L. Mehta, a former ambassador in Washington, replaced him. Mehta maintained close ties with U.S. and World Bank officials, as well as with Indian businesses, including the massive Birla and Tata conglomerates. Former ambassador Chester Bowles condescendingly praised Mehta for having his "heart . . . in the right place"—meaning, in this context, that he favored private enterprise. Woods left his post at the ICICI but peppered Mehta with missives about all manner of policy and practice there. Indeed, Woods maintained powerful control over his former institution by providing the ICICI with lines of credit that gave the World Bank de facto veto power over Mehta's decisions. Woods often used the ICICI to undercut or undermine the official Industrial Finance Corporation, hoping to make the upstart into the standard-bearer for industrial finance in India. *Economic Weekly* cheered on the ICICI in this competition and frequently offered Mehta a public platform; he used the opportunity to agitate for a range of tax and regulatory policies of particular interest to private enterprise. The ICICI, in short, could be both a victim of Western bullying and an Indian bully pulpit.[65]

All in all, the ICICI served as an effective conduit through which Western aid programs, including official American ones, could circumvent the Government of India to promote private-sector industry. The pro-Western Indian press celebrated the ICICI's "dominant position" for precisely this reason. A call to nationalize the corporation in 1969 offered backhanded acknowledgment of its achievements. While the ICICI succeeded at using Western funds to encourage Indian private industry, this particular instrument also came with a disadvantage: the funds were disbursed through indirect mechanisms and were very widely dispersed across many small loans. There was no American counterpart to the public-sector steel plants in the industrial sector. The ICICI, in other words, fit perfectly into the pithy observation of Indian economists that "the United States would be a major supplier, but not a supplier of major projects." It succeeded, furthermore, at building links between the growing India lobby in the United States and the America lobby in India.[66]

Direct Aid Competition over Atomic Power

Many elements of project-based aid competition in India entailed separate spheres: the Soviet Union in public-sector heavy industry, and the United States in industrial finance and agriculture. Yet the two superpowers competed directly in the energy sector, most notably for these purposes in atomic energy. The triangular dynamic over support for India's civilian atomic program demonstrates the deployment of foreign resources in domestic battles but also the structures that prevented that gambit from achieving his desired result.

The brilliant physicist Homi J. Bhabha stood at the center of this effort. Bhabha engaged Meghnad Saha in a battle to shape the future of Indian atomic science—a battle in which both rivals sought to mobilize international networks. After defeating Saha in the battle for atomic supremacy, Bhabha sought to promote an atomic-powered future for India; given the country's size and dispersion of natural resources, he argued, atomic power offered a shortcut to rapid electrification. He also served as India's delegate at the International Atomic Energy Agency, chairing a major conference on peaceful uses of atomic energy in 1955.[67]

The idea of aiding India's civilian atomic projects appealed greatly to American diplomats in India, who were preoccupied with catching up to or surpassing the Soviet Union on the aid publicity front. While some American officials responded to the Bhilai announcement with a plan to win an "American" steel mill in India, other proposals abounded; one pro-Western Indian official argued that steel had already been done, so the best bet for a splashy American project would be an atomic power plant. Atomic aid could celebrate American technological prowess while at the same time flattering Indian pride regarding its own scientific achievements. Expanding Indo-American ties in the atomic realm could also make the Indian project dependent on American technology and fuels, and would allow U.S. officials to keep close tabs on Indian nuclear science.[68]

Indian scientists, for their part, were anxious to develop atomic technologies while avoiding dependence on any foreign powers—and particularly upon the United States. These competing interests shaped the atomic negotiations, which revealed most of the key trends visible in the highest stage of competitive coexistence. Both superpowers sought to curry favor with recipient nations; entrepreneurial Indian officials sought allies in the Soviet Union and the United States and who would help them fight their own domestic battles; and superpower diplomats sought leverage in shaping Indian policies and politics.

Bhabha's ascent did not cheer American observers. Diplomats were convinced that he was politically aligned with the Soviets; their dispatches trafficked in claims about Bhabha's "strong leftist leanings." Indeed, they tried to prevent him from meeting top British scientists for fear that his politics were not just suspicious but contagious. Soviet cultural officials invited Bhabha to Moscow in 1951, which American officials took as a confirmation of Bhabha's political commitments, and they did not revise their opinions when he declined the invitation. Besides, Bhabha spent plenty of time in the West, offering Indian strategic materials to the British and French nuclear establishments in exchange for reactor technology.[69]

By late 1952, however, Bhabha set his sights on cooperation with the United States, by far the world's leader in atomic technology. He offered his American counterparts access to Indian strategic materials, including uranium from the large ore deposits in northeastern India, in exchange for heavy water and technical details on reactor design. Both Bhabha and Nehru spread the word that India was seeking to build a medium-size experimental reactor. American officials were tempted to read Bhabha's new friendliness as a sign of a political shift, though it could just have easily been a straightforward assessment of which nations could aid his efforts to build up Indian atomic capabilities. Even as he approached Americans, for instance, Bhabha hired a Czech research director for his atomic institute at Trombay near Bombay.[70]

By 1955, as the economic cold war heated up, Bhabha was fully engaged in an atomic version of that competition, making dueling visits to the superpowers. He went to Moscow in mid-1955 to meet with Soviet scientists and to visit atomic facilities. Soviet officials had high hopes for the trip because they saw Bhabha as "sympathetic" to the USSR. Bhabha took advantage of these hopes, turning the excursion into a shopping trip and asking—as one of his hosts observed—the price of almost every piece of equipment he saw. But he approached the United States as well as the Soviet Union. He pleaded his case to Secretary of State John Foster Dulles, boasting that India's atomic research far outpaced those of most other nations outside Europe and Japan and thus merited a different kind of relationship than the boilerplate "Atoms for Peace" arrangements.[71]

While concerned about Bhabha's ultimate political allegiance, American diplomats tried to convince U.S. Atomic Energy Commission (USAEC) officials to promote Indo-American atomic cooperation as a means of strengthening diplomatic and economic relations more generally. The enthusiasm of American officials for some kind of atomic cooperation with Bhabha, however, ran up against very strict rules about the export of technology and of fissionable materials, so Indo-American negotiations remained stalemated through 1955 and 1956. All the while, Bhabha kept up negotiations with Soviet atomic officials. The USAEC was determined to hold the line on the safeguards that Bhabha—and Nehru—considered infringements on Indian sovereignty. So Bhabha's negotiations with both superpowers covered conditions for use as well as prices, delivery schedules, and capabilities.[72]

Fortunately for Bhabha, the Canadian nuclear establishment was angling to get into the atomic aid game. Atomic Energy Canada sought international recognition of its design and the chance to advertise Canadian technologies and ultimately boost overseas sales. Canadian aid officials sought something more prestigious than the aluminum or wheat that was the basis of prior Canadian aid. The appeal to India was not just that Canadian officials would provide the reactor over and above its other aid but also that Canadian officials had yet to impose safeguards for nuclear equipment and materials. India's Atomic Energy Commission (AEC) reached an agreement with Canada to build a reactor at the Trombay research facility.[73]

The Canadian aid fed Indian success in navigating between the super-powers. Bhabha triumphantly commissioned the Canadian reactor at the Trombay research facility in 1957, bringing together scientific delegations from thirty nations, including both the Soviet Union and the United States, to celebrate Indian progress. Nehru lauded the peaceful uses of atomic science, while Bhabha promised it would provide "an unending trail into the future." American experts in the audience expressed some skepticism about that future while praising present-day work in Bhabha's research institute. Trombay was dedicated to scientific experimentation, not supplying power, so was only an intermediate point in Bhabha's struggle for atomic power.[74]

Bhabha had long argued that atomic energy was well suited to large countries like India, and indeed used his presidency of the International Conference on the Peaceful Uses of Atomic Energy to make the economic case for atomic power in underdeveloped countries. The Indian Planning Commission, though, had little use for Bhabha's arguments; the Second Plan allocated only small sums for atomic research and none for atomic power. Working through domestic policy channels had not paid off for Bhabha, so he took his struggle abroad.[75]

These international efforts yielded promising results. Only days after the Trombay reactor was inaugurated in 1957, Soviet officials stepped up their efforts to woo him and his colleagues in the Indian atomic establishment. First a Soviet economic official told Nehru that a heavy machinery factory, currently under construction with Soviet aid, could easily provide the equipment necessary for India's atomic aspirations. Days later, a Soviet war hero paid an informal visit to Trombay to demonstrate commitment (without, of course, conceding anything in terms of technology or safeguards). And not long after that Soviet officials offered the Indian government the chance to send students to the USSR for training in atomic physics and engineering—an offer declined because Indian scientists considered Soviet training too "elementary" for their needs. By the late 1950s Indian atomic research was winning laurels in the Soviet press, and visiting Indians like the reliably pro-Soviet planner Mahalanobis were making pilgrimages to Soviet atomic facilities. These efforts produced closer bilateral ties in the atomic sphere, but not a major aid package.[76]

These gestures from the Soviets, combined with the American embassy's concerns about losing the economic cold war in India, spurred the American bureaucracy to action. This political imperative did not, of course, resolve the principal problem behind the stalemate: Indian atomic officials remained steadfastly opposed to the strict safeguards that the USAEC insisted upon. State Department officials in Washington, like their colleagues in Delhi, emphasized the political importance of an Indo-American atomic deal; even pro-Western Indians, they worried, might endorse a Soviet program if American plans fell through. The usually reserved President Eisenhower jumped on the bandwagon, saying that he wanted "something spectacular" that demonstrated American commitment to India. With Eisenhower on their side, American diplomats pressured the USAEC to make a deal with India work. By the time Bhabha brought his proposal to Washington in fall 1959, battle lines within the U.S. government had been drawn. American diplomats optimistically assumed that Bhabha's trip meant that he was willing to yield ground on safeguards. But they also warned, ominously, that "India was made up its mind to have a power reactor and if we won't help them they will turn elsewhere." American officials knew well that "elsewhere" could only mean the Soviet Union.[77]

Bhabha's international engagements once again fed into his domestic battles. His American sojourn opened Washington as a new front in his budget battles, previously limited to New Delhi. He was hoping to increase spending for atomic energy in India's Third Five-Year Plan, then being formulated in the Planning Commission and ministries. Yet his efforts to convert rhetorical enthusiasm into financial support had yet to produce results. By early 1960, he escalated his campaigns, sending a lengthy report to the PC pleading the case for atomic energy as an economically viable power source. The PC, however, still evinced little interest in funding atomic power plants in the Third Plan.[78]

When these budget requests were stuck in limbo, Bhabha turned to external aid. He made clear that aid proposals, running up to $50 million, should be considered "apart from and in addition to" other foreign aid for India's Third Plan. That is, he demanded that atomic power not be subject to the normal process of allocation and economic decision making. After hearing of a possible Canadian deal, for instance, he wrote Nehru imperiously, "I trust that the Third Five Year Plan will not be so frozen as to exclude" an externally funded atomic project.[79]

This condition that Bhabha's project be considered separately from the aid package for the Third Plan raised eyebrows and indeed hackles in American agencies. The USAEC quickly washed its hands of the process, insisting that any program with the Indian atomic establishment could serve only political—and not technical or scientific—aims for the United States. So USAEC staff kicked the decision over to the State Department. Meanwhile officials at State had their own concerns about the politics—namely, that Bhabha was lobbying Washington agencies to evade the planning process in Delhi and that in meeting with the scientist the U.S. embassy flirted with "becoming a middleman between Bhabha and his own Government." The New Delhi embassy overrode these concerns as its officials lobbied American agencies to support Bhabha's atomic aspirations.[80]

This lukewarm reaction did little to slow Bhabha's lobbying efforts, and perhaps even intensified his desire to attract foreign assistance—so much so that it almost backfired. At the end of February, he hosted a technical team from the USAEC, trying once again to convince Americans of great economic advantages of atomic power in India. He also tried, without much success, to explain how the Indian venture would benefit American atomic research, through the provision of strategic minerals like thorium from India and also through the chance to try out American nuclear technology in new climates and circumstances. That delegation arrived while a delegation of Soviet atomic scientists was also present in New Delhi—prompting the Americans' unexpected trip to the Taj Mahal. American embassy officials, though embarrassed by the dueling delegations, nevertheless made the case that the United States simply must support India's atomic program—or else the Soviets would. The final report from the expert team played along, enumerating the many problems with India's proposals before concluding that diplomatic concerns "make it particularly desirable to proceed promptly" with an agreement.[81]

As Bhabha continued his efforts to shop around—and not just among the superpowers—potential donors sought to head off a race to the bottom on safeguards. Bhabha and his AEC staff crisscrossed Western Europe for the best financial deal and the fewest safeguards; one British expert complained that they were "bluffing and playing one country off against another," threatening the British engineering firms that if the UK government did not make concessions about safeguards then they would go across the English Channel to the French. Yet Bhabha's assertiveness ran up against ongoing conversations between potential donors. Assembling in Paris in winter 1960, representatives from France, the Soviet Union, the United Kingdom, and the United States considered joint action regarding safeguards; for all of their differences, these atomic powers reached an agreement to uphold safeguards. This effort at collusion did not bode well for Bhabha's maneuvering between the atomic powers, suggesting that the competitive dynamic of the economic cold war could be contained when it touched on superpowers' mutual interests.[82]

Whether or not Indian officials were aware of this donor cooperation, Prime Minister Nehru staunchly protected Indian interests. In a detailed letter to his British counterpart, Nehru outlined the steps that his government would take to ensure that the atomic technologies or materials were not misused. At the same time, though, he rejected any and all externally imposed safeguards. British trade officials continued to make the case that the United Kingdom should accept Nehru's promises in order to "get export business for our nuclear power plant industry." Unaware of the conclave that might place limits on French and Soviet competitors, they argued that they could not "impose on ourselves a handicap from which our rivals are free." But the trade officials had difficulty convincing American officials, or even other British colleagues, of the wisdom of this approach. Ultimately, the British prime minister overruled the trade officials' proposal and held the line on safeguards.[83]

Bhabha, presumably recovered from the awkward moment of having competing delegations in Delhi at the same time, continued to seek Soviet aid. He led a delegation to Moscow in May 1960, hoping to advance the negotiations begun in Delhi in February. Staff at Bhabha's institute reported that those negotiations were a "flop"; while the Soviets were willing to deliver a small reactor without safeguards, the question of financing for a larger project was still uncertain. He kept up his trips to Moscow even as he met with little success there; senior Soviet atomic officials had rebuffed Indian calls for an atomic power reactor as "premature." Meanwhile, Soviet diplomats received orders that they should under no circumstances offer a guarantee that they would design, build, or supply the reactor that the Indian AEC desired. And Aleksei Kosygin, a heavy industry specialist and devoted friend of India on the Politburo, chided Indian interlocutors for their "misguided focus on atomic energy." Seeking whatever leverage he could get from Soviet negotiations, Bhabha signed a cooperative agreement with the USSR that autumn; Soviet and Indian engineers would build a research reactor using some fissionable materials from the USSR in exchange for Indian atomic minerals. This research reactor was a consolation prize from the Soviets, as well as the means for Bhabha to increase pressure for an American power reactor.[84]

But here again Bhabha was stymied by donor collusion. Both superpowers doubted the economic logic for atomic power, with American calculations pointing to the same conclusion as Soviet ones. He then sought a happier result from the World Bank, hoping that its analysts would endorse his calculations on the economics of nuclear power. The superpowers again compared notes, leading Soviet atomic officials to promise their American counterparts that they would not support such a facility in India. Bhabha's efforts to play competitors against each other might have worked in some realms. But atomic power was different.[85]

Bhabha continued his efforts to internationalize his battle for an atomic-powered India, but faced increasing headwinds. American officials eventually concluded that he flew to Moscow primarily to pry more concessions on his next trip to Washington. This tactic ultimately proved unsuccessful; the stalemate over safeguards remained. The USAEC persisted in rejecting technical or economic assistance unless it could maintain oversight of reactor technology and nuclear fuels. Indian scientists, meanwhile, continued to seek a way around safeguards, which they considered "interference in India's economic and technical development." They proposed an arrangement of "renting" British uranium-235 as an effort to evade the safeguards issue, but British scientists insisted that the safeguard issue would be resolved only when Indians "face[d] reality." So these end-arounds ultimately went nowhere.[86]

Stymied in its approaches to avoid safeguards by negotiating privately with individual nations, the Indian AEC thus publicly sought international tenders to build a reactor. This much-ballyhooed request, often celebrated as a turning point in India's nuclear program, was in fact an admission of defeat for Bhabha. It signified that the USSR was not going to build India's first power reactor, and that Western safeguards were inevitable. Thus when Bhabha approached the Americans yet again, in 1961 and 1962, officials in the administration of President John F. Kennedy optimistically believed that they detected a new willingness to accept some safeguards. American discussions on India were also wrapped up in growing worries (perhaps even obsession) about the potential military and political fallout of a Chinese nuclear test. George McGhee, at that point a senior State Department adviser, floated the idea of helping India build a bomb to preempt a Chinese announcement; though his proposal was roundly rejected, it does demonstrate the intensity of American concerns. But worries over China's nuclear efforts made India's civilian projects more attractive to American policy makers. Thus the USAEC supported American funding of an atomic power station at Tarapur, near Bombay, observing that it could serve as a "major counterweight to Red Chinese atomic energy developments." Supporting civilian power with tight safeguards, American officials hoped, might tamp down Indian interest in a military program; civilian atomic power could become an instrument of non-proliferation. American policy makers also offered a familiar array of arguments about the political benefits of the project, which would have a "great political and public impact in India" and thus would help "keep India on the free world side." American aid for Tarapur, moreover, would make India "dependent indefinitely on the U.S. for its fuel supply." Perhaps to avoid this dependence, Bhabha kept negotiating with French authorities until the last minute; eventually, though, he had little choice but to accept the American offer.[87]

While he lost the battle over safeguards, Bhabha had better luck with budgets. His trips to Moscow and Washington paid off as USAID prepared a large loan—much as Bhabha had hoped, above and beyond other allotments for the Third Five-Year Plan—and the agreement was inked in August 1963. But Bhabha and his institute had made major concessions. General Electric agreed to build the twin reactors with plenty of safeguards in place; the USAEC opened an oversight office in Bombay. The reactor would be built on a turnkey basis, raising the cost (especially the dollar outlay) and reducing the opportunity for Indian training in reactor design and construction. What was more, the Indian side agreed to exclusively use U.S. nuclear fuel. What began as Bhabha's efforts to establish India's economic and political independence, then, ended with reliance on American technology and fuels, much to the regret of some of Bhabha's colleagues and successors.[88]

In using his international contacts to win domestic battles, Bhabha effectively demonstrated the possibilities of development politics. But he also demonstrated the limits of internationalizing his domestic budget dispute, especially in sensitive spheres like atomic energy. Even as the nuclear powers competed on financial terms, they colluded on the question of safeguards. The ultimate cost of circumventing the Planning Commission, then, was higher than Bhabha had initially expected. Playing the donors off each other did not necessarily lead either side into a more generous posture, and so atomic energy helped define the limits of recipient leverage the economic cold war.

Bhabha's pursuit of foreign support from the Cold War East and West marked one of a few arenas in which the two sides competed directly. In other spheres, each side found its own field, its own clientele, and its own institutional base. Taken together, these projects illuminate an important phase of the economic cold war in which the competition took place in terms of projects and enterprises. They show how development politics emerged from this competition, and suggest a number of key lessons about how development aid operated.

Foreign-funded development projects required domestic as well as overseas support. The ability of Indian officials to steer the diplomatic and economic bureaucracies toward their project was the most important determinant for success, as the divergent fates of Bhilai and Suratgarh suggest. There was widespread enthusiasm in India for building a steel plant—so much so that the Soviet plant faced stiff competition from British- and West German–supported ones. In contrast, there were few supporters of Soviet-style agriculture in India, aside from leftist stalwarts like K. D. Malaviya—who as minister of mines and oil had little authority in this realm. American projects like Community Development, PL480, and the ICICI managed to secure their own existence thanks to the operation of international networks with important nodes in India—though the demise of Community Development suggests what happens when foreign support dissipates. The work of local proponents like S. K. Dey for community development and S. K. Patil for PL480 gave the programs important footholds in India. And ditto for Homi J. Bhabha's tireless efforts to build Tarapur.

The origins and the ultimate fate of development projects, furthermore, emerged not just in negotiations between donors and recipients but also in disputes within and across national boundaries. Community development, for instance, pitted proponents like Chester Bowles, S. K. Dey, and Douglas Ensminger against production-oriented officials in both countries. Divergent visions of modern India played an especially prominent role in the debates about Indian industry. Even if the ultimate path was a modern, industrial India, was agriculture the place to start, as many American policy makers and academics insisted? Or could the Indian economy skip straight to heavy industry, from bullock cart to jet plane (in Nehru's famous phrase)? What was the role of the private sector in the Indian economy, and especially in industry? These were contentious questions in India, as in the superpowers, and are too easily dismissed when the economic cold war is conceived as a battle between two superpowers for the hearts and minds of Third World leaders.[89]

Eyeing the competition over aid, well-known Polish economist Michał Kalecki praised India and other nonaligned nations as "clever calves" who could "suckle two cows."[90] To Kalecki, a frequent adviser in India and elsewhere, the contest seemed to be among equals, with each superpower presenting its own vision of modernity and its own version of how to achieve it. American diplomats in India felt acutely that they were playing catch-up with the Soviets, whose high-profile projects like Bhilai had generated so much publicity. Such fears prompted—much as Khrushchev had boasted—American aid for the Third World, not least in high-profile projects as Tarapur. At the root of American fears was a sense that the United States was behind and might not be able to catch up. Such an impression was deceptive, though, as Western aid quickly and decisively came to dominate in government coffers if not in public opinion.

CHAPTER 5

"FREE MONEY" AND THE TILT TOWARD THE WEST

The crisis of the Second Five-Year Plan, which began only months after the plan itself started in April 1956, proved to be a Rorschach test for economists and politicians. Cabinet members looked at the crisis, but each saw a different cause and cure for it, as the figure on the next page shows.

With Prime Minister Jawaharlal Nehru perched on a tree searching for a way out, members of the cabinet each pointed toward a different way out of the woods. Cabinet ministers (and plenty of other politicians and economists not shown in the figure below) diverged in their diagnoses of the economic problems as well as possible solutions—each in line with their respective visions of India's economic future. None of them wanted to waste a good crisis, so each used it as a chance to advance particular economic ideas, pointing forward with a level of certainty unjustified by the circumstances. But two conclusions were clear: any path out of the economic woods would be established by political contest. And every path would involve foreign aid, and thus would involve development politics.

The crisis gave an opening to those opposed to the general orientation of the Second Plan. Prasanta Chandra Mahalanobis had mobilized foreign experts to push through a plan that emphasized public-sector heavy industry and central planning. The foreign exchange crisis of 1956–1958 provided an opportunity for Mahalanobis's opponents who, broadly speaking, favored a more open economy and closer ties with the capitalist West. Since the crisis was acute, but also inaugurated an era of chronic foreign exchange shortages, the initial responses shaped long-term battles over how the Indian economy

Prime Minister Jawaharlal Nehru (in tree) and members of his cabinet search for a way out of the deepening economic crisis of the Second Five-Year Plan, with each pointing in a different direction. Depicted here (left to right) are Commerce and Industry Minister Morarji Desai, Planning and Labour Minister G. L. Nanda, Home Minister G. B. Pant, and Finance Minister T. T. Krishnamachari. *Source:* Cartoon by Keshav Shankar Pillai ("Shankar"), *Shankar's Weekly,* August 18, 1957. Courtesy of Children's Book Trust, New Delhi.

would develop, and who—domestically and internationally—would shape that development.

The foreign exchange crisis of the late 1950s ultimately gave an advantage to the America lobby in New Delhi. And it proved just as useful to the India lobby in Washington, D.C., as well as to those hoping to expand the compass of American aid to the developing world. Indian circumstances had already pushed against the limits of American aid instruments like technical assistance; India would play even a greater role in the late 1950s as American development aid expanded to include larger-scale financing. After the U.S. Congress passed new legislation in 1957, American aid no longer entailed merely the dispatch of a handful of U.S. experts or the support for individual projects (the atomic power station in Tarapur, community development, etc.) that defined the initial phase of the economic cold war. Nor was the United States the only Western institution to shift its emphasis; the World Bank, too, altered both the purposes of its financing and the structures through which it operated.

Especially in the American and Indian governments, but also in the penumbra of other lenders including the World Bank, the dynamic of development politics grew more noticeable. In the short term, the rise of new Western instruments of development finance gave new opportunities to Indian officials promoting closer ties with the West. Since external financing beyond individual projects stood outside Soviet definitions of economic cooperation, those in India hoping for Eastern bloc support faced a major disadvantage. The implications of this unevenness became apparent in subsequent years.

The Origins of the Crisis

Everything about the Indian economic crisis of 1956–1958—how to measure it, what caused it, who was to blame, and how to resolve it—came up for debate. Few diagnoses or descriptions of the crisis stood outside partisan disputes about the recent past and the long-term future of the Indian economy. The dispute over financial versus physical planning offers a convenient starting point. With the help of friendly experts visiting the Indian Statistical Institute (ISI), Mahalanobis won Nehru's endorsement for physical over financial planning—meaning that the plan, in principle, would encompass all production in India rather than just steer government investments to one or another project. The optimism of the Second Five-Year Plan took physical form: the construction of a trio of steel mills that symbolized the arrival of industrial India, power plants under American and Soviet sponsorship, and eager university students spreading the gospel of community development in Indian villages. The Second Plan's boldness was apparent even in the dry tables of official documents. The plan called for a 30 percent increase in agricultural production, aided by a tripling of the coverage of community development programs. Beyond agriculture, the goals were much higher: doubling the generation of electricity, trebling the output of finished steel and aluminum, and quadrupling the production of textile looms and cement machinery. As symbolized by a tome of more than four hundred pages outlining industrial projects in the late 1950s, the Planning Commission (PC) celebrated physical achievements.[1]

Perhaps the PC's relative neglect of financial implications emerged from this emphasis on physical production. In any case, the commission did not fully explain where the substantial resources allocated in the Second Plan would come from. The overall investment figure—4,800 crores rupees, or about $10 billion—far exceeded domestic capacity as well as the limits of foreign aid agencies. The secretary to the PC insisted that the plan's goals could not be reduced to reflect available resources; he nevertheless maintained full confidence that "the necessary national effort should be forthcoming." The plan's projected financing reflected this optimism, as indicated in the table in Chapter 4. About 8 percent would be "covered by [unspecified] additional measures to raise domestic resources"; deficit spending would account for another 25 percent. And without specifying any source or mechanism for external financing, the plan called for raising 17 percent of the funds externally. *Economic Weekly* presciently admonished that "it [was] neither wise nor realistic to count on external assistance of this magnitude."[2]

Planning Commission economists acknowledged the challenging circumstances for external finance, but never reckoned with them. One PC report in 1957 observed that the Second Plan's major increases in investment would involve "a heavy strain on foreign exchange reserves" but insisted that the plan needed to go ahead anyway since the availability of foreign resources "can hardly be determined in advance."[3]

The uncertainties about external resources, alongside the uncertainties about imports and exports, meant that projections of balance of payments in the Second Plan were speculative at best. The PC predicted that India's outflows would exceed inflows by 1,120 crores rupees of the course of the plan, a figure outstripping the country's foreign exchange reserves at the start of the plan (about 750 crores rupees). Jawaharlal Nehru noted the looming foreign exchange challenges but did not want to seek foreign assistance, telling the Lok Sabha (the Parliament's lower house) that "we cannot live in expectation of the bounties of others." Minister of Finance C. D. Deshmukh publicly acknowledged the risks to India's international financial position in late 1955, as the final details of the Second Plan were put into place; he dismissed the notion of floating Indian bonds on the London market but admitted that "there would be a short-fall in the foreign exchange resources" that might—*might!*—eventuate in having to "look around for other sources of financing." (Deshmukh resigned in summer 1956 for reasons unrelated to economic policy.)[4]

Even this vague speculation about seeking foreign aid raised hackles among some Indian ministers. Among them was T. T. Krishnamachari (commonly known as TTK), a Madras-based businessman-cum-Congress-politician whom *Time* magazine gave the awkward but well-intentioned moniker "Private Enterpriser." *Economic Weekly* agreed, calling him the "most self-conscious supporter of private enterprise in the Cabinet." TTK sought to expand Indian engagement in the world economy, but in a way that would serve Indian businesses. He therefore encouraged Indian enterprises to seek foreign investors without yielding operational control. In the name of helping private-sector firms contributing to the industrialization effort, he liberalized imports in 1955–1956 while serving as minister of commerce and industry. After many of his efforts to promote private enterprise faced heavy headwinds, TTK feared that the rise of Mahalanobis and the PC threatened his power and influence. He tendered his resignation, which Nehru refused to accept, leaving TTK in his post through the first months of the plan's operations. While TTK sought closer private-sector connections between India and the West, he viewed foreign aid skeptically. In late 1955, for instance, he proclaimed his opposition to foreign aid to a group of Indian and foreign industrialists. Others in the senior ranks of Indian officialdom opposed TTK on the question of aid. Perhaps the most energetic of those promoting aid was B. K. Nehru, officially the commissioner general for economic affairs in the Ministry of Finance and unofficially the roving economic ambassador for all aid matters. He had been appointed by the pro-Western minister of finance Morarji Desai; the job, Desai recalled, was to "mak[e] arrangements for our foreign exchange requirements"—a fuzzy euphemism for seeking aid in foreign currency. From that ill-defined post, he did more than any other individual to shift the terms of foreign assistance for India.[5]

Foreign Exchange and the Second Plan

The period in which Mahalanobis and the PC formulated the Second Plan (1954–1956) marked a lull in ongoing debates about foreign assistance; the debates returned, however, with a new urgency once the plan got under way in April 1956. India's relatively stable levels of foreign exchange reserves plummeted that spring, beginning a long and steep downward trajectory. Within a few months of the plan's start, the Indian government started burning through its foreign exchange at the unsustainable rate of 6.5 crores rupees ($13.5 million) per week; at that rate reserves would dip below the statutory minimum of 400 crores rupees in less than one year. (One early response was to reduce the minimum to 300 crores rupees, though this solved only the legal—and not the economic—problems.) The decline was steady and precipitous for twenty-eight of the first thirty months of the Second Plan.[6]

The first concerns about foreign exchange came in August 1956—the plan's fifth month—and established the groundwork for future policy debates. Tipped off to the fact that "foreign balances [were] gradually disappearing," the prime minister asked the PC to get better information. A few days later he received a detailed memorandum not from the Planning Commission but from his cousin B. K. Nehru at the Ministry of Finance. That report warned of possible default on international payments unless the government undertook "resolute and immediate action (which will of course be painful)." The prime minister soon informed the chief ministers of India's states, with grave understatement, that India's "foreign exchange position . . . is not a happy one at all." He asked the ministers to do their best to increase food production, which would reduce the need for food imports. But Nehru offered no additional funds for the states to boost agriculture, hoping that intensified efforts alone could yield a 15 percent increase in food crops. By early 1957, Nehru reinstated the foreign exchange budgeting and licensing process that had lapsed in prior years. The cabinet also imposed a "virtual embargo" (Nehru's term) on all new foreign exchange commitments.[7]

The foreign exchange crisis that began in August 1956 and dragged on through the next two years prompted divergent interpretations of the crisis's origins and varied solutions with different domestic and international implications. The Planning Commission, which favored the expansion of public-sector industry, blamed the private sector for overspending its allotments of foreign exchange; it demanded increased responsibility for private-sector transactions. Likewise, the minister of commerce blamed the problem on insufficient attention to exports; he called for programs that would strengthen the government's hand in export promotion—programs that would, naturally, be organized within his ministry.[8]

Not everyone treated the foreign exchange problems with the same seriousness. Master planner Mahalanobis, as responsible as any other individual for the shape of the Second Plan, dismissed the concerns as a failure of nerve. He wrote the Polish economist Oskar Lange that "The present anxiety marks . . . the inevitable difficulties of adjustment to the requirements of a new policy. . . . It will take some time for things to settle down." Mahalanobis thus wanted to continue with the plan as originally formulated. Prime Minister Nehru had some sympathy with this position, noting that such foreign exchange problems were "bound to crop up in an underdeveloped country's economy." Even TTK, a firm supporter of private-sector Indian industry who became finance minister just days before the crisis broke, insisted that the current situation was a "crisis of development, and not a crisis of stagnation or of confidence." He thus called for a solution that would maintain the development program then under way while reducing the demands for foreign exchange. He attributed the problems to "boom" in the private sector. The authoritative Reserve Bank of India, not inclined institutionally toward the Planning Commission's vision, ultimately agreed; its *Bulletin* blamed higher-than anticipated imports of capital goods, primarily by private firms.[9]

The Planning Commission was ready to concede the need for some adjustments to the plan—so long as it got to make them. One PC adviser admitted that the Second Plan had "got off to a rather uncertain start" and called for immediate action "before excessive exuberance" created "a real mess." He proposed slowing down or delaying elements of the plan to reduce the demands for imported capital goods. Signature projects like the steel plants would be exempted from this slowdown, as would smaller projects for which foreign exchange had already been "arranged" through aid agreements. These changes amounted to minor tinkering, he insisted; "the main structure" of the plan would remain "unaltered." The PC stood by the basics of the plan, accepting only minor adjustments to be undertaken by the commission itself.[10]

Other voices came to the defense of Planning Commission prerogatives. Economist D. R. Gadgil shared the view that the commission's formulation of the plan was not the issue—only the ministries' implementation. The main problem, Gadgil wrote, resulted from the "disregard of the definitive policy recommendations"—not from the "structure of the plan" itself. He blamed in particular the dismantling of food price controls on the one hand and "slackness" in import licensing on the other. The answer, therefore, was more and better planning, including closer attention to physical quantities—a return to the battle of physical versus financial planning. Ashok Mitra, a Marxist student of the Dutch econometrician Jan Tinbergen, took up this battle, highlighting the failures of free enterprise. The fact that the government had been unable to stem the outflow of foreign exchange, Mitra argued, "merely emphasizes the hazards of an overwhelming free-enterprise economy." "State policy," he noted angrily, had "to work through an elongated process of compromises and balances." Responses to the crisis occasioned normative statements about the future and not just descriptive statements about the past.[11]

In protracted exchanges in *Economic Weekly* and elsewhere, one consistent approach began from the diagnosis that the foreign exchange problems resulted from excessive import of consumer goods. K. N. Raj, a left-inclined economist at the PC, thus called for strict control over all forms of consumption. Rapid industrialization, Raj implied, required a single-minded focus on production, so the population would need to make sacrifices to see the plan come to fruition. Raj evaluated foreign aid possibilities along these lines, favoring those that boosted production (he cited in particular Soviet aid) over those that fed the growth in consumption (like Food for Peace, PL480). He and his allies favored tighter licensing of imports, especially those that did not contribute directly to industrial development.[12]

Others extended Raj's argument into a larger effort to restrict consumer goods, whether produced domestically or imported. One member of the PC's Panel of Economists came down strongly against consumer goods and called for "greater austerity." A cabinet discussion blamed the crisis on "the lack of will to work hard." The broadest and boldest statement of this view was not intended for Indian audiences. In a presentation to the American Economic Association in 1960, Ashok Mitra defended the Planning Commission's work, but did offer one cutting criticism: "the biggest failure of Indian planning" was the failure to help the Indian population understand the "large quantum of abstinence and sacrifice" necessary for success. Mitra's argument went beyond the economic to include moral undertones.[13]

The Indian right, meanwhile, used the foreign exchange crisis to challenge the Second Plan and its authors at the PC. The Ministry of Finance wasted no time making the argument that "the foreign exchange crisis [was] the result of the Plan itself." And B. R. Shenoy, India's most prominent free-market economist and the sole dissenter on the PC's Panel of Economists, voiced his complaints about the plan and the commission. In his presidential address to the Indian Economic Association in December 1957, Shenoy traced India's economic problems to government spending well in excess of internal resources. Such spending not only caused inflation—a cardinal sin to a monetarist like Shenoy—but also led to excessive imports. This government "over-investment," Shenoy charged, was "the starting point of the trouble" because it deprived the private sector of resources. His criticisms, in other words, went well beyond the balance-of-payments implications of the Second Plan to the whole Indian strategy of rapid industrialization. Shenoy directly dismissed the claims of Nehru and his planners that payments problems were "an essential concomitant of economic development." The ultimate solution, Shenoy proposed, was devaluation of the rupee, which would curb the use of imports (since they would become more expensive) and facilitate exports (since they would be cheaper in international markets). Shenoy, in sum, took the foreign exchange crisis as a sign of the failure of the entire Nehruvian strategy.[14]

A group of officials and industrialists tried to use the crisis to open up the Indian economy to foreign capital. G. D. Birla insisted that the "only solution" to India's current economic predicament was to "prepare a climate" for increased foreign investment in Indian firms. Western-inclined economic officials agreed. Morarji Desai, abstemious and socially conservative, endorsed market oriented policies and closer ties with the West, maintaining a vision of modern India open to U.S. economic ideas even as he was repulsed by the permissiveness of American culture. L. K. Jha, a distinguished civil servant trained at Cambridge and the London School of Economics, worked for decades to expand Indian ties with the West. In an influential report to the Planning Commission, this pair noted the inadequacies of domestically available financing or technology for the demands of industrialization. They thus called for new policies to "encourage the inflow of foreign capital." Morarji Desai and L. K. Jha, like Birla, insisted upon the participation of Indian firms and called for limits on foreign ownership stakes. If those on the left called for redoubling efforts and increasing sacrifices in the name of rapid development, those on the right called for deeper integration into the capitalist world economy.[15]

The blame game combined personalities, politics and institutions, with Jawaharlal Nehru serving as the ultimate, if sometimes reluctant, referee. One key axis of conflict was between the Ministry of Finance and the Planning Commission. Attributing the balance-of-payments problem to the plans as formulated would discredit the PC, while attributing the problem to the execution of stated (and otherwise unproblematic) policies would expose the Ministry of Finance to scrutiny. On this issue the prime minister's response was especially curious. Shortly after learning of the foreign exchange crisis in late summer 1956, Nehru asked the Planning Commission to investigate causes and propose solutions. Perhaps because the commission itself, though an interested party, was not of one mind on the causes or consequences of the problem, its report enumerated many causes but set few priorities. First and foremost, the PC came to the defense of the plan and insisted that the crisis was an inevitable outcome of the plan's boldness. The report stressed factors beyond its writ or control: higher-than-expected defense expenditures, poor weather, higher prices for imports of industrial machinery and raw materials, inflation, and increased consumer goods imports. The report, in other words, had something for everyone. After reading it, Nehru concluded ruefully (and rightly) that "not much thought appears to have been given at the time [of the plan's formulation] as to how to raise the necessary finance." He concluded that the Planning Commission should take a large role, approving any future decisions on external finance.[16] That said, the very nature of the problem favored the ministries. While the PC might set targets, the day-to-day work of licensing imports remained in the ministries of Finance and of Commerce and Industry. Indeed, since the major clients for import licenses were private-sector firms, these remained outside the ambit of the PC, which (notwithstanding the principle of physical planning) took responsibility for plans for government investment.

As skirmishes continued along these lines, TTK, who had served as minister of commerce and industry earlier and had just taken up the post of minister of finance, came in for special criticism. Trying to tamp down that issue, the prime minister concluded that "the responsibility" for the crisis "is shared by all of us." This Solomonic statement only fueled the flurry of accusations, prickly defenses, and counteraccusations. Nehru then tried to shift the blame onto C. D. Deshmukh, by then conveniently out of office; this maneuver allowed him call for more involvement of the PC *and* more direct controls exercised by the Ministry of Finance. As one political scientist concluded, this arrangement marked the dethroning of the Planning Commission, and began a pendulum swing toward having more power residing in the ministries—above all in the Finance Ministry.[17]

Nehru's approach did not, however, resolve the battle between the PC and the Finance Ministry. Nehru's son-in-law Firoze Gandhi was a particularly vehement critic of TTK, railing on the minister's enthusiasm for private enterprise. The left wing of Congress sought his ouster through the time-honored political tradition of scandal-mongering. When TTK weathered the accusations that he had caused the crisis by loosening import licenses, critics shifted gears, publicizing a scandal involving corrupt investments by the government-run life insurance company (under TTK's supervision as minister of finance) that would eventually hit its target. TTK resigned under a cloud of scandal in early 1958.[18]

These shifts in power and influence appeared below the surface; more visible in 1957–1958 was a two-part response to the economic crisis. Stringent restrictions on spending foreign exchange were imposed in January 1957. As the hemorrhaging of foreign currency slowed, the debate soon turned to longer-term implications for economic policy. The Planning Commission was able to hold onto sufficient power (or at least the appearance of power) to issue a revised plan in 1958. That rephasing maintained what the commission called the "hard core" of the plan—the major heavy-industry projects—while deferring many minor projects. Predictably, there was fierce debate about these new goals and new allocations in Parliament, in the National Development Council, and among professional economists. The main targets of the reduced ambitions were agriculture, irrigation / power (each reduced by 10 percent), and social services (reduced by 14 percent); allocations for industry actually *increased* by 14.5 percent—as overall plan expenditures declined by about 6 percent, from 4,800 crores rupees to 4,500 crores rupees.[19]

But even focusing on the "hard core" and reducing the plan's goals could not by themselves refill India's rapidly emptying foreign exchange coffers. So as debates continued over the new shape of the Second Plan, a parallel discussion took place over the possibility of seeking aid from overseas. Ultimately, the crisis helped usher in a group of policy makers—most prominently Morarji Desai (TTK's successor as finance minister) and B. K. Nehru, who took the new post of commissioner general for economic affairs in 1957; while the position had no single overseas base, he spent more time in Washington than in any other capital, possibly including New Delhi.

Wary of foreign investment, the prime minister accepted this shift toward general (rather than project-based) aid, a change that ultimately altered India's relationships with its most important lenders. India had, of course, received foreign aid before the start of the Second Plan. Most such aid, from the Cold War East and West, was organized around stand-alone factories, with lenders providing funds for specific projects, and for specific purchases within those projects. Yet what India needed now was general budget relief and foreign exchange to purchase products (not whole installations) overseas.

The shift away from project aid turned Indian attentions definitively toward the capitalist world. Even left-winger K. N. Raj, who predicted that the fate of the plan would "ultimately be spelled out in terms of dollars and rubles," considered rubles less relevant than dollars. The Soviet Union was facing its own difficulties in foreign economic relations as it underwrote the integration of the Eastern European economies; it had scarce foreign exchange resources and few opportunities to earn significant quantities of dollars, Deutschmarks, or other Western currencies. Sadly, K. N. Raj conceded, the USSR's "capacity to give aid [was] perhaps limited."[20]

Indians partial to the Soviet orientation of economic aid—especially for heavy industry and oil exploration—sought out Soviet financial aid in the hopes of disproving Raj's point. After all, Soviet officials agreed with these Indians on basic economic strategies, including the view that the current situation was an "unavoidable" result of rapid development. So in the middle of final negotiations over an agreement to build a factory, one Indian civil servant asked his Soviet interlocutor about the possibility of receiving an expansion of Soviet credits, and not just products or expertise. The reply was sharply negative: such a request was "unprecedented" and unwanted. The Indian official persisted, writing a follow-up letter detailing the request to allow Soviet aid to be used for items outside contractual agreements; this request, too, went nowhere. As these efforts faltered, those favoring closer economic ties to the USSR found themselves on the defensive—and those interested in American aid on the ascendance.[21]

The Turn toward Economic Aid in the United States

Just as the Indian crisis provided an opportunity for the America lobby in New Delhi to push its cause, so too did it serve well the India lobby in the United States. While the India lobby had long promoted expanding aid programs to the Third World, and especially to India, its members found an increasingly receptive group in the U.S. State Department and the Executive Office of the President. In spite of a general skepticism about India's commitment to the "free world"—and about the reliability and perhaps even the rationality of Jawaharlal Nehru—in the office of Secretary of State John Foster Dulles, increased Soviet attention to India prompted a rethinking of that attitude. Just as important, two of the executive branch's most powerful critics of economic aid to the Third World had both left the government in 1957, paving the way for more figures more sympathetic to India and to economic aid like new undersecretary of state C. Douglas Dillon, a liberal and internationalist Republican who would serve through the administration of President John F. Kennedy. The personnel shuffle cleared away obstacles but did not automatically set American official-dom on the path toward a broader conception of aid.[22]

The India lobby and others interested in expanding the concept of eco-nomic assistance effectively used geopolitical arguments to make their case. A plethora of competing studies circulated in the mid-1950s, each using the logic of Cold War competition. What one member of the lobby proudly called the "cabal" promoting aid took particular inspiration from a report that Massachusetts Institute of Technology (MIT) economists Max Millikan and Walt Rostow prepared for a Senate committee. Rostow later celebrated his role in the "quiet, faintly conspiratorial collaboration" he undertook with sympathetic diplomats and congressional staffers. Both Millikan and Rostow had worked in government, and both maintained close connections with White House staff and senior State Department officials. Rostow considered himself not a detached analyst but the leading member of a group of "development crusaders" seeking to establish more expansive and expensive official aid pro-grams. Though some critics, especially in the House of Representatives, derided the two economists as "cloud nine boys," the leaders of the influential Senate Select Committee on Foreign Aid were deeply impressed.[23]

Millikan and Rostow's report *The Objectives of United States Economic Assistance Programs* (December 1956) used the logic of U.S.-Soviet competi-tion to argue that American aid needed not just quantitative but qualitative change: from military to economic, from the short term to the long term, and from commercial to concessional terms. The authors argued that the so-called Soviet economic offensive in the Third World, combined with the reduction of East-West tensions in Europe, necessitated a new American approach that looked beyond military alliances and year-to-year aid allocations. The only path toward long-term global stability and prosperity, Millikan and Rostow insisted, required a "comprehensive and sustained program of economic assistance over a 20- or 30-year period." With an extraordinary dose of the liberal optimism then abundant in Cambridge, Massachusetts, Millikan and Rostow painted a picture of a beautiful world waiting to be born, should American officials be willing to focus on long-term growth over short-term political gain. Even organizations remote from the liberal politics of Cambridge—including the Brookings Institution in Washington and the University of Chicago's Research Center on Economic Development and Cultural Change—echoed this demand for long-term assistance. The logic for promoting economic aid in all of these studies was geopolitical rather than philanthropic; it was not so much a human response to poverty but the global struggle against communism that justified economic aid.[24]

Though such liberalism was less visible on the banks of the Potomac River than along the Charles, even the Washington policy apparatus appeared more open to economic aid. The private International Development Advisory Board had little of the MIT report's rosy optimism about the future but nevertheless insisted that the best route to supporting "moderate" governments in the Third World was through the creation of a long-term fund to provide "capital investment." Toward that end, the board called on Congress to create an International Development Fund. Even the Mutual Security Program's advisers, though focused upon military aid, conceded the value of capital assistance—at least for those who had joined American military pacts; in South Asia this meant supporting Pakistan but not India. The House Committee on Foreign Affairs also envisioned economic assistance in support of American geopolitical interests.[25]

The development crusaders used these reports to push their case in the White House, ultimately winning a paragraph in President Dwight D. Eisenhower's second inaugural address in January 1957. The president called for the United States to "help . . . fulfill" the aspirations of "needy peoples for some satisfaction of their human wants." Eisenhower's shift reflected changing bureaucratic politics of aid; the replacement of aid opponents with others more sympathetic to aid played a large role, and the agitation of C. D. Jackson, Max Millikan, and Walt Rostow also had an effect. This presidential endorsement proved a crucial step for the pro-aid side, a victory that was soon followed by a handful of reports that circulated (as drafts or leaks) later that winter. Even Secretary of State Dulles, the crusaders' well-placed foe, was ready to countenance "long-term development assistance." In April he publicly proposed a Development Loan Fund (DLF) with an initial capitalization of $750 million that would offer long-term loans at concessional rates for development purposes. Senior administration officials lauded the concept on economic as well as geopolitical grounds, arguing that the DLF would provide "opportunities to utilize the vigor, experience, and inherent strength of American industry" in meeting foreign policy goals. Even with strong administration support, though, the proposed fund barely survived the heated congressional debates that spring and summer. Congressional committees insisted on annual authorizations and cut the amount down to $300 million. Just as the dust began to settle on the Development Loan Fund in summer 1957, Indian requests for economic aid arrived.[26]

American Aid for India

The DLF, even if underfunded, signaled a major change in American aid strategy in at least two dimensions. First, it expanded the repertoire of American aid, no longer limiting aid to technical assistance projects that relied most heavily on importing foreign advisers and imparting expert advice. The DLF provided significant capital funds for the purchase of materials or equipment for individual projects. Second, the DLF expanded the target of American aid, opening up the prospect of nonproject aid (also known as program aid) that would encompass a sector of the economy, rather than one individual project, and could extend over multiple years. While official reports insisted that program aid served only a "subsidiary" purpose for the DLF, it eventually assumed primary importance—at least vis-à-vis India.[27]

For American aid officials the DLF provided a new and better set of tools to influence Indian economic policy. Under project-based technical assistance, U.S. leverage came only by choosing which projects to fund. Thus one senior U.S. aid official insisted that he did not aim to "criticize the [Indian] Government" or dictate its economic policy; he only sought out projects that fit within Indian and American visions. In the case of India, projects emphasizing agriculture (both directly and through the broader community development work) and private-sector industry dominated; projects falling outside those categories rarely received American funding. The new concept of "program aid" opened up the prospect of trying to influence not just individual projects but a whole sector of the economy—a prospect that took shape in future years.[28]

India stood at the center the DLF debate, thanks in large part to the work of the MIT group. With Eisenhower's and Dulles's endorsements of the DLF, even longtime aid skeptics like presidential adviser Clarence Randall got on the bandwagon. He invoked Cold War concerns, arguing that "India's present position in the world justifies a strong effort of support from the United States," and proposed using up to $40 million from the initial DLF budget for India—calibrating the amount that would go "part way to mak[ing] up" India's foreign exchange deficit while "leav[ing] enough need unmet to keep heavy pressure on India." But even this heavy-handed approach referencing geopolitical advantage did not win universal support; the Treasury Department, for instance, "recoiled" at the prospect of a loan fund. Randall's plans won out as the DLF wove its way through the congressional meat grinder. India received the first-ever DLF loan—and received about 25 percent of all DLF funds.[29]

American diplomats in New Delhi joined with the crusaders at MIT to advance the case for American aid. Diplomats welcomed the chance to use these resources to influence Indian economic policy. One dispatch from New Delhi, for instance, hoped that the foreign exchange crisis could lead to "a sound strengthening of [India's] orientation to the West." White House officials echoed this theme, calling for efforts to "gain the maximum influence on India's political economic future" using "aid and investment" as levers of influence. MIT economists, meanwhile, argued that India exemplified the sorts of problems that the DLF was designed to address. After a monthlong tour through India, Max Millikan called for massive and immediate lending to India—through the DLF if it could be done quickly, and through separate legislation if not. The call for aid to India, then, found widening support in American policy circles.[30]

The prospect of a DLF loan also offered new opportunities for the America lobby in India. B. K. Nehru, long a proponent of strengthening economic connections with the West, led this charge. In a meeting with Undersecretary of State Dillon in May 1957, he outlined the dire economic situation and sought whatever form of assistance the United States might provide. Dillon's reply cited some of the recent studies in favor of economic aid and highlighted the ways that India in particular would benefit from the new approach to aid visible in the DLF. The problem was timing; DLF loans would not begin until 1958, and Indian needs were urgent. The prime minister's informal talk with the American ambassador proved no more promising.[31]

The DLF also shifted the terms of Indian economic debates, especially as foreign exchange deficits grew. Midlevel economic officials in India and the United States began discussing possible aid packages even as Congress debated the DLF legislation. B. K. Nehru asked State Department desk officers about the sorts of projects that would be most appropriate for DLF consideration, and must have been relieved that the emphasis on private enterprise did not foreclose aid for India. Even Indian officials wary of American aid seemed more ready to contemplate an American aid package. After the summer of 1957 (which saw a net outflow of over 100 crores rupees, leaving a balance of only

500 crores), even skeptic TTK took up the cause for aid. Prime Minister Nehru grudgingly concluded that only the United States and West Germany had sufficient resources to offer "substantial" assistance. The DLF, in short, expanded the common ground between Indian aspirations and American resources.[32]

Indian diplomats in Washington submitted twenty-five projects for possible DLF funding; most would relieve foreign exchange pressures on the incremental expansion of existing industries, ranging from textile production to cement. The list contained no projects like the Bhilai Steel Plant or community development that could be identified with a single donor. Instead Indian officials wanted the DLF to cover small-scale improvements and updates in industries, using American funds to purchase American machinery. This approach would cede to the Soviet Union and other donors the sorts of large-scale projects that made headlines.[33]

TTK's fund-raising trip in late summer 1957, which made its first, longest, and most important stop in Washington, sought progress on this list of possible DLF loans. His requests totaled $800 million, an amount that far surpassed the total amount that the United States had provided in a full decade since Indian independence—and on far more generous terms. TTK admitted to Dillon that "it was somewhat difficult and embarrassing" for him to acknowledge the extent of Indian needs but that the dire crisis made such conversations necessary. In meetings with Dillon and Secretary of State Dulles, TTK set out the case for a major aid package while also admitting his inexperience: "India has never asked for aid from anyone." Dulles proceeded to outline the impediments in the United States: concerns about U.S. budget shortfalls and a stingy Congress that was deeply suspicious of economic aid, especially to nonaligned nations like India. TTK's initial pessimism about seeking aid had been amply confirmed.[34]

TTK's Washington visit prompted a reconsideration of American aid policies, resulting not so much in a shift of policy as in a clearer articulation of priorities. A U.S. intelligence estimate from early October 1957 predicted political uncertainty—indeed, a likely descent into chaos—if the Indian economy did not stabilize. Such chaos would make the region "far more susceptible to Communist subversion and more likely to adopt authoritarian methods" of rule. An authoritative White House report accepted this prediction, but called on the U.S. government to distance itself from Indian events, being especially careful not to "engage its [own] prestige in the success" of the Second Plan. The United States stood behind Indian efforts at "democratic development"—but far enough behind that it would not risk guilt by association should Indian efforts fail.[35]

While some skeptics within the Indian government had reluctantly turned to U.S. aid, the decision intensified the Indian debate over the value of and need for foreign aid. The announcement of the first American DLF loan to India in March 1958 unleashed a rash of criticism from communist members of Parliament. Nehru tried to calm tempers in the Lok Sabha by reassuring its members that "I think everybody knows, whether in India or the United States, that we do not barter our soul or our policy for money." Even as top Indian officials parried communists' criticisms, they began a quiet rethinking of their approach to aid.[36]

Toward the Aid-India Consortium

B. K. Nehru, in his new post as commissioner general of economic affairs, pondered strategies that could thread the needle of India's aid needs by increasing Western aid without becoming overly reliant on any one source. In top-secret memoranda to his boss Morarji Desai in May 1958, he did not focus on the capital-goods needs of Indian industry (public or private); he argued that they were, by and large, covered by existing aid agreements. India's major need, B. K. Nehru noted, was for "free money usable to finance current imports required for the maintenance of the economy." He called for making this money, not tied to new projects but to support existing enterprises, a top priority for his government. This task, he exhorted with exaggeration, would be "comparable in magnitude to the large peacetime operations that have ever been arranged."[37]

The scale was in fact so great that B. K. Nehru sought to expand Indian horizons by "internationaliz[ing] India's quest for foreign money." He suggested convening current and prospective future lenders under World Bank auspices. Especially since this approach fit well with brewing American ideas about aid to India, it quickly won acceptance and eventually evolved into the Aid-India Consortium (AIC). This consortium remained a major player in foreign aid for more than a dozen years and became a model mechanism replicated elsewhere. Indian circumstances gave rise to innovations in development aid that would spread more widely through the 1960s.[38]

B. K. Nehru's proposal reflected organizational innovation for the purposes of advancing his view of Indian interests. He called for "a combined operation" involving the World Bank, the International Monetary Fund (IMF), and "friendly foreign governments and the money markets." He wanted the World Bank to lead because of its past history (which left the bank "vitally interested in our continued sovereignty"). He was also impressed with the "sympathetic" view of India held by World Bank president Eugene R. Black, who had gradually tied the bank's fate in development lending to India and was deeply invested in Indian economic success. The World Bank's general attitude made it more likely to help than its sister institution, the IMF, which normally handled foreign exchange crises. But B. K. Nehru also hoped that the World Bank would help loosen purse strings in the United States and elsewhere; he cited in particular Black's "very great influence" within the Eisenhower administration, in the U.S. Congress, and among Western allies. He hoped, in short, to deploy the bank and its president as weapons in battles inside the Beltway and beyond.

B. K. Nehru's analysis would require an about-face in World Bank interactions with India. A 1956 World Bank mission, for instance, led to a small dispute within the bank and a major public contretemps in India. The issue emerged after a 1956 bank report on India; after professing a desire to make "constructive criticism," the report challenged almost every major element of the Second Five-Year Plan then just under way. Not stopping at scattershot commentary, the report suggested enforcement mechanisms: World Bank decisions about future loans to India, it concluded, should "be governed by the extent to which the government . . . [took] account of the observations and reservations expressed earlier by the Bank's Mission." The bank's own official historians called this episode "perhaps the strongest attempt the Bank has ever made to use its own leverage . . . to induce changes in aggregative [sic] economic policies in a borrowing country"—though later activities in India were far stronger.[39]

This not-so-veiled threat prompted a debate within the World Bank about the best approach to India. The bank's representative in New Delhi declared his general agreement with the economic diagnosis but dissented from the efforts at conditionality; he did so employing terms that dominated Indian discussions, arguing that the mission's recommendations "might be regarded as attaching strings to the Bank's loans." Especially given the laundry list of policy recommendations included in the committee report, such an approach would likely "lead to an impasse." The debate continued in successive drafts of a formal statement by World Bank president Eugene Black. Composing a letter to Finance Minister TTK, Black railed against India's "ideological" preferences for public sector industry; even after he removed this incendiary language from the final version of the letter, he left standing the direct connection between Indian policy and World Bank beneficence: "We will have to consider," Black wrote, "the pace and scale of our further loan operations in India . . . taking into account the economic policies which are pursued by your Government." As TTK and his cabinet colleagues steamed over the letter, critics of Western aid leaked excerpts into the Indian press. The prime minister ultimately released the full text of both Black's and TTK's letters, prompting a firestorm of criticism of the World Bank from all quarters. Even pro-Western publications like the *Eastern Economist* and *Economic Weekly* called on the bank to retract its criticisms and rethink the logic behind them. The bank apparently retreated in the face of such commentary, funding more public-sector projects than ever in the next few years. Even if loans for these infrastructure projects helped fulfill the goals of the Second Plan, they did not do much to resolve problems with foreign exchange, the reserves of which continued their downward trend in 1957 and 1958.[40]

B. K. Nehru's effort to turn the World Bank into India's economic savior got a sympathetic hearing from Morarji Desai, the newly appointed minister of finance. B. K. Nehru's proposals had important implications for India's economic policy, and in particular for the pursuit of aid. First off, the proposal relegated Soviet aid to the margins, as B. K. Nehru recognized: "What we should do in regard to the USSR is a matter of circumspection, for on the one hand she has told us that she has no more aid to give while on the other asking for aid from her will cause complications with those who are our main sources of external finance and who regard her as their enemy." Taking Soviet aid, in other words, would endanger American aid. The shift from external assistance in the form of projects to "free money" left the Soviet Union on the sidelines.

At the same time, B. K. Nehru also hoped to streamline the pursuit of foreign aid within the Indian government. His 1958 memorandum complained—in a direct criticism of his cousin Jawaharlal Nehru—that requests for foreign aid seemed to come "only from one Ministry and one Minister," as if the rest of the government (including the prime minister) was "little concerned about it one way or another." B. K. Nehru presented this issue as if he wanted to prevent development politics by reining in all the ministries under prime ministerial control. Yet a different dynamic was at play; ultimately, he hoped that his new approach would channel aid requests through the Indian government's principal liaison to the World Bank—in other words, through his own Ministry of Finance. Between seeking to halt the pursuit of Soviet aid and bringing the Ministry of Finance to the center of the process, B. K. Nehru was pursuing his own economic vision and bureaucratic interests. In the end, his proposal was less a critique of development politics than a well-played example of it.

B. K. Nehru did not object strongly to the World Bank's imposition of conditions for its loans, perhaps because he found the general thrust of the conditions to his liking. He was, in other words, ready to incur the significant "non-financial price" that his proposal entailed. Lenders would impose new economic constraints, he acknowledged, including a move away from deficit spending, strict limits on defense expenditures, more welcoming rules for foreign private investment, and possibly even the insertion of Indo-Pakistani relations into aid negotiations. Yet it was no longer possible, B. K. Nehru concluded, to maintain the wariness about large-scale Western aid that had reigned only a few years prior.

American diplomats and legislators found their own reasons to back a collective approach to aiding India. Administration officials had been prodding allies to bear a larger burden of development aid for the Third World—and for India in particular. They argued that fading empires like the United Kingdom, as well as prosperous former antagonists like Japan and West Germany, needed to support development efforts more generously. India also found a new champion in Senator John F. Kennedy, a centrist Democrat who saw economic aid as an opportunity to enhance his prospects in a future presidential campaign. Advised by Walt Rostow and his MIT colleagues, Kennedy saw India as a perfect weapon for attacking the Eisenhower administration for insufficient vigor in prosecuting the global struggle against communism. At the same time, promoting India would help him win over Democrats who doubted Kennedy's liberal bona fides. Picking up one of Rostow's innumerable proposals, Kennedy called for multilateral aid. In a speech to Congress drafted at MIT, he argued for "multilateral solution and joint effort" in India. Such an effort, Kennedy hoped, could "change the whole psychological relationship between India and the Western partners" by empowering pro-Western forces within India. Days later, the head of the International Cooperation Administration privately agreed with Kennedy's suggestion, arguing that a "joint . . . review of India's development plans" might "be helpful to India in providing some 'prestigeful' outside support."[41]

Having won support within both the Indian and American governments, those favoring a consortium set to work creating a lenders' group for India. Representatives from major (or prospective) lenders would meet in Washington under World Bank auspices, and would discuss an assessment of the Indian economy prepared by World Bank staff. India would "not directly ask any government" for aid, and indeed would not even be present at any deliberations. Undersecretary of State Dillon responded enthusiastically, no doubt relieved that he would not need to lead this tortured process.[42]

Capitalizing on his long-standing friendship with Black, B. K. Nehru sought to use the good offices of the World Bank to solve many of India's problems in seeking international aid. First, he wanted the bank to plead India's case within the halls of the State Department and the U.S. Congress. Black's high reputation in Washington became a crucial part of India's lobbying strategy. Once Black brought American policy around to a more generous view of India, B. K. Nehru imagined, American influence might extract aid commitments from Western allies. He hoped, in sum, that "internationalized" aid would use the World Bank to reduce American leverage over India—but then use American sway with its allies to boost development aid.[43]

At first, World Bank efforts worked according to B. K. Nehru's plan. The bank sent a small-scale mission to evaluate current conditions and make to recommendations about future aid to India. B. K. Nehru was confident that the bank's staff was invested in and sympathetic to India's development program. And sending a single mission, the results of which would be available to potential lenders, would save India (in B. K. Nehru's words) from "having to bear our souls to each prospective source of financing separately." The meeting, to discuss "India's Foreign Exchange Situation," was slated to open shortly after India's Independence Day in August 1958; representatives from B. K. Nehru's original list—Canada, Japan, the United Kingdom, the United States, and West Germany and observers from the IMF—received invitations.[44]

If Finance Minister Morarji Desai was correct in asserting that the group constituted "India's best hope of foreign assistance," then there was plenty of scope for concern. The World Bank report echoed earlier analyses and evoked previous controversies; it called for cutting the pace of Indian development and chastised policy makers for slighting the agricultural sector and private enterprise. It proposed that any future aid be "subject to [the World Bank's] achieving appropriate understandings with the Indian Government on its economic and financial policies." When the group convened, Black reiterated this list of criticisms, his effort at subtlety only sowing confusion: "I do not say that the [bank's] advice went unheeded, but it had little effect upon policy." He expected that the ongoing Indian balance-of-payments crisis might force greater adherence to external advice. Black turned this into something of a threat, saying future World Bank lending to India depended upon "the pursuit by India of sound economic and financial policies." Even in the opening session of the first meeting, then, it seemed that the lenders' club might actually concentrate—rather than disperse—policy leverage over India.[45]

Eugene Black's opening talk set the stage for the question for lenders' representatives to discuss how to use their resources to shape Indian policy. The representatives quickly agreed that "they wished to be able to define the remainder" of the Second Plan, but wanted to "avoid listing what India could or could not do." In the end they took a middle road, specifying the "sound economic and financial policies" to which the Government of India should adhere. These included promoting agriculture and the private sector, expanding exports and foreign direct investment, and slowing the pace of future economic growth. The West German representatives considered these goals binding; they expected that it would be made "completely clear" to Indian representatives that "they can only count on more assistance when they observe" those conditions. Others offered more nebulous statements about the relationship between their loans and Indian policy.[46]

The meeting offered mixed results in terms of B. K. Nehru's hopes that the group of lenders together might bring India more aid. Bank staff calculated that India needed $350 million in loans, but the original commitments came in $100 million (!) short. So the second and third days of the meeting were devoted to Black haranguing the participants to raise the total amount they would commit to aid for India. Black's subsequent actions, including peer pressure, backroom discussions, and even a matching increase from the World Bank, ultimately paid off; he announced, with more relief than satisfaction, that the lenders present had met their goal.[47]

In its first meeting, the World Bank lenders' group had delivered a sizable increase in aid and laid the groundwork for a new aid mechanism—though it had not committed to meet again. Lingering just below the surface was a change in the approach to aid. Rather than starting with individual projects in mind and working up to a complete aid package, the group bargained over a total amount without initial regard for the underlying projects. This turn toward program-based aid was hardly the provision of "free money" that B. K. Nehru desired—though neither was it, precisely, business as usual.[48]

Though Black considered his mission accomplished, most of B. K. Nehru's work still lay ahead of him; the lenders' club was not a multilateral mechanism for aid, after all, but more like an extended coffee klatsch at a fancy private club. So his next task was to work out bilateral arrangements with each individual participant. Each participating lender administered its financial commitments differently. American aid, for instance, was split between the Export-Import Bank, the Development Loan Fund, and PL480. West Germany had elaborate paperwork requirements, even more than the DLF's voluminous ones. And the government of Japan, B. K. Nehru complained, "seemed to be doing its best to avoid implementing its promise of credit assistance." Nehru criticized British procedures as well, presumably unaware that British diplomats were on the verge of backing out of the group now that the "crisis atmosphere had dissipated." The spirit of multilateralism was fading fast.[49]

Aiming to turn loose commitments into firm bilateral aid agreements, Finance Minister Morarji Desai soon departed on an extended tour of Western capitals. He got off to a good start, as the U.S. press celebrated the minister as "more pro-Western and anti-Communist" than Nehru. With fainter praise than perhaps intended, *Time* magazine called him "an Indian Estes Kefauver." Yet even a leader of such stature did not find the next step of negotiations easy going. Though at the late August meeting the United States had committed to providing $75 million in aid—less than the World Bank or the United Kingdom—from the DLF, though the sum would not become available until early 1959. Desai's conversations with Dillon could hardly have seemed reassuring; the undersecretary stood ready to enumerate the flaws of Indian economic policy, and to make the case for opening the economy up for foreign capital, but was unwilling to discuss any specifics about the $75 million loan. The tone of Desai's meeting with Eugene Black was similar, with Black making the case that the Indian government should open up oil exploration to Western companies. "Nonfinancial" costs were adding up quickly, just as B. K. Nehru had warned. *Economic Weekly* sounded an alarm, accusing the Indian government of trafficking in "pious generalities about self-reliance" while at the same time moving unthinkingly into new forms of dependence on foreign powers.[50]

The subsequent history of the lenders' club diverged further from B. K. Nehru's goals. In a sign of just how little the group managed to dilute Indian reliance on the United States, the World Bank awaited "clearance" from the State Department before organizing the next meeting. The World Bank report in preparation for that meeting offered a tour d'horizon that brought attention to a different kind of concern: India's overall level of foreign debt. The second meeting, convened in March 1959, focused on debt service levels—with World Bank economists questioning India's capacity to take on any more foreign currency debt. B. K. Nehru was unable to change the topic since he was not in the room where it happened. A roll call about loans to India prompted participants to celebrate their past aid rather than discussing new commitments. And lenders' desires to shape Indian policy remained a key theme: Black threatened that "the readiness of India's friends to continue to provide assistance . . . will be largely influenced by the nature of the preparations being made for the Third Plan." Bringing donors together in the same room, B. K. Nehru was discovering, might streamline the requests for aid, but "nonfinancial" costs could accrue quickly.[51]

Aid Politics in India

These costs changed the internal dynamics of aid requests in India by expanding the role of the Finance Ministry. B. K. Nehru provided his Western interlocutors with his own estimate of Indian capital needs during the Third Five-Year Plan: roughly $1 billion. Strikingly, this estimate came not from the Planning Commission or anyone directly involved in formulating the Third Plan; B. K. Nehru indeed boasted glibly that "made up [his] own mind" about the needs and how to meet them. His next round of requests emerged from that back-of-the-envelope figure, detached though it was from the process of economic policy making in New Delhi.[52]

    Though B. K. Nehru and his colleagues at the Ministry of Finance focused primarily on Western lenders, other Indian officials continued to pursue project-based aid from Moscow, reaching a major aid agreement over the summer of 1959. That agreement, worth almost 180 crores rupees ($375 million) covered dozens of projects in the Third Plan. It placed a heavy emphasis on steel (expanding the Bhilai Steel Plant) and energy; a substantial portion also went to oil and gas exploration. Indo-Soviet economic cooperation seemed unaffected by B. K. Nehru's efforts.[53]

B. K. Nehru's strategy remained focused on the West. He deployed a network of pro-India officials and public figures in the United States to promote aid to India. He took credit for newfound French interest in Indian development, insisting that it came about through his own lobbying efforts. Ditto for another blue-ribbon American advisory committee on foreign aid, whose opposition to economic aid, he bragged, was defanged by his behind-the-scenes efforts. B. K. Nehru also invited more Western delegations to come to India.[54] Most promising was the U.S. Senate, which had a substantial and increasingly powerful India lobby led by Senator Kennedy and a colleague, John Sherman Cooper (R-KY), who had served as ambassador in New Delhi. Kennedy, an increasingly important member of the India lobby, endorsed the dispatch of high-profile experts who could "give a powerful impetus to . . . an international consortium." B. K. Nehru heartily endorsed this approach: "It is obvious that if we expect to get massive aid for the Third Five-Year Plan, we shall have to explain to the prospective aiders what the plan is, what our problems are and how we propose to go about solving them." His first choice was a congressional delegation, but he also endorsed as an alternative a "mission under the auspices of the World Bank composed of unusual personnel like the three wise men proposed by Kennedy." (This notion of the Wise Men caught on so well that even the World Bank's stodgy filing system adopted it.) Kennedy himself lobbied Dillon at State and Black at the World Bank about establishing such a mission in order to "arouse the political energies" of potential donors—or at least to get them to open their wallets. Chester Bowles, a former (and future) ambassador in New Delhi then serving in Congress, followed suit. Industrialist G. D. Birla, who shared B. K. Nehru's interest in promoting Indian economic ties with the United States, offered his assistance both in Washington and in Delhi. The network of pro-India forces in Washington knit ever closer ties with each other and with pro-U.S. forces in New Delhi.[55]

From the start, Indian policy makers (besides B. K. Nehru) expressed reservations about the mission of the Wise Men.[56] As with their biblical namesakes, the group comprised three members. Unlike their predecessors, the modern-day Wise Men were all bankers, by profession and predilection distinctly unsympathetic to Indian economic strategy—and certainly did not arrive bearing gifts. Though officially they comprised an independent fact-finding mission under World Bank auspices, they functioned in practice as emissaries from the State Department, with extensive predeparture briefings from Dillon. In a sign of its continued hostility to the Finance Ministry and to the West, the Planning Commission inhospitably refused to share with the Wise Men any detailed information about the Third Plan it was then formulating.[57]

Armed with little concrete information, the bankers could not pass judgment on the Third Plan; more surprisingly, they did not address deficit financing and offered only vague and anodyne comments on the place of private enterprise. And they concluded with a full-throated endorsement of large-scale and long-term aid. Prime Minister Nehru gloated that even a "team of hard-boiled bankers" managed to take an attitude of "suppressed enthusiasm" for Indian efforts. With tongue firmly lodged in his cheek, Western-inclined economist I. G. Patel called the report "one of the most heartwarming documents in the annals of international relations."[58]

B. K. Nehru tried to parlay this happy outcome into new forms of aid and an enhanced structure for multilateral aid, succeeding more with the former than the latter. He worked with the U.S. State Department to argue for the creation of a soft-loan window at the World Bank, one that could offer loans on terms more advantageous to borrowers. The establishment of the International Development Association (IDA) in 1960 served this purpose, providing a multilateral channel for American aid; American diplomats also hoped it might spur some soft-loan action in Europe. The multilateral aspects of the IDA were, official historians admitted, "an elaborate fiction" since the funds for the IDA would be offered by individual nations, and would be underwritten in a process that gave much more power to the lending countries than did other World Bank loans. India was, from the start, the largest borrower, receiving over half of the original loans. Indeed, it was the raison d'être for the IDA, which quickly earned the nickname Indian Development Association.[59]

Though welcomed by Indian officials, the IDA did not end B. K. Nehru's efforts to bring together the original donors for a reunion. In anticipation of another meeting in late 1960, the World Bank, as usual, sent a mission to evaluate the prospects for the Third Plan. Choosing to share information on the Third Plan that it had withheld from the Wise Men months earlier, the PC was prepared to use the new mission to make the case for substantial aid. The Third Plan offered a significant rhetorical shift from its predecessor, especially in the language describing the importance of agriculture and the need for a strong private sector. Yet in terms of overall investment priorities, the Third Plan was not markedly different from the Second Plan.[60]

India's run of good luck with the World Bank continued with the bank's next mission in spring 1960. This mission seemed impressed with the rhetorical gestures to the private sector, and with a little grumbling about agriculture accepted the basic strategy of industrialization. Though the report noted the heavy needs for foreign exchange (coming to 30 percent of total investments), it foreclosed any discussion about the overall structure and aims of the Third Plan: "to aim any lower would be to admit failure in advance." So B. K. Nehru's focus on the World Bank was starting to pay off; the criticisms had become routine, even routinized, but were not necessarily reflected in aid decisions. His government's rhetorical accommodation preempted major attacks and helped avoid serious alterations to its overall strategy. The success of this approach was evident at the next meeting of the lenders.[61]

That meeting in September 1960 spared India serious criticism of its economic policy but also avoided serious commitment to solving its problems. Representatives from France, Japan, the Netherlands, the United States, the United Kingdom, and West Germany seemed to be busier accusing each other of unfairness than addressing the situation in India. Thus a statement by the authors of the World Bank report that they "accepted the basic theory of Indian plans" was not remarked upon. Even the mission's doubts, which many AIC members shared, did not attract significant discussion. As I. G. Patel remarked with relief, "Gone were the days when our emphasis on the public sector or on public industries was suspect; our getting aid from socialist countries was no longer frowned upon."[62]

Patel's optimism was justified by the statements of American officials in the early 1960s who were willing to countenance Soviet aid to India. A senior diplomat considered India "quite capable of absorbing resources from the Soviet Union" without succumbing to communism; another considered Soviet aid "all to the good"; anything that might improve the Indian economy would be appreciated. Once again, most of the delegates were content to repackage existing aid commitments rather than expanding their efforts; only the United States initiated fresh loans. The World Bank official chairing the meeting expressed his "disappointment" in the results—but nevertheless began making arrangements for a future session.[63]

In what was becoming a ritual, Indian officials once again fanned out after the lenders' club meeting to negotiate bilateral agreements. Once again, the first stop for Finance Minister Morarji Desai was Washington; his results were meager at best. A World Bank vice president celebrated the creation of the IDA, but conceded that its resources were "very modest." A meeting with Dillon at the State Department yielded optimistic statements but nothing specific regarding DLF loans. Desai and Dillon found common ground in complaining about Western European stinginess, but little else. The meeting ended with Dillon's sales pitch to India for Lockheed jets over a domestically built competitor—calling on Indian officials to spend more foreign exchange for an expensive American aircraft. B. K. Nehru had a better reception at the World Bank, where he obtained a tentative commitment to provide up to $100 million in loans for Third Plan projects, almost half of which would be devoted to power generation. As the April 1961 start date for the Third Plan approached, however, Western aid was at a temporary plateau.[64]

The foreign exchange crisis of the Second Five-Year Plan altered the future landscape of economic assistance for India. In India itself, the inauguration of an era of foreign exchange shortage shifted the topic of economic debates, and shifted the locus of power within the top ranks of government. The turn toward what B. K. Nehru called "free money" brought external assistance to the forefront of future discussions about Indian economic policy. While the First and Second Plans devoted little attention to prospects of external assistance for Indian development, the Third Plan placed that topic near the top of its list.

This shift had the effect of promoting the Ministry of Finance in economic deliberations and in the aid process. While industrial ministries and the Planning Commission continued to negotiate with the Soviet Union and other Eastern European programs on specific projects, the Ministry of Finance increasingly took responsibility for negotiating and implementing aid from the West. The Planning Commission still appeared to be regnant—formal policies were released through this body—but the Ministry of Finance had recaptured substantial if contested authority to shape economic policy. In some cases, this authority resulted from hard-fought bureaucratic battles in New Delhi. But much of the Finance Ministry's new authority came from its expanded connections to Western donors. B. K. Nehru's back-of-the-envelope calculations—and not the Draft Plan Frame from the PC—became the basis of Indian pursuit of economic assistance for the Third Plan. And since the plan relied upon foreign assistance for almost one-third of its resources, the availability of aid necessarily affected not just the scale but also the shape of aid. The return of the Finance Ministry also altered the international politics of Indian aid, with more focus on Western nations that could provide aid not tied to individual projects. With more and more aid discussions being about "program" aid and about the terms for repaying loans rather than about the underlying projects, negotiations rested more with the Ministry of Finance than with the Planning Commission. The shift in types of aid reverberated throughout India, and through India's economic relationships with the West. It strengthened the hands of the pro-Western groups in the Indian civil service and cabinet.

The crisis also reshaped the landscape of Western aid for the Third World. An alphabet soup of new organizations—the American DLF, the World Bank's IDA, and soon enough the AIC—all arose in direct response to India's parlous foreign exchange balances. A well-placed India lobby in the United States, alongside Rostow's development crusaders, worked hard to promote their causes and succeeded enough that even the Eisenhower administration established the Development Loan Fund, which went well beyond technical assistance. Across town at the World Bank, two new institutions emerged, showing again the way in which the case of India prompted innovation in development aid. Thanks to efforts from B. K. Nehru on the one hand and the India lobby in the United States on the other, the World Bank sponsored a number of consortia modeled on what became the AIC. The IDA at the World Bank similarly came into being to meet specific problems facing Western (indeed, primarily American) aid to India.

These innovations served many of the purposes that B. K. Nehru had in mind when he made the rounds in New Delhi and then in Washington to promote his ideas. On the one hand, the World Bank had definitely taken a leadership role in aid for India and had created a space for increased American aid—helped also by the energies of the India lobby. By 1960 the World Bank had toned down many of its criticisms over Indian economic policy. This attitude also applied to nonproject aid, which slowly entered discussions with Western lenders. Though hardly providing B. K. Nehru's vaunted "free money," the shift in the mechanisms for aid had both deepened and broadened Western aid available for Indian development. At the same time, though, much as he had warned, the process entailed subjecting Indian economic policy (and occasionally its foreign policy) to public criticism. While the format of the lenders' club served many purposes, it took place without direct Indian representation and thus depended upon friends at the World Bank to promote Indian interests.

Domestically, the turn to the West redounded to B. K. Nehru's benefit; the aid consortium established ever more firmly the links between pro-Western factions in the upper reaches of the Indian government with Western sponsors. These links strengthened the play of development politics in India and also left the group all the more beholden to Western allies.

B. K. Nehru well understood that the turn to Western aid came with "nonfinancial" costs. He accepted those costs in the interests of attracting sufficient funds to resolve the existential crisis in Indian foreign exchange, and to support the ambitious Third Five-Year Plan. Early consortium activities seemed promising; meetings generated plenty of rhetoric about conditionality but few actual conditions. But the ultimate result was increased exposure to the major foreign sponsors of Indian development—including, most notably, the United States. Under the best of conditions this exposure would have been risky, and the events of the early 1960s in South Asia did not provide the best conditions. The Third Plan promised to be difficult enough on its own terms—and that was before military factors created a crisis of the Third Plan that exposed India to new existential threats.

CHAPTER 6

MILITARY SUPPLY AND THE VICISSITUDES OF AID POLITICS

On October 24, 1962, front pages of newspapers around the world spilled over with news about the Soviet-American confrontation in the seas near Cuba. But one White House aide was focused on another conflict some eight thousand miles away and implored his colleagues to share in his concern. "We can't let our other current preoccupations" in the Caribbean, the gruff ex-CIA analyst Robert Komer badgered a busy colleague, "distract us unduly" from the battle in the Himalayas then under way. After all, he insisted, the Sino-Indian conflict in the desolate mountains would be just as important—he would later suggest even more important—than the famous thirteen days of the Cuban Missile Crisis. Komer's insistence that the Himalayan crisis outranked what the Soviet officials called the Caribbean Crisis was not confirmed by subsequent events. But the crisis remade South Asian politics and fed the expansion of development politics there and elsewhere.[1]

The war between Chinese and Indian forces along their contested but desolate border profoundly shaped India's history, especially in its relations with the two superpowers and its onetime colonizer. The conflict's aftermath broke the near monopoly that the United Kingdom held in arms exports to India, speeding its eclipse as supplier to the Indian military, and bringing to the fore aid competition with the superpowers. The crisis also resonated widely and deeply within India. It reduced the prestige and political effectiveness of Prime Minister Jawaharlal Nehru, a process already under way because of his physical decline in the early 1960s. The war and the ensuing rearmament effort stretched the Indian economy further, endangering the success of the Third

Five-Year Plan (1961–1966). The brief war, which ended in a crushing defeat for the Indian armed forces, prompted a reformulation of the sacrosanct posture of nonalignment. The border war, furthermore, revealed the internationalization of domestic Indian disputes over procurement; military aid was subject to the same dynamics of development politics as was economic aid, and with disruptive results.

Military questions were of paramount importance after the first American aid package for Pakistan in 1954; by 1962, the United States and the United Kingdom had sold over $2 billion worth of military equipment to Pakistan. In spite of the emerging South Asian arms race, Nehru and most Indian leaders insisted that nonalignment meant refusing military aid and purchasing military equipment only on the open market. As Nehru declared in Parliament, it contravened Indian "conceptions of dignity" to receive military aid, though his government was ready to purchase arms and production licenses for the best price—that is, on a commercial basis. And yet the distinction between pure commerce and military assistance was difficult to discern. Manufacturers of fighter jets and transport planes, after all, published no price lists. They sold to a small number of purchasers; most of their sales went to their home nation's armed services, with whom they had cozy relationships. Private firms' sales of military equipment abroad involved the respective governments in negotiations. Licensing for overseas production was an even more complex enterprise, tantamount in many cases to an intergovernmental agreement. As one senior Indian officer put it, in direct contradiction to the official line, "All arms sales are the results of political decisions"; there were no purely commercial transactions.[2]

Commerce and Politics in the 1950s

A competition over the purchase of new bombers in 1955–1956 demonstrated the difficulties of defining exactly what constituted a "commercial" transaction. After the sale of American jets to Pakistan in 1954, Prime Minister Nehru outlined a plan to acquire sixty bombers, some through direct purchase and others through a production licensing agreement that would conserve Indian foreign exchange while expanding local manufacturing expertise. A debate broke out at the highest reaches of the Indian government, with different groups favoring different suppliers. Proponents of the Soviet Il-28 praised its technical performance and its price, and especially appreciated the possibility of "liberating [India] from Anglo-American dependence" in defense. Nehru, for his part, had found the Il-28 more appealing on a "purely commercial proposition" than the British Canberra—in large part because the equipment could be purchased using rupees, thus preserving India's precarious foreign-exchange reserves. Yet, as with atomic energy safeguards, the terms of sales and licensing went well beyond pounds and pence; pricing decisions could not be resolved with reference to *Consumer Reports*, the NAPA *Blue Book,* or even *Jane's Aircraft* but entailed politics in one way or another. Strenuous British efforts, including a quiet subsidy to manufacturers to keep the price down, eventually won the contract for the Canberra. British diplomats also won a commitment from Nehru to consult with British officials before concluding other military purchases.[3]

The conclusion of the 1956 Canberra episode—a British firm selling its aircraft to the Indian armed services—might suggest that little had changed from the earlier years of British dominance of the Indian military supply. Yet three features of the episode would augur major changes to come. First and most important was the Soviet offer to sell the Il-28 to India, which was one of its first large-scale offers beyond the people's republics; only the sale of millions of dollars' worth of Czech and Soviet armaments to Egypt preceded it.[4] Second, even as British officials dismissed Indian Air Force (IAF) overtures to the Soviet Union as a tactic to improve the terms of the Canberra deal, they ultimately responded to the tactic by improving their terms dramatically. This was not the last time such a dynamic would emerge. Finally, the Canberra deal was a sign of the increasing influence of Washington, D.C., in Indo-British relations. Because the IAF wanted Canberras armed with advanced weapons that relied on American technology, the Pentagon played an important behind-the-scenes role in these negotiations. Decades of tradition of Indo-British military ties yielded to the high technology and the deep pockets of the American military.

By the end of the 1950s the Indian armed services focused renewed attention on procurement, this time in response to new dangers from China as well as to continued American arms shipments to Pakistan. The fact that some Indian generals wanted to arm the country against China indexes the rapid decline in Sino-Indian relations from the moments of "Hindi-Chini bhai-bhai" (Sino-Indian brotherhood) in the early 1950s. The two nations differed over the status of Tibet—was it independent or was it, per the Chinese official line, "the Tibet region of China"?—and the exact path of their shared twenty-five-hundred-mile border. But in the mid-1950s such disagreements distracted little from warm Sino-Indian relations. Nehru supported the People's Republic of China's bid for membership in the United Nations, and defended the Chinese presence at the Afro-Asian Conference in Bandung in 1955. The following year, Nehru dismissed the possibility of "even the remotest danger" to India from China.[5]

Such a claim was no longer sustainable after 1959, when Tibet moved into open rebellion. American intelligence agencies, looking for ways to challenge the People's Republic of China, made common cause with their Indian counterparts.[6] Chinese diplomats' estimation of India declined further after the Dalai Lama fled Tibet into India; they took little consolation from Nehru's bland assurance that the Dalia Lama "would not wish to do anything that would be embarrassing." Chinese officials expressed their displeasure on the border, as the augmented presence of the People's Liberation Army generated a steady stream of Indian diplomatic protests. American officials, for their part, saw the Tibet turbulence as a "windfall," exulting that Chinese actions there might help cure India's "neutralist mania." Tibet also aggravated Sino-Soviet tensions, as Nikita Khrushchev lectured Mao Zedong and Zhou Enlai that the looming Sino-Indian conflict was a "stupid" dispute over "insignificant patches of land." Mao's reply that Khrushchev was cozying up to imperialism brought ideological differences into stark relief.[7]

Aside from its global implications—building Indo-American ties and challenging Sino-Soviet relations—the events in Tibet and on the Sino-Indian border sent the Indian armed services to the market, seeking especially to expand its capabilities in mountainous regions. These plans to purchase new aircraft were soon enmeshed in increasingly complex Indian domestic politics—a factor that would shape military procurement and much else besides.

Shopping for Air Power, 1960–1962

With the first deadly skirmishes along the Sino-Indian border in late 1959, the military version of development politics escalated in India. Government officials fanned out to the major arms producers, looking to buy fighter jets, transports, and helicopters. Different officials had different agendas, especially as the politics of Indian defense grew more fractious after the appointment of V. K. Krishna Menon as minister of defense in 1957. Widely admired in India (by Nehru in particular) but even more widely reviled at home and abroad, Krishna Menon's enthusiasm for Soviet weapons in the early 1960s became a major point of conflict within and beyond his own ministry. Many uniformed officers saw him as soft on China, chafing at his "apathetic attitude . . . regarding Chinese moves."[8]

The question of military posture quickly bled into questions of defense procurement. Krishna Menon focused on building up defense industries, arguing that self-sufficiency was essential since "foreign countries might withdraw or modify their support for us at any time." Thus he favored licensing agreements over direct purchases of defense equipment; since the U.S. government placed severe restrictions on the licensing of defense technology, this focus meshed well with his general wariness of the United States. The plan to expand domestic production thus gave the Soviet defense industries a leg up in the race for Indian arms sales. As early as 1960, Indian diplomats opened negotiations with the Soviet State Committee for Foreign Economic Connections (Gosudarstvennyi Komitet po Vneshnim Ekonomicheskim Sviaziam—GKES), and its Chief Engineering Administration, which handled military sales, about licensing production of Soviet Mi-4 helicopters. An "urgent" request for similar licensing the Il-14 transport aircraft soon followed.[9]

Overtures to the USSR stirred controversy within the defense establishment. British sources heard rumors that IAF officers were against the purchase of Soviet equipment but expected to be overruled by the civilian leadership. The uniformed military found allies in India's America lobby. Finance Minister Morarji Desai promoted purchases from American firms and seemed ready to countenance U.S. government financing. Roving economic ambassador B. K. Nehru joined Desai in favoring arrangements with the Americans. Citing technological superiority, the pro-American camp nevertheless had a difficult task: American technology might be superior to that available elsewhere, but the financial terms and difficulties in obtaining licenses for domestic manufacture complicated their efforts. In the end, the Ministry of Defence compromised, purchasing a number of used American C-119 transports but also placing major orders for Soviet Mi-4 helicopters, and, at Krishna Menon's insistence, Soviet An-12 transports. British firms were the odd ones out; they could provide neither American technology nor Soviet discounts—and thanks to backlogs could not promise any deliveries for two years. Krishna Menon publicized these Soviet purchases widely, much to the chagrin of Soviet diplomats who worried about exacerbating tensions with their Chinese comrades.[10]

The contest over Indian military procurement soon heated up even further. In March 1961 B. K. Nehru began quietly agitating for Indian purchases from the United States. He was surprised that General B. M. Kaul, whom many uniformed officers resented as a creature of Krishna Menon, aided the cause—even if it meant breaking with his civilian boss. Both B. K. Nehru and General Kaul tried unsuccessfully to convince the prime minister that Krishna Menon's plans for long-term expansion of military industry left India dangerously underequipped to deal with immediate threats from China. True to his political predilections and procurement policy, Krishna Menon underplayed the notion of any such threat. On the other side, B. K. Nehru and General Kaul had a similar logical consistency: the Chinese threat was the grave one, they argued, so the West seemed natural military suppliers. American officials delighted in the inquiries over military supply. Assistant Secretary of State W. Averell Harriman saw a "real opportunity" to "bring India to a more reasonable position," by which he meant into the Western camp. But the Indian minister of defense presented a major roadblock: Pentagon officials warned that he was "undermin[ing] the present strong, Western-oriented military leadership in favor of those more amenable to his personal political thinking," paving the way for "Soviet inroads" in Indian defense.[11]

The battle over defense procurement intensified in 1961. Krishna Menon sent the Indian air marshal to inspect Soviet aviation and production facilities at the exact time that B. K. Nehru initiated discussions about an Indian purchase from the United States. Weeks later, India's ambassador in Moscow approached the military wing the Soviet GKES in the hopes of licensing production of the Soviet RD-9F jet engine for use on an Indian fighter-bomber then in production. At the same time, IAF officers were working around Krishna Menon to maintain ties with Pentagon officials, who in turn were negotiating with companies to bring down prices of American aircraft for Indian purchase. All these efforts, however, did not prevent the IAF's purchases from the USSR.[12]

The Pentagon pursued both political and commercial goals vis-à-vis India, trying to use arms sales to strengthen U.S. connections with Indian generals while undermining its defense minister. A surprising opportunity appeared in March 1962, when Chester Bowles, the former (and future) ambassador in New Delhi then serving (briefly) as an undersecretary of state, returned to his old stomping grounds. Trying to expand his already wide range of contacts, he sought meetings not just with Krishna Menon but also with General Kaul. Keeping to protocol, the general sought Krishna Menon's clearance before meeting with Bowles—to which the defense minister replied sharply, "General, why don't you ask for . . . American citizenship? It will be easier for all concerned." When the general later did meet with Bowles, he asked bluntly whether the United States would "come to India's aid" in the event of a Chinese attack. Bowles immediately assented, at which point the conversation turned to how to open up "secret conversations . . . on contingency plans" with the Indian military—talks that the general insisted should take place "even if not fully sanctioned by Krishna Menon or Jawaharlal Nehru." Bowles first viewed this approach as part of "some obscure [Krishna] Menon play" but slowly came to realize that the offer was sincere. Three days later a secret presidential finding declared that military assistance to India would "strengthen the security of the United States and promote world peace," a legal nicety that cleared the way for American military aid to India. Ambassador John Kenneth Galbraith picked up where Bowles left off, trying to turn a feeler about contingency plans into a reversal of India's "excessive dependence on the Soviets as a source of supply." For his part, General Kaul tried to encourage his defense minister to consider American arms; predictably, Krishna Menon declined. While the Americans may have loved Indian men in uniform (and vice versa), arms procurement decisions remained with that red eminence Krishna Menon.[13]

Fighting Over Fighters: The MiG Purchase of 1962

Krishna Menon had already made up his mind to expand defense ties with the Soviet Union. In April 1962 he presented Soviet ambassador I. A. Benediktov with a fait accompli: the Indian defense establishment, he reported, had already worked out plans to manufacture Soviet-licensed jet engines for military use. This would not have come as a total shock; GKES had already agreed to send specialists to India to study the question, though without any firm commitment. But the defense minister reported to Benediktov that with the plans already under way, anything other than Soviet agreement would create major headaches. At the very least, he argued, a Soviet refusal would "push Indians into the arms of Americans, British or French" for the jet engines; ultimately, larger questions of bilateral relations were at stake. Even more important was

Krishna Menon's prestige, which would be "greatly undermined" by "reactionary forces" if the deal did not go through. As the Soviet Presidium pondered its response to Krishna Menon's demands, it authorized KGB agents in New Delhi to "conduct active-measures operations designed to strengthen [Krishna] Menon's position in India and enhance his personal popularity." The links between military decisions, domestic politics, and geopolitics grew tighter.[14]

The controversies over Indian military purchases in spring and summer 1962 quickly became a thicket of attacks and counterattacks, of threats as well as blandishments. At stake was not just the production of jet engines but also the acquisition of supersonic fighter jets, which generated public as well as secret debates. In conversations with American diplomats, Indian officials emphasized the looming threat from the People's Republic of China, though the process was also driven by upgrades in Pakistan's U.S.-equipped air force. American intelligence grew suspicious of the proposed Indian purchase of the MiG-21, a plane they considered better suited for use against Pakistan than against China. Yet the decision was not based solely upon assessments of military need. Discussing the decision with his intelligence chief, Prime Minister Nehru emphasized the political effects of an arms deal. A purchase from the Americans could help India prosecute a war against China, he said, but a purchase from the Soviets might keep India out of war. As a tangible sign of Soviet commitment to India, the MiG-21 could deter China.[15]

Procurement decisions on military aircraft rested on multiple considerations. On the one hand, basic economic terms of the transaction like cost and currency clearly mattered; Indian resources, especially foreign exchange, were severely limited. But the decision was also a key front in political battles about Indian alignment (or nonalignment) in the Cold War. And military matters, to be sure, were not completely absent: the different supersonic fighters—the Soviet MiG-21, the French Mirage, the British Lightning, and the American F-104, each had different technical capabilities and presented different prospects for production in India.

One group in this dispute apparently felt that confidential consideration did not serve its interests, and told leading American and Indian newspapers that the IAF had agreed to purchase MiG-21 supersonic fighters from the Soviet Union. The deal had many advantages, according to the anonymous sources quoted—not the least of which was that the transaction would take place in rupees, thus preserving India's anemic foreign currency reserves. M. J. Desai, secretary general of the Indian foreign ministry and generally sympathetic to the West, dismissed the reports as "kite flying by some interested party"—either pro-Soviet officials trying to pressure the Soviets to complete the deal or pro-Westerners trying to scotch it. Those in the latter camp, like B. K. Nehru, quickly used the information, once it became public, to push for a generous American offer. Ambassador Galbraith complained that U.S. public opinion would be "allergic" to the MiG-21 purchase, while B. K. Nehru and his allies hoped that the rumors would spur Ambassador Galbraith to push for a better deal.[16]

The currency issue quickly brought up questions that were at once arcane and profoundly political—questions that would shape the competition to supply the IAF with fighter jets. Indian leaders repeated the refrain that the jet purchase would be another "purely commercial" transaction and would not constitute military aid. Soviet willingness to denominate the sale of MiG-21s in rupees, by this logic, made for a better deal in purely commercial terms. The notion that rupee sales were still "commercial" drew heated complaints from American diplomats, who repeatedly insisted that a rupee sale was, like the food acquired through Food for Peace / PL480 (also repaid in rupees), a form of aid. Jawaharlal Nehru disagreed, expressing his annoyance about the American position. Yet even he conceded that the question of Soviet subsidies was literally incalculable; there was no such thing as a "commercial" price for Soviet airplanes. Given this uncertainty, Nehru was surprisingly confident about the details of Western offers, arguing (in the words of British officials) that "if America or Britain were to offer aircraft on comparable terms [as the Soviets] this would involve an element of subsidy." American officials did not balk at the notion of rupee repayment, but could consider such arrangements only within the rubric of the Mutual Security Program—that is, as military aid. The details of the transaction remained a political, and not purely an economic, concern.[17]

The news of a prospective Indian purchase of MiG-21 fighters sparked a major debate within the U.S. government. Galbraith saw the purchase as a referendum on his ambassadorship and worked tirelessly to arrange a competing American deal. He rained short dispatches and long memoranda on Washington, buttonholing anyone he could to explain that a MiG deal would threaten his grand plans for Indo-American relations. Galbraith worked the halls of Indian government just as aggressively; he complained about the unfairness of the United States providing massive economic assistance while being shut out of the military sphere. The ambassador pointed to the controversies whirling around Krishna Menon: "the fundamental problem," he complained to one Pentagon official, "was one of internal Indian politics."[18]

The initial responses to Galbraith's flurry of correspondence suggested that both strategic and personality considerations were at play. Secretary of State Dean Rusk worried that MiGs were a gateway weapon that would soon leave the Indian Air Force addicted to Soviet systems. On the other hand, his assistant secretary argued against an American deal because it might enhance Krishna Menon's prestige. Indian diplomats in Washington, no great friends of the defense minister, were well aware of this dynamic; they compared the American attitude toward Krishna Menon to a "neurosis requiring psychiatric treatment."[19]

As Ambassador Galbraith sprang into action, other American officials urged calm. Robert Komer, head of South Asian affairs at the National Security Council, was also concerned about the way the MiG deal was unfolding but did not see an IAF purchase from the Soviet Union as an unmitigated disaster. He recommended that the U.S. government should "protest . . . vigorously for effect," but need not "break our backs to forestall [the] MiG purchase." He saw a number of advantages to Indian MiG purchases, not least that they might "exacerbate" Sino-Soviet tensions; the Chinese Air Force, after all, did not have such advanced Soviet aircraft and would presumably resent the USSR for equipping its would-be antagonists with them. Countering Soviet offers, Komer continued, might draw the United States into an "undignified" bidding war against the Soviets—which it would likely lose anyway. And winning the deal would cause massive headaches in Pakistani-American relations. The main reason for American "protests," Komer elaborated, was not to win the contract for supersonic fighters, only to "provide some leverage to pro-Westerners in the Indian Cabinet" in their battles against Krishna Menon.[20]

Komer's arguments persuaded President John F. Kennedy of the disadvantages of selling the American F-104 fighter to India. Both agreed, though, that the MiG sale was a "test of strength" for Krishna Menon—a test they hoped to see him fail. The president thus approached British prime minister Harold Macmillan to see whether the British might send supersonic jets to India—either its Lightning jets or possibly even loaning F-104s from Britain's own Royal Air Force. Macmillan rejected the loan concept out of hand, but showed a willingness to sell Lightnings to India—so long as the United States covered the "full cost of the aircraft." This reply shaped the remainder of the negotiations, which focused on a joint Anglo-American agreement with British aircraft and American dollars.[21]

The British government's interest in supporting its arms manufacturers, keeping Soviet weapons out of the IAF, and strengthening Anglo-American ties all argued in favor of such an offer. Macmillan haggled with Kennedy over cost sharing and with his own ministries about the terms. British Treasury officials, for instance, argued that the very notion of a British sale in rupees was Krishna Menon's attempt to "pull our noses out to a ridiculous length." The final British offer would send one squadron of Lightning jets to the IAF priced at roughly half the actual costs of production, and repayable in rupees. Kennedy agreed that the United States would cover most of the expenses.[22]

This hard-wrought offer had much going against it, however. Indian defense experts argued against the Lightning, citing an unspecified "severe technical defect." Prime Minister Nehru also noted that the sophistication of the Lightning would preclude its production in India—and with this even pro-Western diplomats like M. J. Desai agreed. Then there was the vexed question of subsidies. Nehru rejected the loud ministrations of British diplomats and insisted that the MiG purchase would not entail a subsidy, while the Lightning deal would. British diplomats took an aggressive stance, arguing that the MiG purchase endangered future American economic aid to India, which might make "the cheap MiG . . . the most expensive aeroplane the Indians had ever bought." Such threats, however, could easily backfire, drawing resentment even from pro-Western officials like Morarji Desai.[23]

Ironically, the British proponents of the Lightning deal had quite a different agenda from the Americans. President Kennedy, guided by his clever aide Robert Komer, considered a Western offer to India essential, but would not have wept over the MiG deal. The British offer (with quiet support from the Americans) could bolster pro-Western forces in the Indian cabinet irrespective of the ultimate outcome. It might even serve, as Kennedy put it, as a "spoiler" that would allow the cabinet to reject all offers, including the Soviet one.[24]

Pro-Western Indian officials, for their part, were working overtime to derail Krishna Menon's effort to purchase the MiGs. Finance Minister Morarji Desai was the highest-ranking proponent of the Lightning purchase; he worked with American and British diplomats to make the case for the Lighting—and, even more important, against the MiGs. As momentum toward the decision to purchase MiGs gathered, Morarji Desai followed Kennedy's own logic, arguing that India should maintain nonalignment by rejecting both the British and the Soviet offers. He suggested that the United States would readily come to Indian aid in the case of attacks from China—though he warned that the Indian purchase of MiGs might change that. A threat to cut economic aid may actually have backfired. B. K. Nehru, reliably in the camp of seeking American aid, admitted that such threats made it more difficult to back away from the Soviet offer—which would be seen as "yielding to pressure of Western powers." The British threats raised the question, he acknowledged, of "what price we were prepared to pay for economic aid." The assertion, or even the threat, of Western leverage complicated the efforts those in Indian government seeking closer Western ties.[25]

Confronted in July 1962 by new rumors that the MiG deal was going through, American officials conceded the purchase of Soviet fighters. They then shifted to a fallback goal of preventing the licensing of MiGs for Indian production. Meanwhile, the action shifted to Moscow, where a delegation of aviation experts negotiated final details for the MiG purchase.[26]

When Soviet and Indian negotiators signed an agreement in late August 1962, the West finally lost the competition. The final deal promised the delivery of twelve finished MiG-21s in varying configurations. The first four jets would arrive by December 1962, with eight more delivered over the next two years. GKES would also provide technical assistance, training, supplies, and licenses for the production of the jets in India. The total cost would come to four million rubles—payable in rupees.

Since no public announcement appeared, Western officials (along with a surprising number of senior Indian officials) had no inkling that the results were in.[27] Newspaper reports continued in the same vein as they had all summer; Indian and American journalists described Indian inclinations to buy MiG-21s, but did not indicate—even in early September—that an agreement had been signed. Jawaharlal Nehru withheld this information as well; some two weeks after the deal was struck, the prime minister noted only that Indo-Soviet "negotiations had gone a good bit further." He continued to defend a prospective MiG purchase as a "normal commercial transaction without any political implications." As a sign of how closely the information on the final deal was held, some two weeks later Galbraith's friends in the military (including General B. M. Kaul) did not mention the agreement to the ambassador. Galbraith thus expressed his hopes that the MiG deal was "expiring not with a bang but a whimper." In the end it was not the expiration of the deal but its fulfillment that created the "bang."[28]

The Crisis Erupts: Sino-Indian Battles in the Himalayas

Nehru's and Krishna Menon's hopes that the MiG deal might deter Chinese aggression failed immediately. On the very same day that the MiG deal was signed—and, of course, before any public announcement—the leadership of the Chinese Communist Party convened at a beach resort and committed to building up the military presence on the border with India. Tensions had been building since 1960, as diplomatic initiatives spiraled into growing verbal conflicts and deepening mistrust. Military maneuvers—including Chinese reinforcements and road-building and India's so-called forward policy—put border patrols in harm's way, leading to a handful of fatalities and many close calls.[29]

Krishna Menon's stratagem of using a Soviet arms purchase to keep China at bay reached consummation and utter bankruptcy simultaneously. One sign of this fate came from the army itself. Chief of General Staff B. M. Kaul sought out Ambassador Galbraith in early September, offering him a lengthy tale of woe with his defense minister as the chief culprit. The conversation was striking in many ways, not least because neither party seemed to be aware of either of the events of August 29: the MiG deal and the start of the Chinese buildup. General Kaul told the ambassador that the only possible strategy for India was to seek American support, cursing all the more the defense minister's decision to enact "a virtually absolute ban on American material procurement." Deeply worried about the massive military advantage that the Chinese had along its border with India, General Kaul saw only one bright spot in recent events: the Chinese assertiveness of the summer had damaged Krishna Menon's reputation in high political circles.[30]

The growing frequency and intensity of military engagements in September–October 1962 soon became a global and not just a local matter. The clashes endangered Sino-Soviet relations, as the Indian Air Force deployed its new An-12 transports and Mi-4 helicopters against China. Chinese leaders complained vehemently to Soviet diplomats, protesting that the appearance of Soviet aircraft had "a certain effect on the mood of our soldiers." A few days later the Chinese ambassador in Moscow lodged a similar complaint to

Khrushchev, who retorted, "No one has ever fought a war with helicopters and transport planes." Such a rebuttal could not have consoled Khrushchev's Chinese comrades.[31]

Khrushchev quickly moved to shore up the shaky position underlying his bluster. For the leader of world socialism to provide military aircraft to a nonaligned state deploying them against a fraternal socialist one was, at the very least, an awkward situation. Soviet leaders first placed their hopes in an ill-defined Sino-Indian "reconciliation." They then denied the possibility of any future use of the MiGs as deterrence against China, ordering that the MiG deal (then some six weeks old) be kept secret. Khrushchev also tilted supply policy, promising to provide sophisticated versions of the MiG-21s to the Chinese. He postponed the delivery of the fighters just sold to India, telling his Chinese comrades (but not his Indian partners) about the delay. Khrushchev turned against the Indians, ordering his ambassador to take Krishna Menon to task for letting the border troubles escalate into a shooting war. He also obfuscated about the delays, continuing to promise anxious Indian diplomats that the Soviets would "meet their obligations." The Soviet leader, in short, was currying favor with his obstreperous comrades in Beijing at the expense of his friends in New Delhi.[32]

On October 20, as White House aides secretly conferred about the Soviet missiles in Cuba, an all-out Chinese attack across the eastern sector—euphemized as a "self-defensive counterattack"—quickly overran the vastly outnumbered and underequipped Indian forces. The speed and success of the Chinese advance shocked even those Indian generals who had sounded earlier alarms about the limited capability of Indian forces. In a major address on All-India Radio, the prime minister called for national unity amid the heavy burdens imposed by the military crisis. Yet he insisted that the Third Five-Year Plan should continue unabated. The Indian Army was wracked by turmoil among top brass. And a group of politicos leading India's ruling Congress Party hoped to use the crisis to unseat Krishna Menon.[33]

Khrushchev acknowledged from the start that the Sino-Indian conflict could "bring no benefit" to the USSR. American officials shared this view but from a different angle: they wanted to take advantage of the Soviet predicament. Pentagon officials, in conjunction with their friends at Lockheed, saw an opportunity to expand American sales of military transport aircraft—the Lockheed C-130—since the USSR would be unable to ship more An-12s. Even if

Indian orders for big-ticket items did not materialize immediately, pro-Western Indians like M. J. Desai, Morarji Desai, and B. K. Nehru approached their American contacts to procure spare parts for immediate delivery to India. M. J. Desai also cornered Ambassador Galbraith in order to alert him to an impending request for American military equipment.[34]

The most striking plan for engaging American assistance came from General B. M. Kaul, who had long sought to expand military connections with the United States. What Kaul later described laconically as a document listing "what additional weapons and equipment we required" in fact revealed his existential angst. The general called for imposing a dictatorship in India and teaming up with South Korea and Taiwan to launch a U.S.-supported invasion of China. Though this proposal was quickly squelched, it demonstrated in extremis the Western orientation, as well as the deep worries, in senior military ranks.[35]

Though Ambassador Galbraith never got wind of General Kaul's plans, he worked assiduously to strengthen the hands of pro-Western friends like M. J. Desai. He insisted to his colleagues that American aid be plentiful, inexpensive, and free of political strings. He had some success; a State Department report characterized the initial effort as "designed to help a friend, not win an ally." B. K. Nehru delivered to President Kennedy the prime minister's letter seeking American "sympathy and support." The roving ambassador explained that this was as direct as his cousin could be; old habits precluded a more direct request. He also clarified that the official Indian request was for commercial purchases, not aid. The American president was ready to act on any kind of request for weapons, whether cash purchases or military aid, but with one proviso: he wanted Krishna Menon excluded from any discussions about American aid. Kennedy also told B. K. Nehru that it was time for Khrushchev to "put up or shut up" regarding military supplies, likely unaware that the Soviet leader had already put up (but then held up) MiG deliveries.[36]

Meanwhile, Indian officials who had favored Soviet procurement were engaged in similar conversations. A senior Indian diplomat in Moscow pleaded with Soviet officials trying to win Soviet material and political support. Krishna Menon begged the Soviet ambassador to accelerate the delivery of the MiGs so the IAF could use them right away; when the ambassador confirmed blandly that the contract would be honored, the defense minister complained that he was "talking like a lawyer" and not like a friend. But Krishna Menon could do

Shown here in October 1962 with President John F. Kennedy, B. K. Nehru did more than any other single individual to reorient Indian policy toward Western economic aid—and had no small role in changing aid efforts in the United States and at the World Bank. *Source:* Photo by Cecil W. Stoughton, 26 October 1962. Oval office, White House Photographs Collection, John F. Kennedy Presidential Library and Museum, Boston (ST-466-1-62).

little but plead; his gamble on deterrent effects of the MiG-21 had failed both militarily and politically.[37]

The defense minister was well aware that his position was, like that of the Indian forces he oversaw, increasingly precarious. Contacts between Indian and American military officers—so long opposed by the defense minister—grew more frequent and less furtive. And American pressure against Krishna Menon paled in comparison to the intense efforts within the Congress Party to remove him; an American observer termed Congress politicking "political jungle warfare."[38]

Responding to intense pressure from within his party, Prime Minister Nehru relieved Krishna Menon of his Defence Ministry portfolio on Halloween, giving him the portfolio of minister of defense production as a face-saving gesture. Since Krishna Menon was barred from working with the Americans (who already had one thousand tons of supplies en route), or even with the Indian Army's own supply organization, this was not likely to be a successful appointment. The maneuverings continued apace, with Minister of Finance Morarji

Desai telling the prime minister that anger was so intense that Krishna Menon risked being assassinated. In those circumstances, even Krishna Menon's friendship with Nehru was not sufficient to keep him in the cabinet; he was stripped of his new post after only a week.[39]

With Krishna Menon's departure the path toward closer Indo-American military relations was clear. Yet confusion among military and civilian leaders in India ran high in early November. Asked about the Soviet plans for delivery of the MiG-21 fighters, Morarji Desai told one American diplomat that the Indians themselves "would like to know." American diplomats got the impression that even top Indian generals had no information about the MiGs.[40]

Just as American officials sought to press their advantage in India, so too did pro-Western contingents in India seek to strengthen their own hands. B. K. Nehru tried to convince American officials to sell arms for rupees (citing the example of PL480); he no longer fretted over the distinction between commercial transactions and military aid. And B. M. Birla, scion of one of India's great industrial families, made a more general case for American support for India. The generally pro-Western *Economic Weekly* defended the pursuit of military aid by arguing that nonalignment did not preclude receiving such assistance: "the criterion for non-alignment is not the economic terms on which arms are obtained but the political commitments, if any, that go with it." Thus receiving American weapons, even on "favorable terms," did not threaten this bedrock of Indian foreign policy, or so the editorial argued.[41]

These explanations aside, November 1962 proved a difficult month for Indian nonalignment. Galbraith, obviously proud of leading the American response to the crisis, gloated that "much of non-alignment has gone out the window." And in terms of military deliveries, this appeared to be the case; American materiel arrived steadily while Soviet officials remained evasive about their commitments. Khrushchev reassured experienced diplomat T. N. Kaul, the Indian ambassador in Moscow, that the USSR would "fulfill [its] obligations" and deliver the MiGs, but he declined to offer a timetable. Ambassador Kaul recorded, with the utmost diplomacy, that he was impressed by Khrushchev's "down to earth" approach. Jawaharlal Nehru remained optimistic, telling American diplomats that he had "no doubt" that the Soviet MiGs would arrive in December as the agreement stipulated.[42]

Soviet officials fought to contain the damage of the Indo-Soviet conflict. Khrushchev told Ambassador Kaul that the Soviet Union desired a rapid end to the conflict, intimating conspiratorially that "reactionary forces want to prolong this conflict in order to change India's policy, both internal and external." Such statements sounded like Khrushchev's usual bluster, and perhaps they were. But the logic also resonated with American officials like Komer who saw in the Sino-Indian border war a "magnificent opportunity" to bring India into the Western camp. A flurry of internal American correspondence in mid-November 1962 argued that the longer the war went on, the more influence the American government could have upon Indian policy. "Continuance of the war," observed a colleague of Komer's, "may serve important U.S. policy objectives," including improved Indo-Pakistani relations and the demise of nonalignment. Or in the words of a Pentagon consultant, the Sino-Indian conflict, so long as it was "contained within certain limits," offered "potential long-term advantages for the U.S. both in the education of the Indian elite to a clearer understanding of the Communist world threat and in the hard choices that it would press upon the Soviet Union." Ambassador Galbraith agreed, already counting his putative spoils: "We stand on the edge of a great opportunity—reconciliation between India and Pakistan, security for the whole subcontinent, a decisive reverse for communism in its area of its greatest opportunity." Komer called the Himalayan crisis "potentially one of the most crucial events of the decade"; for that very reason "it may not be in our interest to see the Sino-Indian crisis tail off too fast." Komer and his colleagues did not want to waste a good crisis.[43]

Indian officials, even those inclined to the West, seemed well aware of the possible price of American aid. When Foreign Secretary M. J. Desai delivered a wish list of military supplies to Galbraith, for instance, he asked the ambassador to forestall any talk of Kashmir until after "settlement with China." Even while seeking more than $800 million in U.S. weaponry, including the F-104A supersonic fighter, the foreign secretary sought to dictate the terms of the transaction. The pro-Western contingents in New Delhi were no longer shy about their inclinations, and sought a massive infusion of aid from the United States and the United Kingdom. Krishna Menon's successor as minister of defense production, the former finance minister T. T. Krishnamachari (best known as TTK), reiterated the need for American aircraft and for a loan of $500 million or more.[44]

Those in India inclined toward the Soviet Union, however, did not concede defeat. Ambassador T. N. Kaul in Moscow worked frantically to keep Soviet authorities to the schedule to which they had agreed in late August—and even sought additional helicopters, transport aircraft, and the like. He wrote Prime

Minister Nehru that Soviet supplies might have minimal military significance, but would "strengthen the Indian position" politically: they would help isolate China within the Communist world, and could provide at least some Indian leverage in negotiations with the Western powers. But no such equipment was forthcoming.

Nehru was increasingly concerned that aid from the Soviet Union—even the agreed-upon MiG-21s—might not arrive, however beseeching his ambassador's pleas. Even Ambassador Kaul conceded that there was "some lack of clarity regarding the firmness of Soviet commitments." Kaul never slowed or tempered his requests for Soviet assistance, saying that in this moment of existential crisis, "India needed to turn to her friends" for aid. While the ambassador clearly included the USSR among those "friends," many in New Delhi wanted to seek friendship and material support elsewhere.[45]

As the military situation deteriorated in mid-November, Prime Minister Nehru turned decisively toward Western aid. On November 19, he wrote to President Kennedy and Prime Minister Macmillan about the "grim situation" on the border, noting that "a lot more effort, both from us and from our friends, will be required." He hoped that India would "continue to have the support and assistance" of the British and U.S. governments. Only a few hours after sending this request to Washington, the prime minister received word of further military setbacks. Chinese troops were advancing "in massive strength" through territories that India claimed as its own—and were poised, reports indicated, for a major invasion deeper into India. Rather than consulting with the cabinet, or with the Indian Air Force, Nehru met with pro-Western ministers and secretaries like Morarji Desai and M. J. Desai regarding the next steps.[46]

The prime minister then put forth a remarkable proposal for American assistance. In a second letter on November 19, the so-called Midnight Letter, he reported that the situation was "really desperate" and thus called for desperate measures. He requested immediate support from the United States with a level of detail he had earlier avoided. Nehru sought twelve squadrons of supersonic fighters, to be flown and maintained by American personnel—which would entail, he continued, U.S. fighters and transports flown by American pilots. Perhaps even more striking was Nehru's request that U.S. planes "assist" the IAF "in air battles with the Chinese Air Force."[47]

The prime minister's plea—as with Ambassador Kaul's work in Moscow— left open the question of friendship and politics. He admitted that the Indian government had made only rather limited requests for assistance, and had not (until now) asked for "more comprehensive" aid—citing both the global implications and a desire not to "embarrass our friends" in the USSR. Nehru, in other words, hoped to maintain ties to the Soviet Union even as he sought American materiel and combat support. Conceding that he had asked for Soviet military aid before approaching the United States, he reported that Soviet authorities were unable to provide any aid. Soviet officials, for their part, acknowledged the need for Western assistance, pleading with the Indian side only that it avoid a "military alliance or other major alterations" in Indian foreign policy.[48]

American diplomats expressed both shock and concern with the Midnight Letter. Secretary of State Rusk warned that Nehru sought an American commitment "to a fighting war"—a commitment he was not prepared to offer, and one he believed the prime minister would not, by the light of day, desire. There was plenty of room, he noted, to expand American military aid to India without sending American troops into combat. Galbraith was less cautious: he saw in the "overtones of panic" an opportunity to remake Indo-American relations.[49]

And then, abruptly, it was all over. Barely a day after Prime Minister Nehru's panicked letter to President Kennedy, Chinese officials unilaterally declared a cease-fire across all sectors of the border. The decision, one thoughtful analyst later concluded, was not shaped by external aid to India—whether Soviet or Western—but by the Chinese leadership's assessment that it had achieved its objectives: it had embarrassed both India and the Soviet Union and had reclaimed territory that it considered Chinese. With the unexpected cease-fire, India's immediate need for the unprecedented program outlined in the Midnight Letter had passed. But broader questions remained: about India's military future, its connections to the Cold War superpowers, and the meaning of nonalignment.[50]

From Crisis to Competition

The war and its aftermath benefited those seeking closer military, economic, and political ties with the West. With Krishna Menon out of office, the pro-Soviet contingent lost a powerful if polarizing voice. Others invested in Soviet military supplies still faced tough going. Only after the cease-fire did Indian diplomats finally extract an explanation from their Soviet counterparts about the MiG deliveries promised for December. It was more of an excuse, really, and an unconvincing one at that. After weeks of asking everyone he could reach, Ambassador T. N. Kaul was told that an "increase in domestic demand" would delay delivery; in fact, the planes were sent to Iraq. The ambassador's Soviet interlocutors refused to give a revised delivery date, or even a time when they might be willing to discuss the airplanes again. Though Ambassador Kaul and Prime Minister Nehru apparently treated the news about the delayed MiGs with grave concern, others in high Indian government circles reacted differently. Finance Minister Morarji Desai, for instance, expressed his "delight" that the MiG deal was in trouble; he hoped it would (in the words of his British interlocutor), "finally convince any who still doubted it that it was unsafe for India in the future to look to Russia for any important military supplies."[51]

Pressing their advantage, the Western powers sent delegations to India to discuss military matters. U.S. Assistant Secretary of State W. Averell Harriman, distinctly unsympathetic to Indian nonalignment, arrived in December to evaluate the military and political implications of expanding Western military supplies to India. Pro-Western Indians requested from the American delegation an extraordinary range of weaponry in large quantities. TTK, now the minister of economic and defense coordination, observed that Indian generals had made "no attempt . . . to readjust our sights to what is or would be available." Indian diplomats in Washington also got in on the discussions, requesting from the Pentagon a long list of equipment that included cutting-edge Sidewinder air-to-air missiles, torpedoes, and much more. These must have been heady times for those hoping to build military ties to the West—a moment when the crisis seemed to offer a chance for a shopping spree that linked India militarily to the United States and the United Kingdom.[52]

Yet those interested in maintaining Soviet connections kept up the pressure, cautioning Prime Minister Nehru and other members of the cabinet about the costs of Western assistance. Ambassador Kaul warned ominously from Moscow that Western aid would come with "certain conditions." Such alarms were well taken insofar as the Harriman Mission was concerned. President Kennedy wrote Harriman that the Sino-Indian crisis "has given us what may be a one-time opportunity to bring about a Pakistani-Indian reconciliation." Ambassador Galbraith, too, saw military aid as an instrument to force a settlement over Kashmir. The assistant secretary of state needed little convincing on this score, having long promoted using whatever leverage the U.S. could muster to reduce Indo-Pakistani tensions over Kashmir. One sympathetic intelligence official recalled the dilemma, recognizing that the U.S. could not use military aid as a "crude bludgeon" to force a Kashmir settlement, but at the same time predicted that "there would be less aid in the absence of [such a] settlement." Harriman and his colleagues stood ready to play their hand because they argued that the Soviet Union could do little beyond responding "with sorrow more than with anger." Under such circumstances, Harriman arrived in New Delhi ready to lead his Indian interlocutors into a more "cooperative" (critics might read "subservient") position vis-à-vis the United States.[53]

Harriman wasted no time in fulfilling this agenda, expressing disappointment that so many of the Indian officials he met were "unrealistic" regarding Indo-Pakistani tensions—meaning that they were unwilling to compromise on Kashmir in exchange for American aid. In his first meeting with the prime minister, Harriman inquired about Indo-Soviet ties; Nehru reported that the Soviets had acquiesced to India's receiving Western aid but demanded that there would be no "realignment" of Indian foreign relations. Harriman's aim was precisely the opposite: to ensure that Indian nonalignment "underwent a substantive reinterpretation in a manner favorable to our interests." The mission's final report returned again and again to Pakistan in general and Kashmir in particular. Harriman's wishes did not resonate with all of the Indian officials he met on his mission—including some of those generally inclined toward the West.[54]

The Harriman Mission's final report proposed $130 million of military aid in the short term and defense production agreements after that. The mission envisioned a continuing role for the United Kingdom, with details to be worked out at the highest level. And finally, the report called for both donors to apply "continuing strong pressure" to achieve a settlement of the Kashmir conflict. The message from the State Department was clear: American military assistance was possible, but continuing aid depended on progress over Kashmir. Essentially the same message came from London.[55]

The Anglo-American powers got a chance to coordinate their aid—and their pressure—while meeting in Nassau (the capital of the Bahamas) in December 1962. Prime Minister Macmillan and President Kennedy, together with a retinue of advisers eager to talk South Asia rather than sunbathe, shared a basic aim: using the crisis to pursue their long-term goals. Strikingly, those goals meant not letting the crisis resolve itself too quickly: "it is as much in our strategic interest," Komer briefed President Kennedy, "to keep up a high degree of Sino-Indian friction as it is to prevent it from spilling over into large scale war." The two Anglophone powers differed on how much pressure to apply vis-à-vis Kashmir, and who would pay for Indian rearmament, but deferred any moment of reckoning. Instead, they took the less-than-decisive step of suggesting that a joint UK-U.S. expert commission on air defense visit India. This plan would have the advantage of delaying any difficult decisions while still demonstrating firm Western support for India in case China entertained thoughts of additional military engagements.[56]

The Anglo-American discussions at Nassau hardly resolved the issues that had dominated Indian relations with the superpowers for the preceding two years. Even with Krishna Menon out of the cabinet, internal battles about India's relationship with the Western powers continued to rage. One longtime Congress activist insisted to Nehru that he needed to "make the Anglo-Americans feel a sense of definite responsibility" for India. Yet this newfound responsibility, the prime minister replied, should in no way endanger "our basic policy of nonalignment." And Ambassador B. K. Nehru similarly celebrated growing Western commitment to India, but pleaded with Secretary of State Rusk to delink military aid from Kashmir.[57]

Meanwhile, the pro-Soviet groups kept up their fight. Ambassador T. N. Kaul in Moscow devoted himself to prying loose the MiG jets promised earlier—and to seeking additional helicopters and other aircraft. The ambassador's efforts came to little avail; a Soviet general gave plenty of excuses but little reassurance, even as he lashed out against Western military aid to India, which would, he accused, strengthen "reactionary elements in India." Others saw economic (and not just geopolitical) advantages to continuing work with the Soviet Union: while the United States and the United Kingdom were willing to send military assistance, only the Soviet Union had made a commitment to building up Indian defense through production licensing. The Soviet licensing arrangements promised, also, to put significant resources in the hands of the union government, so even as the Soviet deal sat uncomfortably suspended through the winter of 1962–1963, various states angled to host one or another facility related to MiG production.[58]

The Indian government agreed to participate in talks over Kashmir, but neither side in those negotiations was inclined to make concessions. Indian officials debated how closely future military aid would be tied to successful talks with Pakistan; one characterized the ambiguous American position as follows: "while they are at great pains to explain that the supply of military equipment to India is not conditional upon the settlement of the Kashmir problem, it is quite obvious that nothing much is going to be done until the Kashmir settlement is made." Others used blunter language: Western views on Kashmir amounted to "sledgehammer diplomacy."[59]

The visit of key Indian officials to Washington later that spring revealed the extent of differences between the two sides—but at the same time, promoted the ascendance in both governments of those wanting to expand Indo-American military relations. These visits by senior officials from the Ministry of Defence and Economic Coordination (Minister T. T. Krishnamachari and Secretary S. Bhoothalingam) established the contours for U.S. relations with India and the United Kingdom for the coming years. The talks occurred in the context of the collapsing Indo-Pakistani negotiations over Kashmir that had been a key goal of some American and British officials. The message from the top, though, was softening. After receiving a letter from Prime Minister Nehru criticizing the pressure over Kashmir as "ill-considered and ill-conceived," President Kennedy was ready to loosen, if not entirely dispense with, the "strings" about Kashmir. He considered Indian equipment requests far too high (by a factor of five), but in most other respects expressed sympathy for TTK's views.[60]

TTK took the opportunity in his first meeting with President Kennedy to raise Indian complaints about Kashmir; he relayed the prime minister's concern that "the United States was taking advantage" of India's military needs in order to "pressurize her into a settlement of the Kashmir dispute on terms favorable to Pakistan." Indeed, American officials like Harriman and "whiz kid" secretary of defense Robert S. McNamara were hoping to do just that. But the pressure was already abating; President Kennedy had ordered American officials to "prepare to go ahead on military support" even as the Kashmir negotiations faltered. By the time TTK and Bhoothalingam arrived in April 1963, according to Ambassador B. K. Nehru, any American comments about a Kashmir agreement had been transposed into a "much lower key" than earlier. Even after American diplomats wrote off Indo-Pakistani negotiations as a total failure, plans for negotiating defense aid continued apace.[61]

Even if Harriman's Kashmir gambit had failed, the attempted pressure led pro-Western Indians to contemplate military aid from a range of sources. After shepherding TTK through Washington, Ambassador B. K. Nehru conceded that the Indian military needed to fly "as many flags as possible." This plan met with

Soviet approval; according to M. J. Desai, Soviet officials "had no objection" to Western military aid to India. Jawaharlal Nehru continued to argue, publicly and privately, that India would buy weapons from whomsoever it chose, on whatever terms it found most advantageous. Recent military negotiations with the West, he insisted, did not alter that stance.[62]

Though a Kashmir settlement was no longer a quid pro quo for military aid, American officials continued to levy a price for military aid. They lectured Indian defense officials about the need to expand private sector production of materiel—directly contradicting the Indian Industrial Policy Resolution of 1956. Pentagon chief Robert McNamara also sought permission to refuel American spy planes over Indian skies—and to land on Indian airfields. Nehru, in the words of a sympathetic biographer, "allowed his Government to be persuaded" to grant such use of Indian airspace and ground facilities, and to host Voice of America transmitters broadcasting to Vietnam. The bill for American aid was coming due.[63]

TTK's visit ended with an inconclusive meeting with President Kennedy. The president deftly evaded queries about the prospects of Anglo-American air support in the case of another war with China, and spoke positively if vaguely about Indo-American relations. In the sly assessment of Ambassador B. K. Nehru, President Kennedy "really said nothing new, [but] he said it with such charm and grace" that he sounded very sympathetic to the Indian position. Summarizing his visit to Washington and other Western capitals, TTK expressed overall satisfaction. True, he conceded, no concrete aid agreements were signed, but Kashmir had been reduced to a "minor key." And a significant military aid package was in the offing, moving well beyond the plans worked out in Nassau. Perhaps best of all, key American policy makers seemed less worried about the mixing of American and Soviet aircraft and weapons. Indeed, Harriman encouraged TTK to seek military assistance from the Soviet Union; his colleagues went so far as to offer a team of American experts to advise on the optimal deployment of Soviet An-12 transports. This American endorsement came as a welcome relief to pro-Western contingents in New Delhi.[64]

Landing the MiGs

As negotiations with the United States and United Kingdom proceeded in spring 1963, the Indian Air Force still awaited delivery of the four MiG jets due in

December 1962. Thus the top agenda item for the pro-Soviet faction within the Indian government and military was to get the Soviet Union to live up to its agreement. But the Indian position went far beyond the legalities of the situation; the nation sought to entice its Soviet interlocutors to expand the military connections by dangling the prospect of long-term bilateral trade expansion. A top official at the Ministry of External Affairs brought a long list of commodities available for trade, though this did little to spark Soviet movement on any outstanding items: not the delivery of Soviet MiGs, the plans to design and build factories for MiG jets and jet engines, or the request for sophisticated Soviet radar systems. Soviet officials replied blandly and evasively that relevant authorities were busy studying these complicated issues. Indian requests on the political front—namely, asking the Soviets for help in convincing the Chinese leadership to vacate the territories taken during the conflict—garnered the same vague nonresponse.[65]

As winter 1963 turned to spring, Soviet authorities slowly thawed, and began fulfilling the agreement they had signed the previous summer. Ambassador T. N. Kaul made even more explicit the quid pro quo of a long-term trade agreement if his government was satisfied with the progress in military aid. The key elements here were the factories—Indian officials insisted on more than one—for the construction of MiG-21 fuselages and engines. When Soviet experts made a spring 1963 visit, their hosts at the Indian Ministry of Defence and Economic Coordination used the occasion to request the expansion of their work to cover aspects of the design and construction that went beyond the original agreement. Soviet officials generally resisted such requests, but this hardly slowed the pace of Indian efforts to renegotiate the August 1962 agreement.[66]

By summer 1963 the Indian Air Force was operating with both Soviet and Western equipment, so not surprisingly it quickly became a locus of geopolitical maneuvering. Both American and Soviet diplomats had accepted, in principle, that their side would not have an exclusive supply relationship with the IAF. Yet none of these diplomats was entirely satisfied with the IAF's particular mixture of aviation fleets. An official Indian committee to investigate the future of Indian military aircraft took a skeptical attitude toward Soviet equipment—hardly a surprise since industrialist J. R. D. Tata served as committee chair. The Tata Committee came down hard on the MiG-21, which it deemed unsuitable for defense against China. And it recommended suspending the Indo-Soviet agreement for the RD-9F engine. While the Tata Committee questioned prior

Indian purchases, the superpowers themselves were busy angling for future ones. Ambassador Galbraith offered M. J. Desai a joint British-U.S. arrangement for ground radar systems and training—including the long-term loan of two sophisticated mobile radar units and the provision of six permanent radar units to the Indian military. The conversation also made clear that the United States was the major player here, and the United Kingdom was following along, or just following orders.[67]

The Cold War East and West both sought to win an IAF contract to supply of surface-to-air missiles. Soviet diplomats sought to convince S. Bhoothalingam that they could provide the missiles that India desired. An agreement, in fact, had already been reached at the "technical level" before unspecified "problems of a political nature" intervened. Those roadblocks likely involved behind-the-scenes efforts by those sympathetic to American weaponry (and politics) to scrub the Soviet missile deal. But this group did not find much support from American diplomats, who fatalistically conceded the deal to the USSR, debating only the wording of token protests against the arrangement.[68]

The absence of American competition, however, did not always translate into successful Indo-Soviet relations in the military sphere. Indian engineers, for instance, sought to alter agreed-upon specifications for the MiG-21 and related equipment, including a request for engines capable of Mach 2. Soviet counterparts replied huffily that they were "under no obligation" to make such changes and were not inclined to do so. Soviet officials expressed little sympathy for, and more than a little impatience with, the litany of changes that Indian negotiators had requested. Similarly, the two sides differed over the secrecy of the MiG deal. Indian officials wanted their agreements with the USSR widely publicized while Soviet officials, sensitive regarding criticism from their Chinese comrades, wanted to keep the arrangements under wraps. Keeping the agreement quiet would calm roiled Sino-Soviet relations—but would also deprive Indian officials of the chance to use Soviet aid as a bargaining tool vis-à-vis the United States.[69]

To the 1965 War

The possibility of playing the West against the East, even in the military sphere, remained a live option after 1964, even as American officials sought to limit Indian opportunities in this regard. They did so not by outbidding the Soviets but by attaching conditions to their arms deals. As a result, even after President Kennedy forgave the Indian side for failed negotiations in Kashmir, Indo-American military ties never recovered the luster of the darkest days of the crisis. Representatives from the U.S. Air Force and Britain's Royal Air Force tried to tamp down IAF expectations in terms of amounts and capabilities of the airplanes they could provide. When General Maxwell D. Taylor, the chairman of the U.S. Joint Chiefs of Staff, came to New Delhi in December 1963, he promised some aid to meet immediate air defense needs against China—and to entertain requests for a long-term military aid package. While he did not express outright disapproval of the IAF flying both Soviet and Western jets, he did warn his Indian counterparts that his government would consider future American aid in the context of overall Indian defense spending—meaning that Indian military purchases elsewhere (for instance, from the USSR) might lead to the reduction or even cancellation of U.S. aid. Chafing at these conditions, TTK, by this point the minister of finance, replied that he aimed to make India self-sufficient in military supplies—meaning that it could produce all but the most sophisticated electronics domestically. General Taylor cautioned that self-sufficiency in the air force "was a costly business," gently suggesting that the IAF rely upon the "family of nations concerned about the Chinese threat"—that is, on Western aid. Such remarks did not persuade Indian officials, who maintained (in the words of another American general), "an almost pathological desire" to expand military production.[70]

The Indian focus on domestic production, which remained even after Krishna Menon's departure, shaped its dealings with Western powers. Expanded domestic production would likely shut out American and British suppliers, who preferred to sell their equipment than license it for production overseas. Yet production was many years off, so the United States, the United Kingdom, and India seemed headed toward a five-year assistance program worth about $225 million. Defense Minister Y. B. Chavan arranged a trip to Washington in May 1964 to complete the negotiations and sign a Military Assistance Program agreement along those lines.[71]

The 1964 visit, at one level, marked the fruits of the effort to play the two sides against each other. Just before Chavan's arrival, his government signed a secret accord with the USSR establishing a new timetable for the long-delayed MiG-21 deliveries and the construction of production facilities in India. All the while, though, American diplomats were ready to up their offer—even against the recommendation of their own military experts—to forestall a new MiG deal. Any American offer, though, came with numerous conditions; American diplomats warned that they "would have problems" with military and even economic aid if the IAF obtained more MiG jets. Other American conditions soon emerged, expanding well beyond military procurement to overall defense spending (where State Department officials hoped to "impose an austere limit") and to political stipulations regarding Pakistan and Vietnam. Such conditions emerged in the context of what U.S. diplomats euphemistically called security "interdependence"—meaning Indian dependence. Yet even Bowles conceded that his government had "very little leverage" vis-à-vis Indian procurement of Soviet jets.[72]

With the secret Indo-Soviet agreement in his back pocket, Chavan did not have in mind either austerity or interdependence when he arrived in Washington. He wanted supersonic jets, which American experts had long considered beyond India's needs and budget, as well as a wide range of weapons and supplies for the army. Chavan agreed with his American counterpart Robert McNamara about the state of the Indian Air Force—which McNamara (a World War II air forces veteran) undiplomatically compared to a "museum." Top brass in both air forces agreed, and planned for a retirement of the World War II–era aircraft still in service. Though the defense minister blamed Indian dependence on foreign aircraft for the continued presence of vintage planes, his only immediate recourse was to seek new aircraft from abroad. In final negotiations between McNamara, Chavan accepted many conditions for American military aid: a limit on Indian defense expenditures and maintenance of what Americans termed "reasonable force levels"—with Pentagon number-crunchers, of course, serving as the arbiters of reason. With these parameters specified, the two sides set up a formal signing ceremony to take place on May 28—a mundane but ultimately fateful delay. Chavan got word of the death of Prime Minister Nehru on May 27 and returned to New Delhi immediately.[73]

At first Nehru's death did not alter the direction of Indian military procurement. Chavan eventually signed the deal he had worked out with McNamara, which provided a $10 million credit for defense material and a promise to "look with favor" on the long-term Military Assistance Program if India reined it its defense spending. Yet Chavan also learned, much to his chagrin, that the Pentagon would not provide the F-104Gs he had sought. Speaking with the Soviet ambassador that very day, Chavan soon arranged a trip to Moscow. That trip, in August, yielded a more comprehensive deal. What the *Times of India* called Chavan's "shopping" excursion to Moscow was successful indeed: he got commitments for Soviet helicopters and MiG-21 fighters, as well as the promise to facilitate the domestic production of jets in India. Working both sides of the Cold War seemed to be paying dividends for the Indian Air Force.[74]

The changing patterns of Indian defense procurement, especially for its air force, also changed internal dynamics within the West. Though the United Kingdom had long been India's largest military supplier, for instance, Chavan's travels took him first to Washington and Moscow and only then to London. British diplomats chafed at the fact that the Pentagon had been monopolizing Chavan, but they were powerless to prevent this shift. The British government risked, in the words of one diplomat, "becom[ing] even poorer relations than our lesser aid program . . . properly merits" while the Americans "appear[ed] to acquire disproportionate merit." But there was little the British could do to stem the tide other than try to limit Indo-Soviet ties; they had given up on keeping the Americans out. The power shift vis-à-vis Washington also disappointed British officials and executives worried about being supplanted by American defense suppliers. Yet when Chavan did visit London in November 1964, he was met with reticence unusual even by British standards. The Indian Navy, long a British redoubt, did not appreciate the British offer of hopelessly outdated ships and submarines. Meanwhile, Prime Minister Harold Wilson sparred with Chavan over whether military aid would mean pound-for-pound cuts in economic aid. Ultimately, the two sides concluded a modest agreement for some hand-me-down fighters and bombers for use on aircraft carriers. This ungenerous offer, in turn, created an opening for the Soviet suppliers to sell to the Indian Navy.[75]

As the British supply efforts faltered, American officials entered the breach, though were often waylaid by negotiations over the terms and conditions of military sales. Komer identified an ever growing list of stipulations he hoped to see attached to increased military aid; his top priorities were nuclear nonproliferation, changes to economic policy, and "some progress toward Pakistan-Indian reconciliation." Ultimately Indian negotiators were forced to discuss such conditions since their own plans for a domestically built fighter jet had stalled, and they had reluctantly concluded that the MiG-21 had serious limitations in combat situations.[76]

Indo-American military negotiations, and bilateral relations more generally, suffered a bigger blow in April 1965, in the midst of Indo-Pakistani hostilities over territory that had been contested since the Partition of India in 1947: the Gujarat salt marshes known as the Rann of Kutch. The escalation of generalized Indo-Pakistani conflict into actual combat reverberated across South Asia and beyond. Within days of the outbreak of hostilities, the Indian Army gathered what it considered "incontrovertible proof" that Pakistan was deploying American weapons against India. This was a contravention of long-standing promises from top American and British officials that the weapons they were sending to Pakistan would be aimed only at Chinese forces; the fallout in India, and in Indo-American relations, was immediate and severe. As one American briefing paper later noted, "Our past assurances are . . . essentially dead."[77]

The realization of Indian fears in April 1965 quickly heightened wariness about working with the American military, even among those like B. K. Nehru (by then ambassador in Washington) who were generally inclined toward the West. Chester Bowles similarly conceded that the logic for Soviet purchases for the Indian Air Force and Navy, even given past delays, was "rather convincing"; American aid, after all, was also prone to delays—and to conditions imposed both before and after the deal was settled. The Indo-American honeymoon that began in the crisis of fall 1962 had come to an abrupt and definitive end.[78]

American conditions and caveats quickly came to bear in bilateral relations. Though the armed hostilities in April 1965 were only a brief flare-up, the White House nevertheless ordered the Pentagon to examine American military aid to both India and Pakistan with an eye toward what might be most effectively suspended or canceled; this was in anticipation of using aid as incentive (or punishment) should armed hostilities return. Such a moment came sooner than perhaps anyone expected. The late summer and early autumn in South Asia saw a spiral of escalation, of attacks and counterattacks, along various fronts on the Indo-Pakistani border. By early September 1965, the two sides were engaged in full-scale war along a wide front. With the British prime minister publicly siding with Pakistan, the mood in India—public as well as official—was defiant. The United States and the United Kingdom both announced an immediate suspension of military and economic aid to both combatants. For a bipartisan group amounting to about one quarter of the U.S. Congress, this was not enough; after a "volcanic" reaction, they demanded a cutoff of all aid, including PL480 food, to both sides. While this cutoff was a predictable response to the battles raging in Kashmir and Punjab, it reinforced the growing sentiment in Indian official circles that Western powers were not reliable allies. The American cutoff of military sales was essentially permanent; after shipping roughly $95 million (in 1990 dollars) worth of military equipment to India in 1962–1963, the Pentagon shipped only $11 million for the entire decade after 1965.[79]

Though the armed conflict lasted only a few weeks, the U.S. aid suspension permanently undercut those in India who had hoped its military future would be tied to American supplies. Soviet supplies, in contrast, kept flowing through the hostilities in September 1965. In November 1965, not two months after the Western aid cutoff, Finance Minister TTK made a trip to Prague and Moscow to negotiate a new round of military purchases. The experience of 1965 had dramatically increased the Indian request to the USSR, as TTK outlined in a conversation with Aleksei Kosygin. The shape of the battles demonstrated the need for ground support aircraft (in addition to the MiG-21, an interceptor) and for better armor and tanks. Losses of Indian aircraft in combat were magnified by the fact, TTK noted curtly, that the Western aid cutoff eliminated any "prospect of our getting replacements" for the British bombers damaged during the war. Furthermore, the cutoff had reinforced TTK's position that India should be self-sufficient against attacks from Pakistan or, he added in a gesture toward the Chinese threat, "someone else." The visit concluded with a toast from Kosygin for India's military (and not just economic) strength.[80]

From the American perspective, the opportunity that Robert Komer saw in the Sino-Indian crisis of 1962 lasted only briefly. Doing their part to help their allies in the Indian government, American diplomats rejoiced at the demise of V. K. Krishna Menon, who was both a general irritant and a powerful minister who shifted Indian procurement eastward. Yet even his departure from the scene marked only a momentary victory for the United States, as well as for those in Indian government who sought closer Western ties. Hemmed in by continuing military support for Pakistan and always ready to impose new stipulations on aid recipients, the India lobby in the U.S. had little room to maneuver. It eventually gave up on its hopes that military aid could reorient Indian foreign policy, or even its military procurement strategy. Ambassador Chester Bowles bemoaned the failure to bring India closer to the U.S. politically and militarily, calling the 1962–1965 period a "major opportunity . . . missed."[81]

If the original Indian impetus for expanding military purchases from the USSR came from Krishna Menon, the momentum slackened only briefly after his departure. Even Soviet obfuscation and delay over the MiG contract signed in August 1962 only slightly slowed the turn to the east, as the Indian defense ministry never gave up on the prospects of Soviet aircraft and weapons. The events of September 1965 helped plant India staunchly in the Soviet camp in terms of military procurement. In the long haul, the aid cutoff cost the United States close connections in an institution that had rallied toward the West in the early 1960s: the uniformed military. The changing domestic alliances left an opening for Soviet diplomats, who came to share the Western view that the MiG-21 deal held greater political than military significance. They hoped that the new MiG factory might serve the same role that the Bhilai Steel Plant had a decade earlier: as a symbol of Indo-Soviet friendship and cooperation, and a sign of the Soviet commitment to building up Indian capacity.[82]

In their most optimistic moments, members of the America lobby hoped that the turn to Soviet aid would not preclude expanding Indo-American military connections. Diplomats in India insisted that there would be "no conflict" in receiving both American and Soviet military aid. B. K. Nehru argued that military aid was just like economic aid, and could be taken from all who offered. But quickly—and "bluntly"—his interlocutor in the State Department replied that military aid was different. Military aid, American policy makers believed, called for special restrictions and rules and opened up new arenas for policy conditioning: about defense procurement sources, overall defense spending, foreign policy, and so on. This firm stance was, of course, explicable. But it also was costly—not just to American defense industry but especially to those Indian officials seeking to expand ties to the United States. The dynamics of development politics applied to military aid. Reflecting on his country's trying experience with the U.S. military after 1962, Y. B. Chavan told Ambassador Bowles that "The Americans were likely to be good in the big situations, but are impossible in normal dealings." His counterparts in Indian economic ministries soon had the chance to test that proposition.[83]

III

THE BITTER FRUITS OF
DEVELOPMENT POLITICS,
1960–1974

CHAPTER 7

BETS, BARGAINS, AND
THE PRICE OF AMERICAN AID

S. Bhoothalingam, by 1965 capping off a successful government career by serving as secretary of economic affairs in the Indian Ministry of Finance, discreetly advised a senior U.S. Agency for International Development (USAID) official about the tone of their upcoming negotiations. Though originally trained by Joan Robinson, among others, at Cambridge University, Bhoothalingam did not share her aversion to free market–oriented approaches favored by American advisors. He argued for the effectiveness of market operations so long as they were adequately regulated, which in the Indian context put him closer to the Western camp; his words for the American were meant to be friendly. After all, he hoped to use American aid to advance his own economic vision in India. He cautioned his interlocutor that comments resembling a threat (along the lines, he said, of "if you don't change your policies we will not give you any aid") would jeopardize USAID interests—and Bhoothalingam's own. For Bhoothalingam the problem was not so much the Americans' desire to influence Indian policy, nor even the direction of policy changes they sought, but the way they went about it. He was hardly the only member of the America lobby in India to chafe at the pressure tactics employed by USAID and the World Bank in the 1960s; indeed, by 1968, such criticisms echoed throughout Bhoothalingam's Ministry of Finance and elsewhere.[1]

These complaints, from Bhoothalingam and others, only confirmed B. K. Nehru's warning about the "nonfinancial" costs of his strategy of turning to the West. While B. K. Nehru's strategy of seeking "free money" worked to brilliant effect in expanding and redefining American aid, it also opened up plenty of new opportunities for Western agencies—most notably USAID and the World Bank—to offer what Bhoothalingam tactfully called "suggestions" about Indian economic policy. Broadly speaking, the trajectory of American aid in the decade after B. K. Nehru's proposal amply illustrated both the promise and the perils of building closer economic ties with the West. Western aid levels increased dramatically, and an increasing amount of such aid was independent of specific construction projects. Empowered by Western aid, the Ministry of Finance wielded increasing influence in the field of economic assistance and took an even larger role in economic policy. Bolstered by the external support, a number of policy initiatives in the mid-1960s seemed poised to move Indian economic policy away from central planning and import-substitution industrialization. Thus B. K. Nehru's gambit served him and fellow members of his America lobby very well in the short run.

But these new forms of aid came at a price. Demands from the West, and especially from the United States, increased dramatically if not quantifiably. Pressure from USAID and the World Bank placed the lobby's members in an increasingly awkward spot; their success in policy battles owed much to external support, yet the American assertions accompanying such aid threatened their prestige and position. So the arrival of nonproject aid in the 1960s fueled internal debates over Indian economic policy by strengthening those more closely aligned to a Western approach at first—but then weakened them by providing inadequate support. Each of these dynamics impeded the ability of the Indian government to set its own course in economic policy, thus demonstrating the perils of development politics.

Furthermore, the dynamic of Western aid in 1960s India shaped efforts well beyond South Asia. The turn toward nonproject aid accelerated the tendency toward increased donor demands on recipients' overall economic policies, what eventually came to be called conditionality—aid given only on the condition of changes in macroeconomic policy. As USAID and the World Bank worked "in tandem" (in the words of an official World Bank history) they created a version of the Washington Consensus *avant la lettre*.[2] USAID's India chief, John P. Lewis, inaugurated this approach with his so-called Big Push; others promoted "Economic Bargains," or even more stringent if unnamed efforts, to make nonproject aid contingent upon specific economic policies or diplomatic positions. A second channel for increased conditionality made use of Food for Peace (PL480). President Lyndon B. Johnson broke with past patterns (and with virtually all of his advisers) by refusing to sign any multiyear agreements for these concessional food sales. He preferred a form of brinksmanship of one- or two-month extensions. This so-called short tether became a common, indeed constant, reminder of American power. Western powers also imposed conditions through a third channel, the new Aid-India Consortium that operated under World Bank auspices. The Indian experience with the bank and consortium in the mid-1960s served as a precursor to upcoming battles against the bank, its sister institution the International Monetary Fund (IMF), and American policy makers in ensuing decades. Through these three mechanisms—nonproject aid, PL480, and the consortium—the Indian experience introduced macroeconomic conditionality into future aid discussions.

The Aid-India Consortium emerged as a solution to India's foreign-exchange crisis of the Second Five-Year Plan, but soon found new applications for India and far beyond. Promoted by B. K. Nehru as a method of streamlining the aid process, and for mobilizing American influence with its allies, the consortium ultimately disarmed Indian officials by providing leverage to the lenders collectively—leverage they used with increasing frequency over the course of the 1960s. Even the consortium's main weakness—its status of an informal gathering of autonomous lenders—worked against Indian interests. The consortium had no mechanism for enforcement, so general agreements about aid levels did not necessarily generate aid in the agreed-upon amounts—a problem that appeared in dramatic form in the late 1960s.

The transformation of Indian economic relations with the United States and the concomitant empowering and undercutting of India's America lobby came amid a kaleidoscope of global and regional events that shaped the foreign and domestic politics of both nations. A short list of events includes the death of Jawaharlal Nehru in May 1964, the Chinese explosion of a nuclear device in October 1964, the deepening American commitment to the war in Vietnam starting in early 1965, armed conflict between India and Pakistan in April and September 1965, and the unexpected death of Nehru's successor, Prime Minister Lal Bahadur Shastri, in January 1966. Yet the transformation started from a familiar place: competition over a development program.

The Last Gasp for an Industrial Project: Bokaro Steel

From the first rumors in 1955 that the USSR would provide technology and financing for a steel plant in Bhilai, American officials scrambled to find projects that might capture similarly high levels of attention and enthusiasm. They became all the more determined after the British and West German govern-ments signed agreements to finance and build two other steel mills in India, at Durgapur and Rourkela, respectively. How, one British diplomat asked with a mixture of concern and condescension, could Americans get "a Bhilai of their own?"[3]

The pursuit of an American showcase project revealed the debilities that American officials faced in aid competition. United States aid agencies lacked the capacity and even the category for such a large aid program. Focused on small-scale technical assistance programs, the Technical Cooperation Agency and its successors had no mechanism for funding the construction of a major industrial enterprise. Nor were American funds even close to adequate to the task: the Soviet deal for Bhilai amounted to roughly half the amount that American agencies had provided over the better part of a decade. Beyond these loomed other obstacles like policy differences. American aid agencies, much like the World Bank, favored industrial projects in the private sector; while some accommodation might be made for public-sector utilities, a steel plant belonged—so American officials insisted—in the private sector. Yet India's Industrial Policy Resolutions declared that any new plants in major industries—including energy, defense industries and, of course, steel—would end up in the public sector.[4]

In spite of these significant disadvantages, American aid officials sought a way to fund a major project along their preferred lines. In the aftermath of the Bhilai announcement, the U.S. National Security Council recommended funding a private-sector steel mill to the tune of $50 million. Otherwise, Secre-tary of State John Foster Dulles warned, it was "likely that India would accept [another] Soviet steel mill." This was easier said than done; initial American efforts lacked a funding source, an American firm, and most importantly Indian contacts. American diplomats in New Delhi lobbied their colleagues in Washington, D.C., imploring them to consider a range of ownership options for the steel mill.[5]

Observers in India, and even in the Soviet Union, expected that the next steel plant would end up with American funding, though official plans made no such acknowledgment. American efforts—led by White House aide Clar-ence Randall, a former steel executive—focused on the private sector, calling on Minister of Finance Morarji Desai to put forward such a proposal. Kaiser Industries sought to use the new U.S. Development Loan Fund and the World

Bank to finance a steel plant that it would build for the massive Tata conglomerate, which already owned India's oldest steel mill. American diplomats in New Delhi were ecstatic; this would be the "best opportunity we will ever have," one gushed, to raise the profile of American aid in India. Ideally, the diplomat continued, such a steel mill would be in the private sector. But if that would not come to pass, the diplomats implored their colleagues in Washington to support a public-sector enterprise. The U.S. ambassador agreed, arguing that if the private-sector plan failed, his government should support a public-sector project "with whatever tie-in to the private sector" could be salvaged. By autumn 1959 even Randall was ready to bend further on his earlier insistence on free enterprise: "our sympathy should be toward the private sector," he argued, but "we must not be doctrinaire to the point of refusing to help the public sector in industry any further." How far sympathy would extend, though, remained very much up for debate.[6]

Grand American plans for the steel mill soon ran up against Indian ideas. The Planning Commission (PC) insisted that the plant be publicly owned (per the Industrial Policy Resolutions of 1948 and 1956), and that it also would serve as an exemplar of indigenous expertise. It invoked the language of the freedom struggle, arguing that it should be India's *swadeshi* steel mill, a symbol of India's self-sufficiency. A PC note on the eve of the Third Five-Year Plan set out ambitious goals, both actual and symbolic, for the plant. It would provide "maximum opportunity for Indian engineering talent" and would deploy "indigenous equipment to the fullest extent" possible. One sign of this commitment was that the PC anticipated needing only about forty foreign technicians to work on overseeing design and construction; the remainder of the supervisors and engineers would be Indian. By way of comparison, the construction site at Bhilai Steel Plant teemed with some eight hundred Soviet engineers. The principal American contribution, in the Planning Commission's view, was to fund the purchase of equipment from U.S. suppliers as well as to pay the salaries of those few American specialists. Toward that end, Pitamber Pant at the PC proposed hiring the Indian engineering firm Dasturco, whose principal had been trained in the United States. After some internal Indian politicking, the PC identified Bokaro (in Bihar) as the best site for the plant, citing proximity to key supplies and to power from the Damodar Valley hydroelectric project. Yet measures of proximity did not account for the desolate place destined to become Bokaro Steel City: it had no electricity, one road, and no bridge over the key river or link to national railway networks. The first construction office was in a tent, and the first building was a storage shed—and a temporary one at that.[7]

But before facing challenges of construction, getting American approval proved hard enough. The fate of American support for Bokaro soon ended up in the clutches of that deadliest of bureaucratic entities, the interagency committee. When some sixteen officials from seven U.S. departments convened in the first days of 1960 to discuss "Indian steel problems," the representative from the Department of Commerce complained that too many Americans had been "preoccupied with the political desirability" of an American-built steel plant while failing to consider the basic economics.[8]

Impatient to move the process forward, Randall looked beyond the U.S. government, but had little more success there. He turned to his friend and compatriot George Woods at the World Bank to "sound out informally" Indian economic policy makers on how far they would stray from the public-sector steel mill described in Indian policy documents. Randall meanwhile worked on American executives, who were decidedly unenthusiastic. U.S. Steel executives, for instance, told Randall that they were willing to consider investing up to $40 million for a steel plant in India; they noted grudgingly that this was not on the basis of "self-interest" but instead was "in service to the country." Randall ignored such reluctance and celebrated the "immeasurable" positive effect on "world opinion" that a U.S. Steel plant in India would have. Yet these efforts faltered when USAID determined in spring 1961 that any prospective assistance for the Bokaro steel mill would come out of existing U.S. commitments; funding Bokaro would not, in other words, increase the total amount of U.S. development aid.[9]

The American decision to consider support for the steel mill only within the framework of existing aid commitments marked a turning point in Indian policy over Bokaro, one that first introduced the Soviet Union as a possible supporter. As a report to the Indian cabinet observed with frustration, "the realization that foreign finance should be found is one thing, and finding it is another." Should American funding continue to be problematic, the report recommended, the Government of India should consider requesting aid from the Soviet Union. T. T. Krishnamachari (commonly known as TTK), then the minister for economic and military cooperation, was for his part sufficiently irked by American delays to endorse an "entreaty" to the Soviet Union; this turn of events surprised Soviet officials, who still assumed that Bokaro would receive American support. The America lobby had been counting on the plant for support and to bolster its own influence but was undermined by the turn of events in Washington.[10]

The America lobby, led by Desai, faced impediments elsewhere as well. U.S. Steel backed away from its reluctant offer of joint ownership, which (Desai concluded) would in any case have been difficult to arrange in India. Woods still hoped that the "wide range of differences" among top officials would allow him to reach an agreement. The range was so wide, in fact, that Prime Minister Nehru himself quizzed Woods about which ministers held what views. Trying to slow this turn of events, Morarji Desai publicly endorsed American aid, privately indicating that he would go to great lengths to make sure that the Soviets made no further inroads in Indian steel.[11]

The American tide for Bokaro, never strong, soon turned definitively against the project. A USAID feasibility study excoriated almost every element of the Indian plan for Bokaro, including location, construction plans, financing, and management. If that report provided ammunition for American opponents of aid for the steel mill, events unrelated to India provided the guns. USAID as a whole came in for harsh congressional criticism during the so-called Foreign Aid Revolt of 1963. Conservatives, including both Republicans and southern Democrats, consolidated their opposition to any substantial aid program. The liberal Democratic successors to the development crusaders, meanwhile, found fault in the tendency of USAID to support dictators across Latin America. This led, in turn, to strains within the congressional coalition that had supported development efforts like the signature Alliance for Progress only two years earlier. President John F. Kennedy convened a blue-ribbon group with the portentous title Committee to Strengthen the Security of the Free World to overcome such criticisms. But his effort ultimately backfired. While the committee offered tepid support for American aid to India, it concluded that the United States "should not extend aid which is inconsistent with our beliefs, democratic tradition, and knowledge of economic organization and consequences."[12] This last clause, in particular, seemed a barb aimed at countries like India seeking American aid for public-sector projects.

The prospects of an American-funded Bokaro were endangered by this blue-ribbon report but were done in by the critics of foreign aid whom it emboldened. Bokaro stood—in the words of *U.S. News and World Report*—as a "key test" of American aid policy: would taxpayer dollars support "social-ized" steel mills?[13] A *Newsweek* columnist called aid for projects like Bokaro a "direct American subsidy for foreign socialism."[14] The proposed steel mill fared little better in congressional hearings; the USAID administrator faced bruising questions from all quarters and tried to fend off multiple efforts to ban funding for Bokaro.[15] With this growing congressional restiveness, Bokaro became a symbol of everything that was wrong with American for-eign assistance.[16] By the end of August 1963 Prime Minister Nehru discreetly asked President Kennedy if India should withdraw its request for American aid for Bokaro.[17] Reports of a congressperson calling Bokaro "idiotic" may have swayed Kennedy to accept Nehru's offer.[18] Some of the leading Indian figures favoring American funding put a good face on the situation. G. D. Birla consoled American diplomats that even a Soviet-sponsored steel plant at Bokaro would provide plenty of opportunities for the Indian private sector.[19] Minister for Steel and Mines C. Subramaniam celebrated the "breakthrough of Indian talent" that Bokaro might provide.[20] Yet all of this amounted to grasping at straws. The joint effort of the India lobby in Washington and the America lobby in New Delhi had ultimately backfired, leaving both worse off; Bokaro crystallized domestic U.S. opposition to aid programs in general, while the resulting failure to secure funding undercut those in India seeking U.S. assistance.

The demise of the U.S. Bokaro project, furthermore, sounded the death knell for large-scale American project aid to India; increasingly, aid would come in nonproject loans. Front-line diplomats, still hoping for the propaganda splash of a big project, chafed at this turn of events. They feared becoming "a residu-ary source of aid, in which we will be asked to meet general balance of pay-ments deficit[s] after lists of major development projects have been gone over by others and they have made their choice." To end up in such a predicament would be "contrary to . . . [the political] interests of the U.S." Their successors eventually confirmed such fears, as one New Delhi diplomat complained, "Some propaganda advantage may accrue to the Soviets as a Soviet-financed factory is something of a monument to them, while several million dollars' worth of non-ferrous metals financed by the United States will disappear into the industrial maw without a trace." With limited propaganda opportunities in nonproject aid, American officials soon sought other compensations—like the chance to weigh in on economic policy.[21]

Loudly Debating India's Quiet Crisis

Negotiations over increased nonproject loans in the early 1960s came in the context of worsening economic conditions as well as serious Indian debates about economic policy. Even before the Chinese war of autumn 1962, the Third Five-Year Plan (1961–1966) had run into strong headwinds. Large projects with Soviet support consumed significant resources but had not yet come on line. The agricultural sector was still slighted by the Planning Commission—pledges to the Ford Foundation and USAID notwithstanding. Agriculture remained a relatively low priority—14.0 percent in the Third Plan vs. 12.4 percent in the Second. Ultimately, agriculture's contribution to Indian national income, in real terms, had *declined*. While the Third Plan called for a 31.0 percent expansion of national income over its five years, the ultimate result was only 12.5 percent. Even high-priority sectors like mining and manufacturing—the target of significant investments and even more attention—had disappointing results; the plan aimed to increase mining and manufacturing by 70 percent, but came in at less than a third of that figure.[22]

Foreign exchange remained a perennial concern, shaping both domestic policy and approaches to major donors. Stopgap measures in the late 1950s had ended the free fall of foreign exchange; reserves plateaued until 1964 when they plummeted by almost 40 percent. The need to economize on foreign currency was so strong that two cabinet ministers carried on a detailed correspondence about the need for £159 for official travel to Australia and North America—a princely sum ultimately authorized only with the proviso that any unspent funds be returned to the treasury.[23]

By the middle of the Third Plan, proposed solutions to India's economic woes abounded, with a number of influential economists arguing against one or another aspect of import substitution. The rise of an opposition party, Swatantra, at the national level owed much to the worsening economic conditions and the continuing complaints from private business about stultifying economic controls. Swatantra leader C. Rajagopalachari—a giant in the independence movement against Britain—attacked what he called the "permit-quota-license raj that goes by the name of socialism." He called for a sharp reduction of the New Delhi government's role in the economy, for an end to price controls, and for a reorientation of the economy toward agriculture and consumer needs rather than heavy industry. Other criticisms grew louder, even from the bastion of Nehru-Mahalanobis import substitution, the Planning Commission. Official panels to evaluate regulations also recommended the decontrol of licensing and foreign trade even if they lacked the verbal pyrotechnics of Swatantra. Economist Jagdish Bhagwati, then fresh from doctoral studies in international economics at the Massachusetts Institute of Technology (MIT), argued that the push for self-sufficiency encouraged an inflated exchange rate, which in turn made Indian exports less competitive in world markets. Bhagwati argued that the overvalued rupee limited the opportunities for Indian enterprises to earn foreign exchange through exports—while at the same time encouraging inefficient behaviors to game the system of import controls. While Bhagwati conceded that there was a rhetorical interest in increasing exports, in his view "little [was] being done to bring this about." He famously termed this phenomenon "export pessimism." In a trio of articles in the influential *Economic Weekly*, Bhagwati went further, calling for devaluation of the rupee to boost exports.[24]

Similarly, debates about agriculture covered an increasingly wide range of options, many of which departed from the patterns of the 1950s. Official planning documents still prescribed institutional changes—promoting land reform (in spite of the immense electoral risks that had paralyzed the Congress Party vis-à-vis reforms), community development, and so on. The official vision favored cheap food prices and used a complex set of mechanisms to obtain agricultural products at low cost. Yet here, too, new approaches received increasing attention, especially as food shortages continued. Community development received rhetorical support in Third Plan documents, but substantially reduced resources—and focused less on rural transformation and more on agricultural productivity. From his perch in Washington, economic ambassador B. K. Nehru sought foreign financing to build fertilizer plants, which he saw as an opportunity to bolster agriculture while reducing pressure on foreign exchange. Changes were under way, or at least under discussion, in Indian agriculture.[25]

S. K. Patil, the minister of food and agriculture in the early 1960s, sought to end the administrative controls in agriculture and food and to give more play to the free market. Others in Patil's ministry accepted the Ford Foundation's recommendation that India should make a "wager on the strong" in agriculture, focusing its efforts on those areas (and those farmers) with the best prospects for rapid increases in productivity; these areas in the Intensive Agriculture Development Program would receive inputs—most notably fertilizer—and funds for irrigation and mechanization. Even Nehru's last years saw increasing attention to alternative modes of economic organization.[26]

Weak economic results combined with Jawaharlal Nehru's physical decline in the early 1960s, the defeat against China in 1962, and eventually Nehru's death in May 1964 to incite more serious challenges to the economic vision that bore his name. The brief tenure of Nehru's successor Lal Bahadur Shastri (May 1964–January 1966) opened up the possibility that these challenges would find their way into policy. Without the institutional base or charisma of his larger-than-life predecessor, Shastri undertook a number of seemingly minor bureaucratic changes that reverberated in Indian economic policy long after his untimely death. While Nehru's closest companions in the cabinet were leftists like V. K. Krishna Menon (until his fall from grace in autumn 1962) and K. D. Malaviya, Shastri was closer to those on the right, like Morarji Desai and S. K. Patil. Shastri, furthermore, did not share Nehru's passion for planning; while he inherited the mantle of PC chair, he interposed a layer of bureaucracy between the prime minister and the commission. Shastri was, furthermore, sympathetic to the criticisms of business leaders like G. D. Birla, who advised him to shed Nehru's "doctrinaire" thinking about the private sector.[27]

Shastri took an especially active role in agricultural policy. He invited C. Subramaniam, at that point the minister for steel, heavy industry, and mines, to switch to the agriculture portfolio. Subramaniam consented to the change only after the cabinet endorsed a major shift in favor of using economic incentives. Borrowing from pricing strategy he had employed in the steel industry, he proposed new policies that would give agriculturalists incentives to bring their food to market and to undertake productivity-enhancing investments. He also called for reducing food imports, whether through PL480 or those purchased commercially; they depressed prices, he argued, and therefore reduced incentives for Indian agriculturalists. Finally, Subramaniam called for increasing the use of new seed varieties, irrigation techniques, and (above all) fertilizer. Few things excited American officials more than talk of fertilizer: it signaled a new approach to agriculture while at the same time suggesting a new openness to foreign investment. Ambassador Bowles and White House aide Robert Komer celebrated this change as a "coup."[28]

Subramaniam moved quickly to advance his agenda. Within six months he had established the government-owned Food Corporation of India, set up a new committee on food prices with a sympathetic chairman (L. K. Jha), and outmaneuvered the PC to increase investments in agriculture. With the Food Corporation, in particular, the Indian government could maintain fair prices for producers while insuring price stability for consumers; this would entail government subsidies in lieu of government controls. Subramaniam had little to say about community development or rural inequality—but a great many words about fertilizer, which he called "the king-pin of agricultural development in the modern age."[29]

Subramaniam's strategy soon found support, surprisingly enough, from the PC. The commission's deputy chair, Asoka Mehta, had forsaken his long-standing socialist inclinations to endorse this new vision, which he hoped would transform "countless small farms from troughs of self-subsistent activity into . . . economically viable units of production, buying and selling"; the future of Indian agriculture would be in the marketplace. Yet the shift in the PC came at a time when its own powers faced new limits; as a result, the commission faded as a major node in policy debates at the exact time that it shifted rightward in economic policy.[30]

Taken in sum, Indian economic debates during the Third Plan covered a wide spectrum of topics and saw more frequent and more influential criticisms of Nehruvian economic policy. These were, of course, hardly the first criticisms of economic policy, but they found increasing support within the relevant bureaucracies. The result was an economic policy environment in the early and mid-1960s that was in flux. American observers welcomed the stirrings of this market orientation and hoped to encourage such tendencies in the future, working through USAID, the World Bank, and the new Aid-India Consortium.

From Lenders' Club to the Aid-India Consortium

The Aid-India Consortium, which grew directly out of the emergency lenders' club convened in the late 1950s, created some new opportunities for B. K. Nehru and his colleagues, but even more dangers. On the one hand, the group expanded, as Western European nations began to provide development aid. B. K. Nehru's vision of using the consortium as a vehicle for increasing aid from Western powers seemed to be working, as American officials and their neighbors at the World Bank importuned Western donors to expand their aid efforts. On the other hand, though, this enlarged group took a more active role in shaping economic policy, as opposed to simply negotiating over aid projects.[31]

By 1963 the tone of the consortium meetings grew more concerned—and more contentious. The Sino-Indian War of the preceding autumn had wreaked havoc on the Indian economy; defense spending increased drastically, further straining already limited foreign-exchange reserves. Efforts to steer resources toward defense industries entailed new controls and licenses. Meanwhile, economic disruptions had ironically made it more difficult to utilize aid that had already been committed. L. K. Jha, second in command at the Ministry of Finance, promised improvements—including decontrol—in the future, but asked lenders for patience as the Indian economy shifted away from its war footing. He also made the case for increased levels of nonproject aid, and indeed could not enumerate enough projects to cover the extent of aid requested. Consortium members wavered, promising to fulfill existing commitments but nothing more.[32]

Consortium members' talk of steady aid levels came along with ever more bluntly expressed criticisms of the overall direction of the Indian economy the PC attracted particular hostility. World Bank president George Woods communicated these rumblings in a sternly worded letter to Finance Minister Morarji Desai, cataloging in loving detail consortium members' complaints about the planning process, the direction of economic policy, and the recent performance of economy in the Third Plan.[33]

The question of how to shape Indian economic policy writ large emerged with increasing frequency in consortium meetings and side correspondence. Though World Bank economists conceded that there was little chance of a "quick reformation" of Indian economic policy, American diplomats hoped that India might "be required" to promise policy changes before any further discussions at the consortium. Through the tribulations of 1964, World Bank staff balanced their increasing frustration regarding Indian policy with the consolation that there was no point in "trying to do India's planning for her." While they wanted to "keep up the pressure on the Indians," they also worried that increasing assertion on the part of consortium members might come off as if donors were "gang[ing] up" on India. Ideally, in other words, consortium members could induce policy changes without appearing to do so.[34]

Indian officials hoping for stronger Western ties made a series of small concessions to placate their allies. L. K. Jha, who continued to resist efforts to dictate policy, agreed that a small handful of experts might come to India with the limited task of "improving the quality of Indian planning." In June 1964

Woods approached TTK, who had recently taken up the portfolio of finance minister, about sending a "well-qualified economic study team" to India, hinting that future external assistance may hinge on the study results. TTK, like Jha before him, made a small concession that was quickly widened unilaterally by the World Bank; TTK accepted a "small Mission with a . . . limited scope"—but no more. Yet as the temperatures crept upward in Washington that summer, the scope of the study crept outward. Woods, dissatisfied with the bank's in-house experts, recruited economist Bernard Bell to undertake a broad study. Bell quickly made agriculture, heretofore not a particular focus of the World Bank, into a core element; he based this decision on his own inclinations as well as his reading of prior bank studies.[35]

Though the Bell Mission would ostensibly study Indian economic policy in detail, its major conclusions seem foreordained. A number of staff members, preselected for their bluntness, considered devaluation inevitable from the very start. Woods shared some of these a priori conclusions with TTK and L. K. Jha, focusing on defense spending, economic regulation, and population control and quickly eliciting their polite displeasure and defensiveness. Bell's final outline established the broad scope of the inquiry (covering agriculture, industry, exports, population, employment, fiscal policy, and regulation) as well as its high stakes; the report would be "a guide to future Bank lending." With that in mind, Woods predicted that 1965 "would be a year of great decisions" for the bank and the consortium.[36]

From Big Push to Big Pushiness

The decisions of 1965 began with American policy. Economist John P. Lewis took the helm of USAID's huge mission in New Delhi in fall 1964 with a mandate for change. On a prior trip to India while still based in academe, Lewis had expressed outspoken support for nonproject aid—which, he argued, could give India the financial flexibility to purchase the goods it needed for industrialization while also providing U.S. officials with more leverage over Indian policy. Such aid, he argued, could come with new strings—no longer attached to specific projects but about addressing recipients' economic policies more generally. Through the 1950s Lewis wrote, American officials had wrongly considered Indian planning "a *fait accompli* that . . . can be neither gracefully nor usefully cross-examined." In calling for such interrogations,

Lewis acknowledged Indian officials' "residual nervousness about exposing the general objectives and policies . . . to free, protracted discussion." In order to quell such nerves, Lewis endorsed what he euphemized as "before the fact intergovernmental planning." Nonproject aid could allow USAID to shape the overall economic policies by offering incentives that would encourage policy changes by paying for them. Lewis used a fairly straightforward logic: when donors funded individual projects, they could choose between different alternatives. But when they aided the whole economy (through nonproject aid) they could weigh in on overall economic policy.[37]

Lewis soon found others who shared his view: members of a second-generation India lobby favoring aid to India but no longer willing to remain silent about what they saw as India's policy errors. Indeed, the movement to influence Indian economic policy predated Lewis's appointment. One State Department report, for instance, insisted that "we do not . . . want to dictate policy" but nevertheless called for "somewhat more explicit moves to push the Government of India toward improvements in developmental policy." Lewis found support in the White House, where aide Robert Komer endorsed both nonproject aid and the imposition of more conditions. Complaining that American aid officials "have been far too passive in the management of our Indian aid program," Komer wanted to use aid commitments as "levers to get the kind of performance India needs and we want." Komer and Lewis quickly won over Chester Bowles, a charter member of the India lobby then serving in his second stint as ambassador in New Delhi. Bowles quickly took these ideas to heart, celebrating "our growing ability to use aid as an instrument to shape Indian economic policy along more realistic and dynamic lines." By the end of 1964, then, the embassy and USAID mission in New Delhi both endorsed the use of nonproject aid to influence Indian economic policy. They did so precisely as Subramaniam was beginning to remake Indian agricultural policy, and as stirrings about decontrol and devaluation garnered increasing attention. The American chiefs in New Delhi quickly won Washington's approval for additional assistance, to be conditioned upon a "loosening up [of] the Indian controls which now seem to restrict the natural vigor of the economy."[38]

Calling his approach the "Big Push," Lewis wanted to use promises of increased aid as incentives for policy changes; as he put it, "The idea is that if India will effect certain reforms, we could increase our assistance." He borrowed the term from development economics but altered the meaning. MIT economists had used "the big push" to describe the effort to get a developing nation into a phase of sustainable growth but Lewis reimagined the object of the push as the recipient nation's policies, not its economy.[39]

India's growing economic woes gave Lewis, Bowles, and Komer a chance to put their plans into action. A large-scale review of American aid strategy for India endorsed the "fundamental principle" of "tak[ing] a more active part in influencing Indian policies" and enumerated the policies (in order of priority) targeted for change; agriculture, rural welfare, and "use of the market mechanism" topped the list. As a starting point, the review proposed using $100 million in aid as an incentive; if the Indian government would agree to policy changes, USAID would convert $100 million from aid to specific projects to nonproject aid; this would increase flexibility but not funding levels. In a long memorandum, "Betting on India" (January 1965), Lewis called for expanding the American aid commitment to India—and, in a veteran bureaucratic move, enlarging the USAID mission too. He lauded the economic decontrols already undertaken but doubted that more would be forthcoming without a substantial increase in aid. A quantum increase in aid, he underscored, could "*extract very much improved performance* from the Indians." He offered a long (and familiar) list of what higher aid levels could "buy"—all of which would, he hoped result in a much higher growth rate. Ambassador Bowles quickly jumped on the Big Push bandwagon; he hoped to "take advantage of the urgency of the present situation" to promote devaluation and regulation. These policies for purchase, it should be noted, were all in the economic aisle. As one leading USAID official put it later in categorical terms, "I don't think you can use aid . . . to exact a political price."[40]

Even a Big Push proponent like Komer admitted, however, that betting on India entailed risks.[41] S. Bhoothalingam, the secretary of the Ministry of Finance, was well aware of the risks on his side, pointedly reminding an American diplomat that the policies under discussion—like import liberalization— would require a multiyear commitment from donors. And at the same time, Bhoothalingam cautioned USAID officials on the need for tact, so that policy "suggestions" did not come off as "dictation." Ignoring such appeals, American policy makers turned the Big Push into pushiness, applying it to PL480 food aid as well as nonproject loans.[42]

Yanking on the Short Tether: PL480 Food as Bargaining Chip

As Robert Komer contemplated how to exact this leverage, he quickly fixed on commodities provided through the Food for Peace program, PL480. The 1963 agreement—the one that cost Food and Agriculture Minister S. K. Patil his job—was set to expire at the end of June 1965. Rather than uphold the usual pattern, in which negotiations over a new pact began a few months before the current agreement expired, Komer wanted to use PL480 "to ensure that the Indians face up to their agrarian problems with greater imagination and energy." To do so he wanted to apply the approach of the Big Push: dangle multiyear food agreements in exchange for policy changes. Brinksmanship, he argued, "creat[ed] a tolerable degree of uncertainty" about the future of PL480 so that Indian negotiators would feel compelled to take American stipulations seriously. Thus American officials dragged their feet on a new PL480 agreement over the winter, even as food prices increased as much as 8 percent in a single quarter.[43]

The arrival of spring did not liberate the PL480 request from the deep freeze. Responding to a barrage of inquiries and pleadings from New Delhi in June, a top White House aide told Ambassador Bowles that a two-year agreement was off the table because it "might deprive us of major leverage before we have fully worked out what we want to Indians to do in return." As the expiration date loomed, the USAID chief warned that delivery delays could led to "instability" and political dangers—a warning repeated numerous times in the coming years; National Security Adviser McGeorge Bundy made similar pleas to the president. Shastri gently reminded Johnson about the PL480 agreement, asking the president to "intervene personally" to expedite the new agreement—unaware, of course, that it was the president himself who was holding up a PL480 deal.[44]

When B. K. Nehru made the case for an extension after the original agreement expired, President Johnson introduced a new factor into the PL480 process: the legislative branch. Johnson "insisted that Congress must share . . . responsibility" for a future agreement—though he already knew that congressional leaders favored the one-year PL480 arrangement. Yet according to Johnson's budget chief, no congressional approval was required by either PL480 legislation or past practice. As another aide later put it, with apparent

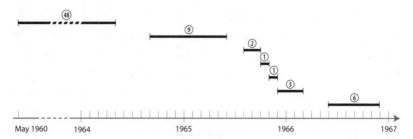

PL480 Agreements in the Era of the Short Tether

Sources: Reports in FRUS 1964–1968, 25:266, 399–400, 443–444, 455; Mitchel B. Wallerstein, *Food for War—Food for Peace: United States Food Aid in a Global Context* (Cambridge: Massachusetts Institute of Technology Press, 1980), 185–193; and "Pact for More U.S. Food Aid Signed," TOI, May 28, 1965, 1.

frustration, Johnson was "asking Congress for authority" that he already had. Indeed, reflecting on his presidency later, Johnson admitted this circumstance: he already had the necessary authority, he recalled, but sought congressional approval "as a matter of principle"; what particular principle he was upholding he did not specify.[45]

By invoking congressional approval, well beyond what the law required or his predecessors had done, Johnson brilliantly strengthened his own hand in negotiations. An extraordinarily effective Senate leader before he joined the 1960 ticket as John F. Kennedy's vice president, Johnson was the world's leading expert on manipulating the U.S. Congress. By inserting congressional approval into the PL480 process, he shifted the terrain from the expertise of diplomats (American or Indian) to his own specialty. Positioning himself between U.S. Congress and the Indian government, furthermore, gave him the leeway *not* to act, ostensibly in deference to congressional opinion. This ploy gave the president the upper hand over the foreign policy experts he had inherited, uneasily, from President Kennedy.

Johnson used this newly accrued power to enact a version of the leverage that his aides had proposed—indeed, to enact it much more aggressively than they had imagined. For the next two years, until the long-term PL480 agreement was signed in June 1967, Johnson would act (as one junior diplomat would later put it) as "his own desk officer" for PL480 food, approving individual shipments. The policy quickly earned many nicknames, most coined by critics of the policy in the United States ("short-tether" or "ship-to-mouth") and India ("short leash"). Criticism quickly mounted, even from those aid officials who had encouraged the use of American aid as leverage to or impose policy changes in India. John Lewis, the leading proponent of the Big Push strategy, quickly got cold feet. Less than three weeks after the expiration of the old PL480 agreement, Lewis threatened that an "explosion" of Indian political instability and anti-Americanism would ensue unless food was released within forty-eight hours. (A two-month extension followed a week after his dispatch.) Lewis insisted that "food was different" from nonproject aid and must have been "accidentally" caught up with other forms of aid that Lewis was hoping to use for leverage in his Big Push. Johnson seemed to take missives such as Lewis's as signs that his government was full of "India lovers" who were busier defending that nation's interests than their own. Such pleas seemed only to harden the president's determination to continue the month-to-month PL480 agreements.[46]

Furthermore, Johnson's strategy called on Indian officials to play up the danger of famine in order to help Congress understand the need for American food. He enlisted B. K. Nehru, telling him to "make a special case . . . [that] there is starvation and famine" in order to win attention and sympathy from U.S. Congress. The famine stood permanently poised in the immediate future—always imminent but never actually arriving. Scholarship has incisively described this famine as human-made—not in the sense of being the result of human action but of being a fiction invented by Indian and American officials more attuned to statistical abstractions than to actual conditions. But it was the threat of impending famine, not calorie counts, that energized American bureaucrats and legislators. This process of anticipatory crisis came into play before Johnson's congressional ploy emerged, but became a dominant element in official American discussions over Indian conditions. A report from two Department of Agriculture officials in May 1965, for instance, set the parameters for future discussion; it contained a lengthy critique of Indian policies, and especially their neglect of agriculture, before concluding that the situation was "serious, and . . . could soon become critical." A few months later, a *Washington Post* reporter described parts of India "trembling near [the] brink of famine" if the monsoons did not arrive in the next fortnight. White House aides privately concurred, noting that the effects of the famine would not be visible until

October. Bowles issued similar warnings. The famine was a looming threat, not an actual event.[47]

Colliding Crises: War and Famine

The permanently looming famine took on a growing sense of urgency with escalating Indo-Pakistani tensions in 1965. After brief clashes at the Rann of Kutch in the spring, Indian and Pakistan armies engaged in full-scale armed conflict in September. The war led to an American aid cutoff—with the threat of ending economic aid voiced (if not voted upon) in the U.S. Congress. PL480 food continued flowing, at least in principle, after the aid cutoff in September 1965—a suspension that lasted much longer than the brief conflict itself. Komer, responding to plaintive prompts from the New Delhi Embassy about the next PL480 authorization (the current authorization would expire in late September), replied that he wanted to keep the governments of India and Pakistan "worried." Meanwhile, anxious projections about a future famine circulated around Washington. One CIA report warned that the military situation could "threaten famine." With Komer's calculations in mind, President Johnson authorized the next one-month PL480 extension in the last days of September. Yet this last-minute action, coming amid the mood of patriotism and crisis in India, did not head off harsh public criticisms about PL480, including statements from both Prime Minister Shastri and Jawaharlal Nehru's daughter Indira Gandhi (then a junior cabinet minister) that the Indian government would forgo any aid, even food aid, that came with political strings attached.[48]

Food aid quickly returned to status quo ante bellum. Komer warned the president that "some famine and starvation seem inevitable." Even the president conceded—in a secret memorandum likely intended for widespread circulation—that there was a "looming Indian famine problem." Memos flew around New Delhi and Washington warning of serious risks if the next PL480 extension was not quickly authorized. And inevitably the authorization arrived uncomfortably close to (or just after) the previous deal expired.[49]

The end of the armed conflict in late September led some American diplomats to worry that the Big Push could backfire. Ambassador Bowles worried that his allies in India would have "grave doubts" about relying on foreign assistance. And indeed, the PC redoubled its emphasis on a policy of import substitution in the wake of the conflict, and focused on policies that would "yield quick results" in agriculture and industry—in lieu of the longer-term approach that American officials were promoting. Asoka Mehta at the Planning Commission announced publicly that the PC had already made "alternate plans" to do without aid. Even those behind the Big Push called on the president to approve food aid more quickly; the typical form was to flatter the president by noting how well the short-tether had worked—but then calling on him to loosen up. Yet for the time being, such pleas for more food generated little from the Oval Office except increased obstreperousness.[50]

The repetition of this pattern did little to improve the moods or ease the loads of Indian bureaucrats and policy makers. The last-minute approvals greatly complicated logistical planning. Even those seeking American aid to advance their own position resented the process. S. Bhoothalingam, for instance, took a gimlet eye to Johnson's protestations about Congress, rightly identifying them as negotiating tactics. He accused his American interlocutors of a "breach of faith" for using aid to "pressuriz[e] India" about Kashmir. Those more skeptical of American aid entertained gloomier thoughts. Indira Gandhi, then serving as minister of information and broadcasting, worried that the PL480 delays portended "the beginning of a new dark age." The United States, she concluded, would "give PL480 food aid and everything at a price. The manner of execution will be so deft and subtle that no one will realize it until it is too late and India's freedom of thought and action will both have been bartered away." Few of her colleagues, or for that matter her American counterparts, considered Johnson's approach either deft or subtle.[51]

For Whom Bernard Bell Tolls

Western pressure operated not only through the monthly cycles of worry about PL480, but also through the new Aid-India Consortium's discussions of non-project aid. The U.S. government played a major role, in conjunction with the World Bank as well as consortium partners; indeed, the proliferation of actors profoundly affected the aid dynamic. Bernard Bell led twenty specialists to India in 1964; they blanketed the country, visiting top officials in New Delhi as well as obscure offices in out-of-the-way ministries and enterprises all across India. A few high-level opponents of the mission managed to contain such thorough interrogations; for instance, no employee of the Ministry of Steel—generally hostile to Western aid—met officially with Bernard Bell or his associates.[52]

For all of the information Bell and his colleagues gathered in India, the results could have been predicted well in advance. From the start, World Bank president George Woods saw the Bell Mission as an instrument to change Indian policies; as he told TTK wistfully, "I cannot help thinking that considerably greater progress could have been made if policies and practices in the Government of India . . . had been different."[53] The list of problems was familiar from earlier World Bank analyses: lagging agricultural production, an overvalued rupee, overspending on defense, neglect of population control, inefficiency of public enterprise, hostility to foreign investment, and excessive regulation. The report devoted a volume or more to each of these topics.

The penultimate drafts of the report circulated in late summer 1965, arriving in India just before the Pakistani Army and carrying about as much disruptive potential. Senior Indian officials made pilgrimages to Washington to plead their respective ministries' cases. The conversations must have been a little awkward given Bell's lengthy list of recommendations: the final report, spread over fourteen volumes and some seventeen hundred pages, was thorough in its documentation of the ostensible failings of the Indian economy. In firm, directive tones it enumerated sixteen "major actions required on the part of India." Unless and until these actions were undertaken, Bell argued, external assistance could not have the desired effects, and therefore should not be offered. Even the most controversial of policy changes—devaluation—found plenty of support in Indian ministries, though key details about the process and the extent of devaluation remained subjects for negotiation. Bank officials were optimistic that they could get the devaluation they desired by promising "a substantial increase" in foreign aid over the next five to ten years.[54]

Indian officials accepted much of this long list of policy recommendations, in large part because contingents within the Indian government were already endorsing (or implementing) many of them well in advance of Bernard Bell's arrival. Ambassador Bowles reported with his usual optimism that his friends and allies in the Indian cabinet were "receptive" to the recommendations. Predictable supporters like C. Subramaniam (now of the Ministry of Food and Agriculture) and Asoka Mehta (of the Ministry of Planning) were open to the general thrust of the proposals. But the report, in its extent and tone as well as its specific recommendations, also provoked its share of opponents, including TTK (by then minister of finance), as well as the ministers of steel and commerce. Given this opposition, it is highly unusual that elements of the report did not make its way into the boisterous English-language media that fed on leaks.[55]

In the weeks following the submission of the report in fall 1965, World Bank officials seemed to be trying their hardest to alienate their Indian supporters. Barely had the report been received when Bernard Bell and George Woods began organizing a follow-up mission. Indian officials would barely have a chance to read Bell's report, let alone implement its recommendations, before hosting the second mission. Ostensibly the follow-up mission would be oriented toward the Fourth Plan (slated to start in April 1966), though in its charge and its personnel it was a sequel to the original Bell Mission. As with the first mission, some of the conclusions seem to be determined a priori; before departure, one World Bank officer had already concluded that the Fourth Plan was "a colossal exercise in delusion." Though bank economists purported to be sensitive to how their work might "hurt [the] sensibilities" of Indian officials, they dove in to the second mission with more gusto than tact. They were right about the sense of injury.[56]

Indian officials bristled at this latest affront. "It was a sad day," mourned planner Tarlok Singh, "when our creditors go to the length of cross-examining our Departmental Heads about . . . the propriety of their programs." Pitamber Pant, a Planning Commission member still favoring import substitution, protested poetically about the World Bank. "For whom does Bell toil?," he asked, "For the great tycoons of international oil or for the impoverished sons of Indian soil?" Such criticisms came from the relatively unsympathetic quarters of the PC. Those with inclinations toward the West had even harsher words, perhaps because their own ideas and their own prestige were on the line. I. G. Patel, for instance, bemoaned the continued pressure from Bernard Bell: "Most of us involved in the dialogue," Patel recalled, "were convinced of the wisdom of much of Bell's advice, but Bell turned what could have been a civilized dialogue into a slanging match." A battering ram—in the form of a multivolume catalog of Indian economic problems—was not the ideal instrument with which to promote policy changes.[57]

The Agricultural Front and the Treaty of Rome

Bernard Bell's focus on agricultural policy was hardly a voice in the wilderness; the rural sector became something of an obsession for American and World Bank officials. The Bell Report's three hefty volumes on agriculture endorsed a capital-intensive approach to agriculture, along the lines of what Subramaniam had been calling the "new strategy." It entailed a "package" of inputs including irrigation, pest control, and high-yield seeds, but especially fertilizer. USAID India chief John Lewis wanted to increase Indian usage of chemical fertilizer, which he considered the single most important element of a new agricultural policy. He promoted projects with major U.S. firms like Bechtel and Standard Oil of New Jersey. Lewis recognized, also, that significant imports would be required before domestic plants could come online. When the Indian talks with Bechtel stalled in spring 1965, Indian officials were so concerned about USAID pressure that they quietly inquired whether the failure to reach a deal would mean an immediate reduction in economic assistance. Arguing that the fertilizer plant projects came with financial terms "prejudicial to India's economic independence," TTK persuaded the Cabinet to reject these proposals. A former business executive, he did not share the antipathy for the private sector that was common in government circles but at the same time often sought to protect Indian businesses from foreign (and especially American) competition. TTK did not stand alone in his skepticism about the pressure over fertilizers; even sympathetic Indian ministers like Asoka Mehta later wondered aloud whether the United States had reduced the new agriculture strategy to the construction of American fertilizer plants in India.[58]

Fortunately for Indo-American relations, at least some American policy makers looked beyond fertilizer. Secretary of Agriculture Orville Freeman, a liberal Democrat, sought a wider package of policy changes, devoting months of conversation and correspondence with his Indian counterpart, C. Subramaniam, about Indian agricultural policy. The discussions between "friends"—as they referred to one another—could be distinctly formal, with wonkish back-and-forth about specific Indian reforms. These were, by and large, the issues that Subramaniam (whom Bowles called "vigorously pro-American") had already been promoting since taking the agriculture portfolio in spring 1964. By late summer 1965, amid deepening tensions in Kashmir, the Indian minister sent Freeman a seven-page letter outlining the policy reforms already under way—pricing, high-yield seeds, fertilizer, and food distribution—for American endorsement. Freeman aimed high; as he later put it in a hopelessly mixed metaphor, he wanted to put his friend Subramaniam "over a barrel" and then "squeeze"—excused by the troubling logic that his Indian counterpart "didn't object very much." Freeman's second goal was more effective, and fit more readily into the dynamics of development politics; he hoped to provide Subramaniam "a stack of promises and penalties" to deploy against opponents of agricultural reform.[59]

Freeman foisted this stack of goodies, along with his long list of policy recommendations, on Subramaniam while they both attended a conference in Rome. Subramaniam quickly agreed with the recommendations, in large part because they drew echoed so closely his own plans for Indian agriculture, in topics ranging from government spending to fertilizer consumption to rural credit facilities to prices. It was remarkably specific, down to annual breakdowns of fertilizer use by nutrient type (nitrogen, potassium, phosphorus), and specific spending figures. What Freeman later puffed up as the "Treaty of Rome" amounted to a binding Indian commitment about its overall policy framework as well as many details.[60]

In recognition of the so-called treaty, President Johnson signed off on a new aid agreement in December, the first since the September war. It included a three-month PL480 extension—which in the era of the short tether, would have to qualify as a long-term agreement. It also included a $50 million non-project loan for the purchase of fertilizer. In informing his principal Indian contact, S. Bhoothalingam at the Ministry of Finance, Lewis indicated that the loan would go through only if India agreed to a list of stipulations running to five single-spaced pages. After Subramaniam gave a public performance of that acceptance in the Lok Sabha, the text of his speech ricocheted around Washington as evidence that the agriculture minister planned to make good. Yet even this declaration proved insufficient; Secretary Freeman insisted that PL480 aid could continue only if Indian officials sent weekly (!) reports on grain distribution and hosted American inspectors.[61]

Lewis, like many of his colleagues, cheered Subramaniam's performance, quickly if unduly crediting the Big Push for "help[ing] engineer" Indian reforms. He also boasted that American pressure had been so deftly applied that the Indian cabinet was by and large unaware of the Big Push. All of these signs pointed to the success of the strategy, and, he believed, to the future growth of the Indian economy. American officials celebrated the Treaty of Rome as proof of how well the Big Push could work. As Robert Komer gloated to the president, "Subramaniam has . . . told Freeman all the things we want to hear." Yet such performances did not stop Secretary of Agriculture Freeman for asking for more.[62]

American officials saw no limits to the "Big Push." In preparation for Prime Minister Shastri's upcoming visit to Washington, Lewis sent a lengthy to-do list, with the overall goal of "convinc[ing] the President that it is worth betting on India." Making that case, though, would be a tall order; Komer identified ten criteria on which Shastri would be evaluated, including a new "fact of life in Washington" in 1965: Vietnam. The aide underscored, both literally and figuratively, that *"Shastri's statement and actions on Vietnam will be just as important as his economic promises."*[63] What started as the Big Push on economic issues had expanded to encompass political ones.

This list of criteria, however, soon made its way into the Indian radical press, most likely leaked by TTK to hinder an Indo-American agreement. The full text of the letter appeared under the headline "Yankee Moghul's Fatwa" in early January 1966. Even before the article appeared, however, Shastri fired TTK; the prime minister wanted to move ahead with devaluation, so removed one of the highest-ranking obstacles: the finance minister, who had called devaluation "no answer to our problems." American aid and the conditions for it continued to shape Indian politics.[64]

In the years after 1966, as the new agricultural strategy took hold in the Indian countryside, Americans and Indians alike sought to take credit. USAID administrator William Gaud lauded Subramaniam's "new strategy," crediting his agency's pressure. Gaud coined the term "Green Revolution" in explicit contradistinction to the "violent Red Revolution" in Russia and the Shah of Iran's authoritarian "White Revolution" of the early 1960s. The Green Revolution would spread agricultural plenty around the world—thanks in large part to USAID spreading the ideas and technologies involved. Gaud explicitly credited the pressure tactics that USAID and the World Bank had employed in India; thanks to American conditioning, he said, "the message has been getting through."[65]

Indian officials, even those favoring the new agricultural strategy, considered this American celebration uncouth if not uncalled for. Subramaniam recalled derisively that President Johnson "had the feeling that he was working the Indian agricultural miracle from the White House." Shastri's secretary, L. K. Jha, later complained that American policies were far more forceful than necessary; USAID officials were not swaying policy so much as they were "leaning against open doors." Given Subramaniam's policy preferences, and the distinct lack of subtlety behind American efforts, the effect was more like battering down the "open door." Deaf to such concerns, American officials made even more muscular and wide-ranging efforts to shape Indian policy. The crucial moments would come in Washington, starting with Shastri's visit scheduled for early 1966.[66]

From Bets to Bargains

American officials hoped that Shastri's planned visit to Washington in February 1966 would induce policy change and cement relationships between the U.S. government and the America lobby in New Delhi. A year into the Big Push and the "short tether," the pressure from American officials was meant to arm Indian allies with a "stack of promises" for use in domestic politics. Allies like S. Bhoothalingam, Asoka Mehta, and C. Subramaniam took advantage of these resources to promote policy changes. But American pressure tactics also included a "stack" of "penalties" that undercut these very same allies, who had to scramble monthly for PL480 extensions and had to defend themselves against criticisms of kowtowing to foreign pressure. The leaked publication of John Lewis's "yard-long" list of conditions indicated that even quiet pressure ran risks of explosive publicity.[67]

Before Shastri could meet with President Johnson to work out the future of Indo-American relations, though, other events intruded. By the time *Blitz* obtained and published Lewis's memo, Shastri was out of the country, in the USSR to negotiate a peace treaty between India and Pakistan in the aftermath of the September war. Aleksei Kosygin welcomed Prime Minister Shastri and Pakistan's president Mohammad Ayub Khan to the Central Asian city of Tashkent just after New Year's Day 1966. Over the course of the next week, Kosygin led a herculean effort to conclude the so-called Tashkent Declaration, which returned the regional rivals to status quo ante bellum and achieved promises to improve economic and political relations over the coming years. Before any "spirit of Tashkent" could take hold—indeed, before news of the declaration had reached many quarters—came the shocking news that Shastri had died.[68]

A brief but intense struggle ensued within the Congress Party. Morarji Desai, who had sought the prime minister's post after Jawaharlal Nehru's death in 1964 but withdrew under pressure from party chiefs, was not going to throw away his shot again two years later. But he ran up against Shastri's minister of information and broadcasting, Indira Gandhi, who waged a shrewd campaign. Ironically, the organization of state party leaders, led by Congress president K. Kamaraj and known as the Syndicate, preferred Gandhi because they considered her an "innocuous person" who posed no threat to their power.[69]

Though Indira Gandhi was markedly less enthusiastic about American-style economic reforms than her predecessor, the bilateral aid relationship changed little with her succession. American diplomats took consolation in reports that she intended to continue Subramaniam's agricultural strategy. They also noted with appreciation her desire to visit Washington as soon as was practicable. This trip, set for late March 1966, would bring into a single conversation all of the different forms of leverage exercised by American officials—nonproject assistance, PL480 food, and the consortium—and the long (and by now familiar) list of policy changes desired: agricultural policy, deregulation, devaluation, defense spending and Vietnam. With such a full agenda, Komer exclaimed (with his usual overstatement) that Gandhi's visit with Lyndon Johnson would rank in importance to international relations right up there with the Kennedy-Khrushchev summit in Vienna in 1961.[70]

Officials expressed American aims for the summit in blunt terms. Johnson described the purpose of his meeting as a chance to see what India could do to "help us," insisting that there would be no "one-way deal." President Johnson complained to B. K. Nehru about his increasingly difficult relations with the U.S. Congress, hinting that the right statements from Indian leaders could calm roiled waters. Such concerns about dealing with the legislative branch became Johnson's refrain through the conversation. So when the ambassador sought emergency nonproject aid to keep the economy moving, Johnson worried that he would not be able to "borrow on his own prestige by going ahead without Congress." Johnson decided to once again don voluntary congressional handcuffs in order to maximize his control. The circumstances added handily to the anxieties of Ambassador Nehru and his colleagues—and to the frustration of Indian lobbyists like Chester Bowles, who called the short tether a "cruel performance" undertaken so that the president could watch Indian leaders "fawn." Such ex post facto criticisms aside, however, even Bowles argued for "taking advantage of the urgency of the present situation" to bring about devaluation in India.[71]

President Johnson's list of conditions incorporated Lewis's leaked "fatwa" and indeed expanded upon it. Domestically the president sought serious progress on food production, population control, and the removal of "shackles of interference of state control" from the economy. In the international arena he sought a more accommodating attitude toward Pakistan and more help in combating "Chinese expansionism" (a circumlocution for Vietnam). Komer focused especially on this last point, telling Ambassador Bowles that "nothing would convince the president more of India's *bona fides* more than a forthright stand on Vietnam."[72]

Agriculture remained a particular focus of American policy makers—and an arena in which they had support from their friends at the World Bank. Building on the results of its Bell Report, bank officials prepared suggestions on Indian agricultural policy that took a directive form, each one preceded by a condescending "we trust that. . . ." The policies themselves lined up with the Bell Mission's recommendations, and with American promotion of Green Revolution technologies—especially fertilizers.[73]

American diplomats in New Delhi had hoped to convince Shastri about their proposals for Indian economic policy; they knew they had a harder sell with his successor and thus ratcheted up the pressure all the more. The graphomaniac American ambassador Bowles dispatched some thirty-five pages of overheated prose expounding on the American position. Bowles's chief economic officer went so far as to script the prime minister's upcoming conversations with President Johnson. In a series of imperative statements, each beginning with "The Prime Minister should . . . ," the junior diplomat outlined the usual set of American demands. He was particularly pointed about the need for devaluation, one of the conclusions of the Bell Mission Report some months earlier: "While neither [President Johnson] nor the American Government," an Indian diplomat recorded, "were positively advocating this step of devaluation, he felt that this was the only real method of resolving our problems." The conversation went well beyond the economic counselor's writ, touching also on Pakistan and Vietnam. President Johnson was only slightly more subtle in a meandering talk with Ambassador Nehru on the eve of the prime minister's arrival, scheduled for March 28. Secretary of State Dean Rusk termed the new conditions "The Economic Bargain with India"; it amounted to a rechristened Big Push, once again incorporating a set of policy prescriptions that Indian officials had already

Prime Minister Indira Gandhi shares a smile with President Lyndon Baines Johnson at the White House in March 1966. Despite her own reservations about expanding Indian reliance on American aid, Gandhi convinced Johnson to loosen the purse strings after the meeting. *Source:* Photo by Yoichi Okamoto, 28 March 1966, Oval Office, White House Photo Office Collection, Lyndon Baines Johnson Presidential Library, Austin (A2186–7A).

begun: trade liberalization, population control, and agricultural intensification (measured, as usual, by production and consumption of fertilizer). Nor was the bargain strictly economic; it also called for India to step up vis-à-vis Vietnam and step back vis-à-vis Pakistan.[74]

Indira Gandhi and her adviser P. N. Haksar sought an agreement with the United States even as they had to overcome their political instincts to do so; both prime minister and adviser had long expressed ambivalence about relying too much on the United States. Haksar wanted to expand a "direct relationship" with the United States primarily as way to limit Indian dependence on the United Kingdom, but chafed at the specter of "dependence on the United States." The prime minister, in spite of her reservations, described her mission to Washington as a fine balance—trying "to get both food and foreign exchange without appearing to ask for them."[75]

Given both sides' determination to make sure that any agreement was not simply a "one-way street," the summit went surprisingly well. The prime minister followed the script that American diplomats had written a few weeks earlier, appending a reminder that she risked criticism for selling out to the United States. She noted the difficult food situation, though her advisers insisted that the issue was not "dead bodies on the streets" so much as an imminent "famine . . . averted." Conversation ranged across the usual American demands about Indian policy.[76]

The summit with Indira Gandhi finally led President Johnson to act on the barrage of requests from the India lobby within the U.S. government. He moved with alacrity to apply both the carrot and the stick, using the various channels within the U.S. government in addition to working closely with the World Bank. Only days after Gandhi's departure, the president released a message to Congress warning that India stood on "the threshold of a great tragedy" and required as much aid as Congress could provide. With this message, the president finally took the congressional delay tactic off the table, offering fulsome praise when Congress passed a nonbinding joint resolution, portentously titled "To Support the United States Participation in Reliving Victims of Hunger in India and to Enhance India's Capacity to Meet the Nutritional Needs of Its People." Though the resolution did not offer any new funds or programs, it served as the congressional green light that Johnson had demanded.[77]

Toward Devaluation

Whatever the congressional resolution meant for American aid, it did not reduce the force behind the Big Push. American officials like Robert Komer still looked for ways to keep "working over India," either via USAID or in conjunction with the World Bank. Meanwhile, the unlucky Indian official who had to reckon with this new effort was Minister of Planning Asoka Mehta, who was soon dispatched to Washington. By 1966 Mehta's socialist years—both in and out of Congress—had passed, and he had become a firm supporter of the market-oriented approach promoted in Washington.[78]

Mehta's response in Washington provided one more indication of how American pressure undercut the efforts of those most inclined toward Western economic policy. He had, after all, already endorsed the overall policy thrust, and many of the specific policies, in the Bell Report. Yet both the State Department and the World Bank prepared for his visit as if it entailed the dressing-down of a delinquent schoolchild. Bernard Bell, for instance, wanted Mehta to give the bank's Delhi office a larger role in Indian economic policy making. Rusk's Economic Bargain strayed even further from purely economic concerns to include military spending and political conditions (related to Pakistan and Vietnam). After Secretary Rusk raised the question of Indo-Pakistani relations Mehta was sufficiently worried that he asked Walt Rostow point-blank whether future American assistance was contingent on peace in South Asia.[79]

Mehta's visit took place in an atmosphere of self-deception on the part of American officials. State Department functionaries closely followed the negotiations with George Woods and Bank staff even while they wanted to "maintain the appearance that we do not know the content of the talks between Mehta and the bank." American officials, from the president on down, repeated the fiction that they were just offering friendly advice to a friendly government, not imposing conditions. As President Johnson told Mehta with no apparent irony, "We had made no request of the Prime Minister or Subramaniam nor had we demanded conditions."[80]

World Bank dealings with the sympathetic Mehta produced a document as striking in its length as it was in the breadth of its coverage and the depth of its detail. A thirty-two-page summary of Mehta's meetings enumerated sixty (!) policy recommendations, neatly divided into eleven policy areas. Most recommendations echoed earlier discussions: increasing fertilizer imports and eventually fertilizer production, deregulation, population control, and the like. But it entered new (and ever narrower) arenas like tourism and transportation. Mehta tetchily insisted that the policies in question were not imposed from without, but "were those which the Indian Government wished to pursue if it could."[81]

Even this thorough list of "recommendations" was not comprehensive since it omitted the single most important and immediate Western demand for reform: currency devaluation. The World Bank took the lead here, even though currency issues usually rested with its sister institution, the International Monetary Fund. But the IMF, with little leverage in India, gratefully if quietly supported World Bank efforts.[82]

During his visit Mehta stressed that the notion of an Economic Bargain cut two ways. Lewis's Big Push, which dangled nonproject aid as incentive for policy change, began from a similar premise. Mehta repeatedly made this understanding explicit, insisting for instance that import liberalization would occur only if "the necessary aid for this purpose would be made available."

Similarly, he promised a British interlocutor that his government would adopt the enumerated reforms so long as "it could be given adequate resources to justify it in doing so." Mehta's views, derived directly from the comments made by American and World Bank officials and were shared with others in his government. In late 1965, for instance, B. K. Nehru told the USAID chief in Washington that he was willing to promote deregulation and trade liberalization "if we can be assured by the world community of the financing we will need over the next several years to carry through these policies." Policy changes, the argument went, would merit additional aid. Officials from all sides—the World Bank headquarters, the State Department, and the Indian Cabinet—had accepted this logic.[83]

This common understanding left unspecified crucial details about amounts and timing, however. American officials voiced suspicion that Mehta had been exaggerating the foreign aid needs for India's Fourth Five-Year Plan, but eventually agreed upon a sum of $900 million nonproject aid from the consortium members for the coming year. This figure marked a substantial increase over previous aid commitments, especially because the nonproject aid would be over and above existing pledges. What would happen after the first year was left vague; Mehta, for instance, accepted the $900 million figure for the first year but also "required assurance that adequate support will be available" in subsequent years. This formulation did not catch on, however; only days after Mehta's statement, USAID officials neglected to mention any aid whatsoever beyond the first year. John Lewis, thousands of miles away from the action, later recalled that the commitment was for two or three years, but he cited no evidence anyone in Washington concurred. This ambiguity soon haunted Indian relations with its major Western donors—and ultimately Indian domestic and international politics.[84]

Rupee Diplomacy

The test of Western commitment to India—and of Indian commitment to policy change—centered around an explosive economic reform: devaluation. The exchange rate was not a new question by the time Indira Gandhi and Asoka Mehta came to Washington in spring 1966. Through the early 1960s, Indian economists like Jagdish Bhagwati and Manmohan Singh had promoted devaluation as a means to increase exports, formulate appropriate prices for imported goods, and properly align the Indian rupee in the international arena. But exchange rates were a fraught topic, tantamount in Indian popular opinion (according to S. Bhoothalingam) to "self-diminution." For George Woods at the World Bank, the topic was not something for polite company—"like talking to a man about the virtue of his wife," in the words of one staffer. Bernard Bell, in a bulldozer fashion, had flattened any resistance to the topic in his mission for the bank; the report had ultimately called for devaluation but did not specify a target level. One of the key opponents of devaluation in the cabinet through 1965, T. T. Krishnamachari, was out of office by the time Indira Gandhi became prime minister. A number of journalists reported rumors that Asoka Mehta and C. Subramaniam had convinced Shastri of the need to devalue—but that he died in Tashkent before he could take concrete steps. Some observers reported that Prime Minister Gandhi had already accepted in principle the need for devaluation, even as she remained vexed by its political ramifications. On the eve of her visit, a key aide described the internal discussions about devaluation as a dispute about timing and amount; the fact of devaluation itself was a foregone conclusion.[85]

True to the dynamics of development politics, Prime Minister Gandhi seemed more immersed in the politics than the economics of devaluation—who would win and who would lose by the decision? For domestic politics, she consulted leading economists, including proponents like Bhagwati and skeptics like K. N. Raj and D. R. Gadgil. Raj, well informed about the secret bargaining, came out forcefully against capitulating to American demands. Invited to meet the prime minister, Bhagwati recalled preparing a lengthy economic argument for devaluation, only to find that her first question was purely political: if she devalued the rupee, she asked, who would be against her? Senior policy makers in India, including proponents like C. Subramaniam, feared that devaluation would be an act of political suicide for the prime minister. Political criteria outweighed economic ones, and everyone she consulted—except Bhagwati— staunchly opposed devaluation. Worried about leaks, the prime minister moved quickly after Mehta's return from Washington. She quizzed the head of the IMF about the appropriate level for the rupee. As if setting the price for a trinket at the bazaar, the IMF chief replied that 6 rupees to the dollar (20.5 percent devaluation from the previous level of 4.76) would be "good," 7 to the dollar (32.1 percent) "better," and 7.5 to the dollar (36.7 percent) "fantastic." Yet this created a new problem: Indian and foreign proponents of devaluation alike expected it to take place in conjunction with trade liberalization and changes to licensing. To undertake devaluation without other elements of the policy package had major economic and ultimately political risks.[86]

Prime Minister Gandhi did not shy away from those risks. On a quiet Sunday morning—so that she could inform the IMF before announcing the decision—she brought the question of devaluation to the cabinet. By the end of the day—June 6, the anniversary of D-Day—devaluation without other reforms got under way. In spite of rushed efforts to put a positive spin on devaluation, the decision was widely and loudly criticized from all sides within India. The pages of the *Times of India* the following day cataloged only a small portion of the response: the Communist Party cried betrayal, many Congress politicians called the decision a sign of Indians' new status as "economic vassals" of the West; Morarji Desai, a proponent of devaluation but an opponent of Indira Gandhi, maintained a stony silence. Elsewhere TTK offered muted opposition. Communist members of Parliament directly accused the prime minister of setting Indian policy in consultation with "the World Bank and other American agencies," rather than with the Parliament. Against this barrage, the finance minister's calm insistence that the decision resulted from "careful study" had just as little effect as his ministry's handy Q&A brochure. The critics had a point: devaluing the rupee without undertaking other reforms would hurt Indian foreign-currency flows without providing the desired realignment of incentives for exports and disincentives for imports. The other measures were not taken at the same time as devaluation, and the strong blowback against that decision made such measures even harder to institute. Thus, while Indian diplomats in Washington reported resentfully about the "jubilant" attitude there, Gandhi faced dual economic and political crises—and only eight months before a general election.[87]

Those who favored devaluation remained apprehensive that the donors might not live up to their part of the bargain. Would they send enough aid to steady the economy before the February elections? Devaluation, by all accounts, would stretch Indian foreign-exchange reserves in the short term, and thus required significant inflows of foreign currency in order to keep India solvent. B. K. Nehru summarized the Indian predicament with characteristic directness: "devaluation will be a good move only if India can 'get a lot of money' to make it work prior to elections." In the aftermath of the devaluation, the Ministry of Finance swung into action, dispatching representatives to the World Bank and to development agencies in the United States and the United Kingdom. The pro-American L. K. Jha remained wary in his talks with Ambassador Bowles; as the American note-taker recorded, "While Jha was profoundly relieved that the devaluation decision had been taken, he was at the same time deeply concerned that the scope and timing of Bank-Consortium-U.S. support has not been officially confirmed to the Government of India." Much to the dismay of B. K. Nehru, L. K. Jha, and their compatriots, such concerns proved prescient. Their erstwhile Western allies ultimately undercut their position by failing to live up to their part of the bargain.[88]

Living Up to the Bargain

American policies focused on what concessions they expected to wring from the Government of India, not on what they would deliver if India met the stringent conditions of USAID and the World Bank. As originally conceived, John Lewis's Big Push and Dean Rusk's Economic Bargain asked a great deal of India—but promised aid in return; Rusk, for instance, offered "assurances of substantial Consortium financial support" in exchange for policy changes. The Bell Mission, similarly, offered the "assurance of finance on an increased scale for the next few years" in exchange for Indian economic reforms.[89]

For those like B. K. Nehru and L. K. Jha who were apprehensive about the funding, the months after devaluation in June 1966 provided an unfortunate confirmation. The American government was not the main problem—at least not at first. President Johnson approved a major expansion of lending to India after Rostow and USAID leaders convinced him that Prime Minister Gandhi had lived up to her end of the bargain; it was now time, Rostow argued, to move ahead "with our part of the economic deal." With President Johnson's approval, the initial American commitment was assured.[90]

From the start, however, there was an agency problem: the United States and the World Bank could exercise only moral suasion to solicit contributions from the consortium members. Even though no consortium member questioned Indian adherence to the reforms specified in the Bell Report, few ponied up sufficiently to meet the assurances already offered to Indian officials. The initial figure of $900 million in consortium nonproject aid divided responsibility based on past commitments—but right at the outset the German and Japanese representatives announced that their respective governments would not meet those goals. George Woods asked USAID to make up the shortfall (of some $16 million) but was rebuffed. Even in the flush of devaluation in June 1966, the consortium fell short.[91]

Indian officials expressed immediate and deep apprehension over the delays in consortium funding, reminding their interlocutors (in the words of one American diplomat) that India's liberalization program was undertaken on the understanding that it would "be supported through India's Fourth Five Year Plan," then slated for 1966–1971. But 1971 seemed impossibly far off when the consortium had not even settled its commitments for 1967. At the next consortium meeting in November 1966, even the usually optimistic Bernard Bell warned that without "sympathetic, adequate, and early support" the Indian reforms could fail. While most delegations were "impressed" by the Bell Report, consortium members, led by the West German representatives, argued that Indian economic performance—reforms or no—did not merit additional aid. World Bank economists took a more positive view, endorsing the reforms undertaken, and noting for the record that these had been based upon the Indian government's "expectation" of additional nonproject aid of about $900 million per year "for the next year or two"—a shorter duration than earlier bank statements about "a few years."[92]

As doubts about Western commitments grew in winter 1966–1967, the political risks of devaluation and economic reform became all the more apparent. The results of the February 1967 election exceeded even the gravest fears of Indira Gandhi and her advisers. While Congress narrowly maintained its majority in the Lok Sabha in New Delhi, it lost control of a number of once-reliable states. In the postelection shuffle, Gandhi reluctantly appointed her most powerful Congress foe, Morarji Desai, to his second stint as minister of finance—and his first as deputy prime minister. Desai had stood in firm support of Western aid and Western-style economic policies since his first term as finance minister (1958–1963), and not surprisingly began his second stint with the same posture; among his first acts was to try to defang the Planning Commission. The electoral results weakened the Congress Party and its prime minister and contributed to growing division at the top and increased friction throughout the government.[93]

Yet Morarji Desai and his pro-Western allies were soon dealt another blow when a consortium working group met in March 1967. Though its Economic Committee recommended that the bank proceed with financing its part of the earlier bargain, the meeting itself all but ignored discussion of new commitments in favor of technical details for loans, and some conversation about rescheduling existing development loans. The full consortium convened in early April 1967 and quickly agreed in principle to provide another $900 million in nonproject aid to India for the coming year. Yet practice diverged sharply from principle. Consortium members insisted that the figure include both debt relief and food relief—and even with these additions, the total consortium commitment came to barely $600 million of the $900 million promised. Such weak results prompted the session chair, George Woods, to suspend rather than adjourn the meeting, holding the delegation heads for detention to chastise them for failing to come even remotely close to the aid that they had promised. Woods's shakedown of consortium members, however, yielded meager results. The German representative demurred on any formal commitment, whereupon a number of other delegates indicated that any higher levels of support would be contingent on German action. So the group agreed to meet again six weeks later, hoping again to gather the pledges that they had already made to India.[94]

Amid the fight to meet the promised aid levels, the details evolved in ways that ultimately worked against the Indian government. The World Bank president allowed that about half of the $900 million could take the form of debt relief rather than new loans.[95] There was a logic here beside the obvious desire to move the goal line closer; reducing loan repayment would reduce the foreign-exchange burdens on the Indian government, and would thus leave the funds open for use along the lines of nonproject aid. Unfortunately for the Indians hoping for more from the World Bank, consortium partners typically favored debt rescheduling (which kept the same obligations but pushed them further into the future) to debt relief (reducing / canceling repayment amounts), but still considered either act a form of "aid."

In the aftermath of the consortium's dismal April discussions, Finance Minister Morarji Desai invited George Woods to New Delhi to make the World Bank president answer publicly for his institution's actions and inaction. Desai lambasted Woods privately about exposing the Indian government—and pro-Western forces within it—to significant political risk. Yet Woods could offer little other than hope that consortium members would fulfill their commitments. In the unenviable position of defending the bank and the consortium at a press conference in New Delhi, Woods expressed confidence that the goals "can be achieved," but admitted under questioning that the consortium might

Aid to India Consortium Commitments
(in millions of current dollars)

	US	UK	W GER.	BANK / IDA	OTHER	TOTAL
1966–1967	$382	$90	$63	$215	$152	$901
1967–1968	116	82	63	25	184	469
1968–1969	9	84	63	15	148	318
1969–1970	394	91	63	235	173	955

Source: GOI Department of Economic Affairs, EA 1978–1979, 270–271.

need another five months or more (i.e., until well into the fall) to meet 1967 commitments. Yet the future kept getting pushed back: the next meeting was postponed until September 1967, but it again focused more on debt relief than on new nonproject aid. Furthermore, the fine print on debt relief made it seem more like debt rescheduling than actual relief, thus offering only delaying the moment of reckoning and not really providing much development assistance.[96]

The next consortium meeting two months later was even more problematic; members focused on criticizing Indian economic performance rather than evaluating reforms and on penalties rather than aid. Performance criteria proved especially problematic for recipients like India; no longer would simply making the agreed-upon reforms be sufficient for increased aid; the failure of reforms to yield anticipated effects—whether due to foot-dragging on the part of recipient governments, external shocks, or other reasons—became a justification for denying promised aid. While American representatives praised Indian persistence in the face of economic challenges, most others expressed "dismay" or "disappointment" about Indian economic performance. They focused in particular on the Indian export sector, which had not expanded anywhere near as much or as quickly as they had hoped. They also criticized the remaining restrictions on imports as unduly interfering with free trade—a marked change from tolerance for protections of selected Indian domestic sectors from foreign competition that was part of the 1966 Economic Bargain. The participants' pledges came to a meager $350 million, nowhere near the $900 million target.[97]

Consortium meetings in 1968 went even more poorly for Indian representatives—and for those in the Indian government who had hitched their fate to substantial Western aid. The first session, in March, focused on debt relief—which, consortium members had convinced themselves, was a form of nonproject aid—but aimed for only $300 million over three years. The May session observed India's "grim" balance-of-payments situation, but provided little direct relief for it—and indeed imposed new burdens on India's still meager foreign-exchange reserves. Early surveys of the group indicated that aid pledges for the following year would drop even lower than in 1967–1968; the U.S. representatives managed to up their figures by including PL480, for the first time, in their calculations. The year 1968 was capped off by an unpleasant visit to India by World Bank president Robert S. McNamara, fresh from the Pentagon. While in Delhi he heard every form of sniping and backstabbing from Indian and American interlocutors alike. John Lewis, still head of the USAID mission, had lost faith in two Indian leaders whom he had previously championed (Morarji Desai and I. G. Patel); they had also lost faith in him. Asoka Mehta badmouthed the whole Indian political establishment, telling McNamara's assistant he "would not lend a cent" to current Indian leaders. This infighting seemed a fitting conclusion to a disastrous year in India's relationship with the World Bank.[98]

In the thirty months after the dramatic devaluation of June 1966, then, the notion of providing major commitments of new nonproject aid to support economic liberalization had receded into the background. Indian officials found themselves on the wrong end of a catch-22; they had undertaken major economic reforms at heavy economic and political costs. Yet the external assistance to pay for the reforms came first too late—and then too little and in the wrong form. Even as they failed to meet their own commitments, consortium members voiced ever-louder disapproval of Indian economic performance, as if their own inability to meet the target aid amounts had no relation to India's continuing economic troubles.[99]

Indian observers, even those generally sympathetic to the United States, began to wonder if the Economic Bargain went only one way; it obligated the Indian government without obligating the Western donors. Even World Bank economists later conceded that the institution "mucked up" on delivering the aid promised. Such skepticism was voiced more frequently and was more bluntly expressed even by those Indian officials who had long endorsed the shift to Western-oriented economic policies and had defended the World Bank and USAID Economic Bargain against domestic critics. By early 1968 Morarji Desai's tone had grown caustic; in a scathing letter to bank president McNamara he noted the shortfall of aid and enumerated his government efforts to obtain the loans expected through the Economic Bargain. New loans, he protested, were frequently promised but rarely provided, and the promises themselves seemed forever to recede into the future. The finance minister protested that he knew of no complaint that the Indian government had that backtracked on its promises of reform; delays and postponements in financing, he concluded, amounted to a failure of the World Bank to live up to its end of the bargain. He had similarly withering views of American aid, complaining to American diplomats that the failure to deliver aid meant that political support for the Green Revolution had "been shot out from under" its proponents.[100]

I. G. Patel, Desai's colleague at the Ministry of Finance and a civil servant with long and deep connections to the World Bank and IMF, adopted a tone of wounded betrayal. Though he had earlier described performance conditioning in sympathetic terms, by 1968 he took the offensive against the World Bank. After the 1968 consortium meetings failed to yield anything resembling the aid figures discussed prior to devaluation, Patel returned to India declaring that India had been "swindled." He recommended that Indian policy makers make future plans without accounting for such aid, which rarely arrived in the amounts and time frame promised. The only way to avoid disappointment, in his view, was to lower expectations. By the time he wrote his memoirs, Patel's attitude had soured further; he bemoaned the "shriller and shriller" demands for economic performance and the "inequitable application" of those criteria "to suit the political compulsions of the donors." Morarji Desai and I. G. Patel, in short, felt abandoned by the Western donors with whom they had found common cause. The effects were economic as well as political; two experts close to the situation concluded that devaluation and its aftermath "had a lasting influence on the management of the economy"—and not for the better.[101]

Lengthening the Short Tether

As the Economic Bargain focused on devaluation and trade liberalization, Western efforts to use food as a weapon unfolded on a parallel track. The short tether for PL480 shipments continued, in the process still undercutting India's proponents of Western approaches to agriculture—even as Indian policies moved toward American visions. C. Subramaniam's effectiveness in promoting Indian agricultural reforms had, by June 1966, satisfied various constituencies in Washington, but the familiar dynamic within the U.S. government continued: various officials, including India lobbyists like Chester Bowles, would plead with President Johnson to release the next shipment of wheat. The president requested additional information—conditions in India, wheat prices in the United States, the status of one or another ship—or simply ignored the query. Meanwhile the tether remained short. The head of USAID forcefully rejected the notion that "the withholding of aid or of food supplies . . . can possibly improve Indian performance in the agricultural sector." For his part, Johnson was just as frustrated and even "disappointed" by the drumbeat of requests. He raised again the specter of congressional approval, telling Agriculture Secretary Freeman that he was "not going to do anything unless Congress does." Toward that end, National Security Adviser Walt Rostow hastily dispatched a congressional delegation and a team of USDA experts to study Indian conditions first-hand. The USDA report repeated the familiar position that famine, food shortage, and political turmoil were just around the corner without immediate shipments of food aid. Johnson once again deferred to Congress, saying he would wait until after the return of the congressional delegation.[102]

John Lewis, who had proposed increasing pressure on India in the first place, protested that the short-tether policy was undermining American allies in India. It might be "brutally humane," he admitted, but was hurting America's best friends in the leadership and endangering India's political stability. The short tether, and not the famine, in other words, was the greater threat to India. President Johnson, meanwhile, came up with new delaying tactics; in addition to congressional approval, he sought to widen responsibility for feeding India to include other nations. Indian officials took American importuning to diversify their food aid sources to heart, seeking aid from all quarters, including the USSR. Yet they grew increasingly frustrated with the American delays and pressure—which they complained about incessantly even as they had to deny publicly that there was any such pressure whatsoever. Low-level American diplomats sympathized with the predicament of pro-American leaders in India, but could not reduce U.S. pressure or extend the duration of the PL480 deals.[103]

As the process dragged through 1967 and well into 1968, practically every American adviser called for easing up on the short tether, leading the president to complain that his administration employed more people working for India than for the United States. Rostow argued, to no avail, that there "was nothing

This cartoon, printed on the twentieth anniversary of Indian independence, identifies some of the economic problems threatening India. PL480 food aid sits squarely in the middle as a hot water bottle, easing economic pains—or is it a weight threatening the patient's health? *Source:* Cartoon by Keshav Shankar Pillai ("Shankar"), *Shankar's Weekly,* August 14, 1967. Courtesy of Children's Book Trust, New Delhi.

we want from [India] which we haven't already received or could possibly receive." But even this did not stop Johnson, who by this point seemed determined to teach a lesson to his own government's officials as well as Indian ones. Thus he added yet one more criterion, insisting that food aid depended upon cutting defense spending. In a muddled effort at clarification, Secretary of State Dean Rusk told Ambassador Bowles that food aid would "not be contingent" on reduced defense spending but followed this statement with the threat that

"Indian actions in this field will weigh heavily" on all aid decisions, specifically including PL480. Other conditions continued to pile up through the final days of the Johnson administration in January 1969.[104]

After leaving the presidency, Johnson waxed nostalgic about South Asian affairs to an Indian friend: "I shall always remember the times when I followed, week by week, the course of the monsoons. And I shall continue to follow the programs of agricultural development and family planning which the Indian government has mounted and on which so much of India's future depends."[105] No doubt the recipient of the letter—and many of his colleagues in the Indian government—would always remember those times too, but with less fondness. And the notion that Johnson would continue to "follow" Indian programs would likely have been a distressing one, mitigated only by the fact that he could no longer influence American policy.

By the time Lyndon Johnson left office in January 1969, many Indian officials and politicians who had consistently sought to deepen ties with the West were fed up with the increasing leverage calls on the part of American aid donors. Morarji Desai and I. G. Patel had been friends of the United States; both envisioned an Indian economy that was less industrial, less regulated, less planned, and less isolated than the Nehruvian model. They worked hard throughout the 1960s to see that come to pass, using Western aid to win support for their vision, yet the continually receding goal line and the heavy-handed pressure imposed by the United States left them exasperated. Other officials sympathetic with the West, like S. Bhoothalingam, Asoka Mehta, and C. Subramaniam, had been through the same wringer. The America lobby in New Delhi, which had gained strength from the promise of major infusions of Western nonproject aid and continuing food supplies, ended up in precarious political circumstances. Ironically the ranking member of the America lobby, Morarji Desai, was in the most difficult position. Imposed on a prime minister with whom he had both political and personal conflicts, he faced not only diminished prestige but also the prime minister's increased anger over the unhappy results of liberalization and devaluation. The dynamics of development politics, then, exacerbated the long-standing clash between the prime minister and her deputy.

Within the lending agencies, different—less existential—lessons from these experiments with conditionality emerged. A dissenting strain within the

World Bank chafed at the stipulations and argued against such strenuous conditioning. Even as the episode ended unhappily from the bank's perspective, the mechanisms—conditionality and consortia—proved resilient and long lasting. Within the U.S. government, the short tether unified otherwise warring bureaucrats. By the time it ended, President Johnson alone stood in favor; just about every adviser in every agency opposed him. So it was little surprise that Johnson's successor found such a receptive bureaucratic audience as he sought to end such micromanagement.

In 1965, as the Big Push became pushier, TTK (then serving as finance minister) strongly resisted what he called the increasing "political overtones" of Western aid. He confided in one international leader that he was "not comfortable" with the growing dependence on Western aid and sought above all to "diversify this dependence." He did not want to expand the consortium (in fact, he wanted to abandon it) but instead wanted to seek more aid from beyond the West. That TTK—*Time* magazine's "private enterpriser"—had turned from the West demonstrates the ability of the aid relationship to alter the Indian political landscape.[106] Irate at the increasing pressure from USAID and the World Bank, especially over devaluation, TTK became a fierce opponent of the conditions for Western aid. This stance cost him his job as finance minister at the end of 1965. But it also revealed the extent to which American officials had repulsed some of those most sympathetic to their views. Further evidence of this comes in TTK's interlocutor as he called for diversifying Indian dependence: Chairman of the Soviet Council of Ministers Aleksei Kosygin. But reliance on the USSR, events of the 1960s would demonstrate, came with its own political dangers.

CHAPTER 8

SOVIET AID FROM INSPIRATION TO ARMORY

Economic aide extraordinaire S. Bhoothalingam once quipped that the public sector "took on an almost religious significance" in Jawaharlal Nehru's India. Having rejected religion as the opiate of the people, Soviet officials could talk only in terms of ideology, not theology. Hence Foreign Minister Andrei Gromyko intoned that his government "regard[ed] with deep sympathy" Indian efforts to build its public sector. Soviet officials appreciated also the political effects of financing government-owned industry, which supported "progressive elements" and emphasized the contrast between Soviet and Western aid. The ministries and enterprises of the public sector came to rely on aid from the USSR and the socialist nations of Eastern Europe—and, true to the dynamics of development politics, used that aid to bolster their own position in Indian political economy.[1]

Expanding the Indian public sector, however, came at a price. While planners celebrated the benefits of coordination, the Indian experience of the 1960s also revealed its costs; the virtues of an integrated public sector could quickly turn to vices, as confusion and delay in one enterprise rippled through the whole sector. As Indian economic performance sank to the level of Soviet stagnation, the costs of public enterprise created political difficulties for its proponents—and for its sponsors. Indo-Soviet tensions rose as the problems of India's public sector deepened. To resolve (or evade) the economic concerns, Soviet and Indian officials sought to expand bilateral trade—not so much for the purposes of comparative advantage as to become a buyer of last resort for Indian industrial products.

Project aid remained the bedrock of Indo-Soviet economic relations. While American assistance tilted away from projects in the 1960s, Soviet aid doubled down on this form of aid. Building on high-profile projects like the Bhilai Steel Plant, Soviet aid to India in the Third Five-Year Plan (1961–1966) continued very much as it had in the Second Plan: through industrial projects in the public sector. Both sides proudly announced a major package of Soviet credits (1.5 million rubles, or 180 crores rupees) for the Third Plan in 1959, including the expansion of the Bhilai Steel Plant, oil and gas exploration, an oil refinery, heavy equipment manufacturing, and much more. Even as they basked in their own generosity, Soviet officials were well aware that their aid paled in comparison with Western aid—but they claimed it held a special significance beyond its limited extent. Privately, Soviet aid chief S. A. Skachkov of the State Committee for Foreign Economic Connections (Gosudarstvennyi Komitet po Vneshnim Ekonomicheskim Sviaziam—GKES) congratulated his country for the sacrifices made in the name of "humanitarianism."[2]

The next Indo-Soviet economic cooperation agreement, signed in 1966, committed the Soviets to a larger sum—250 crores rupees—for a similar range of projects, with a strong emphasis on oil and power sectors. By the time that later agreement was inked, Indo-Soviet aid relations had expanded to incorporate a new dimension: military supply. Over the course of the 1960s, military aspects became an increasingly important element in Indo-Soviet relations—with both geopolitical and economic implications.

Finding Common Ground in Public-Sector Projects

Soviet-aided projects in India ran into problems well beyond the amount of aid or the limits of Soviet humanitarianism—and in ways that reveal the antinomies of the public sector. In Soviet aid to the oil sector, as in aid to industries like steel and heavy equipment, the trajectory from optimism to disillusionment unfolded because the two partners had different priorities. Indian proponents envisioned the public sector as a means to the end of *swadeshi* (self-sufficiency), which could be more quickly and easily obtained through government-owned enterprises. Their Soviet counterparts, in contrast, expected the new industrial installations to serve as physical manifestations of Soviet generosity and industrial prowess. What seemed like a united front for the public sector turned out to contain not just multitudes but also contradictions.

The Indian National Congress had long promoted the public sector, and for a variety of reasons. From the very founding of the Indian National Congress, its leaders expressed the concern that privately owned foreign firms had exploited India. The strong interest in planning, furthermore, favored the public sector; planners could work more readily with government-owned enterprises than private firms. Core elements of the Industrial Policy Resolutions of 1948 and 1956 established expansive boundaries for the public sector, and limited the role of the private sector in core industries. The 1955 declaration that Congress sought to build a "socialistic pattern of society" gave further impetus to expanding the public sector. Official policy lined up accordingly. Whether mobilizing in poetry, then, or governing in prose, the Congress Party placed high hopes in government-owned industry.

Soviet aid officials and scholars had their own case for promoting the public sector in the Third World. The emergence of "state capitalism" as a useful category of economic analysis highlighted the "progressive" nature of industrial enterprises under public ownership. State-owned enterprises, the theory went, had advantages in planning, management, and even trade, especially for underdeveloped nations. Scholars at the Institute for Oriental Studies similarly promoted the public and cooperative sectors as the best use of Soviet (and domestic) resources for economic growth. The party apparat agreed, stressing in its programmatic statements that heavy industry in the public sector would be "the highest priority" for Soviet aid to the Third World.[3]

Both Indian and Soviet proponents of the public sector also contemplated less lofty motives. As the Indian Planning Commission (PC) noted, the public sector did not just improve Indian economic prospects but limited the wealth in private hands and increased the power of the state.[4] Soviet apparatchiks made parallel arguments: building public-sector industry would help the USSR's friends in India while marginalizing "reactionary circles" aligned with the West—thus advancing the "anti-imperialist struggle." They even named individual Indian politicians whose standing would be helped or hurt by the expanding public sector.[5]

Given their respective ideological commitments, political positions, and economic practices, many Indian officials agreed with the Soviet efforts to expand the public sector. Yet fundamental tensions soon emerged. Was the public sector, as many if not all Indian economic officials indicated, an instrument to achieve economic self-sufficiency? Or was it, as Soviet officials usually implied, an end in itself? GKES chief Skachkov argued that the virtue of Soviet technical assistance was that it would create Soviet-style economies through the expansion of the public sector. A larger public sector was, ipso facto, an indicator of economic and political progress.[6]

Supporting industrial facilities in the public sector, GKES remained dedicated to project aid. Not only were Soviet plans operated on similar terms, but Soviet planning could more easily accommodate a handful of large projects than the smaller transactions nonproject aid entailed. Indian economic officials intermittently sought to expand the compass of Soviet aid to include credits not for a specific use, but made no headway. Soviet interlocutors rebuffed everyone from midlevel officials to Prime Minister Jawaharlal Nehru, even when the request was framed as an attempt to reduce Indian dependence on Western aid. Yet these demurrals did little to stanch the flow of Indian requests. Soviet aid chief Skachkov came down particularly hard on diplomat T. N. Kaul, calling his request for nonproject aid a "violation of the principles of [Soviet] aid to developing countries." Undeterred, Kaul soon enough put the question to Aleksei Kosygin, receiving a similarly resounding rebuff, albeit in more diplomatic language. A visiting Indian delegation declared nonproject aid "the *highest priority*" for its visit to Moscow, preparing a twenty-six-page list of possible purchases with such aid—all to no avail. Soviet officials were far more welcoming of project requests, and Soviet aid helped remake Indian oil, manufacturing, and steel.[7]

Battling Big Oil via Vertical Integration

The case for Soviet aid for the Indian oil industry was a simple one. Visions of modern and self-sufficient India featured industrial behemoths; these had to be powered by products not readily available in India. Since the Industrial Policy Resolutions of 1948 and 1956 reserved minerals for the public sector, such plans awaited government initiative. A cadre of Indian officials sought to challenge the primacy of the global, vertically integrated Western firms known as the Seven Sisters, a goal readily supported by GKES. While Indo-Soviet cooperation in oil seemed a natural fit, many contingencies came into play. The individuals involved—especially longtime energy minister K. D. Malaviya—had a clear predisposition for government ownership, and indeed for the USSR more generally. Early Indian agreements with affiliates of the Seven

Sisters established in a dramatic fashion the hefty price of relying on foreign oil—and gave Malaviya plenty of ammunition for his argument for building a domestic oil industry.

The Seven Sisters' preeminence in India dated back to the colonial period, but a flurry of activity in 1951 continued, and even expanded, the firms' dominant place in India. Feeling an urgent need for oil, the Government of India signed agreements to have regional subsidiaries of the Seven Sisters build refineries in India. The Burmah Shell Oil Company and Stanvac (Mobil and Standard Oil of New York) agreed to build at Trombay, just outside Bombay, while Caltex (a joint venture of Texaco and Standard Oil of California) signed on to build a refinery on the east coast at Visakhapatnam. Boosters saw the agreements as part of a major expansion and redirection of the world's oil industry toward India—while others saw the refineries as a potential source of patronage and jobs, and lobbied accordingly. But even those responsible for the deals admitted that they were very favorable to the foreign companies in terms of pricing, taxes, and tariffs.[8]

Later oil deals further entrenched the advantage for the Seven Sisters. A 1954 agreement provided Stanvac with the opportunity to prospect in a very promising ten-thousand-square-mile area in West Bengal. Though the agreement provided a 25 percent equity share to the Indian government, it gave full managerial responsibility to Stanvac and allowed sufficient accounting loopholes that Stanvac could keep most of the profits but offload most of the risk. This prospecting agreement, the first in independent India, prompted controversy. Even the Indian civil servant who signed the agreement later acknowledged that it was "weighted very much in favor of the oil companies"; Indian officials were in too much of a hurry to press for a better bargain. This deal, however, opened up an intense debate within the Ministry of Natural Resources and Scientific Research. K. D. Malaviya, then a secretary in the ministry, began (in the words of an adoring biographer) to "elbow his way more and more" into matters of oil exploration. He criticized the Stanvac plans, in particular, for doing little to advance indigenous capacities in the oil industry. The young secretary exhorted the prime minister not to "give away our best known oil areas to foreigners," and called instead for a major domestic program of exploration under government auspices. Set against Malaviya, then as always favoring public-sector enterprise, was a network of Indian economic officials favoring the expansion of oil exploration and production in the private sector. Led by Morarji Desai, many Ministry of Finance staffers took this view; they were joined by some at the PC, and even one from the scientific wing of Malaviya's own ministry. Taken together, they provided a formidable challenge to Malaviya's vision, but the secretary had on his side the Industrial Policy Resolution of 1948. He also had the backing of Prime Minister Nehru.[9]

Such endorsements, however helpful, did not make the process automatic; oil exploration was a risky, capital-intensive business that required skills and equipment not readily available in India. So Malaviya sought out the expertise and financing necessary to "break the foreign monopoly" on oil. To do this, ironically, Malaviya looked overseas; he approached many governments, including those of the United States, Great Britain, and Mexico, for assistance in developing Indian oil. Yet the only expressions of interest came from the Cold War East—specifically from Romania, then the largest oil producer in Europe, and the USSR.[10]

Malaviya led a small Indian delegation to the Soviet Union in summer 1955, shortly after Prime Minister Nehru's higher-profile visit. He discussed arrangements for buying equipment for oil exploration, for sharing technical know-how, and for training Indian engineers and technicians. The delegation also stopped over briefly in the United Kingdom, but to discuss a much more circumscribed set of topics: purchasing some specialized equipment from British suppliers and hiring British technical personnel to work on contract in India. Much like Prasanta Chandra Mahalanobis's work with foreign economists, Malaviya arranged the visits to advance his cause. He reported that his delegation was impressed by what they learned of the Soviet oil industry and had invited a team of Soviet technical experts to India. At the same time, pro-Western Indian diplomats undercut Malaviya, bad-mouthing Soviet imperiousness and Romanian technology while favoring an agreement with Austria.[11]

Malaviya managed to evade the diplomats' opposition by inviting a Soviet delegation to India. During their tour in December 1955, the Soviet experts endorsed a broad mandate for the new public-sector Oil and Natural Gas Directorate. Disappointed by the Planning Commission's decisions, Malaviya took to the offensive, insisting that the proposed allocation for oil exploration was "wholly inadequate" and calling on the prime minister to overturn the PC's recommendations. But he (like Homi J. Bhabha) ultimately relied on the presence of Soviet experts to make the case. He invoked them to insist that the public sector—that is, his new directorate—get exclusive exploration rights.

PC members, sensing a challenge to their powers, fought back. Malaviya, however, was interested not just in more funds for his ministry but also in making India "oil-minded in a proper way," a task that required, among other things, increased PC allocations. The Soviet delegation thus provided plenty of ammunition for internal Indian disputes over the direction and management of India's oil policy.[12]

Once his directorate was created, Malaviya had two principal goals: to expand public-sector exploration and production, and to deepen ties with the USSR and the Cold War East. To a large degree, Malaviya's economic and political goals were compatible. He made the case that oil could prove more important for the Indian economy, and for Indo-Soviet relations, than steel—a bold statement in 1956, while the afterglow the Bhilai agreement shone brightly. Yet even for Malaviya, building ties with the Soviet Union was secondary to building up public-sector oil. Thus, while Malaviya negotiated broad technical and economic assistance agreements with Soviet and Romanian officials, other parts of the ministry pursued a mission of training with a variety of partners. Some 140 Indian technicians were shipped off to train overseas; their destinations included Czechoslovakia and Romania—but also North America and Western Europe. And even as his missions and missives did not yield new domestic resources for oil and gas exploration, foreign assistance from both Romania and the USSR provided for the import of advanced oil rigs and for the training of Indian technical personnel.[13]

Malaviya's second overseas tour, in autumn 1956, reflected his determination to expand what soon became the Oil and Natural Gas Commission (ONGC)— but also his openness to accepting help from all quarters. He led a delegation to the Canada, France, and the United States in order to compare public- and private-sector oil industries in those nations. He took to heart the advice from the chief of Gulf Oil, who encouraged Malaviya to integrate vertically. Malaviya operated similarly at home, inviting experts from all over the world to advise him on the technical, economic, and managerial aspects of the oil industry. He began with an invitation to Soviet experts, but when their trip was postponed he imported expertise from elsewhere. A pair of German experts produced a ranked list of possible sites for prospecting, for instance, as did engineers from the Institut français du pétrole. The newly reconstituted Ministry of Mines and Oil thus worked with a wide group of experts to expand the activities in the public sector, using funds and expertise from any willing source.[14]

A series of events in 1957 made that year a turning point for Malaviya's efforts to compete with foreign firms. Since Malaviya's boss (Swaran Singh, the minister of steel, mines, and fuel) feared collusion among the Seven Sisters, he stalled in approving their plans, thus confirming British worries of Indian "prejudice" against Western firms. Yet Malaviya's desire to create a vertically integrated public-sector enterprise also played a role; he hoped to use promising discoveries in Assam as leverage to wring concessions from the Western firms. Though Minister of Finance T. T. Krishnamachari (commonly known as TTK) did not necessarily share Malaviya's leftist leanings, the two did have a common antipathy of foreign oil firms. TTK rued that "we cannot at the moment get rid" of foreign firms but hoped at least to force them to refine Assam oil at the new Caltex refinery; this would minimize the strain on balance of payments. Western firms bluntly rejected such queries. Such maneuvers contributed to the steadily worsening relationships between the Indian government and foreign oil firms.[15]

Malaviya and Singh hoped that rapid progress in their own oil exploration would prove a greater threat to the Seven Sisters, imploring Soviet prospectors to emphasize speed above all. Arguing that "even one dry hole" could be politically "risky," the Indians were ready to temporarily abandon exploration in Assam when another site seemed especially promising. Meanwhile, Soviet geologists counseled patience in Assam. The time pressure also led Malaviya to work, once again, with all countries, not just with Romania and the USSR. His 1958 European tour, for instance, took him to Moscow (where he negotiated for the first Soviet-built refinery in India) and across Eastern Europe, but also to Italy and Switzerland, and he discussed possible refinery deals with American, Austrian, and Italian firms. Back in New Delhi, Malaviya explored an American connection, at least until the American ambassador quickly squelched any plans. And meanwhile he sought Austrian and Romanian deals; only when the former collapsed did he turn in earnest to the USSR.[16]

Malaviya's negotiations with the USSR revealed the interests and motivations on both sides. Intrabureaucratic conflicts were key: Malaviya's Indian critics complained that Soviet prices were unreasonably high. He defended the Soviet arrangement with a touch of pathos: "no body [else] helped us at a time when we wanted help." Meanwhile, GKES representatives agreed, accusing Soviet industrial enterprises of price gouging and ultimately winning the Indian side lower prices. Agreements on price, however, did little to ensure that production deadlines would be met. One Soviet apparatchik, trying to work around the continuing delivery delays, even raised the possibility of substituting American equipment for the held-up Soviet supplies. His comrades quickly and firmly corrected him. The two sides ultimately completed an agreement to build a refinery at Barauni in Bihar; it became the largest single item in the 1959 Soviet aid package for the Third Indian Five-Year Plan. Yet Soviet officials in India continued to worry that their compatriots in the USSR would not deliver; one geologist noted that the many delays and defects in Soviet equipment "attracted foreign companies" eager for new business.[17]

With the firm support of Soviet officials and scientists in India, Malaviya faced down significant internal opposition to his strategy of vertical integration. Planning Commission members had a bureaucratic concern: a vertically integrated enterprise, by virtue of its internal accounting, would wrest some control over its activities from oversight bodies like their own. The Seven Sisters had perfected using internal transfer pricing to reduce tax liability, and similar maneuvers could help public-sector enterprises maintain control over revenues. Others on the Commission pooh-poohed investments in oil, arguing that the carbon age was already in eclipse and the atomic age in ascendance. (Or perhaps that was just an excuse; the PC did not fund a major atomic energy program either, much to Homi J. Bhabha's frustration.) The issues came to the fore in a fight in the PC in November 1959 over allocations in the Third Five-Year Plan. Malaviya's ONGC received about one-third of its request for oil exploration, leading him to seek even more foreign assistance from all possible external sources, socialist or otherwise.[18]

Malaviya pursued collaboration with Western firms in an effort to speed the ONGC's vertical integration—advice he heard in the United States but now associated primarily with the socialist world. Indian oil might be socialist in orientation but could still be global in practice; the ONGC tried to convince American, French, and German firms to undertake exploration on behalf of the public sector. Meanwhile, at the next step up the vertical integration ladder, construction on the Soviet-financed refinery in Barauni as well as the Romanian-aided one in Gauhati continued apace through the early 1960s. Aware of this competition, Soviet diplomats in New Delhi tried to crack the whip on Soviet enterprises—as much as they could do so at long distance. Their immediate goal was again political: to provide physical instantiation of Soviet support for India. Meanwhile, Malaviya's opponents in the Indian government continued their attacks, demanding that the ONGC submit itself to standard budgeting and planning procedures.[19]

To fight against these internal critics while carrying on his battles against the Seven Sisters, Malaviya sought additional foreign aid. In 1960–1961 he explored importing Soviet oil to India to create what he called "regular competition" for oil. He pursued imports from Italy's government-owned oil enterprise as well. The lack of refining capacity, however, stymied such efforts. By the terms of agreements of the early 1950s, the privately owned refineries had the authority to purchase oil from whomever they wanted—meaning in most cases that they purchased only from other companies under the same corporate umbrella. Since the ONGC had no completed refineries of its own, it could not seal the deal to import Soviet oil. But Malaviya's Soviet gambit was not a total failure; shortly after the query, the Western firms relented and cut their prices.[20]

The Western firms' hardball tactics soon managed to unite in opposition Malaviya and his adversaries in the Planning Commission and the Ministry of Finance. When the cabinet appointed an Oil Price Enquiry Committee in 1961, Western observers saw the move, rightly, as a tool to attack the Seven Sisters. World Bank president Eugene R. Black criticized the cabinet for "putting prestige ahead of real need" and for "refusing to accept [the] productive capital" of foreign companies. The committee did not mince words in its criticism of the Western firms; it slammed the companies' secrecy about their own prices with a coruscating incredulity, accusing the firms of abusing internal pricing to enrich themselves. The committee recommended seeking immediate discounts on oil products in India and requiring Western firms to process Soviet crude. Western firms responded to this proposal by threatening to cut off all shipments to India. Indian officials took this threat as more than a negotiating tactic, and they quietly asked Soviet officials to backstop oil supplies should the Western firms make good on their bluster. Publicly Malaviya offered a counterthreat of his own: without a satisfactory solution, the Ministry of Oil and Gas would nationalize the Western firms. Privately, though, the ONGC offered a less extreme choice to the Western firms: either agree to refine Soviet crude oil or reduce prices. After lobbing their own threats, and lobbying hard for the status quo, the firms ultimately made significant price concessions in exchange for assurances that the government maintain its prior commitments not to nationalize them. Yet the conflict had set Malaviya and the ONGC on a new path: controlling the imports of crude oil into India rather than leaving such decisions up to the Western owners of the refineries.[21]

The Assam oil fields had the potential to help the public-sector Oil Corporation of India, but only if it had the means to refine the oil. Thus the plans for a second Soviet-built refinery, at Koyali in Gujarat, proceeded; the project would eventually be incorporated into the Soviet aid package for India's Fourth Five-Year Plan. While the state of Indian engineering precluded turning a refinery into a swadeshi facility (like Indian hopes for the Bokaro Steel Plant), the Koyali refinery was based primarily on Indian design work and initial engineering. One Indian official went so far as to boast (to a Soviet diplomat, no less) that Koyali offered a chance at "liberation from foreign dependence"— which included dependence on the USSR. Time pressures also created tensions between Indian and Soviet interests in building Koyali as a familiar story of Soviet delays and Western suppliers unfolded. When the delivery of Soviet cranes was delayed, Indian construction engineers purchased substitutes from England. The same phenomenon also appeared in exploration efforts, with the ONGC purchasing drilling platforms and heavy-duty cranes from Dutch firms. Indeed, as Indian exploration turned to the offshore site known as Bombay High, ONGC engineers considered Soviet equipment ill-suited for the task and sought Western technology.[22]

These troubles with Soviet-financed projects should not, however, undercut the overall effectiveness of joint Indo-Soviet efforts in the oil sector. Indian consumption of oil had tripled in the dozen or so years after 1954, with almost all of the increase supplied from the public sector. Even before the nationalization of the oil industry in the mid-1970s, the public-sector enterprises accounted for ever-increasing shares of oil production, refining, and distribution. In keeping with the high Indian priority on self-sufficiency, the oil fields exploited thanks to Soviet exploration (Assam and Bombay High, in particular) accommodated much of the increased demand. The various forms of Soviet involvement in the Indian oil sector—financing and building refineries, undertaking significant exploration, and later selling crude oil—all helped limit the market power of the Western firms operating in India.[23]

The Indo-Soviet relationship in the oil sector revealed some of the antinomies of economic self-sufficiency. Soviet officials made strong connections in India's expanding public-sector oil industry thanks to shared interests and commitments. But shared interests did not mean identical ones; the long-term goal for Malaviya was swadeshi, not Soviet, oil. In the early stages of the ONGC, these aims did not diverge much, but as the industry grew, new tensions emerged.[24]

Integrating Heavy Industry

Soviet aid to the Indian oil industry helped construct a vertically integrated public-sector enterprise that could challenge similarly organized Western firms. Even without such external challenges and threats, Indian economic policy favored a parallel integration in other parts of the economy, including capital goods industry—producing machinery and equipment for factories. Given the enthusiasm for heavy industry within GKES, Soviet officials followed up their assistance to the steel plant at Bhilai with other heavy industrial projects. Indeed, the two major Soviet economic assistance credits with India in the late 1950s had a strong concentration on heavy industry (37 percent of the funds) and oil / natural resources (42 percent).[25]

New factories required new equipment, so the Indo-Soviet agreement covered the government-owned Heavy Engineering Corporation (HEC). The substantial investments in heavy industry fit with the Nehru-Mahalanobis model of import substitution; without an HEC, the argument went, any effort at industrialization would drain investment capital and foreign exchange. Toward that end, Indian officials hoped that local companies would design the plant—though Soviet managers overruled them. The fact that the plant was in the public sector facilitated connections to potential users of its products, which were, by and large, also publicly owned. Thus Soviet and Indian managers alike noted with pride that the Durgapur and Ranchi factories would be supplying equipment for the expansion of the Bhilai Steel Plant during the Third Five-Year Plan. The decision to locate in Bihar put the HEC facility not just near supplies (like steel) but also close to potential customers.[26]

HEC built upon Soviet connections in Indian industrial ministries. Nehru seems to have been especially taken by the prospect—raised by a visiting Soviet apparatchik—that a heavy-machine building plant could be useful for the nascent Indian work in civilian atomic energy; the proposed site of Ranchi (Bihar, near West Bengal), was in a region rich in atomic materials. Ranchi was also near major industrial facilities like the British-aided steel plant in Durgapur; it was, furthermore, only about one hundred kilometers from Bokaro, the presumed site of the next public-sector steel mill. A group of Western-oriented ministers in the cabinet challenged this proposal, hoping instead to build four smaller plants dispersed around the country, not coincidentally near British-aided facilities. The principle of dispersion, in other words, was hard to disentangle from a call to expand Indo-British ties; by the same token, the principle of concentration—ultimately victorious—linked closely with those building Indo-Soviet ties. The international competition of development politics played out as domestic disputes over technical arrangements.[27]

When the Ranchi plant began production in late 1963, Indian attention turned toward obtaining orders for this newfound capacity. Indian bureaucrats hoped that HEC could supply the fourth steel mill at Bokaro and had made this a recurring theme in the negotiations; Bokaro, in other words, fell into Soviet laps just in time to provide a raison d'être for HEC's new plant. Soviet diplomats pressured HEC to draw up ten-year plans of production, an arrangement that favored public-sector firms (with their lengthy planning process) and might therefore keep HEC products out of the private sector. Soviet officials saw the expansion of public-sector heavy industry as an end in itself, focusing on the ability to supply steel plants. Indian counterparts, in contrast, were more likely to see public-sector industry as means to one of many ends—self-sufficiency above all.[28]

These two visions would clash again over the largest project of Indo-Soviet economic cooperation of the 1960s and 1970s: the Bokaro Steel Plant. Soviet officials justified the HEC plants they financed in Durgapur and Ranchi with reference, first and foremost, to the needs for of the expanding steel industry. Augmenting steel production required heavy industrial equipment that would in turn require additional steel. The Soviet case rested, in other words, on an integrated heavy industry sector that generated supplies (like metals) as well as demand (for finished equipment purchased for use in the plant's construction). It all worked well in theory but not necessarily in practice.

Bokaro, India's "Magnificent Obsession"

The steel plant at Bokaro became the capstone and symbol of this integrated public sector under Soviet sponsorship. Once the eight-year American effort to fund the Bokaro plant collapsed in fall 1963, the Soviet GKES quickly moved in. Though the Ministry of Steel and Mines had also invited bids on the project from Japan, the United Kingdom, and West Germany, it gave a leg up to the USSR. Even before the deal was consummated, Indian officials expressed optimism and gratitude. One toast to a Politburo member compared Bokaro to "Russian caviar, a good appetizer before a meal"; the main course would be closer Indo-Soviet economic ties.[29]

Negotiating a package for a large steel mill was, however, substantially more complicated than ordering caviar off a menu, and it soon stalled on the question of just how indigenous Bokaro would be. Indian officials emphasized their determination to make Bokaro their swadeshi steel plant while their Soviet counterparts sought to make Bokaro a monument to Soviet industrial might. These two broad visions came into conflict in many places—first and foremost in the question of who would design and supervise the construction of the plant. Many Indian officials promoted the Calcutta-based firm Dasturco, which had already produced the preliminary feasibility study back in 1958. Ambassador T. N. Kaul regaled GKES head Skachkov with paeans to Dasturco, not so subtly commenting upon Dasturco's importance "in the political sphere." Skachkov retorted that having a public-sector factory built under the supervision of a private firm was "a little strange." From the perspective of Indian negotiators, swadeshi was the overriding concern and the public-sector orientation simply the means to get there; their Soviet counterparts focused on public ownership above all. Dasturco's head, trained and employed in the United States until Jawaharlal Nehru recruited him to return to India, took the unusual step of offering to convert his engineering firm into a public-sector enterprise in order to keep the contract. But Soviet officials continued to assert their responsibility for all aspects of the project. Dastur took his case to Prime Minister Indira Gandhi, who "blew her top" in a cabinet meeting (in the words of American diplomats) but declined to argue Dasturco's case before the Soviets.[30]

Dasturco's travails were not just bluster over blueprints; the company revealed some of the core stakes for the Indian and Soviet sides. Even more than other projects, the Indo-Soviet conflicts over the construction of Bokaro became no-holds-barred battles. Senior managers at the Soviet enterprise tasked with producing many of the largest components for Bokaro accused Indian counterparts of trying to discredit the Soviets by repeatedly making requests of Soviet enterprises and then complaining when those were not met. Another executive successfully enlisted GKES representatives to get his Indian nemeses dismissed. Meanwhile, delays on the project mounted, quickly leading to even more mutual recriminations. Ships laden with equipment were held back in Odessa for problems with paperwork. Other equipment could not be shipped to the construction site because of a holdup in building a warehouse in which they could be safely stored. As delays mounted, the Indian director at Bokaro opted for a Potemkin mill strategy, pleading with Soviet officials to build some small structures, even if unimportant, to show progress and forestall any accusations that construction was delayed. He also filled both diplomatic as well as technical channels with a full-court press on GKES to get supplies delivered more rapidly from the Soviet Union. Indian managers' level of desperation suggests not just the desire to minimize the delays—but also an acknowledgment that delays would undercut their own position as well as the broader case for public-sector heavy industry.[31]

In some cases, Indian executives went beyond the agreement itself rather than face further delays and additional criticism from those skeptical of the public sector. As with the Bhilai plant, electrical equipment remained a particular concern; when such equipment was not available from the USSR, Bokaro Steel Ltd. arranged with General Electric as well as a Swiss firm to obtain the necessary supplies. Similarly, after Soviet and Indian public-sector enterprises proved unable to deliver freight cars that met the specifications, Indian managers anointed a firm in the massive Tata conglomerate as supplier by default.[32] As with Bhilai, the conflict between Soviet and Indian sides over supplying the plant revealed different priorities: Soviet engineers favored their equipment to showcase Soviet superiority and public-sector enterprises to demonstrate their effectiveness. Meanwhile, Indian officials were quicker to look to Western firms and to private Indian firms to get the goods they wanted. The USSR was making a statement; the Indians were building a steel plant—even to the point of using privately produced equipment to demonstrate the effectiveness of the public sector.

Another source of delays demonstrated the dangers of the joint Indo-Soviet strategy of linking Bokaro to other Soviet projects in India. From the start of negotiations over Bokaro, the project planned to use equipment produced by the HEC. Other supplies would come from Soviet-built factories in Durgapur (mining and related equipment) and Hardwar (heavy electrical equipment). The design was elegant from both economic and political standpoints: purchasing the products of these plants would reduce the foreign-exchange needs for Bokaro while at the same time highlighting both Soviet beneficence and Indian self-sufficiency. Yet the elegant linkage also had its vulnerabilities, as

Skachkov and his GKES staff soon discovered: when problems emerged at these factories, they held back the flagship Soviet project. Problems and delays at Bokaro accumulated over 1967 and 1968, starting from Ranchi and spreading outward—prompting pilgrimages to the site and complaints by both Soviet ambassador and by Indian and Soviet construction chiefs. The delays at Ranchi were almost incomprehensibly large: the plant was supposed to produce about 82,000 pieces of metal equipment weighing 29,000 tons, but had delivered only 1,200 pieces weighing 500 tons. And delays for mining equipment—destined for public-sector mines—were even worse: equipment deliveries totaled only 100 tons of the 16,000 tons expected.[33]

Despite the growing problems in the public sector, both the Soviet GKES and the Indian Planning Commission remained officially committed to five-year plans and to heavy industry in the public sector. The economic cooperation agreement of December 1966 bore out this claim, with the bulk of Soviet credits devoted to expanding Soviet-built facilities (Bhilai and Bokaro steel works, power stations, etc.) and continuing Soviet assistance in oil exploration; new projects included an aluminum smelter, some iron mines, and a fertilizer facility, all under government ownership.[34]

Even such a firm commitment to the strategy of an integrated public sector did not in and of itself improve its performance. As delays at HEC's Ranchi plant sent Bokaro engineers looking for equipment from other sources, HEC lost the chance to sell to other heavy industry facilities, depriving the firm of its intended market as well as its raison d'être. One skeptical observer, in fact, argued that the expansion of Bokaro was intended as much to make use of newly built heavy equipment plants as it was related to the production of steel. K. D. Malaviya confirmed this when he told a journalist that the future of his enterprise lay in Bokaro's construction (then under way) and its future expansion. Bokaro, he said, would "take care" of HEC's orders for the foreseeable future—suggesting that Bokaro served HEC as much as the other way around.[35]

The HEC delays thus had two effects on the Bokaro plant construction. First and most obviously, tardy deliveries set the steel plant's construction off schedule—eighteen months and growing by 1968. And second, efforts to avoid further delays by purchasing equipment elsewhere cost HEC some of the sales that it had been counting on—and for which it had been built in the first place. The pitfalls of integration were growing clearer. The first blast furnace, for instance, was completed almost three years late, and the cold rolling mill—a core reason for building Bokaro in the first place—lagged a remarkable six years behind schedule.[36]

Even if the schedule did not work out as planned, the Bokaro plant scored better on meeting Indian goals for self-sufficiency. Bhilai was mostly built with foreign components; Indian supplies accounted for only one-fifth of the plant's structure, and as little as one-twentieth of specialized materials used in the foundries. The Bokaro plant marked a sharp contrast, with 95 percent of the plant structure and over half of the foundries supplied from within India. In obtaining domestic supplies, Indian managers were happy to look beyond the public sector, as they had at Bhilai. This was especially true in the equipment used in the construction of Bokaro: plant records indicate that almost half of the Indian supplies were purchased from private-sector firms. Bokaro thus hewed closer to the Indian vision of a swadeshi steel mill than to the Soviet vision of a public-sector steel mill.[37]

Observers at the time and since have fit the financing and construction of the Bokaro Steel Plant into varied narratives, from a heroic epic of building the first swadeshi steel mill to sweeping criticisms of the futility of the public sector. Such broad views, of course, situate Bokaro into long-running arguments about economic development in Nehruvian India and after—debates that have hardly waned a half century after Nehru's death. Yet close examination of the process of construction suggests alternatives to these sweeping narratives. The tensions over building Bokaro, the failed American effort as well as the Soviet one, indicate the ideological stakes in economic aid programs. Though some U.S. economic officials pursued a private-sector plant more energetically than others, the legislative branch proved the greatest obstacle. Soviet officials, though immune from any kind of parallel obstacles, nevertheless responded with staunch ideological positions; they offered vigorous challenges to Indian efforts to rely on private-sector firms, though they could not prevent such purchases.

The project at Bokaro reveals, finally, both the promise and the problems of building an integrated public sector. Soviet and Indian officials hoped that the linked projects would create a positive feedback loop: public-sector steel plants would supply the heavy industry plants (also in the public sector), and the expansion of steel would provide a market for the output of plants like Ranchi. Yet this virtuous circle could turn vicious: problems at Ranchi could endanger the whole sector by leaving the steel expansion to purchase supplies from private firms, Indian or otherwise. This turn of events threatened the prestige and even the position of some of India's most influential proponents of the public sector—especially as performance came under attack not just from those skeptical of the public sector but even from Soviet sponsors.

The Indian Public Sector under Attack

The extravagant delays at Bokaro, the HEC, and elsewhere in the public sector fueled growing criticism within Indian economic and political circles. These debates constituted just the latest front in ongoing battles over the form and fixtures of the Indian economy. Faltering public-sector performance contributed to the three-year "plan holiday" between the conclusion of the Third Plan (in March 1966) and the start of the Fourth Plan (in April 1969), though of course it was hardly the only factor. In spite of her general sympathy for the public sector, Prime Minister Indira Gandhi reconstituted the government's Administrative Reforms Commission expressly to evaluate its efficiency. The commission's report on public-sector undertakings, released in October 1967, recommended extensive reorganization, seeking to devolve both authority and responsibility downward to the enterprise level; as the commission chair put it, "The best way to enable an undertaking to be run with the greatest efficiency is to confer on it the maximum possible autonomy and hold it accountable for performance." Accountability would be reinforced, according to the report, by creating an extensive network of audit agencies and by strengthening the Bureau of Public Enterprises. *Economic and Political Weekly* shared this view and used choice words to make the point: one editorial prescribed "a controlled degree of brutality" to overcome "flabby" management in the public sector. Through fall 1968, Congress Party organs, as well as the Cabinet and the Planning Commission, debated these proposals to improve the Indian economy, with a particular focus on its burgeoning but bogged-down public sector.[38]

But just as Planning Commission members joined these debates, they faced additional challenges to their power and prestige. In 1968 the PC was intact and was still chaired by the prime minister though it had already suffered setbacks that circumscribed its role. The foreign-exchange crises of the late 1950s marked an early victory for the Ministry of Finance in the supervision of everyday economic activity. During his brief premiership, Lal Bahadur Shastri placed the PC at further bureaucratic remove from the prime minister—and from centers of power. He created ancillary planning bodies, including a Business

Advisory Council, that diluted the impact of the commission proper. Indira Gandhi, whose sympathies lay closer to the ideas of the PC, further contributed to its marginalization. The commission faced sharp criticisms about its priorities, its privileges, and even its "intellectual bankruptcy." Prime Minister Gandhi promised to "revitalize" it intellectually by shunting it to the political margins. Following the recommendations of the Administrative Reforms Commission, Gandhi turned the PC into an expert advisory body without any "executive" responsibilities for managing the economy. These changes index the weakening of institutions at the center. Key allocation decisions devolved to the Indian states, which received union money in block grants to be used for a wide range of purposes.[39]

What had once been the hallmark of Indian planning—the powerful role for the center—gave way to decentralization and to new forms of conflict; in the words of one observer, "planning became a process of competition and struggle over resources, goals, strategies, and patronage without an overall design, a piece of patchwork rather than a coherent structure." Plans and planning continued after the three-year "holiday" of 1966–1969, but even those tasks once entrusted to it—investment allocation decisions within the public sector—faced new obstacles. The reconfiguration also left the PC ill positioned to continue its once prominent role in discussions of external economic aid—a role its members, especially those with Soviet contacts, relished.[40]

The Soviet Challenge

In that context the mounting Soviet criticism of the Indian public sector must have been particularly unwelcome. Such criticisms emerged from a longer-term broader reconsideration of its aid, and also as a more immediate response to local Indian conditions. Only a few years after the era of economic cooperation began, Skachkov identified some of its potential political risks; delays and defects in Soviet-supplied material, he warned, could create not just economic but also political problems for aid recipients in the Third World. Such doubts, as initially expressed, focused on headaches of relying on a Soviet system that was rigid and inefficient. But over time it also called into question the very premises of Soviet aid—that it would be helpful to the extent it could reproduce Soviet-style economies elsewhere. Soviet scholars, removed from the daily drama of supply crises, began to express similar doubts about the ideological certainties that had brought the USSR into the foreign aid arena in the first place. A May 1963 economists' *diskussiia,* for instance, revealed how much Soviet faith in the public sector had diminished; even R. A. Ul'iankovskii, the doyen of Soviet Indology, rejected the optimistic views of the public sector dominant only a few years earlier. The public sector still had value, to be sure, but it was not a cure-all: "not all undertakings in the state sector," a leading Soviet scholar observed with understatement, "operate satisfactorily and profitably." Another participant in that diskussiia questioned both the economic and political benefits of relying on the public sector. Ultimately, he argued, what mattered was not just who owned a given enterprise but whether it could increase production. As the public sector faltered, its flaws shaped Soviet theories of foreign aid.[41]

Skepticism about Soviet activities in the Third World extended from practice to theory. An undercurrent of Soviet analysis on east-south relations in the early 1960s called into question the benefits of Soviet aid on either political or economic grounds. These reached the highest levels of Soviet rule when Leonid Brezhnev led the Politburo putsch against Nikita Khrushchev in 1964. The bill of particulars included harsh words about the "chaos" (*proizvol*) reigning in this sphere: "an absence of thoughtful political steps [or] an account of effectiveness" had given free rein to "the subjective wishes of Comrade Khrushchev." As a result, Soviet budgets were overstretched and the Communist Party was unable to provide the "necessary" improvements in Soviet citizens' living conditions. Aid could continue, Brezhnev and his coconspirators insisted, but only along a "strictly political line." While Khrushchev exuberantly imagined a bright future for world socialism, and was ready to spend his way to get there, Brezhnev emphasized "actually existing socialism" and domestic stability. The influential head of the Oriental Studies Institute emphasized a similar theme, complaining about the lack of "socio-economic and political accounting" of aid to the Third World, let alone "determination of what the outcomes [*rezul'taty*] were for us." He singled out the Bhilai project for special criticism, asking what the "advantage" was for the "world revolutionary process." This new search for political or economic payoff in Soviet–Third World relations was joined to the Soviet push for efficiency and productivity in the domestic economy as well as in those economies receiving significant aid.[42]

Soviet views of India also reflected the economic slowdown in the USSR and the efforts to overcome it. The so-called Kosygin reforms of 1965 called for a major overhaul of Soviet economic planning and policy in the interests of improving efficiency. The reforms maintained the overall structure of central planning but shifted important powers and responsibilities down the chain of command. The key economic unit, once the ministry or the republic, now became the enterprise itself. Enterprise directors like factory heads had more autonomy but also new responsibilities; enterprises were held to account in terms of productivity and profits, no longer just production. This imperative also applied to wages; bonuses would be tied to increases in productivity at all levels: enterprise, shop, and individual worker. The pursuit of economic efficiency came through decentralization, reversing earlier approaches.[43]

When Skachkov and his GKES colleagues arrived in India, they carried the baggage of domestic reforms. They soon arrogated for themselves the role of economic advisers on a wide spectrum of issues, at times going well beyond the elements aided directly by their organization. Much like Western officials used nonproject aid to expand the compass of their inquiries into Indian economic policy, Soviet aid officials used the travails of the Indian public sector to claim a similar role. The advisory role began with small-bore operations questions and expanded into "technical management questions" like wage structure, bonuses, and the like. After 1965 such commentary accelerated and expanded. In the aftermath of the Kosygin reforms, the Soviet Foreign Ministry instructed its diplomats in India to dedicate themselves to "increasing the economic efficiency" of the factories built with Soviet assistance. They expressed—with no apparent irony—the hopes that Indian public-sector enterprises could learn from the Soviet experience. Skachkov used a visit to India in late 1966 to see how well this message was sinking in. He complained that Indian ministries and enterprises were slow to adopt Soviet-style reforms to improve efficiency (*effektivnost'*). The reforms even led Skachkov and Soviet diplomats to seek out closer ties to the Indian private sector, which they considered a bastion of relative economic efficiency. A Soviet economist touring India in early 1968 cataloged the growing troubles of capital accumulation and profitability (*pribyl'nost'*) in India's public sector. The mid-1960s, then, saw a sea change in the language of Soviet advice. The public sector was no longer sacrosanct, an end in itself. "Productivity" (*proizvoditel'nost'*) became a new buzzword. And wage incentives and bonuses were seen as the best route to productivity. Soon enough the term "profit" (*pribyl'*) joined the lexicon.[44]

During a trip to India in November–December 1968, Skachkov put heavy pressure on his Indian interlocutors to straighten out the public sector; he sought not just to improve the Indian economy but also to maintain the Soviet position in India. The prime minister's private secretary P. N. Haksar warned his boss that the GKES chief had arrived in a "very troubled and even agitated state of mind." Skachkov intimated to Haksar, whose economic ideas were inclined toward the public sector, his own "dark forebodings" that a conspiracy was afoot in India to make Soviet-built projects look bad and thereby undermine Indo-Soviet friendship. Over the years such rumors had floated around from many Indian sources, including Malaviya's successor at the Oil and Natural Gas Commission. In the same vein, Skachkov blamed the poor performance of the Bhilai Steel Plant on "partisan" civil servants who favored the private sector. The stakes, he warned, were high: without drastic improvements, he told the Minister of Industry, the entire public sector in India would be "discredited"—and Soviet prestige would suffer a similar blow. Skachkov's mood was hardly improved by the sight of economist D. R. Gadgil, then deputy chairman of the Planning Commission, arriving in a Boeing jet for a tour of Soviet-built facilities.[45]

Haksar reassured Skachkov of his government's desire to improve the Indian public sector and to follow Soviet recommendations in doing so. Skachkov and his colleagues obliged by providing detailed and sharply critical recommendations. Visiting the Bhilai Steel Plant, he excoriated Soviet advisers about a workforce that had "no interest in working"; Skachkov's proposed solution (lifted from the Kosygin reforms) was to restructure wages in order to "stimulate productivity." In speaking with finance minister / deputy prime minister Morarji Desai, Skachkov blasted the low levels of productivity, complaining that far too many workers were doing far too little work. Soviet experts also levied more general criticism about the inefficiencies of Indian enterprises, and demanded that the ministries invest more authority in the enterprise managers—a solution proposed both in the Kosygin reforms and by India's Administrative Reforms Commission. The language of profit and profitability peppered the conversations. The Soviet delegation had a clear and consistent plan for India's economic future—one that echoed in many ways the optimistic plans for a brighter Soviet economic future.[46]

Soviet criticism also addressed the core problem of the Indian public sector: excess capacity (or perhaps insufficient demand). Unused capacity for capital goods stood at a respectable 14 percent in the early 1960s, but soared to 34 percent in the late 1960s and to 40 percent in the early 1970s. Skachkov expressed dismay that major public-sector enterprises had idled some of their production lines because of a lack of orders. Many of the heavy industry projects had been built to maximize interconnection, but these connections amounted to a kind of dependence; once the construction projects had taken place, or after engineers at Bokaro had turned to alternative suppliers, the HEC had trouble finding other purchasers. Skachkov drilled home this point to the Indian minister in charge of steel. Soviet projects like Bhilai and Bokaro were essential capstones to the heavy industry strategy—and were not just dependent upon HEC but essential to its existence.[47]

Given that the problems with the integrated public sector were related to its very integration, GKES economists took a comprehensive approach to promoting change. Toward that end, they sent a thirty-five-page list of recommendations to improve the "economic effectiveness" of Soviet-sponsored factories in India; labor relations, management, inventories, and manufacturing processes all came under the Soviet microscope. The document was, no doubt, received gratefully and graciously by the Indian ministries. In subsequent years groups of Indian managers and engineers traveled to socialist countries in order to improve management techniques and labor relations; what Indian public-sector enterprises could learn from Eastern European labor relations was left unspecified. The overall effect, however, was to expand the ambit of Soviet advice regarding the Indian economy. Much as the American "push" toward nonproject aid ultimately gave U.S. officials license to comment upon overall Indian economic aims, so too did the events of the late 1960s provide Soviet counterparts with an equivalently broad license.[48]

Indian managers, meanwhile, persisted in seeking alternative solutions to the demand problem. The reliably pro-Soviet and pro–public sector K. D. Malaviya, long departed from the Ministry of Oil and Gas but in 1968–1969 serving a brief term as HEC chairman, serves as a case in point. While the Soviet GKES, along with its Czech counterpart, had provided the financing and technology for the HEC plant's construction and expansion, delays in designing and installing rolling equipment from these sources led HEC managers to evaluate other options, including purchases from American firms. Soviet officials joined with Malaviya to sideline such efforts, demanding that HEC stick with Eastern European engineers and suppliers. Malaviya's struggles with the Ministry of Steel shows the internal divisions within Indian officialdom. Some in the industrial ministries saw a public-sector HEC as the way to industrialize India quickly and were happy to purchase the goods they needed from whatever seller they chose. Others, including Malaviya, used their connections to the Soviet Union to promote the socialization of the economy, building up the public sector as an autonomous element of the Indian state.[49]

Trade as a Form of Aid

As public-sector travails deepened, Malaviya also called on the Soviet Union to help with another HEC problem: creating a market for its products. The extensive delays had sent potential customers, including other public-sector industries, in search of other suppliers (much as what had happened to HEC itself vis-à-vis delayed Soviet supplies)—and thus reduced the firm's potential market. Malaviya and sympathetic ministers and planners raised the problem of excess supply with Soviet interlocutors in 1968, offering specifics about railway wagons and other Indian manufactures that might make suitable exports to the USSR. Skachkov arranged for Soviet ministries to purchase as many as twenty-five thousand Indian railway wagons over five years, the largest effort to use trade to solve the problems of Soviet-aided plants. But the possibility of solving problems of Soviet-aided projects through trade would soon get fuller exploration.[50]

The turn to trade came from unexpected quarter: the industrial ministries that had long favored import substitution and heavy industry. They expressed a kind of "export optimism"—an unrealistic one—in proposing trade as the solution to demand problems of the Indian public sector. Many Indian proponents of the public sector had expressed wariness about foreign trade in general. Soviet aid could be a boon to Indian self-sufficiency by changing India's place in world trade flows; in the words of one Indian diplomat, only with Soviet aid was there "the possibility of creating and developing an independent national economy for India." Soviet aid officials shared that view, arguing that Soviet aid for Indian projects was designed to build the basis for economic independence. The foreign-exchange constraints of both nations encouraged a kind of barter arrangement: Indian imports from the USSR would be matched against Indian exports to the USSR so that on net there would be only negligible flows of currency from one country to another. Soviet trade officials, furthermore, preferred to work within the parameters of a multiyear trade agreement, which fit naturally into the Soviet planned economy; this had the added advantage of privileging large Indian public-sector enterprises, also organized around long-term (if long-delayed) production plans. Thus trade, aside from its core economic functions, promised political benefits; as one Soviet official declared: trade could be an "important means of the future development of political relations between the Soviet Union and India."[51]

At the same time as both sides found advantage in trade deals, they had to reckon with conflicting interests. Yes, Soviet and many Indian officials sought to liberate India from dependence on the West. But after that they diverged, with Indian officials seeking economic independence full stop while Soviet counterparts could accept a dependence that shifted eastward. Soviet scholars and officials often proclaimed their interest in helping ex-colonies achieve economic independence, though their recommendations and goals were most often about integrating India (and other trading partners) into a world socialist economy. They railed against Western arrangements of free trade as "nothing more than an attempt to conceal the dependent position" of the underdeveloped nations and the "economic domination" of developed ones. They envisioned a world economy in which Third World nations would continue to export primary goods—but to the USSR. Academic R. A. Ul'ianovskii oriented his recommendations for agrarian reform in terms of the ability of Indian primary products to compete in international markets. While he and his colleagues may have criticized the West's "colonial" relationship with nations like India, they had little different to offer.[52]

India's bilateral trade with the USSR was in many ways typical of Soviet–Third World relations. By one tally, almost 70 percent of Soviet imports from those nations were primary products and about 60 percent of nonmilitary exports to those nations were machinery, iron, steel, or oil. The principal Indian exports to the Soviet Union were commodities and agriculture products, with tea, iron ore, raw hides, and jute at the top of the list; these four alone accounted for about half of Indian exports; other commodities pushed the overall share of raw materials to over 90 percent of total trade volume. Conversely, Soviet exports to India were almost entirely finished products such as equipment and metals. Typical was the Soviet scholar who, after offering a ritual denunciation of the "international capitalist division of labor," sang the praises of the "international socialist division of labor." Given the patterns of Soviet trade with India and other Third World nations, outside observers might be forgiven for being unable to distinguish between these two concepts.[53]

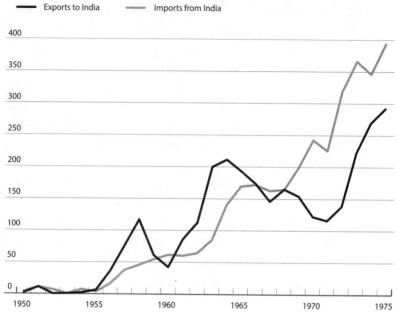

Soviet Trade with India, 1950–1975

Source: VTSSSR, various years.

When Skachkov in late 1968 heard Malaviya's proposals that Indian public-sector enterprises sell their products to the USSR, he was not thinking of the long-term construction of the international socialist division of labor but about the short-term problem of finding purchasers for the products of Indian heavy engineering enterprises in the public sector. And selling Indian industrial goods to the USSR would help solve his problem. Just before his departure from New Delhi in late December 1968, Skachkov agreed to reduce the barriers for exporting Indian industrial products—at least those from the Soviet-financed enterprises—to the Soviet Union. The bureaucratic barriers fell away, but economic ones remained; Soviet trade negotiators—who did not share GKES's vision of what trade could accomplish—declined to pay competitive prices for Indian industrial goods, in some cases offering less than the costs of production. Indo-Soviet trade was thus subject to extensive dispute within Soviet economic organs as well as between the two governments.[54]

Soviet trade was becoming a solution to problems of Soviet aid. Soviet imports from India increased sixfold over the 1960s, and India's share of Soviet imports doubled—though ending only at under 2.5 percent of total Soviet imports. But even as the amount of trade grew, and as the balance of trade began to shift in India's favor in the late 1960s, the composition of trade changed only slowly. As Skachkov had promised, Soviet imports of Indian machinery increased dramatically, peaking in 1971. Yet other trade increased as well, so that foods, raw materials and textiles still accounted for 80–90 percent of imports from India. Soviet exports did not keep pace with imports, allowing India to begin to repay the level loans then coming due.[55]

This increased trade, however much celebrated in the Soviet Ministry of Foreign Trade, worked at cross-purposes with GKES. Most primary products like jute, spices, tea, wool, and leather were produced outside the public sector. Other Indian exports—consumer goods like shoes, textiles, and handicrafts—were likewise produced in sectors dominated by private firms. Thus the Ministry of Foreign Trade's goal of expanding imports from India came at the expense of GKES efforts to isolate India's private enterprises.[56]

Growing Military Cooperation

The state of Indo-Soviet economic relations also had to account for military sales, which accounted for a rapidly increasing portion of bilateral flows of goods. While such sales dated back to the early 1960s, the Indo-Pakistani War in September 1965 marked a watershed in Indian military procurement. The subsequent aid cutoff from the West abruptly ended the brief but intense period of American involvement that had begun during the Sino-Indian border dispute of 1962. British officials intended to weather this storm and hoped that Indian purchases from the United Kingdom would bounce back once the "irritation with the West" and "euphoria towards Russia" dissipated. If the respective moods of irritation and euphoria faded, however, the general tendencies did not: the Soviet Union quickly became the dominant supplier for the Indian military—especially for its air force and navy. The British remained important suppliers for the army, and the United States all but disappeared. Soviet arms transfers to India edged British transfers by about 10 percent in the early 1960s, but by the end of that decade Soviet transfers were about triple those of the British. The Indian military drew most of its sustenance from the USSR, which accounted for over 80 percent of Indian arms imports for the decade starting in 1967. For the Indian Air Force in particular, procurement from the USSR boomed, as the air fleet incorporated hundreds of Soviet fighters and fighter-bombers. (British fighters still remained part of the air force plans, though in smaller numbers.) The Indian Navy, too, took the preponderance of its submarine fleet and torpedoes from the USSR. A steady stream of military agreements during the mid-1960s turned into a flood by the late 1960s—nine between 1968 and 1970 alone. These agreements covered more than one hundred fighter jets, two hundred tanks, plus torpedoes, artillery, radar, submarines, and much else. The Soviet Union sent at least twenty-two hundred military personnel to train and repair such equipment, with a handful more arriving from the people's republics of Eastern Europe.[57]

The expansion of the Indo-Soviet military relationship did not come at the cost of economic aid. When visiting Moscow in November 1965, after all, TTK heard Kosygin toast both India's military and economic strength. Kosygin demanded total secrecy regarding any military supplies—trying to keep Sino-Soviet tensions from escalating, but at the same time depriving those most enthusiastic about Indo-Soviet relations of publicity to help their cause. Once the conversations on military aid were completed, TTK used the occasion to seek additional economic aid. He mentioned a possible aid package from the Western Aid-India Consortium, explaining that it would come with hefty demands, including the enforced promotion of "free enterprise"; "surely," he threatened Kosygin, "you do not want us to accept this offer."[58] The threat helped inspire Soviet generosity for its major 1966 economic cooperation agreement with India. Soviet economic aid during the turmoil of late-1960s India kept moving along well-established project-by-project lines enshrined most recently in the 1966 agreement that covered a range of public-sector industrial projects for the Fourth Plan.

The changing balance of Soviet military and economic aid for India reflected a larger trend. In the late 1960s, Soviet military aid quickly caught up with, and in many years surpassed, economic aid not just in India but around the Third World. With the exception of 1962 (which saw massive deliveries of Soviet weapons to Cuba in the buildup to the Cuban Missile Crisis), Soviet economic aid had far outpaced military aid to the nonsocialist world. In the late 1950s, for instance, Soviet economic aid to the Third World dwarfed military aid by a factor of six or more; a similar ratio appeared as late as 1966. But in 1967 Soviet

military aid for the Third World exceeded economic aid, and would continue
to do so in most future years. By 1979 the ratio had almost reversed. The Soviet
Union, whose economic practices had inspired so many in the Third World,
was in the middle of its shift to becoming an armory for the Third World. This
global trend played out—indeed in many ways had begun—in India.[59]

By New Year's Day 1969, after Skachkov's mission had left a burned-over district in the halls of the economic ministries in Udyog Bhawan, Indo-Soviet
economic relations looked very different from what they had been a decade
earlier. Soviet economic hopes for India were in disarray. The Indian public
sector, a top Soviet priority, was under harsh criticism not just from Indian free
marketeers but even from Indian economists and officials long sympathetic to
the Nehruvian approach of public-sector heavy industry—not to mention from
Soviet aid officials themselves. Skachkov and his colleagues, to be sure, were
not interested in privatizing Indian enterprises, but they expressed many of
the same criticisms of those factories and ministries that could be heard from
the increasingly restive Indian opposition. Such criticisms, joined to Western
calls to overthrow the so-called permit-quota-license raj allowed some public-
sector enterprises to make their own economic decisions. These policies, in
turn, undercut the claims about the superiority of central planning by pushing
authority and responsibility down to the enterprises; if enterprises were acting
as their own centers of profit and loss—language found increasingly in Soviet
commentary—then what purposes did central planning serve?[60]

The growing criticisms of the public sector, furthermore, suggested that the
Indian strategy of building a public sector was reaching a point of exhaustion.
The rampant delays, woeful inefficiencies, and growing national concern about
the public sector in general increasingly drew fire from those who had been
its fiercest supporters, both politically and financially. So just as the laggard
performance of public-sector enterprises increased the stress on the political
system, changes to the central economic apparatus left it poorly equipped to
improve performance. In addition, searching questions about those enterprises
limited the possibilities of a unified political response. By the late 1960s growing turmoil in the public-sector enterprises and those who supported them
reduced the capacity of Indian economic organs to steer national policy. This
reduced capacity coincided with growing economic and political crises that

required more engagement—at the exact moment when the political system was itself debilitated. Development politics, then, weakened the political apparatus just as new challenges emerged.

The trajectory of Soviet aid to the Indian public sector in the 1960s reveals the difficult position of Indian economic policy makers—especially of those enamored of the Soviet example. The right wing of the Congress Party and critics outside Congress continued their criticisms of public ownership, joined by unlikely allies from GKES. Thus the Soviet victories in aid competition that had piled up in the 1950s and 1960s—from the steel plant at Bhilai to the HEC facilities at Ranchi and Durgapur, to oil exploration in Assam and the refinery at Barauni—did not have the desired political or economic effects. Even as Soviet-financed enterprises bolstered the Indian public sector, the sector itself came in for harsh criticism at Soviet hands. And the growing delays of projects like Bokaro and Ranchi went a long way to doing just what Skachkov had feared: discrediting those who shared the Soviet vision of India's economic future. Poor performance, combined with Soviet criticism, undercut the position of pro-Soviet and pro–public sector individuals and groups within India. The only bright spots on their horizons were the growing military relationship and the prospects of expanded trade. Whether these would be sufficient to improve Indo-Soviet ties remained an open question in late 1968.

CHAPTER 9

INDIA'S DOUBLE CRISIS
AND THE PRICE OF AID

A fall 1970 meeting between Indian prime minister Indira Gandhi and U.S. secretary of state William S. Rogers inadvertently summed up the state of their countries' bilateral relations. According to Indian notes from the meeting, the prime minister complained about "a large number of USAID officials who were floating around Delhi going from Ministry to Ministry and suggesting changes in policies, and even in the objectives of our development." The American notes on the meeting, meanwhile, expressed a mixture of condescension and consternation. They recorded that the prime minister "made oblique and unspecific accusations" about "U.S. interference in India's internal affairs"; Rogers's efforts "to elicit specific charges," the American notes continued with a schoolmarm's smug impatience, "were unavailing." This brief misunderstanding—an inability even to agree on what they were disagreeing about—symbolized a larger shift in Indo-American economic relations. Within a few years of this otherwise forgettable conversation, American aid to India had changed in scope and structure. Gone were the days of funding technical assistance or capital projects; in their place came negotiations over financial transfers in the form of nonproject aid or, increasingly, debt relief. Meanwhile, both sides paid unprecedented (and perhaps undue) attention to the prospects of bilateral trade.[1]

As American aid to India was financialized over the course of the early 1970s, Soviet aid was militarized. Soviet delegations still came to India to celebrate the behemoths of Indo-Soviet cooperation in heavy industry. But they offered no new aid packages for an entire decade after their 1966 agreement, which funded industrial projects in the Fourth Five-Year Plan. Meanwhile, deepening problems in the Indian public sector, the main prompt for the unpleasant visit in late 1968 by S. A. Skachkov, chief of the State Committee for Foreign Economic Connections (Gosudarstvennyi Komitet po Vneshnim Ekonomicheskim Sviaziam), led to increased Soviet criticism of the overall direction of the Indian economy as well as the exploration of new forms of bilateral economic relations—especially trade. But the headline story was military aid; Soviet military equipment arrived in India with ever-increasing frequency and in increasingly larger amounts over the late 1960s and early 1970s.

The transformations of Indian aid relationships with the superpowers, undertaken in an effort to promote Indian economic growth, ultimately accomplished little on that score. Average per-capita growth during the Fourth Plan period (1969–1974) clocked in at only 1.2 percent, an improvement over the corresponding figure for the crisis-filled Third Plan (1961–1966) of 0.3 percent but anemic compared with, say, South Korea's rate of 8.7 percent. Economist K. N. Raj referred to this low figure as the "Hindu rate of growth," as if it reflected an essential Indianness. Though agricultural production expanded as capital-intensive approaches took hold in some regions, the troubled heavy industrial sector weighed on overall growth figures. A rapidly expanding population diluted the economic gains that did take place.[2]

The political impact of the changed aid relationships weakened the ability of the Indian government to respond to the era's crises in electoral politics—what political scientist Atul Kohli termed India's deepening "crisis of governability." This crisis had its origins in the changing landscape of electoral politics and Congress Party structures—not in India's relationships with the superpowers—but development politics eroded the ability of the political system to respond in at least two ways. First, the separate enclaves of support for different aspects of the Indian economy, which had been growing through the late 1950s and early 1960s, contributed to the general tendency toward "deinstitutionalization" that marked Indian politics in the era of Indira Gandhi. Second, the transformations of the late 1960s and early 1970s—American financialization and Soviet militarization—limited the opportunities for resolving the economic crises using outside support.[3]

The tumultuous events of the early 1970s represented the fruits of development politics. External aid relationships became flash points in the crises of the late 1960s, starting with devaluation promoted by the West in 1966 and continuing through the Indo-Soviet Treaty of Peace, Friendship and Cooperation in 1971. Struggles for political power took the form of disagreements over economic policies between entrenched groups within the ministries. The changing nature of Indian politics, furthermore, placed external pressures on a public sector that could not even handle its own internal strains. India's aid relationships had contributed to these problems and were ill suited for providing solutions. Soviet aid—in India as across the Third World—came to focus increasingly on the military dimension. American aid, meanwhile, underwent its own streamlining to focus increasingly on financial dimensions, ultimately symbolized by the expulsion of the large U.S. Agency for International Development (USAID) mission in New Delhi. The changed dynamics of aid competition, furthermore, meant the end of the initial phase of the economic cold war. After 1975 finance and trade came to dominate discussion of north-south relations, a process visible in India as elsewhere.

The Public Sector and the "Double Crisis" in Economics and Politics

The travails of the Indian public sector shaped what political scientist Francine Frankel called India's "double crisis" of the late 1960s and early 1970s: economic stagnation and political instability. The fruits of development politics had created a substantial presence of Soviet-supported contingents in the industrial ministries and public-sector undertakings, contributing to the ongoing fragmentation of politics and administration. And the economic performance of the public sector contributed handily to the economic stagnation that hung over the whole era. Heavy industry, Jagdish Bhagwati and coauthor Padma Desai wrote, performed at a "dismal" level, with negligible returns on capital in spite of years of heavy domestic and foreign investment. Some of the most prominent enterprises like the Heavy Engineering Corporation (HEC) and Hindustan Steel ran consistent losses or barely made it into the black. Labor costs depressed profitability of public-sector enterprises, which generally paid higher wages for unskilled work and employed more workers than comparable private-sector firms and yet faced more labor stoppages than their counterparts in the private sector. The rising levels of labor unrest and organized movements in the countryside combined to paralyze West Bengal and other regions, with national economic and political effects.[4]

The state and the fate of the public sector became common touchpoints in the political battles of the mid- to late 1960s—battles that raged at first within the Congress Party and eventually across parliamentary and electoral politics more broadly. Long-standing divisions over the structure as well as the aims of the Congress Party festered without Jawaharlal Nehru as a guiding force—or at the very least, as a mediator. State party leaders joined in a powerful informal group known as the Syndicate to promote their interests during the succession battles after Nehru's death (in May 1964) as well as that of Lal Bahadur Shastri (in January 1966). The Syndicate's rise tracked the growing power of state leaders within the party at the expense of the union government in New Delhi. It tried to shape the post-Shastri succession that pitted Morarji Desai, who had already contested unsuccessfully in the post-Nehru succession, against Indira Gandhi. Led by Tamil politician and Congress Party president K. Kamaraj, the Syndicate acted for reasons having little to with economic ideas or policies but sought a weak union government in New Delhi that would leave power in the states.[5]

Within months of Gandhi's ascension to prime minister in January 1966, internal Congress battles soon played out in the sphere of economic policy and economic aid, most notably over devaluation. On the one hand, Morarji Desai (then between cabinet positions) and Indira Gandhi agreed about the need for devaluation, but disagreed about most everything else.

Thanks in part to the powers of persuasion of T. T. Krishnamachari (commonly known as TTK), Kamaraj opposed devaluation. When the prime minister made the decision without formally consulting party leadership, Kamaraj was incensed. Aside from the economics of the issue, the Congress president was aghast that the decision was made without him. He organized two meetings of party officials to castigate the decision to devalue—and especially the prime minister who made it. Criticisms of devaluation came fast and furious and were intended to score political points, as if (in the phrase of one journalist) "every harsh word was meant to be a stiletto pointed at Mrs. Gandhi." Contemporary reports suggested that the rupee devaluation had "devalued [the] political authority of the Centre." Yet the issue ultimately demonstrated the strength of the Centre and its prime minister over the states; even if Kamaraj rued his decision to support Gandhi in January 1966, he had no opportunity to rescind it six months later. One well-connected journalist called the episode a "watershed" in relations between Congress's president and its prime minister.[6]

The Congress Party's very poor showing in the general election of February 1967 escalated the dispute between the center and the states, and between the prime minister and the party president; it ultimately transformed the Indian political system. A number of divergent opposition parties shared the slogan "Congress Hatao" (Remove Congress). They met partial success: Congress lost control of eight state legislatures and had its slimmest-ever majority in the union Lok Sabha. Many Congress stalwarts lost their seats, including pro-Western officials like onetime food minister S. K. Patil and Syndicate leader Kamaraj. In the postelection finger-pointing, Indira Gandhi came in for tough criticism and had to compromise on a number of personnel decisions. She reluctantly acceded to the appointment of rival Morarji Desai as finance minister and deputy prime minister. What contemporary observers had called the "Congress System," in which most of the major policy debates took place *within* the Congress Party rather than *between* Congress and other parties, gave way to a system that had disputes both within and between parties.[7]

The prime minister, aided by her personal secretary P. N. Haksar, tried to convert Congress from a parliament of Indian opinion into an ideologically consistent party. And the former diplomat Haksar's predilections, honed in radical circles of Indian students in Depression-era London, were toward the left. His sharp tactical instincts gave those views added influence, as Haksar quickly sought to marginalize or expel figures on the Congress right; Morarji Desai sat at the top of that list. Toward that end, the prime minister circulated a ten-point economic plan that Haksar drafted shortly after the election, a plan heavy on left-oriented and / or populist proposals, including a call for land reform, increased economic regulation, and the nationalization of banks and insurance companies. Congress leadership expressed doubts about the public sector, at which point Indira Gandhi doubled down; she stressed the value of the public sector for helping attain self-sufficiency. "Many countries were trying to influence India," she argued, and only more investment in the public sector could free India from external meddling, especially from the West. The public sector could be both economically and political advantageous; the prime minister celebrated its contribution to broader national purposes not reducible to double-entry bookkeeping, even as she hoped to improve its profitability.[8] She made the case for the public sector at a Congress Party gathering, using the forum to appeal to those at the bottom of the socioeconomic ladder. Her speeches functioned brilliantly for this purpose, even as they provided only limited policy guidance. This was one step in the deinstitutionalization of Indian politics, relying more on the charisma and the power of individual politicians than on the party apparatus upon which they had once relied.

Internal disputes consumed the Congress Party for two years after the 1967 elections in ways that brought economic issues—and especially the troubled public sector—to the fore. As a result of the increasingly intense political and personal disputes within Congress, the prime minister relied heavily on votes from the non-Congress left in Parliament, including but not limited to the Communist Party of India. She told one journalist that her move to the left was not a sign of her true commitments but an effort to "take the wind out of the sails of the Communists," arguing that she was working to "contain" communists and to ensure that India did not "go red." In any case, the leftward turn helped her establish a parliamentary alliance with the Communist Party and simultaneously boost popular support. At the urging of her top advisers, Gandhi turned her personal battles into ideological ones, bringing (in their words) her "own ideological image directly to the people." As her struggle to maintain her place atop an increasingly fractious party continued, she stuck with the advice of Haksar and others to "convert the struggle for personal power into an ideological one." Along the lines of her Ten-Point Program of 1967, the prime minister put forward some "Notes on Economic Policy" in 1969 that promised more of the same, calling in particular for the strengthening of the public sector. On flimsy grounds of respect for Morarji Desai's own predilection for the private sector, she stripped him of the Ministry of Finance portfolio, precipitating his resignation from the deputy premiership. Soon thereafter she maneuvered a split within the Congress Party, turning her Congress (R) faction into its own party. Not invoking the public sector directly, Gandhi and her supporters nevertheless portrayed her faction as a force "for Socialism, for change" as against her opponents' preference "for the status quo."[9]

Though the prime minister invoked the public sector as a pretense for firing Morarji Desai, her interest in it went beyond this purpose; it also became an important electoral tool. In a speech to Congress leading up to the party split, for instance, she cited the value of the public sector in "removing regional imbalances"—in other words, locating new industries in poorer areas of the country with the admirable goal of reducing inequality, but at the same time placing such considerations above economic factors like transportation links and resource endowments. Her discussions over a new public-sector steel plant, for instance, seemed directly responsive to political alignments. Similarly, soon after the nationalization of banks, branches sprung up all over rural India, physical manifestations of the prime minister's commitment to the rural population that did not rely on party machinery.[10] As one economist later observed, the public sector, which had expanded for "ideological" reasons in the 1950s, had become a source of "autonomous economic"—not to mention political—power in the 1960s.[11]

The end result of these electoral and party machinations was the renewed importance of the public sector as a political resource at the same time that the mechanisms for controlling the public sector's economics withered. The Planning Commission had lost any decision-making authority; its members included more economists but fewer with any political sway. Soviet sponsors of the Indian public sector began, especially after Skachkov's 1968 trip, to distance themselves from it so that its problems would not damage Soviet prestige.

The Militarization of Soviet Aid

Skachkov devoted more time in his 1968 trip to identifying the problems with the Indian public sector than seeking bold new programs. This time allocation reflected the lack of any new aid packages after the 1966 agreement to support public-sector industrial projects for the period of the Fourth Five-Year Plan (originally slated for 1966–1971, but ultimately in effect 1969–1974). In the same period, though, Soviet military aid to India increased dramatically. Transfers increased by about 75 percent between 1963 and 1964, and by another 60 percent between 1964 and 1968. Soviet military sales to India in 1968 and 1969, in fact, exceeded British arms sales for the whole period 1960–1967. These military sales agreements stepped up dramatically in 1968–1969, thanks to both regional and bilateral concerns. Increased arms sales helped placate Indian officials' anger over Soviet decisions to sell weapons to its archrival Pakistan— though sales to India dwarfed those to Pakistan by a factor of eight or more.[12]

Military aid could serve as diplomacy by other means. Soviet diplomats hoped to use the growing military relationship to sway their Indian counterparts to sign a bilateral friendship treaty. On a brief trip to Delhi in early 1969, for instance, the Soviet minister of defense, General Andrei Grechko, used the promise of Soviet support as an enticement for India to consider enshrining this arrangement in a treaty—a proposition regarded warily by even the most sympathetic Indian diplomats. Through spring 1969, Soviet officials kept up pressure for an Indo-Soviet treaty; one Indian diplomat wearied by such requests concluded that the Soviet side was "extremely keen that we should enter into such an agreement." Ambassador D. P. Dhar responded enthusiastically to this news, beseeching his foreign minister for permission to proceed. The prime minister's secretary, P. N. Haksar, saw these approaches as an excellent chance to sanctify closer Indo-Soviet ties with a treaty—especially if it contained a security guarantee against China. Meanwhile, Foreign Secretary T. N. Kaul, whose long stint as ambassador to Moscow left him particularly open to warmer Indo-Soviet ties, saw the Soviet initiative as an important opportunity. Taking note of the escalation of Sino-Soviet tensions—to the point of shooting on their shared border—Kaul recommended "cashing in" on the Soviet offer; a treaty would be a small price to pay for access to more sophisticated aircraft and weapons. As Soviet prime minister Aleksei Kosygin kept up the pressure on his Indian counterpart through the spring of 1969, Kaul's advice loomed large in Prime Minister Gandhi's thinking. She made desultory and abstract comments about the treaty's language, but spoke at length and in loving detail about India's defense needs. At the same time, though, she declined to push ahead with the treaty, brushing aside the draft texts provided by Kosygin and his compatriots and ultimately ordering Ambassador Dhar in Moscow to listen mutely to any Soviet entreaties; she explicitly denied him the authority to negotiate about any kind of pact. The Indian prime minister apparently calculated that Soviet authorities were sufficiently determined to conclude a pact that they might provide weapons over the course of negotiations over the treaty—meaning that she might be able to obtain military materiel without actually signing a treaty at all.[13]

Gandhi's approach had the added advantage of not forcing a decision within the divided diplomatic corps. Internal critics of an Indo-Soviet treaty argued that it would mean a rejection of the long-standing Indian posture of nonalignment. In response, Haksar underscored that the treaty under discussion would be about "friendship and cooperation" rather than a formal alliance; the treaty, he continued, would not restrict Indian freedom of action in the international sphere. Besides, he maintained, India could similarly conclude a similar treaty with any other nation in the world, most certainly including the United States. For that reason, he suggested, the treaty could be a means of obtaining military supplies without signing a military pact. As the Indian foreign service went into a holding pattern, Haksar successfully fended off (albeit with increasing annoyance) a steady stream of queries from the Soviet ambassador in New Delhi; each time he tried to steer their exchanges from talk of a treaty to concrete needs for military equipment. Haksar's goals were clear; as he wrote Ambassador Dhar in Moscow, "We have no repeat *no* other source of supply than to rely upon Soviet readiness to understand and respond to our needs"; that statement was attached to a lengthy list of such needs, ranging from tanks to bombers to carrier-based fighters.[14]

As these discussions unfolded, American diplomats considered the implications of the steady flow of Soviet weapons and materiel. All in all, American intelligence analysts and desk officers agreed, closer Indo-Soviet military ties were better than any of the alternatives. The growing connections reflected the Soviet interest in securing India against China and saved the United States from the constant frictions that came with providing weapons to both India and Pakistan. Even the high-profile sales of Soviet ships and submarines to the Indian Navy, American diplomats reassured each other, would not compromise American interests in the region.[15]

For much of the late 1960s the focus of Indo-Soviet economic relations was upon improving the Indian public sector and especially its greatest problem child, the HEC's large plant at Ranchi. His half-hearted protestations to the contrary, Skachkov worried that Soviet prestige was riding on a solution to the HEC's failings. He explored a variety of different efforts to save the Indian public sector. On a trip back to India in 1970 to celebrate the fifteenth anniversary of the Bhilai agreement, Skachkov signed off on Soviet financing for the expansion of the Bokaro Steel Plant, finally making good on aid promised in 1966. It was likely not the passage of time but the HEC's problems that prompted the agreement; without the expansion of Bokaro, one Soviet report predicted, the machine-building plant at Ranchi would have a completely empty order book within a matter of months. Even new Soviet projects, then, were as much about keeping old public-sector projects like the HEC on life support. On that same trip, Skachkov also agreed to a second strategy to bolster demand for the Indian public sector: tripartite agreements by which GKES could finance third-country purchases of equipment from the HEC and its sister enterprises. For the next few years these efforts would become part of ongoing Soviet aid negotiations with Iran, Turkey, and other countries.[16]

Though these demand-oriented efforts for the most troubled segments of the Indian public sector continued, Indo-Soviet economic relations focused increasingly on bilateral trade rather than aid. Both sides had made rhetorical commitments to increased trade over the prior decade; from 1960 to 1968,

Indian exports to the USSR increased by a factor of 2.5. The preponderant share (about 95 percent) of Indian exports, though, remained primary products. Trying to change the composition, and not just the quantity, of trade, one delegation of Indian planners went to Moscow to agitate for the export of Indian manufactures. Citing the increasingly industrial character of the Indian economy, the delegates demanded a "new framework of industrial cooperation" between the two countries. The question of foreign exchange weighed heavily on the Indian delegation, which noted that about half of Indian exports to the USSR went to cover payments on past development loans. The delegation proposed reducing that figure by increasing the export of Indian manufactured goods to the Soviet Union.[17]

The combination of Soviet dissatisfaction with the Indian public sector and Indian dissatisfaction with bilateral trade led to a form of "aid through trade." Soviet officials began to arrange purchases of goods from Indian heavy-industry installations that suffered from excess capacity. The Soviet-built Mining and Allied Machinery Corporation, for instance, predicted excess capacity of 25 percent or more within the next four years, and even those figures included some dubious "likely orders." One sympathetic journal editor wrote Skachkov calling for more Soviet purchases: "We are just like soldiers fighting in the battlefield—and we are fighting YOUR battle," she exhorted; to win it, and to quell doubts planted by "vested interests," Indian public-sector undertakings needed more sales. Indian diplomats took a subtler but no less insistent tack: they continued their pleas for aid, but also proposed that they could boost Soviet-aided industrial installations by exporting such products to the USSR. Indian attempts to organize "aid through trade" were not limited to the Soviet purchase of products of Indian heavy industry, or to prospective joint ventures in third countries. The Indian ambassador in Moscow, D. P. Dhar, tried to arrange for Indian processing of Soviet cotton into textiles that would then be reexported to the Soviet Union. In promoting the plan Dhar exhorted his Indian colleagues to contemplate the "vast potential [of the] Soviet market."[18]

The focus on trade did mean the abandonment of pursuing aid. Indian diplomats attempted yet again to steer GKES toward nonproject aid, arguing that even enhanced Indo-Soviet trade could not solve India's economic woes. Indian trade officials argued that Indian needs in the Fourth Plan era went increasingly in the direction of fertilizers and petrochemicals, areas in which the "sophisticated machinery" that India required were "not readily available" in the Soviet Union—thus, nonproject aid would be most useful. Meanwhile, the rapid expansion of the Indian industrial sector, thanks in large part to Soviet assistance, meant that the goods that Soviet organs wanted to provide were increasingly being produced in India. Indian utilization of the large Soviet package from 1966 lagged in dramatic form, as delays in construction and operation meant delays in drawing on Soviet financing.[19]

The answer, Indian diplomats argued, was to shift the form and nature of Soviet aid, moving away from "complete projects" toward nonproject aid—to shift from sales of equipment to materials, spare parts, and commodities that could feed India's industrial sector. This move would have brought Soviet aid more closely in line with aid from the World Bank–sponsored Aid-India Consortium, which increasingly took the form of financing for maintenance imports rather than full projects. Yet such efforts met the same fate as their predecessors' attempts. Discussions about Soviet aid continued very much along the same project-based lines as they had since the Bhilai agreement of 1955.[20]

Failing to achieve any progress on nonproject aid, Indian trade officials settled for a new and expanded trade treaty—the preferred Soviet modus operandi. The schedules of goods for trade differed from prior agreements; the list of Indian exports, for instance, led off with "machinery and equipment manufactured at industrial enterprises built in India with the assistance of the USSR," including the railway wagons that Skachkov had earlier offered to purchase. Most of the remaining fifty-some items were primary products (e.g., tea and spices) or products of light industry (e.g., shoes and garments). Soviet officials talked about a bright future but could not shake off past patterns.[21]

By the start of the 1970s, then, Indo-Soviet relations had undergone significant change, including increased attention to military supplies on the one hand and to trade on the other. The tumultuous year of 1971, which began with Indira Gandhi's authoritative electoral victory and included the signing of a treaty that was a long time coming, ended with a major regional conflagration over Bangladesh. That year also saw an even more fundamental transformation of Indian economic and political relations with the other superpower.

The Financialization of American Aid

The shift of U.S. aid to India from project support (and a brief but intense episode involving military aid) to financial transfers materialized as a result of events in both nations. The drastic loss in prestige of the America lobby in New Delhi (the likes of B. K. Nehru and I. G. Patel) in the aftermath of devaluation, and the unfulfilled Economic Bargain proposed by U.S. secretary of state Dean Rusk, left American aid officials with fewer opportunities to sway Indian policy. The multilateral channel for influence had been significantly reduced, as the visit of World Bank president Robert S. McNamara in December 1968 confirmed. He faced a uniformly hostile reaction; even his erstwhile allies publicly berated the consortium's failure to meet the promises upon which devaluation was premised.

The changes in the Indian political landscape also played an important role. Indira Gandhi's political strategy to cement an alliance between the Congress left and the non-Congress left led to increasingly vocal criticism of American actions, especially in India and Vietnam. And in the United States, the election of Richard M. Nixon brought to bear a new vision of American relations with the Third World along with a substantial stock of his own resentments in Indo-American relations. Pushed into a narrower range of options, those in India and the United States favoring closer bilateral relations pursued a counterintuitive path of trying to reduce the intensity of those interactions on a day-to-day basis.

The India lobby hoped against hope that Indo-American relations could improve in spite of all of these countervailing factors. After Nixon's imposing electoral victory in November 1968, Ambassador Chester Bowles made the case for continued American commitment to India in terms of strategic importance, prior investment (which he calculated at $9 billion), and "simple morality"—this last, perhaps, a sign that he did not understand his new boss well. Yet even Bowles had to concede that all was not well in India; his economic reporting presented a generally troubling picture in which even the optimistic ambassador had to squint to find glimmers of hope.[22]

Bowles faced an uphill battle in the new administration. Nixon's skepticism about India ran deep and was directed precisely at people like Bowles. The new president thought that American intellectuals' "love affair" with India was a "prime example of liberal softheadedness." In the brilliantly understated phrase of National Security Adviser Henry Kissinger, Nixon "was less susceptible to Indian claims of moral leadership" than his Democratic predecessors had been. Nixon's experiences in South Asia had only confirmed these views. As Indian diplomats bitterly noted, Nixon had helped engineer the original alliance with

Pakistan in 1954 while serving as Dwight D. Eisenhower's vice president. He also took offense at his treatment in New Delhi during a world tour in 1967; Morarji Desai hosted an abstemious lunch (vegetarian and nonalcoholic) for Nixon—while Pakistani leaders feted him in a boisterous dinner soon thereafter. The visits did little to improve his view of India.[23]

While Nixon held a particular animus against India, his policies toward the world's largest democracy fit neatly with his worldview and broader foreign policy ideas. The Nixon Doctrine, announced incongruously at a refueling stop in Guam while en route to Asia, called for a new American approach to the continent, and indeed to the whole world beyond Europe. In its most basic form, the Nixon Doctrine marked a retreat from direct American engagement in Asian affairs; as the president put it in Guam, "we should assist, but we should not dictate." The doctrine soon enough came to encompass, at least in the abstract, an overall American posture toward the Third World: the United States would defer to regional allies rather than involving itself directly in their disputes. Well before Nixon issued a formal statement drawing out the implications of his nascent doctrine for foreign aid programs the following year, he aimed to reshape American aid, de-emphasizing bilateral aid, technical assistance, and project-based aid. India became an early arena for this new approach, which did not so much end the notion of aid as channel it into financial transactions.[24]

India made an early test case for the Nixon Doctrine in economic aid, since those most dedicated to close Indo-American economic ties had been working in those directions for their own reasons. Even Ambassador Bowles, ever the energetic proponent of all things Indian, contemplated the end of "the era of orthodox, projectized technical assistance." He cited the growing Indian reluctance to seek technical assistance, as well as the increased numbers of Indian experts qualified to undertake the sorts of advising that previously required importing foreign experts. Bowles continued to agitate for increased American aid to India, but called for aid to take the form of program (nonproject) loans; he also maintained his steadfast optimism that with one more round of generous funding India could be fully self-sufficient in a decade or less. But even on the final lap toward self-sufficiency, Bowles suggested, U.S. assistance should have a reduced footprint. For the India lobbyists, this meant not ending aid but channeling it into nonproject aid that would involve fewer Americans on the ground in India.[25]

Even before landing in New Delhi on the same world tour that started in Guam, President Nixon sought to make a distinctive mark on his policies toward India. He quickly approved a substantial package based on Food for Peace (PL480), in large part (as Kissinger put it) because it contrasted sharply with President Lyndon B. Johnson's approach. In many other ways, the Nixon administration continued business as usual. The president's briefing papers for the trip, for instance, included scripted exhortations calling on the Indian government to reduce military expenditure, expand family planning efforts, and continue investments in Green Revolution technology—familiar refrains carried over practically verbatim from the Johnson presidency. And an internal report called for using development aid to "press or help the Indian government toward more effective development policies."[26]

Upon landing in New Delhi days after his Guam announcement, Nixon set about implementing his new doctrine. The president and key members of his administration took pride in rising above the fuzzy and emotion-laden diplomacy that, they argued, had plagued their predecessors. Bowles's successor as ambassador, liberal Republican Kenneth Keating, set the tone when he told a British diplomat that it was time for Americans to "control the itch we feel to lean over the shoulders of Indian officials and tell them what to do." And a top official at the South Asia desk in Washington, D.C., similarly called on his colleagues to abandon to "great myth" of American influence in India.[27]

Indian officials espoused similar sentiments, calling for a new kind of economic relationship in general but making specific requests that were familiar if not hackneyed. In meetings with Henry Kissinger during the July 1969 presidential visit, for instance, top Indian advisers called for a reformulated aid relationship but at the same time sought continued PL480 food aid and nonproject economic assistance. The one novelty, or perhaps concession, was a newfound emphasis on "increas[ing] the commercial content" of Indo-American relations—that is, to focus on ways to increase Indian exports to the United States.[28]

The reorientation of Indo-American economic relations toward trade and financial flows and away from USAID-administered projects had to reckon with the legacies of prior American assistance. Almost all of the aid of the 1950s and 1960s came in the form of loans on concessional terms, meaning loosened underwriting terms, low interest rates, and relatively generous terms for repayment. As these loans came due in the mid-to late 1960s, Indian aid repayments to the United States and other lenders began to grow steadily.

External Aid vs. Debt Service

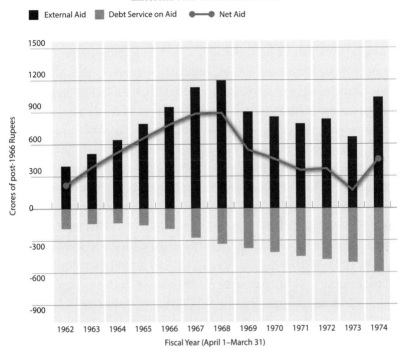

Sources: GOI Ministry of Finance, *Economic Survey, 1965–66* (New Delhi: Ministry of Finance, 1966), 42; GOI Ministry of Finance, *Economic Survey, 1969–70* (New Delhi: Ministry of Finance, 1970), 53; and GOI Ministry of Finance, *Economic Survey, 1975–76* (New Delhi: Ministry of Finance, 1976), 49.

Because American aid was shrinking, India might approach negative aid flows, in which it sent out more dollars to pay for past loans than it was receiving in new development financing. World Bank economists predicted a similar situation would soon emerge with other lenders in the Aid-India Consortium. Soviet aid, though denominated in rupees, also ran the risk of going negative—which would affect budgets but not foreign exchange. The question of repaying Soviet debts quickly became the source of political disputes between I. G. Patel and the World Bank and, domestically, between Morarji Desai and Indira Gandhi.[29]

A second and more convoluted legacy of foreign aid was the large and growing balance of American-owned rupees that accumulated through the PL480 program. The original PL480 legislation allowed for recipient nations to repay the United States in local currencies to protect their limited foreign-exchange holdings. It blithely anticipated that U.S.-owned funds would be used to pay for official U.S. government expenses (for instance, maintaining the embassy buildings, employing local staff, etc.) or for components of development projects, including a special program to support private-sector firms. In addition to the proceeds from the sale of grain to India, U.S. government receipt of rupees (an additional one-eighth of the proceeds) came under U.S. government control. U.S. spending of its rupees was a complex, even fraught, issue. Indian policy makers remained cautious of these funds because they feared U.S. leverage over India through its rapidly accumulating holdings of Indian rupees, but they also feared that spending those rupees would create inflationary pressures. John P. Lewis, before he had gone into government service, dismissed such concerns with the wave of a hand but little evidence: "We may be fairly sure that the United States government is not really going to own a third of the Indian money supply." Events soon disproved this optimistic forecast; in the last half of the 1960s American rupee holdings increased sevenfold, ultimately approaching $5 billion, or 40 percent of the Indian money supply. India topped the list of what one American report called "super-excess currency" countries. While the local currency problem was not unique to India, that nation did account for about half of the total PL480 funds owned by the United States.[30]

Reducing this massive stockpile did not come easily. The two earlier concerns (leverage versus inflation) were joined to two more wrinkles, each of which reflected tense bilateral relations. The uses for U.S.-owned rupees anticipated in the original legislation—local expenses for U.S. diplomatic representation or programs to bring American experts for technical assistance or educational purposes—each faced significant headwinds. Paying diplomatic expenses with PL480 funds would deprive the Indian government of dollar resources that the Department of State paid for the costs of U.S. representation—an ostensibly routine commercial transaction that in fact served as a form of disguised foreign-exchange relief. More problematic was the notion that U.S.-held rupees might pay for more foreign visitors. This notion had been a nonstarter since it was first broached in the mid-1950s; a substantial segment of Indian officialdom resented the size of the permanent American presence, so augmenting their numbers was hardly appealing.[31] By the time of Nixon's inauguration in January 1969, the USAID mission alone included 440 Americans, most of whom were serving on technical assistance missions. Another 1,300 Peace Corps volunteers were dispersed across India. Anti-American groups in India had longed raised the specter that visiting Americans were really CIA agents, accusations that had already led to the expulsion of the Massachusetts Institute of Technology's economic advising project a few years earlier.[32] A new round of revelations in 1967 documented covert CIA support for many nongovernmental and scholarly organizations, including the Asia Foundation; this news reverberated in India, attracting the ire of Indira Gandhi, among others. P. N. Haksar acknowledged his own increasingly "xenophobic" tendencies as he worried more and more about the "tentacles of U.S. foundations spreading far and wide." He stepped up his complaints about the "reckless" use of PL480 funds, citing in particular the "bitter pill" of American academic institutions opening study centers in India. Haksar also had his hand in a drawn-out controversy regarding a Soviet cultural center in left-leaning Kerala, the ironic and circuitous result of which was the closure of five American cultural centers. The results thrilled anti-American circles in India just as it frustrated pro-India circles in the United States. In that context, it is hardly a surprise that given the options of using the rupees to cover American in-country expenses, or especially using them to bring more Americans to India, the official Indian position was "none of the above." Secretary of State Rogers felt similarly, concluding that "problems abound whether we hold on to them or whether we try to use them."[33]

Others within the State Department, however, tried to address these problems head on, commissioning Raymond Saulnier, a conservative economist who had chaired President Dwight D. Eisenhower's Council of Economic Advisers, to resolve the rupee issue once and for all. The resulting report dwelled upon the technical details of the rupee problem in the way that only an academic economist could love, but ultimately proposed a mechanism for solving the rupee problem over the next decade. Without action, the report warned, the current balances of $4.8 billion would accrue interest so that the problem would last, according to Saulnier's careful calculations, "for something a little less than forever." The report proposed that the United States government use its rupee balance to cover local expenses (embassy, local employees, etc.), while also offering annual grants for development purposes. The agreement had something for everyone: it would cost the Indian government some of the foreign exchange it had previously received for embassy expenses, but only for a limited time. And the annual rupee grants would facilitate some development projects, minimizing the inflationary potential of such grants by spreading them out over many years. And most important, Saulnier's proposal would put an expiration date on a major and recurrent obstacle to closer Indo-American relations. Saulnier's report marked the first serious effort to solve (rather than just complain about) the excess rupee problem that had been growing over the previous dozen or more years.[34] Implementing the recommendations required Herculean efforts on the part of American and Indian negotiators over the next three years.

If the problem of PL480 rupees focused less on food and more on financial transactions, so too did a surprising change in the position of members of the America lobby who had been stalwart supporters of closer Indo-American relations. Many of the strongest Indian proponents of American aid programs emphasized their disagreements with, rather than their gratitude toward, American aid organizations. G. L. Mehta, who facilitated the rapid buildup of American aid during his stint as ambassador in Washington in the 1950s, expressed wariness about American aid, an attitude honed by the experience with USAID and the Aid-India Consortium a few years earlier. He called for "heart-searching" on the part of both donors and recipients, especially as recipients might feel pressured into "barter[ing] away their sovereignty and self-respect for a few quick bucks of aid."[35]

American diplomats heard from a number of their Indian counterparts—including those who sought aid from America—that they hoped to extricate India from dependence on unreliable donors, very much including the United States. Those skeptical about American aid expressed their views even more bluntly; the prime minister, for instance, told the visiting USAID chief that "foreign aid did not make a significant impact" on the Indian economy. The call to reduce American aid to India also, and more surprisingly, came from those generally enthusiastic about Indo-American relations. Washington ambassador L. K. Jha, for instance, talked of taking concrete steps to improve Indo-American relations—but doing so through reduced aid. Soon thereafter, he argued that the best way to deal with economic aid was to "agree on a program for phasing it out." Similarly, I. G. Patel called on American officials to review the deployment of American experts with an eye toward shrinking their numbers dramatically. He wanted India to "disengage ourselves from U.S. aid without necessarily complicating further the overall relationship with the

United States"—a very fine balance indeed. American diplomats readily agreed to this plan.[36]

A parallel process unfolded in American policy circles, where institutions and individuals long associated with expanding the American presence in India ultimately promoted reductions in aid personnel. For instance, Ambassador Keating agreed wholeheartedly with the call to reduce staff, connecting it directly to the Nixon Doctrine. Internal State Department studies, even those undertaken by analysts and diplomats firmly committed to aiding India, similarly recommended "a gradual and deliberate reduction of bilateral aid to India and of the number of USAID personnel in India." Such reports cited prominently the Nixon Doctrine's push to reduce the overseas footprint of the United States. By their dialectical logic, the diminution of aid would restore American ability to "exercise political influence" by reducing a source of frequent friction. Sharp reductions in technical assistance personnel reflected a similar effort to reduce tensions, and the report went so far as to suggest a staff reduction of 80–90 percent in relatively short order. Finally, the report offered a blunt calculation that improved Indo-American relations would be worth cutting down aid—even if those cuts slowed Indian economic growth. The fact that the recommendations to cut back on aid came from individuals and from quarters that had long been fervent supporters of aid to India marked a striking departure and a new element in the aid relationship.[37]

By early 1971, then, high-level groups within both the American and Indian governments began working toward a new basis for bilateral economic ties, this time denominated in dollars and rupees, not projects, experts, or commodities. Yet these efforts to reformulate Indo-American relations faced constant challenges from sources within the two governments. One area all could agree on—those who wanted to expand Indo-American relations and those who wanted to curtail them—was a reduction in the number of American personnel in India. Proponents of closer ties saw the staff reductions as a way of reducing tensions and providing less ammunition to anti-American forces. And opponents, of course, were glad to see Americans leave. By the first weeks of 1970, USAID officials were contemplating which projects would go on the chopping block to reduce the American presence. Yet this reduction did not necessarily mean that American aid efforts in India were winding down; they were just taking a different shape. As the cuts got under way, Indian officials underscored their openness to additional—financial—aid from USAID.[38]

The Electoral and Geopolitical
Transformations of 1971

The year 1971 saw an acceleration of India's changing aid relationships with the superpowers, a process that began with the December 1968 visits of S.A. Skachkov on the one hand and World Bank president Robert McNamara on the other. Prime Minister Indira Gandhi consolidated her political power by calling elections for the union government in the spring of that year. And brewing trouble to India's northeast—what would become the Bangladesh crisis—confirmed the changed relationships that the Indian government maintained with the superpowers.

The electoral changes came first, as Gandhi prepared for a general election in March 1971. Wary of the growing power of state and regional parties, she separated the election to union posts from that for state governments, with the latter deferred for a year; this complicated the efforts of the Syndicate, whose power lay especially in the states. Economic issues remained prominent in the Congress campaign, as she continued to invoke the public sector in her populist appeals. Her Congress (R) faction contested this election along the lines that Haksar had suggested earlier, providing an ideological gloss on what were otherwise struggles for power. Her opponents took the opposite tack, personalizing the electoral battles by criticizing her "personality cult" standing apart from party and state. Adapting the "Congress Hatao" slogan from the 1967 elections, they argued that the best opposition to Indira Gandhi's Ten-Point Program was "a one-point program: Indira Hatao" (Remove Indira). The deinstitutionalization of Indian politics had reduced election campaigns to a contest over personalities. Sticking to Haksar's guidance, the prime minister replied: while her opponents call for "Indira Hatao," she favored "Garibi Hatao" (Eliminate Poverty)—a vague slogan that served her populist purposes well, and was soon bolstered in the academic realm by pathbreaking studies of Indian poverty.[39]

The 1971 election was a referendum on Indira Gandhi's populist maneuvers, but also one that had important implications for the public sector. Her Congress (R) platform emphasized the public sector, calling for further nationalizations, including general insurance (a holdover from the Ten-Point Program of 1967); a greater role for state industries in general, and in the food sector in particular; increased state role in foreign trade; and restrictions on large private businesses. A large public sector, after all, proved politically indispensable; enterprises provided patronage to co-opt officials as well as a means of large-scale employment to shore up support in one or another region. Congress (R) won commanding electoral victories in New Delhi, regaining some of the ground lost in 1967. Gandhi's political strategy had proven itself successful, and had brought new attention to the public sector in the process.[40]

While the elections of March 1971 consolidated the prime minister's power in India, the political situation in Pakistan was headed in the opposite direction. A national election at the end of 1970 posed a fundamental challenge to the basic governance structures of Pakistan—structures that had grown increasingly fragile since the Partition of British India in 1947. That partition created Pakistan out of Muslim-majority territories in Bengal and Punjab. Partition was catastrophic enough, with massive population transfers as Hindus in East Bengal and northern Punjab fled to India while millions of Indian Muslims left for Pakistan. But further complicating matters was the fact that the two Muslim-majority territories that constituted Pakistan were noncontiguous, separated by a large swath of Indian territory. The distance between East and West Pakistan, furthermore, was ethnolinguistic as well as geographic: the bulk of the population in West Pakistan was Punjabi, while the bulk in East Pakistan was Bengali. Punjabis / West Pakistanis dominated the succession of unstable civilian and military governments of Pakistan, over time giving rise to a Bengali movement for autonomy in East Pakistan. After the 1970 election the growing strength of the Bengali movement prompted more assertive repression from the central government, including militarized campaigns that led thousands and eventually millions of Bengalis to flee from East Pakistan into the Indian state of West Bengal and neighboring states. The result was a humanitarian and political crisis. Pakistan accused India of not just harboring the East Pakistan resistance, but providing direct and indirect military support to the movement in East Bengal. President Nixon, never a friend of India or of Indira Gandhi, strongly favored Pakistan, and repeatedly excused or ignored accusations that the American-supplied Pakistan Army had mistreated the population of East Pakistan. He and Kissinger mockingly disparaged American dispatches from the East Pakistan capital of Dacca, including one alleging "genocide" that soon leaked into the press.[41]

Kissinger made a brief trip to India and Pakistan in July 1971, hoping to quell rising international tensions. Much of his daylong stopover in New Delhi dealt with Indian requests for emergency aid for the millions of refugees streaming into northern India, as well as defending himself from Indian criticisms of U.S. support for Pakistan. He and his Indian interlocutors also found common ground over the threat posed by China, with Kissinger promising that the United States "would take a very grave view of any Chinese move against India."[42]

Kissinger's next ports of call after Delhi, however, represented a radical and momentous departure. He left India for the Pakistan capital of Islamabad for a day of meetings. Though he called in sick the next day, in fact he played a daring form of hooky, sneaking to Beijing for top-secret talks with Chinese prime minister Zhou Enlai. Kissinger's dependence on the good offices of the Pakistani government gave him further incentive to soft-pedal criticisms of Pakistan's activities in the East. The fruits of Kissinger's surreptitious travels—Sino-American rapprochement—dramatically reshaped not just superpower relations but also South Asian regional politics.[43]

Indo-American relations became collateral damage in Kissinger's China gambit. Only ten days after his meetings with members of the Indian cabinet in New Delhi, Kissinger called in the Indian ambassador in Washington, L. K. Jha, to make clear that his blanket promise to help India against China no longer applied. Kissinger apparently told the Indian diplomat that "the United States Government would consider any Chinese invasion in India in response to any Indian action in the Bangladesh conflict as entirely different from the Chinese invasion in 1962, and that the U.S. Government would provide no support to India, either military or political, in that event." This new position carved out a significant exception in what had been a long-standing American guarantee to come to the aid of India in the case of a Chinese attack. Now such a guarantee would apply only outside the brewing Indo-Pakistani tensions over East Pakistan—in which armed conflict was, in Indian estimations, a distinct possibility. The question was not an entirely new one, as Ambassador Jha had worried about such caveats months earlier, only to receive vigorous reassurances from Kissinger. In mid-July, however, Indian diplomats in Washington and in New Delhi received confirmation from their sources about this new limit upon American support. In the aftermath of this conversation, P. N. Haksar tried to maintain equanimity about Sino-American rapprochement, but conceded that it would nevertheless be difficult for India to adjust diplomatically. This adjustment would entail, as the State Department analysts well knew, moving closer to the Soviet Union.[44]

For those like Haksar favoring closer Indian ties to the USSR, Kissinger's announcement, while worrisome, had a bright side: the evaporation of any internal opposition in reaching out to the Cold War East. Already those Indian diplomats favoring closer Indo-Soviet ties expressed increasing impatience for action—as did Soviet diplomats who pleaded that whenever Indian representatives were ready for a treaty, they "would not find the Soviet government wanting." D. P. Dhar in Moscow and P. N. Haksar in Delhi maintained steady contacts with Soviet representatives but preferred to focus on concrete military equipment rather than vague platitudes about friendship and cooperation. T. N. Kaul pushed for Indian action but was insufficiently persuasive or powerful to clinch the deal.[45]

Indian diplomats more inclined toward the West, meanwhile, sought to leverage the unrequited talk of an Indo-Soviet treaty into building bridges to the United States. They excavated a long paper trail about failed negotiations with the United States over the treaty of friendship and navigation, a sporadic exchange over the early 1950s that had petered out a dozen years earlier. Ambassador L. K. Jha argued that only by signing treaties with both superpowers could Indian nonalignment survive. Growing Indian dissatisfaction with American policy vis-à-vis Pakistan led many leading Indian diplomats to argue against an American treaty, which was quickly shelved.[46]

The Indian turn toward the treaty came with whiplash-inducing speed. Only weeks before, Foreign Minister Swaran Singh, who had replaced his unrelated namesake Dinesh Singh, spent a few days in Moscow dodging any talk of the treaty. That attitude dissipated as soon as Indian diplomats learned of Kissinger's gambit in China in July. Indian diplomats scurried to finalize the agreement that had been under sporadic and noncommittal discussion for the previous two years. D. P. Dhar, who had completed his stint as ambassador in Moscow, quickly returned there, this time with the authority to negotiate a final deal. Even as the two sides rushed toward an agreement, however, differences emerged. Soviet minister of foreign affairs Andrei Gromyko sought to bask in a public glow, proposing a state visit for Indira Gandhi, while Dhar tried to scale things down and speed them up. After Kissinger's mid-July declaration about the limits of American support for India against China, internal critics of the treaty were few; as Foreign Secretary T. N. Kaul told the prime minister,

Kissinger's message "has changed the whole perspective in which the Soviet proposal has to be considered." Citing the need for a "reliable friend" as troubles mounted vis-à-vis East Pakistan, Kaul insisted that there was "no alternative" to the treaty. Dhar used his time in Moscow to advance the treaty and also to push further requests for military aid. Toward that end, he requested that Gromyko bring along senior military and intelligence officials on his trip to New Delhi.[47]

Kaul also tried to preempt those foreign-policy experts who worried that the treaty marked the end of the Nehruvian posture of nonalignment. Kaul started with the insistence that the treaty "does not conflict with our concept of non-alignment," which was open to treaties with all nations. Indeed, Kaul argued that the agreement would give India "greater credibility in the world" and, somewhat less persuasively, that it would "increase and strengthen" Indian bargaining power vis-à-vis other countries." For months afterward, the pro-American contingents within the Indian Ministry of External Affairs made the dubious case that the Indo-Soviet treaty created new opportunities for rebuilding, even expanding, the Indo-American aid relationship.[48]

The Treaty of Peace, Friendship and Cooperation came into effect only days after Dhar's trip to Moscow. Gromyko quickly flew to New Delhi—without the military and intelligence officers that Dhar had requested—and signed the treaty with his counterpart Swaran Singh on August 9. The treaty invoked the grandest of principles and the broadest of good intentions, but ultimately contained few specific commitments on either side. The most important clauses obligated each side to stay clear of the other in armed conflicts; the parties agreed "not [to] enter into or participate in any military alliance directed against the other" or to allow "the use of its territory for the commission of any act which might inflict military damage on the other." Most notably, the treaty obligated the two parties to "abstain providing any assistance to any third party that engages in armed conflict" with the other; Indian officials hoped that this would curtail Soviet support for Pakistan should a new war with India break out. Should either party enter into armed conflict, the two sides called only for "mutual consultations"—hardly the most profound of commitments.[49]

Though originally the product of the pro-Soviet officials in the highest ranks of Indian government and foreign service, the treaty was greeted enthusiastically across the Indian political spectrum. T. N. Kaul, as foreign secretary the senior civil servant in the Ministry of External Affairs, concluded that the treaty marked a new stage of Indian nonalignment; his boss, Foreign

Minister Swaran Singh, was similarly enthusiastic. Kaul also boasted to the American ambassador that the treaty would lay the groundwork for a new kind of Indo-Soviet economic relationship along more equal lines; he cited in particular the prospects for a joint Indo-Soviet economic commission. Outside government, too, the treaty won wide praise. The Communist Party of India, not surprisingly, celebrated the treaty as a major contribution to peace and as a sturdy element of defense against Pakistan. Even a roundup by the skeptical *Times of India* included expressions of support from many quarters. One member of Parliament bemoaned the end of nonalignment but was "very happy we have at least one military ally on our side." Others focused on the treaty's deterrent effect vis-à-vis Pakistan. Congress elder statesman C. Rajagopalachari, a long-standing supporter of ties with the West and founder of the Swatantra Party that contested elections in the 1960s, similarly expressed "great gratification" about the treaty's potential to strengthen India's geopolitical position.[50]

Some members of the America lobby in India nevertheless continued their sharp opposition. Washington ambassador L. K. Jha shared his negative views on the treaty with American diplomats. He blamed, above all, Dinesh Singh, who had served as in senior foreign ministry roles through the 1960s, including a brief stint as minister of external affairs in 1969–1970. Jha insinuated that Dinesh Singh had been on the Soviet payroll. Ambassador Jha also criticized Haksar, whom he considered "very much under Soviet influence," as well as Foreign Secretary Kaul. He speculated wishfully to Kissinger that Haksar was already "on his way out" as a result of the treaty, and that Kaul was likely to follow. Jha placed his hopes in a backlash from the treaty that would remove the major sources of pro-Soviet foreign policy from the top ranks of the Indian government. Thousands of miles away, Jha could entertain such hopes. A few of his accusations had echoes in New Delhi; S. K. Patil, the pro-Western former minister of food and agriculture, for instance, claimed that Indira Gandhi's appointments were subject to Soviet approval. Meanwhile, top military brass in India sought to sow Indo-Soviet discord through leaks to Western journalists that described the Soviet Union as desperate to strengthen ties in spite of opposition within the upper echelons of the Indian government. The battles between civilian and uniformed leadership got play even a decade after V. K. Krishna Menon's unceremonious ouster in 1962.[51]

Indian hopes to use the treaty to expand military aid came through clearly. As T. N. Kaul put it to Indologist R. A. Ul'ianovskii and other Soviet functionaries, the treaty "had solemnized our friendship and cooperation," but only expanding military relations could invest it with "real content and meaning." A steady stream of high-level military delegations—seven in 1972 alone—soon provided such meaning. The treaty, in other words, though not a formal military alliance, emerged out of and contributed to the militarization of Soviet relations with India.[52]

American Aid after 1971: Financialization and Trade in "Mature" Relations

Though some portion of the America lobby in India approved of the treaty, American officials took a more skeptical view; the treaty proved a great obstacle, and even greater distraction, to Indo-American aid relations. For one thing, it put the India lobby in Washington on the defensive, making it harder to justify continued American aid to a country that had just declared its commitment to "friendship and cooperation" with the Soviet Union. Though startled, some optimistic American diplomats did not panic; they saw the treaty as a "dramatic demonstration" of the current state of Indo-Soviet relations, not a dramatic departure. They even hoped that the treaty might even put the USSR in a position to moderate India's actions toward Pakistan. Senior Nixon administration officials who were India doubters expressed even stronger criticism. Kissinger later called the treaty a "bombshell," and mixing his explosive metaphors, a "lighted match" thrown into a "powder keg." He then reversed course and petulantly dismissed the treaty as a "matter of secondary concern," repeating for good measure the threat that an Indian attack on Pakistan would result in a total cutoff of economic aid.[53]

The State Department set to work planning to make good on Kissinger's threat. Within a week of the treaty, U.S. diplomats warned their bosses that American leverage regarding Indian policy was minimal. They outlined a number of measures to restore American influence, but most of these were punishments—like the reduction of American aid—rather than incentives. One group argued that "restrictive use of aid" would help American-inclined policy makers in India far more than an aid cutoff.[54]

The continuing crisis in East Pakistan soon interposed itself directly in Indo-American relations. American officials repeated their warnings that India should not intervene militarily in Pakistan's ongoing crisis. Without much enthusiasm or commitment, they politely asked Pakistan's leaders—to whom they had been indebted over the approach to China, and whom Nixon and Kissinger viewed as more reliable—to end the repression in East Pakistan. Meanwhile, America's diplomats in chief used an impressive stock of undiplomatic language to refer to India and its prime minister, ranging from the obscene to the offensive to the merely misguided. Despite their striking profanity, these insults hardly constituted a foreign policy departure; American attitudes toward India became more vulgar, but economic and political relations continued much as they had.[55]

When Indo-Pakistani conflict escalated into war on December 3–4, 1971, American officials quickly put into place the plans for an aid cutoff that they had been discussing for months. Top American officials had little interest in sorting out the subtleties of Indo-Pakistani hostilities; they had decided before the event that India would be held responsible, and stuck to that position. The fact that the Indian government extended diplomatic recognition to the new nation of Bangladesh only confirmed their suspicion that India intended to dismember Pakistan. To underscore American dissatisfaction, the U.S. Navy sent a carrier group into the Bay of Bengal, immediately raising the pitch of Indian anti-Americanism several notches. Midlevel specialists at the State Department who argued against this position—much like those who had warned of impending genocide in East Pakistan—quickly found themselves on the margins of policy debates. Kissinger announced from the start that he and President Nixon wanted to "tilt toward Pakistan" and that they expected every government agency to follow suit. Thanks to leaks from American officials who disagreed with this view, the top-secret conversation over the tilt soon appeared in the *Washington Post*. Public disclosure did not weaken Nixon and Kissinger's desire to punish India.[56]

Kissinger soon made good on his threats. He hoped to use this conflict, in his words, to "start throttling the economic aid program to India." Even before the Indo-Pakistani War, he argued, the United States received nothing in return for its aid to India; the recent conflict, coming after American calls for restraint, demonstrated just how little India heeded American wishes. USAID halted all forms of economic aid to India, including some $87 million that had been authorized and committed and was already in the pipeline.[57]

The speed and efficiency of the aid cutoff, ironically, complicated the longer-running effort to reduce American aid to India. The cancellation of already

committed loans prompted loud protests from Indian diplomats, further isolat-
ing those Indian officials pushing for closer ties to the United States. Kissinger
and Nixon seemed to revel in such protests. State Department desk officers
asked opposite numbers in India to refrain from criticizing American policy,
unpersuasively dangling the possibility of restoring "the old pattern" of Indo-
American political and economic relations. Even the most optimistic Indian
diplomats doubted the prospects for such a return. Outside the Indian Foreign
Service, too, the American move garnered opposition even from those generally most enthusiastic about ties to the United States, including industrialist
J. R. D. Tata. The cutoff damaged the prestige of those favoring American aid
within India.[58]

Meanwhile, American foreign-policy makers enthusiastic about India continued their long-standing efforts to reduce the presence of American personnel in India. But—responding to blunt messages from the White House—they
now claimed to be doing so out of a desire to punish India. In this sense, the
logic of USAID policy reversed course, from preserving relations to punishing
India. But the policy itself remained constant: the reduction of the American
footprint in India. What American officials had earlier celebrated eagerly as
an overhaul of Indo-American aid relations to improve political relations now
became the opposite: officials defended the reductions in aid as punishment
for purported Indian misbehavior vis-à-vis Bangladesh and Pakistan. Indian
diplomats played along with this new arrangement, approaching their American counterparts with their hopes for attaining rapid economic self-sufficiency.
The ambassador heartily endorsed such a move, citing the stated purpose of
American aid to "enable aided countries to stand on their own feet." Or, in the
words of a later dispatch, the American aid cutoff had "sharpened" the Indian
desire for *swadeshi* (self-sufficiency).[59]

American officials joined their Indian counterparts in reconsidering the
nature of the bilateral aid relationship, with an eye toward advancing their own
ideas. Not surprisingly, the top echelons at USAID saw economic assistance as
a key element in reconfiguring relations. A "partial resumption" of aid, USAID
argued, would "remove the immediate and symbolic thorn" in bilateral relations by "calm[ing] nationalist indignation"—while at the same time preventing a recurrence of the "take the United States for granted" syndrome. The aid
resumption, not coincidentally, reestablished USAID's role in U.S. deliberations
over India. The Department of State insisted, from the start, that American

aid played only a limited role in the Indian economy, and thus could not serve as effective leverage. And it similarly doubted the ability of economic assistance—either extending offers or threatening cutoffs—to shape political behavior such as official Indian criticisms of American policy in Vietnam. "There is little prospect," the State Department concluded, "of getting India to modify its position" on any issue, and American policy needed therefore to remove the aid arrow from its quiver of policy options.[60]

Official Indian statements vilifying American policy did not abate in 1972, as Indira Gandhi supported left-leaning Congress (R) candidates in state-level elections. She emphasized the importance of achieving economic self-sufficiency right away. And she sharply criticized economic aid in general, calling it a misnomer since it came only in the form of long-term credits that burdened the recipient's economy and created a sense of dependency. The prime minister focused her ire on American aid, which was used to "pressure the Government of India to 'toe [the American] line of thinking in conflict with our internal and foreign policies.'" Or, as Foreign Secretary T. N. Kaul told a group of Indian industrialists, "aid is a dirty word" that typically benefited donor nations more than recipients. He called—no doubt to the delight of the audience—for earning foreign exchange through increased exports rather than new rounds of aid. While American diplomats at first dismissed the escalating criticism of aid as electioneering, the end of the campaign hardly put an end to Indian complaints.[61]

By May 1972 Indian dissatisfaction with USAID found new—and bolder—expression. Preliminary steps to decrease the size of American aid mission in India had begun before war in Bangladesh, but these became more substantial and blunter. Then, in a move that caught American diplomats by surprise, a junior official from the Ministry of External Affairs informed the head of the USAID mission that the Indian government requested the removal of "all Americans working on economic aid" within one month; he cited the recent congressional criticisms of India and especially the December 1971 aid suspension. He clarified that the reduction in personnel did not amount to a rejection of assistance per se; the Government of India would welcome the release of the previously suspended loan for $87 million, as well as offers for new loans, but sought to have those loans handled on a purely financial basis, obviating the need for USAID experts in New Delhi or elsewhere in India.[62]

Though the announcement came precipitously, American diplomats acted as if it had always been part of their plans for the financialization of aid to

India. They chose to credit the departure of American personnel to India's increased capacity for self-sufficient growth and its own growing ranks of locally educated experts—much as Bowles had done a few years earlier. The change, they argued, came about thanks to the success of the decades of American assistance to India. This narrative sidestepped any of the specific criticisms made by Indian officials.[63]

Redefining American aid was a complex affair, so the two sides set right to sorting out logistical concerns, ranging from the retrenchment of many Indian local hires working for USAID to the status of the building, which was ultimately donated to the government of India. As the negotiations wound down, a less-than-grand total of twenty-seven USAID technical experts would remain in India after September 1972—and those only for a year. This amounted to only 5 percent of peak levels. The Peace Corps faced a slower but steady demise from its peak strength of 1,300 volunteers in 1968. Even before the Indo-Pakistani War, the group was down to 567—and by the end of 1972, it would be only one-third of that figure. The Peace Corps headquarters had already planned such reductions, to continue into the early 1970s, but in May 1972 India imposed an upper limit so low that the organization decided to cease operations there completely. The new era of American assistance to India might involve dollars, but would not involve people—either trained specialists or enthusiastic Peace Corps volunteers.[64]

USAID officers slowly and reluctantly accommodated themselves to this new relationship, which made their own organization less relevant to bilateral relations. USAID proposals focused on nonproject aid rather than technical assistance, and the organization sought to create a "more collaborative assistance style" that freed the remaining bilateral relations from an unequal donor-recipient dynamic; its proposals offered little indication of how USAID could effect this change of tone. The proposals, however, revealed a sharp contrast with the approaches of the 1960s—Big Push, Economic Bargain, "short tether"—each of which sought to use assistance for leverage and influence. The new aid relationship, in short, would reduce the scale and the stakes of American economic assistance.[65]

At the same time, USAID attempted to move Indo-American aid relations into a multilateral context—which meant, first and foremost, focusing on the World Bank's Aid-India Consortium. But ultimately the work of that group only exacerbated already fraught Indo-American tensions. As the consortium devoted increasing attention to debt rescheduling and relief, it accelerated the turn toward financialization. The consortium continued to be dominated by American preferences; it was a source of problems, not solutions, for Indian relations with Western lenders. When U.S. representatives single-handedly sunk a debt rescheduling exercise in the Aid-India Consortium, economist I. G. Patel angrily accused the Americans of "torpedoing" the whole process.[66]

The planned closure of the USAID mission hardly diminished Indira Gandhi's animosity toward American aid. She used a courtesy farewell session with Ambassador Kenneth Keating to launch an attack on American activities in India, economic assistance most certainly included. She railed against the "anti-Indian" activities of American diplomats in New Delhi and singled out in particular the work of USAID officials and visiting experts. "India," she concluded with a combination of pride and anger, "will survive and progress with or without help from the United States." Ambassador L. K. Jha, now in the unenviable position of explaining a rising tide of Indian anti-Americanism to officials in Washington, hinted that the recent activities of the Aid-India Consortium had sparked Gandhi's wrath. Midlevel Indian officials expressed their dissatisfaction through actions rather than words. Quotidian elements of bilateral economic relations—money transfers, requests for relocation, housing, and the like—faced inordinate delays, with even the most routine transaction requiring "additional study" on the part of Indian authorities. American officials theorized that such "abrasive" delays had the explicit purpose of expressing official Indian annoyance with American aid. And a number of sympathetic Indian interlocutors seemed to confirm this notion.[67]

As the financialization of the Indo-American aid relationship continued, India's America lobby joined with its American counterpart to explore bilateral trade relations. Their campaign emphasized low expectations, employing watchwords expressing newfound modesty. American officials in particular called for a "more mature economic assistance relationship," by which they meant that aid could be administered in an "unobtrusive" manner. The balance of responsibility would shift toward India, which would have an enhanced role "in program direction and implementation" supported only by a very small USAID contingent housed at the embassy. State Department officials took an even stronger stance about the need to lower expectations, recommending that USAID refrain from even informal advice about the Indian economy. One sign of the precariousness of the new aid relationship was the call to add a new criterion in USAID evaluations of aid projects: whether the proposed program "lends itself to misunderstandings and accusations." Avoiding offense became a principal consideration—more important even than the economic impacts of any given program. President Nixon's newly appointed ambassador in New Delhi, Democratic politico-cum-academic Daniel Patrick Moynihan, used his trademark irony to describe the situation: "Our relations are certainly improving," he reported after meeting with Prime Minister Gandhi, "but mostly because they were diminishing."[68]

To add to the irony, ending the old relationship required completing it. So the Nixon administration smoothed the path to a "mature relationship" by releasing the $87 million in aid that had been suspended two years earlier, at the outbreak of the Indo-Pakistani War in December 1971. This release of aid, however, did little to improve overall Indo-American relations, since it was paired with the disclosure of a large shipment of military supplies to Pakistan. Even so, the release of the long-suspended aid removed one more obstacle to reconfiguring Indo-American aid relations.[69]

The last U.S. technical assistance program in India concluded in the middle of 1973—one more step in establishing the new aid relationship. With the departure of the last American experts, the American embassy memorialized "the end of an era in bilateral Indo-U.S. economic assistance." Conversations then turned to financial questions. Indian diplomats made clear that the end of technical assistance did not necessarily mean the end of economic aid; they expected to expand maintenance loans—purely financial transactions—in the place of project loans that required significant in-country staffs. But American officials hoped to defer any serious discussions over the nature and levels of economic aid for some time. They wanted, first, to resolve the PL480 rupee balance problem, then to focus on expanding trade and investment. To establish aid as "clearly subordinate to . . . trade and investment," they refused to even discuss the topic until after these other issues were resolved. Indeed, one top aide expected that any future aid would be "little more than symbolic."[70]

Resolving the financial implications of PL480 thus became a top priority. In Ambassador Moynihan's words, the PL480 rupees were the sole remaining issue before "conclusion of that period [of extensive economic aid] and of many of the assumptions that fostered it." The indiscreet diplomat indicated to the Indian foreign secretary that solving the rupee crisis had more to do with Washington politics than with broader foreign policy goals. He sought a settlement "for which Mr. Nixon would take some credit" and wanted to move expeditiously since he worked "only for this president and not for future presidents." Meanwhile, politics on Capitol Hill complicated the agreement in predictable ways. In a split indicative of the interest-group alignments, the members of the House and Senate committees on foreign relations enthusiastically greeted a potential rupee agreement, while those concerned about agriculture, fearing that it might augur the end of PL480, stood opposed. Cognizant of congressional opinion, American diplomats negotiated with their Indian counterparts over how much debt the American government would write off, and how quickly. Indian negotiators sought to use the discussions as a chance to promote Indian exports—specifically, by proposing that the U.S. government commit to purchasing Indian goods.[71]

The bilateral agreement, signed in February 1974, offered a neat prelude to future economic relations: the financial issues were satisfactorily solved, but American negotiators balked on any promise of U.S. government purchases of Indian exports. Under the terms of the agreement, roughly one-third of the rupee balance—7,500 crores rupees, or $1 billion—would cover American embassy costs over the next two decades. The remaining amount—16,640 crores rupees, or $2.05 billion—would become a "grant" to the Government of India for development purposes; true to American priorities, most of the funds went toward agriculture, though roughly 10 percent was earmarked for power generation in the state sector. Moynihan, always one to appreciate the political angles and potential ironies, arranged to have the grant delivered in the form of a check for the full 16,640 crores rupees delivered at the official ceremony. He then wrote to the *Guinness Book of World Records* to certify this transaction as "the greatest amount paid by a single check." The delivery of this well-publicized check marked another symbol of the end of bilateral aid.[72]

With PL480 rupees—one more vestige of the old Indo-American aid relationship—out of the way, talk turned to establishing a new bilateral economic relationship featuring trade. T. N. Kaul, who left the foreign secretary post in late 1972 to become Indian ambassador in Washington, told Kissinger of his hopes for a new era of "economic cooperation." Kissinger responded positively to this notion, perhaps unknowingly offering praise for the nomenclature long used for Soviet economic aid. Kaul took the conversation as a sign that Kissinger genuinely sought closer Indo-American relations, one with reduced scale and increased distance. American experts and officials became less directly involved in Indian economic decision making and would adopt other trimmings of formal equality.[73]

Trade remained central to "mature" Indo-American economic relations. Indian minister of finance Y. B. Chavan shared with his American interlocutors a commitment to expanding trade. T. N. Kaul made the same point when speaking to American business executives; it was time, he reported, to "look beyond the Aid relationship," focusing instead on trade. He sought help in increasing Indian exports to the United States, hoping unrealistically that they could double in the next year or two. Privately Kaul asked for Kissinger's help in "substitut[ing] trade for aid"—which required "some encouragement" from the U.S. government. He and other Indian diplomats continued to press for increased trade over the next year, but with little net effect.[74]

In spite of Kissinger's noncommittal reply, American diplomats saw trade as a symbol of new Indo-American relations—a key element of President Nixon's call to create a "mature [Indo-American] relationship founded on equality, reciprocity, and mutual interests." Such "maturity" was a leitmotif in Nixon's foreign policy pronouncements, appearing a dozen times in his 1973 foreign policy report to Congress and in numerous internal reports. In many such accounts, trade symbolized a "more mature and business-like economic relationship," helping to bury the "patron / client relationship" that U.S. aid had created in the 1950s. Aiming to increase trade, Ambassador Moynihan contemplated resurrecting long-moribund negotiations for a treaty of commerce and navigation. Such a treaty, Moynihan hoped, would make manifest American hopes for trade as a new foundation of Indo-American relations.[75]

American economic officials did not share diplomats' enthusiasm for increasing U.S. imports of Indian goods. One report concluded that there was little hope of "substantially expanding" American trade with and investment in India—but that American diplomats needed to keep negotiating in order to preempt Indian finger-pointing for the likely failure of such efforts. Another analysis argued that a navigation treaty without any real prospect of increased trade smacked of desperation to match the Soviets treaty-for-treaty. One wearied and skeptical American economic official in New Delhi doubted the sincerity of the Indian trade campaign: "To the Government of India, trade not aid means in effect aid in the form of trade." Ambassador Moynihan publicly promoted trade but expressed his private concerns to Kissinger: the two sides

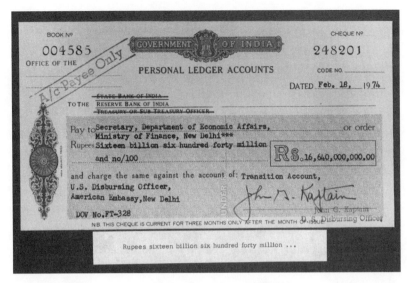

The amount of this check (over $2 billion) indicates the magnitude of U.S.-owned rupee holdings through PL480. But the fact that this photo made it into the *Guinness Book of World Records* also reveals Ambassador Daniel Patrick Moynihan's sensibilities. *Source:* Visual materials from the Daniel P. Moynihan Papers Library of Congress Prints and Photographs Division, PR 13 CN 1004 / 123, container 29 (LC-DIG-ds-10241).

turned to trade, he suggested, only because neither side could conceive of a continuing economic relationship based on anything else.[76]

Indo-Soviet Economic Relations

Indo-Soviet aid continued along the same lines—militarization, with increased attention to trade—but accelerated after the Friendship Treaty. The industrial project orientation of Indo-Soviet relations remained as strong as ever in principle, if not in practice. Indo-Soviet aid transactions in the early 1970s amounted to funding some of the projects originally approved in the large 1966 agreement for the Fourth Five-Year Plan. Thus GKES provided loans and equipment for another expansion of the Bhilai Steel Plant—"one of the most valued symbols of Indo-Soviet friendship"—even though the two sides haggled over the costs. And an event marking the commissioning of the first blast furnace at the Bokaro Steel Plant, Prime Minister Gandhi celebrated it as a "major milestone on the quest for self-reliance," and a "fine example of swadeshi." Celebrations of self-sufficiency outranked those of Soviet generosity.[77]

Following from the logic and the advice of S. A. Skachkov during his 1968 visit, Soviet officials promoted nationalization as a solution to the problems of the Indian public sector. On the one hand, nationalization would render civil servants' partisanship for private enterprise (a large part of the reason for Skachkov's foul mood) irrelevant; there would be no point in favoring a private coal company, for instance, if coal came under government control. And it would be harder for HEC's potential customers to look elsewhere—as they had been doing—if the government controlled purchasing decisions. The power of ownership, then, could achieve what economic logic had failed to do: create an integrated heavy industrial sector under government control. By the time of Skachkov's return to India in 1970, the nationalization of the steel industry had not come to pass. But Indian policy makers found new ailments that Skachkov's prescription could cure.[78]

After Indira Gandhi's commanding electoral victory in 1971—a campaign that included planks celebrating the public sector and promising the nationalization of more industries—encomiums for the public sector were heard more frequently. Forming her new government after the election, the prime minister installed a number of leftist ministers who had long favored this approach to expanding the public sector. Indira Gandhi herself publicly emphasized the economic logic of the public sector, which could promote development and provide financing that would otherwise be dissipated as individual profit. Along different economic lines, the new minster for steel and mines, a one-time Communist Party member, made the case for the nationalization of the coal industry. He criticized the private-sector collieries for mistreatment of workers and for low productivity, making the case that nationalization would promote economic efficiency and fair opportunities for workers. He rebutted arguments that damned the public sector for the performance of the HEC; the problem with the HEC was not government ownership, he insisted, but the lack of expert oversight. In a speech at Avadi (fittingly, where Congress first affirmed the "socialistic pattern" plank), the minister called for the creation of expert-led holding companies that would bear profit-and-loss responsibility for public enterprises. The holding company, he declared, could create a sharp "line of demarcation" between political decisions and economic ones. He created the Steel Authority of India, Limited (with the grand acronym SAIL) as such a holding company—though without adding to its portfolio through nationalization. He also initiated the phased nationalization of the coal industry in 1972–1973, eventually creating Coal India as a holding company for that enterprise; this followed the prime minister's nationalization of the insurance industry—ostensibly to protect consumers, but also to improve government access to investment capital. Soon thereafter, some textile plants were nationalized as well. A fierce interministerial battle broke out over efforts to nationalize wholesale food grains distribution, though the agriculturally oriented states ultimately joined forces with the Ministry of Finance to push back the effort.[79]

The pattern of these nationalizations suggests the futility of official claims that the public sector could be insulated from politics. The neutering of the Planning Commission in the late 1960s created a vacuum for systematic economic analysis of the public sector. The rising power of Prime Minister Gandhi and her secretary P. N. Haksar moved more decisions out of the hands of economists. Proponents of each of these reforms followed a similar script; they paid obeisance to an economic logic while arguing that social considerations predominated. One telling 1970 exchange made multiple but incompatible cases for the public sector: some economists insisted that the public sector had values not captured by the "smug government accounting" of return on investment while others insisted that such accounting would prove the value of publicly owned industries. The Indian president similarly defended public-sector enterprises on social and political grounds, not just economic ones. Soviet analysts like R. A. Ul'ianovskii, meanwhile, were increasingly skeptical, noting that nationalization was not the answer to all economic problems of the Third World.[80]

These social considerations—economic equality, dispersion of development gains, and the like—were quickly overwhelmed by the political possibilities of the public sector. Location decisions quickly got caught up in rent-seeking behavior as states and cities vied for enterprises to bolster their own positions, prestige, or pocketbooks. Before long, decisions on pricing, product mix, and distribution faced similar pressures. Employment, especially in heavy industry and textiles, became an especially difficult area on which to impose an economic logic. Organized labor, which had supported nationalization, was an "intended beneficiary" of the new program according to one disapproving economist. Even the sympathetic D. P. Dhar concluded that the public-sector unions fell victim to "economism," seeking higher wages rather than identifying ideologically with the public sector. By measure of market share, sales, investment, and employment, the Indian public sector expanded rapidly in the first half of the 1970s, with investment increasing by 50 percent in the quinquennium after 1969. Scholars and observers in India and abroad focused on the political economy of the public sector, stressing the centrality of political decisions rather than economic ones, the "irresponsible introduction of ideology," and the arrival of "demand politics" in which decisions are made to satisfy constituencies rather than on economic criteria. While the dynamic for this repurposing of the public sector emerged out of domestic electoral and partisan concerns, the Indian public sector itself remained closely tied to the Soviet agencies that had helped expand it through financing, technology, and exhortation.[81]

Soviet analysts, too, formulated new languages and concepts to understand the political economy of India and other Third World nations. In a series of books and articles, economist A. I. Levkovskii described the situation as "multistructural" (*mnogoukladnyi*): India had no dominant economic structure (like capitalism, state capitalism, socialism, etc.), but contained within it a complex and varied set of economic relations. By Marxist tenets, the varied and competing economic structures led necessarily to an "eclectic" politics. This approach could underwrite a new approach to winning friends and influencing people in the Third World, though the sharp criticism of more orthodox scholars limited the ultimate effects of this conceptual innovation.[82]

The problems of the HEC, including labor disputes and shortages of raw materials, prompted another new direction in Soviet aid policy. Unreliable and frequently delayed production once again left the HEC's potential customers to seek alternative sources of supply. GKES representatives treated the problem as a major political crisis, ultimately offering a Soviet-style crutch to the Indian factory. GKES arranged to deliver premade components to Ranchi, which could then resell them to Indian steel plants. This plan allowed the HEC to deliver on its orders in spite of the delays at its Ranchi plant—but it also undermined celebrations of swadeshi and hindered the long-term goals of a robust and self-sufficient heavy industrial sector under government ownership. The Ministry of Heavy Industry continued trying to rescue the HEC and its Ranchi plant, recognizing that the importance of "establish[ing] credibility in the eyes of our workers and the people of our country"; its representatives thus continued to promote Soviet loans to third countries to offload HEC products. Even the industrial projects, then, began seeing international trade as a means to success—or at least survival. Given these trends, Soviet diplomats' assessment that the Indian public-sector projects were "standing on their own two feet" seems delusional, or at best recklessly optimistic.[83]

As the HEC episode suggests, the aftershocks of Skachkov's cranky 1968 visit continued to reverberate through the early 1970s, especially in the use of bilateral trade. Indo-Soviet efforts to rescue public-sector industries relied not just on quick fixes (ubiquitous in planned economies) and improved management (much rarer) but also turned increasingly to trade—handled, for the most part by Indian industrial ministries. But prospects for trade went beyond a public-sector bailout. Soviet planners met with their Indian counterparts with the hopes of establishing and strengthening export-oriented industries. Most bilateral trade, meanwhile, entailed a conventional flow of goods, with India exporting raw materials to and importing manufactured goods from the Soviet Union. The oil shocks of 1973 only exacerbated this pattern, with a spike in Indian imports of Soviet oil; 1974 oil imports exceeded the total for the previous six years combined, and 1975 imports were higher still. The mushrooming imports of oil ran against a main purpose of Indo-Soviet trade, which was to keep the rupee repayments to the Soviet Union flowing back into Indian coffers. Increased Indian exports of pig iron and steel, which served little economic purpose for the Soviet economy, hardly made up for this major hit to the balance of payments. But the contemplation of Soviet aid for Indian exports, and the general shift toward an export orientation, potentially marked a lasting change. Even this new direction, however, focused on the usual Soviet ministerial and bureaucratic contacts in the industrial ministries and public-sector undertakings.[84]

Joint Commissions: Structures without Content

Though India's economic relations with the superpowers in the mid-1970s moved along very different trajectories, they converged on similar mechanisms. Over the course of a few years, Indian officials set up an Indo-Soviet Joint Commission and its American counterpart. Joint commissions could symbolize equality without actually creating it. Though the notion of a joint commission had circulated in the late 1960s (and indeed, Prasanta Chandra Mahalanobis had proposed close Indo-Soviet cooperation in economic planning in the mid-1950s), the 1971 treaty provided a new impetus to bring the commission into being. Serious negotiations unfolded over the course of 1972, with a writ to discuss a range of bilateral commercial and scientific concerns. At its first meeting in February 1973, the commission discussed means to increase bilateral trade and to undertake closer cooperation in production. Through the Joint Commission the Soviet Union got its much-awaited long-term agreement on trade and economic cooperation, signed during Leonid Brezhnev's fall 1973 visit to India; that fifteen-year agreement identified the usual set of aid priorities (headlined by the expansion of the Bhilai and Bokaro plants) and hoped to increase bilateral trade. For all the talk of trade, however, the Indian approach to the Soviet Union involved as much political as economic calculation; indeed, diplomat D. P. Dhar worried that bilateral relations might be "unduly influenced by commercial factors." Indian economic officials hoped that Soviet authorities could help solve ongoing problems in the public-sector enterprises built with Soviet assistance; too much attention to the economic costs and benefits might jeopardize these efforts.[85]

The Joint Commission added little to the substance of Indo-Soviet discussions, though it did provide a convenient setting for discussing familiar themes like trade, third-party exports, and so on—and to a friendly crowd of Indian bureaucrats and politicians oriented toward the USSR in the first place. Indian economic officials hoped that trade would solve their problems with public-sector overcapacity and balance-of-payments deficits. But they faced a similar calculation by their Soviet interlocutors, who likewise hoped to use Indo-Soviet trade to boost their own country's economic prospects. Thus the Joint Commission meetings simply provided a new venue for old-fashioned haggling over trade, with each side angling to increase exports to the other— and, one Soviet trade official underscored, purely on a commercial basis. The Joint Commission became the venue for proposing all kinds of new areas for trade, including services and electronic computers. Ultimately, however, it produced more press releases than economic progress.[86]

The Joint Commission also hosted further conversations on the prospect of joint ventures in third countries, an extension of Soviet financing of Indian exports to third countries that had begun earlier. Such arrangements might have Indian and Soviet enterprises building new installations in countries like Afghanistan and Turkey. Both sides agreed that the Heavy Equipment Corporation had the most excess capacity and therefore (perversely) the greatest chance of success in this venture. These efforts achieved little, though they strengthened the connections between Soviet ministries and the Indian industrial ministries and public-sector undertakings; indeed, the new topics for discussion expanded the base of Soviet agencies to include not just GKES but also the Ministry of Foreign Trade, which had previously worked at cross-purposes. Yet the overall scope of direction of Soviet efforts had changed little from the heyday of the economic cold war in the 1950s—heavy industry in the public sector.[87]

The Joint Indo-American Commission, similarly, could provide a venue for ongoing discussions about expanding trade, investment, and scientific-technical cooperation. Hearing that their compatriots were busy organizing an Indo-Soviet Joint Commission, pro-Western officials like L. K. Jha initiated conversations with American diplomats about an analogous Indo-American body and found a receptive audience in the New Delhi embassy. Moynihan, with a keen eye for the power of symbolism, proposed such a commission shortly after arriving in New Delhi, hoping it could become a mechanism to ensure "increasingly close and correct relations with the American economy." Kissinger, however, wanted to aim even lower than "correct" relations, cautioning Moynihan against being too "specific" about how such a commission might operate.[88]

When T. N. Kaul arrived in Washington as ambassador in 1973, he tried to keep the cause alive, attempting to build institutional mechanisms for closer relations and intimating that his side expected that such a commission must be "more than just a symbolic empty shell." Kissinger's indifference did not dent Kaul's optimism, which was based, he declared, on his view that "America needs the friendship of India as much as India needs the friendship of America." (It seems unlikely that even the most devoted India lobbyists in the U.S. would have shared this assessment.) American diplomats, for their part, used the talk of a commission to push for trade over aid; they replied that they could not even discuss future economic aid until the establishment of a subcommission on trade and investment.[89]

The State Department grudgingly inched toward the establishment of an Indo-American commission. One internal study called the commission a symbol of "mature" bilateral ties, but also a means to make India feel "special" since only a handful of other such commissions existed. Kaul's hopes for a meaningful body did not come to pass; Kissinger, for instance, promised Chinese officials that there would be no financial commitments through the commission. The first meeting of the Indo-American Joint Commission took place in January 1975 and produced about as little as pessimists had predicted: formal statements but little real progress. And when the next downturn in political relations came in 1975, the New Delhi embassy praised the Joint Commission as a way to keep some semblance of an economic relationship under way—at least on paper—until political conditions improved.[90]

The Indo-American Joint Commission, in sum, offered more symbol than substance; it did little to expand relations in anything beyond formal terms. The commission meetings generated some newspaper articles but did little to deepen bilateral ties. Similarly, the new tone of Indo-American relations, invoking "maturity" as a constant theme, was more correct than close. Indeed, one transition brief prepared to edify incoming president Gerald Ford (who took over after Nixon's resignation amid the Watergate scandal in August 1974) made this particularly clear. That document noted defined the new, "more mature" relationship as a "less intimate" one; for whatever that may say about the link between age and intimacy in general, the overall implication seems clear: "mature" Indo-American relations would be more distant.[91]

Ultimately the dueling joint commissions symbolized the division of labor that had taken place, thanks to development politics, over the preceding decades. The Indo-Soviet Joint Commission was led by D. P. Dhar, superbly equipped for the role, and not just because of his leftist inclinations. Dhar had, after all, served as ambassador to the USSR, helped negotiate the Friendship Treaty after leaving Moscow, and at the time of his leadership of the new commission was deputy chairman of the Planning Commission and minister for planning in the Cabinet. From his time in Moscow to his work in the one of the great redoubts for planning and heavy industry, Dhar found the Joint Commission a perfect spot from which to encourage closer Indo-Soviet economic cooperation.[92]

Development politics worked in similar ways on the Indo-American Joint Commission. Y. B. Chavan, who had long favored closer economic ties to the United States, served as chair. Other commission participants had long experience in expanding economic relations with the United States, and served in ministries closely tied to the West, including the Ministry of Finance and the atomic projects at the Ministry of Defence. The joint commissions became the instantiations of long-standing patterns and preferences, providing a new institutional structure for evolving debates about India's economic future. They harkened back, in a way, to the proliferating subcommittees of the pre-1947 National Planning Committee; each gathered sympathizers for its own particular cause, but with no overarching group to assess the competing claims. These commissions carried a heavier symbolic than operational load, ostensibly enacting new economic relationships between equals. In the process, the joint commissions also symbolized the final stage of development politics, where different groups within the Indian government built connections to different external powers. Financial resources did not generally flow through these commissions, but technical and symbolic resources still did.[93]

The peregrinations of external aid contributed to the emergence and the deepening of what political scientist Francine Frankel called India's "double crisis" of economic stagnation and political instability in the late 1960s and early 1970s. The long-standing debates over the future of the Indian economy became all the more wrapped up in electoral politics with the ascent of Indira Gandhi to the head of the Congress Party and the premiership in 1966. Increasingly intense intraparty disputes took shape as debates over economic issues of the late 1960s—devaluation, agriculture, and the public sector. These issues were, not coincidentally, at the center of the Indian government's relationships with its largest foreign donors. Once in office as prime minister, Indira Gandhi used economic issues to distance herself from her political rivals. By the end of 1971, with her impressive electoral victory in February and the plaudits she received for resolving the Bangladesh crisis in India's favor, Gandhi had reconfigured Indian politics.

In the process of attaining such a strong domestic position, the prime minister also transformed India's economic relationships with the superpowers, turning slow-moving trends into hard-and-fast patterns. Indo-Soviet relations had focused increasingly on military aid in the aftermath of the Indo-Pakistani War and the attendant Western suspension of aid. But the events of 1971—Sino-American rapprochement in July, the Soviet treaty in August, and the Indo-Pakistani War in December—furthered that trend. As went India so went the Third World, where Soviet military aid caught up with and surpassed economic aid across most developing countries.

Indo-American relations, meanwhile, reached a new, and low, plateau in 1971, as the treaty and disagreements over Bangladesh soured already testy relations. The early 1970s marked the death knell for the brief but intense American efforts to influence Indian economic policy. The Big Push and the Economic Bargain departed from the policy portfolio shortly after President Lyndon Johnson left the White House. The expulsion of the USAID mission in 1972–1973 could easily be seen as an act of Indian hostility, an interpretation belied by the fact that proponents of closer bilateral ties in both India and the United States. The USAID mission, at one point boasting over a thousand employees, was a symbol of a bygone era when the superpowers went toe-to-toe over aid projects. The expulsion instead clarified a long-standing trend in American (and, more broadly, Western) aid to India, favoring negotiations over financial transfers to debates about specific projects.

Trade became more central to Indian economic relations with both superpowers. American officials hoped that trade would eventually supplant aid, while Soviet officials saw trade as a solution to some of the problems of the Indian public sector. These grandiose monuments to heavy industry made great backdrops for speeches about India's industrial future, but they were economic drains. Industrial capacity greatly outran domestic demand, and yet the products were not competitive in the international markets. So if the Americans sought trade, not aid, the Soviets ended up with aid through trade; Soviet enterprises purchased Indian manufacturers in large part to keep the Indian public-sector factories running.

For both superpowers, dealings with India both symbolized and shaped their future interactions in development aid. For the United States, the change was particularly abrupt. Nixon came into office expecting to reduce American commitments to the Third World and hoping to make India into an example. Disdainful of American liberals' enthusiasms for India (and of American liberals in general), American policy toward India debuted themes that would soon emerge in Nixon's relations with the underdeveloped world. Focusing on trade over aid, and punishing Indian expressions of anti-American sentiment, Nixon oversaw the reduction of the Indo-American relationship to a shell of its former self. What T. N. Kaul called American "aid-weariness" took its toll on even the most sympathetic USAID officials and State Department diplomats.[94]

And yet for all of these changes, old dynamics endured. Soviet aid organs persisted in their devotion to public-sector industry; the talk of trade was primarily to provide a lifeline for heavy industry, and so their principal contacts remained the ministries and enterprises that had long been Soviet interlocutors. American aid changed more substantially, but only to emphasize the focus on financial matters from nonproject aid to debt rescheduling. The joint commissions, established in 1973–1974, provided homes for each camp. Even as superpower aid changed shape, development politics remained, pulling the Indian government in different directions.

DEVELOPMENT POLITICS AND THE PRICE OF AID

By the time the Indo-American and Indo-Soviet joint commissions convened in the mid-1970s, development politics had been well entrenched in Indian institutions and continued its corrosive effects on the union government in New Delhi. The process had come a long way since 1950, when pro-planning groups within the Indian government sought help from planning impresario Solomon Trone while those hoping for deeper engagement in the capitalist world economy invited a World Bank mission. The linkages between the Soviet Union and the Indian industrial ministries, and between the United States and the Indian Ministry of Finance, had grown stronger through the heyday of the economic cold war of the late 1950s and through the 1960s. The joint commissions, though hardly at the core of Indian state power, reflected the divisions at the highest reaches of government.

The Price of Aid has documented the many steps, from the one-off pursuit of outside support in 1950 to networks so firmly established that they appeared in organizational charts and official registers a quarter century later. The uneven flow of events, of bureaucratic and diplomatic moves and countermoves, created the circumstances of the early 1970s. Yet within this flow a few moments played outsize roles and would have disproportionate downstream effects. Of course, these turning points came after leading Indian officials accepted the need for external funding, which itself was a battle fought for the first half of the 1950s. Once the pursuit of aid became an element of Indian economic policy, the door to development politics opened up. But the doorway grew wider—and the scope and impact of development politics expanded all the more—thanks to efforts to expand and reshape aid relationships.

The first such turning point came as early as 1958, amid the foreign exchange crisis of the Second Five-Year Plan. Economic ambassador B. K. Nehru wanted to replace project-by-project funding in favor of what he called, alluringly, "free money" unattached to any particular project. And at the same time, he wanted to reorganize his government's pursuit of aid, as he complained to his boss, Minister of Finance Morarji Desai: "We have suffered in the past from the feeling among those who are potentially our greatest source of external finance that the request for foreign aid really comes only from one Ministry and one Minister of Government without the rest of the Government, including the PM [Prime Minister], being greatly concerned about it one way or another." Prime Minister Jawaharlal Nehru bristled defensively at his cousin's accusation that he was inattentive to foreign aid. But the prime minister did not dispute B. K. Nehru's description of the dynamics of aid, in which a donor built connections to one ministry rather than to the Government of India as a whole.[1]

Though B. K. Nehru claimed to offer a critique of development politics, he really provided a well-played example of it. Though he mentioned a desire to make sure that aid did not become the exclusive province of subsidiary groups within the Indian government, his memorandum was ultimately a gambit to expand the aid relationships he favored—with the Cold War West—at the expense of those favoring closer ties to the Soviet Union. What appeared to be an effort to transcend development politics, then, was in fact a play to use foreign aid to win domestic battles.

B. K. Nehru won that round, but only by incurring unexpectedly high "non-financial" costs that came due at the next turning point: the American "Big Push" in India.[2] The proponent of this effort, U.S. Agency for International Development (USAID) mission chief John P. Lewis, seized on the idea of providing so-called free money—but only at a price. Such aid might be liberated from projects, but it came tethered to new and more stringent conditions imposed by donors. The Big Push was ultimately not so much a single episode as the opening volley in a major effort to subject Indian economic policy writ large—not to mention key aspects of foreign policy—to negotiations. Over the course of the mid-1960s, the scope and instruments of U.S. leverage swelled. Lewis's list of changes that aid could "buy" (termed the "Yankee Mogul's fatwa" by the left-wing newspaper *Blitz*) was followed by Secretary of State Dean Rusk's

"Economic Bargain," by President Lyndon Johnson's "short tether" for food aid through Food for Peace (PL480), and by the efforts to promote devaluation and other reforms in the aftermath of Bernard Bell's study for the World Bank. These efforts annoyed Indian officials sympathetic to the West, but the American failure to live up to its part of Rusk's Economic Bargain infuriated them—and cost them dearly in political capital. This process exposed Indian officials to ever-increasing pressures, as American officials considered even the most fundamental aspects of Indian policy up for negotiation.

Meanwhile, the expansion of Indo-Soviet aid soon exposed Indian officials favoring publicly owned and centrally planned heavy industry to new pressures, providing a third turning point. While Soviet aid officials took offense at Indian requests for nonproject aid, they nevertheless expanded the scope of leverage and advice over the course of the 1960s. The call for political and economic payoffs for overseas aid predated the putsch against Nikita Khrushchev and in fact helped precipitate it. And Aleksei Kosygin's reforms of the mid-1960s soon found their way abroad, as consideration of profit soon entered Indo-Soviet negotiations. Nowhere was this clearer than in the final crucial moment: the visit of Soviet aid chief S. A. Skachkov to India in December 1968. Unlike B. K. Nehru's call for free money, or John Lewis's Big Push proposal, Skachkov's visit was not so much the formulation of a policy change as it was the announcement of it to concerned Indian officials. The new approach to aid that Skachkov announced on his grumpy visit followed from the Kosygin reforms, but also—like the emerging American approach—expanded the ambit of Soviet leverage. His interventions were no longer limited to improving the functioning of one or another project but extended to the operation of the Indian public sector as a whole. Investing the economic performance of the Indian public sector with newfound political significance, Skachkov asserted the authority to shape the sector as a whole, not just individual projects. Just as those inclined to the West reckoned with the price of the aid over the course of the 1960s, so too did those in India who favored Soviet aid projects.

These turning points in economic aid intersected, of course, with other events in Indian foreign relations—usually in ways that increased the pressures on the Indian government while at the same time weakening it. The Indian debacle in its war with China in 1962 opened up the possibility of a competition for military aid from both superpowers, at the same time spelling the end of British dominance in this sphere. But the next Indian war—against Pakistan in 1965—abruptly ended the military competition, as the Western aid cutoff left the USSR as the primary outfitter of the Indian Air Force, with its navy not far behind. Similarly, the dramatic events of 1971—steps toward Sino-American rapprochement, the Indo-Soviet friendship treaty, and the creation of Bangladesh—realized the disadvantages of offending the Americans without the advantages of a true alliance with the Soviet Union. Soviet aid to India had become increasingly militarized as the Indian military grew more and more reliant upon Soviet (and eventually Russian) equipment.

India

True to the precepts of development politics, these crucial events shaped Indian politics and governance, contributing to the political and economic crises of the late 1960s and early 1970s. The superpowers' division of development labor, building since the start of the economic cold war in India in the 1950s, contributed to what political scientists called the "deinstitutionalization" of Indian politics and administration, where formally constituted bodies like the Cabinet and the Planning Commission ceded authority to informal networks around charismatic leaders. Development politics did not create this devolution but fueled divisions within the Indian National Congress during Indira Gandhi's first premiership (1966–1977). The continuing pursuit of external aid, furthermore, impinged on the capacity of the Indian government to respond to this "double crisis" of economic stagnation and political instability. Foreign aid affected the shape and the timing of these crises while at the same time reducing the capacity of the Indian government to respond to them.[3]

India's economic policies in the early 1970s did not solve its growing economic problems. At the same time as the public sector was increasingly used for instrumental purposes, the authorities that once shaped overall economic policy atrophied. The restrictions on the Planning Commission's powers, combined with the centralization of authority in the Prime Minister's Secretariat, reduced economic oversight. Not surprisingly, location and production decisions came to fulfill political and not economic aims. The creation of holding companies could, in principle, have returned the focus of the public sector to economic returns. Yet the overriding sense of public-sector advocates was that government-owned enterprises answered to a higher logic than mere economic returns—a logic that made decision making fundamentally political in nature.

Meanwhile, increasing regulation of foreign trade in 1973–1974 prompted new efforts to game the licensing of imports and exports. (The regulations took on great importance in the economics profession, occasioning the term "rent-seeking" in one influential analysis.) The oil shocks of 1973 soon placed added strains on the Indian economy and led to increased reliance on International Monetary Fund (IMF) credit facilities, which came with their own sets of conditions and restrictions.[4]

The latter half of the 1970s brought more political turmoil and more economic difficulties. Indira Gandhi's unprecedented declaration of the Emergency in 1975 shook up Indian politics dramatically. Two years later, when she ended the Emergency by announcing elections, the opposition Janata Party prevailed, putting Gandhi's longtime rival Morarji Desai in the prime minister's office. Three years of continued economic difficulty and political gridlock, however, helped Congress retake parliament in 1980. Upon her return to the premiership, Gandhi shifted rightward in economic policy, marginalizing some of her left-oriented advisers in favor of centrist technocrats. By the mid-1980s, Congress governments under Indira Gandhi and her son and successor Rajiv openly discussed plans for economic liberalization, including relaxation of import controls and deregulation. The changing complexion of the economic policy apparatus in the early 1980s facilitated such changes, especially after economist Manmohan Singh became deputy chairman of the Planning Commission in 1985. Yet internal debates about the best solution to India's deepening economic crisis made such efforts (in the apt words of one political scientist at the time) "half-hearted liberalization."[5]

A more thoroughgoing set of economic reforms came in 1991, when Manmohan Singh took the Ministry of Finance portfolio for the Congress government. A longtime proponent of trade liberalization, he spent the 1970s and 1980s in an ascending succession of posts in Indian and international economic bureaucracies. By 1991 the political circumstances had changed and Indian conditions had worsened. When the IMF demanded economic liberalization (in terms that echoed the devaluation episode a quarter century earlier), this pressure provided sufficient external resources for Singh to act on long-held beliefs about opening up India to the world economy and allowing for the freer play of market forces domestically. In one fell swoop he led his government to reduce tariffs, open up longtime monopolies to competition, loosen restrictions on foreign direct investment, and devalue the rupee—a very familiar list of policies, but this time implemented as a package. True to the form of development politics, such changes came about in conjunction with foreign agencies that demanded major changes as a condition for a bailout of India's desperate foreign-exchange position. Development politics ushered out an era of state-led development that it had, decades earlier, ushered in.[6]

The United States

The peregrinations of American aid policy in India both reflected and shaped economic aid practices. U.S. economic assistance to India underwent a drastic contraction in the early 1970s. Adjusting for inflation, aid to India halved between 1966 (the peak year) and 1969, then declined by an additional 80 percent by 1972, never again reaching anything near peak levels. Much of the remaining aid was in the form of agricultural exports under PL480. While India accounted for as much as one-eighth of total U.S. overseas aid at its mid-1960s peak, a decade later the figure was more like one-eightieth.[7]

This declining share of aid aside, the Indian situation did not diverge from the broader tendencies of American assistance policy. The financialization of American aid reflected bilateral Indo-American relations—most notably the concerns of top Indian officials about too many Americans roaming the Indian countryside or the halls of the economic ministries in New Delhi. The expulsion of the USAID mission symbolized the end of the era of "projectized" assistance, in the awkward phrase of former ambassador Chester Bowles. With the conclusion of the rupee agreement, generating what the *Guinness Book of World Records* certified as the world's largest check, even PL480 aid was substantially reduced. With few new projects on the horizon and no more food aid, conversations in the Indo-American Joint Commission revolved around trade and investment rather than aid. The commission did not, however, handle the largest elements of Indo-American economic relations, debt relief and rescheduling; these remained the province of the Indian Ministry of Finance and the U.S. departments of State and the Treasury.

These changes vis-à-vis India prefigured a broad shift toward USAID as a financial entity disbursing checks to others rather than as an agency that undertook its own development projects. Discussions in Washington in the early 1970s, spurred by USAID as well as by private organizations that lobbied for American aid, promoted an overhaul of the Foreign Assistance Act in 1973. That act promised "New Directions" in American assistance programs: a focus on poverty alleviation, renewed emphasis on multilateral aid, an acknowledgment of the authority of the recipient countries to establish their own priorities, and the rejection of what critics called trickle-down aid that focused on overall economic growth. These ideas had been percolating, in official correspondence and blue-ribbon task forces, since the early days of the administration of President Richard M. Nixon. The beauty of the New Directions proposal was that all stakeholders could find something they wanted in it. For USAID personnel it represented a change in the procedures for allocating funds. For aid lobbyists it offered the chance to maintain funding by presenting aid as something new and improved. Liberals in and out of government praised the emphasis on poverty reduction. Critics of foreign aid appreciated the attention to trade. Others may not have thought New Directions amounted to much at all; after interviewing a number of congressional representatives and staffers, one researcher concluded that they remained only dimly aware of the extent of changes they legislated in the 1973 act.[8]

The initial effects of the revised Foreign Assistance Act were structural, not fiscal; they did not lead in the short term to reduced levels of aid. USAID slowly began to reconfigure itself, concerned less with direct administration of aid and more with channeling funds to projects managed by others. They bolstered relations with nongovernmental organizations, which soon became prominent fixtures in the aid landscape. A second means for USAID to remove itself from direct engagement in projects was to channel more aid through multilateral organizations: the World Bank, its International Development Association (IDA), and the growing ranks of regional development banks. The poverty alleviation goal soon evolved into USAID's Basic Human Needs mandate of the late 1970s, focusing on nutrition, housing, and income for the poorest citizens of the poorest nations—fields well suited to the growing number of NGOs receiving USAID funds. India, home to more than one-third of the world's poor, remained prominent in these discussions.[9]

The expansion of multilateral aid fit neatly with Robert S. McNamara's plans for the World Bank after he became its president in 1968. The former U.S. secretary of defense announced right away his plan to increase bank lending, which he quickly accomplished. Over the course of his years at the bank (1968–1982), he spearheaded a tenfold increase in lending and a remarkable thirtyfold increase in the concessional lending of the IDA. He aimed to remake the World Bank as a development agency and, over time, succeeded; a focus on poverty reduction replaced an emphasis on macroeconomic growth—the same turn away from trickle-down development visible in the American aid policy at the time. The bank became a development institution, ironically, just as USAID was becoming a financing agency.[10]

The Soviet Union

The Soviet engagement with the Third World, meanwhile, shifted in part according to its experiences in India. The general tendency was away from ideological prescriptions—about the public sector in developing countries, about the dangers of international trade and investment—in favor of more practical calculations. One top apparatchik celebrated the "gradual overcoming of the illusions that had begun in euphoria" under Khrushchev. By the 1970s, he added, Soviet leaders held a "weakening attraction to their own ideology," for which they compensated by turning to nationalism and state building. These tendencies were evident in S. A. Skachkov's recommendations for India during and after his 1968 visit. The debates about "multistructurality" (*mnogoukladnost'*) in the 1970s demonstrated the ebbing of Soviet optimism that revolution was around the corner, or that it could be readily achieved through the expansion of government-owned heavy industry or through other economic steps. In the meantime, even Soviet observers who had long measured India's progress toward communism by the size of its public sector conceded that it would not become a panacea for Third World economic problems.[11]

Changing Indian political economy threw up obstacles in economic relations with the USSR. The stock-in-trade of Soviet development aid—credits for large-scale heavy industry projects—declined in importance; indeed, India went from 1966 to 1977 without a new agreement for Soviet credits. Even the use of existing credits was on the decline as Indian industry produced more and more of the kinds of products that had once been part of cooperation agreements. The USSR helped establish the very industries that rendered many of its projects obsolete.[12]

Given such travails in the economic sphere, it is little surprise that Soviet economic aid to India and to other parts of the nonaligned Third World comprised a shrinking portion of Soviet activity while military aid grew dramatically. The militarization of the Indo-Soviet relationship paralleled a global trend. Soviet deliveries of military aid to the nonaligned Third World spiked in the early 1970s. Through the late 1960s, military aid hovered around $500 million per year, at roughly one and a half times the levels of economic aid. Military deliveries to the Third World doubled in short order, as did the ratio of military to economic aid. By 1973, the absolute amount doubled again and the ratio of military to economic aid approached five to one. Soviet arms sales to India were not quite as volatile but also increased over the 1970s. As one analysis convincingly suggests, Soviet officials had retreated from the earlier basis of aid—building socialist economies in the hopes of creating socialist states. Instead, they aimed to build and defend "states of socialist orientation" and hoped that socialist economies would follow.[13]

Yet military aid, with its less advantageous financing terms, amplified India's growing financial dilemmas. As early as the mid-1960s Soviet scholars promoted an "international socialist division of labor" that relied on trade. By the early 1970s, trade expansion became a possible solution to India's public sector woes, as Skachkov negotiated with Indian economic ministers about the Soviet purchase of Indian industrial production that found no domestic buyers. The establishment of the Indo-Soviet Joint Commission provided a venue for further efforts to expand trade; one of its first tasks was to implement the trade agreement signed in 1973. Development loans also contributed to the need for Indian exports to the USSR. While its debts could be repaid in rupees, they were handled on a "clearing basis," meaning that the debts would be essentially be covered by the export of Indian goods to the USSR. Thus, even as trade expanded in the early 1970s, these higher levels of Indian exports to the USSR mostly covered repayment of past development loans or purchases of military equipment. India, in fact, faced the prospect of a negative aid flow with the USSR in the 1970s, with more funds going from India to the USSR to cover repayments than were going the opposite direction as development assistance.[14]

The Soviet enthusiasm for trade resonated more widely as trade became a heated issue in north-south relations in the 1970s. The UN Conference on Trade and Development (UNCTAD), founded in 1964, became a venue for poorer countries to make claims for the reconfiguration of the international economic system in their favor. Calls to improve their place in the international economy acknowledged trade as the fundamental international economic relationship of the era; recalibrated trade relations, proponents argued, would set the Third World on the path to prosperity. The process culminated in the proposal for a New International Economic Order (NIEO) on the floor of the UN General Assembly in 1974—a document that focused primarily on trade as the solution to global economic inequality.

The NIEO placed the Soviet Union in an unusual position. Soviet statements repeated familiar condemnations of neocolonialist exploitation. But subtle shifts in wording suggested that Soviet officials were increasingly reconciled to participating in a single world economy and even saw their own economic interests threatened by the NIEO. Soviet delegations to UNCTAD distanced themselves from the demands of the NIEO's most vocal proponents; in the words of one Western observer, the Soviet Union had long cast itself as "the outsider who trumpeted Third World grievances and sought to refashion . . . international economic institutions" but had "become a proponent of depoliticized, pragmatic polices." Comparative advantage and the international division of labor, previously bugbears of capitalist exploitation, had become routine elements of Soviet foreign economic policy.[15]

Legacies

By the mid-1970s the core dynamics that had energized the economic cold war had shifted. American-Soviet antagonisms continued to ebb and flow, of course, but key elements of aid competition had diminished. Both superpowers turned increasingly to trade—and, more specifically, to trade within the world capitalist economy. The Soviet vision of an "international socialist division of labor" had given way to a socialist bloc participating in the international division of labor. The integration of the socialist states into the world economy exacerbated some of the planned economies' greatest woes. These deepening economic problems also made the aid competition all the more one-sided. American economic assistance globally had always exceeded comparable Soviet figures, but American aid levels grew twice quickly as Soviet levels over the 1970s.[16]

The Soviet Union had managed to compete for the hearts and minds of the Third World despite its massive resource disadvantage by invoking visions of a modern economy—industrial, publicly owned, and centrally planned—that appealed widely to leaders of the Third World. Such an economy, leaders of the new nations hoped, would provide for its population while building the apparatus of the postcolonial state. But as this vision foundered, in India as elsewhere, the USSR was left to compete only in terms of economic performance—which was, by all calculations, weak. Indeed, economic stagnation led Soviet agencies to abandon many of the precepts that had attracted such international enthusiasm in the first place. Labor productivity replaced the language of "progressive forces"; returns on investment came to matter as much as revolutionary potential. The USSR had started the economic cold war as an underresourced competitor that could nevertheless provide an inspiration to Third World leaders; it presented appealing structures of domestic political economy and a possible alternative to Western capitalism. By the 1970s the Soviet Union was less of an inspiration and more of an armory—and was itself increasingly enmeshed in the capitalist world order. By this time, then, the dynamics of the economic cold war had given way to new forces, including the rise of what would come to be called globalization.[17]

The Cold War paradox of the global project of development—it both enshrined the sovereign state and weakened governance structures—gave way to more complex and (for poorer nations) more vexing circumstances in the 1990s. Cheerleaders for accelerated economic globalization celebrated not state boundaries and centralized power but decentralization, integration, and hybridity—"the dance of flows and fragments," in historian Frederick Cooper's inimitable phrase. In doing so, they questioned the future of state sovereignty in world politics.[18] Development aid, in this brave new world, was no longer Janus-faced, both sustaining and undermining recipient nations' sovereignty; it became more corrosive than constructive of state power. Its organization and purposes had changed, with NGOs taking on tasks that once were the primary responsibility of states (both donors and recipients). The result was what historian Gregory Mann cleverly termed "nongovernmentality," an uneven decline of state sovereignty in the face of encroachments by international NGOs. Even beyond such extreme cases, though, development aid came at the cost of state power; development politics disrupted domestic politics in relatively stable and institutionalized states like India.[19]

Even at the height of the Cold War, scholars and practitioners alike began to reckon the domestic political impacts of foreign assistance. The firsthand experiences of many Indian officials, regardless of their political predispositions or economic visions, led them to wonder whether their pursuit of foreign aid brought new burdens that outweighed aid's new possibilities. While many foreign aid skeptics within the superpowers worried primarily about the impact on their own country, others questioned whether aid produced results commensurate with its costs. While Soviet bureaucrats demanded a "sociopolitical accounting" of foreign aid, at least one important American scholar had even a deeper criticism. In the heyday of the economic cold war, Hans Morgenthau—the twentieth century's most important theorist of international relations—tried to reckon with the emerging phenomenon of foreign aid; of all the new foreign policy instruments of the modern age, he wrote in 1962, "none has proven more baffling." Morgenthau was perplexed by the variety of contradictory claims for what such aid could accomplish, as well as by the mismatch between stated purposes and actual results. Unlike many American observers, he concerned himself with the effects of foreign aid on recipients' political structures—which, he argued, would be dramatically altered by the infusion of external funds. Aid was sought and delivered in the name of self-sufficiency, political stability, and helping recipient nations "stand on their own two feet"—but too often could have the opposite effect: "foreign aid for economic development," Morgenthau concluded awkwardly, "can be counter-productive if the . . . goal of the giving nation is the recipient's social and political stability." Aid programs, in other words, did not necessarily create more stable nations or a more stable international system. Closely attuned to the political effects of foreign assistance, Morgenthau was starting to calculate the price of aid—a bill that would soon enough come due in India and beyond.[20]

NOTE ON SOURCES

ABBREVIATIONS

NOTES

ACKNOWLEDGMENTS

INDEX

Note on Sources

As the notes to the preceding text indicates, this book builds not only on a wide-ranging archival source base but also on an extraordinarily insightful and empirically rich set of published scholarship. While of course any direct references are duly cited, the notes do not fully reflect my reliance on a number of key works that provided crucial orientation to their respective topics and helped shaped the ideas of *The Price of Aid*. These works were, literally, at my desk as I wrote the book.

Since I began the project with no professional knowledge of Indian history and politics, I relied heavily on scholarly accounts to get me started. Most important was Francine R. Frankel's extraordinary *India's Political Economy* (1978 / 2005); Ramachandra Guha's broad account, *India after Gandhi* (2007) also offered an indispensable introduction. Analytical accounts like Paul R. Brass, *The Politics of India since Independence* (1987 / 1994) and Atul Kohli, *Democracy and Discontent* (1990) offer compelling interpretations of Indian politics. For Indian economics and political economy, Pranab K. Bardhan, *The Political Economy of Development in India* (1984), Lloyd I. Rudolph and Suzanne Hoeber Rudolph, *In Pursuit of Lakshmi* (1987), and Vivek Chibber, *Locked in Place* (2003), were especially helpful. On the study of economics in India, T. J. Byres, *The Indian Economy* (1998) offers a thoughtful reflection and analysis; for other retrospectives by those in the field, see Jagdish Bhagwati and Sukhamoy Chakravarty, "Contributions to Indian Economic Analysis," *American Economic Review* (1969) and V. N. Balasubramanyam, *Conversations with Economists* (2001). The planning moment of midcentury India has been the subject of especially rich analysis; see David Ludden, "India's Development Regime" (in Nicholas Dirks, ed., *Colonialism and Culture*, 1992); and the essays in Terence J. Byres, ed., *The State and Development Planning in India* (1994). Raghabendra

Chattopadhyay's remarkable dissertation ("The Idea of Planning in India," Australian National University, 1985) remains unpublished, though Benjamin Zachariah, *Developing India* (2005) examines an important portion of that story. While archive-based accounts of Indian foreign relations are few, Srinath Raghavan's impressive accounts—*War and Peace in Modern India* (2010) and *1971* (2013)—are both analytical incisive and empirically rich. I have also learned from Mithi Mukherjee, *India in the Shadows of Empire* (2010) and Manu Bhagavan, *The Peacemakers* (2012).

Life stories of key Indian figures also proved helpful for varying permutations of empirical details and analytical frameworks. Ashok Rudra wrote about his teacher in *Prasanta Chandra Mahalanobis* (1996); H. N. Kaul wrote admiringly in *K. D. Malaviya and the Evolution of India's Oil Industry* (1991); Sarvepelli Gopal's three-volume official biography, *Jawaharlal Nehru* (1976), remains important. Medha Kudaisya's *The Life and Times of G. D. Birla* (2003) interweaves the life of its main subject with Indian political economy in his time. Memoirs and recollections provide another avenue into the topics: T. N. Kaul's *Diplomacy in Peace and War* (1979) initiated his second career as a memoirist. B. K. Nehru's *Nice Guys Finish Second* (1997) revises Leo Durocher's famous exhortation but is lively and informative. I. G. Patel's *Glimpses of Indian Economic Policy* (2002) is a very helpful retrospective; for an American view of the same events, John P. Lewis's *India's Political Economy* (1995) combines retrospection and archival research, as does George Rosen's *Western Economists and Eastern Societies* (1985). Unfortunately, Amit Das Gupta's thorough biography of Foreign Secretary Subimal Dutt, *Serving India* (2017), arrived in time to admire but too late to use fully.

U.S. relations with India have been well analyzed in a pathbreaking book by Robert McMahon, *The Cold War on the Periphery* (1994); Paul McGarr, *The Cold War in South Asia* (2013) updates and expands the story with new archival materials. On early Indo-British relations, see Anita Inder Singh, *The Limits of British Influence* (1993). Dennis Merrill's *Bread and the Ballot* (1990) may well be the first archivally based history of U.S. development efforts anywhere; that he chose India made the work even more significant. Giles Boquérat's *No Strings Attached?* (2003) studies similar events from an Indian perspective. Histories of U.S. development efforts have become more and more numerous in recent years. Nick Cullather wrote pioneering articles as well as an insightful book, *Hungry World* (2010); Matt Connelly's *Fatal Misconception* (2008) offers a rich account of a topic adjacent to economic development. Corinna Unger's account of U.S. and West German aid proved helpful when it appeared in the late stages of my writing: *Entwicklungspfaden in Indien* (2015). Vernon W. Ruttan's *United States Development Assistance Policy* (1996) provides a very thorough account of the domestic and bureaucratic politics of American aid over a long haul, while Burton I. Kaufman's *Trade and Aid* (1982) analyzes the debates of the administration of President Dwight D. Eisenhower. The World Bank is well analyzed in an official history—Edward S. Mason and Robert E. Asher's *The World Bank since Bretton Woods* (1973)—and a more recent account, Devesh Kapur, John P. Lewis, and Richard Webb's *The World Bank* (1997).

The study of the Soviet Union in the Third World was primarily the province of political scientists, but excellent historical studies have emerged—and are still emerging. Some of the contemporaneous studies of published scholarship have proved remarkably incisive: Steven Clarkson, *The Soviet Theory of Development* (1978), and Jerry Hough, *The Struggle for the Third World* (1985); see also Robert Remnek's earlier and more modest *Soviet Scholars and Soviet Foreign Policy* (1975). For a review of the field as of 2010–2011 see Tobias Rupprecht, "Die sowjetische Gesellschaft in der Welt des Kalten Kriegs," *Jahrbücher für Geschichte Osteuropas* (2010). The essays in Andreas Hilger's edited volume *Die Sowjetunion und die Dritte Welt* (2009) expand our knowledge of this once-neglected topic. Oscar Sanchez-Sibony's *Red Globalization* (2014) offers a sharp argument on economic aspects of Soviet–Third World relations. Vojtech Mastny's "The Soviet Union's Partnership with India," *Journal of Cold War Studies* (2010) pulls together an extraordinary range of sources. Unfortunately Andreas Hilger's *Sowjetisch-indische Beziehungen, 1941–1968* did not appear in time to engage in this text—though I have learned a great deal from his articles and document collections. All of these works provided indispensable information and insight for *The Price of Aid*. Unless otherwise noted, all translations are my own.

List of Archives Cited

Antioch College Library
    Arthur E. Morgan Papers

Archive of the Foreign Policy of the Russian Federation (AVPRF)
    fond 90 / 090—India Desk (Referantura po Indii)

Archive of the Polish Academy of Sciences
    Oskar Lange Papers

Archive of the Russian Academy of Sciences (ARAN)
   fond 499—Division of Economic, Philosophical, and Legal Sciences
   fond 579—Foreign Department
   fond 1978—Institute of International Economics and World Politics

British Library
   India Office Records

Dwight D. Eisenhower Presidential Library (DDEL)
   Ezra Taft Benson Papers
   John Foster Dulles Papers
   Dennis A. FitzGerald Papers
   Christian A. Herter Papers
   Thomas Mann Papers
   Office of the Staff Secretary Records
   Office of the Special Assistance for National Security Affairs Records
      (OSANSA)
      National Security Council Files (NSC)
      Operations Coordinating Board Files (OCB)
   Joseph Rand Papers
   Clarence Randall Journals
   Donald Paarlberg Papers
   James H. Smith Papers
   Staff Secretary Records
   U.S. Committee on Foreign Economic Policy Records (USCFEP)
      Office of the Chairman Records
   White House Central Files (WHCF)
      Confidential Files
      Official Files
      Subject Files
   White House Office Records (WHO)
      NSC Staff Records
   Ann Whitman Files (AWF)
      Legislative Files
      National Security Council Records (NSC)

Gerald R. Ford Presidential Library (GRFL)
  National Security Advisor Files
    International Economic Affairs Staff Files (NSAD—IEAS)
    NSC Middle Eastern and South Asian Affairs Staff Files
      (NSAD—NSC-MESA)
    Presidential Transition File (NSAD—Transition)
    Presidential Country Files–Middle East and South Asia (PCF-MESA)

Foundation Archives of Parties and Mass Organizations of the GDR, Federal
  Archive of Germany (SAPMO)
    DY30—Central Committee of the SED Records

Hoover Institution Archives
  Milton Friedman Papers

Lyndon B. Johnson Presidential Library (LBJL)
  Robert Komer Papers
  National Security Files (NSF)
    Country Files
    McGeorge Bundy Files
    Edward Hamilton Files
    Charles E. Johnson Files
    Robert Komer Files
    NSC Histories
    W. W. Rostow Files
    Harold Saunders Files
  White House Administrative Histories

John F. Kennedy Presidential Library (JFKL)
  C. Douglas Dillon Papers
  John Kenneth Galbraith Papers
  Roger Hilsman Papers
  National Security Files (NSF)

Library of Congress Manuscript Reading Room (LC)
  W. Averell Harriman Papers
  Loy Henderson Papers
  Daniel Patrick Moynihan Papers
  Prints and Photographs Collection

Mahalanobis Memorial Museum and Library, Indian Statistical Institute (ISI)
  Planning Commission Records (PC / ISI)
  Visitor Records

Massachusetts Institute of Technology Archives (MIT)
  Center for International Studies Records (CIS)
  Max F. Millikan Papers

National Archives of India (NAI)
  Cabinet Secretariat Records
  Education Department Records
  Finance Department Records
  Legislative Department Records
  Ministry of External Affairs Records (MEA)
  Ministry of Food and Agriculture Records
  Ministry of Home Affairs Records
  Planning Commission Records (PC / NAI)
  Prime Minister's Office Records (PMO)
  Private Papers
      G. L. Nanda Papers

National Security Archive (NSA)
  Russian and Eastern European Document Database (READD)

Nehru Memorial Museum and Library (NMML)
  Subimal Dutt Papers
  P. N. Haksar Papers (Installments I–II, III)
  T. N. Kaul Papers (Installments I–III)
  T. T. Krishnamachari Papers
  J. C. Kumarappa Papers
  K. D. Malaviya Papers
  M. O. Mathai Papers
  G. L. Mehta Papers (Installments I–II, III–IV)
  Asok Mitra Papers
  K. M. Munshi Papers
  B. K. Nehru Papers
  R. K. Nehru Papers
  Vijayalakshmi Pandit Papers (Installments I, II)
  Pitamber Pant Papers

C. Rajagopalachari Papers (Installments VI–XII)
Meghnad Saha Papers (Installments I–IV, V, VII)
Purshotamdas Thakurdas Papers
K. S. Thimayya Papers

Richard Nixon Presidential Library (RMNL)
National Security Files—Country Files (NSF—Country)

Pitamber Pant Papers (Privately held—donated to NMML)

Political Archive of the Foreign Office, Berlin (PAAA)
New Office Records

Seeley G. Mudd Manuscript Library, Princeton University
John Foster Dulles Papers
Albert O. Hirschman Papers

Rockefeller Archive Center (RAC)
Ford Foundation Records (FF)

Russian State Archive of the Economy (RGAE)
fond 29—State Committee for Aviation Technology, 1957–1965
fond 298—Committee for Military Technology / Department of Foreign
Relations, 1957–1965
fond 365—Institutions for Foreign Economic Connections
fond 413—Ministry of Foreign Trade
fond 4372—State Planning Committee (Gosplan)
fond 9480—State Committee for Science and Technology

Russian State Archive for Contemporary History (RGANI)
fond 1—Congresses of the Communist Party of the Soviet Union
fond 5—Apparatus of the Central Committee
opis' 17—Department of Science and Culture
opis' 28—International Department
opis' 30—General Department
opis' 35—Department of Science and Higher Education
Institutions

Russian State Archive of Socio-Political History (RGASPI)
fond 82—V. I. Molotov Papers
fond 558—I. V. Stalin Papers

State Archive of the Russian Federation (GARF)
  fond R-5446—Council of Ministers
    opis' 120—A. I. Mikoian

Harry S. Truman Library (HSTL)
  Dean Acheson Papers
  Matthew J. Connelly Papers
  Henry F. Grady Papers
  George McGhee Papers
  President's Secretary's Files (PSF)
  Psychological Strategy Board Records (PSB)
  White House Central Files (WHCF)—Official Files

UK National Archives (UKNA)
  Atomic Energy Authority Records (AEA)
  Cabinet Records
  Commonwealth Relations Office Records (CRO)
  Foreign Office Records (FO)
  Ministry of Defence Records (MOD)
  Prime Minister's Office (PMO)
  Treasury Records

U.S. National Archives (USNA)
  Record Group 59—Department of State
    Central Foreign Policy File (CFPF)
      entry A1-1134A: Ex–Top Secret Files, 1964–1966
    State Department Decimal File (SDDF)
    entry A1-558CA: Policy Planning Staff Records
    entry A1-1330: General Subject Files Related to South Asia, 1957–1959
    entry A1-3008A: General Records Relating to Atomic Energy
      Matters, 1948–1962
    entry A1-3139: Near Eastern Affairs / South Asia Division / Records of
      the Director, 1960–1961
    entry A1-5026: Policy Planning Subject and Country Files, 1965–1969
    entry A1-5041: Policy Planning Subject Files, 1963–1973
    entry A1-5254: Near Eastern Affairs / India-Nepal-Ceylon Country
      Director / Records Relating to Indian Economic Affairs, 1964–1966

entry A1-5255: Near Eastern Affairs / India-Nepal-Ceylon
Country Director / Records Relating to Indian Political Affairs,
1964–1966

entry A1-5640: Near Eastern Affairs / India-Nepal-Ceylon Country
Director / Records Relating to India, 1966–1975 (assembles
twenty-one related lot files)

Record Group 286—USAID

entry P266: Executive Secretary / Country and Regional
Correspondence, 1964–1971

entry P270: Office of the Executive Secretary / Country and Regional
Files, 1961–1966

entry P409: Classified Country and Regional Files, 1965–1986

entry P475: Mission to India / Office of the Director / Records
Relating to Program Liaison with Government of India, 1957–1963

Record Group 326—U.S. Atomic Energy Commission (USAEC)

entry 67-B1: Office of the Secretary / General Correspondence,
1951–1958

Record Group 330—Office of the Secretary of Defense

entry A1-1025: Office of the Assistant Secretary of Defense for
International Security Affairs / General Files, Secret and Below,
1962 (OASD-ISA)

Record Group 469—Records of the U.S. Foreign Assistance Agencies
(RUSFAA), 1948–1961

entry P268B: International Cooperation Agency / U.S. Operations
Mission to India / Office of the Director / Classified Subject File,
1953–1959

entry P271: International Cooperation Agency / U.S. Operations
Mission in India / Office of the Director / Classified General
Correspondence, 1953–1956

entry P273: Foreign Operations Administration / U.S. Operations
Mission to India / Classified Central Subject Files, 1952–1962

entry P274: U.S. Operations Mission in India / Development
Division / Classified Subject Files, 1951–1960

entry UD181: Office of the Director / Geographic Files, 1948–1955

entry UD191A: International Cooperation Agency / Executive
Secretariat / Subject Files of the Director, 1952–1960

entry UD600A: Office of Near East and South Asia / South Asia
Division / India Project Files, 1952–1958
Record Group 490—Peace Corps
entry P16: Office of International Operations / Country Plans,
1966–1985

University of Oslo, Department of Economics Archive
Ragnar Frisch Papers

World Bank Group Archives (WBGA)
Bernard R. Bell Papers
Country Files (fond 1)
Benjamin B. King Papers
Robert S. McNamara Papers
George Woods Papers
Copies from Columbia University Collection (CU / WBGA)
Personal Papers

Yale University Library, Rare Books and Manuscripts
Chester Bowles Papers
Douglas Ensminger Papers
William Gaud Papers

Oral Histories / Interviews

Author Interviews
Jagdish Bhagwati, Cambridge, Mass., July 1, 2011
Thomas Weisskopf, Ann Arbor, Mich., March 12, 2014

Lyndon Baines Johnson Presidential Library (LBJL)
Orville Freeman, February 14, 1969
Robert Komer, January 30, 1970

Nehru Memorial Museum and Library (NMML)
M. A. Menshikov, July 1967
Gunnar Myrdal, January 20, 1974

Center for Oral History, Columbia University (CCOH)
Arthur F. Burns, 1967

Earl L. Butz, 1968
I. G. Patel, March 9, 2001
Harold E. Stassen, 1967
George Votaw, April 30, 1985

World Bank (WBGA)
Bernard Bell, November 13, 1985
Benjamin B. King, August 14, 1991

Electronic Collections

Central Intelligence Agency FOIA Reading Room: www.cia.gov/library
/readingroom

Cold War International History Project (CWIHP): digitalarchive.wilsoncenter
.org/

Declassified Documents Retrieval System (DDRS): subscription service

Digital National Security Archive (DNSA): subscription service
China 1960–1968
Henry Kissinger Transcripts
Nuclear Proliferation
Presidential Directives

International Monetary Fund (IMF) Archives: archivescatalog.imf.org/

Miller Center Presidential Recordings: millercenter.org
/presidentialrecordings

National Security Archive (NSA): nsarchive.gwu.edu
The Tilt: The U.S. and the South Asian Crisis of 1971

Organization for Economic Cooperation and Development
Query Wizard for International Development Statistics: stats.oecd.org/qwids

Parallel History Project (PHP): www.php.isn.ethz.ch
India-Soviet Bloc Relations: The View from India
Indo-Soviet Relations

Stockholm International Peace Research Institute (SIPRI): www.sipri.org
  Importer / Exporter TIV Tables
  Trade Registers

USAID Development Experience Clearinghouse: dec.usaid.gov

USAID Explorer: explorer.usaid.gov

World Bank Archives Online Collections: www.worldbank.org/en/about
  /archives

Abbreviations

Archives

ARAN	Arkhiv Rossiiskoi Akademii Nauk (Archive of the Russian Academy of Sciences)
AVPRF	Arkhiv vneshnei politiki Rossiiskoi Federatsii (Archive of Foreign Policy of the Russian Federation)
CCOH	Columbia Center for Oral History, Columbia University Libraries
CWIHP	Cold War International History Project
DDEL	Dwight D. Eisenhower Presidential Library
DDRS	Declassified Document Reference System
DNSA	Digital National Security Archive
GARF	Gosudarstvennyi arkhiv Rossiiskoi Federatsii (State Archive of the Russian Federation)
GRFL	Gerald R. Ford Presidential Library
HSTL	Harry S. Truman Presidential Library
JFKL	John F. Kennedy Presidential Library
LBJL	Lyndon Baines Johnson Presidential Library
LC	Library of Congress
NAI	National Archives of India
NMML	Nehru Memorial Museum and Library
NSA	National Security Archive (George Washington University)
PAAA	Politisches Archiv des Auswärtigen Amtes (Political Archive of the Foreign Office), Germany
PHP	Parallel History Project
RAC	Rockefeller Archive Center

RGAE	Rossiiskii gosudarstvennyi arkhiv ekonomiki (Russian State Economic Archive)
RGANI	Rossiiskii gosudarstvennyi arkhiv noveishei istorii (Russian State Archive of Contemporary History)
RGASPI	Rossiiskii gosudarstvennyi arkhiv sotsial'no-politicheskoi istorii (Russian State Archive of Socio-Political History)
RMNL	Richard M. Nixon Presidential Library
SAPMO	Stiftung Archiv der Parteien und Massenorganisationen (Foundation Archives of the Party and Mass Organizations of the GDR)
UKNA	UK National Archives
USNA	U.S. National Archives
WBGA	World Bank Group Archives

Collections

AWF	Ann Whitman Files (DDEL)
CFPF	Central Foreign Policy Files (USNA)
CIS	Center for International Studies (MIT)
CREST	CIA Records Search Tool (USNA)
CRO	Commonwealth Relations Office (UKNA)
FCO	Foreign and Commonwealth Office (UKNA)
FF	Ford Foundation Records (RAC)
FO	Foreign Office (UKNA)
IEAS	International Economic Affairs Staff (GRFL)
MEA	Ministry of External Affairs (NAI)
MOD	Ministry of Defence (UKNA)
NSAD	National Security Adviser (GRFL)
NSC	U.S. National Security Council
NSC-MESA	National Security Council—Middle East and South Asia (GRFL)
NSF	National Security Files (JFKL, LBJL)
OASD-ISA	Office of the Assistant Secretary of Defense for International Security Affairs (USNA)
OCB	Operations Coordinating Board (DDEL)
OSANSA	Office of the Special Assistant for National Security Affairs (DDEL)

PC	Planning Commission (ISI, NAI)
PCF-MESA	President's Country Files—Middle East and South Asia (GRFL)
PMO	Prime Minister's Office (NAI, UKNA)
PSB	Psychological Strategy Board (HSTL)
PSF	President's Secretary's Files (HSTL)
READD	Russian and Eastern European Documents Database (NSA)
RUSFAA	Records of U.S. Foreign Assistance Agencies (USNA)
SDDF	State Department Decimal Files (USNA)
SDR	State Department Records (USNA)
USCFEP	U.S. Committee on Foreign Economic Policy (DDEL)
WHCF	White House Central Files (DDEL)
WHO	White House Office (DDEL)

Publications

AR	*Asian Reporter*
CWMG	M. K. Gandhi, *Collected Works of Mahatma Gandhi,* 100 vols. (Delhi: Publications Division, 1958–1994)
EA	Ministry of Finance, Department of Economic Affairs, *External Assistance* (New Delhi: Ministry of Finance, various years)
EE	*Eastern Economist*
EPW	*Economic and Political Weekly* (1966–)
EW	*Economic Weekly* (1949–1965)
FRUS	U.S. Department of State, Office of the Historian, *Foreign Relations of the United States,* various vols. (Washington, D.C.: U.S. Department of State, various years)
IJPRVD	*Indian Journal of Power and River Valley Development*
LCM	Jawaharlal Nehru, *Letters to Chief Ministers, 1947–1964,* ed. G. Parthasarathi (New Delhi: Jawaharlal Nehru Memorial Fund, 1985)
NYT	*New York Times*
PPP	*Public Papers of the Presidents,* various vols. (Washington D.C.: Office of the Federal Register, various years)

SWJN1	Jawaharlal Nehru, *Selected Works of Jawaharlal Nehru*, [1st series,] ed. S. Gopal, 15 vols. (New Delhi: Jawaharlal Nehru Memorial Fund, 1972–1982)
SWJN2	Jawaharlal Nehru, *Selected Works of Jawaharlal Nehru*, 2nd series, ed. S. Gopal, 67 vols. (New Delhi: Jawaharlal Nehru Memorial Fund, 1984–)
TOI	*Times of India*
VTSSSR	*Vneshniaia torgovlia Soiuza SSR,* various vols. (Moscow: Ministerstvo vneshnei torgovli SSSR, various years)

Miscellaneous

AEC	Atomic Energy Commission (India)
AIC	Aid-India Consortium
AICC	All-India Congress Committee
CC-CPSU	Central Committee of the Communist Party of the Soviet Union
CD	community development
CPI	Communist Party of India
CU	Columbia University
DLF	Development Loan Fund
DVC	Damodar Valley Corporation
ECAFE	Economic Commission for Asia and the Far East
FAO	Food and Agriculture Organization
FICCI	Federation of Indian Chambers of Commerce and Industry
FOA	Foreign Operations Administration
FOIA	Freedom of Information Act
GIU	Chief Engineering Administration (of GKES)
GKES	State Committee for Foreign Economic Connections (Gosudarstvennyi Komitet po Vneshnim Ekonomicheskim Sviaziam)
GOI	Government of India
HC	High Commission
HEC	Heavy Engineering Corporation (India)
ICICI	Industrial Credit and Investment Corporation of India
IAF	Indian Air Force

IBRD	International Bank for Reconstruction and Development (World Bank)
IDA	International Development Association (of the World Bank)
IMF	International Monetary Fund
INC	Indian National Congress
I-O	input-output (analysis)
ISI	Indian Statistical Institute
LBJ	Lyndon Baines Johnson
LSE	London School of Economics
MID	Ministry of Foreign Affairs (USSR)
MIT	Massachusetts Institute of Technology
NGO	nongovernmental organization
NIEO	New International Economic Order (United Nations)
NPC	National Planning Committee (India, 1938–1949)
ONGC	Oil and Natural Gas Commission (India)
PC	Planning Commission (India, 1950–2014)
TCA	U.S. Technical Cooperation Administration
TTK	T. T. Krishnamachari
TVA	Tennessee Valley Authority
UNCTAD	UN Conference on Trade and Development
USAID	U.S. Agency for International Development
USAEC	U.S. Atomic Energy Commission
USAF	U.S. Air Force

Notes

Introduction

1. "Spravka o sotrudnichestve s Respublikoi Indii v oblasti izpol'zovaniia atomnoi energii v mirnykh tseliakh," December 30, 1971, RGAE, 9480 / 9 / 1712 / 1–4 (on the U.S. delegation, see Byron Kratzker to John Hall, April 12, 1960, SDR, USNA, RG 59, entry A1-3008A, box 498); unnamed newspaper, quoted in New Delhi Embassy to U.S. State Department, February 29, 1960, Staff Secretary Records, DDEL, International Subseries, box 7; "Soviet Atom Scientist," *TOI*, February 29, 1960, 3; "Russian Help Assured," *TOI*, March 9, 1960, 7.

2. Michał Kalecki, "Observations on Social and Economic Aspects of 'Intermediate Regimes' (1964)," in *Developing Economies*, ed. Jerzy Osiatyński (Oxford: Clarendon Press, 1993), 10.

3. USAEC meeting with U.S. Department of State officials, November 5, 1959, SDR, USNA, RG 59, entry A1-3008A, box 496.

4. On the scientists' dissatisfaction, see M. R. Srinivasan, *From Fission to Fusion: The Story of India's Atomic Energy Programme* (New Delhi: Viking, 2002), 181–183.

5. *EA 1978–1979*, 222–225. On "two feet" see, for instance, Joseph Rand to Clarence Randall, July 10, 1959, USCFEP, Office of the Chairman Staff Series, DDEL, box 4; and S. A. Skachkov to Central Committee, September 7, 1959, RGANI, 5 / 30 / 305 / 116–117.

6. Vijay Joshi and I. M. D. Little, *India: Macroeconomics and Political Economy, 1964–1991* (Washington, D.C.: World Bank, 1994), 107.

7. For a like-minded genealogy of UN development efforts, see Daniel Speich Chassé, "Technical Internationalism and Economic Development at the Founding Moment of the UN System," in *International Organizations and Development, 1945–1990*, ed. Marc Frey, Sönke Kunkel, and Corinna R. Unger (Houndmills, England: Palgrave Macmillan, 2014), 21–45.

8. On population, see Susan Greenhalgh, "The Social Construction of Population Science: An Intellectual, Institutional, and Political History of Twentieth-Century Demography," *Comparative Studies in Society and History* 38:1 (1996): 26–66; and Susan Greenhalgh, "On the Crafting of Population Knowledge," *Population and Development Review* 38:1 (2012): 121–131. On economic measures, see Timothy Mitchell, "Economists and the Economy in the Twentieth Century," in *The Politics of Method in the Human Sciences: Positivism and Its Epistemological Others*, ed. George Steinmetz (Durham, N.C.: Duke University Press, 2005), 126–141; Daniel Speich, "The

Use of Global Abstractions: National Income Accounting in the Period of Imperial Decline," *Journal of Global History* 6:1 (2011): 7–28; and Dirk Philipsen, *The Little Big Number: How GDP Came to Rule the World and What to Do about It* (Princeton, N.J.: Princeton University Press, 2015). For additional citations on economic measurement, see David C. Engerman, "American Knowledge and Global Power," *Diplomatic History* 31:4 (2007): 599–622.

9. For varied perspectives on conceptions of "backwardness," see Alexander Gerschenkron, *Economic Backwardness in Historical Perspective: A Book of Essays* (Cambridge, Mass.: Harvard University Press, 1962), especially the 1952 title essay. See also Johannes Fabian, *Time and the Other: How Anthropology Makes Its Object* (New York: Columbia University Press, 1983); and Jeremy Adelman, "Development and the Global History of Distributive Justice," Mellon-Sawyer Seminar Series "Reinterpreting the Twentieth Century," Boston University, 2014, http://www.wbur.org/worldofideas/2015/06/07/adel.

10. See, for instance, Gilbert Rist, *The History of Development: From Western Origins to Global Faith* (London: Zed Books, 1997).

11. Teodor Shanin, *Russia as a "Developing Society"* (London: Macmillan, 1985); Tim McDaniel, *Autocracy, Modernization, and Revolution in Russia and Iran* (Princeton, N.J.: Princeton University Press, 2014); Nathan J. Citino, "The Ottoman Legacy in Cold War Modernization," *International Journal of Middle East Studies* 40:4 (2008): 579–597. Frederick Cooper, *Decolonization and African Society: The Labor Question in French and British Africa* (Cambridge: Cambridge University Press, 1996).

12. Manu Goswami, *Producing India: From Colonial Economy to National Space* (Chicago: University of Chicago Press, 2004); Benjamin Zachariah, *Developing India: An Intellectual and Social History, c. 1930–50* (New Delhi: Oxford University Press, 2005); David Ludden, "Development Regimes in South Asia: History and the Governance Conundrum," *EPW*, September 10–16, 2005, 4042–4051; David Ludden, "India's Development Regime," in *Colonialism and Culture*, ed. Nicholas B. Dirks (Ann Arbor: University of Michigan Press, 1992), 247–287; Raghabendra Chattopadhyay, "An Early British Government Initiative in the Genesis of Indian Planning," *EPW*, January 31, 1987, PE19–PE29.

13. Montagu Butler note in George Schuster, "Notes on Economic Policy, 1930," Finance Department Records, NAI, 15-I-F.

14. This paragraph builds on David C. Engerman, "Ideology and the Origins of the Cold War, 1917–1962," in *The Cambridge History of the Cold War*, ed. Melvyn P. Leffler and Odd Arne Westad (Cambridge: Cambridge University Press, 2010), 1:20–43.

15. Mark Mazower, *Governing the World: The History of an Idea* (New York: Penguin Press, 2012); Charles S. Maier, *Once within Borders: Territories of Power, Wealth, and Belonging since 1500* (Cambridge, Mass.: Harvard University Press, 2016), chapter 6. A trio of articles by John D. Kelly and Martha Kaplan make an especially effective case; see John D. Kelly and Martha Kaplan, "'My Ambition Is Much Higher than Independence': U.S. Power, the UN World, and Its Critics," in *Decolonization: Perspectives from Now and Then*, ed. Prasenjit Duara (New York: Routledge, 2004), 131–152; John D. Kelly and Martha Kaplan, "Legal Fictions after Empire," in *The State of Sovereignty: Territories, Laws, Populations*, ed. Douglas

Howland and Luise White (Bloomington: Indiana University Press, 2009); and John D. Kelly and Martha Kaplan, "Nation and Decolonization: Toward a New Anthropology of Nationalism," *Anthropological Theory* 1:4 (2001): 419–438.

16. Partha Chatterjee, *Nationalist Thought and the Colonial World: A Derivative Discourse?* (London: Zed Books, 1986), remains an essential starting point. See also Manu Goswami, "Rethinking the Modular Nation Form: Toward a Sociohistorical Conception of Nationalism," *Comparative Studies in Society and History* 44:4 (2002): 770–799; Manu Goswami, "Imaginary Futures and Colonial Internationalisms," *American Historical Review* 117:5 (2012): 1461–1485 (which cites a growing strand of scholarship on anticolonialism that did not necessarily take the nation-state as its end point); Itty Abraham, *How India Became Territorial: Foreign Policy, Diaspora, Geopolitics* (Stanford, Calif.: Stanford University Press, 2014); and Benjamin Zachariah, *Playing the Nation Game: The Ambiguities of Nationalism in India* (New Delhi: Yoda Press, 2011).

17. Mazower, *Governing the World,* chapter 10; Partha Chatterjee, "Development Planning and the Indian State," in *The State and Development Planning in India,* ed. Terence J. Byres (New Delhi: Oxford University Press, 1994), 51–72; Sugata Bose, "Instruments and Idioms of Colonial and National Development: India's Historical Experience in Comparative Perspective," in *International Development and the Social Sciences: Essays on the History and Politics of Knowledge,* ed. Frederick Cooper and Randall M. Packard (Berkeley: University of California Press, 1997), 45–63; Nick Cullather, " 'Fuel for the Good Dragon': The United States and Industrial Policy in Taiwan, 1950–1965," *Diplomatic History* 20:1 (1996): 1–26.

18. Steven Rodriguez, "Intervention by Other Means: The U.S., Cuba, and the Rockefeller Foundation International Health Division, 1929–1946" (MA Thesis, Brandeis University, 2017); Stephen Macekura, review of David C. Engerman, "Development Politics and the Cold War," June 9, 2017, H-Diplo, https://networks.h-net.org/node/28443/discussions/182361/h-diplo-article-review-703-"development-politics-and-cold-war".

19. The essential starting point is James Ferguson, *The Anti-Politics Machine: "Development," Depoliticization, and Bureaucratic Power in Lesotho* (Cambridge: Cambridge University Press, 1990), esp. 267–277. For more recent works in this insightful field, see Tania Li, *The Will to Improve: Governmentality, Development, and the Practice of Politics* (Durham, N.C.: Duke University Press, 2007); and David Mosse, "The Anthropology of International Development," *Annual Review of Anthropology* 42 (2013): 227–246. For works on India, see the essays in Carey Anthony Watt and Michael Mann, eds., *Civilizing Missions in Colonial and Postcolonial South Asia from Improvement to Development* (London: Anthem Press, 2011); Harald Fischer-Tiné and Michael Mann, eds., *Colonialism as Civilizing Mission: Cultural Ideology in British India* (London: Anthem Press, 2004); and Richard Harry Drayton, *Nature's Government: Science, Imperial Britain, and the "Improvement" of the World* (New Haven, Conn.: Yale University Press, 2000).

20. I am indebted to Bruce Schulman for this formulation.

21. Peter Evans, *Embedded Autonomy: States and Industrial Transformation* (Princeton, N.J.: Princeton University Press, 1995), 19.

22. Timothy Nunan, *Humanitarian Invasion: Global Development in Cold War Afghanistan* (Cambridge: Cambridge University Press, 2016), 71–74; Thomas C. Field, *From Development to Dictatorship: Bolivia and the Alliance for Progress in the Kennedy Era* (Ithaca, N.Y.: Cornell University Press, 2014); Amy C. Offner, "Anti-Poverty Programs, Social Conflict, and Economic Thought in Colombia and the United States, 1948–1980" (PhD diss., Columbia University, 2012); Michelle Grisé, "What Makes the Nation Strong? Rockets, Reactors, and Scientific Development in Pakistan, 1947–1998" (PhD diss., Yale University, 2017), cited with permission. For the battle between Vice President Jaramogi Oginga Odinga and Minister Tom Mboya see, for instance, Poppy Cullen, " 'Kenya Is No Doubt a Special Case': British Policy towards Kenya, 1960–1980" (PhD diss., Durham University, 2015), chapter 2.

23. Carol Lancaster, *Foreign Aid: Diplomacy, Development, Domestic Politics* (Chicago: University of Chicago Press, 2007).

24. Oded Eran, *Mezhdunarodniki: An Assessment of Professional Expertise in the Making of Soviet Foreign Policy* (Ramat Gan, Israel: Turtledove Publishers, 1979); Nisha Sahai-Achuthan, "Soviet Indologists and the Institute of Oriental Studies," *Journal of Asian Studies* 42:2 (1983): 323–343; Nils Gilman, *Mandarins of the Future: Modernization Theory in Cold War America* (Baltimore: Johns Hopkins University Press, 2003); Zachary Lockman, *Field Notes: The Making of Middle East Studies in the United States* (Stanford, Calif.: Stanford University Press, 2016), chapters 1–3.

25. John Foster Dulles conversation with Citizen Advisors on the Mutual Security Program, October 25, 1956, in FRUS *1955–1957,* 10:118; Michael R. Adamson, " 'The Most Important Single Aspect of Our Foreign Policy': The Eisenhower Administration, Foreign Aid, and the Third World," in *The Eisenhower Administration, the Third World, and the Globalization of the Cold War,* ed. Kathryn C. Statler and Andrew R. Johns (Lanham, Md.: Rowman & Littlefield, 2006), 48.

26. L. M. Kaganovich (against) and A. I. Mikoian (for), in Politburo meeting, December 16, 1955, in *Prezidium TsK KPSS 1954–1964,* ed. A. A. Fursenko (Moscow: Rosspen, 2003), 1:71–72.

27. Matthew Connelly, *A Diplomatic Revolution: Algeria's Fight for Independence and the Origins of the Post–Cold War Era* (Oxford: Oxford University Press, 2002); Ryan M. Irwin, *Gordian Knot: Apartheid and the Unmaking of the Liberal World Order* (Oxford: Oxford University Press, 2012); Paul Thomas Chamberlin, *The Global Offensive: The United States, the Palestine Liberation Organization, and the Making of the Post-Cold War Order* (Oxford: Oxford University Press, 2012).

28. For an exhaustive criticism of the adage, attributed to Senator Arthur Vandenberg, see Julian E. Zelizer, *Arsenal of Democracy: The Politics of National Security in America from World War II to the War on Terrorism* (New York: Basic Books, 2010).

29. Nick Cullather, *The Hungry World: America's Cold War Battle against Poverty in Asia* (Cambridge, Mass.: Harvard University Press, 2010); Matthew James Connelly, *Fatal Misconception: The Struggle to Control World Population* (Cambridge, Mass.: Harvard University Press, 2008); Erez Manela, "A Pox on Your Narrative: Writing Disease Control into Cold War History," *Diplomatic History* 34:2 (2010): 299–323. See also the essays in Peter A. Hall,

ed., *The Political Power of Economic Ideas: Keynesianism across Nations* (Princeton, N.J.: Princeton University Press, 1989).

30. Nick Cullather, "The Third Race," *Diplomatic History* 33:3 (2009): 507–512.

31. On the NIEO, see especially the special issue introduced by Nils Gilman, "The New International Economic Order: A Reintroduction," *Humanity* 6:1 (2015): 1–16. For more on economics and the Cold War, see Diane B. Kunz, *Butter and Guns: America's Cold War Economic Diplomacy* (New York: Free Press, 1997); and David C. Engerman, "The Romance of Economic Development and New Histories of the Cold War," *Diplomatic History* 28:1 (2004): 23–54. See, more broadly, Thomas W. Zeiler, "Opening Doors in the World Economy," in *Global Interdependence: The World after 1945*, ed. Akira Iriye (Cambridge, Mass.: Harvard University Press, 2014), 203–361. For the world economy from a Soviet perspective, see Oscar Sanchez-Sibony, *Red Globalization: The Political Economy of the Soviet Cold War from Stalin to Khrushchev* (Cambridge: Cambridge University Press, 2014).

32. Arne Westad's now-classic account expanded the geographic and analytical horizons of Cold War history; see Odd Arne Westad, *The Global Cold War: Third World Interventions and the Making of Our Times* (Cambridge: Cambridge University Press, 2005). For an impressive recent work, see Jeremy Scott Friedman, *Shadow Cold War: The Sino-Soviet Split and the Third World* (Chapel Hill: University of North Carolina Press, 2015).

33. For useful historiographic reviews, see Corinna R. Unger, "Histories of Development and Modernization: Findings, Reflections, Future Research," December 9, 2010, H-Soz-Kult http://www.hsozkult.de/literaturereview/id/forschungsberichte-1130; Joseph Morgan Hodge, "Writing the History of Development (Part 1: The First Wave)," *Humanity* 6:3 (2015): 429–463; and Joseph Morgan Hodge, "Writing the History of Development (Part 2: Longer, Deeper, Wider)," *Humanity* 7:1 (2016): 125–174. For a sophisticated overview, see Nick Cullather, "Development and Technopolitics," in *Explaining the History of American Foreign Relations*, 3rd ed., ed. Frank Costigliola and Michael J. Hogan (Cambridge: Cambridge University Press, 2016), 102–117.

34. For snapshots of the first historical approaches to the USSR in the Third World, see Tobias Rupprecht, "Die sowjetische Gesellschaft in der Welt des Kalten Kriegs: neuen Forschungsperspektiven," *Jahrbücher für Geschichte Osteuropas* 58:3 (2010): 381–399; David C. Engerman, "The Second World's Third World," *Kritika* 12:1 (2011): 183–211; and Michael David-Fox, "The Implications of Transnationalism," *Kritika* 12:4 (2011): 885–904. For later approaches, see "Across and Beyond: Rethinking Transnational History," *Kritika* 17:4 (2016): 715–720; and the special issue introduced by Christine Philliou, "USSR South: Postcolonial Worlds in the Soviet Imaginary," *Comparative Studies of South Asia, Africa and the Middle East* 33:2 (2013): 197–200.

35. Some examples of published research on aspects of Soviet–Third World relations are Ragna Boden, *Die Grenzen der Weltmacht: sowjetische Indonesienpolitik von Stalin bis Brežnev* (Stuttgart: F. Steiner, 2006); Tobias Rupprecht, *Soviet Internationalism after Stalin: Interaction and Exchange between the USSR and Latin America during the Cold War* (Cambridge: Cambridge University Press, 2015); Guy Laron, *Origins of the Suez Crisis:*

Postwar Development Diplomacy and the Struggle over Third World Industrialization, 1945–1956 (Washington, D.C.: Woodrow Wilson Center Press, 2013); Alessandro Iandolo, "The Rise and Fall of the 'Soviet Model of Development' in West Africa, 1957–64," *Cold War History* 12:4 (2012): 683–704; Alessandro Iandolo, "Imbalance of Power: The Soviet Union and the Congo Crisis, 1960–1961," *Journal of Cold War Studies* 16:2 (2014): 32–55; Vojtech Mastny, "The Soviet Union's Partnership with India," *Journal of Cold War Studies* 12:3 (2010): 50–90; Antonio Giustozzi and Artemy M. Kalinovsky, *Missionaries of Modernity: Advisory Missions and the Struggle for Hegemony in Afghanistan and beyond* (London: C. Hurst, 2016); Artemy M. Kalinovsky, "Not Some British Colony in Africa: The Politics of Decolonization and Modernization in Soviet Central Asia, 1955–1964," *Ab Imperio* 2013:2 (2013): 191–222; and S. V. Mazov, *Politika SSSR v zapadnoi Afrike, 1956–1964: neizvestnye stranitsy istorii Kholodnoi Voiny* (Moscow: Nauka, 2008). See also Andreas Hilger, *Sowjetisch-indische Beziehungen 1941–1966: Imperiale Agenda und nationale Identität in der Ära von Dekolonisierung und Kaltem Krieg* (Cologne: Böhlau Verlag, forthcoming, 2018).

36. Sugata Bose and Kris Manjapra, eds., *Cosmopolitan Thought Zones: South Asia and the Global Circulation of Ideas* (Houndmills, England: Palgrave Macmillan, 2010); Ali Raza, Franziska Roy, and Benjamin Zachariah, eds., *The Internationalist Moment: South Asia, Worlds, and Worldviews, 1917–1939* (New Delhi: SAGE India, 2014); Carolien Stolte and Harald Fischer-Tiné, "Imagining Asia in India: Nationalism and Internationalism (ca. 1905–1940), *Comparative Studies in Society and History* 54:1 (2012): 65–92; and Manu Goswami, "Imaginary Futures and Colonial Internationalisms," *American Historical Review* 117:5 (2012): 1461–1485.

37. Francine R. Frankel, *India's Political Economy, 1947–1977: The Gradual Revolution* (Princeton, N.J.: Princeton University Press, 1978); Ramachandra Guha, *India after Gandhi: The History of the World's Largest Democracy* (New York: Ecco, 2007); Vivek Chibber, *Locked in Place: State-Building and Late Industrialization in India* (Princeton, N.J.: Princeton University Press, 2003); Atul Kohli, *State-Directed Development: Political Power and Industrialization in the Global Periphery* (Cambridge: Cambridge University Press, 2004); Lloyd I. Rudolph and Susanne Hoeber Rudolph, *In Pursuit of Lakshmi: The Political Economy of the Indian State* (Chicago: University of Chicago Press, 1987). Pranab K. Bardhan, *The Political Economy of Development in India* (Oxford: Basil Blackwell, 1984).

38. Up through 1974–1975, U.S. loans amounted to 5,850 crores rupees, UK loans 1,300 crores rupees, World Bank / International Development Association loans 3,470 crores rupees, and the Soviet Union 1,020 crores rupees—out of total loans of 13,100 crores rupees. (In dollars these figures are U.S. loans $7.8 billion, UK loans $1.8 billion, World Bank loans $4.6 billion, and USSR loans $1.4 billion out of a total of $17.5 billion.) These figures are calculated in 1971 rupees; see *EA 1978–1979*, 222–225.

39. On British aid, see Michael Lipton, "Growing Mountain, Shrinking Mouse? Indian Poverty and British Bilateral Aid," *Modern Asian Studies* 30:3 (1996): 481–522; and Saskia Enthoven, "The Indo-British Aid Relationship: From Its Reluctant Beginning to Its Controversial End (1958–2015)" (PhD diss., Kings College London, in process). For West Germany, see especially Corinna R. Unger, *Entwicklungspfade in Indien: eine internationale*

Geschichte, 1947–1980 (Göttingen, Germany: Wallstein Verlag, 2015). On European overseas development efforts more generally, see Véronique Dimier, *The Invention of a European Development Aid Bureaucracy: Recycling Empire* (Basingstoke, England: Palgrave Macmillan, 2014).

40. Frankel, *India's Political Economy*, 388.

1. Debating Development and Discovering India

1. Jawaharlal Nehru, "Tryst with Destiny," in *SWJN2*, 3:135–136.

2. See especially M. R. Masani, "Ideologies That May Dominate Future India," *TOI*, August 15, 1947, 14.

3. Montagu Butler, quoted in George Schuster, "Notes on Economic Policy" (1930), Finance Department Records, NAI, 15-I-F, 1930; Bipan Chandra, *The Rise and Growth of Economic Nationalism in India; Economic Policies of Indian National Leadership, 1880–1905* (New Delhi: People's Publishing House, 1966); Sumit Sarkar, *The Swadeshi Movement in Bengal, 1903–1908*, 2nd ed. (Ranikhet, India: Permanent Black, 2010); Tirthankar Roy, "The British Empire and the Economic Development of India," *Revista de Historia Económica* 34:2 (2016): 1–28.

4. M. K. Gandhi, "Speech at Ellore," April 3, 1921, in *CWMG*, 19:510–514. See also the essays in M. K. Gandhi, *The Gospel of Swadeshi*, ed. Anand T. Hingorani (Mumbai: Bharatiya Vidya Bhavan, 1993).

5. Girish Mishra, *Nehru and the Congress Economic Policies* (New Delhi: Sterling Publishers, 1988); Sarvepalli Gopal, *Jawaharlal Nehru: A Biography* (Cambridge, Mass.: Harvard University Press, 1976), 1:106–109; Jawaharlal Nehru, "The Fascination of Russia," April 3, 1928, in *SWJN1*, 2:381–383; Jawaharlal Nehru, *Toward Freedom* (New York: John Day, 1942), 230–231.

6. A. Mukherjee, "Indian Capitalist Class and Congress on National Planning and Public Sector 1930–47," *EPW*, September 2, 1978, 1516–1528.

7. "Bombay Business Men Denounce Nehru's Ideas," *TOI*, May 30, 1931, 11; B. R. Tomlinson, *The Indian National Congress and the Raj, 1929–1942: The Penultimate Phase* (Toronto: Macmillan of Canada, 1976), chapter 2; David Lockwood, *The Indian Bourgeoisie: A Political History of the Indian Capitalist Class in the Early Twentieth Century* (London: I. B. Tauris, 2012), chapter 6; Benjamin Zachariah, *Developing India: An Intellectual and Social History, c. 1930–50* (New Delhi: Oxford University Press, 2005), chapter 4. On business leaders, see Claude Markovits, *Indian Business and Nationalist Politics, 1931–1939: The Indigenous Capitalist Class and the Rise of the Congress Party* (Cambridge: Cambridge University Press, 1985); and Stanley A. Kochanek, *Business and Politics in India* (Berkeley: University of California Press, 1974), chapter 10.

8. G. D. Birla, "A Plea for Planning," April 1, 1934, in *The Path to Prosperity: A Collection of the Speeches & Writings of G. D. Birla* (Allahabad, India: Leader Press, 1950), 11; M. P. Gandhi, "Economic Planning for India—A Supreme Necessity," *Indian Journal of Economics* 15:4 (1935): 397–408; N. R. Sarkar, quoted in Raghabendra Chattopadhyay, "Indian Business and Economic Planning, 1930–56," in *Business and Politics in India: A Historical Perspective*, ed. Dwijendra Tripathi (New Delhi: Manohar Publishers, 1991), 323. See also Raghabendra

Chattopadhyay, "An Early British Government Initiative in the Genesis of Indian Planning," *EPW*, January 31, 1983, PE19–PE29. On Western interest in Soviet planning, see David C. Engerman, *Modernization from the Other Shore: American Intellectuals and the Romance of Russian Development* (Cambridge, Mass.: Harvard University Press, 2003), chapters 6–7. M. Visvesvaraya was a well-known engineer and proponent of industrialization in the early twentieth century; see M. Visvesvaraya, *Planned Economy for India* (Bangalore City, India: Bangalore Press, 1934), 217, 220, 279.

9. Tomlinson, *Indian National Congress*, 30; David Washbrook, "The Rhetoric of Democracy and Development in Late Colonial India," in *Nationalism, Democracy and Development: State and Politics in India*, ed. Sugata Bose and Ayesha Jalal (New Delhi: Oxford University Press, 1997), 37.

10. AICC at Bombay, April 1931, and Congress at Karachi, March 1931, both in Indian National Congress, *Resolutions on Economic Policy, Programme, and Allied Matters (1924–1969)* (New Delhi: All-India Congress Committee, 1969), 3–6, 6–9; Jawaharlal Nehru, "Presidential Address," December 26, 1936, in *SWJN1*, 7:598–614.

11. "Congress-British Round Table Conference," *TOI*, October 15, 1938, 13; "All-India National Planning Commission to Be Formed," *TOI*, October 4, 1938, 6; INC National Planning Committee, *National Planning Committee: Being an Abstract of Proceedings and Other Particulars Relating to the National Planning Committee* (Bombay: Indian National Congress, 1939), 9–12; Subhas Chandra Bose, quoted in Pramit Chaudhuri, "The Origins of Modern India's Economic Development Strategy," in *The Indian National Congress and the Political Economy of India, 1885–1985*, ed. Mike Shepperdson and Colin Simmons (Aldershot, England: Avebury, 1988), 276–277; "A Plan for Industry," *TOI*, October 7, 1938, 8.

12. "National Planning Committee," *TOI*, October 18, 1938, 7; "All-India National Planning Commission to be Formed," *TOI*, October 4, 1938, 6; Jawaharlal Nehru to Kunwar Jagdish Prasad, June 20, 1939, and H. Dow to Jawaharlal Nehru, July 24, 1939, both in Legislative Department Records, NAI, 246 / 39 C&G; Chairman's Note on Congress Policy, December 21, 1938, in INC National Planning Committee, *Report of the National Planning Committee, 1938* (New Delhi: Indian Institute of Applied Political Research, 1988), 43.

13. Jawaharlal Nehru to K. T. Shah, May 13, 1939, in *SWJN1*, 9:373–374; Markovits, *Indian Business*, 141–144; Bidyut Chakrabarty, "Jawaharlal Nehru and Planning, 1938–41: India at the Crossroads," *Modern Asian Studies* 26:2 (1992): 283; M. K. Gandhi to Jawaharlal Nehru, August 11, 1939, in *CWMG*, 70:86; M. K. Gandhi to Amrit Kaur, June 29, 1939, in *CWMG*, 69:383–384; Sunil Amrith, "Food and Welfare in India, c. 1900–1950," *Comparative Studies in Society and History* 50:4 (2008): 1021.

14. INC National Planning Committee, *Mining and Metallurgy: Report of the Sub-Committee* (Bombay: Vora, 1948); INC National Planning Committee, *Industrial Finance: Report of the Sub-Committee* (Bombay: Vora, 1948); INC National Planning Committee, *Power and Fuel: Report of the Sub-Committee* (Bombay: Vora, 1949), 49–50; INC National Planning Committee, *Engineering Industries and Scientific Instruments Industries. Reports of the Sub-Committees: Engineering Industries* (Bombay: Vora, 1948), 17–29.

15. G. D. Birla, "Preliminaries for Planning," April 20, 1945, in *Path to Prosperity*, 45.

16. Purshotamdas Thakurdas, a well-regarded business leader in Bombay, spearheaded this effort. Quotations in this and subsequent paragraphs are from a note circulated to the initial meeting of the self-proclaimed Committee on Post-War Economic Development on December 11, 1942, Purshotamdas Thakurdas Papers, NMML, subject 291.

17. Purshotamdas Thakurdas, *A Brief Memorandum Outlining a Plan of Economic Development for India* (Harmondsworth, England: Penguin, 1945), 7, 9, 29, 31–32, 34; Lord Wavell to L. Amery, June 12, 1944, quoted in Sanjoy Bhattacharya and Benjamin Zachariah, "'A Great Destiny': The British Colonial State and the Advertisement of Post-War Reconstruction in India, 1942–45," *South Asia Research* 19:1 (1999): 81–82; Reconstruction Committee of Council, "Brief Record of an Informal Conference with the Authors of 'A Plan of Economic Development for India,'" April 20, 1944, Purshotamdas Thakurdas Papers, NMML, subject 260.

18. B. N. Banerjea, G. D. Parikh, and V. M. Tarkunde, *People's Plan for Economic Development of India* (Delhi: A. K. Mukerjee, 1944); S. N. Agarwal, *The Gandhian Plan of Economic Development for India* (Bombay: Padma Publications, 1944), 52; Birla, "Preliminaries for Planning," 71; Congress Working Committee, "Election Manifesto" (1945), in *The Foundations of Indian Economic Planning: An Attempt at Reshaping the Destiny of 600 Million Indians,* ed. A. M. Zaidi (New Delhi: Chand, 1979), 70–74.

19. INC National Planning Committee, *National Planning, Principles & Administration,* ed. K. T Shah (Bombay: Vora, 1948), 1. Meetings of the National Planning Committee, September 17, 1945, and November 8–10, 1945, and Revised Instructions and Directives to Sub-Committees, November 17, 1945, all in INC National Planning Committee, *Report of the National Planning Committee, 1938,* 63, 237, 242–243; H. Venkatasubbiah, *Enterprise and Economic Change: 50 Years of FICCI* (New Delhi: Vikas Publishing House, 1977), chapter 3.

20. GOI Advisory Planning Board, *Report of the Advisory Planning Board* (New Delhi: Government of India, 1946), 4–7, 16–17, 28, 30–64 (K. T. Shah dissent).

21. INC National Planning Committee, *National Planning, Principles & Administration,* 46, 55–56, 73, 92, 121, emphasis in the original; Final Meeting of the NPC, March 26, 1949, in INC National Planning Committee, *Report of the National Planning Committee, 1938,* 250–255.

22. Tariq Omar Ali, "The Envelope of Global Trade: The Political Economy and Intellectual History of Jute in the Bengal Delta, 1850s to 1950s" (PhD diss., Harvard University, 2012), chapter 5.

23. Rajni Kothari, "The Congress 'System' in India," *Asian Survey* 4:12 (1964): 1161–1173; W. H. Morris-Jones, "From Monopoly to Competition in Indian Politics," in *Politics Mainly Indian* (Bombay: Orient Longman, 1978), 144–159; C. A. Bayly, "The Ends of Liberalism and the Political Thought of Nehru's India," *Modern Intellectual History* 12:3 (2015): 605–626.

24. Daya Shankar Nag, *A Study of Economic Plans for India* (Bombay: Hind Kitabs, 1949), 141; AICC, Delhi Meeting, November 1947, in Zaidi, ed., *Foundations,* 74–88; S. Bhoothalingam, *Reflections on an Era: Memoirs of a Civil Servant* (Delhi: Affiliated East-West Press, 1993), 39; L. K. Jha, "The Concept of Mixed Economy," in *Towards Commanding Heights,*

ed. R. C. Dutt and Raj K. Nigam (New Delhi: Standing Committee of Public Enterprises, 1975), 248; Howard L. Erdman, "The Industrialists," in *Indira Gandhi's India: A Political System Reappraised,* ed. Henry Cowles Hart (Boulder, Colo.: Westview Press, 1976), 129; V. B. Singh, *Indian Economy, Yesterday and Today,* 2nd enl. ed. (Delhi: People's Publishing House, 1970), 138–146. As Vivek Chibber notes, this resolution shared much with its colonial predecessor; see Vivek Chibber, *Locked in Place: State-Building and Late Industrialization in India* (Princeton, N.J.: Princeton University Press, 2003), 134–137.

25. Jawaharlal Nehru, "The Primacy of Production," in *SWJN2,* 4:571–579; Jawaharlal Nehru, "The Crisis in Production," January 18, 1948, in *SWJN2,* 5:353–356.

26. Jawaharlal Nehru, "India's Foreign Policy," March 8, 1948, in *SWJN2,* 5:495–507; Mithi Mukherjee, " 'A World of Illusion': The Legacy of Empire in India's Foreign Relations, 1947–62," *International History Review* 32:2 (2010): 253–271; Jawaharlal Nehru, "Foreign Policy for India," December 4, 1947, in *SWJN2,* 4:594–603.

27. Venkatasubbiah, *Enterprise and Economic Change,* 43–49, 61.

28. A. D. Shroff, quoted in U.S. Department of State, *Proceedings and Documents of United Nations Monetary and Financial Conference, Bretton Woods, New Hampshire, July 1–22, 1944* (Washington, D.C.: Government Printing Office, 1948), 2:1173. See also Eric Helleiner, *Forgotten Foundations of Bretton Woods: International Development and the Making of the Postwar Order* (Ithaca, N.Y.: Cornell University Press, 2014), chapter 8; and Catherine R. Schenk, *Britain and the Sterling Area from Devaluation to Convertibility in the 1950s* (New York: Routledge, 1994), chapter 2.

29. Walter Bedell Smith to U.S. Department of State, March 20, 1948, and Robert Lovett conversation with G. S. Bajpai, April 2, 1948, both in *FRUS 1948,* 5:499–500, 506–508; "What Price American Aid?" *EE,* June 26, 1948, 1122–1124; "A New Drive for Dollars," *EW,* January 15, 1949, 1–2; Jawaharlal Nehru to K. P. S. Menon, August 12, 1948, in *SWJN2,* 7:629–630.

30. W. A. B. Iliff to N. Sundaresan, December 17, 1948, W. A. B. Iliff to Loan Committee, December 14, 1948, and A. S. G. Hoar, "General Outline of Indian Government's Development Plans," January 25, 1949, all in Country Files, WBGA, folder 1840724; Anton Basch conversation with John Mathai, March 1, 1949 (memorandum date April 5, 1949), A. S. G. Hoar conversation with Jawaharlal Nehru, March 4, 1949, and "Report of the Mission to India," May 31, 1949, all in Country Files, WBGA, folder 1840725.

31. Jawaharlal Nehru, "Statement on Foreign Investments," April 6, 1949, in *SWJN2,* 10:49–51. *Capital,* September 22, 1949, quoted in Michael Kidron, *Foreign Investments in India* (Oxford: Oxford University Press, 1965), 105.

32. K. M. Pannikar to Vijayalakshmi Pandit, May 25, 1949, in Vijayalakshmi Pandit Papers I, NMML, subject 50; "What about Trone's Report?" *EW,* February 12, 1950, 147–148; Solomon Trone to Jawaharlal Nehru, September 12, 1949, October 4, 1949, and November 21, 1949, all in P. N. Haksar Papers III, NMML, subject 187, capitalization in the original; Tarlok Singh, "Jawaharlal Nehru and the Five-Year Plans" (1964), in *Towards an Integrated Society; Reflections on Planning, Social Policy and Rural Institutions* (Westport, Conn.: Greenwood Press, 1969), 251–265; Jawaharlal Nehru, "On a No-War Declaration," January 6, 1950, in *SWJN2,*

14.1:10–30. On the unusual life and adventures of Solomon Trone, see Michael Chanan, "The American Who Electrified Russia: Synopsis," http://www.mchanan.com/the-american -who-electrified-russia-synopsis/. For press coverage, see K. C. K., "Delhi Diary," *TOI*, September 18, 1949, 8; "American Planning Expert in Bombay," *TOI*, October 15, 1949, 4.

33. Jawaharlal Nehru to Vallabhbhai Patel, February 20, 1950, in Sardar Patel, *Sardar Patel's Correspondence*, ed. Durga Das (Ahmedabad, India: Navajivan Publishing House, 1972), 10:1–6; Michael Brecher, *Nehru: A Political Biography* (Oxford: Oxford University Press, 1959), 514–516; G. L. Nanda, quoted in Stanley A. Kochanek, *The Congress Party of India: The Dynamics of One-Party Democracy* (Princeton, N.J.: Princeton University Press, 1968), 140; Raghabendra Chattopadhyay, "The Idea of Planning in India, 1930–1953" (PhD diss., Australian National University, 1985), 322.

34. "Planning Commission," *TOI*, March 16, 1950, 6; Jawaharlal Nehru, quoted in "A Clean Slate," *TOI*, March 14, 1950, 6; Jawaharlal Nehru to Chief Ministers, April 1, 1950, *LCM*, 2:55. The text of the resolution, dated March 1950, appears in GOI PC, *The First Five Year Plan* (New Delhi: Manager of Publications, 1952), 1.

35. "Planning Commission or Super-Cabinet," *EW*, March 25, 1950, 297–298; K. M. Munshi, quoted (without citation) in S. Ambirajan, *A Grammar of Indian Planning* (Bombay: Popular Book Depot, 1959), 7; "Grave Misgivings on Delhi Pact," *TOI*, June 3, 1950, 1; "Cause of Dr. Matthai's [sic] Exit from Cabinet," *TOI*, June 6, 1950, 1; John Mathai to Jawaharlal Nehru, June 17, 1950, quoted in Medha Kudaisya, " 'A Mighty Adventure': Institutionalising the Idea of Planning in Post-Colonial India, 1947–60," *Modern Asian Studies* 43:4 (2009): 951; Jawaharlal Nehru, letters to John Mathai, May–June 1950, in *SWJN2*, 14:227–250; Jawaharlal Nehru to Vijayalakshmi Pandit, June 5, 1950, Vijayalakshmi Pandit Papers I, NMML, subject 50; V. K. Krishna Menon, quoted in Michael Brecher, *India and World Politics: Krishna Menon's View of the World* (New York: Praeger, 1968), 268; G. L. Nanda, notes on PC meeting, July 1, 1950, G. L. Nanda Papers, NAI—Private, 21/Planning/74.

36. GOI PC, *First Five Year Plan*, 3; Jawaharlal Nehru, "Socialistic Pattern of Society," January 22, 1955, in *SWJN2*, 27:279–283.

37. GOI PC, *First Five Year Plan*, chapter 30; G. L. Nanda, questions for discussion, July 3, 1950, G. L. Nanda Papers, NAI—Private, 21/Planning/74; I. G. Patel, "The Landscape of Economics," *Indian Economic Journal* 45:1 (1997): 30; I. G. Patel oral history, March 9, 2001, CCOH, 19–20. On "export pessimism," see Jagdish N. Bhagwati and T. N. Srinivasan, *Foreign Trade Regimes and Economic Development: India* (New York: Columbia University Press, 1975), 59.

38. GOI PC, *The First Five Year Plan: A Draft Outline* (New Delhi: Manager of Publications, 1951), 159–160; GOI PC, *First Five Year Plan*, 26–27; GOI PC, *The First Five Year Plan: People's Edition* (New Delhi: Manager of Publications, 1952), 201. On the dating of the plan documents, see Francine R. Frankel, *India's Political Economy, 1947–1977: The Gradual Revolution* (Princeton, N.J.: Princeton University Press, 1978), 85.

39. A. A. Zhdanov conversation with S. A. Dange, August 16, 1947, in *Indo-Russian Relations, 1917–1947: Select Documents from the Archives of the Russian Federation*, ed. Purabi Roy, Sobhanlal Datta Gupta, and Hari S. Vasudevan (Calcutta: Asiatic Society, 1999), 2:348–358.

40. Karl Marx, "The British Rule in India," *New York Daily Tribune,* June 25, 1853, in Karl Marx, *Karl Marx on India,* ed. Iqbal Husain (New Delhi: Tulika Books, 2006), 16–17; V. I. Lenin, *Imperialism, the Highest Stage of Capitalism* (New York: International Publishers, 1939); "Appeal of the Council of People's Commissars to the Moslems of Russia and the East," December 3, 1917, in *Soviet Documents on Foreign Policy,* ed. Jane Tabrisky Degras (Oxford: Oxford University Press, 1951), 1:16.

41. K. M. Troianovskii, *Vostok i revoliutsiia: popytka postroeniia novoi politicheskoi programmy dlia tuzemnykh stran Vostoka—Indii, Persii i Kitai* (Moscow: Izdatel'stvo Vserossiiskago Tsentral'nago Komiteta Sovetov Rabochikh, Sluzhaiushchikh i Krest'ianskikh Deputatov, 1918), 29, 40–41; Joseph Stalin, "Do Not Forget the East," November 24, 1918, in *Soviet Russia and the East, 1920–1927,* ed. Xenia Joukoff Eudin and Robert Carver North (Stanford, Calif.: Stanford University Press, 1957), 156–157; Leon Trotsky to the Central Committee, August 5, 1919, in Leon Trotsky, *The Trotsky Papers, 1917–1922,* ed. Jan Marinus Meijer (The Hague: Mouton, 1964), 1:620–627.

42. Stalin Speech at Communist University for Toilers of the East, May 18, 1925, in Degras, ed., *Soviet Documents,* 2:48; Nikolai Bukharin speech at Fifteenth Party Congress, December 10, 1927, in Eudin and North, eds., *Soviet Russia,* 391; Eugen Varga, "Economics and Economic Policy in the Fourth Quarter of 1927," *International Press Correspondence* 8:15 (1928): 290–292; Comintern to the All-India Conference of Workers' and Peasants' Parties, December 2, 1928, in *The Communist International, 1919–1943: Documents,* ed. Jane Tabrisky Degras (London: Frank Cass, 1971), 2:561.

43. Ernst Thälmann, "The Economic Struggles, Our Tactics, and the Tasks of the Communist Parties," *International Press Correspondence* 9:55 (1929): 1203; Dmitrii Manuilskii (1929), quoted in Robert H. Donaldson, *Soviet Policy toward India: Ideology and Strategy* (Cambridge, Mass.: Harvard University Press, 1974), 38.

44. G. Dimitrov and A. Paniushkin to V. M. Molotov, July 28, 1945, RGASPI, 82/2/1196/8–10—PHP.

45. Eugen Varga, *Izmeneniia v ekonomike kapitalizma v itoge vtoroi mirovoi voiny* (Moscow: Gosizdatel'stvo Politliteratury, 1946), 219.

46. V. M. Molotov to "Druzhkov" [Stalin], September 30, 1946, RGASPI, 558/11/306/1–2; "K ustanovleniiu diplomaticheskikh otnoshenii mezhdu Sovetskim Soiuzom i Indiei," *Pravda,* April 14, 1947, 4.

47. Alexei Kojevnikov, "Rituals of Stalinist Culture at Work: Science and the Games of Intraparty Democracy circa 1948," *Russian Review* 57:1 (1998): 13; Eugen Varga, quoted in Leo Gruliow, trans., *Soviet Views on the Post-War World Economy: An Official Critique of Eugene Varga's "Changes in the Economy of Capitalism Resulting from the Second World War"* (Washington, D.C.: Public Affairs Press, 1948), 7, 211. The original transcript appeared in E. S. Varga, "Diskussiia po knige E. S. Vargi 'Izmeneniia v ekonomike kapitalizma v itoge vtoroi mirovoi voiny,'" *Mirovoe khoziaistvo i mirovaia politika* 1947:11, supplement (1947). Future citations will be to the English translation. See also E. Varga, "Bor'ba i sotrudnichestvo mezhdu SShA i Angliei," *Mirovoe khoziaistvo i mirovaia politika* 1947:8 (1947): 13; and

William Curti Wohlforth, *The Elusive Balance: Power and Perceptions during the Cold War* (Ithaca, N.Y.: Cornell University Press, 1993), 79 (and also 112). For an important analysis of key *diskussii* of the late 1940s and early 1950s, see Ethan Pollock, *Stalin and the Soviet Science Wars* (Princeton, N.J.: Princeton University Press, 2006).

48. K. V. Ostrovitianov, A. N. Shneierson, and V. V. Reikhardt, quoted in Gruliow, trans., *Soviet Views*, 90, 19–20, 21.

49. A. M. D'iakov, "K sobytiiam v Indii," *Pravda*, October 21, 1946, 4 (D'iakov was responding to Jawaharlal Nehru, "Free India's Role in World Affairs," September 7, 1946, in *swjn2*, 1:404–408); V. V. Balabusevich, "Indiia posle razdela," *Mirovoe khoziaistvo i mirovaia politika* 1947:12 (1947): 49, 53, 54–55, 72; V. V. Balabushevich, "Rabochii klass i rabochee dvizhenie v sovremennoi Indii," in USSR. Academy of Sciences, Pacific Ocean Institute, *Uchenye zapiski Tikhookeanskogo Instituta,* (Moscow: Izdatel'stvo Akademii Nauk SSSR, 1949), 2:5–28; E. M. Zhukov, "K polozheniiu v Indii," *Mirovoe khoziaistvo i mirovaia politika* 1947:7 (1947): 10–11.

50. A. A. Zhdanov, "O mezhdunarodnom polozhenii," September 1947, *Pravda*, October 22, 1947, 22; E. M. Zhukov, "Obostrenie krizisa kolonial'noi sistemy posle vtoroi mirovoi voiny," in *Krizis kolonial'noi sistemy; Natsional'no-osvoboditel'naia bor'ba narodov vostochnoi Azii,* ed. E. M. Zhukov (Moscow: Izdatel'stvo Akademii Nauk SSSR, 1949), 18.

51. Ramachandra Guha, *India after Gandhi: The History of the World's Largest Democracy* (New York: Ecco, 2007), 108–110; Clare Lindgren Wofford and Harris Wofford, *India Afire* (New York: John Day, 1951), chapter 6; A. D'iakov, "Anglo-amerikanskie plany v Indii," *Pravda*, November 25, 1949, 3; A. M. D'iakov, "Krizis angliiskogo gospodstva v Indii i novyi etap osvoboditel'noi bor'by ee narodov," in *Krizis kolonial'noi sistemy*, 10; E. M. Zhukov, "Voprosy natsional'no-kolonial'noi bor'by posle vtoroi mirovoi voiny," *Voprosy ekonomiki* 1949:9 (1949): 58–59.

52. S. M. Mel'man, "Ekonomicheskie posledstviia vtoroi mirovoi voiny dlia Indii," in USSR Academy of Sciences, ed., *Uchenye zapiski Tikhookeanskogo Instituta,* 29–53; E. S. Varga, "Sotsializm i kapitalizm za tridsat' let," *Mirovoe khoziaistvo i mirovaia politika* 1947:10 (1947): 4–24; Kyung Deok Roh, "Stalin's Think Tank: The Varga Institute and the Making of the Stalinist Idea of World Economy and Politics, 1927–53" (PhD diss., University of Chicago, 2010), chapter 5.

53. Zhukov, "Obostrenie krizisa," 18–19.

54. Russian Embassy in India, "On Establishing Diplomatic Relations between the Soviet Union and India," December 4, 2014, http://rusembindia.com/the-embassy-and-its-history /6894-k-ustanovleniyu-diplomaticheskikh-otnoshenij-mezhdu-sovetskim-soyuzom-i -indiej; Jawaharlal Nehru, conversation with Pandit and Novikov, September 12, 1948, Vijayalakshmi Pandit Papers I, nmml, subject 54; "Indo-Soviet Food Pact," *toi*, April 27, 1949, 3, K. C. Neogy, quoted in "India's Economy Sound," *toi*, June 24, 1949, 1.

55. Joseph Stalin conversation with Sarvepalli Radhakrishnan, January 14, 1950, rgaspi, 558 / 11 / 306 / 5–12; Joseph Stalin to Jawaharlal Nehru, July 16, 1950, in Joseph Stalin, *Sochineniia*, ed. Robert McNeal (Stanford, Calif.: Hoover Institution Press, 1967), 16:172; I. V. Gaiduk, *Divided Together: The United States and the Soviet Union in the United Nations, 1945–1965*

(Washington, D.C.: Woodrow Wilson Center Press, 2012), 164–177. Joseph Stalin conversation with Comrades Rao, Dange, Ghosh, and Punnaya, February 9, 1951, RGASPI, 558 / 11 / 310 / 71–86—PHP / CWIHP.

56. Chester Bowles 1963 oral history, Columbia Center for Oral History, quoted in Howard B. Schaffer, *Chester Bowles: New Dealer in the Cold War* (Cambridge, Mass.: Harvard University Press, 1993), 37.

57. U.S. Central Intelligence Agency, "Review of the World Situation as It Relates to the Security of the United States," September 12, 1947, DDRS, document CK2349267236.

58. "Review of Current Trends of U.S. Foreign Policy" (PPS / 23), February 24, 1948, in *FRUS 1948*, 1:510–529, esp. 523–526.

59. "Appraisal of U.S. National Interests in South Asia" (SANACC 360 / 14), April 19, 1949, in *FRUS 1949*, 6:8–31; U.S. Central Intelligence Agency, "India-Pakistan" (SR-21), September 16, 1948, PSF, HSTL, box 220.

60. Robert A. Pollard, *Economic Security and the Origins of the Cold War, 1945–1950* (New York: Columbia University Press, 1985); Henry Grady to Stephen Bechtel, October 16, 1947, Stephen Bechtel to Henry Grady, October 21, 1947, and Stephen Bechtel to H. W. Morrison and C. P. Dunn, April 20, 1948, all in Henry F. Grady Papers, HSTL, 2:7; Henry Grady, "Indo-American Trade Relations" (Speech to Indian Council on World Affairs), March 23, 1948, Henry F. Grady Papers, HSTL, box 4; Loy Henderson speech at Hindu University of Benares, January 12, 1949, in Loy Henderson Papers, LC, box 22; George McGhee meeting of December 12, 1949, in George Crews McGhee, *Envoy to the Middle World: Adventures in Diplomacy* (New York: Harper & Row, 1983), 100 (McGhee's language echoes—and at time replicates—Loy Henderson's account; see Loy Henderson to U.S. Department of State, January 12, 1950, George McGhee Papers, HSTL, box 2); Rapporteur D. R. Gadgil describing the conversation on "Economic Relations between the United States and India," in Indian Council of World Affairs, *Indian-American Relations, Proceedings of the India-America Conference Held in New Delhi in December 1949* (New Delhi: Indian Council of World Affairs, 1950); "Policy Statement: India," December 1, 1950, in *FRUS 1950*, 5:1476–1481; Economic Committee of the Cabinet, September 20, 1952, Cabinet Secretariat Records, NAI, 7–11 / ECC / 52; Chester Bowles to William Benton, November 21, 1951, Chester Bowles Papers, Yale University Library, 81:16; Shirkar to Gonsalves, April 11, 1953, M. R. Pillai note, March 31, 1954, and R. S. Mani report, June 4, 1954, all in MEA Records, NAI, S / 52 / 1841 / 70-II.

61. Gordon Gray, *Report to the President on Foreign Economic Policies* (Washington, D.C.: Government Printing Office, 1950), 13; NSC Executive Secretariat, "The Position of the United States with Respect to South Asia" (NSC 98), January 5, 1951, PSF, HSTL, 182:80.

62. John Foster Dulles, quoted in editorial note, in *FRUS 1947*, 3:139–140; Henry S. Villard to John Foster Dulles, January 23, 1947, and John Foster Dulles to Henry S. Villard, January 27, 1947, both in John Foster Dulles Papers, Seeley G. Mudd Library, Princeton University, box 32; Merrell to U.S. Department of State, January 21, 1947, and January 22, 1947, in *FRUS 1947*, 3:138–140; Loy Henderson to James Webb, October 3, 1949, quoted in Dennis Merrill, *Bread and the Ballot: The United States and India's Economic Development, 1947–1963* (Chapel Hill: University of North Carolina Press, 1990), 40.

63. Harry S. Truman Inaugural Address, January 20, 1949, in *PPP: Harry S. Truman 1949*, 112–115.

64. Stephen Macekura, "The Point Four Program and U.S. International Development Policy," *Political Science Quarterly* 128:1 (2013): 148–150; Dean Acheson, *Present at the Creation: My Years in the State Department* (New York: W. W. Norton, 1969), 265.

65. U.S. Council of Economic Advisers, *Economic Report of the President: 1950* (Washington, D.C.: Government Printing Office, 1950), 124–125; TCA Press Release, October 22, 1952, Chester Bowles Papers, Yale University Library, 95:267.

66. Subir Sinha, "Lineages of the Developmentalist State: Transnationality and Village India, 1900–1965," *Comparative Studies in Society and History* 50:1 (2008): 57–90; Sunil S. Amrith, *Decolonizing International Health: India and Southeast Asia, 1930–65* (Houndmills, England: Palgrave Macmillan, 2006), chapter 3; C. H. Willson to Chester Bowles, January 3, 1952, Chester Bowles Papers, Yale University Library, 108:460; Chester Bowles to Harry S. Truman, January 31, 1952, Chester Bowles Papers, Yale University Library, 96:287; Chester Bowles to Eric Johnstone, November 29, 1952, Chester Bowles Papers, Yale University Library, 95:263; J. Rucinski conversation with Loy Henderson, October 6, 1949, Country Files, WBGA, folder 1840726; TCA-India, "Description of India's Handicaps and Opportunities" (1952), Chester Bowles Papers, Yale University Library, 109:466.

67. Henry Grady to U.S. Department of State, July 9, 1947, in *FRUS 1947*, 3:160–161; Henry Grady, "Adventures in Diplomacy," in Henry F. Grady Papers, HSTL, box 2, p. 182.

68. New Delhi Embassy to U.S. Department of State, October 3, 1949, quoted in Robert J. McMahon, *The Cold War on the Periphery: The United States, India, and Pakistan* (New York: Columbia University Press, 1994), 54; New Delhi Embassy to U.S. Department of State, January 12, 1950, George McGhee Papers, HSTL, box 2; Dean Acheson conversation with Harry S. Truman, August 28, 1950, in *FRUS 1950*, 5:180–181 (see also McGhee, *Envoy to the Middle World*, chapters 18, 21); Indian Embassy in Washington, "Political Report for 1950," July 23, 1951, MEA Records, NAI, 34-20 / 51-AMS.

69. Gray, *Report to the President*, 69, 54, 13–14. Nelson Rockefeller chaired the group; see International Development Advisory Board, *Partners in Progress: A Report to the President* (Washington, D.C.: Government Printing Office, 1951), 69, 1.

70. Report on South Asia Conference (Colombo), February 26–March 3, 1951, George McGhee Papers, HSTL, box 2, pp. 3, 67–70; Humelsine to Bruce, June 9, 1952, and Glick to Tate, January 28, 1953, both in *FRUS 1952–1954*, 1:248–254, 258–263.

71. Albert O. Hirschman, "The Rise and Decline of Development Economics," in *Essays in Trespassing: Economics to Politics and Beyond* (Cambridge: Cambridge University Press, 1981), 1–24.

72. P. N. Haksar, "Public Sector: Hope or Despair?," in *Towards Commanding Heights*, ed. R. C. Dutt and Raj K. Nigam (New Delhi: Standing Conference of Public Enterprises, 1975), 27.

2. Inventing Development Aid

1. Y. D. Gundevia, *Outside the Archives* (Hyderabad: Sangam Books, 1984), 89–90; C. D. Deshmukh, *Economic Developments in India, 1946–1956: A Personal Retrospect* (Bombay: Asia Publishing House, 1957), 29–31; U.S. Department of State, "Background Memoranda on Visit to the United States of Pandit Jawaharlal Nehru," October 3, 1949, PSF, HSTL, box 158.

2. For the challenges (political and otherwise) of provisioning in independent India's first years, see Sunil S. Amrith, "Food and Welfare in India, c. 1900–1950," *Comparative Studies in Society and History* 50:4 (2008): 1010–1035; Taylor C. Sherman, "From 'Grow More Food' to 'Miss a Meal': Hunger, Development and the Limits of Post-Colonial Nationalism in India, 1947–1957," *South Asia* 36:4 (2013): 571–588; and Benjamin Siegel, " 'Fantastic Quantities of Food Grains': Cold War Visions and Agrarian Fantasies in Independent India," in *Decolonization and the Cold War: Negotiating Independence,* ed. Leslie James and Elisabeth Leake (London: Bloomsbury, 2015), 21–42.

3. George McGhee, quoted in Robert J. McMahon, *The Cold War on the Periphery: The United States, India, and Pakistan* (New York: Columbia University Press, 1994), 87.

4. K. M. Munshi, quoted in Loy Henderson to U.S. Department of State, November 6, 1950, and George McGhee to Dean Acheson, December 15, 1950, both in Robert J. McMahon, "Food as a Diplomatic Weapon: The India Wheat Loan of 1951," *Pacific Historical Review* 56:3 (1987): 356, 357; Siegel, "Fantastic Quantities," 25; Jawaharlal Nehru, quoted in Deshmukh, *Economic Developments,* 29–30; C. D. Deshmukh, *The Course of My Life* (New Delhi, 1974), 182–183; Loy Henderson to U.S. Department of State, December 17, 1950, cited in McMahon, *Cold War,* 91.

5. George McGhee to the President, August 28, 1950, and Dean Acheson conversation with Harry S. Truman, August 28, 1950, both in *FRUS 1950,* 5:178–181. George McGhee to Dean Acheson, July 25, 1950, and Dean Acheson to Harry S. Truman, September 9, 1950, both cited in McMahon, "Food as a Diplomatic Weapon," 354–355; "Factors Entering into Consideration of Indian Request for Food Grains," December 29, 1950, Dean Acheson Papers, HSTL, box 67; "India's Request for Food Grains: Political Considerations," January 24, 1951, and Loy Henderson to U.S. Department of State, January 27, 1951, both in *FRUS 1951,* 6:2103, 2090–2091.

6. Senator Tom Connally, January 26, 1951, quoted in McMahon, "Food as a Diplomatic Weapon," 360; executive sessions of the Senate Foreign Relations Committee, discussed in McMahon, "Food as a Diplomatic Weapon," 361–365.

7. On the wartime network, which included Eleanor Roosevelt and future ambassadors Henry Grady and Chester Bowles, see M. S. Venkataramani, *Bengal Famine of 1943: The American Response* (Delhi: Vikas, 1973), chapter 4; see the list in "Famine Relief Group Formed to Aid India," *NYT,* November 23, 1943, 7. The postwar group also included China expert Pearl Buck and others. See also Devki Nandan Prasad, *Food for Peace: The Story of U.S. Food Assistance to India* (Bombay: Asia Publishing House, 1980), 23; McMahon, "Food as a Diplomatic Weapon," 359; and "Week by Week," *Commonweal* 53 (1951): 318. The

term "India lobby," invoking the mid-century China lobby, appears also in Nick Cullather, *The Hungry World: America's Cold War Battle against Poverty in Asia* (Cambridge, Mass.: Harvard University Press, 2010), 138.

8. "Message to Congress on the Indian Food Crisis," *Department of State Bulletin* 24 (1951), 349–351; McMahon, *Cold War*, 95; House Report No. 185, 33–34, cited in McMahon, "Food as a Diplomatic Weapon," 367; F. W. Marten to Roger Makins, February 20, 1951, FO Records, UKNA, FO 371 / 93195; Nehru, "Fighting Famine," April 29, 1951, and Nehru, "The War against Famine," May 1, 1951, both in *SWJN2*, 16:37–43; Dean Acheson, quoted in Cabinet Notes, April 9, 1951, Matthew J. Connelly Papers, HSTL, 2:27.

9. "China Raises Rice Offer to India; Would 'Sell' Second 50,000 Tons," NYT, March 31, 1951, 3.

10. Sarvepalli Gopal, *Radhakrishnan: A Biography* (New Delhi: Oxford University Press, 1989), 238–239; Gundevia, *Outside the Archives*, 91.

11. "Russian Wheat for India: Agreement Reached," TOI, May 11, 1951, 1; "Soglashenie mezhdu Ministrom vneshnei torgovli SSSR i pravitel'stvom Indii o postavkakh pshenitsy v obmen na dzhut, shelk, tabak i chai," June 22, 1951, RGAE, 413 / 13 / 6724 / 48–63.

12. "U.S. Aides in India See Prestige Loss," NYT, May 13, 1951, 8; "Soviet to Sell India 50,000 Tons of Wheat," *Washington Post,* May 11, 1951, 3; "Russian Wheat for India: Agreement Reached," 1; R. P. Rao, *The Helping Hand* (New Delhi: Eurasia Publishing House, 1964), 20–21; K. M. Munshi to G. J. Watamull, October 29, 1951, K. M. Munshi Papers, NMML, file 115; McMahon, "Food as a Diplomatic Weapon," 377. See also Gilles Boquérat, *No Strings Attached? India's Policies, and Foreign Aid 1947–1966* (New Delhi: Manohar, 2003), 139–140.

13. Hubert H. Humphrey, quoted in George C. McGhee, *Envoy to the Middle World: Adventures in Diplomacy* (New York: Harper & Row, 1983), 52. Figures included Norman Cousins, among others; see Philip Coombs to Chester Bowles, December 31, 1952, Chester Bowles Papers, Yale University Library, 84:47. On Representative Jacob Javits and his brother, see G. L. Mehta conversation with Benjamin Javits, February 5, 1952, Cabinet Secretariat Records, NAI, 14(1)-ECC / 52. On the operation of the India Lobby, see Donald Kennedy to Chester Bowles, February 29, 1952, Chester Bowles Papers, Yale University Library, 95:265.

14. C.D. Deshmukh speech, February 28, 1951, in Deshmukh, *Economic Developments*, 79.

15. GOI PC, *The First Five Year Plan: A Draft Outline* (New Delhi: Manager of Publications, 1951), 50; GOI PC, *The First Five Year Plan: People's Edition* (New Delhi: Manager of Publications, 1952), 34; GOI PC, *The First Five Year Plan* (New Delhi: Manager of Publications, 1952), 61–62. On the Colombo Plan, see B. R. Tomlinson, " 'The Weapons of the Weakened': British Power, Sterling Balances, and the Origins of the Colombo Plan," in *The Transformation of the International Order of Asia: Decolonization, the Cold War, and the Colombo Plan,* ed. Shigeru Akita, Gerold Krozewski, and Shoichi Watanabe (London: Routledge, 2014), 34–48; and Saskia Enthoven, "The Indo-British Aid Relationship: From Its Reluctant Beginning to Its Controversial End (1958–2015)" (PhD diss., Kings College London, in process).

16. "Indo-American Technical Cooperation Agreement," January 5, 1952, USAID Records, USNA, RG 286, entry P475, box 1; Jawaharlal Nehru to Chief Ministers, June 5, 1952, and February 1, 1954, both in *LCM*, 3:5, 491; Jawaharlal Nehru, "The Challenge of Development,"

to heads of Indian missions, June 19, 1953, in *SWJN2*, 22:77; "Scope of the Five Year Plan," October 6–7, 1953, and Jawaharlal Nehru to TTK, October 12, 1953, both in *SWJN2*, 24:125, 142–143; Jawaharlal Nehru to G. L. Mehta, June 7, 1954, G. L. Mehta Papers I–III, NMML, subject 1. On American diplomats' efforts to persuade Nehru through the U.S. allies Deshmukh and Foreign Secretary G. S. Bajpai, see New Delhi Embassy to U.S. Department of State, June 7, 1951, in *FRUS 1951*, 6:2167–2168.

17. N. A. Kuznetsova and L. M. Kulagina, *Iz istorii sovetskogo vostokovedeniia, 1917–1967* (Moscow: Nauka, 1970), 115, 128, 134–139; V. I. Avdiev, "Novye zadachi Instituta Vostokovedeniia Akademii Nauk SSSR," *Vestnik Akademii Nauk SSSR* 1951:2 (1951): 57–60; Kuznetsova and Kulagina, *Iz istorii sovetskogo vostokovedeniia*, 134–139; Oded Eran, *Mezhdunarodniki: An Assessment of Professional Expertise in the Making of Soviet Foreign Policy* (Ramat Gan, Israel: Turtledove Publishers, 1979), 55–59.

18. USSR Academy of Sciences, Oriental Studies Institute, "O kharaktere i osobennostiakh narodnoi demokratii v stranakh vostoka," *Izvestiia Akademii Nauk SSSR. Seriia istorii i filosofii* 1952:1 (1952): 81; an English-language account of the debate appeared as USSR Academy of Sciences, Oriental Studies Institute, "On the Character and Attributes of People's Democracy in Countries of the Orient," *Current Digest of the Soviet Press* 20:4 (1952): 3–7, 84–87.

19. Karl Marx and Friedrich Engels, *The Communist Manifesto,* ed. David McLennan (Oxford: Oxford University Press, 1992), 16; Vladimir Lenin, quoted in John Riddell, ed., *Workers of the World and Oppressed Peoples Unite! Proceedings of the Second Congress* (New York: Pathfinder Press, 1991), 1:215; Valia, "The Struggle for Indian State Independence: A Condition of Success for the English Proletariat," *Communist International* 8:20 (1931): 698; P. Prager, "K postanovke voprosa nekapitalisticheskom razvitii otstal'nikh stran (chast' I)," *Proletarskaia revoliutsiia* 1930:5 (1930): 55–94. Engels would reconsider his position in light of the experience in Russia; on his debates with Russian populists in the 1870s and 1880s, see Andrzej Walicki, *The Controversy over Capitalism: Studies in the Social Philosophy of the Russian Populists* (Oxford: Clarendon Press, 1969).

20. All quotations in this paragraph are from USSR, Academy of Sciences, Oriental Studies Institute, "O kharaktere i osobennostiakh narodnoi demokratii," 85–86.

21. Joseph Stalin, *Economic Problems of Socialism in the U.S.S.R.* (New York: International Publishers, 1952), 31; Ethan Pollock, *Stalin and the Soviet Science Wars* (Princeton, N.J.: Princeton University Press, 2006), 190–191; Richard B. Day, *Cold War Capitalism: The View from Moscow, 1945–1975* (Armonk, N.Y.: M. E. Sharpe, 1995), 82–84.

22. Eugen Varga, *Osnovnye voprosy ekonomiki i politiki imperializma posle vtoroi mirovoi voiny* (Moscow: Gosudarstvennoe izdatel'stvo politicheskoi literatury, 1953), 368, 371, 384, 375.

23. André Mommen, *Stalin's Economist: The Economic Contributions of Jenö Varga* (New York: Routledge, 2011), 215.

24. These requests are summarized in M. Bakhitov, "K voprosu zondazha indusov o zakliuchenii ekonomicheskogo soglasheniia mezhdu SSSR i Indiei i o poezdke Neru v SSSR," June 29, 1951, RGASPI 82/2/1196/90–91—PHP.

25. "Spravka," n.d. (June 1951), RGASPI 82/2/1196/93—PHP; N. Martynov, "The Singapore Economic Conference," *News (Moscow)*, October 31, 1951, 30–31; S. Borzenko, "Promyshlennaia vystavka v Indii," *Pravda*, January 7, 1952, 3; "Uspekh sovetskogo pavil'iona na mezhdunarodnoi promyshlennoi vystavke v Bombee," *Pravda*, January 22, 1952, 3; "Indiiskaia obshchestvennost' trebuet ukrepleniia sviazi s SSSR," *Izvestiia*, January 17, 1952, 4; "Russia Seeks Economic Ties with India," *TOI*, January 22, 1952, 3; "Mr. Malik's Speech and India's Reaction," *TOI*, January 22, 1952, 4; "Soviet Desire for Closer Trade Ties with India," *TOI*, January 11, 1952, 5. See also Surendra K. Gupta, *Stalin's Policy towards India, 1946–1953* (New Delhi: South Asian Publishers, 1988), 249–250.

26. Alec Cairncross, "The Moscow Economic Conference," *Soviet Studies* 4:2 (1952): 114; "Industrialization of the Underdeveloped Countries," *New Times* 1952:21 (1952): 1–3; V. Matveyev, "Trade Contacts Will Be Broadened," *News (Moscow)*, April 15, 1952, 7–11; M. V. Nesterov, "Speech at the International Economic Conference," *News (Moscow)*, April 15, 1952, 10–16.

27. Joseph Stalin conversation with Sarvepalli Radhakrishnan, April 5, 1952, RGASPI 558/11/306/30–35.

28. G. M. Malenkov, "Otchetnyi doklad," *Pravda*, October 6, 1952, 6; K. P. S. Menon, *The Lamp and the Lampstand* (Bombay: Oxford University Press, 1967), chap. 2; Il'ia Ehrenburg, quoted in "Kongress narodov zashchitu mira: rech' Il'i Erenburga," *Pravda*, December 17, 1952, 3.

29. Selig S. Harrison, *India: The Most Dangerous Decades* (Princeton, N.J.: Princeton University Press, 1960), 146–150, 264–266; Robert H. Donaldson, *Soviet Policy toward India: Ideology and Strategy* (Cambridge, Mass.: Harvard University Press, 1974), 108–109. A. Vyshinskii to Stalin, February 9, 1952, RGASPI 558/11/306/37; K. P. S. Menon diary entry, February 18, 1953, in K. P. S. Menon, *The Flying Troika* (Oxford: Oxford University Press, 1963), 26–32; Gupta, *Stalin's Policy*, 250.

30. "Informatsiia o prebyvanii v SSSR Indiry Gandi, docheri prem'er-ministra Indii Neru," July 7, 1953, RGANI, 5/28/94/75–79; Indira Gandhi and Jawaharlal Nehru, *Two Alone, Two Together: Letters between Indira Gandhi and Jawaharlal Nehru 1940–1964*, ed. Sonia Gandhi (London: Hodder and Stoughton, 1992), 592–594. Malenkov gave his speech on August 8, 1953; see G. M. Malenkov, "Speech at Supreme Soviet of the USSR," *New Times*, 1953:33, supplement (1953): 15.

31. Richard B. Remnek, *Soviet Scholars and Soviet Foreign Policy: A Case Study in Soviet Policy towards India* (Durham, N.C.: Carolina Academic Press, 1975), 11; Jawaharlal Nehru conversation with M. A. Men'shikov, July 20, 1953, in *SWJN2*, 23:495; M. A. Men'shikov, *S vintovkoi i vo frake* (Moscow: Mezhdunarodnye otnosheniia, 1996), 173. Biographical information on Men'shikov comes from the CIA Daily Digest, November 15, 1951, CIA FOIA Electronic Reading Room, https://www.cia.gov/library/readingroom/document/cia-rdp79t01146a000500250001-0.

32. Robert Trumbull, "Indians Reaffirm a Middle Position," *NYT*, December 5, 1953, G3; Bimal Prasad, *Indo-Soviet Relations, 1947–1972: A Documentary Study* (Bombay: Allied Publishers,

1973), 73–83; V. P. Nikhamin, *Ocherki vneshnei politiki Indii, 1947–1957 gg.* (Moscow: Gosu-darstvennoe izdatel'stvo politicheskoi literatury, 1959), 176–185; Girish Mishra, *Nehru and the Congress Economic Policies* (New Delhi: Sterling Publishers, 1988), 137; K. V. Novikov speech characterized by K. P. S. Menon, in K. P. S. Menon to R. K. Nehru, April 30, 1954, MEA Records, NAI, D/3042/Eur—PHP.

33. Bowles, "The Indo-American Development Program: Problems and Opportunities," March 5, 1952, MEA Records, NAI, S/52/1911/70; Jawaharlal Nehru Notes, April 14, 1954, and March 4, 1954, and Jawaharlal Nehru to Krishna Menon, March 4, 1954, both in SWJN2, 25:489–493.

34. "American Personnel in India during Each Fiscal Year" (1957?), RUSFAA, USNA, RG469, entry P268B, box 1.

35. Rohan D'Souza, "Damming the Mahanadi River: The Emergence of Multi-Purpose River Valley Development in India (1943–46)," *Indian Economic and Social History Review* 40:1 (2003): 81–105; Peter Sutoris, *Visions of Development: Films Division of India and the Imagination of Progress, 1945–75* (Oxford: Oxford University Press, 2016), 147; Megh-nad Saha, "Symposium on Power Supply" (1938), and Meghnad Saha, "Multipurpose River Scheme (Lok Sabha, April 6, 1954), both in Meghnad Saha, *Collected Works of Meghnad Saha,* ed. Santimay Chatterjee (Calcutta: Saha Institute of Nuclear Physics, 1982), 2:231, 2:181; David Gilmartin, "Imperial Rivers: Irrigation and British Visions of Empire," in *Decentring Empire: Britain, India, and the Transcolonial World,* ed. Durba Ghosh and Dane Kennedy (New Delhi: Orient Longman, 2006), 76–103. Engineer Kanwar Sain also fit well in this group; see Kanwar Sain, *Reminiscences of an Engineer* (New Delhi: Young Asia Publications, 1978), 37–39. On Saha, see Satyendra Nath Sen, *Professor Meghnad Saha: His Life, Work and Philosophy* (Calcutta: Meghnad Saha Sixtieth Birthday Committee, 1954), 43–47. On Sen, see Sudhir Sen, *Wanderings: In Search of Solutions of the Problem of Poverty* (Madras: Macmillan, 1989), 2–3, 29–32, 37. On Lilienthal, see David Ekbladh, *The Great American Mission: Modernization and the Construction of an American World Order* (Princeton, N.J.: Princeton University Press, 2010). More generally, see Daniel Klingensmith, *"One Valley and a Thousand": Dams, Nationalism, and Development* (New Delhi: Oxford University Press, 2007), esp. 114–119.

36. Klingensmith, *"One Valley,"* 109–110; P. R. Greenough, *Prosperity and Misery in Modern Bengal: The Famine of 1943–1944* (Oxford: Oxford University Press, 1982); Enquiry Commit-tee and Lord Wavell instructions to British Embassy in Washington, cited in Henry Cowles Hart, *New India's Rivers* (Bombay: Orient Longman, 1956), 65–66; William Voorduin, memorandum, quoted (without date) in DVC Enquiry Committee, *Report of the Damodar Valley Corporation Enquiry Committee (1952–53)* (New Delhi: DVC Enquiry Committee, 1953), 11; G. H. Baxter conversation with R. G. Casey, October 8, 1945, India Office Records, British Library, L/E/9/381.

37. DVC Enquiry Committee, *Report,* 12. See also New Delhi Embassy to U.S. Department of State, April 30, 1946, SDDF, USNA, RG 59, 845.646/4-3046; Advisory Planning Board minutes, November 8, 1946, Finance Department Records, NAI, 6(13), 1945; Merrill R. Goodall, "River Valley Planning in India: The Damodar," *Journal of Land and Public Utility*

Economics 21:4 (1945): 375; Lord Wavell to the Secretary of State for India, January 14, 1947, and February 19, 1947, and Pethwick-Lawrence to Lord Wavell, January 12, 1947, all in India Office Records, British Library, L / PO / 10 / 24.

38. Kanwar Sain, "Importance and Necessity of Combined Resource Development of a River Valley Multi-Purpose Project," *Irrigation and Power,* July 1951, 499–506; Sain, *Reminiscences of an Engineer,* vii; Meghnad Saha with K. Ray, "The Training of the Tennessee River" (1944), in Saha, *Collected Works,* 2:113–114. See also Klingensmith, *"One Valley,"* 148.

39. Arthur Morgan to George McGhee, October 13–14, 1949, Leonard Elmhirst to Jawaharlal Nehru, December 17, 1949, and Arthur Morgan to DVC, August 29, 1949, all in Arthur E. Morgan Papers, Antioch College, India Universities Commission series, box 2.

40. Sudhir Sen, "Developing the Damodar Valley: The TVA Approach and Its Possibilities in India," *Capital,* January 31, 1946, supplement, 29–31; Lord Wavell to Secretary of State for India, January 14, 1947, India Office Records, British Library, L / PO / 10 / 24; "India and the TVA Method" (editorial), *IJPRVD* 2:11, DVC issue (1952): 55–58; "The Basic Issue" (editorial), *IJPRVD* 5:6 (1955): 77–78; Sudhir Sen, "DVC: What Benefits to Bihar?" *IJPRVD* 3:8 (1953): 1–5; DVC Enquiry Committee, *Report,* 54–57, 114–115. The chairman was S. N. Mozumdar; see Klingensmith, *"One Valley,"* 170–172, 185.

41. Sudhir Sen, "Why a Steam Power Station?" *IJPRVD* 211 (1952): 11–18; "United States Aid to India, 1951–54," n.d., MEA Records, NAI, S / 54 / 1756 / 70-I; David Eli Lilienthal, entry for March 3, 1951, in *The Journals of David E. Lilienthal* (New York: Harper & Row, 1964), 3:115; Donald Kennedy conversation with S. N. Mazumdar, December 22, 1952, SDDF, USNA, RG 59, 891.2614 / 12-2252; HC-New Delhi to CRO, CRO Records, UKNA, DO 142 / 107; Calcutta Consulate-General to U.S. Department of State, April 12, 1961, SDDF, USNA, RG 59, 891.00 / 4-1261. Total World Bank loans by 1959 were about $52 million; see James P. Grant to Director, October 12, 1959, RUSFAA, USNA, RG 469, entry UD191A, box 47; On Soviet equipment, see N. Firiubin conversation with K. P. S. Menon, September 29, 1958, RGAE, 365 / 2 / 1974 / 3. On British efforts to win contracts away from American firms, see Washington Embassy to Foreign Office, June 29, 1959, FO Records, UKNA, FO 371 / 75566.

42. See, for instance, Arundhati Roy, *Power Politics* (Cambridge, Mass.: South End Press, 2001); and Alf Gunbald Nilsen, *Dispossession and Resistance in India* (London: Routledge, 2010).

43. Ford Foundation, *The Ford Foundation and Foundation Supported Activities in India* (New Delhi: Ford Foundation, 1955), 29–30; United Nations Economic and Social Council, "Community Development and Related Services" (1956), quoted in Cullather, *Hungry World,* 86; Nicole Sackley, "Village Models: Etawah, India, and the Making and Remaking of Development in the Early Cold War," *Diplomatic History* 37:4 (2013): 749–778; Subir Sinha, "Lineages of the Developmentalist State: Transnationality and Village India, 1900–1965," *Comparative Studies in Society and History* 50:1 (2008): 57–90.

44. Daniel Immerwahr, *Thinking Small: The United States and the Lure of Community Development* (Cambridge, Mass.: Harvard University Press, 2015), 73, and chapter 3; Jawaharlal Nehru to Albert Mayer, June 17, 1946, in Albert Mayer, *Pilot Project, India: The Story*

of Rural Development at Etawah, Uttar Pradesh (Berkeley: University of California Press, 1958), 7–8; Eleanor Roosevelt, *India and the Awakening East* (New York: Harper, 1953), 122. Even the industrially inclined M. Visvesvaraya promoted rural reform as a means to free up labor; see M. Visvesvaraya, *Rural Reconstruction in India: An Outline of a Scheme* (Bangalore City, India: Bangalore Press, 1931). The urban planner turned community developer was Albert Mayer.

45. Chester Bowles, *Ambassador's Report* (New York: Harper, 1954), 198–200; Chester Bowles, "Tentative Proposal for Economic Aid and Development," November 22, 1951, in Chester Bowles Papers, Yale University Library, 98:323. Mayer, *Pilot Project*, 31; Nicole Sackley, "Foundation in the Field: The Ford Foundation New Delhi Office and the Construction of Development Knowledge, 1951–1970," in *American Foundations and the Coproduction of World Order in the 20th Century*, ed. John Krige and Helke Rausch (Göttingen, Germany: Vandenhoeck and Ruprecht, 2012), 232–260.

46. S. K. Dey memorandum, February 12, 1952, Ministry of Food and Agriculture Records, NAI, 5-2 / 52 G.M.F.; Eugene S. Staples, *Forty Years, a Learning Curve: The Ford Foundation Programs in India, 1952–1992* (New Delhi: Ford Foundation, 1992), 12; Jawaharlal Nehru, "This Sacred Work," October 2, 1952, in *Jawaharlal Nehru on Community Development, Panchayati Raj and Co-Operation* (Delhi: Publications Division, 1965), 15 (this speech does not appear in SWJN2); GOI PC, *Review of the First Five Year Plan* (Delhi: Manager of Publications, 1957), 110; S. K. Dey, *Community Development: A Chronicle, 1954–1961* (Delhi: Ministry of Information and Broadcasting Publications Division, 1962), 61n; Cabinet Meeting Minutes, September 14, 1956, Ministry of Home Affairs Records, NAI, 3 / 16 / 56—Public.

47. Draft of Memorandum to Jawaharlal Nehru, n.d. (November 1951?), Chester Bowles Papers, Yale University Library, 98:323; TCA press release, January 7, 1952, and John P. Ferris to Chester Bowles, February 20, 1952, both in Chester Bowles Papers, Yale University Library, 109:469; Staples, *Forty Years*, 7; H. Parker to Willson, August 6, 1952, Chester Bowles Papers, Yale University Library, 108:460; S. K. Dey, *Community Development* (Allahabad, India: Kitab Mahal, 1960), v; K. R. Damle (secretary in the Ministry of Food and Agriculture), quoted in Willard J. Hertz, *Roots of Change: The Ford Foundation in India* (New York: Ford Foundation, 1961), 18–19. Ferris did not retain such optimism; by 1955 he admitted that CD's main results were "intangible"; see John P. Ferris, "Some Lessons of the U.S.-India Foreign Aid Program," *Public Administration Review* 15:2 (1955): 91.

48. Edward L. Taylor, comments on Chester Bowles memorandum of April 7, 1952, PSB Records, HSTL, 6:91; Chester Bowles, "The Crucial Problem of India," February 4, 1952, PSF, HSTL, 158:6; Chester Bowles to Donald Kennedy, December 15, 1952, Chester Bowles Papers, Yale University Library, 95:268; Nicole Sackley, "The Village as Cold War Site: Experts, Development, and the History of Rural Reconstruction," *Journal of Global History* 6:3 (2011): 492–493.

49. "U.S. Aid to India, 1951–1954," MEA Records, NAI, S / 54 / 1756 / 70; Bowles, *Ambassador's Report*, 202; "American Personnel in India during Each Fiscal Year" (1957?), RUSFAA, USNA, RG469, entry P268B, box 1; Ford Foundation, *Ford Foundation in India*, 18–35; GOI PC, *Review of the First Five Year Plan*, 2–3; State Department Office of Intelligence Research,

"Results of the Technical Assistance Program—India," December 6, 1951, RUSFAA, USNA, RG 469, entry P274, box 1; Technical Cooperation Mission / New Delhi, "Background Paper— Community Development," May 7, 1956, RUSFAA, USNA, RG 469, entry UD600A, box 1; S. K. Dey to J. C. Kumarappa, November 21, 1956, J. C. Kumarappa Papers, NMML, subject 20. U.S. records suggest a far lower figure over the 1950s: barely \$1.5 million per year, or 2.7 percent of total technical assistance between 1951 and 1957; see Charles Wolf, *Foreign Aid: Theory and Practice in Southern Asia* (Princeton, N.J.: Princeton University Press, 1960).

50. Srirupa Roy, *Beyond Belief: India and the Politics of Postcolonial Nationalism* (Durham, N.C.: Duke University Press, 2007), 20; Nick Cullather, "'The Target Is the People': Representations of the Village in Modernization and U.S. National Security Doctrine," *Cultural Politics* 2:1 (2006): 29–48.

51. Bureau of the Budget, "The Difference between Ambassador Bowles and the State Department on the Amount of Aid for India in Fiscal 1953," February 25, 1952; Philip H. Coombs to Bowles, February 26, 1952, both in Chester Bowles Papers, Yale University Library, 84:46. Jonathan Bingham to Bowles, March 12, 1952, Chester Bowles Papers, Yale University Library, 94:234. Bowles, "A Progress Report from India," April 7, 1952, PSB Records, HSTL, 6:91; Chester Bowles to Harry S. Truman, May 22, 1952, PSF, HSTL, 158:5.

52. Representative James Davis, in 98 Cong. Rec. 82nd Cong., 2nd Sess. (1952), part 7, 8488–8489; Chester Bowles to Harry S. Truman, July 5, 1952, and W. Averell Harriman and Dean Acheson to Harry S. Truman, June 1952, both in PSF, HSTL, 158:5; Chester Bowles to Dean Acheson, December 6, 1951, PSF, HSTL, 158:6. Bowles's own TCA staff remained skeptical; see E. A. Midgely conversation with J. P. Ferrers, January 15, 1952, Treasury Records, UKNA, T 236/3163.

53. U.S. Central Intelligence Agency, "NIE-23: India's Position in the East-West Conflict," September 4, 1951, in *FRUS 1951*, 6:2174–2175, 2179; Chester Bowles to Harry S. Truman, September 11, 1951, in WHCF Official File, HSTL, box 1278; James Webb to W. Averell Harriman (draft), October 25, 1951, Chester Bowles Papers, Yale University Library, 94:234.

54. Dean Acheson to Chester Bowles, January 8, 1953, in *FRUS 1952–1954*, 11:1682–1684.

55. Richard M. Nixon, report on Far East trip, December 24, 1953, AWF-NSC, DDEL, 5:177. Dean Acheson conversation with Ambassador G. L. Mehta, January 13, 1953, Dean Acheson Papers, HSTL, box 71.

56. "Nehru Suggests Ending U.S. Help," *NYT*, March 7, 1954, 1; Jawaharlal Nehru, "Problems of Accepting American Aid" (note), April 24, 1954, in *SWJN2*, 25:494–496.

57. K. P. S. Menon to R. K. Nehru, April 30, 1954, MEA Records, NAI, D/3042/Eur—PHP; C. D. Deshmukh, quoted in "Scope of Foreign Aid," *The Hindu*, June 7, 1954, 5; Michael Kidron, *Foreign Investments in India* (Oxford: Oxford University Press, 1965), 100.

58. Dwight D. Eisenhower, "The Chance for Peace," April 16, 1953, in *PPP: Dwight D. Eisenhower 1953*, 179–188; John Foster Dulles, "Report on the Near East," June 1, 1953, *Department of State Bulletin* 28:729 (1953): 831–835; John Foster Dulles press conference at New Delhi embassy, May 22, 1953, John Foster Dulles Papers, Seeley G. Mudd Manuscript Library, Princeton University, box 7.

59. U.S. Commission on Foreign Economic Policy, *Report to the President and Congress,* U.S. Congress Serial Set, 83rd Cong., 2nd sess., House Document 290 (1954), 12; Clarence B. Randall, *A Foreign Economic Policy for the United States* (Chicago: University of Chicago Press, 1954), 19, 27–28.

60. Walter Bedell Smith to Gabriel Hauge, February 10, 1954, and Thorsten Kalijarvi to John Foster Dulles, March 18, 1954, both in *FRUS 1952–1954,* 1:50–52, 57–62; C. D. Jackson, description of his March 25, 1954, meeting with Dulles, quoted in W. W Rostow, *Eisenhower, Kennedy, and Foreign Aid* (Austin: University of Texas Press, 1985), 95–96; Dennis Merrill, *Bread and the Ballot: The United States and India's Economic Development, 1947–1963* (Chapel Hill: University of North Carolina Press, 1990), 110–111; Dwight D. Eisenhower, "Special Message to Congress on Foreign Economic Policy," March 30, 1954, in *PPP: Dwight D. Eisenhower 1954,* 352–363.

61. C. D. Jackson to John Foster Dulles, April 9, 1954, quoted in Rostow, *Eisenhower, Kennedy, and Foreign Aid,* 245–249; "Transcript of a Conference held at the Princeton Inn under the auspices of Time, Inc.," May 15–16, 1954, Max F. Millikan Papers, MIT Archives, 8:226; Bureau of Economic Affairs, "Foreign Economic Relations of the United States," May 17, 1954, in *FRUS 1952–1954,* 1:65–82; Dennis A. FitzGerald to John H. Stambaugh, June 2, 1954, Dennis A. FitzGerald Papers, DDEL, box 35.

62. Rostow, *Eisenhower, Kennedy, and Foreign Aid,* 97; Merrill, *Bread and the Ballot,* 111–113; Stephen E. Ambrose, *Eisenhower* (New York: Simon & Schuster, 1983), 2:204; Burton Ira Kaufman, *Trade and Aid: Eisenhower's Foreign Economic Policy, 1953–1961* (Baltimore: Johns Hopkins University Press, 1982), 49; memorandum of internal State Department discussion, August 24, 1954, in *FRUS 1952–1954,* 1:83–86. Harold Stassen was director of the Foreign Operations Administration.

63. Russell Edgerton, *Sub-Cabinet Politics and Policy Commitment: The Birth of the Development Loan Fund* (Syracuse, N.Y.: Inter-University Case Program, 1970), 32–33; John Foster Dulles conversation with Dwight D. Eisenhower, October 27, 1954, John Foster Dulles Papers, DDEL, White House Memoranda Series, box 1. Clarence Randall to President, December 7, 1954, in *FRUS 1952–1954,* 1:105–108. The committee chair was Undersecretary of State Herbert Hoover Jr.

64. "New Front in the Cold War," *Time,* December 13, 1954; Walt W. Rostow to C. D. Jackson, December 27, 1954, in Rostow, *Eisenhower, Kennedy, and Foreign Aid,* 252–254; Merrill, *Bread and the Ballot,* 112.

65. Wolf, *Foreign Aid,* 121–122.

66. See especially the records of the Academy of Sciences Foreign Department, ARAN, fond 579, opis' 3, dela 504, 535, 537.

67. S. S. Sokhey to A. I. Mikoian, October 26, 1957, GARF, R-5446 / 120 / 1269 / 92–102; P. N. Kaul, "Report on Trade Relations from India's Moscow Embassy," n.d. (April 1954?), MEA Records, NAI, D / 3042 / Eur—PHP. Dr. S. S. Sokhey won the Stalin Prize in 1953; see S. S. Sokhey, "Memorandum on Enlisting the Technical Aid of the Soviet Union for Setting up Industry to Make India Self-Sufficient," September 16, 1954, RGAE, 365 / 2 / 1503 / 282–266.

68. I. Plyshevskii, "Za razvitie ekonomicheskikh sviazei stran Azii i dal'nego vostoka," *Pravda*, February 18, 1954, 4; M. A. Men'shikov conversation with R. K. Nehru, March 21, 1954, M. A. Men'shikov conversation with Lanka Sandaram, April 9, 1954, and M. A. Men'shikov conversation with Sarvepalli Radhakrishnan, April 16, 1954, all in AVPRF, 090 / 16 / 44 / 8 / 28–32, 49–51, 59–63; M. A. Men'shikov to V. A. Zorin, May 12, 1954, AVPRF, 090 / 16 / 44 / 14 / 44–48; "Spravka," n.d. (December 1954?), ARAN, 579 / 3 / 504 / 68–70. See also the correspondence in V. Iu. Afiani and V. D. Esakov, *Akademiia Nauk v resheniiakh TsK KPSS: Biuro Prezidiuma, Prezidium, Sekretariat TsK KPSS* (Moscow: Rosspen, 2010), 94–98.

69. U.S. Central Intelligence Agency, *Current Intelligence Bulletin*, December 12, 1954, CIA FOIA Electronic Reading Room, https://www.cia.gov/library/readingroom/document /cia-rdp79t00975a001800380001-0; Jawaharlal Nehru, note, August 28, 1954, in SWJN2, 26:517–520; H. V. R. Iyengar to M. A. Men'shikov, July 31, 1954, RGAE, 413 / 13 / 7429 / 60, 67–68; S. P. Sen to H. V. R. Iyengar, December 12, 1954, RGAE, 413 / 13 / 7624 / 48–50. M. A. Men'shikov conversation with H. V. R. Iyengar, July 30, 1954, and August 3, 1954, AVPRF, 090 / 16 / 44 / 8 / 76–80, 93; "Russia Will Not Be Able to Help India," *TOI*, December 10, 1954, 1; "Report on Russia Termed Ill-Timed and Biased," *TOI*, December 21, 1954, 6.

70. INC National Planning Committee, *Report of the National Planning Committee, 1938* (New Delhi: Indian Institute of Applied Political Research, 1988), 65; GOI Planning and Development Department, Office of the Industrial Advisor, *First Report of the Iron and Steel (Major) Panel* (New Delhi: Government of India Press, 1946), 11, 31–32; Ved Mehta, "Development: The Pulsating Giant," *New Yorker*, February 14, 1970, 68; Board of Trade– New Delhi to Board of Trade–London, October 29, 1949, Treasury Records, UKNA, T 263 / 3163; All-India Congress Committee, *Report of the Economic Programme Committee* (Delhi: Indian National Congress, 1948), 19–21. A jumbled report from a British consultant appears in Meghnad Saha Papers VII, NMML, subject 7. References to American visitors in 1948 appear in T. F. Moffitt report, October 1, 1956, in RUSFAA, USNA, RG 469, entry 273, box 9.

71. C. D. Deshmukh to Jawaharlal Nehru, October 7, 1952, TTK Papers, NMML, subject 8A; "World Bank Loan to Indian Iron," *TOI*, December 30, 1952, 4.

72. Jawaharlal Nehru to C. D. Deshmukh, October 13, 1952; TTK to Jawaharlal Nehru, October 26, 1952; TTK, "Review of the Government's Activities in the Economic and Industries Field since May 1952," n.d. (June 1953?), TTK to Jawaharlal Nehru, July 5, 1953, and Jawaharlal Nehru to TTK, December 29, 1953, all in TTK Papers, NMML, Correspondence—J. Nehru. Nehru rejected the claim of "super-cabinet" explicitly in his reply to TTK; see TTK to Jawaharlal Nehru, and Jawaharlal Nehru to TTK, both December 30, 1953, both in TTK Papers, NMML, Correspondence—J. Nehru.

73. "Report of the Mission Sent to U.S.A. in Connection with the Expansion of the Steel Project," December 28, 1952, and George Woods Statement, July 1, 1952, both in George D. Woods Papers, WBGA, folder 1453124; Klaus Röh, *Rourkela als Testfall für die Errichtung von Industrieprojecten in Entwicklungsländern* (Hamburg: Verlag Weltarchiv, 1967), 80–82; "Loans for Indian Iron and Steel Co.," *TOI*, December 26, 1952, 4; "World Bank Loan to Indian Iron: 'Unique Aid,' " *TOI*, December 30, 1952, 4; B. B. Lal, *Profit Planning and Control*

in Public Enterprises in India (New Delhi: Atlantic Publishers, 2000), 162; Memorandum to Warren Iliff, March 1, 1952, Country Files, WBGA, folder 1840727.

74. Lal, *Profit Planning,* 162; "New Steel Factory," *TOI,* August 19, 1953, 7; "Vast Progress by German Firm," *TOI,* October 7, 1953, 5; Mission Report no. 3, September 5, 1953, Country Files, WBGA, folder 1840728; Amit Das Gupta, *Handel, Hilfe, Hallstein-Doktrin: Die bundesdeutsche Südasienpolitik unter Adenauer und Erhard 1949–1966* (Husum, Germany: Matthiesen, 2004), 82–83; S. Bhoothalingam, *Reflections on an Era: Memoirs of a Civil Servant* (New Delhi: Affiliated East-West Press, 1993), 83–84.

75. B. M. Birla to TTK, February 3, 1954, Jawaharlal Nehru to TTK, July 3, 1954, and Jawaharlal Nehru to TTK, September 27, 1954, all in TTK Papers, NMML, Correspondence—J. Nehru; G. D. Birla plans for American-supported steel mill, February 10, 1955, TTK Papers, NMML, subject 7; Eugene Black conversation with A. D. Shroff, October 15, 1954, Country Files, WBGA, folder 1840728; London Embassy to U.S. Department of State, November 10, 1954, SDDF, USNA, RG 59, 891.33/11-1054.

76. Iu. Ershov, "Torgovye i ekonomicheskie otnosheniia mezhdu SSSR i Indiei," September 23, 1954, RGANI, 5/28/243/2–10; Robert S. Walters, *American and Soviet Aid: A Comparative Analysis* (Pittsburgh: University of Pittsburgh Press, 1970), 111.

77. GOI Lok Sabha, Committee on Public Undertakings, *Thirtieth Report: Bhilai Steel Plant of Hindustan Steel, Ltd.,* CPU 44 (New Delhi: Lok Sabha Secretariat, 1966), 1–2; M. A. Men'shikov conversation with Mahalanobis, November 6, 1954, M. A. Men'shikov conversation with Lanka Sundaram, April 9, 1954, and M. A. Men'shikov conversation with Iyengar and S. Bhoothalingam, December 22, 1954, all in AVPRF, 090/16/44/8/49–51, 178–181, 206–211; V. A. Zorin conversation with K. P. S. Menon, July 19, 1954, and Government of India aide-memoire, July 19, 1954, both in AVPRF, 090/15/43/6/16–18, 19–20; HC–New Delhi to CRO, January 28, 1955, and E. A. Midgely to F. Doy, February 7, 1955, both in FO Records, UKNA, FO 371/116720.

3. The Geopolitics of Economic Expertise

1. Gunnar Myrdal, oral history, January 20, 1974, Transcripts, NMML, 2. This paragraph draws on information on visitors and on Mahalanobis's travels, each of which merited a section of the ISI *Annual Report.* Among the early Nobel laureates in economics who had conducted extended trips in India were Ragnar Frisch, Simon Kuznets, and Jan Tinbergen. Other prominent Western economists visiting India include George Akerlof, Milton Friedman, Anne Krueger, and Wassily Leontief Jr.

2. John Kenneth Galbraith, *A Life in Our Times: Memoirs* (Boston: Houghton Mifflin, 1981), 328; Johannes Rudolph, "Bericht über meine Arbeit im Indian Statistical Institute . . . ," September 1957–March 1958, SED Zentrale komitete—Abteil für internationale Verbindungen, SAPMO, Bundesarchiv-Lichterfelde, DY30/IV 2/20/321, B1, 49–50.

3. V. K. R. V. Rao founded the Delhi School; see V. K. R. V. Rao, "Memorandum for Submission to the University Grants Committee on the Proposed Delhi School of

Economics," March 16, 1948, Purshotamdas Thakurdas Papers, NMML, folder 259. See also P. N. Dhar, "The Early Years," in *D School: Reflections on the Delhi School of Economics*, ed. Dharma Kumar and Dilip Mookherjee (New Delhi: Oxford University Press, 1995), 7–23.

4. Jawaharlal Nehru, "Socialistic Pattern of Society," January 22, 1955, and Jawaharlal Nehru, "Towards a Socialist Society," November 9, 1954, both in *SWJN2*, 27:279–283, 373; C. D. Deshmukh, *Economic Developments in India, 1946–1956: A Personal Retrospect* (Bombay: Asia Publishing House, 1957), 85; Prasanta Chandra Mahalanobis, quoted in Ashok Rudra, *Prasanta Chandra Mahalanobis: A Biography* (New Delhi: Oxford University Press, 1996), 432.

5. Johanna Bockman and Gil Eyal, "Eastern Europe as a Laboratory for Economic Knowledge: The Transnational Roots of Neoliberalism," *American Journal of Sociology* 108:2 (2002), 310–352; British Tory, quoted in Daniel Ritschel, *The Politics of Planning: The Debate on Economic Planning in Britain in the 1930s* (Oxford: Clarendon Press, 1997), 48; Tony Judt, *Postwar: A History of Europe since 1945* (London: Penguin, 2005), 67–73; George Schuster, "Notes on Economic Policy" (1930), Finance Department Records, NAI, 15-I-F. This paragraph is drawn from David C. Engerman, "The Rise and Fall of Central Planning," in *Cambridge History of World War II*, ed. Michael Geyer and Adam Tooze (Cambridge: Cambridge University Press, 2015), 3:575–598.

6. Prasanta Chandra Mahalanobis report on his 1946 visit, dated January 2, 1947, in Education Department Records, NAI, 63-8/46EI. Prasanta Chandra Mahalanobis to Pitamber Pant, June 24, 1954, in Pitamber Pant Papers, NMML. Prasanta Chandra Mahalanobis to Oskar Lange, March 18, 1953, Visitor Records, ISI, folder Lange.

7. Prasanta Chandra Mahalanobis to Pitamber Pant, June 24, 1954, Pitamber Pant Papers, NMML.

8. American Marxist Paul Baran was also in Mahalanobis's sights; see Prasanta Chandra Mahalanobis to Pitamber Pant, June 24, 1954, Pitamber Pant Papers, NMML. Baran, Bettelheim, Frisch, and Tinbergen were among the early visitors to the ISI.

9. G. F. Aleksandrov to K. V. Ostrovitianov, February 23, 1954, RGANI, 5/30/70/1–10.

10. Prasanta Chandra Mahalanobis to Pitamber Pant, July 17, 1954, July 7, 1954, and July 16, 1954, all in Pitamber Pant Papers, NMML; emphases in the originals. E. N. Komarov conversation with Prasanta Chandra Mahalanobis, July 12, 1954, ARAN, 579/3/535/8–13.

11. G. F. Aleksandrov to K. V. Ostrovitianov, February 23, 1954, RGANI, 5/30/70/1–10. On Mahalanobis's official role, see I. Kovalenko to S. G. Korneev, May 29, 1962, ARAN, 579/1/1158/139. Indeed, Mahalanobis told one Soviet scholar that the ISI functioned like a government agency; see G. V. Aleksandrov to N. P. Pospelov, July 7, 1954, RGANI, 5/30/71/94–100.

12. V. P. D'iachenko to A. N. Nesmeianov, July 3, 1954, ARAN, 579/3/504/58–59; M. G. Pervukhin conversation with Prasanta Chandra Mahalanobis, August 30, 1957, RGAE, 365/2/65/171–177; Prasanta Chandra Mahalanobis to Pitamber Pant, July 7, 1954, Pitamber Pant Papers, NMML.

13. A. N. Nesmeianov to M. A. Suslov, February 26, 1954, RGANI, 5 / 28 / 242 / 7–8; Gosplan celebrated by Asoka Mehta in conversation with P. F. Lomako, May 5, 1965, RGAE, 365 / 2 / 2169 / 82–105. Pant was especially interested in the 1920s; see V. P. D'iachenko, "Otchet o poezdke v Indiiu," November 12, 1955, ARAN, 579 / 1 / (1956) 81 / 40–41.

14. "Direktivnye ukazaniia sovetskim uchenym, vyezzhaiushchim v Indiiu dlia okazaniia pomoshchi indiiskomu statisticheskomu institutu," February 1954, RGANI, 5 / 28 / 242 / 9–10.

15. I. A. Ershova, "Otchet o prebyvanii v Indii, 7 noiabr'ia—26 dekabr'ia 1954 g.," n.d. (December 1954), ARAN, 579 / 3 / 536 / 12; K. V. Ostrovitianov, "Scientific Principles of the Planning of the National Economy of the USSR," ISI Studies Relating to Planning for National Development no. 18, January 22, 1955, in PC Records, ISI, folder 15; D. D. Degtiar' to P. N. Pospelov, May 24, 1955, RGANI, 5 / 30 / 117 / 4–38; G. F. Aleksandrov and K. V. Ostrovitianov to Central Committee, September 25, 1954, RGANI, 5 / 30 / 70 / 67–68. Other Soviet economists at the ISI with Rubinshtein included D. D. Degtiar' and I. Iu. Pisarev.

16. M. I. Rubinshtein, "Razvitie sovremennoi tekhniki i ee sotsial'nye posledstviia," September 2, 1954, ARAN, 499 / 1 / 333 / 12–13.

17. Prasanta Chandra Mahalanobis report on travels, April 15, 1947, Education Department Records, NAI, 63-8 / 46EI. Ragnar Frisch to Prasanta Chandra Mahalanobis, August 8, 1953, in Ragnar Frisch Papers, University of Oslo Department of Economics; Ragnar Frisch, *Planning for India: Selected Explorations in Methodology* (New York: Asia Publishing House, 1960), 1, emphasis in the original; ISI, *Annual Report, 1954–55* (Calcutta: ISI, 1955), 162; Ragnar Frisch, "Planning for Economic Development in India: A Memorandum on the Broad Macroeconomic Aspects of the Problem," November 26, 1954, PC Records, ISI, folder 15.

18. Prasanta Chandra Mahalanobis to Ragnar Frisch, January 13, 1955, and Ragnar Frisch to Prasanta Chandra Mahalanobis, July 12, 1954, and January 14, 1955, all in Visitor Records, ISI, folder Frisch. New Delhi Embassy to U.S. Department of State, "Political Considerations in Connection with the Proposed Electronic Computer Project for the Indian Statistical Institute," April 11, 1957, RUSFAA, USNA, RG 469, entry P279, box 1. On I-O analysis and Wassily Leontief Jr., see Raymond Goldsmith, ed., *Input-Output Analysis: An Appraisal* (Princeton, N.J.: Princeton University Press, 1955); and Mary S. Morgan, "Economics," in *The Cambridge History of Science,* ed. Theodore M. Porter and Dorothy Ross (Cambridge: Cambridge University Press, 2003), 7:275–305. On computers, see Prasanta Chandra Mahalanobis to Pitamber Pant, June 23, 1954, Pitamber Pant Papers, NMML; and M. A. Men'shikov conversation with Prasanta Chandra Mahalanobis, March 30, 1954, AVPRF, 090 / 16 / 44 / 8 / 37–42.

19. Ragnar Frisch, "A Short Memorandum on a Technique for Elaborating the New Five-Year Plan for India," ISI Studies Relating to Planning for National Development, Working Paper no. 5, December 11, 1954, 3, 7–8, in PC Records, ISI, folder 15. Frisch apparently brought a draft of this essay with him to India; a fragment of "Scheme of a Model of Reasoning for the Elaboration of the Second Five-Year Plan of India" is dated October 29, 1954, before his November 1954 arrival in India—see PC Records, ISI, folder 109. See also Ragnar Frisch, "The Methodology of Planning in an Underdeveloped Country," ISI Studies Relating to Planning for National Development, Working Paper no. 20, January 23, 1955, PC Records, ISI, folder 15.

20. D. D. Degtiar' to P. N. Pospelov, May 24, 1955, RGANI, 5 / 30 / 117 / 4–38; Jawaharlal Nehru, "Approach to the Second Plan," December 25, 1954, in SWJN2, 27:379–382; J. J. Anjaria and Tarlok Singh, "Planning Studies at the Indian Statistical Institute, Calcutta," December 31, 1954, PC Records, ISI, folder 116 (this report was approved by the PC in a meeting that same day; see PC Minutes, December 31, 1954, PC Records, ISI, folder 116); Jawaharlal Nehru to V. T. Krishnamachari, January 8, 1955, in SWJN2, 27:383, 384–385 (V. T. Krishnamachari served as PC deputy chairman; he is not related to T. T. Krishnamachari). Nehru's notes on his ISI visit appear in SWJN2, 27:379–382, and a copy appeared, translated into Russian, in the records of the International Department of the Communist Party of the Soviet Union's Central Committee; see RGANI, 5 / 28 / 344 / 94–97.

21. Prasanta Chandra Mahalanobis to Oskar Lange, July 28, 1952, in Oskar Lange Papers, Archive of the Polish Academy of Sciences, folder 130; thanks to Malgorzata Mazurek for this document.

22. ISI, *Annual Report, 1954–55*, 162; ISI, *Annual Report, 1955–56* (Calcutta: ISI, 1956), 53; Planning Commission Minutes, February 1, 1955, PC Records, ISI, folder 116; Oskar Lange, "Some Observations on Input-Output Analysis," *Sankhyā* 17:4 (1957): 305–336, quotation on 306; Oskar Lange, "Agrarian Reform in Poland," Studies Relating to Planning for National Development, no. 33, March 11, 1955, and Oskar Lange, "Some Data on the Economic Development of Poland," Studies Relating to Planning for National Development, no. 28, March 4, 1955, both in PC Records, ISI, folder 15. Lange's ideas are quoted (without citation) in Widzaj Soni, "Oskar Lange i planiwanie w Indii," *Polityka*, November 27, 1965, 10; see also Janusz Zaręba, *Reforma w testamencie: Rzecz o Oskarze Langem* (Warsaw: Młodzieżowa Agencjia Wydawnicza, 1985), 145–146.

23. Ashwani Saith, "Joan Robinson and Indian Planning: An Awkward Relationship," *Development and Change* 39:6 (2008): 1115–1134; Prasanta Chandra Mahalanobis to Pitamber Pant, June 24, 1954, Pitamber Pant Papers, NMML; Joan Robinson, "Review of Ragnar Frisch, Planning for India," *Journal of the Royal Statistical Society,* ser. A (general), 125:3 (1962): 505; Robinson, "India 1955: Unemployment and Planning," in *Collected Economic Papers,* 2nd ed. (Oxford: Blackwell, 1975), 3:182–191; Geoffrey Harcourt, *Joan Robinson* (Houndmills, England: Palgrave Macmillan, 2009), 86, 141–142; Prasanta Chandra Mahalanobis questionnaire, n.d. (1955?), PC Records, ISI, folder 97.

24. ISI, *Annual Report, 1953–54* (Calcutta: ISI, 1954), 417; ISI, *Annual Report, 1954–55,* 161; ISI, *Annual Report, 1955–56,* 52; [Charles Bettelheim,] "A Note on the Economic Policy, December 12, 1954, in Frederic P. Bartlett to U.S. Department of State, January 14, 1955, in SDDF, USNA, RG 59, 891.00 / 1-1455. On Kaldor, see Taya Zinkin, "The Kaldor Report," *EW,* December 15, 1956, 1467; "Progressive Taxation for India Essential," *TOI,* September 2, 1955, 9; "Expenditure Tax Proposal under Study: Idea Discussed with British Economist," *TOI,* September 12, 1955, 7; "Measures to Reduce Disparity in Income," *TOI,* May 26, 1956, 7; and "U.K. Expert's View on Tax," *TOI,* May 27, 1956, 1. On Bettelheim, see Francois Denord and Xavier Zunigo, "'Révolutionnairement Vôtre': Économie Marxiste, Militantisme Intellectual et Expertise Politique Chez Charles Bettelheim," *Actes de la Recherche en Sciences Sociales* 158 (2005): 8–29; Charles Bettelheim, "Some Observations on Social and Economic Policy,"

December 13, 1954; and Charles Bettelheim, "Scheme of a Model of Reasoning for the Elaboration of the Second Five-Year Plan in India," November 19, 1954, both in Charles Bettelheim, *Some Basic Planning Problems* (New York: Asia Publishing House, 1961), 1–34, 41–42.

25. Prasanta Chandra Mahalanobis, "Planning Targets," September 18, 1954, PC Records, ISI, folder 97; P. C. Mahalanobis, "Some Observations on the Process of Growth of National Income," *Sankhyā* 12:4 (1953): 307–312, esp. 309.

26. Jawaharlal Nehru speech, December 21, 1954, in *Lok Sabha Debates* (New Delhi: Lok Sabha Secretariat, 1954), column 3692; "Draft Resolution for Avadi Congress," January 9, 1955, and "Tasks before the Congress," January 10, 1955, both in SWJN2, 27:255–261, 261–278; Congress resolution at Avadi session, January 1955, in A. M. Zaidi, ed., *The Foundations of Indian Economic Planning: An Attempt at Reshaping the Destiny of 600 Million Indians* (New Delhi: Chand, 1979), 142–145.

27. Jawaharlal Nehru speech at Avadi Congress session, January 21, 1955, in SWJN2, 27:279–283. Economist I. G. Patel credits J. J. Anjaria, a Bombay-trained economist connected to both the National Planning Committee and the Planning Commission, with this strategic dilution; see I. G. Patel, "The Landscape of Economics," *Indian Economic Journal* 45:1 (1997): 31.

28. I. G. Patel, *Glimpses of Indian Economic Policy: An Insider's View* (New Delhi: Oxford University Press, 2002), 38, 39; "Preparing Next 5-Year Plan: Panel of Leading Economist," *TOI*, January 22, 1955, 5; "Weekly Notes: Panel of Economists," *EW*, February 5, 1955.

29. [Prasanta Chandra Mahalanobis,] "Notes for the Meeting with Economists, January 27–28," PC Records, ISI, folder 97.

30. Ragnar Frisch to Prasanta Chandra Mahalanobis, January 11, 1955 [letter mistakenly dated 1956], Visitor Records, ISI, folder Frisch; PC Minutes, February 1, 1955 (Lange), February 3, 1955 (Degtiar'), and March 4–5, 1955 (Frisch), all in PC Records, ISI, folder 116; New Delhi Embassy to U.S. Department of State, February 15, 1955, SDDF, USNA, RG 59, 891.00 Five Year / 2-1555; J. J. Anjaria, "Summary Record of the Standing Committee of the Panel of Economists," March 1, 1955, PC Records, ISI, folder 116; K. Subbaroyan, "Studies to Be Undertaken: Formulation of Second Plan," *TOI*, March 3, 1955, 1. See also the minutes of the eight meetings that the Planning Commission held with the ministries of Natural Resources and Scientific Research, Commerce and Industry, Health, Production, Education, Transportation, and Irrigation and Power, February 8–10, 1955, PC Records, ISI, folder 116.

31. Prasanta Chandra Mahalanobis, Notes for Panel of Economists, January 27, 1955, PC Records, ISI, folder 97; "The Fourth NDC Meeting," May 6, 1955, in GOI PC, *Five Decades of Nation-Building (Fifty NDC Meetings)* (New Delhi: Planning Commission, 2005), 1:59. For examples of the invocation of foreign experts, see Jawaharlal Nehru to Chief Ministers, January 13, 1955, in SWJN2, 27:568. For later invocations, as the plan began, see Jawaharlal Nehru, "Changes in the Soviet Union," March 24, 1956, in SWJN2, 32:452; Jawaharlal Nehru, "India and the International Situation," May 4, 1956, in SWJN2, 33:15; and Jawaharlal Nehru, "Approval of the Second Plan," May 23, 1956, in SWJN2, 33:71.

32. "Recommendation for the Formulation of the Second Five-Year Plan," March 17, 1955, in P. C. Mahalanobis, *Talks on Planning* (New York: Asia Publishing House, 1961), 19, 21–22, 41, 35–36. A second document, "The Second Five-Year Plan: A Tentative Framework" (a working paper prepared by the Economic Division of the Ministry of Finance and the Economic Division of the Planning Commission in consultation with the Central Statistical Organization and the ISI on March 23, 1955) also emerged from the work at the ISI; even though it had a wider sponsorship, Mahalanobis's plan-frame was the basis of further public and private discussion. Both documents are reproduced in GOI PC, *Papers Relating to the Formulation of the Second Five Year Plan* (Delhi: Planning Commission, 1955).

33. Francine R. Frankel, *India's Political Economy, 1947–1977: The Gradual Revolution* (Princeton, N.J.: Princeton University Press, 1978), 122; Jawaharlal Nehru to V. T. Krishnamachari, January 8, 1955, in SWJN2, 27:383; Jawaharlal Nehru to Bisnuram Medhi, March 10, 1955, in SWJN2, 28:364; Jawaharlal Nehru to Chief Ministers, June 5, 1955, in LCM, 4:188; Jawaharlal Nehru, "The Tasks before Congress," January 10, 1955, in SWJN2, 27:267; Thomas Balogh to M. O. Mathai, July 11, 1956, PMO Records, NAI, 32(31) / 56-PMS. For a sampling of public criticisms, see S.N.G., "The Story behind 'Physical' Planning," *Thought* (Delhi) 7 (1955): 4; and Hannan Ezekiel, "The Dangers of Physical Planning," *Freedom First* 35 (1955): 1–2. The debate continued within the Planning Commission for many years; see conversation with Paul Rosenstein-Rodan, March 14–15, 1960, Country Files, WBGA, folder 1837562.

34. "The Second Five Year Plan: Basic Considerations Relating to the Plan Frame," in GOI PC, *Papers Relating to the Formulation,* 1, 13–14. Compare these "basic considerations" to some of the articles published in the same volume, for instance: A. K. Das Gupta, "Notes on Objectives, etc. of the Second Five-Year Plan," 111–115, and B. K. Madan, "The Second Five-Year Plan: Problems of Resource Mobilization," 466–474. See also "Major Changes Needed in Administrative Set-Up: Economists on Success of Second Plan," TOI, May 18, 1955, 11.

35. I. G. Patel, *Essays in Economic Policy and Economic Growth* (Basingstoke, England: Macmillan 1986), 39–41; Medha Kudaisya, " 'A Mighty Adventure': Institutionalising the Idea of Planning in Post-Colonial India, 1947–60," *Modern Asian Studies* 43:4 (2009): 939–978; Aye-a-Sigh [pseud.], "The Pity of It, Iago . . . ," EW, June 18, 1955, 727–729. American diplomats cataloged complaints from prominent economists like D. R. Gadgil, V. K. R. V. Rao, and C. N. Vakil; see New Delhi Embassy to U.S. Department of State, January 12, 1955, SDDF, USNA, RG 59, 891.00 / 1-1255.

36. C. N. Vakil and P. R. Brahmananda, *Planning for an Expanding Economy: Accumulation, Employment and Technical Progress in Underdeveloped Countries* (Bombay: Vora, 1956); "Economic Conference at Poona," EW, January 7, 1956, 11–12.

37. Patel, *Glimpses,* 41; Patel, "Landscape of Economics," 29; Tarlok Singh, *The Planning Process and Public Policy: A Reassessment* (Bombay: Orient Longman, 1979), 7.

38. The attack was launched most effectively by K. C. Neogy (PC member) and C. D. Deshmukh (minister of finance and chair of the Panel of Economists). PC Minutes, May 2, 1955, PC Records, ISI, folder 116.

39. Jawaharlal Nehru, "The Second Five-Year Plan," May 6, 1955, in SWJN2, 28:369, 371; "The Fourth NDC Meeting," in GOI PC, *Five Decades*, 1:57–65; C. D. Deshmukh, *The Course of My Life* (New Delhi: Orient Longman, 1974), 220.

40. Frankel, *India's Political Economy*, 128–129. For a review of press accentuating the positive feedback, see Frederic Bartlett dispatch, May 2, 1955, SDDF, USNA, RG 59, 891.00 Five-Year Plan / 5-255. For criticisms, see "Not a People's Plan," *EW*, June 18, 1955, 701–702; Asoka Mehta, "From Plan-Frame to a Popular Plan," *EW*, June 18, 1955, 697–698; and "Towards a Communist Pattern?" *Freedom First* 36 (1955): 1–2, 6–7.

41. Milton Friedman, "The Methodology of Positive Economics," in *Essays in Positive Economics* (Chicago: University of Chicago Press, 1953), 3–34; Angus Burgin, *The Great Persuasion: Reinventing Free Markets since the Depression* (Cambridge, Mass.: Harvard University Press, 2012), chapter 5; Harold Stassen conversation with C. D. Deshmukh, March 2, 1955, in Stassen's report on India Trip, March 21, 1955, DDRS, CK3100389521; New Delhi Embassy to U.S. Department of State, April 20, 1955, SDDF, USNA, RG 59, 891.00A / 4-2055.

42. Milton Friedman and Rose D. Friedman, *Two Lucky People: Memoirs* (Chicago: University of Chicago Press, 1998), 257–262. The Rockefeller Foundation work in India at that point was limited almost exclusively to medical and public health programs; it is a stretch to read those policies as pro-central planning. See, for instance, relevant issues of the Rockefeller Foundation *Annual Reports* as well as its agreement with the Government of India, April 12, 1956, in MEA Records, NAI, 67(4)-AMS / 58.

43. Alvin Roseman to John Hollister, August 4, 1955, in RUSFAA, USNA, RG469, entry UD181, box 22; Jeffrey J. Jones conversation with Milton Friedman, August 23, 1955, SDDF, USNA, RG 59, 891.00 / 8-2355; George Allen conversation with Milton Friedman, August 23, 1955, SDDF, USNA, RG 59), 891.00A / 8-2355. Friedman was joined in this last conversation—as in his trip to India—by University of California–Los Angeles economist Neil H. Jacoby, who had recently completed a stint on President Eisenhower's Council of Economic Advisers. See Friedman, "Notes on Conferences—New Delhi, India, October–November 1955" and Milton Friedman to D. A. FitzGerald, November 22, 1955, both in Milton Friedman Papers, Hoover Institution Archives, 226:12, emphasis in the original; and Friedman, "The Indian Alternative," *Encounter*, January 1957, 71–73.

44. H. Rowan Gaither Jr. to Julius Stratton, July 27, 1951, "Proposal for a Research Program on Economic Development and Political Stability," 1952, and Economic Workshop Report, June 13, 1952, all in FF Records, RAC, reel 115, grant file 52-152; Donald L. M. Blackmer, *The MIT Center for International Studies: The Founding Years, 1951–1969* (Cambridge, Mass.: MIT Center for International Studies, 2002), 67–85. The very earliest plans did not center on India but on Iran (in addition to Italy and Indonesia); see Hans Speier to Rowan Gaither, September 18, 1951, FF Records RAC, reel 115, grant file 52-152. Economist Walt Rostow was seeking I-O analysis from an early date, but only in 1954 did the project endorse it as a core aim; see Walt Rostow to Max Millikan, September 4, 1952, CIS Records, MIT Archives, 10:11; and "Proposal for Completion of the Economic and Political Development Research Program," March 1954, CIS Records, MIT Archives, 2:2.

45. Simon Kuznets commentary on MIT proposal, March 26, 1954; Carl B. Spaeth to Don K. Price, April 7, 1954, John B. Howard memorandum to files, May 26, 1954, and Clarence Thurber conversation with Max Millikan and Wilfred Malenbaum, February 8, 1955, all in FF Records, RAC, reel 116, grant file 54-88; Lowry Nelson to Carl B. Spaeth, July 23, 1952, FF Records, RAC, reel 115, grant file 52-152; Max Millikan to Douglas Ensminger, March 31, 1953, Douglas Ensminger to Carl B. Spaeth, April 20, 1953, and Douglas Ensminger, "MIT Reconnaissance Survey," December 15, 1953, all in FF Records, RAC, reel 116, grant file 53-73; J. J. Anjaria to Max Millikan, November 19, 1953, CIS Records, MIT Archives, 2:2; D. Ghosh to Prasanta Chandra Mahalanobis, April 27, 1957, Max Millikan to Prasanta Chandra Mahalanobis, April 25, 1957, and Prasanta Chandra Mahalanobis to Max Millikan, April 27, 1957, all in PC Records, ISI, folder 42. The University of Bombay would agitate successfully to join the project later; see M. O. Dantwalla to D. Ghosh, May 21, 1957, and Prasanta Chandra Mahalanobis to D. Ghosh, June 16, 1957, both in PC Records, ISI, folder 42. For a full list of MIT economists, see CIS Records, MIT Archives, 9:22. See also the harsh assessment in the letter of the Australian economist Trevor Swan (employed by MIT), March 23, 1959, quoted in Blackmer, *MIT Center*, 88–89.

46. Wilfred Malenbaum, "Some Comments on the Second Five-Year Plan Draft Memorandum," December 27, 1955, PC Records, ISI, folder 109; Harold Stassen memorandum of conversation with Planning Commission, March 1, 1955, DDRS, CK310024999; Wilfred Malenbaum, *India and China: Development Contrasts*, CIS Report C/55–28 (Cambridge, Mass.: Center for International Studies, MIT, 1955), 48 (and compare Wilfred Malenbaum, "India's Economic Progress under the Plan," *EW*, September 11, 1954, 1016–1018); Clarence Thurber memorandum to files, February 5, 1955, and Douglas Ensminger to John B. Howard, February 17, 1955, both in FF Records, RAC, reel 116, grant file 54-88. For the growing concerns in Cambridge about this distance from the ISI, see Nicole Sackley, "Passage to Modernity: American Social Scientists, India, and the Pursuit of Development, 1945–1961" (PhD diss., Princeton University, 2004), 261.

47. Jan Tinbergen, "Capital Formation and the Five Year Plan," *Indian Economic Journal* 1:1 (1953): 1–5 (quotation herein on 5). See also Jan Tinbergen, "An International Economic Policy," *Indian Journal of Economics* 38:248 (1957): 11–16; Jan Tinbergen, Jan R. Magnus, and Mary S. Morgan, "The ET Interview: Professor J. Tinbergen," *Econometric Theory* 3:1 (1987): 134–135; Jan Tinbergen, *The Design of Development* (Baltimore: Johns Hopkins University Press, 1958), 5–6. Marcel Boumans, *A Case of Limited Physics Transfer: Jan Tinbergen's Resources for Re-shaping Economics* (Amsterdam: Thesis Publishers, 1992).

48. Jan Tinbergen, "A Note on Employment Policy," n.d. (1956?), and "Note for Professor Mahalanobis on the Influences on the Process of Industrialization Exerted by 'Accounting Interest Rates' and 'Accounting Wage Rates,'" March 31, 1956, both in Visitor Records, ISI, folder Tinbergen; ISI *Annual Report 1955–56*, 53.

49. ISI *Annual Report, 1955–56*, 52; Galbraith, "Economic Planning in India: Four Comments," March 20, 1956, in M. O. Mathai Papers, NMML, Speeches/Writings by Others, 5; Richard Parker, *John Kenneth Galbraith: His Life, His Politics, His Economics* (New York: Farrar, Straus and Giroux, 2005), 277–281. For correspondence related to Galbraith's initial

travels, see the correspondence in John Kenneth Galbraith Papers, JFKL, box 38. For one of a handful of direct references to India, see Galbraith, *The Affluent Society* (Boston: Houghton Mifflin, 1958), 242.

50. Ian M. D. Little, *Economic Development: Theory, Politics, and International Relations* (New York: Basic Books, 1982), 50; Stuart Rice to William F. Ogburn, August 20, 1951, SDDF, USNA, RG 59, 891.00TA / 2-1753; Jawaharlal Nehru, "Engagement of Foreign Experts," May 9, 1953, in *SWJN2*, 22:300.

51. Prasanta Chandra Mahalanobis, "Studies of the Problems of Industrialization in the Underdeveloped Countries," 1959, in *Talks on Planning*, 138–141; "Etot plan otkryvaet Indii dorogu v budushchee: interviu d-ra Makhalanobisa," *V zashchitu mira* 58:3 (1956): 75; military metaphor quoted (without citation) in Stephen Clarkson, *The Soviet Theory of Development: India and the Third World in Marxist-Leninist Scholarship* (Toronto: University of Toronto Press, 1978), 267; Prabhakar Padhye, "Planning for Freedom," *Freedom First* 38 (1955): 8–9; "The Unfolding of the Plan," *EW*, June 18, 1955, 679–680; "Towards a Communist Pattern?," *Freedom First* 36 (1955): 1–2; Jawaharlal Nehru to Mailas Nath, May 23, 1954, in *SWJN2*, 25:264n3; Jawaharlal Nehru to Prasanta Chandra Mahalanobis, August 2, 1956, in *SWJN2*, 34:180. For a sympathetic account of Satya Brata Sen, one such communist working for the ISI, see Ashok Mitra, "A Rare Man," *EPW*, October 12, 1996, 2789–2790.

52. Prabhat Patnaik, "Delhi School Days," in Kumar and Mookherjee, eds., *D School*, 115; Amartya Sen, "On the Delhi School," in Kumar and Mookherjee, eds., *D School*, 101; Brijeshwar Singh, "Memories," in Kumar and Mookherjee, eds., *D School*, 158; S. R. Sen, quoted in George Rosen, *Western Economists and Eastern Societies: Agents of Change in South Asia, 1950–1970* (Baltimore: Johns Hopkins University Press, 1985), 52; Gurcharan Das, *India Unbound* (New Delhi: Viking, 2000), 107. See also V. N Balasubramanyam, *Conversations with Indian Economists* (Basingstoke, England: Palgrave, 2001), 62 (A. M. Khusro), 138 (Jagdish Bhagwati), and 185 (Bimal Jalan).

53. Amartya Kumar Sen, "A Note on the Mahalanobis Model of Sectoral Planning," *Arthaniti* 1:2 (1958): 26–33; Jagdish Bhagwati, "Deficit Financing and Economic Development," *Indian Economic Review* 3:2 (1956): 40–60; Man Mohan Singh, "Monetary Policy and Economic Expansion," *Indian Economic Review* 4:3 (1959): 45–56; Ignacy Sachs, "My Education in Delhi," in Kumar and Mookherjee, eds., *D School*, 69; Sen, "On the Delhi School," 93.

54. Amartya Sen, "Theory and Practice of Development," in *India's Economic Reforms and Development: Essays for Manmohan Singh*, ed. Isher Judge Ahluwalia and Ian Malcolm David Little (New Delhi: Oxford University Press, 1998), 79. Econometrician T. N. Srinivasan taught at Yale, and Meghnad Desai at the University of Pennsylvania and the LSE. For a thoughtful overview of Indian economics in the 1950s and 1960s, see T. J Byres, ed., *The Indian Economy: Major Debates since Independence* (New Delhi: Oxford University Press, 1998), chaps. 1–3.

55. Rudra, *Prasanta Chandra Mahalanobis*, 319; David Webster, "Development Advisors in a Time of Cold War and Decolonization: The United Nations Technical Assistance Administration, 1950–59," *Journal of Global History* 6:2 (2011): 264–265; Ragnar Frisch to Prasanta Chandra Mahalanobis, February 9, 1955, Visitor Files, ISI, folder Frisch. For an alternative

use of the term "brain irrigation," see Kris Manjapra, "Knowledgeable Internationalism and the Swadeshi Movement, 1903–1921," *EPW*, October 20, 2012, 53–62. Paul Streeten applies the notion of import substitution to the pursuit of economic expertise, but with the caveat that scholarly protectionism would result in an inferior or overpriced product; see Paul Streeten, *The Limits of Development Studies* (Leeds: Leeds University Press, 1975), 19. Similarly, B. S. Minhas noted India's "self-sufficiency" in economic expertise, in discussion of Gustav Papenek, "Foreign Advisors and Planning Agencies"; see Mike Faber and Dudley Seers, *The Crisis in Planning* (London: Chatto and Windus, 1972), 1:185.

56. Balasubramanyam, *Conversations with Indian Economists*, 91 (Manmohan Singh); Jagdish Bhagwati, interview with the author, Cambridge, Mass., July 1, 2011; Rosen, *Western Economists*, 121–125. For a full list of visiting scholars, see James Dorsey to Martha Sue McConnell, June 16, 1966, CIS Records, MIT Archives, 9:22. See also Douglas Ensminger, oral history (1971–1972), FF Records, RAC, finding aid 744, box 1. Further details on Ford Foundation support are in FF Records, RAC, reel 905, grant file 58-30 (Delhi School of Economics); reel 906, grant file 58-217 (ISI); and reel 4833, grant file 58-267 (University of Calcutta—largely to smooth feathers ruffled by Amartya Sen's appointment to a professorship at the age of twenty-four). See also Ford Foundation, *Annual Report 1955* (New York: Ford Foundation, 1956), unpaginated appendix; and Ford Foundation, *Annual Report 1959* (New York: Ford Foundation, 1957), 146–149. Recipients included D. R. Gadgil's Gokhale Institute; see Rockefeller Foundation, *Annual Report 1955*, 237; and Ford Foundation, *Annual Report 1961* (New York: Ford Foundation, 1962), 208–209.

57. Marie Scot, *La London School of Economics and Political Science, 1895–2010: Internationalisation universitaire et circulation des savoirs* (Paris: Presses universitaires de France, 2011), annexe 5; Balasubramanyam, *Conversations with Indian Economists*, 30 (P. R. Brahmananda); untitled memorandum on foreign students to Central Committee, December 18, 1956, RGANI, 5 / 35 / 42 / 181–184.

58. Sunil Khilnani, *The Idea of India* (New York: Farrar, Straus and Giroux, 1998), 96.

4. The Aid Project and Cold War Competition

1. N. S. Khrushchev, "Rech' na zasedanii parlamenta Indii," February 11, 1960, in *O vneshnei politike Sovetskogo Soiuza, 1960 god* (Moscow: Gosudarstvennoe izdatel'stvo politicheskoi literatury, 1961), 73–74; I. A Benediktov, *Bonds of Friendship* (Moscow: Novosti Press Agency, 1973), 22–23; K. S. Likhachev memorandum, n.d. (March 1960), and N. V. Goldin conversation with Swaran Singh, February 27, 1960, both in AVPRF, 090 / 22 / 72 / 25 / 65–67, 86–88.

2. See, for instance, the series Studies in Competitive Coexistence, in which appeared Wilfred Malenbaum, *East and West in India's Development* (Washington, D.C.: National Planning Association, 1959); for a Soviet version, see A. S. Kodachenko, *Sorevnovanie dvukh sistem i slaborazvitye strany* (Moscow: Izdatel'stvo sotsial'no-ekonomicheskoi literatury, 1960).

3. George Allen note regarding Prasanta Chandra Mahalanobis Statement, August 2, 1955, SDDF, USNA, RG59, 791.5-MSP / 8-255; Lazar Kaganovich quoted in Protokol 175,

December 16, 1955, in A. A. Fursenko, ed., *Prezidium TsK KPSS 1954–1964* (Moscow: Rosspen, 2003), 71–72.

4. C. D. Deshmukh press conference, November 2, 1955, quoted in "Planning and Resources," *AR* 1:44 (1955): 488.

5. TTK at Associated Chambers of Commerce, December 12, 1955, quoted in "Associated Chambers of Commerce," *AR* 1:51 (1955): 566.

6. *EA 1960–1961,* appendix 2, and *EA 1966–1967,* appendix 2. These figures lump loans together with a small number of grants. See also Asha Laxman Datar, *India's Economic Relations with the USSR and Eastern Europe, 1953 to 1969* (Cambridge: Cambridge University Press, 1972), 263.

7. "Indo-Soviet Pact on Steel Plant Signed," *TOI,* February 3, 1955, 1; "Vazhnoe ekonomicheskoe soglashenie," *Pravda,* February 15, 1955, 4; K. Novikov conversation with K. I. Koval' (regarding the criticisms of Lok Sabha member Lanka Sundaram), February 10, 1955, AVPRF, 090 / 16 / 51 / 27 / 3–4.

8. M. A. Men'shikov oral history, July 1967, Transcripts, NMML, 11.

9. N. S. Khrushchev, TsK KPSS report, February 14, 1956, and A. I. Mikoian speech, February 16, 1956, both in *XX s"ezd Kommunisticheskoi Partii Sovetskogo Soiuza, 14–15 fevralia 1956 g.: stenograficheskii otchet* (Moscow: Gosudarstvennoe izdatel'stvo politicheskoi literatury, 1956), 1:39–40, 314–315. Indeed, early drafts of his foreign policy speech were more declarative in tone, with succeeding drafts adding qualifiers and passive voice to weaken these paragraphs; see the drafts of December 28, 1955, and January 18, 1956, and the final version on February 14, 1956, RGANI, 1 / 2 / 3 / 59–61, 198–200.

10. Modeste Rubinstein, "A Non-Capitalist Path for Developing Countries (1)," *New Times,* July 5, 1956, 3–6; Modeste Rubinstein, "A Non-Capitalist Path for Developing Countries (2)," *New Times,* August 2, 1956, 6–9.

11. D. Degtiar', "Otchet o poezdke v Indiiu sovetskikh spetsialistov, rabotavshikh v Indiiskom statisticheskom institute, g. Kalkutte," June 1, 1955, RGANI, 5 / 28 / 344 / 64–93; M. I. Rubinshtein, "Ob ekonomicheskom razvitii sovremennoi Indii," *Voprosy ekonomiki* 1955:10 (1955): 124–125; Karl Marx, *Capital* (Moscow: International Publishers, 1970), 1:13.

12. M. I. Rubinshtein, *Ekonomicheskoe razvitie Respubliki Indii* (Moscow: Znanie, 1956), 26, 56.

13. Rubinstein, "Non-Capitalist Path (1)," 6.

14. N. Gudtsov, "O podlinnykh i mnimykh druz'iakh Indii," *Literaturnaia gazeta,* March 28, 1955, 2; S. A. Skachkov conversation with T. N. Kaul, April 2, 1964, RGAE, 365 / 2 / 2142 / 1b-4; New Delhi Embassy to U.S. Department of State, February 10, 1958, SDDF, USNA, RG 59, 891.331 / 2-1058; "O razshirenii ekonomicheskikh sviazei s Indiei," November 14, 1955, AVPRF, 090 / 17 / 51 / 23 / 3–11; N. S. Khrushchev, speech to the Presidium of the Communist Party of the Soviet Union, December 29, 1955, in *Missiia druzhby: prebyvanie N. A. Bulganina i N. S. Khrushcheva v Indii, Birme, Afganistane,* ed. Pavel Alekseevich Satiukov (Moscow: Pravda, 1956), 353; P. C. Mahalanobis to Pitamber Pant, May 7, 1959, Pitamber Pant Papers (privately held).

15. Joe Miller, a Yale University librarian, recalling Edward R. Murrow's reports, cited in Ramachandra Guha, *India after Gandhi: The History of the World's Largest Democracy* (New York: Ecco, 2007), 219; Calcutta Consulate-General to U.S. Department of State, April 25, 1955, in SDDF, USNA, RG 59, 891.331/4-2555; discussion at the 248th Meeting of the National Security Council, May 12, 1955, AWF-NSC (DDEL), NSC, box 6; memorandum of June 21, 1955, cited in Anita Inder Singh, *The Limits of British Influence: South Asia and the Anglo-American Relationship, 1947–56* (New York: St. Martin's Press, 1993), 198.

16. Corinna R. Unger, "Rourkela, Ein 'Stahlwerk im Dschungel': Industrialisierung, Modernisierung, und Entwicklungshilfe im Kontext von Dekolonisation und Kaltem Krieg (1950–1970)," *Archiv für Sozialgeschichte* 48 (2008): 372–374; HC–New Delhi to CRO, December 17, 1955, PMO Records, UKNA, PREM 11/1303; C. J. M. Alport briefing, June 22, 1959, CRO Records, UKNA, DO 35/8528; GOI Lok Sabha, Committee on Public Undertakings, *Twenty-Ninth Report: Durgapur Steel Plant of Hindustan Steel, Ltd. Ministry of Steel and Heavy Engineering* (New Delhi: Lok Sabha Secretariat, 1966), 1; K. Novikov conversation with K. I. Koval', February 10, 1955, AVPRF, 090/17/51/27/3–4; William Turnage to Thorsten Kalijarvi, January 13, 1955, SDDF, USNA, RG 59, 791/5-MSP/1-1355; Medha M. Kudaisya, *The Life and Times of G. D. Birla* (New Delhi: Oxford University Press, 2003), 333.

17. C. D. Jackson to Nelson Rockefeller, November 10, 1955, WHCF, DDEL, Confidential Files, Subject Series, box 61.

18. Colin Clark, "Development Economics: The Early Years," in *Pioneers in Development*, ed. Gerald M. Meier and Dudley Seers (Oxford: Oxford University Press, 1984), 64 (Paul Rosenstein-Rodan, an eminent economist long involved in the MIT India project, used similar language; see his preface to Padma Desai, *The Bokaro Steel Plant: A Study of Soviet Economic Assistance* [Amsterdam: North-Holland Publishing, 1972], vii); Zbigniew Brzezinski, "The Politics of Underdevelopment," *World Politics* 9:1 (1956): 60. Indian officials chafed at such descriptions; see, e.g., C. Subramaniam, "The Case for Steel," 1963, in *India of My Dreams* (New Delhi: Orient Longman, 1972), 81. See also W. W. Rostow, "Marx Was a City Boy: Or, Why Communism May Fail," *Harper's*, February 1955, 25–30.

19. OCB Report on South Asia, November 9, 1960, OSANSA Records, DDEL, NSC Series, Policy Papers Subseries, box 19.

20. Nikita Khrushchev, *Khrushchev Remembers: The Last Testament*, ed. Strobe Talbott (Boston: Little, Brown, 1974), 301.

21. "O poseshchenie prim'er-ministrom Dzh. Neru," December 16, 1957, RGAE, 365/2/1976/8. The phrase, as the Soviet observer recorded it, was, "znamenie Indii budushchego."

22. These Soviet reports did not enumerate the equipment needs, but measured them only by weight. Conversation with V. Sergeev, N. A. Smelov, B. B. Khlebnikov, and N. V. Godin, October 19, 1956, RGAE, 365/2/1545/2–3; T. F. Moffitt report, October 1, 1956, RUSFAA, USNA, RG 469, entry P273, box 9; "Otchet gruppy proektnogo nadzora na ianvar' mesiats 1958 g.," January 1958, RGAE, 365/2/1976/61–62; N. A. Smelov conversation with S. Bhoothalingam, September 11, 1957, RGAE, 365/2/1951/63–61; A. G. Sheremet'ev conversation with S. Bhoothalingam, January 7, 1958, RGAE, 365/2/1955/5–11; Bombay Consulate-General to

U.S. Department of State, January 21, 1959, SDDF, USNA, RG 59, 891.331/1-2159; Marshall I. Goldman, *Soviet Foreign Aid* (New York: Praeger, 1967), 89–90.

23. Bernard D'Mello, "Soviet Collaboration in Indian Steel Industry, 1954–84," *EPW*, March 5, 1988, 476; N. A. Smelov and V. Sergeev conversation with Swaran Singh, September 13, 1957, and N. A. Smelov conversation with S. Bhoothalingam, September 25, 1955, both in RGAE, 365/2/65/70–71, 139–140; report from John Scott, in New Delhi Embassy to U.S. Department of State, September 18, 1957, SDDF, USNA, RG 59, 891.331/9—1857 (journalist Scott wrote an important account of the construction of the Soviet steel plant at Magnitogorsk); A. G. Sheremet'ev conversation with Vaidyanathan, January 30, 1958, RGAE, 365/2/112/13–15; E. Zabordin to A. G. Sheremet'ev, September 11, 1958, RGAE, 365/2/1955/23; "O sostoianii stroitel'stva Indiiskogo metallurgicheskogo zavoda v Bkhilai," October 16, 1958, RGAE, 365/2/1976/245; K. D. Malaviya conversation with A. I. Mikoian, October 24, 1958, K. D. Malaviaya Papers, NMML, subject 85. Swaran Singh to S. A. Skachkov, August 25, 1960, RGAE, 365/2/223/91–95.

24. N. A. Smelov conversation with S. Bhoothalingam, September 11, 1959, RGAE, 365/2/65/50–52; N. S. Srivastava (director general for construction), quoted in A. N. Kosygin conversation with Soviet and Indian specialists, February 26, 1961, RGAE, 365/2/277/85–91; report on Morarji Desai's visit to Bhilai, January 29–30, 1960, RGAE, 365/2/223/46 (the report quoted Desai as using the word *trudoliubivy*); "O sostoianii stroitel'stva Indiiskogo metallurgicheskogo zavoda v Bkhilai," October 16, 1958, RGAE, 365/2/1976/250–251.

25. New Delhi Embassy to U.S. Department of State, February 10, 1958, and New Delhi Embassy to U.S. Department of State, October 30, 1959, both in SDDF, USNA, RG 59, 891.331/2-1058, 10-3059; Central Committee to M. A. Men'shikov, March 22, 1960, AVPRF, 090/22/71/15/59–60; I. A. Benediktov to N. S. Khrushchev, March 19, 1960, AVPRF, 090/22/72/18/95–96.

26. Jawaharlal Nehru to Swaran Singh, October 21, 1957, and Jawaharlal Nehru to Foreign Secretary and others, October 21, 1957, both in SWJN2, 39:126, 691–692; P. Ratnam to Secretary of Ministry for Iron and Steel, March 11, 1957, MEA Records, NAI, 26(116)-Eur/56; N. K. Grigorev conversation with Ratnam and Das Gupta, January 5, 1957, and N. A. Smelov and V. Sergeev conversation with Swaran Singh, September 13, 1957, both in RGAE, 365/2/65/2–4, 69–71; record of meeting with S. Bhoothalingam, N. A. Smelov, and V. Sergeev, September 26, 1957, RGAE, 365/2/1951/231–226, 199–195.

27. A. G. Sheremet'ev, GKES Protocol, November 29, 1957, RGAE, 365/2/1956/180–166; N. A. Smelov memorandum of conversation with S. Bhoothalingam, September 11, 1957, RGAE, 365/2/1951/63–61; Calcutta Consulate-General to U.S. Department of State, May 21, 1966, CFPF, USNA, RG 59, AID 6 INDIA.

28. The journalist John Scott, famous for his reports from the construction of the Soviet steel plant at Magnitogorsk in the 1930s, visited Bhilai in 1957. See his report in New Delhi Embassy to U.S. Department of State, September 18, 1957, SDDF, USNA, RG 59, 891.331/9-1857. Other dispatches on Bhilai appear in New Delhi Embassy to U.S. Department of State, April 23, 1958, and February 10, 1958, both in SDDF, USNA, RG 59, 891.331/4-2358, 2-1058.

29. Pitamber Pant, "The Bokaro Steel Project: Possible Patterns of Indo-U.S. Collaboration," October 26, 1961, CIS Records, MIT Archives, 11:19; Bombay Consulate-General to U.S. Department of State, April 16, 1959, SDDF, USNA, RG 59, 891.331/4-1659; A. G. Sheremet'ev and F. Iakobovskii, "O sostoianii stroitel'stva Indiiskogo metallurgicheskogo zavoda v Bkhilai," October 16, 1958, and "O poseshchenii prem'er-ministrom Dzh. Neru," December 16, 1957, both in RGAE, 365/2/1976/236–253, 7 (Nehru visit with Burmese prime minister U Nu); J. G. P. MacKenzie, "The Durgapur Steel Project," January 27, 1960, CRO Records, UKNA, DO 35/8529; V. Sergeev to N. A. Mukhitdinov, June 16, 1961, RGANI, 5/30/372/245–247; A. I. Mikoian conversation with TTK and C. Subramaniam, July 24, 1962, AVPRF, 090/24/82/18/40–44; report on Soviet delegation trip to India and Nepal, February 8, 1960, AVPRF, 090/22/72/19/22–37.

30. Taya Zinkin, *Challenges in India* (London: Chatto and Windus, 1966), 130–131; D'Mello, "Soviet Collaboration"; K. Krishna Moorthy, *Technology Transfer: India's Iron & Steel: An ICRIER Research Study with Experts' Comments* (Madras: Technology Books, 1987), 53; Santosh K. Mehrotra, *India and the Soviet Union: Trade and Technology Transfer* (Cambridge: Cambridge University Press, 1990), 101; Calcutta Consulate-General to U.S. Department of State, February 6, 1959, SDDF, USNA, RG 59, 891.331/2-659; William Turnage to Thorsten Kalijarvi, January 13, 1955, SDDF, USNA, RG59, 791.5-MSP/1-1757; Bombay Consulate-General to U.S. Department of State, February 20, 1957, SDDF, USNA, RG59, 891.00/2-2057.

31. See the special issue of *Indian Journal of Agricultural Economics* 4:1 (1949)—especially D. Krishna Iyengar, "Economics of the Mechanization of Agriculture," 179–181 (on American and Soviet models) and V. M. Paranjape, "Mechanization of Agriculture," 172–174 (on unemployment).

32. "Direktivnye ukazaniia sovetskim uchenym, vyezzhaiushchim v Indiiu dlia okazaniia pomoshchi indiiskomu statisticheskomu institutu," February 1954, RGANI, 5/28/242/9–10. GOI Delegation to China on Agricultural Planning and Techniques, *Report of the Indian Delegation to China on Agricultural Planning & Techniques* (New Delhi: Ministry of Food and Agriculture, 1956); GOI PC, *Report of the Indian Delegation to China on Agrarian Cooperatives* (New Delhi: Planning Commission, 1957), 86–87, 183–184; P. N. Rosenstein-Rodan notes on meetings with Planning Commission staff, March 14–15, 1960, Country Files, WBGA, folder 1837562.

33. Andrei Gromyko to Central Committee, April 19, 1960, AVPRF, 090/22/71/15/66. The area would be irrigated with the completion of the Bhakra-Nangal dam project; see "Waterless Area to Become Granary of State," *TOI*, August 15, 1956, 24. While there is no good overview of the Suratgarh farm, the first five years are well summarized in "Gosudarstvennaia tsentral'naia mekhanizirovannaia sel'sko-khoziaistvennaia ferma v Suratgarkhe," 1961, attached to V. Sergeev to N. A. Mukhitdinov, June 16, 1961, RGANI, 5/30/371/249–254; unless otherwise noted, general information on the Suratgarh farm comes from this report.

34. Jawaharlal Nehru and Nikita Khrushchev meeting transcript, March 1, 1960, Subimal Dutt Papers, NMML, subject 24—PHP; Indian cabinet minutes about Khrushchev visit, January 31, 1960, MEA Records, NAI, 13(3)Eur(E)/60; Benediktov, *Bonds of Friendship*, 49–50; "As the Plan Moves," *Yojana* 5:4 (1961): 30; Srirupa Roy, *Beyond Belief: India and the Politics*

of Postcolonial Nationalism (Durham, N.C.: Duke University Press, 2007), 47; V. Bol'shakov and A. Selivanov, "Spravka o tsentral'noi mekhanizirovannoi ferme v Suratgarkhe," January 1961, RGAE, 365 / 2 / 2026 / 1–5; GOI Ministry of Food and Agriculture, *The Desert Blooms* (New Delhi: Ministry of Food and Agriculture, 1961).

35. D. V. Ter-Avanesian conversation with T. S. Krishnamurthi, December 31, 1958, RGAE, 365 / 2 / 169 / 1–2.

36. Jawaharlal Nehru conversation with N. A. Mukhitdinov, March 18, 1959, Subimal Dutt Papers, NMML, subject 1; "The Suratgarh Farm," EE, October 21, 1960, 717; D. V. Ter-Avanesian and V. A. Sergeev to N. A. Mukhitdinov, "O gosudarstvennoi tsentral'noi mekhanizirovannoi ferme v Suratgarkhe," March 4, 1959, RGAE, 365 / 2 / 1997 / 2–15; V. Sergeev and A. A. Skachkov to V. V. Matskevich and I. A. Benediktov, July 25, 1960, V. Bol'shakov and A. Selivanov, "Spravka o tsentral'noi mekhanizirovannoi ferme v Suratgarkhe," January 1961, and I. D. Kutovoi, "Spravka o rabote gruppy sovetskikh spetsialistov na TsMF v Suratgarkhe," October 11, 1960, all in RGAE, 365 / 2 / 2026 / 24–44, 71–121, 1–5; I. Kutuva, "Spravka o rabote gruppy sovetskikh spetsialistov na TsMF v Suratgarkhe," October 11, 1960, RGAE, 365 / 2 / 2026 / 104. The limits of Soviet forms of labor mobilization abroad were also visible in a high-profile Soviet project, the Aswan High Dam in Egypt; see Elizabeth Bishop, "Talking Shop: Egyptian Engineers and Soviet Specialists at the Aswan High Dam" (PhD diss., University of Chicago, 1997).

37. K. D. Malaviya to Jawaharlal Nehru, January 21, 1960, K. D. Malaviya Papers, NMML, subject 13; Ministry of Food and Agriculture note, February 5, 1959, Cabinet Secretariat Records, NAI, 7 / CF / 59; "Suratgarh-Type Farms," TOI, February 11, 1961, 5.

38. "A Woeful Paradox," TOI, August 4, 1959, 6; "Fifty Million Acres," TOI, October 24, 1959, 6; Times of India, *Directory and Year Book Including Who's Who 1963–64* (Bombay: Times of India, 1964), 37, 946; GOI PC, *Third Five Year Plan* (Delhi: Manager of Publications, 1961), 323; R. K. Karanjia, *The Mind of Mr. Nehru: An Interview with R. K. Karanjia* (London: Allen & Unwin, 1960), 54; " 'Unrealistic Estimates,' " TOI, April 13, 1956, 7; "Suratgarh-Type Farms Urged in States," TOI, March 11, 1961, 9; GOI Ministry of Food and Agriculture, *First Report of the Committee on Large-Sized Mechanised Farms* (New Delhi: Ministry of Food and Agriculture, 1961), 11. The new farm was at Jetsar. See also "Suratgarh: No Prototype," EW, March 18, 1961, 467–468; and Theodor Bergmann, "Problems of Mechanization in Indian Agriculture," *Indian Journal of Agricultural Economics* 18:4 (1963): 20–31. And compare, for instance, the purposes noted in GOI Ministry of Food and Agriculture, *Making the Desert Bloom* (New Delhi: Ministry of Food and Agriculture, 1959), 5; GOI Ministry of Food and Agriculture, *The Desert Blooms*, 3. Unfortunately, I was unable to obtain a copy of GOI Ministry of Food and Agriculture, *The Central Mechanised Farm at Suratgarh, 1956–1958* (New Delhi: Ministry of Agriculture, 1960?), so instead relied on the analysis of it in Harold H. Mann, "Progress at Suratgarh," EW, December 17, 1960, 1827–1828.

39. I. Karnaukov, "Itogi raboty 'tsentral'noi mekhanizirovannoi fermy' v Suratgarkhe v 1962–63 godu," February 6, 1964, RGAE, 365 / 2 / 2155 / 1–19; N. P. Firiubin to A. Kosygin, December 31, 1966, RGAE, 365 / 2 / 2245 / 3; "Spravka o polozhenii na Tsental'noi mekhanizirovannoi

sel'sko-khoziaistvennoi ferme v Suratgarkhe," April 25, 1966, RGAE, 365 / 2 / 2274 / 2–9; GOI Administrative Reforms Commission, *Report of the Study Team on Agricultural Administration* (New Delhi: Manager of Publications, 1967), 704–705; K. Kalinin, "Komandirovka na suratgarkhskuiu gosudarstvennuiu mekhanizirovannuiu fermy," November 7, 1969, RGAE, 365 / 9 / 43 / 154–161.

40. S. K. Dey, *Community Development: A Chronicle, 1954–1961* (Delhi: Ministry of Information and Broadcasting, 1962), 61n; GOI PC Program Evaluation Organization, *Evaluation Report on Second Year's Working of Community Projects* (New Delhi: Planning Commission, 1955), 5; Asok Mitra, *The New India, 1948–1955: Memoirs of an Indian Civil Servant* (Bombay: Popular Prakashan, 1991), 96–97. For a brief summary of this episode, see GOI Ministry of Food and Agriculture, *Report of the Foodgrains Enquiry Committee* (New Delhi: Ministry of Food and Agriculture, 1957), 32–33. On the evasion of land reform, see Francine R. Frankel, *India's Political Economy, 1947–1977: The Gradual Revolution* (Princeton, N.J.: Princeton University Press, 1978), 136.

41. GOI PC, *Second Five Year Plan* (Delhi: Manager of Publications, 1956), chapter 13.

42. For the report of the Balvantray Commission, named for chair Balvantray Mehta (the chief minister of Gujarat), see GOI Committee on Plan Projects, *Report of the Team for the Study of Community Projects and National Extension Service* (New Delhi: Manager of Publications, 1957), 33, 110 (compare the 1956 and 1958 versions of GOI PC Program Evaluation Organization, *Evaluation Report on Working of Community Projects and N.E.S. Blocks,* Douglas Ensminger Papers, Yale University Library, 14:B21; "Success of Community Projects: Comparatively or Not Particularly?," *EW,* January 18, 1958, 68–70; D. R. Gadgil, "Prospects for the Second Plan-Period" (1957), in *Planning and Economic Policy in India* (New York: Asia Publishing House, 1961), 56.

43. Dey, *Community Development,* 62, 75, 121; M. J. Coldwell, René Dumont, and M. Read, *Report of Community Development Evaluation Mission in India, 23 November 1958–3 April 1959* (New York: UN Commissioner for Technical Assistance, 1959), 51; U.S. Department of Agriculture, *India: A Review of Selected Technical Assistance Programs* (Washington, D.C.: U.S. Department of Agriculture, 1961), 17–18; Ford Foundation Agricultural Production Team, *Report on India's Food Crisis and Steps to Meet It* (New Delhi: Ford Foundation, 1959), 6–7; John Kenneth Galbraith, entry for September 17, 1961, in *Ambassador's Journal: A Personal Account of the Kennedy Years* (Boston: Little, Brown, 1969), 182. Funding levels come from Ford Foundation, *Annual Reports, 1956–1965* (New York: Ford Foundation, 1956–1965). For a report on the conclusions of the Sixth Development Commissioners' Conference, April 1957, see GOI Ministry of Food and Agriculture, *Report of the Foodgrains Enquiry Committee,* 33.

44. George Jacobs, foreword, and "Group I Report," both in *Objectives of Community Development: Its Role in National Development,* ed. U. C. Ghildyal (Hyderabad, India: National Institute for Community Development, 1967), 7, 27.

45. Nick Cullather, *The Hungry World: America's Cold War Battle against Poverty in Asia* (Cambridge, Mass.: Harvard University Press, 2010), esp. 89; for a similar argument

about Indian economic policy makers, see Frankel, *India's Political Economy*, 101–105; and Ashutosh Varshney, *Democracy, Development, and the Countryside: Urban-Rural Struggles in India* (Cambridge: Cambridge University Press, 1995), 34.

46. Earl L. Butz oral history, 1968, CCOH, 20; George McGovern, quoted in Devki Nandan Prasad, *Food for Peace: The Story of U.S. Food Assistance to India* (Bombay: Asia Publishing House, 1980), 103.

47. Legislative Leadership Meeting, February 4, 1958, AWF, DDEL, Legislative Meetings, box 3; Arthur F. Burns oral history, 1967, CCOH, 15–16; Christian Herter to Dwight D. Eisenhower, August 5, 1960, Christian Herter Papers, DDEL, Official Correspondence, box 20; Christian Herter to Clarence Randall, May 15, 1957, Christian Herter Papers, DDEL, Official Correspondence, box 20. For a detailed account of the bureaucratic politics, see especially Trudy Huskamp Peterson, *Agricultural Exports, Farm Income, and the Eisenhower Administration* (Lincoln: University of Nebraska Press, 1979); Sherman Adams on John Foster Dulles quoted in Peterson, *Agricultural Exports*, 10.

48. CFEP Working Group Report, December 30, 1957, Staff Secretary Records, DDEL, Subject Series, White House Subseries, box 5; Hubert H. Humphrey, *Food and Fiber as a Force for Freedom* (Report to U.S. Senate Committee on Agriculture and Forestry (Washington, D.C.: Government Printing Office, 1958); Vernon W. Ruttan, *United States Development Assistance Policy: The Domestic Politics of Foreign Economic Aid* (Baltimore: Johns Hopkins University Press, 1996), 159.

49. Jagdish N. Bhagwati and Padma Desai, *India, Planning for Industrialization: Industrialization and Trade Policies since 1951* (Oxford: Oxford University Press, 1970), 210; Sundara Rajan, quoted in R. P. Rao, *The Helping Hand* (New Delhi: Eurasia Publishing House, 1964), 55 (see also 80–81 on counterpart projects). The private-sector projects were funded by so-called Cooley loans, named after Rep. Harold Cooley (D-NC), chairman of the House Agriculture Committee for most of the 1950s; see Peterson, *Agricultural Exports*, 66–68.

50. U.S. Department of Agriculture, Economic Research Service, *P.L. 480 Concessional Sales*, Foreign Agricultural Economic Reports 142 (Washington, D.C.: U.S. Department of Agriculture, 1977), 11. See also in R. K. Jain, ed., *US-South Asian Relations, 1947–1982* (Atlantic Highlands, N.J.: Humanities Press, 1983), vol. 1, appendix 4, 619–623.

51. A. P. Jain, quoted in Prasad, *Food for Peace*, 46 (see also 45); R. N. Chopra, *Evolution of Food Policy in India* (Delhi: Macmillan India, 1981), 92. For more on the domestic context and the implications for politics broadly construed, see Benjamin Siegel, " 'Self-Help Which Ennobles a Nation': Development, Citizenship, and the Obligations of Eating in India's Austerity Years," *Modern Asian Studies* 49:3 (May 2016): 975–1018. Minister of Food and Agriculture A. P. Jain made the trip; see Nehru to MEA Secretary General, May 10, 1956, in *SWJN2*, 33:457.

52. Editorial Note, in *FRUS 1955–1957*, 8:318n5. Thomas Mann to Representative Gathings, October 30, 1959, Thomas Mann Papers, DDEL, box 2; Dennis Merrill, *Bread and the Ballot: The United States and India's Economic Development, 1947–1963* (Chapel Hill: University of North Carolina Press, 1990), 130; GOI Ministry of Food and Agriculture,

Report of the Foodgrains Enquiry Committee, 73–74; IBRD, Department of Operations—Asia and the Middle East, *Current Economic Position and Prospects of India: Report of Bank Mission to India,* August 31, 1956, WBGA online, http://documents.worldbank.org/curated/en/101071468268800453/India-Current-economic-position-and-prospects, 59; Jawaharlal Nehru, talks with Soviet ambassador M. A. Men'shikov, May 31, 1957, in *SWJN2,* 38:745.

53. GOI Ministry of Food and Agriculture, *Report of the Foodgrains Enquiry Committee,* 185, 94–95, 77, 86; "India May Purchase More Grains Soon," *TOI,* November 15, 1957, 1; "Further Supply of U.S. Wheat," *TOI,* February 14, 1958, 7; Dwight D. Eisenhower conversation with John Foster Dulles and others, November 12, 1957, in *FRUS 1955–1957,* 8:404–406; B. R. Tomlinson, *The Economy of Modern India, 1860–1970* (Cambridge: Cambridge University Press, 1993), 199.

54. GOI Ministry of Food and Agriculture, *Report of the Foodgrains Enquiry Committee,* 94–95; Mordecai Ezekiel, "Apparent Results in Using Surplus Food for Financing Economic Development," *Journal of Farm Economics* 40:4 (1958): 918; V. M. Dandekar, *Use of Food Surpluses for Economic Development* (Pune, India: Gokhale Institute, 1956); Food and Agriculture Organization, *Uses of Agricultural Surpluses to Finance Economic Development in Under-Developed Countries: A Pilot Study in India* (Rome: FAO, 1955).

55. Chopra, *Evolution of Food Policy,* 120. R. N. Chopra was chair of the public-sector Food Cooperation of India.

56. Rao, *Helping Hand,* 81; B. K. Nehru to Jawaharlal Nehru, October 11, 1960, in B. K. Nehru Papers, NMML, subject 97-II; Frederic Bartlett conversation with B. K. Nehru, March 3, 1959, SDR, USNA, RG59, entry A1-1330, box 24; S. R. Sen, "Impact and Implications of Foreign Surplus Disposal on Underdeveloped Economies: The Indian Perspective," *Journal of Farm Economics* 42:5 (1960): 1031; New Delhi Embassy to U.S. Department of State, May 29, 1958, and New Delhi Embassy to U.S. Department of State, August 26, 1958, both in *FRUS 1958–1960,* 15:430–431, 446–447.

57. Narindar Singh, "P L 480: An Appraisal," *EW,* May 30, 1959, 720; "India-Key Points," November 1, 1957, Ezra Taft Benson Papers, DDEL, box 21; S. K. Patil, *My Years with Congress* (Bombay: Parchure Prakashan Mandir, 1991), 96; "Background Information on Multi-Year Title I Program for India," February 11, 1960, and New Delhi Embassy to U.S. Department of State, October 3, 1959, both in Paarlberg Papers, DDEL, box 13; New Delhi Embassy to U.S. Department of State, January 8, 1958, and U.S. Department of State to New Delhi Embassy, March 17, 1958, both in *FRUS 1958–1960,* 15:475, 380.

58. H. N. Mookerjee, in Lok Sabha, March 1960, quoted in Prasad, *Food for Peace,* 93; K. D. Malaviya to Jawaharlal Nehru, January 9, 1960, K. D. Malaviya Papers, NMML, Correspondence: J. Nehru; B. R. Shenoy, "Aid under P.L. 480," *TOI,* January 28, 1960, 8; B. R. Shenoy, "P.L. 480 Imports," *TOI,* February 17, 1960, 6.

59. Merrill, *Bread and the Ballot,* 144; D. R. Gadgil, "Price Policy: Report to Panel of Economists," October 1960, in *Planning and Economic Policy,* 199; V. K. Krishna Menon, quoted in K. C. Arora, *V. K. Krishna Menon: A Biography* (New Delhi: Sanchar Publishing House,

1998), 265; B. R. Shenoy, "P.L. 480 Counterpart Funds and Inflation," *Economic Times,* March 27–29, 1963.

60. "Mistaken Zeal," *TOI,* May 17, 1963, 6; "Premature," *TOI,* May 18, 1963, 6; "Bewildering," *TOI,* May 29, 1963, 6; "'Foundation' Laid for Talks on New P.L. 480 Agreement," *TOI,* June 25, 1963, 8; "Planning Body Not for New P.L. 480 Pact," *TOI,* May 17, 1963, 1; Frankel, *India's Political Economy,* 226–227.

61. Joseph Rucinski to J. Burke Knapp, March 25, 1957, Country Files, WBGA, folder 1840730.

62. "Industry Program Review 1959," RUSFAA, USNA, RG 469, entry P268B, box 1, capitalization in the original; U.S. Comptroller General, *Examination of Economic and Technical Assistance Program for India, International Cooperation Administration, Department of State, Fiscal Years 1955–1958; Report to the Congress of the United States* (Washington, D.C.: Government Printing Office, 1959), 26.

63. *EA 1966–1967,* annexures 23-A through 23-I; Technical Cooperation Mission Contracts, February 3, 1956, RUSFAA, USNA, RG469, entry P271, box 1. Major projects aided by American financing included the Orissa Iron Ore Project; the Chandarapura, Durgapur, Kanpur, and Sharavathy Thermal Power Projects; and the Trombay Fertilizer Plant. See the detailed list in *EA 1977–1978,* annexures 23-A through 23-I. See also U.S. Information Service (New Delhi), *Fact Sheet: United States Economic Assistance to India, June 1951–April 1971,* Fact Sheet 23 (New Delhi: U.S. Information Service, 1971), 23–26.

64. J. C. de Wilde conversation with John Ferris, September 28, 1953, Country Files, WBGA, folder 1840728; Robert W. Oliver, *George Woods and the World Bank* (Boulder, Colo.: Lynne Reimer, 1995), 127; C. Douglas Dillon conversation with Ramaswami Mudaliar, June 13, 1958, C. Douglas Dillon Papers, JFKL, box 16; Joseph Rand to Clarence Randall, April 22, 1959, U.S. Committee on Foreign Economic Policy—Chairman Papers, DDEL, Clarence Randall Series, Agencies Subseries, box 1; Harold E. Stassen oral history, 1967, CCOH, 58; Jawaharlal Nehru to G. L. Mehta, n.d. (September 1957?), TTK Papers, NMML, Correspondence—J. Nehru.

65. G. L. Mehta to George Woods, June 28, 1958, George Woods Personal Papers, WBGA, folder 1215037; Chester Bowles to Donald Kennedy, October 13, 1952, Chester Bowles Papers, Yale University Library, 95:267; George Woods to G. L. Mehta, December 8, 1958, George Woods Papers, CU / WBGA, folder 1215239; George Woods to G. L. Mehta, December 22, 1959, George Woods Papers, CU / WBGA, folder 30178041; "Five Years of ICICI," *EW,* March 5, 1960, 405; "Six Years of ICICI," *EW,* February 25, 1961, 352; G. L. Mehta, "The Industrial Credit and Investment Corporation of India Limited: Statement by the Chairman, Shri G. L. Mehta," *EW,* March 5, 1963, 421–423. See also the correspondence between G. L. Mehta, George Woods, and J. Burke Knapp, April–May 1960, George Woods Papers, CU / WBGA, folder 30178042.

66. "Five Years of ICICI," *EW,* March 5, 1960, 405; GOI Department of Industrial Development, *Report of the Industrial Licensing Policy Inquiry Committee* (New Delhi: Manager of Publications, 1969), 195; GOI Lok Sabha, Committee on Public Undertakings, *Forty-Ninth Report: Industrial Finance Corporation of India* (New Delhi: Lok Sabha Secretariat, 1969), 19; R. K. Hazari and S. D. Mehta, *Public International Development Financing in India* (Bombay: Asian Studies Press, 1968), 78.

67. The physicist Homi J. Bhabha, like the literary scholar Homi K. Bhabha, was born in Bombay's Parsi community; the two are otherwise unrelated. For basic biographical information on Bhabha and Saha, see especially Robert S. Anderson, *Nucleus and Nation: Scientists, International Networks, and Power in India* (Chicago: University of Chicago Press, 2010), chapter 12; and Jahnavi Phalkey, *Atomic State: Big Science in Twentieth-Century India* (New Delhi: Permanent Black, 2013). On Saha's use of international networks, see Anderson, "Meghnad Saha's Two International Faces: Politics as Science and Science as Politics between the Wars," in *The Internationalist Moment: South Asia, Worlds, and World Views, 1917–1939*, ed. Ali Raza, Franziska Roy, and Benjamin Zachariah (New Delhi: SAGE India, 2014), 229–262.

68. H. V. R. Iyengar (governor of the Reserve Bank of India), cited in E. J. Schuyten to George Woods, April 4, 1960, George D. Woods Papers, CU / WBGA, folder 3017855; J. Robert Schaetzel to Philip Farley, April 17, 1959, SDR, USNA, RG 59, A1-3008A, box 496.

69. New Delhi Embassy to U.S. Department of State, October 3, 1950, SDDF, USNA, RG59, 791.001 / 10-350; Bombay Consulate-General to U.S. Department of State, November 28, 1950, SDDF, USNA, RG59, 700.561 / 11-2850. The scientist in question was John Cockcroft; see M. W. Perkin to R. C. C. Hunt, February 22, 1951, FO Records, UKNA, FO 371 / 93195; Bombay Consulate-General to U.S. Department of State, April 10, 1951, SDDF, USNA, RG 59, 561.91 / 4-1051; "Spravka na Prof. Bkhabkha Kh.," n.d. (1955), ARAN, 579 / 1 / 61 / 80; Washington Embassy to FO, February 20, 1951, Paris Embassy to FO, October 31, 1951, Washington Embassy to FO, May 31, 1951, and J. D. Cockcroft to Homi J. Bhabha, March 12, 1951, all in FO Records, UKNA, FO 371 / 83195. For details on the French relationship, see Jayita Sarkar, *From the Peaceful Atom to the Peaceful Explosion: Indo-French Nuclear Relations in the Cold War, 1950–1974*, Woodrow Wilson Center Nuclear Proliferation International History Project 3 (Washington, D.C.: Woodrow Wilson Center, 2013).

70. "Atomic Energy Problems in India," April 3, 1953, in SDR, USNA, RG 59, entry A1-3008A, box 496; C. H. Reichardt to H. S. Traynor, January 18, 1955, USAEC Records, USNA, RG 326, entry 67-B1, box 130. See also Itty Abraham, *The Making of the Indian Atomic Bomb: Science, Secrecy and the Postcolonial State* (London: Zed Books, 1998), 61.

71. N. M. Sisakian to M. A. Suslov, June 25, 1955, RGANI, 5 / 17 / 509 / 208–209; "Pribytie v Moskvu," *Pravda*, August 31, 1955, 4; John Foster Dulles conversation with Homi J. Bhabha, October 14, 1955, SDR, USNA, RG 59, entry A1-3008A, box 496; "Informatsiia o prebyvanii v SSSR delegatsii indiiskikh uchenykh vo glave s Khomi Baba," August 31, 1955, ARAN, 579 / 3 / 535 / 181–182; "Spravka na Prof. Bkhabkha Kh.," n.d. (1955), ARAN, 579 / 1 / 61 / 80; Homi J. Bhabha to M. A. Men'shikov, December 12, 1955, RGAE, 365 / 2 / 1553 / 1; "Atoms for India," *Time*, February 7, 1955; Briefing for the President, 1956, WHCF, DDEL, Subject Series, box 72; press conference after Bhabha-Dulles talks, AR 1:42 (1955): 471.

72. J. B. Hamilton note, February 16, 1956, and Gerard C. Smith to John Hall, January 30, 1956, both in USAEC Records, USNA, RG 326, entry 67-B1, box 130; Bruce Hamilton to Gerard C. Smith, October 26, 1956, SDR, USNA, RG 59, entry A1-3008A, box 496; I. P. Bardin to Central Committee, August 26, 1955, RGANI, 5 / 17 / 509 / 218; Minutes of USAEC Meeting, September 25, 1956, USAEC Records, USNA, RG326, entry 67-B1, box 134. On

Nehru, see Briefing for the President, December 7, 1956, WHCF, DDEL, Subject Series, box 72.

73. Robert Bothwell, *Nucleus: The History of Atomic Energy of Canada Limited* (Toronto: University of Toronto Press, 1988), 352–355, 369.

74. "India Will Not Use Atomic Power for Evil Purposes," *TOI*, January 21, 1957, 5; Homi J. Bhabha speech, January 20, 1957, and General K. D. Nichols to Lewis Strauss, February 14, 1957, both in USAEC Records, USNA, RG 326, entry 67-B1, box 130. See also "Notes on the Bombay Visit of the Brookhaven Team," April 24, 1957, RUSFAA, USNA, RG 469, entry P273, box 1.

75. Agenda for Planning Commission meeting of January 23–24, 1956, PC Records, ISI, folder 109; GOI PC, *Second Five Year Plan*, chapter 24; TTK speech in Lok Sabha, September 12, 1956, in GOI Lok Sabha, *Lok Sabha Debates 1956* (New Delhi: Lok Sabha Secretariat, 1956), columns 6915–6916. On Bhabha's case at Geneva, see his speeches in Jagdish P. Jain, *Nuclear India* (New Delhi: Radiant Publishers, 1974), 2:19–26.

76. Jawaharlal Nehru to TTK, January 29, 1957, in SWJN2, 36:174–176; "Soviet Offer for Atomic Training Not Accepted," *TOI*, September 2, 1958, 8; V. Vladimirov, "Indiia i problema ispol'zovaniia atomnoi energii," *Mirovaia ekonomika i mezhdunarodnaia otnosheniia*, 1959:3 (1959), 118–119; Prasanta Chandra Mahalanobis to Pitamber Pant, May 7, 1959, Pitamber Pant Papers (privately held); Marshal G. K. Zhukov's visit is described in "One-Day Trip to Bombay Planned," *TOI*, January 29, 1957, 3.

77. New Delhi Embassy, "Soviet Economic Offensive in India," May 12, 1959, *FRUS 1958–1960*, 15:488–489; Philip Farley to John Hall, March 3, 1958, SDR, USNA, RG 59, entry A1-3008A, box 497; Dwight D. Eisenhower conversation with Lord Plowden, November 13, 1959, Nuclear Proliferation Collection, DNSA, NP-602; Robert Winfree to Philip Farley, October 18, 1959, SDR, USNA, RG 59, entry A1-3008A, box 496.

78. Abraham, *Making of the Indian Atomic Bomb*, 107; GOI Department of Atomic Energy, "Additional Nuclear Stations for the Third Plan," February 1, 1960, attached to New Delhi Embassy to U.S. Department of State, April 8, 1960, SDDF, USNA, RG 59, 891.2614/4-860; summary record, Fourteenth Meeting of the National Development Council, March 19–20, 1960, in GOI PC, *Five Decades of Nation Building* (New Delhi: Planning Commission, 2005), 1:506; GOI PC, *Third Five Year Plan* (New Delhi: Manager of Publications, 1961), 618–619, 628–629.

79. John A. McCone (USAEC) conversation with Homi J. Bhabha, November 21, 1960, D. D. Kennedy (U.S. Department of State) conversation with Homi J. Bhabha, November 5, 1959, and Lynn Stambaugh (Export-Import Bank) conversation with Homi J. Bhabha, November 9, 1959, all in SDR, USNA, RG 59, entry A1-3008A, box 496; Homi J. Bhabha to Jawaharlal Nehru, December 9, 1960, PMO Records, NAI, 17/411/1960-PMS.

80. Philip Farley, memorandum for the files, November 16, 1959, meeting report, November 5, 1959, and John A. McCone to Christian Herter, February 3, 1960 (referring to Ambassador Bunker's dispatch of December 17, 1959), all in SDR, USNA, RG 59, entry A1-3008A, box 496.

81. G. Lewis Jones to Christain Herter, February 12, 1960, SDR, USNA, RG 59, entry A1-3008A, box 496. U.S. Department of State to New Delhi Embassy, April 8, 1960, SDDF, USNA, RG 59, 891.261/4-860. On the Soviet delegation, see "Spravka o sotrudnichestve s Respublikoi Indii v oblasti izpol'zovaniia atomnoi energii v mirnykh tseliakh," December 30, 1971, RGAE, 9480/9/1712/1–4; and "Russian Help Assured," *TOI*, March 9, 1960, 7. On the American delegation, see New Delhi Embassy to U.S. Department of State, February 29, 1960, Staff Secretary Records, DDEL, International Series, box 7. On the American response, see Myron Kratzer to John Hall, April 12, 1960, SDR, USNA, RG 59, entry A1-3008A, box 498; and New Delhi Embassy to U.S. Department of State, February 29, 1960, Office of the Staff Secretary, DDEL, International Series, box 7. While this latter memorandum expressed surprise, other American officials were well aware that an atomic expert would be joining Khrushchev in his February 1960 visit; see R. P. Terrill to Undersecretary of State, February 12, 1960, and G. Lewis Jones to Christian Herter, February 12, 1960, both in SDR, USNA, RG 59, entry A1-3008A, box 496; and Kratzer Team Report, April 1960, quoted in Abraham, *Making of the Indian Atomic Bomb*, 93.

82. M. I. Michaels to J. E. C. Macrae, February 3, 1960, and aide-memoire regarding Paris meeting of January 20, 1960, both in FO Records, UKNA, FO 371/149461.

83. Jawaharlal Nehru to Harold Macmillan, June 23, 1960, draft telegram, FO, to Washington Embassy, June 1960, and Reginald Maulding to Harold Macmillan, June 30, 1960, all in FO Records, UKNA, FO 371/149467.

84. "Spravka o sotrudnichestve s Respublikoi Indii v oblasti izpol'zovaniia atomnoi energii v mirnykh tseliakh," December 30, 1971, RGAE, 9480/9/1712/1–4; New Delhi Embassy to U.S. Department of State, August 10, 1960, SDDF, USNA, RG 59, 861.2614/8-1060; USAEC report, October 19, 1960, Nuclear Proliferation Collection, DNSA, NP-701; "Sovetsko-indiiskoe sotrudnichestvo v oblasti ispol'zovaniia atomnoi energii v mernykh tseliakh," July 26, 1960, AVPRF, 090/22/72/23/43–50; GOI PC, "A Note on Discussions with Mr. A. N. Kosygin," February 21 and March 3, 1961, MEA Records, NAI, 13(123)/Eur.E/60. A copy of the agreement (dated October 6, 1960) appears in MEA Records, NAI, WI/110(1)/66. V. S. Emel'ianov expressed his skepticism to USAEC member John A. McCone earlier; see McCone memorandum to file, October 2, 1959, Nuclear Proliferation Collection, DNSA, document NP-592.

85. Norman L. Gold, "Regional Economic Development and Nuclear Power in India," February 19, 1957, SDDF, USNA, RG 59, 891.00/4-457; L. K. Jha to Homi J. Bhabha, January 17, 1961, PMO Records, NAI, 17/411/1960-PMS; McCone-Emel'ianov conversation, mentioned in Roger Makins conversation with John McCone, November 30, 1960, FO Records, UKNA, FO 371/149472.

86. New Delhi Embassy to U.S. Department of State, February 6, 1961, SDDF, USNA, RG 59, 861.1901/2-661; C. L. Henderson to Bromley Smith, November 6, 1961, and Glenn Seaborg to McGeorge Bundy, November 6, 1961, both in NSF Files, JFKL, box 106; "Brief for Sir Alan Hitchman on Paper AEX(60)183, Supply of U235 to India," December 1, 1960, AEA Records, UKNA, AB 16/2828; Roger Makins to F. F. Turnbull, June 28, 1961, AEA Records, UKNA, AB 38/54.

87. New Delhi Embassy to U.S. Department of State, May 4, 1961, SDDF, USNA, RG 59, 861.1901/5-361; Robert W. Komer to President, June 5, 1962, NSF Files, JFKL, box 107. On concerns about China, see George McGhee, "Anticipatory Action Pending Chinese Communist Demonstration of Nuclear Capability," September 13, 1961, China 1960–1968 Collection, DNSA, CH-6; George Perkovich, *India's Nuclear Bomb: The Impact on Global Proliferation* (Berkeley: University of California Press, 1999), 49–59; and William Burr and Jeffrey T. Richelson, "Whether to 'Strangle the Baby in the Cradle': The United States and the Chinese Nuclear Program, 1960–1964," *International Security* 25:3 (2000–2001): 54–99. On U.S. engagements with India, see A. A. Wells to Glenn Seaborg, June 3, 1963, A. A. Wells to Charles Johnson, June 28, 1963, AEC Military Division to Director, July 16, 1963, and AEC Biweekly Report, August 13, 1963, all in NSF—Charles E. Johnson Files, LBJL, box 34. On the French angle, see Bertrand Goldschmidt, "Les problèmes nucléaires indiens," *Politique étrangère* 47:3 (1982): 617–631; my thanks to Jayita Sarkar for this citation.

88. A. A. Wells to Charles Johnson, June 28, 1963, and excerpt from AEC Biweekly Report, August 13, 1963, both in NSF—Charles E. Johnson Files, LBJL, box 34; A. S. Friedman to David T. Schneider, January 16, 1973, Daniel Patrick Moynihan Papers, LC, 371:4. On critics of the deal, see M. R. Srinivasan, *From Fission to Fusion: The Story of India's Atomic Energy Programme* (New Delhi: Viking, 2002), 52–54, 181–183; and Perkovich, *India's Nuclear Bomb*, 56–57. The text of the Indo-American agreement is in Jain, *Nuclear India*, 2:114–124.

89. Jawaharlal Nehru, "Bullock Cart, Motor Lorry, Jet Plane," December 14, 1953, in SWJN2, 24:129–136.

90. Michał Kalecki, "Observations on Social and Economic Aspects of 'Intermediate Regimes' (1964)," in *Developing Economies,* ed. Jerzy Osiatyński (Oxford: Clarendon Press, 1993), 10.

5. "Free Money" and the Tilt toward the West

1. GOI PC, *Second Five Year Plan* (New Delhi: Manager of Publications, 1956) 21 (where the problems are enumerated) and 58–61 (where quantitative targets are listed); GOI PC, *Programmes of Industrial Development, 1956–61* (New Delhi: Planning Commission, 1956).

2. GOI PC, *Second Five Year Plan,* 51–52, 77–78; V. T. Krishnamachari note, April 28, 1956, PC Records, NAI, Plan 24/4/56; "External Assistance," EW, January 14, 1956, 29–30.

3. GOI PC, *Approach to the Second Five-Year Plan* (New Delhi: Planning Commission, 1957), 94, 105.

4. GOI PC, *Second Five Year Plan,* 95; Reserve Bank of India, *India's Balance of Payments, 1948–49 to 1961–62* (Bombay: Reserve Bank of India, 1963), 138; Lok Sabha discussion, May 23, 1956, in SWJN2, 33:82; C. D. Deshmukh news conference, November 2, 1955, AR 1:44 (1955): 488–489; C. D. Deshmukh, *The Course of My Life* (New Delhi: Orient Longman, 1974), chapter 6.

5. "Private Enterpriser," *Time,* February 14, 1955, 30; "Will TTK Quit?" EW, February 5, 1955, 101; B. K. Nehru, *Nice Guys Finish Second* (New Delhi: Viking, 1997), 292. TTK to Associated

Chambers of Commerce, December 12, 1955, AR 1:51 (1955): 566–567; Morarji R. Desai, *The Story of My Life* (Oxford: Pergamon Press, 1979), 2:112. On import controls, see the monthly updates in the *Bulletin of the Reserve Bank of India*, especially June and October 1953, September 1954, and January and July 1956.

6. H. M. Patel press conference, October 31, 1957, AR 3:45 (1957): 1713; "Prospects of Foreign Assistance," EW, November 2, 1957, 1403–1404; Reserve Bank of India, *India's Balance of Payments, 1948–49 to 1961–62* (Bombay: Reserve Bank of India, 1963), 138–139; see also *Bulletin of the Reserve Bank of India*, May 1955, May 1956, May 1957, May 1958, May 1959.

7. Jawaharlal Nehru to V. T. Krishnamachari, August 12, 1956, in SWJN2, 34:45; B. K. Nehru, note of August 22, 1956, quoted in Jawaharlal Nehru to C. D. Deshmukh, January 13, 1958, TTK Papers, NMML, subject 8B; Jawaharlal Nehru to Chief Ministers, August 27, 1956, LCM, 4:425–431; V. K. Ramaswami (of the Ministry of Commerce), "Import Trade Control and Industrialization," EW, January 19, 1957, 98–100; Jawaharlal Nehru at budget debate in Lok Sabha, March 18, 1958, in SWJN2, 41:118; Jawaharlal Nehru, memorandum to cabinet ministers, January 9, 1957, in SWJN2, 36:172–173.

8. Planning Commission meeting, October 30, 1957, in SWJN2, 39:130; D. P. Karmarkar in "Exports and Foreign Exchange," EW, April 20, 1957, 806–807.

9. Prasanta Chandra Mahalanobis to Oskar Lange, February 27, 1957, Visitor Files, ISI, folder Lange; Jawaharlal Nehru, "Stop Indulging in Petty Squabbles," October 26, 1957, in SWJN2, 49:44; TTK to All-India Congress Committee, September 1, 1957, AR 3:36 (1957): 1618–1619; TTK budget speech to Lok Sabha, March 19, 1956, AR 1:64 (1956): 1365–1368; TTK memorandum of December 3, 1956, cited in Jawaharlal Nehru to Y. N. Sukthankar, December 3, 1956, in SWJN2, 36:163; TTK speech to Council on Foreign Relations, September 25, 1957, in T. T. Krishnamachari, *Speeches: Second Series* (New Delhi: Ministry of Information and Broadcasting, 1957), 7; "India's Balance of Payments: First Half, 1956–57," *Bulletin of the Reserve Bank of India*, December 1956, 1238–1245.

10. Penderell Moon, a rare Briton who stayed on in independent India, gave a broadcast that is quoted extensively in K. N. Raj, "The Foreign Exchange Crisis and the Plan," EW, February 23, 1957, 291. See also "The Plan Shall Not Be Whittled Down—Mr. Krishnamachari," TOI, March 24, 1957, 9.

11. D. R. Gadgil, "On Rephasing the Second Five-Year Plan," *Indian Economic Journal* 5:4 (1958): 355–357; Ashok Mitra, *Foreign Exchange Crisis and the Plan,* National Council of Applied Economic Research Occasional Papers 1 (New Delhi: National Council of Applied Economic Research, 1957), 8; Ashok Mitra, *A Prattler's Tale* (Calcutta: Samya, 2007), 161–163.

12. K. N. Raj, "The Foreign Exchange Crisis and the Plan," EW, February 23, 1957, 291–294. See also H. C. Malkani, "Recent Cut in Imports Analyzed," EW, annual number, January 19, 1957, 179–180.

13. B. N. Ganguli, "The Outlook for India's Balance of Payments: Re-examination of Trade Policy Necessary," EW, January 19, 1957, 125–128; cabinet meeting, June 4–5, 1958, in SWJN2, 42:119; Ashok Mitra, "India: Plan and Performance," paper presented to the American Economic Association, December 28–30, 1960, Country Files, WBGA, folder 1837563.

14. Ministry of Finance note on Planning Commission report, n.d., TTK Papers, NMML, Correspondence: J. Nehru 1958; B. R. Shenoy, "The Indian Economic Scene," *Indian Economic Journal* 5:4 (1958): 338, 340–341.

15. G. D. Birla to Eugene R. Black, May 21, 1958, Country Files, WBGA, folder 1840731; L. K. Jha and Morarji Desai, "Policy towards Foreign Capital," September 11–12, 1960, in PC Records, ISI, folder 109.

16. Nehru summarizes the report's findings in Jawaharlal Nehru to C. D. Deshmukh, January 13, 1958, and Jawaharlal Nehru to V. T. Krishnamachari, January 24, 1958, both in SWJN2, 41:190–194, 194–195.

17. Jawaharlal Nehru to C. D. Deshmukh, January 13, 1958, TTK to Jawaharlal Nehru, January 11, 1958, and TTK to C. D. Deshmukh (draft, January 1958), all in TTK Papers, NMML, subject 8B; TTK to Jawaharlal Nehru, January 11, 1958, and C. D. Deshmukh to Jawaharlal Nehru, January 4, 1958, both in TTK Papers, NMML, Correspondence: J. Nehru. See the helpful annotations in Jawaharlal Nehru to C. D. Deshmukh, January 13, 1958, in SWJN2, 41:190–194. See also Vivek Chibber, *Locked in Place: State-Building and Late Industrialization in India* (Princeton, N.J.: Princeton University Press, 2003), 196–212.

18. Nasir Tyabji, *Forging Capitalism and the State* (New Delhi: Oxford University Press, 2015), chapter 6; R. Tirumalai, *TTK, the Dynamic Innovator* (Madras: TT Maps & Publications, 1988), 84–98. For a useful retrospective, see Inder Malhotra, "The Mundhra Affair," *Indian Express,* December 12, 2008. See also the parliamentary debates of September 12, 1956, in GOI Lok Sabha, *Lok Sabha Debates 1956* (New Delhi: Lok Sabha Secretariat, 1956), columns 6803–6807.

19. Gadgil, "On Rephasing the Second Five-Year Plan"; B. R. Shenoy, "Professor Gadgil on Rephasing the Plan," *Indian Economic Journal* 6:4 (1958): 62–72; GOI PC, *Appraisal and Prospects of the Second Five Year Plan* (Delhi: Manager of Publications, 1958), 23. See the debates of April 16–17, 1958, in GOI Lok Sabha, *Lok Sabha Debates 1958* (New Delhi: Lok Sabha Secretariat, 1958), columns 10295–10546. For the NDC, see in particular the meetings of June 3, 1957 and May 5, 1958, both in GOI National Development Council, *Five Decades of Nation-Building: Fifty NDC Meetings* (New Delhi: Planning Commission, 2005), vol. 1. For background, see Francine R. Frankel, *India's Political Economy, 1947–1977: The Gradual Revolution* (Princeton, N.J.: Princeton University Press, 1978), 147–153.

20. K. N. Raj, "The Foreign Exchange Crisis and the Plan," *EW,* February 23, 1957, 293; Oscar Sanchez-Sibony, *Red Globalization: The Political Economy of the Soviet Cold War from Stalin to Khrushchev* (Cambridge: Cambridge University Press, 2014), chapter 3.

21. "Obzor ekonomiki Indii za 1959 g.," June 1960, RGAE, 365 / 2 / 1996a / 104. See also, "Obzor ekonomiki Indii za 1957 g.," April 1958, RGAE, 365 / 2 / 1957 / 4–5. N. Smelov conversation with S. S. Khera (Secretary, Ministry of Production), September 17, 1957, RGAE, 365 / 2 / 65 / 90. S. S. Khera to N. Smelov, September 18, 1957, RGAE, 365 / 2 / 1951 / 136.

22. W. W. Rostow, *Concept and Controversy: Sixty Years of Taking Ideas to Market* (Austin: University of Texas Press, 2003), 245. Dillon replaced Undersecretary of State Herbert Hoover Jr. (who shared his father's conservatism), and Secretary of the Treasury George

Humphrey was replaced by the more open-minded Robert B. Anderson; see W. W. Rostow, *Eisenhower, Kennedy, and Foreign Aid* (Austin: University of Texas Press, 1985), 125. For lineups of pro- and anti-aid groups in the administration, see Russell Edgerton, *Sub-cabinet Politics and Policy Commitment: The Birth of the Development Loan Fund,* (Syracuse, N.Y.: Interuniversity Case Program, 1970).

23. Russell Edgerton, "The Creation of the Development Loan Fund (DLF)" (Ph.D. diss., Columbia University, 1967), 139 (Hart Perry, "cabal," May 8, 1964), 196, 153; Rostow, *Concept and Controversy,* 245; Rostow, *Eisenhower,* 121.

24. MIT Center for International Studies, "The Objectives of United States Economic Assistance Programs," December 1956, Max F. Millikan Papers, MIT Archives, 10:344; Burton Ira Kaufman, *Trade and Aid: Eisenhower's Foreign Economic Policy, 1953–1961* (Baltimore: Johns Hopkins University Press, 1982), 97–99.

25. U.S. International Development Advisory Board, *A New Emphasis on Economic Development Abroad: A Report to the President of the United States on Ways, Means and Reasons for U.S. Assistance to International Economic Development* (Washington, D.C.: Government Printing Office, 1957), 16, 18–19; U.S. President's Citizens Advisers on the Mutual Security Program, *Report to the President, March 1, 1957* (Washington, D.C.: Government Printing Office, 1957), 3, 13, 8–9, 14. Steel executive Benjamin Fairless chaired the committee. For a summary of the reports and their reception, see Kaufman, *Trade and Aid,* 96–101.

26. Rostow, *Eisenhower,* 121 (Eisenhower address, January 20, 1957) and 129–130 (Dulles congressional testimony, April 8, 1957); Michael R. Adamson, "'The Most Important Single Aspect of Our Foreign Policy'? The Eisenhower Administration, Foreign Aid, and the Third World," in *The Eisenhower Administration, the Third World, and the Globalization of the Cold War,* ed. Kathryn C Statler and Andrew L Johns (Lanham, Md.: Rowman & Littlefield, 2006), 58–60; Kaufman, *Trade and Aid,* 104, 108–112; Christian Herter to Westmore Willcox, August 22, 1957, Christian Herter Papers, DDEL, box 2. See also Thomas Mann to John Foster Dulles, March 22, 1958, Thomas Mann Papers, DDEL, box 1.

27. U.S. Congress, House of Representatives, Committee on Government Operations, *Operations of the Development Loan Fund* (Washington, D.C.: Government Printing Office, 1960), 9–10.

28. Speech by J. S. Hollister (director of the International Cooperation Administration), February 20, 1956, AR 1:61 (1956): 1306–1307.

29. Clarence Randall to Sherman Adams, July 17, 1957 (summarizing a State Department report of July 15, 1957), in *FRUS 1955–1957,* 8:362; Kaufman, *Trade and Aid,* 111; U.S. Congress, House of Representatives, Committee on Government Operations, *Operations of the Development Loan Fund,* 4.

30. New Delhi Embassy to U.S. Department of State, October 28, 1956, SDDF, USNA, RG 59, 891.10 / 10-2856; Operations Coordinating Board, "Progress Report on 'United States Policy toward South Asia' (NSC 5409)," November 28, 1956, in *FRUS 1955–1957,* 8:17; Max Millikan to Christian Herter, June 20, 1960, SDDF, USNA, RG 59, 891.00 Five Year / 6-2060.

31. C. Douglas Dillon conversation with B. K. Nehru, May 31, 1957, in *FRUS 1955–1957*, 8:344–348; William Turnage conversation with P. Govindan Nair, June 5, 1957, SDDF, USNA, RG 59, 791.5-MSP / 6-557; Jawaharlal Nehru talks with Ambassador Bunker, May 8, 1957, in *SWJN2*, 38:734

32. William Turnage conversation with B. K. Nehru, June 20, 1957, SDDF, USNA, RG 59, 791.5-MSP / 6-2057; Reserve Bank of India, *India's Balance of Payments*, 138–139; Jawaharlal Nehru to Vijayalakshmi Pandit, September 17, 1957, in *SWJN2*, 39:109–111.

33. P. Govindan Nair to Rufus Burr Smith, September 18, 1957, SDDF, USNA, RG 59, 891.00 / 9-1857.

34. Calcutta Consulate-General to U.S. Department of State, September 18, 1957, and Christian Herter conversation with TTK, September 25, 1957, both in SDDF, USNA, RG 59, 891.10 / 9-1857, 9-2557; U.S. Department of State to New Delhi Embassy, October 15, 1957, and John Foster Dulles and C. Douglas Dillon conversation with TTK, September 25, 1957, both in SDDF, USNA, RG 59, 891.10 / 10-1557. President Eisenhower's briefing on the meeting is in John Foster Dulles to Dwight D. Eisenhower, October 7, 1957, DDRS, CK2349166275.

35. CIA, *Consequences of Economic Crisis in India*, NIE 51-57, October 8, 1957, WHO-NSC Staff, NSC Registry Series, DDEL, box 18; Operations Control Board, "Recommendations for United States Action to Assist India in Realizing Its Economic Development Objectives," September 18, 1957, in *FRUS 1955–1957*, 8:384–386.

36. S. A. Dange, March 11, 1958 in *Lok Sabha Debates* (New Delhi: Lok Sabha Secretariat, 1958), cols. 4341–4360; Jawaharlal Nehru comments in Lok Sabha budget debate, March 18, 1958, in *SWJN2*, 41:108.

37. B. K. Nehru to Morarji Desai, May 14, 1958, and May 21, 1958, both in PMO Records, NAI, 37 / 437 / 58-PMS. Another copy, without the prime minister's annotations, appears in M. O. Mathai Papers, NMML, Other Papers, 11. Unless otherwise noted, quotations in the next three paragraphs come from this document.

38. Amit Das Gupta, "Development by Consortia: International Donors and the Development of India, Pakistan, Indonesia, and Turkey in the 1960s," *Comparativ* 19:4 (2009): 96–111.

39. Thomas McCittrick to C. D. Deshmukh, June 30, 1956, Country Files, WBGA, folder 1840728; criticisms quoted in "Second Plan—Black-Krishnamachari Letters," *AR* 1:94 (1956): 1073–1076; Thomas McCittrick, mission report (draft), quoted in Antonin Basch to John de Wilde, August 5, 1956, Country Files, WBGA, folder 1840729; *Current Economic Position and Prospects of India* (final mission report), August 1956, WBGA Online, http://documents. worldbank.org/curated/en/101071468268800453/India-Current-economic-position-and -prospects; Edward S. Mason and Robert E. Asher, *The World Bank since Bretton Woods* (Washington, D.C.: Brookings Institution Press, 1973), 372–373, 455. The statement dates to 1973, and perhaps no longer holds about the bluntest use of conditionality, but it may well have been the first.

40. McCittrick mission report (draft), quoted in Antonin Basch to John de Wilde, August 5, 1956, and drafts of Eugene R. Black to TTK, August 27, 1956, and September 5, 1956, all in Country Files, WBGA, folder 1840729; Jawaharlal Nehru to Chief Ministers, October 14,

1956, in *LCM,* 4:456–457; "The Bank and the Plan," *EE,* October 12, 1956, 537–538; "On the Carpet," *EW,* October 13, 1956, 1200–1201. There is no indication that Indian officials sought or received World Bank permission before releasing the letters.

41. Herbert Hoover Jr. memorandum, July 18, 1955, SDDF, USNA, RG 59, 791.5-MSP / 7-1855; Dwight D. Eisenhower conversation with John Foster Dulles, George Anderson, Richard Nixon, Sherman Adams, and others, November 12, 1957, in *FRUS 1955–1957,* 8:404–406; Rostow, *Concept and Controversy,* 204, 189; speech (misquoted, about a "lenders' club under the sponsorship of the World Bank") in J. Burke Knapp conversation with John F. Kennedy, February 26, 1959, Country Files, WBGA, folder 1844596; Fred Holborn to Max Millikan, February 15, 1958, and John F. Kennedy to Wilfred Malenbaum, April 1, 1958, both in CIS Records, MIT Archives, 9:15; J. H. Smith to C. Douglas Dillon, March 11, 1958, SDDF, USNA, RG 59, 891.00 / 3-1158. For the full text of Kennedy's speech of March 25, 1958, see 104 Cong. Rec., 85th Cong., 2nd sess. (1958) part 4, 5246–5253 (quotation herein from 5250).

42. O. S. Kamanu, "India Consortium," July 10, 1968, Country Files, WBGA, folder 1844750; B. K. Nehru, "The Way We Looked for Money Abroad," in *Two Decades of Indo-U.S. Relations,* ed. Vadilal Dagli (Bombay: Vora, 1969), 20–21.

43. Nehru, *Nice Guys,* 344–352.

44. B. K. Nehru to Morarji Desai, May 21, 1958, M. O. Mathai Papers, NMML, Other Papers, 11.

45. "India Expects Foreign Aid after World Bank Meeting," *TOI,* August 14, 1958, 1; IBRD, "Current Economic Position and Prospects of India," July 28, 1958, and "Meeting on Foreign Exchange Situation: Text of Statement by Mr. Eugene R. Black," August 25, 1958, both in Country Files, WBGA, folder 1844595.

46. "Minutes of Meeting on India's Foreign Exchange Situation," August 25–27, 1958, and "Meeting on India's Foreign Exchange Situation: Report of Proceedings," August 27, 1958, both in Country Files, WBGA, folder 1844595; "Aufzeichnung: Die Konferenz von Washington vom 25.-27. August 1958 über die Wirtschafts- und Finanzlage Indiens," September 2, 1958, Auswärtigen Amt-Neues Amt, PAAA, B61-411#114.

47. "Minutes of Meeting on India's Foreign Exchange Situation," August 25–27, 1958, Country Files, WBGA, folder 1844595.

48. Mason and Asher, *World Bank,* 514–516.

49. C. Douglas Dillon conversation with B. K. Nehru, August 26, 1958, in *FRUS 1958–1960,* 15:449–451; B. K. Nehru to Eugene R. Black, March 16, 1959, Country Files, WBGA, folder 1844596; Frederic P. Bartlett conversation with B. K. Nehru, March 3, 1959, SDR, USNA, RG59, entry A1-1330, box 24; C. Douglas Dillon conversation with B. K. Nehru, March 13, 1959, and C. Douglas Dillon conversation with Lord Cromer, March 13, 1959, both in C. Douglas Dillon Papers, JFKL, box 17.

50. Jawaharlal Nehru press conference, September 7, 1958, in *SWJN2,* 44:112; "Meeting on India's Foreign Exchange Situation: Report of Proceedings," August 27, 1958, Country Files, WBGA, folder 1844595; C. Douglas Dillon conversation with Morarji Desai, September 9, 1958, C. Douglas Dillon Papers, JFKL, box 16; C. Douglas Dillon conversation with Morarji Desai, September 8, 1958, in *FRUS 1958–1960,* 15:461–464; Eugene R. Black conversation with

Morarji Desai, September 7, 1958, Country Files, WBGA, folder 1840732; "Use and Abuse of Foreign Aid," EW, November 29, 1958, 1473–1474. Estes Kefauver was on the national Democratic Party ballot twice, both times losing to the Eisenhower-Nixon ticket; see "Billion-Dollar Troubles," *Time,* September 1, 1958, 25.

51. Antonin Basch to J. Burke Knapp, January 5, 1959, "Recent Economic Developments and Current Prospects of India," February 20, 1959, "Meeting on India's Foreign Exchange Situation: Text of Mr. Black's Statement at the Opening Session," March 16, 1959, "Second Meeting on India's Foreign Exchange Situation: Report of Proceedings," March 19, 1959, and "Meeting on India's Foreign Exchange Situation: Text of Mr. Black's Statement at the Opening Session," March 16, 1959, all in Country Files, WBGA, folder 1844596.

52. B. K. Nehru to Morarji Desai, May 11, 1959, B. K. Nehru Papers, NMML, Correspondence: Desai.

53. "Obzor ekonomiki Indii za 1959 g.," June 1960, RGAE, 365 / 2 / 1996a / 5–6; A. G. Sheremet'ev conversation with Vaidyanathan, September 1959, RGAE, 365 / 2 / 1955 / 62–63. See also EA 1977–1978, 150–156.

54. B. K. Nehru to Morarji Desai, May 11, 1959, B. K. Nehru Papers, NMML, Correspondence: Desai.

55. John F. Kennedy speech, March 25, 1958, 104 Cong. Rec., 85th Cong., 2nd sess. (1958) part 4, 5250; B. K. Nehru to Morarji Desai, May 11, 1959, B. K. Nehru Papers, NMML, Correspondence: Desai; J. Burke Knapp conversation with John F. Kennedy, February 26, 1959, Country Files, WBGA, folder 1844596; C. Douglas Dillon conversation with B. K. Nehru, May 5, 1959, in *FRUS 1958–1960,* 15:481–483; John F. Kennedy to Eugene R. Black, October 17, 1959, correspondence between Kennedy staffer Fred Holborn and J. Burke Knapp, summer and fall 1959, Chester Bowles to Eugene R. Black, December 17, 1959, and G.D. Birla to Eugene R. Black, January 6, 1960, all in Country Files, WBGA, folder 1837568. Senator Cooper had been ambassador in New Delhi in 1955–1956.

56. Harry G. Curran to Eugene R. Black, March 21, 1960, Country Files, WBGA, folder 1837569.

57. J. Burke Knapp to Allan Sproul, February 2, 1959, and Allan Sproul to Eugene R. Black, February 1, 1959, both in Country Files, WBGA, folder 1837568; Donald D. Kennedy and James M. Wilson to C. Douglas Dillon, n.d. (January 1960?), SDR, USNA, RG59, entry A1-3139, box 1. The members were Hermann Abs (Deutsche Bank); Oliver Franks (Lloyds Bank); and Allan Sproul (Federal Reserve Bank of New York).

58. "Bankers' Mission to India and Pakistan, February–March 1960," March 21, 1960, Country Files, WBGA, folder 1837569 (the information on the Third Plan made available to them is on 10–11); Jawaharlal Nehru note, August 28, 1960, PMO Records, NAI, 17 / 411 / 1960-PMS; I. G. Patel, *Foreign Aid* (Bombay: Allied Publishers, 1968), 14. On internal differences, see especially Allan Sproul to Eugene R. Black, October 13, 1960, Country Files, WBGA, folder 1837569; C. Douglas Dillon conversation with Allan Sproul, March 30, 1960, RUSFAA, USNA, RG 469, entry UD191A, box 47; and "Aufziechnung: 3. Indischer Fünfjahresplan," April 1, 1960, Auswärtigen Amt-Neues Amt, PAAA, B61-411#114.

59. J. Burke Knapp conversation with B. K. Nehru, April 22, 1960, and J. Burke Knapp to Eugene R. Black, June 3, 1960, both in Country Files, wbga, folder 1844957. For preliminary (premature?) discussions, see John Foster Dulles conversation with Dwight D. Eisenhower and Hubert H. Humphrey, December 9, 1955, John Foster Dulles White House Memoranda, in *The Papers of John Foster Dulles and of Christian A. Herter, 1953–1961: The White House Correspondence and Memoranda Series* (Frederick, Md.: University Publications of America, 1986), reel 2. On early loan data, see James H. Weaver, *The International Development Association: A New Approach to Foreign Aid* (New York: Praeger, 1965), 128–131; and *EA 1978–1979*, 256–275. For ida background, see Robert W. Oliver, *George Woods and the World Bank* (Boulder, Colo.: Lynne Reiner, 1995), 131; Mason and Asher, *World Bank,* 682; Jason A. Kirk, *India and the World Bank: The Politics of Aid and Influence* (New York: Anthem Press, 2010), 8–9; and Mason and Asher, *World Bank,* 380–403.

60. goi pc, *Third Five Year Plan* (Delhi: Manager of Publications, 1961), 59.

61. ibrd, "India's Third Five-Year Plan: Report of Bank Mission to India," August 10, 1960, wbga Online, http://documents.worldbank.org/curated/en/918871468033330261/India-Third-five-year-plan.

62. "Notes on the Third Meeting on India's Foreign Exchange Situation," September 12–14, 1960, Country Files, wbga, folder 1844597; Patel, *Foreign Aid,* 14–15.

63. George Ball and Henry Labouisse, quoted in M. S. Venkataramani, "Indo-American Relations," *Commerce,* December 1962, annual number, A48; "Notes on the Third Meeting on India's Foreign Exchange Situation," September 12–14, 1960, Country Files, wbga, folder 1844597.

64. Morarji Desai to Jawaharlal Nehru, October 11, 1960, B. K. Nehru Papers, nmml, Subject 97-II; C. Douglas Dillon conversation with Morarji Desai, September 26, 1960, sddf, usna, RG 59, 791.5-MSP / 9-2660; J. Burke Knapp conversation with B. K. Nehru, November 3, 1960, Country Files, wbga, folder 1844597.

6. Military Supply and the Vicissitudes of Aid Politics

1. Robert Komer to Phillips Talbot, October 24, 1962, oasd-isa Records, usna, RG 330, entry A1-1025, box 87; Robert Komer to Carl Kaysen, November 16, 1962, nsf—nsc Histories, lbjl, box 24.

2. "Prime Minister's Reply to Rajya Sabha Debate on Foreign Affairs," August 23, 1961, *Foreign Affairs Record* (1961): 242; unnamed "senior military officer" on commercial terms, in a 1978 interview quoted in Surjit Mansingh, *India's Search for Power: Indira Gandhi's Foreign Policy, 1966–1982* (New Delhi: sage Publications, 1984), 159. Here and throughout the chapter, arms transfer and sales data from the Stockholm International Peace Research Institute's sipri Arms Transfers Database, https://www.sipri.org/databases/armstransfers.

3. hc-New Delhi to cro, December 17, 1955, cro to Cabinet, January 28, 1955, Cabinet minute, January 31, 1955, hc-New Delhi to Anthony Eden, April 19, 1956, Jawaharlal Nehru to Anthony Eden, March 23, 1956, and Anthony Eden to Jawaharlal Nehru, March 29, 1956, all

in PMO Records, UKNA, PREM 11/1399; "O razshirenii ekonomicheskikh sviazei s Indiei," November 14, 1955, AVPRF, 090/17/51/23/7; Jawaharlal Nehru conversation with Selwyn Lloyd, March 4, 1956, and Jawaharlal Nehru to Anthony Eden, March 23, 1956, both in SWJN2, 32:290–291, 372–374; New Delhi Embassy to U.S. Department of State, March 13, 1956, and London Embassy to U.S. Department of State, June 11, 1956, both in SDDF, USNA, RG 59, 791.5622/3-1356 and 6-1156.

4. For the political history, see Uri Ra'anan, *The USSR Arms the Third World: Case Studies in Soviet Foreign Policy* (Cambridge: Massachusetts Institute of Technology Press, 1969), part 1.

5. Jawaharlal Nehru conversation with Zhou Enlai, October 20, 1954, M. O. Mathai Papers, NMML, subject 35; Jawaharlal Nehru, "The World Scenario and National Security," March 13, 1956, in SWJN2, 32:489–498.

6. This is a fraught topic in Indian politics and history; see Srinath Raghavan, *War and Peace in Modern India: A Strategic History of the Nehru Years* (New Delhi: Permanent Black, 2010), 249–252; One head of Indian intelligence alludes to Indo-American cooperation; see B. N. Mullik, *My Years with Nehru: The Chinese Betrayal* (Bombay: Allied Publishers, 1971), 194. And American records provide ample suggestion—but few concrete details—of American subversive activity in Tibet. See, for instance, the documents in OSANSA-OCB Records, DDEL, Subject Files, box 6; Bruce O. Riedel, *JFK's Forgotten Crisis: Tibet, the CIA, and Sino-Indian War* (Washington, D.C.: Brookings Institution Press, 2015); and Gyalo Thondup, *The Noodle Maker of Kalimpong: The Dalai Lama's Brother and His Struggle for Tibet* (New York: PublicAffairs, 2015), chapter 21.

7. "Message to be Conveyed by Shri P. N. Menon on Behalf of the Prime Minister to the Dalai Lama," April 29, 1959, Subimal Dutt Papers, NMML, subject 6; Colonel Edwin F. Black to Karl G. Harr Jr. and Bromley Smith, March 31, 1959, OSANSA-OCB Records, DDEL, Subject Files, box 6; memorandum to Robert Komer, March 30, 1959, Records of the President's Committee to Study the U.S. Mutual Security Program, DDEL, box 20; Nikita Khrushchev conversation with Mao Zedong, October 2, 1959, in Vladislav Zubok, "The Mao-Khrushchev Conversations, 31 July–3 August 1958 and 2 October 1959," *Cold War International History Project Bulletin* 12–13 (2001): 265–266; A. A. Brezhnev, *Kitai: ternistyi put' k dobrososed-stvu: vospominaniia i razmyshleniia* (Moscow: Mezhdunarodnye otnosheniia, 1998), 70–72; Andrei Gromyko to K. E. Voroshilov, F. R. Kozlov, and E. A. Furtseva, December 31, 1959, RGANI, 5/30/301/257–258; V. Likhachev, "Ob indo-kitaiskikh otnosheniiakh," December 24, 1959, RGANI, 5/30/303/73–91; Chen Jian, "The Tibetan Rebellion of 1959 and China's Changing Relations with India and the Soviet Union," *Journal of Cold War Studies* 8:3 (2006): 54–101; Lorenz M. Lüthi, "Sino-Indian Relations, 1954–1962," *Eurasia Border Review* 3 (2012): 93–119. See also the correspondence in Rajendra Kumar Jain, ed., *China South Asian Relations, 1947–1980* (Atlantic Highlands, N.J.: Humanities Press, 1981), 1:112–183; and *US Policy toward South Asia*, NSC 5701, May 22, 1959, OSANSA-NSC Records, DDEL, Policy Papers, box 19.

8. Brij Mohan Kaul, *The Untold Story* (Bombay: Allied Publishers, 1967), 215–225; General K. S. Thimayya to Jawaharlal Nehru, August 31, 1959, and September 1, 1959, and General K. S. Thimayya conversation with Jawaharlal Nehru, n.d., all in K. S. Thimayya Papers, NMML,

Correspondence—J. Nehru. On the prime minister's friendship with Krishna Menon, see Sarvepalli Gopal, *Jawaharlal Nehru: A Biography*, 3 vols. (Cambridge, Mass.: Harvard University Press, 1976), 3:130–132.

9. Kaul, *Untold Story,* 320–321, 337; Major General M. Sergeichik, "Spravka po voprosam sovetsko-indiiskogo sotrudnichestva v voennoi oblasti," September 4, 1961, AVPRF, 090 / 23 / 77 / 20 / 85–89. On Il-14s, see G. M. Pushkin to Subimal Dutt, June 22, 1960, AVPRF, 090 / 22 / 70 / 3 / 6–7.

10. HC-New Delhi to CRO, July 18, 1960, HC-New Delhi to CRO, October 5, 1960, and Ministry of Aviation note, November 3, 1960, all in MOD Records, UKNA, DEFE 7 / 692; CRO memorandum, September 18, 1959, Prime Minister's Office Records, UKNA, PREM 11 / 4304; Major General M. Sergeichik, "Spravka po voporosam sovetsko-indiiskogo sotrudnichestva v voennoi oblasti," September 4, 1961, AVPRF, 090 / 23 / 77 / 20 / 85–89; Soviet agreement of winter 1961 discussed in P. Sergeev to F. B. Iakubskii, November 21, 1963, RGAE, 365 / 2 / 2120 / 4; N. S. Khrushchev conversation with K. P. S. Menon, March 27, 1961, AVPRF, 090 / 23 / 77 / 16 / 55–65; John Kenneth Galbraith to U.S. Department of State, February 24, 1962, SDDF, USNA, RG 59, 791.6522 / 2-2462. MID South Asia Department to Central Committee, n.d. (February–March 1961), AVPRF, 090 / 23 / 76 / 13 / 50. They were also joined by the Indian ambassador in Washington, M. C. Chagla; see, for instance, Christian Herter conversation with M. C. Chagla, January 27, 1960, SDDF, USNA, RG 59, 791.5-MSP / 1-2760;

11. Kaul, *Untold Story,* 320–322; B. K. Nehru, *Nice Guys Finish Second* (New Delhi: Viking, 1997), 385–386; W. Averell Harriman conversation with Jawaharlal Nehru, March 24, 1961, W. Averell Harriman Papers, LC, box 526; W. Averell Harriman to Dean Rusk and John F. Kennedy, March 24, 1961, in *FRUS 1961–1963,* 19:30–32; Lee Metcalf conversation with D. N. Chatterjee, May 19, 1961, SDDF, USNA, RG 59, 791.5-MSP / 5-1961. Roswell Gilpatric to Chester Bowles, June 12, 1961, in *FRUS 1961–1963,* 19:57–58.

12. Major General M. Sergeichik, "Spravka po voporosam sovetsko-indiiskogo sotrudnichestva v voennoi oblasti," September 4, 1961, AVPRF, 090 / 23 / 77 / 20 / 85–89; Roswell Gilpatric to Chester Bowles, September 13, 1961, in *FRUS 1961–1963,* 19:96–98.

13. U.S. Department of State to Islamabad Embassy, December 8, 1961, in *FRUS 1961–1963,* 19:150–151; Kaul, *Untold Story,* 340; Brigadier General Stephen Fuqua to William Bundy, March 6, 1962, and Alfred Rubin to S. O. Fuqua, October 30, 1962, both in OASD-ISA Records, USNA, RG 330, entry A1-1025, box 87; Chester Bowles, *Promises to Keep: My Years in Public Life, 1941–1969* (New York: Harper & Row, 1971), 474; New Delhi Embassy to U.S. Department of State, March 22, 1962, NSF, JFKL, box 106A; Mullik, *My Years,* 338.

14. Major General M. Sergeichik, "Spravka po voporosam sovetsko-indiiskogo sotrudnichestva v voennoi oblasti," September 4, 1961, AVPRF, 090 / 23 / 77 / 20 / 85–89; I. A. Benediktov conversation with Krishna Menon, April 18, 1962, AVPRF, 090 / 24 / 5 / 80 / 207–209, in READD, NSA; Presidium resolution of May 16, 1962, summarized in Christopher M. Andrew and Vasili Mitrokhin, *The World Was Going Our Way: The KGB and the Battle for the Third World* (New York: Basic Books, 2005), 314–315.

15. Paul M. McGarr, *The Cold War in South Asia: Britain, the United States and the Indian Subcontinent, 1945–1965* (Cambridge: Cambridge University Press, 2013), 219; Defense Intelligence Agency Technical Intelligence Report, July 2, 1962, OASD-ISA Records, USNA, RG 330, entry A1-1025, box 88; M. J. Desai conversation with John Kenneth Galbraith, May 18, 1962, in T. N. Kaul Papers I–III, NMML, subject 15; Kaul, *Untold Story,* 343; K. C. Arora, *V. K. Krishna Menon: A Biography* (New Delhi: Sanchar Publishing House, 1998), 210; Mullik, *My Years,* 450.

16. "U.S. Is Concerned by Reports That India Will Buy Soviet Jets," *NYT,* May 5, 1962, 10; "Soviet MiG Jets for India Soon," *TOI,* May 6, 1962, 1; M. J. Desai conversation with John Kenneth Galbraith, May 4, 1962, B. K. Nehru to M. J. Desai, May 5–6, 1962, M. J. Desai to B. K. Nehru, May 8, 1962, B. K. Nehru to M. J. Desai, May 14, 1962, and M. J. Desai conversation with John Kenneth Galbraith, May 4, 1962, all in B. K. Nehru Papers, NMML, subject 17.

17. U.S. Department of State to New Delhi Embassy, June 2, 1962; and New Delhi Embassy to U.S. Department of State, June 25, 1962, both in NSF, JFKL, box 107; Edwin Duncan Sandys to Harold Macmillan, June 17, 1962, Treasury Records, UKNA, T 317/362; William Bundy conversation with John Kenneth Galbraith, June 1, 1962, OASD-ISA Records, USNA, RG 330, entry A1-1025, box 87.

18. New Delhi Embassy to U.S. Department of State, May 9, 1962, SDDF, USNA, 791.6522/5-962; M. J. Desai conversation with John Kenneth Galbraith, May 5, 1962, B. K. Nehru Papers, NMML, subject 17; John Kenneth Galbraith, *Ambassador's Journal: A Personal Account of the Kennedy Years* (Boston: Houghton Mifflin, 1969), 527.

19. Dean Rusk to John F. Kennedy, June 1, 1962, in *FRUS 1961–1963,* 19:259–260; Phillips Talbot to Dean Rusk, June 5, 1962, NSF, JFKL, box 420; Washington Embassy, Fortnightly Political Report, May 1–15, 1962, MEA Records, NAI, WII/101(5)/61.

20. Robert Komer to McGeorge Bundy, May 9, 1962, in *FRUS 1961–1963,* 19:242–243; Robert Komer to John F. Kennedy, May 16, 1962, and H. P. Wriggins, "Implications to U.S. Policy toward South Asia of a Soviet MiG Deal with India," May 26, 1962, both in NSF, JFKL, box 420; W. W. Rostow memorandum, May 29, 1962, SDR, USNA, RG59, entry A1-558CA, box 38; Robert Komer to McGeorge Bundy, May 22, 1962, NSF, JFKL, box 419.

21. John F. Kennedy to Harold Macmillan, June 10, 1962, and Harold Macmillan to John F. Kennedy, June 13, 1962, both in PMO Records, UKNA, PREM 11/3836; Harold Macmillan conversation with Edwin Duncan Sandys and Harold Atkinson, June 12, 1962, Cabinet Records, UKNA, CAB 21/5685.

22. Edward Haslam to Paul Milner-Barry, June 13, 1962, Treasury Records, UKNA, T317/362; CRO Briefing, June 22, 1962, and Harold Macmillan to John F. Kennedy, July 24, 1962, both in FO Records, UKNA, FO 371/164881; "Fighter Offer," n.d. (likely June 17, 1962), CRO Records, UKNA, DO 121/239; Harold Macmillan to John F. Kennedy, July 23, 1962, Cabinet Records, UKNA, CAB 21/5685.

23. M. E. Hedley-Miller to L. Pliatzky, June 4, 1962, Treasury Records, UKNA, T 317/362; Jawaharlal Nehru, cited in John Kenneth Galbraith to John F. Kennedy, June 20, 1962, in *FRUS 1961–1963,* 19:281–282; M. J. Desai, cited in HC-New Delhi to CRO, July 28, 1962, and Harold

Macmillan to John F. Kennedy, July 23, 1962, both in Cabinet Records, UKNA, CAB 21/5685; Edwin Duncan Sandys notes, June 15, 1962, CRO Records, UKNA, DO 121/239; George Ball conversation with Morarji Desai, September 19, 1962, NSF, JFKL, box 107A.

24. B. K. Nehru to M. J. Desai, June 14, 1962, B. K. Nehru Papers, NMML, subject 17; CRO Note, "MiGs for India," June 22, 1962, FO Records, UKNA, FO 371/164881.

25. HC-New Delhi to CRO, July 25, 1962, PMO Records, UKNA, PREM 11/4307; London to U.S. Department of State, July 7, 1962, NSF, JFKL, box 107; B. K. Nehru to Jawaharlal Nehru, June 14, 1962, and July 25, 1962, both in B. K. Nehru Papers, NMML, subject 17.

26. Robert Komer to McGeorge Bundy, July 26, 1962, NSF, JFKL, box 107. M. J. Desai to B. K. Nehru, July 27, 1962, B. K. Nehru Papers, NMML, subject 17; summary of delegation aims (translated from English), RGAE, 29/1/2369/63–65; S. A. Skachkov conversation with Indian delegation, August 4, 1962, RGAE, 29/1/2369/86–87.

27. Protocol no. 49, August 20, 1962, in A. A. Fursenko, ed., *Prezidium TsK KPSS 1954–1964* (Moscow: Rosspen, 2003), 1:1005. The full agreement from August 29, 1962—with side letters—appears in RGAE, 29/1/2369/115–134. See also the useful summary in Andrei Gromyko and S. A. Skachkov to CC-CPSU, October 26, 1962, AVPRF, 090/24/81/14/57–61. On the RD-9F sale (denominated in dollars) dated June 26, 1962, see E. G. Kovtun conversation with Krishnaswami, June 27, 1962, RGAE, 29/1/2369/45–47.

28. "India May Buy a Squadron: No Production of MiGs Here Now," *TOI*, September 12, 1962, 7; "MiG's Seen Favored by Indian Experts," *NYT*, September 4, 1962, 8; Jawaharlal Nehru, quoted in Bureau of Near Eastern and South Asian Affairs, "Status of Indian Negotiations for MiGs," September 19, 1962, in *FRUS 1961–1963*, 19:325–326; John Kenneth Galbraith reports on conversations with General B. M. Kaul and A. K. Sen, September 14, 1962, SDDF, USNA, RG 59, 691.93/9-1462.

29. Roderick MacFarquhar, *The Origins of the Cultural Revolution* (New York: Columbia University Press, 1974), 3:299–303; Steven A. Hoffmann, *India and the China Crisis* (Berkeley: University of California Press, 1990), 113; Raghavan, *War and Peace*, 271–277, 287–292; Anton Harder, "Defining Independence in Cold War Asia: Sino-Indian Relations 1947–1962" (PhD diss., London School of Economics, 2015), chapter 5.

30. John Kenneth Galbraith to U.S. Department of State, September 2, 1962, SDDF, USNA, RG 59, 691.93/9-262.

31. MacFarquhar, *Origins of the Cultural Revolution*, 3:312; Sergey Radchenko, *Two Suns in the Heavens: The Sino-Soviet Struggle for Supremacy, 1962–1967* (Stanford, Calif.: Stanford University Press, 2009), 29–30; Niu Jun, "1962: The Eve of the Left Turn in China's Foreign Policy," Working Paper 48, Cold War International History Project, Washington, D.C., 2005.

32. Protocol no. 58a, October 11, 1962, and Prezidium Protocol no. 59, October 14, 1962, both in Fursenko, *Prezidium TsK KPSS*, 1:596, 616–617; V. V. Kuznetsov to CC-CPSU, October 18, 1962 (citing CC-CPSU decision of October 12, 1962), AVPRF, 090/24/81/14/56; Radchenko, *Two Suns*, 29–30; MacFarquhar, *Origins of the Cultural Revolution*, 3:313; I. A. Benediktov report on meeting with Jawaharlal Nehru, n.d. (not later than October 17, 1962), in Fursenko,

Prezidium TsK KPSS, 3:336–338; T. N. Kaul notes on meeting with Nikita Khrushchev, November 24, 1962, T. N. Kaul Papers I–III, NMML, Speeches / Writings by Him 11.

33. "Time of Trial and Testing for All," *TOI*, October 23, 1962, 9; John W. Garver, "China's Decision for War with India in 1962," in *New Approaches in the Study of Chinese Foreign Policy*, ed. Robert S. Ross and Alistaire Iain Johnston (Stanford, Calif.: Stanford University Press, 2006), 122. For a thorough overview on the changing military situation, see Hoffmann, *India and the China Crisis*, part 4.

34. Protocol No. 59, October 14, 1962, in Fursenko, *Prezidium TsK KPSS*, 1:616–617; William Bundy to Phillips Talbot, October 12, 1962, OASD-ISA Records, USNA, RG 330, entry A1-1025, box 88. William H. Brubeck (U.S. Department of State) to McGeorge Bundy, October 15, 1962, in *FRUS 1961–1963*, 19:340–343; Galbraith, *Ambassador's Journal*, 374–375.

35. Kaul, *Untold Story*, 397; S. S. Khera, *India's Defence Problem* (Bombay: Orient Longman, 1968), 230–231; Mullik, *My Years*, 403–404.

36. New Delhi Embassy to U.S. Department of State, October 23, 1962, SDDF, USNA, RG 59, 691.93 / 10-2362; John Kenneth Galbraith to Dean Rusk, November 1, 1962, U.S. Department of State, "Report on Current Activity on the Sino-Indian Border and Estimate of Future Developments," November 3, 1962, John Kenneth Galbraith to Dean Rusk, October 25, 1962, and Carl Kaysen to John F. Kennedy, October 26, 1962, all in *FRUS 1961–1963*, 19:361–362, 367, 351–352; Jawaharlal Nehru to John F. Kennedy, October 26, 1962, NSF, JFKL, box 111; Nehru, *Nice Guys*, 453. The American transcript reflects a similar sentiment if not the exact phrasing: Kennedy complained that Khrushchev "has never had to put up. I think he ought to either give you some equipment, or he ought to be of some political help, or he ought to be discredited"; John F. Kennedy conversation with B. K. Nehru, October 26, 1962, in *John F. Kennedy: The Great Crises*, ed. Timothy J. Naftali, Philip Zelikow, and Ernest May (New York: W. W. Norton, 2001), 2:337–342.

37. V. V. Kuznetsov conversation with R. Jaipal, October 22, 1962, AVPRF, 090 / 24 / 80 / 3 / 1–5; Arora, *V. K. Krishna Menon*, 232.

38. New Delhi Embassy to U.S. Department of State, October 27, 1962, SDDF, USNA, RG 59, 791.5 / 10-2762; U.S. Department of State to New Delhi Embassy, October 28 (or 27?), 1962, SDDF, USNA, RG 59, 691.93 / 10-2862.

39. New Delhi Embassy to U.S. Department of State, November 1, 1962, NSF, JFKL, box 108; Michael Brecher, "Non-Alignment under Stress: The West and the India-China Border War," *Pacific Affairs* 52:4 (1979): 616; William Bundy to Robert S. McNamara, November 9, 1962, OASD-ISA Records, USNA, RG 330, entry A1-1025, box 87; Morarji R. Desai, *The Story of My Life* (Oxford: Pergamon Press, 1979), 2:204; Gopal, *Jawaharlal Nehru*, 3:227.

40. New Delhi Embassy to U.S. Department of State, November 1, 1962, and November 7, 1962, both in NSF, JFKL, box 108.

41. U.S. Department of State to New Delhi Embassy re Phillips Talbot meeting with B. K. Nehru, November 8, 1962, NSF, JFKL, box 108; Phillips Talbot conversation with G. D. Birla, November 7, 1962, SDDF, USNA, RG 59, 691.93 / 11-762; "Magnificent Response," *EW*, November 17, 1962, 1749–1750.

42. John Kenneth Galbraith to John F. Kennedy, November 13, 1962, in John Kenneth Galbraith, *Letters to Kennedy* (Cambridge, Mass.: Harvard University Press, 1998), 114–116; T. N. Kaul, *Diplomacy in Peace and War: Recollections and Reflections* (New Delhi: Vikas, 1979), 124; T. N. Kaul notes on meetings with Nikita Khrushchev, November 9, 1962, T. N. Kaul Papers I–III, NMML, Speeches / Writings by Him 11; New Delhi Embassy to U.S. Department of State, November 10, 1962, SDDF, USNA, RG 59, 791.6522 / 11-1062.

43. T. N. Kaul notes on meetings with Nikita Khrushchev, November 9, 1962, T. N. Kaul Papers I–III, NMML, Speeches / Writings by Him 11; Robert Komer to Chester Bowles, September 16, 1963, DDRS, CK3100040457; Carl Kaysen to John F. Kennedy, November 16, 1962, and New Delhi Embassy to U.S. Department of State, November 17, 1962, both in *FRUS 1961–1963*, 19:387, 389; F. R. Colburn (RAND Corporation) to William Bundy, November 16, 1962, OASD-ISA Records, USNA, RG 330, entry A1-1025, box 87; Robert Komer to Carl Kaysen, November 16, 1962, NSF, JFKL, box 108; Robert Komer to McGeorge Bundy, December 7, 1962, NSF—NSC Histories, LBJL, box 24.

44. New Delhi Embassy to U.S. Department of State, November 15, 1962, NSF, JFKL, box 108; Galbraith, *Ambassador's Journal*, 417.

45. T. N. Kaul to Jawaharlal Nehru, November 16, 1962, T. N. Kaul Papers I–III, NMML, subject 15. CIA information report, November 20, 1962, and Foy Kohler conversation with T. N. Kaul, November 19, 1962, both in NSF, JFKL, box 108; MID to O. A. Troianovskii, November 20, 1962, AVPRF, 090 / 24 / 81 / 15 / 182.

46. Jawaharlal Nehru to John F. Kennedy, in New Delhi Embassy to U.S. Department of State, November 19, 1962, and U.S. Department of State to John Kenneth Galbraith, both in SDDF, USNA, RG 59, 691.93 / 11-1962; D. K. Palit, *War in High Himalaya: The Indian Army in Crisis, 1962* (London: Hurst, 1991), 375. On the cabinet, see Brecher, "Non-Alignment under Stress," 617.

47. U.S. Department of State to John Kenneth Galbraith, November 19, 1962, SDDF, USNA, RG 59, 691.93 / 11-1962; Nehru, *Nice Guys*, 453–454.

48. U.S. Department of State to John Kenneth Galbraith, November 19, 1962, SDDF, USNA, RG 59, 691.93 / 11-1962; John Kenneth Galbraith to Dean Rusk and John F. Kennedy, November 20, 1962, NSF, JFKL, box 108.

49. Dean Rusk to John Kenneth Galbraith, November 20, 1962, in *FRUS 1961–1963*, 19:400–402; John Kenneth Galbraith to Rusk, November 21, 1962, NSF, JFKL, box 108.

50. Hoffmann, *India and the China Crisis*, 210.

51. Andrei Gromyko and S. A. Skachkov to CC-CPSU, October 26, 1962, AVPRF, 090 / 24 / 81 / 14 / 57–61; Ia. A. Malik conversation with T. N. Kaul, November 23, 1962, AVPRF, 090 / 24 / 80 / 3 / 9–12, in READD, NSA, box 17; W. Averell Harriman conversation with M. J. Desai, November 24, 1962, W. Averell Harriman Papers, LC, 537:7; TTK conversation with John Kenneth Galbraith, November 24, 1962, TTK Papers, NMML, Speeches / Writings by Him 3; HC-New Delhi to CRO, November 26, 1962, PMO Records, UKNA, PREM 11 / 4307.

52. "Report of the W. Averell Harriman Mission," November 22–30, 1962, W. Averell Harriman Papers, LC, 536:6; TTK to Y. B. Chavan, November 28, 1962, TTK Papers, NMML, subject 24;

William Bundy Conversation with R. P. Sarathy, November 26, 1962, OASD-ISA Records, USNA, RG 330, entry A1-1025, box 88. On the British mission, see McGarr, *Cold War*, 177.

53. T. N. Kaul to Jawaharlal Nehru, November 30, 1962, T. N. Kaul Papers I-III, NMML, Correspondence—J. Nehru; T. N. Kaul to B. K. Nehru, November 29, 1962, T. N. Kaul Papers I-III, NMML, Correspondence—B. K. Nehru; John F. Kennedy to W. Averell Harriman, November 25, 1962, W. Averell Harriman Papers, LC, 538:1. Roger Hilsman memorandum on W. Averell Harriman meeting with Jawaharlal Nehru, November 22, 1962, and "Soviet Reaction to U.S. Military Aid to India (RSB-184)," November 21, 1962, both in Roger Hilsman Papers, JFKL, 1:17; Roger Hilsman, *To Move a Nation: The Politics of Foreign Policy in the Administration of John F. Kennedy* (Garden City, N.Y.: Doubleday, 1967), 337; New Delhi Embassy to U.S. Department of State, November 24, 1962, W. Averell Harriman Papers, LC, 536:7.

54. New Delhi Embassy to U.S. Department of State, November 24, 1962, W. Averell Harriman Papers, LC, 536:7; Roger Hilsman memorandum on W. Averell Harriman meeting with Jawaharlal Nehru, November 22, 1962, Roger Hilsman Papers, JFKL, 1:17; "Report of the W. Averell Harriman Mission," November 22–30, 1962, W. Averell Harriman Papers, LC, 536:6.

55. "Report of the W. Averell Harriman Mission," November 22–30, 1962, W. Averell Harriman Papers, LC, 536:6; U.S. Department of State to New Delhi Embassy, December 8, 1962, and Harold Macmillan to John F. Kennedy, December 13, 1962, both in *FRUS 1961–1963*, 19:423–425, 430–432.

56. John F. Kennedy conversation with Harold Macmillan, December 20, 1962; and Robert Komer to John F. Kennedy, December 16, 1962, both in *FRUS 1961–1963*, 19:434–435, 455–460. For an overview of this issue, see McGarr, *Cold War*, 180–182.

57. Sudhir Ghosh to Jawaharlal Nehru, December 31, 1962, NSF, JFKL, box 418; Jawaharlal Nehru to Sudhir Ghosh, January 5, 1963, cited in Raghavan, *War and Peace*, 309; Dean Rusk conversation with B. K. Nehru, December 27, 1962, NSF, JFKL, box 418.

58. T. N. Kaul conversation with Marshal R. Ia. Malinovskii, December 17, 1962, T. N. Kaul Papers I-III, NMML, subject 15; HC-New Delhi to CRO (reporting on conversation with Defence Secretary P. V. R. Rao), January 9, 1963, Cabinet Records, UKNA, CAB 21 / 5685; TTK to Jawaharlal Nehru (re correspondence with Lal Bahadur Shastri), n.d. (March 1963), TTK Papers, NMML, Correspondence—J. Nehru.

59. Sudhir Ghosh to Jawaharlal Nehru, March 15, 1963, TTK Papers, NMML, subject 37; diplomat Y. D. Gundevia, quoted in Palit, *War in High Himalaya*, 406.

60. Jawaharlal Nehru to John F. Kennedy, April 21, 1963, quoted in Gopal, *Jawaharlal Nehru*, 3:259.

61. B. K. Nehru to Jawaharlal Nehru, May 17, 1963, TTK Papers, NMML, subject 37 (note that there are multiple letters between these two correspondents on this date); Robert Komer to John Kenneth Galbraith (re Robert S. McNamara), May 4, 1963, NSF, JFKL, box 418; W. Averell Harriman to Dean Rusk and Chester Bowles, May 17, 1963, W. Averell Harriman Papers, LC, 472:3; McGeorge Bundy memorandum for the record, April 25, 1963, NSF—NSC Histories, LBJL, 24:1; President's meeting on India, April 25, 1963, and notes by Secretary of State Rusk, May 5, 1963, both in *FRUS 1961–1963*, 19:561–565, 575–577.

62. B. K. Nehru to Jawaharlal Nehru, May 17, 1963, TTK Papers, NMML, subject 37. M. J. Desai memorandum, n.d. (May 1963), TTK Papers, NMML, Correspondence—M. J. Desai; Nehru speech in Lok Sabha, March 22, 1963, quoted in Philip J. Eldridge, *The Politics of Foreign Aid in India* (London: Weidenfeld & Nicolson, 1969), 33.

63. M. J. Desai conversation with Robert S. McNamara, May 1963, TTK Papers, NMML, Correspondence—M. J. Desai; Paul Nitze conversation with S. Bhoothalingam, April 25, 1963, and Defense Production Subcommittee conversation with S. Bhoothalingam, April 26, 1963, both in NSF, JFKL, box 419; TTK to Jawaharlal Nehru, May 20, 1963, in TTK Papers, NMML, subject 37. See also Gopal, *Jawaharlal Nehru*, 3:254.

64. U.S. Department of State to New Delhi Embassy, May 18, 1963, and John F. Kennedy conversation with TTK, May 20, 1963, both in *FRUS 1961–1963*, 19:598–604; M. J. Desai memorandum, May 22, 1963, TTK Papers, NMML, Correspondence—M. J. Desai; B. K. Nehru to Jawaharlal Nehru, May 21, 1963, and TTK summary, June 22, 1963, both in TTK Papers, NMML, subject 37. William Bundy, the assistant secretary of defense for international security affairs and brother of National Security Adviser McGeorge Bundy, offered assistance.

65. G. M. Pushkin conversation with T. N. Kaul, January 9, 1963, AVPRF, 090 / 25 / 84 / 3 / 1–4.

66. S. G. Lapin conversation with T. N. Kaul, May 22, 1963, AVPRF, 090 / 25 / 84 / 3 / 13–16; P. Guzdenko and A. Gliukin to A. A. Belianskii and G. S. Sidorovich, June 17, 1963, RGAE, 29 / 1 / 3002 / 47–49. On the distribution of production facilities, see GOI Lok Sabha, Committee on Public Undertakings, *Eighth Report: Hindustan Aeronautic, Ltd., Ministry of Defence Production* (New Delhi: Lok Sabha Secretariat, 1968), 8–20.

67. TTK provided a copy of this report to William Bundy in Jonathan Moore memo, May 9, 1963, CFPF, USNA, RG 59, DEF 1–4; M. J. Desai (?) conversation with John Kenneth Galbraith, July 9, 1963, T. N. Kaul Papers I-III, NMML, subject 15. British reticence to deepen the military relationship with the Indian Air Force is evident in John Boyd-Carpenter to Edwin Duncan Sandys, July 19, 1963, PMO Records, UKNA, PREM 11 / 4307.

68. S. G. Lapin conversation with S. Bhoothalingam, July 27, 1963, AVPRF, 090 / 25 / 84 / 3 / 17–18; Foy Kohler conversation with R. Jaipal, reported in Moscow to U.S. Department of State, August 21, 1963, CFPF, USNA, RG 59, DEF INDIA-US; New Delhi Embassy to U.S. Department of State, July 12, 1963, CFPF, USNA, RG 59, AID-6.

69. "Spravka ob obiazatel'stvakh sovetskoi storony v sootvetstvii s dogovorom ot 29-go oktiabr'ia 1962 g.," October 9, 1963, A. I. Mikoian to B. V. Kupirianov, August 26, 1963, and I. Arkhipov, P. V. Dement'ev, V. Kalmykov, and Marshal R. Ia. Malinovskii to Central Committee, October 9, 1963, all in RGAE, 29 / 1 / 2981 / 115–119, 76–78, 246–255; A. Kobzarev to M. A. Sergeichik, July 26, 1963, RGAE, 29 / 1 / 2980 / 302; A. Khokhlov and A. Sobolev, "Tekhnicheskoe zadanie," May 22, 1963, RGAE, 298 / 1 / 3828 / 107–111; delegation report, August 17, 1963, RGAE, 298 / 1 / 3828 / 189–221; A. Guliukin to A. A. Belianskii, October 10, 1963, RGAE, 29 / 1 / 3002 / 92–93.

70. William Bundy to Robert S. McNamara, March 30, 1963, NSF, JFKL, box 419 (the visitor was General Maxwell Taylor; see Dean Rusk to LBJ, December 9, 1963, NSF—Robert Komer Papers, LBJL, box 26); General Maxwell Taylor conversation with TTK, December 17, 1963,

CFPF, USNA, RG 59, DEF 1–3; Cabinet Secretariat (Emergency Wing), résumé of discussions with General Maxwell Taylor, n.d. (December 1963), B. K. Nehru Papers, NMML, subject 18; General Maxwell Taylor to Robert S. McNamara, January 13, 1964, NSF—Robert Komer Papers, LBJL, box 41; B. K. Nehru to Y. D. Gundevia, December 19, 1963, B. K. Nehru Papers, NMML, subject 17; General Maxwell Taylor conversation with TTK, December 20, 1963, CFPF, USNA, RG 59, DEF 1–3; General Paul D. Adams, as characterized in Carol Laise to Turner Cameron Jr., April 17, 1964, SDR, USNA, RG 59, entry A1-5255, box 2.

71. Chester Bowles to McGeorge Bundy, December 21, 1963, and Chester Bowles to LBJ, December 27, 1963, both in NSF—Country Files, LBJL, box 134.

72. I. Arkhipov to P. V. Dement'ev, May 23, 1964, and intergovernmental agreement, May 9, 1964, both in RGAE, 29 / 1 / 3578 / 210–218, 219–221. Andrei Gromyko memorandum, May 26, 1964 (re M. J. Desai visit to start the following day), AVPRF, 090 / 26 / 89 / 17 / 61–69; P. V. R Rao conversation with Peter Solbert, May 14, 1964, and Peter Solbert to Robert S. McNamara, May 21, 1964, both in SDR, USNA, RG59, entry A1-5255, box 1; U.S. Department of State to New Delhi Embassy (recounting a conversation between Phillips Talbot and P. V. R. Rao), May 7, 1964, CFPF, Ex–Top Secret, USNA, RG 59, DEF 19-3; M. J. Desai to B. K. Nehru, February 29, 1964, B. K. Nehru Papers, NMML, subject 18; Robert Komer to McGeorge Bundy, March 6, 1964, NSF—Robert Komer Files, LBJL, box 23; "Courses of Action for Discussion with Indian Defense Officials," April 9, 1964, NSF—Robert Komer Files, LBJL, box 23; "US-Indian Defense Talks," May 20, 1964, SDR, USNA RG 59, entry A1-5255), box 2; New Delhi Embassy to U.S. Department of State, May 7, 1964, NSF—Robert Komer Files, LBJL, box 24; Chester Bowles to Robert Komer, May 11, 1964, NSF—Robert Komer Files, LBJL, box 41.

73. Y. B. Chavan to Jawaharlal Nehru, May 22, 1964, B. K. Nehru Papers, NMML, subject 18; U.S. Department of State to New Delhi Embassy, May 22, 1964, NSF—Robert Komer Papers, LBJL, box 41; Y. B. Chavan, *1965 War, the Inside Story: Defence Minister Y. B. Chavan's Diary of India-Pakistan War,* ed. R. D. Pradhan (New Delhi: Atlantic Publishers, 2007), xiii–xiv; USAF conversation with IAF officers, February 18, 1965, and Robert S. McNamara conversation with Y. B. Chavan, May 22, 1964, both in NSF—Komer Papers, LBJL, box 24; T. V. Kunhi Krishnan, *Chavan and the Troubled Decade* (Bombay: Somaiya Publications, 1971), 98–99.

74. Hollis B. Chenery to David Bell, June 10, 1964, USAID Records, USNA, RG 286, entry P266, box 7; Y. B. Chavan conversation with I. A. Benediktov, June 6, 1964, B. K. Nehru Papers, NMML, subject 18; Chester Bowles to McGeorge Bundy, July 18, 1964, NSF—McGeorge Bundy Files, LBJL, box 16. Dean Rusk to Robert McNamara, July 17, 1964, CFPF, USNA, RG 59, DEF 1–3; Robert S. McNamara to Dean Rusk, July 2, 1964, CFPF Ex–Top Secret, USNA, RG 59, DEF 19-8; "Defence Shopping," *TOI,* September 23, 1964, 8.

75. "Chavan Outlines Defence Aid from the Big-Three," *TOI,* September 22, 1964, 1; R. D. Pradhan, *Debacle to Revival: Y. B. Chavan as Defence Minister, 1962–65* (New Delhi: Orient Longman, 1999), chapters 20–22; Mansingh, *India's Search,* 160–62; N. Pritchard memorandum, March 19, 1964, and H. A. F. Rumbod to R. H. Belcher, June 5, 1964, both in CRO Records, UKNA, DO 164 / 124; "Defence Assistance to India," n.d. (October 1964?), Arthur Bottomley conversation with Y. B. Chavan, November 12, 1964, and Harold Wilson conversation with Y. B. Chavan, November 13, 1964, all in CRO Records, UKNA, DO 164 / 125.

76. Robert McNamara to Dean Rusk, July 2, 1964, CFPF Ex–Top Secret, USNA, RG 59, DEF 19-8; Robert Komer to Chester Bowles, March 20, 1965, NSF—Robert Komer Files, LBJL, box 13; Y. B. Chavan conversation with Chester Bowles, March 6, 1965, B. K. Nehru Papers, NMML, subject 18; Harold Saunders to Robert Komer, March 15, 1965, NSF—NSC Histories, LBJL, 24:3.

77. Dean Rusk conversation with B. K. Nehru, May 8, 1965, in *FRUS 1964*, 25: 249–252 (this American document quotes Ambassador Nehru about the proof); Robert J. McMahon, *The Cold War on the Periphery: The United States, India, and Pakistan* (New York: Columbia University Press, 1994), 324–325; John P. Lewis to David Bell, May 7, 1965, USAID Records, USNA, RG 286, entry P409, box 6; "Military Assistance Policy in India and Pakistan," n.d. (March 1966?), SDR, USNA, RG 59, entry A1-5255, box 14.

78. Chester Bowles diary entry, September 21, 1965, Chester Bowles Papers, Yale University Library, 395:168.

79. Robert S. McNamara to LBJ, July 6, 1965, NSF—Robert Komer Files, LBJL, box 41; McGarr, *Cold War*, 324–326; McMahon, *Cold War*, 329–330. For an Indian overview, see Sumit Ganguly, *The Origins of War in South Asia: The Indo-Pakistani Conflicts since 1947,* 2nd ed. (Boulder, Colo.: Westview Press, 1994), chapter 3.

80. "India's Defence Requirements" (for Czechoslovakia), "Requirements for Indian Defence" (for the USSR), "Brief for Discussions on Military Hardware from USSR and Czechoslovakia," TTK conversation with Aleksei Kosygin, November 12, 1965, and summary records of discussions during the visit of the Indian finance minister to the USSR, November 9–17, 1965, all in TTK Papers, NMML, subject 43. (The first three documents are undated but presumably from fall 1965.)

81. Chester Bowles, "America and Russia in India," *Foreign Affairs* 49:4 (1971): 642; James Hershberg, "Quietly Encouraging Quasi-Alignment: US-Indian Relations, the Sino-Indian Border War of 1962, and the Downfall of Krishna Menon," *Eurasia Border Review* 3 (2012): 121–158.

82. A. I. Mikoian conversation with Y. B. Chavan, June 20, 1964, AVPRF, 090 / 26 / 89 / 17 / 84–86.

83. T. N. Kaul conversation with Chester Bowles, March 7, 1964, T. N. Kaul Papers I–III, NMML, subject 15; B. K. Nehru to Y. D. Gundevia, December 19, 1963, B. K. Nehru Papers, NMML, subject 17; Y. B. Chavan, quoted in Chester Bowles diary entry, September 21, 1964, Chester Bowles Papers, Yale University Library, 395:168.

7. Bets, Bargains, and the Price of American Aid

1. C. Tyler Wood discussions with S. Bhoothalingam and others, July 26–31, 1965, USAID Records, USNA, RG286, entry P409, box 23; Ravi Bhoothalingam, "Philosophy of an Economist-Civil Servant," *The Hindu*, April 9, 2010, www.thehindu.com/opinion/op-ed /Philosophy-of-an-economist-civil-servant/article16364972.ece; S. Bhoothalingam, *Plain Speaking: Selected Writings on the Indian Economy and Administration* (New Delhi: Affiliated East-West Press, 1994), 80–82.

2. Devesh Kapur, John Prior Lewis, and Richard Charles Webb, *The World Bank: Its First Half Century* (Washington, D.C.: Brookings Institution Press, 1997), 1:463–464.

3. W. Turnage to E. Kalijarvi, January 13, 1955, SDDF, USNA, RG 59, 791.5-MSP / 7-1757; Conversation with S. Bhoothalingam, December 9, 1959, CRO Records, UKNA, DO 35 / 8529.

4. *EA 1966–1967*, 102, 115.

5. Minutes of 248th NSC meeting, May 12, 1955, AWF-NSC, DDEL, box 6, and W. R. Herod to Harold Stassen and John Hollister, June 7, 1955, both in White House Office Records, DDEL, NSC Staff Series, OCB Central File Subseries, box 37; Herbert Hoover Jr. to Glen Edgerton, June 6, 1955, in *FRUS 1955–1957*, 8:288–289; Nelson Rockefeller to Dwight D. Eisenhower, October 29, 1955 (two letters), and Herbert Hoover Jr. and W. Randolph Burgess to Sherman Adams, November 29, 1955, all in White House Confidential Files, DDEL, Subject Series, box 61.

6. "Ekonomicheskoe polozhenie i vneshnee ekonomicheskie sviazi Indii," February 9, 1960, RGAE, 365 / 2 / 2017 / 24; GOI PC, *Third Five Year Plan* (Delhi: Manager of Publications, 1961), 457–467; GOI PC, *Programmes of Industrial Development, 1961–66* (New Delhi: Planning Commission, 1962), 14–15; James H. Smith to Dennis FitzGerald, John Bill, and Walter Schaefer, September 10, 1958, in James H. Smith Papers, DDEL, box 5; Tata Iron and Steel Company conversation with Tarlok Singh, n.d. (early 1959?), George Woods Papers, CU / WBGA, folder 30178055; George Anderson conversation with Morarji Desai, October 9, 1958, in *FRUS 1958–1960*, 15:471; Chad Calhoun to Clarence Randall, July 10, 1959, and New Delhi Embassy to U.S. Department of State, June 19, 1959, both in USCFEP Chairman Records, DDEL, Clarence Randall Series, Subject Subseries, box 6; Ellsworth Bunker conversation with William Turnage, August 5, 1959, in *FRUS 1958–1960*, 15:510–511; Clarence Randall to Andrew Goodpaster, November 19, 1959, Office of the Staff Secretary Records, DDEL, Subject Series, White House Subseries, box 5.

7. Unfortunately, I was unable to obtain a copy of this report, so am quoting it through secondary sources. Padma Desai, *The Bokaro Steel Plant: A Study of Soviet Economic Assistance* (Amsterdam: North-Holland Publishing, 1972), 3, 85, chapter 3; S. S. Sidhu, *The Steel Industry in India: Problems and Perspective* (New Delhi: Vikas, 1983), 15, 35, 36; Peter Lande to Daniel Patrick Moynihan, October 31, 1973, Daniel Patrick Moynihan Papers, LC, 372:4; Asha Laxman Datar, *India's Economic Relations with the USSR and Eastern Europe, 1953 to 1969* (Cambridge: Cambridge University Press, 1972), 64; Pitamber Pant, "Bokaro Steel Project," October 26, 1961, CIS Records, MIT, 11:19; Ross Knox Bassett, *The Technological Indian* (Cambridge, Mass.: Harvard University Press, 2016), 202–210; GOI Lok Sabha, Committee on Public Undertakings, *Sixty-Eighth Report: Bokaro Steel Ltd—Minister of Steel and Heavy Engineering* (New Delhi: Lok Sabha Secretariat, 1970), 1. On the overall politics, see J. R. D. Tata conversation with Tarlok Singh, n.d. (1959?), George Woods Papers, CU / WBGA, folder 30178055; and N. R. Srinivasan, *The History of Bokaro* (Bokaro Steel City, India: Steel Authority of India, Ltd., 1988), 37.

8. Minutes of interagency meeting, January 6, 1960, Joseph Rand Papers, DDEL, box 5; entry for January 6, 1960, Clarence Randall Journals, DDEL, box 6; memorandum of January 6, 1960, Dennis A. FitzGerald Papers, DDEL, box 37.

9. Vance Brand to Ellsworth Bunker, January 29, 1960, and Woods notes from meeting with B. K. Nehru, March 21, 1960, both in George Woods Papers, CU / WBGA, folder 30178055; George Woods notes from meetings with L. K. Jha, Morarji Desai, and S. Bhoothalingam, February 19, 1960, George Woods Papers, CU / WBGA, folder 30178055; Jawaharlal Nehru conversation with Nikita Khrushchev, March 1, 1960, Subimal Dutt Papers, NMML, subject 24—PHP. Entries for June 29, 1960 and October 6, 1960, both in Clarence Randall Journals, DDEL, box 6; confidential cabinet memorandum "Bokaro Steel Plant," enclosed in New Delhi Embassy to U.S. Department of State, May 23, 1961, SDDF, USNA, RG 59, 891.331 / 5-2361.

10. Confidential cabinet memorandum "Bokaro Steel Plant," enclosed in New Delhi Embassy to U.S. Department of State, May 23, 1961, SDDF, USNA, RG 59, 891.331 / 5-2361; TTK to cabinet secretary, August 16, 1962, TTK Papers, NMML, subject 23. Kuznetsov conversation with R. Jaipal, October 12, 1962, RGAE, 4372 / 64 / 445 / 42–45. See also Indian note, October 12, 1962, RGAE, 365 / 2 / 339 / 148.

11. L. D. Battle to Ralph Dungan (discussing both U.S. Steel and Morarji Desai), November 13, 1961, NSF, JFKL, box 106; George Woods to Edgar Kaiser, February 20, 1960, George Woods Papers, CU / WBGA, folder 30178055; "Increase in Size of Third Plan by Rs. 250 Crores," TOI, June 11, 1960, 1; John Kenneth Galbraith to U.S. Department of State (reporting on conversation with Morarji Desai on June 23, 1961), June 27, 1961, SDDF, USNA, RG 59, 791.5-MSP / 6-2761.

12. The USAID study was based on prior work by U.S. Steel: *Techno-Economic Survey of a Proposed Integrated Steel Plant at Bokaro, Bihar State, India,* March 1963; the report is summarized in James Peter Stillman, "Foreign Aid, Ideology and Bureaucratic Politics: The Bokaro Steel Mill and Indian-American Relations" (PhD diss., Columbia University, 1975), appendix 10. See also Robert David Johnson, *Congress and the Cold War* (Cambridge: Cambridge University Press, 2006), 94–95. The committee was led by General Lucius Clay; see U.S. Committee to Strengthen the Security of the Free World, *The Scope and Distribution of United States Military and Economic Assistance Programs: Report to the President of the United States* (Washington, D.C.: Department of State, 1963), 5–6. For more details on the committee, see especially Andrew David and Michael Holm, "The Kennedy Administration and the Battle over Foreign Aid: The Untold Story of the Clay Committee," *Diplomacy and Statecraft* 27:1 (2016): 65–92.

13. "Key Test of U.S. Aid—'Socialized' Steel for India," *US News and World Report,* April 15, 1963, 75–76.

14. Henry Hazlitt, "The Foreign-Aid Folly," *Newsweek,* July 8, 1963, 77.

15. Robert B. Rakove, *Kennedy, Johnson, and the Nonaligned World* (Cambridge: Cambridge University Press, 2013), 188. Representative Otto Passman led the attack, as he did on many elements of President Kennedy's foreign assistance plans; see U.S. Congress, House of Representatives, Committee on Appropriations, Subcommittee on Foreign Operations, *Foreign Operations Appropriations, Part IV,* Pub. No. Y4.Ap6 / 1:F76 / 3 / 964 / part 4 (1963), 1397–1398 (July 16–17, 1963).

16. That did not, of course, stop Galbraith from continuing to lobby; see John Kenneth Galbraith, "Proposal for Steel Mill in India Strikes Iron Resistance," *Washington Post,* August 18, 1963, E4.

17. Jawaharlal Nehru to John F. Kennedy, August 28, 1963, NSF, JFKL, box 111.

18. Representative William Minshall, quoted in "Blow at Bokaro," *Newsweek*, September 2, 1963, 64.

19. W. Averell Harriman conversation with G. D. Birla, June 3, 1963, USAID Records, USNA, RG 286, entry P266, box 7.

20. C. Subramaniam, speech to Lok Sabha, quoted in "Bokaro without U.S. Aid," *EW*, September 14, 1963, 1543.

21. New Delhi Embassy to U.S. Department of State, June 21, 1959, USCFEP Chair Records, DDEL, Clarence Randall Series, Subject Subseries, box 6; Carol Laise to Raymond Hare, July 12, 1966, in SDR, USNA, RG59, entry A1-5254, box 10.

22. GOI PC, *Third Five Year Plan*, 59. Public spending on the rural sector did increase more dramatically from the Second to the Third Plan. GOI PC, *Fourth Five Year Plan: A Draft Outline* (New Delhi: Manager of Publications, 1965), 3, 419–420; GOI PC, *Third Five Year Plan*, 55.

23. GOI Ministry of Finance, *Economic Survey, 1969–70* (New Delhi: GOI, 1970), 117; TTK to Morarji Desai, April 9, 1963, TTK Papers, NMML, subject 35.

24. C. Rajogopalachari, quoted in "Mahatab to Join Swatantra Party?" *Hindustan Times*, June 26, 1961, 12; M. R. Masani, *Why Swatantra?* (Bombay: Popular Prakashan, 1966), chapter 3; this document, released for the February 1967 elections, reflected the core philosophy of Swatantra in earlier years; see Howard L. Erdman, *The Swatantra Party and Indian Conservatism* (Cambridge: Cambridge University Press, 1967), chapter 6. The Swaminathan Committee released its report; see GOI Ministry of Industries, *Final Report of the Committee on Industries Development Procedures* (Delhi: Manager of Publications, 1964); and GOI Ministry of Commerce and Industry, *Report of the Import and Export Policy Committee* (New Delhi: Ministry of Commerce and Industry, 1962). For a brief overview, see Jayati Ghosh, "Liberalization Debates," in *The Indian Economy: Major Debates since Independence*, ed. T. J Byres (New Delhi: Oxford University Press, 1998), 312. See also Jagdish Bhagwati, "Indian Balance of Payments Policy and Exchange Auctions," *Oxford Economic Papers*, new ser., 14:1 (1962): 51–68 (quotation on 56); and Jagdish Bhagwati, "The Case for Devaluation," *EW*, August 4, 1962, 1263–1266. Pranab Bardhan and A. K. Das Gupta wrote critiques; see Pranab Bardhan, "The Case against Devaluation," and A. K. Das Gupta, "Export Promotion through Devaluation," both in *EW*, September 8, 1962, 1446–1448. Bhagwati rejoined with "More on Devaluation," *EW*, October 6, 1962, 1581–1584, and "Further Notes on Devaluation," *EW*, March 23, 1963, 523–525.

25. GOI PC, *Third Five Year Plan*, chapters 3–5; G.J. MacMahon conversation with B. K. Nehru, February 7, 1957, CRO Records, UKNA, DO 35 / 8528.

26. For a useful, if skeptical, overview, see Francine R. Frankel, *India's Green Revolution: Economic Gains and Political Costs* (Princeton, N.J.: Princeton University Press, 1971), chapter 1.

27. Michael Brecher, *Nehru's Mantle: The Politics of Succession in India* (New York: Praeger, 1966), 114–116. G. D. Birla note for Lal Bahadur Shastri, n.d. (May–June 1964?), quoted in

Medha M. Kudaisya, *The Life and Times of G. D. Birla* (New Delhi: Oxford University Press, 2003), 341. For general context of Shastri's economic policies, see especially Medha M. Kudaisya, "'Reforms by Stealth': Indian Economic Policy, Big Business and the Promise of the Shastri Years, 1964–1966," *South Asia* 25:2 (2002): 205–229; and Francine R. Frankel, *India's Political Economy, 1947–1977: The Gradual Revolution* (Princeton, N.J.: Princeton University Press, 1978), chapter 7.

28. C. Subramaniam, "New Policy for Steel," April 15, 1963, in *India of My Dreams* (New Delhi: Orient Longman, 1972), 63–75; C. Subramaniam, *The New Strategy in Indian Agriculture: The First Decade and after* (New Delhi: Vikas, 1979), chapter 1; GOI Ministry of Food and Agriculture, Department of Agriculture, *Agricultural Production in the Fourth Five-Year Plan: Strategy and Programme* (New Delhi: Ministry of Food and Agriculture, 1965), 3–5, 23; Robert Komer to Chester Bowles, October 9, 1964, NSF—Komer Files, LBJL, box 13; Chester Bowles to David Bell, September 21, 1964, Robert Komer Personal Papers, LBJL, box 10. For a general overview of the rise (and fall) of the Bechtel negotiations, see especially Ashok Kapoor, *International Business Negotiations: A Study in India* (New York: New York University Press, 1970).

29. Foodgrains Price Committee, *Report of the Jha Committee on Foodgrain Prices for the 1964–65 Season* (New Delhi: Ministry of Food and Agriculture, 1965); summary of the Twenty-First Meeting of the National Development Council (October 27–28, 1964), in GOI National Development Council, *Five Decades of Nation-Building: Fifty NDC Meetings* (New Delhi: Planning Commission, 2005), 2:284–304; "Implementation of Foodgrains Price Policy, 1964–65," n.d., PC Records, NAI, 1/108/64-CDN; C. Subramaniam, "The Concept of the Food Corporation," January 14, 1965, and "Increasing Food Production," November 28, 1964, both in C. Subramaniam, *A New Strategy in Agriculture: A Collection of Speeches* (New Delhi: Indian Council of Agricultural Research, 1972), 281–286, 21. For an insightful overview of the policy changes in agriculture, see Ashutosh Varshney, "Ideas, Interest and Institutions in Policy Change: Transformation of India's Agricultural Strategy in the Mid-1960s," *Policy Sciences* 22:3–4 (1989): 289–323.

30. V. K. R. V. Rao, "Self-Reliance in Agricultural Production," *Yojana,* October 10, 1965; Mehta, "Breakthrough in Agriculture," n.d. (1964–1965?), in *Economic Planning in India* (New Delhi: Young India Publications, 1970), 67.

31. Véronique Dimier, *The Invention of a European Development Aid Bureaucracy: Recycling Empire* (Basingstoke, England: Palgrave Macmillan, 2014); Marc Frey and Sönke Kunkel, "Writing the History of Development: A Review of the Recent Literature," *Contemporary European History* 20:2 (2011): 215–232; O. S. Kamanu, "India Consortium," July 10, 1968, Country Files, WBGA, folder 1844850. B. K. Nehru to Morarji Desai, May 21, 1958, M. O. Mathai Papers, NMML, Other Papers 11. E. P. Wright conversation with William S. Gaud, January 4, 1968, Country Files, WBGA, folder 1844603. For helpful overviews of the shifting mood of the Aid-India Consortium, see Bruce Muirhead, "Differing Perspectives: India, the World Bank and the 1963 Aid-India Negotiations," *India Review* 4:1 (2005): 1–22; and Shigeru Akita, "The Aid-India Consortium, the World Bank, and the International Order of Asia, 1958–1968," *Asian Review of World Histories* 2:2 (July 2014): 217–248.

32. E. Peter Wright to Escott Reid, November 3, 1963, Country Files, WBGA, folder 1844608; consortium proceedings, April 30–May 1, 1963, Country Files, WBGA, folder 1844604.

33. Gregory Votaw to Escott Reid, May 9, 1963, Country Files, WBGA, folder 1844604; E. P. Wright to Escott Reid, June 11, 1963, Country Files, WBGA, folder 1844605; George Woods to Morarji Desai, June 20, 1963, Country Files, WBGA, folder 1844602.

34. E. P. Wright to Alexander Stevenson, Country Files, WBGA, folder 1844608; Gregory Votaw to Escott Reid, March 14, 1964, and Escott Reid to George Woods, March 6, 1964, both in Country Files, WBGA, folder 1844609.

35. L. K. Jha, quoted in Escott Reid to George Woods, March 19, 1964, Country Files, WBGA, folder 1844609; George Woods to TTK, June 4, 1964, and TTK to George Woods, June 27, 1964, both quoted in Robert W. Oliver, *George Woods and the World Bank* (Boulder, Colo.: Lynne Rienner, 1995), 132–133; David Bell to William Macomber (re conversation with Edward Mason / IBRD), August 6, 1964, USAID Records, USNA, RG 286, entry P409, box 7; Bernard Bell oral history, November 13, 1985, WBGA online, http://documents.world bank.org/curated/en/726021468050068737. Of particular interest was Charles Lindblom's USAID study of food grain production; see Charles Lindblom to Chester Bowles, April 1964, Albert O. Hirschman Papers, Seeley G. Mudd Manuscript Library, Princeton University, 45:7.

36. Romano Pantalini to E. P. Wright, July 31, 1964, J. Kraske memo, September 25, 1964, Holland to Bernard Bell, November 27, 1964, and "Statement on the Bank Study of the Indian Economy, 1964–65," August 27, 1964, all in Bernard R. Bell Papers, WBGA, folder 1850796; Bernard Bell oral history, November 21, 1990, WBGA online, http://oralhistory. worldbank.org/person/bell-bernard-r, 4; Gregory Votaw oral history, April 30, 1985, CCOH, 43; George Woods conversation with TTK, August 24, 1964, Country Files, WBGA, folder 1844611; Phillips Talbot conversation with George Woods, November 12, 1964, SDR, USNA, RG 59, entry A1-5254, box 1.

37. John Prior Lewis, *Quiet Crisis in India: Economic Development and American Policy* (Washington, D.C.: Brookings Institution Press, 1962), 301–303, emphasis in the original.

38. "U.S. Private Position for Ninth [Aid-India] Consortium Meeting," March 17, 1964, SDR, USNA, RG 59, entry A1-5254, box 1; Robert Komer to Chester Bowles, October 28, 1964, NSF—Robert Komer Papers, LBJL, box 13; Chester Bowles to David Bell, August 4, 1964, USAID Records, USNA, RG286, entry P409, box 7; Harold H. Saunders memorandum for the record (summarizing conversation between William Macomber, William S. Gaud, David Bell, Robert Komer, and others), October 19, 1964, NSF—Robert Komer Files, LBJL, box 23. See also the account by journalist Barbara Ward, an honorary foreign member in the U.S. India lobby: Barbara Ward, *The Plan under Pressure: An Observer's View* (New York: Asia Publishing House, 1963).

39. David Schneider to Raymond Hare, October 14, 1965, SDR, USNA, RG 59, entry A1-5254, box 8. Lewis credits economist Hollis Chenery, at that point a senior USAID official, for the "big push" approach that the two shared; see John Prior Lewis, *India's Political Economy: Governance and Reform* (New Delhi: Oxford University Press, 1995), 94. And indeed, Chenery brought USAID to consider performance and policy conditioning more seriously in USAID

Program Coordination Staff, *Principles of Foreign Economic Assistance* (Washington, D.C.: USAID, 1963). See also Paul N. Rosenstein-Rodan, *Notes on the Theory of the "Big Push,"* CENIS Economic Development Series, C/57-25 (Cambridge, Mass.: MIT Center for International Studies, 1957). The notion of discontinuous growth as countries industrialized was a common one in those years; see, for instance, Donald N. McCloskey, "Kinks, Tools, Spurts and Substitutes: Gerschenkron's Rhetoric of Relative Backwardness," in *Patterns of European Industrialization: The Nineteenth Century*, ed. Richard E. Sylla and Gianni Toniolo (London: Routledge, 1991), 92–105.

40. John Prior Lewis, "Betting on India," January 14, 1965, NSF—NSC Histories, LBJL, 25:6; John Prior Lewis, *India's Political Economy*, 94–95, emphasis in the original; Chester Bowles to David Bell, March 8, 1965, USAID Records, USNA, RG 286, entry P409, box 6. William S. Gaud oral history, November 26, 1968, William S. Gaud Papers, Yale University Library, 3:53.

41. Robert Komer to McGeorge Bundy, April 30, 1965, in NSF—NSC Histories, LBJL, box 24.

42. C. Tyler Wood discussions with S. Bhoothalingam, July 26–31, 1965, USAID Records, USNA, RG286, entry P409, box 23.

43. Harold Wriggins to Phillips Talbot, November 18, 1964, NSF—Robert Komer Files, LBJL, box 13; "India: Long-Term Review," October 9, 1964, USAID Records, USNA, RG286, entry P409, box 7. All-India food prices jumped 8 percent in the third quarter of 1964, and another 8 percent in the subsequent year; see GOI Ministry of Finance, *Economic Survey, 1966–67* (New Delhi: Ministry of Finance, 1967), figure 5-2.

44. McGeorge Bundy to Chester Bowles, April 28, 1965, McGeorge Bundy to LBJ, June 28, 1965, and Lal Bahadur Shastri to LBJ, July 9, 1965, all in *FRUS 1964–1968*, 25:240–241, 284–285, 301n2 (summary). The USAID administrator was David Bell (no relation to Bernard Bell, then employed by the World Bank); see David Bell to LBJ, June 16, 1965, USAID Records (USNA, RG286, entry P409), box 7.

45. LBJ conversation with B. K. Nehru, July 13, 1965, in *FRUS 1964–1968*, 25:300–303; Charles L. Schultz to LBJ, July 15, 1965, NSF—Robert Komer Files, LBJL, box 24. Richard Reuter, March 21, 1966, quoted in Kristin L. Ahlberg, " 'Machiavelli with a Heart': The Johnson Administration's Food for Peace Program in India, 1965–1966," *Diplomatic History* 31:4 (2007): 693; Lyndon Baines Johnson, *The Vantage Point: Perspectives of the Presidency, 1963–1969* (New York: Holt, Rinehart and Winston, 1971), 226–227. On congressional approval, see Bernard Bell to LBJ, June 16, 1965, USAID Records, USNA, RG286, entry P409, box 7.

46. Dennis Kux, *Estranged Democracies: India and the United States, 1941–1991* (Thousand Oaks, Calif.: SAGE Publications, 1994), 243; John Prior Lewis memorandum, July 18, 1965, and John Prior Lewis memorandum, July 18, 1965, both in USAID Records, USNA, RG286, entry P409, box 23. An agreement of July 26, 1965, was mentioned in Chester Bowles to LBJ, September 16, 1965, and an editorial note (regarding a telephone call between LBJ and Secretary of Agriculture Orville Freeman, November 27, 1966), both in *FRUS 1964–1968*, 25:399–400, 765. See also Robert Komer oral history, January 30, 1970, LBJL, 40–41.

47. LBJ conversation with Thomas C. Mann, July 13, 1965, Harold Sunders to McGeorge Bundy, August 23, 1965, and Chester Bowles to LBJ, September 16, 1965, all in *FRUS*

1964–1968, 25:299–300, 340–341, 399–400; Nick Cullather, *The Hungry World: America's Cold War Battle against Poverty in Asia* (Cambridge, Mass.: Harvard University Press, 2010), chapter 8; Martin Abel and Lester Brown, "An Evaluation of India's Fourth Five Year Plan—the Agricultural Sector," May 13, 1965, NSF—Robert Komer Files, LBJL, box 24; Selig S. Harrison, "India Trembling Near Brink of Famine," *Washington Post*, August 22, 1965, A25.

48. Chester Bowles to Robert Komer, September 12, 1965, NSF—Country Files, LBJL, box 134; Robert Komer to McGeorge Bundy, September 13, 1965, and Raymond Hare to Dean Rusk, October 2, 1965, both in *FRUS 1964–1968*, 25:393, 443–444; U.S. Central Intelligence Agency, *Warfare Aggravates Indian Food Shortages* (special report), September 24, 1965, NSF—Robert Komer Files, LBJL, box 24; Paul M. McGarr, *The Cold War in South Asia: Britain, the United States and the Indian Subcontinent, 1945–1965* (Cambridge: Cambridge University Press, 2013), 324–326; Robert J. McMahon, *The Cold War on the Periphery: The United States, India, and Pakistan* (New York: Columbia University Press, 1994), 329–330.

49. Robert Komer to LBJ, December 2, 1965, and "Critical Indian Food Situation," National Security Action Memorandum 339, December 17, 1965, both in *FRUS 1964–1968*, 25:484–486, 513–514; W. W. Rostow conversation with B. K. Nehru, December 1, 1965, SDR, USNA, RG 59, entry 5255, box 8.

50. Chester Bowles to Thomas C. Mann, September 30, 1965, CFPF 64, USNA, RG 59, AID(US); "Emergency Committee of Secretaries Meeting" (late 1965), citing Planning Commission report to National Development Council, September 6, 1965, Asok Mitra Papers, NMML, subject 64. Asoka Mehta, quoted in Raymond Hare to Dean Rusk, October 5, 1965, and editorial note regarding LBJ telephone conversation with Orville Freeman, February 2, 1966, both in *FRUS 1964–1968*, 25:443–444, 553–555. See also the discussion at the National Development Council meeting in GOI National Development Council, *Five Decades*, 2:334–336; and Robert Komer to LBJ, November 30, 1965, NSF—Robert Komer Files, LBJL, box 25.

51. Robert H. Johnson to Walt Rostow, December 21, 1965, SDR, USNA, RG 59, entry A1-5026, box 303. S. Bhoothalingam report on visit to Washington, New York, London and Paris, November 8, 1965, MEA Records, NAI, WII / 122 / 13 / 66; Indira Gandhi to P. N. Haksar, November 10, 1965, P. N. Haksar Papers I–II, NMML, Correspondence: Indira Gandhi.

52. David Denoon, *Devaluation under Pressure: India, Indonesia, and Ghana* (Cambridge: Massachusetts Institute of Technology Press, 1986), 39. The Planning Commission kept close tabs on the Bell Mission staff; see the reports in PC Records, NAI, 1 / 108 / 64-CDN.

53. George Woods to TTK, May 28, 1965, Country Files, WBGA, folder 1844613.

54. Bernard Bell to George Woods, August 31, 1965, Bernard R. Bell Papers, WBGA, folder 1859706; Bernard R. Bell, *Report to the President of the International Bank for Reconstruction and Development and the International Development Association on India's Economic Development Effort*, October 1, 1965, WBGA online, http://documents.worldbank.org/curated /en/726021468050068737, 1:32–36; R. R. Neild, report on conversation with Andre de Lattre and Bernard Bell, September 28, 1965, Treasury Department Records, UKNA, T 317 / 735.

55. Chester Bowles to Thomas C. Mann, August 26, 1965, NSF—Robert Komer Papers, LBJL, box 23; Denoon, *Devaluation under Pressure*, 39.

56. "Fourth Plan Appraisal Mission—Terms of Reference," October 25, 1965, Country Files, WBGA, folder 1837536; R. Picciotto commentary, August 26, 1965, and B. Walstedt to Kenneth A. Bohr, October 7, 1965, both in Benjamin B. King Papers, WBGA, folder 1848515; Denoon, *Devaluation under Pressure*, 41.

57. Tarlok Singh to Asoka Mehta, September 10, 1966, PMO Records, NAI, 37 / 161 / 1966-PMS. Pitamber Pant, quoted in Thomas Weisskopf, interview with the author, Ann Arbor, Mich., March 12, 2014; I. G. Patel, *Glimpses of Indian Economic Policy: An Insider's View* (New Delhi: Oxford University Press, 2002), 104.

58. New Delhi Embassy to U.S. Department of State, November 24, 1965, NSF—Robert Komer Files, LBJL, box 24; Chester Bowles to Dean Rusk, May 20, 1965, NSF—Edward Hamilton Files, LBJL, box 2. Irving Friedman conversation with Asoka Mehta, April 18–19, 1967, Country Files, WBGA, folder 1837392. Reports on this meeting, with W. Averell Harriman, vary; the American report noted laconically that "TTK seemed reluctant to take up opportunities to discuss Indian economic matters"; see New Delhi Embassy to U.S. Department of State, March 4, 1965, W. Averell Harriman Papers, LC, 543:16. A scholar who interviewed Indian officials, however, heard that Indian officials were "thoroughly incensed" by Harriman's "rough treatment"; see Kapoor, *International Business Negotiations*, 159. TTK's views on the economics of fertilizer are described in C. Subramaniam, *Hand of Destiny: Memoirs* (Bombay: Bharatiya Vidya Bhavan, 1993), 175.

59. Chester Bowles to Orville Freeman, November 15, 1965, in *FRUS 1964–1968*, 25:467–468; C. Subramaniam to Orville Freeman, August 30, 1965, MEA Records, NAI, WI / 103 / 11 / 65; Orville Freeman oral history, July 21, 1969, LBJL Online, www.lbjlibrary.net/collections/oral-histories/freeman-orville.html, 9; Robert L. Paarlberg, *Food Trade and Foreign Policy: India, the Soviet Union, and the United States* (Ithaca, N.Y.: Cornell University Press, 1985), 148. Serious conversations began after Freeman's 1964 visit to India; see Orville L. Freeman, *World without Hunger* (New York: Praeger, 1968), chapter 9.

60. Orville Freeman to LBJ, November 26, 1965, in *FRUS 1964–1968*, 25:476–479.

61. Robert Komer to LBJ, November 30, 1965, and transcripts of C. Subramaniam speech, December 7, 1965, both in NSF—Robert Komer Files, LBJL, box 24 (transcripts also appear in Country Files, WBGA, folder 1845052); U.S. Department of State to New Delhi Embassy, December 9, 1965, and Orville Freeman to C. Subramaniam, December 22, 1965, both in *FRUS 1964–1968*, 25:498–499, 520–521; John Prior Lewis to S. Bhoothalingam, December 18, 1965, MEA Records, NAI, WII / 122 / 13 / 66 (the first and last pages of this letter, plus fragments of three others, are contained in this file); B. G. Verghese, "New Agricultural Policy," TOI, December 10, 1965, 8. *Economic Weekly* made only passing note of the speech; see "With Only PL 480," EW, December 11, 1965, 1807–1809.

62. John Prior Lewis to Robert Komer, December 28, 1965, NSF—NSC Histories, LBJL, box 24 (this memorandum is also excerpted in Lewis, *India's Political Economy*, 113–115). Robert Komer to LBJ, November 30, 1965, NSF—Robert Komer Files, LBJL, box 24; Orville Freeman to LBJ, February 3, 1966, USAID Records, USNA, RG286, entry P409, box 23.

63. Robert Komer to John Prior Lewis, January 4, 1966, NSF—Robert Komer Files, LBJL, box 22, emphasis in the original.

64. "Shocking Document Lays Bare Our Abject Surrender to US on Economic Front," *Blitz*, January 8, 1966, 9; C. P. Srivastava, *Lal Bahadur Shastri, Prime Minister of India, 9 June 1964–11 January 1966: A Life of Truth in Politics* (New Delhi: Oxford University Press, 1995), chapter 30; Kuldip Nayar, *India: The Critical Years* (Delhi: Vikas, 1971), 90; TTK quoted in Rabindra Chandra Dutt, *Retreat of Socialism in India: Two Decades without Nehru, 1964–1984* (New Delhi: Abhinav, 1987), 44. Lewis attributed the leak to soon-to-be-ousted finance minister TTK; see Lewis, *India's Political Economy*, 115n19.

65. William S. Gaud, "The Green Revolution—Accomplishment and Apprehensions," March 8, 1968, William S. Gaud Papers, Yale University Library, 3:43.

66. Henry Kissinger conversation with C. Subramaniam, July 7, 1971, CFPF, USNA, RG 59, POL INDIA-US; Robert S. McNamara conversation with C. Subramaniam, November 23, 1968, Robert McNamara Papers, WBGA, folder 1771074; L. K. Jha, "Comment: Leaning against Open Doors?," in *The World Bank Group, Multilateral Aid, and the 1970s*, ed. John Prior Lewis and Ishan Kapur (Lexington, Mass.: Lexington Books, 1973), 97–101.

67. Paarlberg, *Food Trade*, 148.

68. For the text of the declaration, signed on January 10, 1966, see Srivastava, *Lal Bahadur Shastri*, 383–386.

69. K. Kamaraj, quoted in Ramachandra Guha, *India after Gandhi: The History of the World's Largest Democracy* (New York: Ecco, 2007), 389–391, 405–406.

70. Dean Rusk to LBJ, January 28, 1966, and Robert Komer to LBJ, March 27, 1966, both in *FRUS 1964–1968*, 25:549–550, 593–595; New Delhi Embassy to U.S. Department of State, January 19, 1966, NSF—Country Files, LBJL, box 131.

71. Editorial note regarding LBJ telephone conversation with Orville Freeman, and LBJ conversation with B. K. Nehru, February 2, 1966, both in *FRUS 1964–1968*, 25:553–555, 555–560; Chester Bowles journal entry, February 6, 1966, in Chester Bowles, *Promises to Keep: My Years in Public Life, 1941–1969* (New York: Harper & Row, 1971), 534; Chester Bowles to David Bell, March 8, 1965, USAID Records, USNA, RG 286, entry P409, box 6.

72. P. K. Banerjee conversation with Robert Komer, February 4, 1966, MEA Records, NAI, WII/104/18/66; Robert Komer to Chester Bowles, February 9, 1966, NSF—Robert Komer Files, LBJL, box 24, emphasis in the original.

73. George D. Woods to Morarji Desai (draft), February 14, 1966, Country Files, WBGA, folder 1844619.

74. Chester Bowles, "Must India Choose between Growth and Justice?" February 8, 1966, and Chester Bowles, "Differing Indo-American Attitudes on Key Foreign Policy Questions," February 12, 1966, both in NSF—Robert Komer Files, LBJL, box 13; director of the Americas Division conversation with Leonard Weiss, n.d. (March 1966), MEA Records, NAI, WII/102(2)66; LBJ conversation with B. K. Nehru, March 22, 1966, and Dean Rusk to LBJ, March 26, 1966, both in *FRUS 1964–1968*, 25:585–586, 588–589. Rusk communicated this outline to B. K. Nehru a week earlier; see B. K. Nehru to MEA, March 13, 1966, MEA Records, NAI, WI/122(8)/66.

75. P. N. Haksar to Indira Gandhi, February 13, 1966, Indira Gandhi to P. N. Haksar, February 21, 1966, and P. N. Haksar to Indira Gandhi, March 4, 1966, all in P. N. Haksar Papers I–II, NMML, Correspondence: Gandhi; Inder Malhotra, *Indira Gandhi: A Personal and Political Biography* (Boston: Northeastern University Press, 1991), 95.

76. See the meeting summaries in *FRUS 1964–1968*, 25:596–603.

77. "Special Message to the Congress Proposing an Emergency Aid Program for India," March 30, 1966, and LBJ, "Statement by the President upon Signing Resolution Supporting U.S. Participation in Food Relief for India," April 19, 1966, both in *PPP: Lyndon B. Johnson 1966*, 1:366–369, 425–426; David Bell to LBJ, March 29, 1966, USAID Records, USNA, RG286, entry P409, box 23.

78. Robert Komer to LBJ, March 29, 1966, in *FRUS 1964–1968*, 25:605–606; Frankel, *India's Political Economy*, 230, 253. American documents typically referred to Asoka Mehta as Ashok Mehta.

79. U.S. Department of State to New Delhi Embassy, April 6, 1966, Walt Rostow to LBJ, April 18, 1966, and U.S. Department of State to New Delhi Embassy, April 25, 1966, all in *FRUS 1964–1968*, 25:611–612, 614–615, 622–624; B. R. Bell, "Visit of Asoka Mehta," April 11, 1966, Country Files, WBGA, folder 1844619; William J. Handley to Dean Rusk, April 25, 1966, USAID Records, USNA, RG 286, entry P409, box 11; Rostow conversation with Asoka Mehta, April 28, 1966, NSF—Harold Saunders Files, LBJL, box 13.

80. U.S. Department of State to New Delhi, April 24, 1966, USAID Records, USNA, RG 286, entry P409, box 11; LBJ conversation with Asoka Mehta, May 4, 1966, in *FRUS 1964–1968*, 25:637–639.

81. K. S. Sundara Rajan to Bernard R. Bell, May 9, 1966, Country Files, WBGA, file 1844620 (this document was, according to one scholar, "highly classified" in the World Bank for many years; see Denoon, *Devaluation under Pressure*, 75); A. A. Dudley conversation with Asoka Mehta, May 7, 1966, CRO Records, UKNA, DO 189 / 501.

82. Bernard Bell oral history, November 13, 1985, WBGA online, http://oralhistory.worldbank .org/person/bell-bernard-r; Praveen K. Chaudhry, Vijay L. Kelkar, and Vikash Yadav, "The Evolution of 'Homegrown Conditionality' in India-IMF Relations," *Journal of Development Studies* 40:6 (2004): 59–81. British diplomats speculated that Mehta was not authorized to discuss devaluation; see Alan Dudley conversation with Stern, May 6, 1966, CRO Records, UKNA, DO 189 / 501.

83. K. S. Sundara Rajan to Bernard R. Bell, May 9, 1966, Country Files, WBGA, folder 1844620; A. A. Dudley conversation with Mehta, May 7, 1966, CRO Records, UKNA, DO 189 / 501. B. K. Nehru, quoted in David Bell to Dean Rusk, December 29, 1965, USAID Records, USNA, RG286, entry P409, box 23.

84. U.S. Department of State to New Delhi, April 24, 1966, USAID Records, USNA, RG 286, entry P409, box 11; U.S. Department of State / USAID to New Delhi, May 8, 1966, in *FRUS 1964–1968*, 25:644–646; William MacComber to David Bell, May 11, 1966, USAID Records, USNA, RG286, entry P409, box 23; Lewis, *India's Political Economy*, 149.

85. Manmohan Singh, *India's Export Trends and the Prospects for Self-Sustained Growth* (Oxford: Clarendon Press, 1964), 332–335; Jagdish Bhagwati, "The Case for Devaluation," *EW,*

August 4, 1962, 1263–1266; S. Bhoothalingam, *Reflections on an Era: Memoirs of a Civil Servant* (Delhi: Affiliated East-West Press, 1993), 142; George Votaw oral history, April 30, 1985, CCOH, 43; Benjamin B. King oral history, August 14, 1991, WBGA online, http://oralhistory. worldbank.org/person/king-benjamin-b, 3; Oliver, *George Woods,* 134; Frankel, *India's Political Economy,* 287; "Rupee Not to Be Devalued," *TOI,* July 18, 1965, 1–2; D. P. Mishra, *The Post-Nehru Era: Political Memoirs* (New Delhi: Har-Anand Publications, 1993), 36; Nayar, *India,* 91–92; I. G. Patel oral history, March 9, 2001, CCOH, 16; E. A. Midgley conversation with L. K. Jha, March 18, 1966, CRO Records, UKNA, DO 189 / 501.

86. *The International Monetary Fund, 1966–1971: The System under Stress* (Washington, D.C.: International Monetary Fund, 1976), 469–470; K. N. Raj, "Food, Fertilizer, and Foreign Aid," *Mainstream,* April 30, 1965, 10–12, 24; K. S. Krishnaswamy, "Some Influential Contributions," in *A Passionate Humanitarian: V. K. R. V. Rao,* ed. S. L. Rao (New Delhi: Academic Foundation, 2008), 232; Patel, *Glimpses,* 112–113; Jagdish Bhagwati, interview with the author, Cambridge, Mass., July 1, 2011; Chester Bowles to U.S. Department of State, May 31, 1966, CFPF, USNA, RG 59, Ex–Top Secret Files, box 3; David Bell to LBJ, June 10, 1966, NSF—Harold Saunders Files, LBJL, box 13; New Delhi Embassy to U.S. Department of State, June 8, 1966, CFPF, USNA, RG 59, AID(US) 9 INDIA. On the discussion of new rupee values, see Gregory Votaw oral history, April 30, 1985, CCOH, 47.

87. Memorandum to Executive Board, "India—Par Value," June 4, 1966, EBS / 66 / 135, IMF online, http://archivescatalog.imf.org/detail.aspx?parentpriref=125045148; Bhoothalingam, *Reflections on an Era,* 144–145; "Devaluation Decision Taken after Careful Study," *TOI,* June 7, 1966, 11; Kuldip Nayar, *Between the Lines* (Bombay: Allied Publishers, 1969), chapter 3; Indira Gandhi to TTK, June 8, 1966, TTK Papers, NMML, Correspondence: Indira Gandhi; Tridib Kumar Chaudhuri and Bhupesh Gupta to Indira Gandhi, August 30, 1966, PMO Records, NAI, 17(696) / 66-PMS; "Devaluation of the Rupee—Some Questions Answered," June 7, 1966, Asok Mitra Papers, NMML, subject 16; Rahul Mukherji, "India's Aborted Liberalization—1966," *Pacific Affairs* 73:3 (2000): 375–392; New York Consulate-General to MEA, June 29, 1966, MEA Records, NAI, WII / 202 / 7 / 66. For a helpful if partisan overview, see Jagdish N. Bhagwati and T. N. Srinivasan, *Foreign Trade Regimes and Economic Development: India* (New York: Columbia University Press, 1975), chapter 10.

88. B. K. Nehru, paraphrased and quoted in U.S. Department of State to New Delhi Embassy, June 7, 1966, in *FRUS 1964–1968,* 25:668–670; HC-New Delhi to Ministry of Overseas Development, June 10, 1966, CRO Records, UKNA, DO 189 / 501; New Delhi Embassy to U.S. Department of State, June 8, 1966, CFPF, USNA, RG 59, AID(US) 9 INDIA.

89. Dean Rusk to LBJ, March 26, 1966, in *FRUS 1964–1968,* 25:588–589; G. M. Wilson to M. L. Hoffman, April 1, 1966, Country Files, WBGA, folder 1844619.

90. Walt Rostow to LBJ, June 11, 1966, in *FRUS 1964–1968,* 25:677–679; David Bell to LBJ, June 10, 1966, USAID Records, USNA, RG 286, entry P409, box 19.

91. Howard Wriggins to Walt Rostow, July 22, 1966, NSF—Harold Saunders Files, LBJL, box 13; Lewis, *India's Political Economy,* 150–151.

92. Briefing regarding Minister of Finance Sachindra Chaudhuri's visit to Washington, September 26–29, 1966, SD, USNA, RG 59, entry A1-5640, box 3; Bernard Bell quotation as noted by an American diplomat in Paris Embassy to U.S. Department of State, November 8, 1966, CFPF, USNA, RG 59, AID-9; chairman's report of proceedings, India Consortium Meeting, November 7–8, 1966, in Bernard R. Bell Papers, WBGA, folder 1850873; R. Dayal (Paris) to S. Bhoothalingam, November 15, 1966, MEA Records, NAI, WII / 104 / 11 / 66; "India: Policy Memorandum," June 14, 1966, Country Files, WBGA, folder 1844620.

93. Medha Kudaisya, "Developmental Planning in 'Retreat': Ideas, Instruments, and Contestations of Planning in India, 1967–1971," *Modern Asian Studies* 49:3 (2015): 725–726; Morarji Desai to George Woods, January 16, 1968, Country Files, WBGA, folder 1844848.

94. Economic Policy Committee meeting, March 1, 1967, Country Files, WBGA, folder 1837392; chairman's report of proceedings, India Consortium Working Party meeting, March 8–9, 1967, Country Files, WBGA, folder 1844625; annex X to chairman's report of proceedings, India Consortium, April 4–6, 1967, Country Files, WBGA, folder 1844626; chairman's report of proceedings, India Consortium, April 25, 1967, Bernard R. Bell Papers, WBGA, folder 1859873.

95. Meeting of India Consortium heads of delegation, April 6, 1967, Bernard R. Bell Papers, WBGA, folder 1850873. Rostow put a positive spin in this for President Johnson; see Walt Rostow to LBJ, April 8, 1967, in *FRUS 1964–1968*, 25:839–840.

96. George Woods conversation with Morarji Desai, May 1, 1967, and "Proceedings of the Press Conference Held by Mr. George Woods," May 9, 1967, both in Country Files, WBGA, folder 1844844; chairman's report of proceedings, India Consortium, September 7–8, 1967, Country Files, WBGA, folder 1844845.

97. Chairman's report of proceedings, India Consortium, November 13–14, 1967, Bernard R. Bell Papers, WBGA, folder 1850874.

98. Chairman's report of proceedings, India Consortium, March 4–5, 1968, and chairman's report of proceedings, India Consortium, May 23–24, 1968, both in Bernard R. Bell Papers, WBGA, folder 1850875. Chester Bowles to Robert S. McNamara, April 11, 1968, USAID Records, USNA, RG 286, entry P266, box 35; Paul Streeten and Roger Hill, "Aid to India," in *The Crisis of Indian Planning: Economic Planning in the 1960s*, ed. Paul Streeten and Michael Lipton (Oxford: Oxford University Press, 1968), 324; John Prior Lewis and Asoka Mehta quotations as reported in Mary S. Olmsted report on McNamara visit, December 13, 1968, SDR, USNA, RG 59, entry A1-5640, box 6.

99. I. P. M. Cargill conversation with Indian delegation to World Bank, September 13, 1967, Country Files, WBGA, folder 1844845.

100. Benjamin B. King oral history, August 14, 1991, WBGA online, http://oralhistory.worldbank.org/person/king-benjamin-b, 19–20; Morarji Desai to Robert S. McNamara, April 12, 1968, Country Files, WBGA, folder 1844849; New Delhi Embassy to U.S. Department of State, September 24, 1968, CFPF, USNA, RG 59, AID(US)INDIA.

101. I. G. Patel, "How to Give Aid: A Recipient's Point of View (1968)," in *Essays in Economic Policy and Economic Growth* (Basingstoke, England: Macmillan, 1986), 185–194; I. G. Patel, quoted (without citation) in Lewis, *India's Political Economy,* 154–157; I. G. Patel, *Foreign Aid* (Bombay: Allied Publishers, 1968), 23, 27; Patel, *Glimpses,* 127–128; Vijay Joshi and I. M. D. Little, *India: Macroeconomics and Political Economy, 1964–1991* (Washington, D.C.: World Bank, 1994), 75.

102. Harold Wriggins to LBJ, August 24, 1966, Walt Rostow to LBJ, September 15, 1966, Walt Rostow to LBJ, September 26, 1966, Walt Rostow to LBJ, October 15, 1966, Orville Freeman to LBJ, November 7, 1966, editorial notes on LBJ telephone conversations with Orville Freeman, November 10, 1966, and November 27, 1966, and Orville Freeman to LBJ, November 28, 1966, all in *FRUS 1964–1968,* 25:732–751, 758–759, 763–766, 770–772; William S. Gaud to Walt Rostow, October 8, 1966, NSF—Harold Saunders Files, LBJL, box 13; New Delhi Embassy to U.S. Department of State, November 14, 1966, NSF—Walt Rostow Files, LBJL, box 3; William Macomber to Walt Rostow, November 25, 1966, NSF—Harold Saunders Files, LBJL, box 13; Saunders memorandum re LBJ conversation, December 9, 1966, NSF—Harold Saunders Files, LBJL, box 12.

103. John Prior Lewis to Charles L. Schultze and Gardiner Ackley, December 19, 1966, USAID Records, USNA, RG 286, entry P266, box 19; LBJ, "Special Message to the Congress on Food for India and on Other Steps to Be Taken in an International War on Hunger," February 2, 1967, in *PPP: Lyndon B. Johnson 1967,* 1:121–128; N. Firiubin conversation with Kewal Singh, June 21, 1967, AVPRF 090 / 29 / 104 / 4 / 56–57; I. Klimenko to N. Firiubin, July 25, 1967, AVPRF 090 / 29 / 106 / 17 / 33–34; P. N. Haksar to Kewal Singh, August 31, 1967, P. N. Haksar Papers III, NMML, subject 117; P. N. Haksar to B. K. Nehru, May 1967, P. N. Haksar Papers III, NMML, subject 112; Mary S. Olmsted to Arnold, June 19, 1967, SDR, USNA, RG 59, entry A1-5640, box 2.

104. Walt Rostow to LBJ, May 8, 1968, and U.S. Department of State to New Delhi Embassy, October 22, 1967, in *FRUS 1964–1968,* 25:970–974, 908; Orville Freeman and William S. Gaud to LBJ, November 22, 1967, included in "U.S. Agency for International Development," White House Administrative Histories, LBJL, box 2. See also Dean Rusk to LBJ, September 18, 1968, NSF—Harold Saunders Files, LBJL, box 12.

105. LBJ to P. K. Banerjee, February 11, 1969, P. N. Haksar Papers III, NMML, subject 197.

106. TTK conversation with Aleksei Kosygin, November 12, 1965, TTK Papers, NMML, subject 43; "Private Enterpriser," *Time,* February 14, 1955, 30.

8. Soviet Aid from Inspiration to Armory

1. S. Bhoothalingam, *Plain Speaking: Selected Writings on the Indian Economy and Administration* (New Delhi: Affiliated East-West Press, 1994), 1, 9; Andrei Gromyko to Central Committee, April 26, 1964, AVPRF, 090 / 26 / 89 / 17 / 61–69; K. Voroshilov, F. Kozlov, and E. Furtseva to Central Committee, n.d. (February 1960), AVPRF, 090 / 22 / 72 / 19 / 22–37.

2. "Press Communique Issued by the Indian Ministry of Finance," July 30, 1959, in *Soviet-South Asian Relations, 1947–1978,* ed. R. K. Jain (Atlantic Highlands, N.J.: Humanities Press,

1979), 1:264–265. For the projects funded in the agreement of December 10, 1966, see *EA 1974–1975*, 152–155; Val'kov, "Sovetsko-indiiskie politicheskie, ekonomicheskie, i torgovye otnosheniia," August 30, 1961, AVPRF, 090 / 23 / 77 / 20 / 58; S. A. Skachkov to Central Committee, September 12, 1959, RGANI, 5 / 30 / 305 / 122.

3. Stephen Clarkson, *The Soviet Theory of Development: India and the Third World in Marxist-Leninist Scholarship* (Toronto: University of Toronto Press, 1978), chapter 4; A. Kutsenkov, "Vtoroi piatiletnii plan i problemy razvitii vneshnei torgovli Indii," *Vneshniaia torgovlia* 1959:7 (1959): 12–17; "Nekotorye predlozheniia po razvitiiu ekonomicheskikh sviazei SSSR so slaborazvitymi stranami (odobreny ekonomicheskoi sektsii soveshchaniia uchenykh-vostokovedov)," October 29–November 1, 1958, RGANI, 5 / 30 / 272 / 176–186; "Spravka ob ekonomicheskom i tekhnicheskom sotrudnichestve Sovetskogo soiuza so slaborazvitymi v ekonomicheskom otnoshenii stranami," September 7, 1959, RGANI, 5 / 30 / 305 / 123–127.

4. GOI PC, *Third Five Year Plan* (Delhi: Manager of Publications, 1961), 14; Partha Chatterjee, "Development Planning and the Indian State," in *The State and Development Planning in India*, ed. Terence J. Byres (New Delhi: Oxford University Press, 1994), 51–72.

5. V. Rymalov, "Economic Aspects of the Current Stage of the Liberation Revolution," *International Affairs (Moscow)* 1967:5 (1967): 61; K. Voroshilov, F. Kozlov, and E. Furtseva to Central Committee, n.d. (February 1960), AVPRF, 090 / 22 / 72 / 19 / 22–37.

6. S. A. Skachkov to Central Committee, September 7, 1959, RGANI, 5 / 30 / 305 / 120.

7. N. Smelov conversation with S. S. Khera (secretary, Ministry of Production), September 17, 1957, RGAE, 365 / 2 / 65 / 90; S. A. Skachkov conversation with Jawaharlal Nehru, February 13, 1959, RGAE, 365 / 2 / 169 / 12–13; A. I. Mikoian conversation with Morarji Desai, July 7, 1960, summarized in A. I. Mikoian to Central Committee, July 19, 1960, AVPRF, 090 / 22 / 71 / 18 / 45; D. D. Degtiar' conversation with P. C. Mahalanobis, March 29, 1961, RGAE, 365 / 2 / 277 / 93–94; Pitamber Pant, "Soviet Aid for the Fourth Soviet Five-Year Plan," February 8, 1963 (drafted for R. K. Nehru's upcoming trip to Moscow), AVPRF, 090 / 26 / 90 / 19 / 134–149 (the cover note indicates that the report came to the Soviet embassy in New Delhi through CPI comrades, most likely working in the PC); S. A. Skachkov conversation with T. N. Kaul, April 2, 1964, RGAE, 365 / 2 / 454 / 180–182; Aleksei Kosygin conversation with T. N. Kaul, February 22, 1965, AVPRF, 090 / 27 / 95 / 16 / 8–12; "Non-project Imports from USSR," n.d. (May 1965?), RGAE, 365 / 2 / 2169 / 56–81; "Economic Cooperation, 1966–1971," n.d. (fall 1965), TTK Papers, NMML, subject 43, emphasis in the original.

8. "Erection of Oil Refineries," *TOI*, November 30, 1951, 7; "Centre of World Oil Industry," *TOI*, December 29, 1951, 4; B. C. Roy to Jawaharlal Nehru, February 27, 1952, Cabinet Secretariat Records, NAI, 9(5)ECC / 52; H. N. Kaul, *K. D. Malaviya and the Evolution of India's Oil Policy* (New Delhi: Allied Publishers, 1991), 6–14.

9. R. Vedavalli, *Private Foreign Investment and Economic Development: A Case Study of Petroleum in India* (Cambridge: Cambridge University Press, 1976), 123–124; C. C. Desai, "Looking Back at the Controversial Refinery Agreements," in *India Petroleum* (New Delhi: Lifeline Publications, 1963), 73–75; Kaul, *K. D. Malaviya*, 40 (quoting K. D. Malaviya to Jawaharlal Nehru, February 16, 1954), 95–97, 103. On S. S. Bhatnagar in Malaviya's ministry,

see K. D. Malaviya to Jawaharlal Nehru, July 13, 1954, and Jawaharlal Nehru note, August 18, 1955, both in K. D. Malaviya Papers, NMML, Correspondence: J. Nehru.

10. Kaul, *K. D. Malaviya*, 55–56; Vedavalli, *Private Foreign Investment*, 147–49; J. H. Bamberg, *The History of the British Petroleum Company* (Cambridge: Cambridge University Press, 1994), 113.

11. Delegation brief, n.d. (August 1955?), K. D. Malaviya Papers, NMML, subject 49; K. D. Malaviya trip report, October 20, 1955, and Rajeshwar Dayal report, November 1, 1955, both in K. D. Malaviya Papers, NMML, subject 74.

12. K. D. Malaviya undated notes (late 1955), in K. D. Malaviya Papers, NMML, subject 74; Kaul, *K. D. Malaviya*, 61–62; K. D. Malaviya to Jawaharlal Nehru, December 16, 1955, V. T. Krishnamachari to Jawaharlal Nehru, March 17, 1956, and K. D. Malaviya to Jawaharlal Nehru, April 13, 1956, all in K. D. Malaviya Papers, NMML, subject 77.

13. A. I. Mikoian conversation with K. D. Malaviya, March 27, 1956, GARF, R-5446/120/143/7–20; Kaul, *K. D. Malaviya*, 57, 62.

14. W. L. Mellon (Gulf Oil), quoted in Kaul, *K. D. Malaviya*, 63; "Otchet za dekiabr' mesiats i za ves' 1957 god," RGAE, 365/2/1275/19; W. Schott and G. Richter-Bernberg report, April 16, 1957, and Ministry of Mines and Oil officials' conversation with Messrs. Moulin and Trumpy, November 30, 1957, both in K. D. Malaviya Papers, NMML, subject 79.

15. S. N. Visvanath, *A Hundred Years of Oil: A Narrative Account of the Search for Oil in India* (New Delhi: Vikas, 1989), 103; Swaran Singh conversation with Sinclair, August 29, 1957, K. D. Malaviya Papers, NMML, subject 83; Malcolm MacDonald to Gilbert Laithwaite, May 17, 1957, and Gilbert Laithwaite to M. MacDonald, July 16, 1957, both in CRO Records, UKNA, DO 35/5769; TTK to K. D. Malaviya, July 31, 1957, K. D. Malaviya Papers, NMML, subject 77. This episode is recounted from the perspective of the Seven Sisters in Michael Tanzer, *The Political Economy of International Oil and the Underdeveloped Countries* (Boston: Beacon Press, 1969), part 2.

16. Swaran Singh conversation with N. A. Kalinin, December 20, 1957, K. D. Malaviya Papers, NMML, subject 79; N. A. Kalinin conversation with Swaran Singh, December 20, 1957, and Tagiev, "Doklad i rekomendatsii po rabote gosudarstvennoi komissii po nefti i prirodnomy gazy pravitel'stva Indii," July 28, 1958, both in RGAE, 365/2/1275/3–6, 116–138; K. D. Malaviya to Jawaharlal Nehru, n.d. (1958), K. D. Malaviya Papers, NMML, subject 85; K. D. Malaviya diary entry, August 14, 1958, K. D. Malaviya Papers, NMML, subject 86; Kaul, *K. D. Malaviya*, 80.

17. K. D. Malaviya diary entry, June 1959, K. D. Malaviya Papers, NMML, subject 86; A. G. Sheremet'ev conversation with K. P. S. Menon, April 21, 1959, S. A. Skachkov conversation with K. P. S. Menon, August 3, 1959, and S. A. Skachkov conversation with K. P. S. Menon, November 16, 1959, all in RGAE, 365/2/169/19–20, 36–38, 93–96. "Spravka po voprosu tsen na burovye ustanovki tipa Uralmash 3D i Uralmash 5D," May 6, 1959, S. S. Khera, quoted in Antropov conversation with Swaran Singh, May 29, 1959, and "Pamiatka voprosov, podlezhashchikh razresheniiu v Goskomitete i v V/O Tekhnoeksport," March 12, 1960, all in RGAE, 365/2/1994/11–13, 102, 30–31; "Stenogramma soveshchaniia v GKES o

nepoladkakh v razvedke nefti i gaza v Indii v sviazi s pis'mom Menona," November 26, 1959, and excerpts from N. A. Kalinin to Minister of Geology Antropov, n.d. (mid-1959?), both in RGAE, 365 / 2 / 2012 / 65; EA 1977–1978, annexure 21; "Press Communique Issued by the Indian Ministry of Finance on Soviet Credit of 1500 Million Roubles (Rs. 180 crores)," July 30, 1959, in Jain, ed., *Soviet–South Asian Relations*, 1:264–265.

18. K. D. Malaviya diary entries, March 3, 1959 and November 16, 1959, both in K. D. Malaviya Papers, NMML, subject 86; V. T. Krishnamachari to K. D. Malaviya, May 5, 1958, K. D. Malaviya Papers, NMML, subject 77.

19. K. D. Malaviya diary entry, February 2, 1959, K. D. Malaviya Papers, NMML, subject 86; "Ekonomicheskoe polozhenie i vneshnie ekonomicheskie sviazi Indii," February 9, 1960, RGAE, 365 / 2 / 2017 / 20–33; V. I. Likhachev to N. Firiubin, April 21, 1960, AVPRF, 090 / 22 / 72 / 25 / 89–90; Morarji Desai to K. D. Malaviya, August 4, 1960, K. D. Malaviya Papers, NMML, subject 83.

20. I. A. Benediktov, quoted in *Free Press Journal* (Bombay), December 2, 1960, quoted in Kaul, *K. D. Malaviya*, 171; I. Popov, "Spravka: Sovetsko-indiiskoe sotrudnichestvo v razvitii neftiannoi promyshlennosti Indii," January 14, 1961, AVPRF, 090 / 23 / 77 / 20 / 9–17; Vedavalli, *Private Foreign Investment*, 28n29; K. D. Malaviya to Morarji Desai, July 29, 1960, K. D. Malaviya Papers, NMML, subject 83; Marshall I. Goldman, *Soviet Foreign Aid* (New York: Praeger, 1967), 96–97. On Malaviya's trip, see ONGC, "Report of the Delegation Led by K. D. Malaviya," January 1961, MEA Records, NAI, 13(47)EurE / 60.

21. Vedavalli, *Private Foreign Investment*, 19 (describing Eugene R. Black letter, quoted in *Commerce*, May 6, 1961), 47; S. S. Khera, *Oil: Rich Man, Poor Man* (New Delhi: National, 1979), 187, 67; "Minister Deplores Oil Firms' Stand," TOI, November 21, 1961, 9; S. S. Khera conversation with V. S. Romanov, cited in S. A. Skachkov to A. I. Mikoian, November 2, 1961, AVPRF, 090 / 23 / 77 / 20 / 108; "Sobrazheniia MVT po voprosam sovetsko-indiiskikh torgovykh otnoshenii dlia vkliucheniia v pamiatku," n.d. (1961), AVPRF, 090 / 23 / 77 / 18 / 117–118; "Centre May Seek Russian Products," TOI, November 17, 1961, 1; "No Nationalisation of Oil Companies," TOI, December 2, 1961, 1; "Impasse May Be Resolved," TOI, November 21, 1961, 1; Kaul, *K. D. Malaviya*, 230–233. While I was not able to obtain a copy of the full report of the so-called Damle Committee, press coverage quoted from it extensively; see "More Light on Oil Pricing," EW, October 21, 1961, 1627–1628; "Oil Firms Should Not Insist on Source of Crude," TOI, October 4, 1961, 7; Kaul, *K. D. Malaviya*, 225–229.

22. V. A. Sergeev conversation with R. Jaipal, April 16, 1963, RGAE, 365 / 2 / 396 / 7; S. A. Skachkov conversation with R. K. Nehru, AVPRF, 090 / 25 / 85 / 14 / 4–7; P. E. Volkov to R. Jaipal, October 1963; N. M. Siluianov to V. A. Sergeev, December 9, 1963. "K peregovorom s Kuveitom o sotrudnichestve v oblasti neftiannoi promyshlennosti," February 3, 1964, and Besoslov to V. A. Sergeev, August 28, 1964, all in RGAE, 365 / 2 / 2120 / 2, 5, 25, 100; F. V. Pavlov conversation with N. N. Kash'ian, February 17, 1966, and Soviet specialists' conversation with O. S. Alagezan and P. R. Naik, March 3, 1966, both in RGAE, 365 / 2 / 2204 / 11, 20; P. N. Haksar to D. P. Dhar, June 4, 1969, Haksar Papers III, NMML, subject 140.

23. GOI PC, *Report of the Working Group on Energy Policy* (New Delhi: Planning Commission, 1979), 4, 74. By the 1970s, over 98 percent of refinery capacity was in the public sector.

24. Ajit Mitra, "Soviet Collaboration in Development of Oil Industry in India," in *Indo-Soviet Cooperation and India's Economic Development*, ed. R. K. Sharma (New Delhi: Allied Publishers, 1982), 90; Clarkson, *Soviet Theory*, 171–177.

25. *EA 1974–1975*, 150–153.

26. "Materialy besedy mezhdu sovetskimi and indiiskimi ekspertami otnositel'no stroitel'stva zavoda tiazhelogo elektrooborudovaniia," May 4, 1961, RGAE, 365 / 2 / 2055 / 18; B. S. Romanov conversation with Rao, May 22, 1965, RGAE, 365 / 2 / 2142 / 9–10.

27. Jawaharlal Nehru to TTK, January 29, 1957, in *SWJN2*, 36:176; B. G. Verghese, "Machine Building in Two Stages," *TOI*, February 7, 1957, 1; "Meeting Demand for Plant and Machinery," *TOI*, February 23, 1957, 1; Manubhai Shah to S. A. Skachkov, March 13, 1961, RGAE, 365 / 2 / 291 / 8–10.

28. Kedarnath Prasad, *Economics of Industrialization* (New Delhi: Sarup and Sons, 2004), 396–397. B. S. Romanov conversation with Krishnamurthy, May 5, 1964, RGAE, 365 / 2 / 2142 / 9–10; I. A. Benediktov conversation with C. Subramaniam, October 29, 1963, AVPRF, 90 / 25 / 48 / 6 / 99–101; O. N. Misra to P. S. Besolov, July 16, 1964, RGAE, 365 / 2 / 2124 / 68–72; A. I. Mikoian conversation with TTK, June 20, 1964, AVPRF, 090 / 26 / 89 / 17 / 79–83; GOI PC, *Programmes of Industrial Development, 1956–61* (New Delhi: Planning Commission, 1956), chapter 4.

29. Peter Lande to Daniel Patrick Moynihan, October 31, 1973, Daniel Patrick Moynihan Papers, LC, 372:4; C. Subramaniam, *Hand of Destiny: Memoirs* (Bombay: Bharatiya Vidya Bhavan, 1993), 2:34; "Bokaro with Soviet Aid," *EW*, May 9, 1964, 796; L. K. Jha, quoted in A. I. Mikoian conversation with TTK, June 20, 1964, AVPRF, 090 / 26 / 89 / 17 / 79–83.

30. N. M. Silianov conversation with S. Subramaniam, May 7, 1964, S. A. Skachkov conversation with T. N. Kaul, July 24, 1964, and M. N. Dastur to Sanjiv Reddy, December 3, 1964, all in RGAE, 365 / 2 / 2121 / 29, 77–81, 131–136; B. S. Romanov conversation with Krishnamurthy, May 5, 1964, RGAE, 365 / 2 / 2142 / 9–10; A. I. Mikoian conversation with TTK, June 20, 1964, AVPRF, 090 / 26 / 89 / 17 / 79–83; N. R. Srinivasan, *The History of Bokaro* (Bokaro Steel City: Steel Authority of India, Inc., 1988), 11–12; Ross Knox Bassett, *The Technological Indian* (Cambridge: Massachusetts Institute of Technology Press, 2016), 202–210; Pitamber Pant, "Bokaro Steel Project," October 26, 1961, CIS Records, MIT, 11:19; "An Inferiority Complex," *TOI*, December 1, 1964, 8; S. A. Skachkov to Council of Ministers, December 4, 1964, RGAE, 365 / 2 / 507 / 186–196; "Less Scope for Dastur & Co.," *TOI*, October 4, 1964, 12; Indira Gandhi to T. N. Kaul, May 13, 1966, T. N. Kaul Papers I-III, Correspondence: Indira Gandhi; New Delhi Embassy to U.S. Department of State, June 16, 1966, CFPF, USNA, RG 59, AID 9.

31. "Vystuplenie predstavitelia Uralmashzavoda na soveshchanii v otdele IuVA GKES," June 3, 1963, and I. Naidich to V. N. Pashin, July 31, 1967, RGAE, 365 / 2 / 2261 / 94–95, 65; "Godovoi otchet o rabote predstavitel'stva general'nogo postavshchika i gruppy avtorskogo nadzora na stroitel'stve metallurgicheskogo zavoda v Bokaro za 1967 g.," December 1967, RGAE, 365 / 2 / 2263 / 3; O. M. Grigor'ev conversation with K. N. George, November 27, 1967,

RGAE, 365 / 2 / 2262 / 151; S. A. Skachkov conversation with Kewal Singh, August 2, 1967, RGAE, 365 / 2 / 2245 / 22–28.

32. V. M. Eremenko, "Otchet o komandirovka v Indiiu glavnogo inzhenera proekta instituta Energoset'proekt," November 14–December 13, 1966, and O. M. Grigor'ev conversation with K. N. George, November 24, 1967, both in RGAE, 365 / 2 / 2262 / 137–141, 146.

33. "HEC Can Fabricate Steel Plant," TOI, June 16, 1965, 1; N. M. Pegov and V. N. Pashin conversation with Ali Ahmed, December 8, 1967, and S. A. Skachkov conversation with K. N. George, August 16, 1967, both in RGAE, 365 / 2 / 2245 / 125, 62; "Godovoi otchet o rabote predstavitel'stva general'nogo postavshchika i gruppy avtorskgo nadzora na stroitel'stve metallurgicheskogo zavoda v Bokaro za 1967 g.," December 1967, RGAE, 365 / 2 / 2263 / 7–8.

34. EA 1977–1978, annexure 21.

35. S. A. Skachkov conversation with P. C. Sethi, December 13, 1968, RGAE, 365 / 2 / 708 / 1–6; Padma Desai, The Bokaro Steel Plant: A Study of Soviet Economic Assistance (Amsterdam: North-Holland Publishing, 1972), 43; "Delays in Supply of HEC Units to Bokaro Admitted," TOI, November 22, 1968, 12; "Bokaro Delay until 1973 Forecast," Statesman, December 23, 1968, 1, 16; A. S. Eroian, "Otchet o stroitel'stve metallurgicheskogo zavoda v g. Bokaro Indiia za 1968 g," February 7, 1969, RGAE, 365 / 2 / 2306 / 1–4, 67.

36. N. I. Konstantinov conversation with N. N. Wanchoo, December 10, 1968, RGAE, 365 / 2 / 708 / 15–22. A useful chronology—without reference to original plans—appears in Srinivasan, History of Bokaro, 153; a useful comparison of planned and actual benchmarks is available in M. N. Dastur, Purchase of Capital Goods and Technology in the Iron and Steel Sector: The Case of Bokaro, India (New York: United Nations Conference on Trade and Development, 1978), 16.

37. "Swadeshi Steel," TOI, October 30, 1965, 6; Dastur, Purchase of Capital Goods, 5, annex 3. Information in this paragraph derived from the data in Srinivasan, History of Bokaro, 30.

38. GOI Administrative Reforms Commission, Report on Public Sector Undertakings (New Delhi: Manager of Publications, 1967), 11, 29; K. Hanumanthaiya, quoted in "ARC Urges Regrouping of Govt. Projects," TOI, October 21, 1967, 11; Romesh Thapar, "The Backlash—Now and in the Future," EPW, May 25, 1968, 802; Francine R. Frankel, India's Political Economy, 1947–1977: The Gradual Revolution (Princeton, N.J.: Princeton University Press, 1978), 307.

39. Medha Kudaisya, "Developmental Planning in 'Retreat': Ideas, Instruments, and Contestations of Planning in India, 1967–1971," Modern Asian Studies 49:3 (2015): 717–722; "Revitalise the Planning Commission," and D. K. Rangnekar, "Second Thoughts on Indian Planning," both in EPW, February 1967, annual number, 89–91, 273–278; A. H. Hanson, "Power Shifts and Regional Balances," in The Crisis of Indian Planning: Economic Planning in the 1960s, ed. Paul Streeten and Michael Lipton (Oxford: Oxford University Press, 1968), 47–48; GOI Administrative Reforms Commission, Report: Machinery for Planning (New Delhi: Manager of Publications, 1968), i; Medha M. Kudaisya, " 'Reforms by Stealth': Indian Economic Policy, Big Business and the Promise of the Shastri Years, 1964–1966," South Asia 25:2 (2002): 205–229; Akhil Gupta and K. Sivaramakrishnan, "Introduction: The State in India after Liberalization," in The State in India after Liberalization: Interdisciplinary

Perspectives, ed. Akhil Gupta and K. Sivaramakrishnan (New York: Routledge, 2011), 7–8; Rabindra Chandra Dutt, *Retreat of Socialism in India: Two Decades without Nehru, 1964–1984* (New Delhi: Abhinav Publications, 1987), 64–65; GOI PC, *Fourth Five Year Plan, 1969–74* (New Delhi: Manager of Publications, 1970), 54–57; Frankel, *India's Political Economy*, 250, 308–312, 268–269.

40. Paul R. Brass, *The Politics of India since Independence*, 2nd ed. (Cambridge: Cambridge University Press, 1994), 278.

41. S. A. Skachkov to Central Committee, July 17, 1961, RGANI, 5 / 30 / 371 / 191–208; R. A. Ul'ianovskii, quoted in "Stenogramma diskussii: Bor'ba dvukh sistem i osobennosti sotsial'no-ekonomicheskogo razvitiia osvobodivshikhsia stran," May 13, 1963, ARAN, 1978 / 1 / 134 / 4–5; R. A. Ul'ianovskii, "Sotsializm, kapitalizm, slaborazvitye strany (1)," *Mirovaia ekonomika i mezhdunarodnaia otnosheniia* 1964: 4 (1964): 119; V. Rymalov, "The Social Preconditions for Economic Independence," *International Affairs (Moscow)* 9:6 (1963): 19–24.

42. "Doklad prezidiuma TsK KPSS na oktiabr'skom plenume TsK KPSS," n.d. (not later than October 13, 1964), in *Nikita Khrushchev. Stenogrammy plenuma TsK KPSS i drugie dokumenty*, ed. A. N. Artizov (Moscow: Mezhdunarodnyi fond "Demokratiia," 2007), 200; B. Gafurov to Leonid Brezhnev, March 12, 1966, RGANI, 5 / 30 / 489 / 149; I. Beliaev and F. Burlitskii, "V poiskakh reshenii," *Pravda*, May 29, 1966, 4.

43. George R. Feiwel, *The Soviet Quest for Economic Efficiency: Issues, Controversies and Reforms* (New York: Frederick A. Praeger, 1967), chapters 5–6; Abraham Katz, *The Politics of Economic Reform in the Soviet Union* (New York: Frederick A. Praeger, 1972), chapters 8–9; Jerry F. Hough, *The Soviet Prefects: The Local Party Organs in Industrial Decision-Making* (Cambridge, Mass.: Harvard University Press, 1969).

44. E. Dundukova to V. N. Novikov, May 19, 1965, RGAE, 365 / 2 / 508 / 5; "Summary Record of Discussions during the visit of Finance Minister, India to the USSR from the 9th to the 17th November, 1965," TTK Papers, NMML, subject 43; overview (including discussion of S. A. Skachkov trip) in L. Eiranov to M. A. Maksimov, May 7, 1967, AVPRF, 090 / 29 / 106 / 17 / 25–29; I. I. Egorov, "Otchet o komandirovke v Indiiu," March 6–June 26, 1968, ARAN, 579 / 2 / 243 / 98–116; G. P. Semenov conversation with Ali Ahmed, March 11, 1968, and N. M. Pegov conversation with Ali Ahmed, March 20, 1968, both in RGAE, 365 / 2 / 2298 / 49, 66–67.

45. "Skachkov in Delhi: Talks on Trade," TOI, November 28, 1968, 4; P. N. Haksar note, December 18, 1968, Haksar Papers III, NMML, subject 138; I. A. Benediktov conversation with P. R. Naik (ONGC), February 8, 1964, AVPRF, 90 / 26 / 52 / 6 / 39–40; D. R. Gadgil recalled in Kuldip Nayar, *Between the Lines* (Bombay: Allied Publishers, 1969), 126; S. A. Skachkov conversation with Fakhruddin Ali Ahmed, December 10, 1968, RGAE, 365 / 2 / 708 / 10–14; Skachkov, for instance, complained that wages at Bhilai were too low compared with competing private firms; see S. A. Skachkov to Swaran Singh, March 9, 1961, RGAE, 365 / 2 / 291 / 3.

46. P. N. Haksar note, December 16, 1968, Haksar Papers III, NMML, subject 138; S. A. Skachkov conversation with Soviet specialists at Bhilai, December 6, 1968, S. A. Skachkov

conversation with Morarji Desai, December 6, 1968, S. A. Skachkov conversation with N. N. Wanchoo, December 10, 1968, and S. A. Skachkov conversation with Ali Ahmed, December 10, 1968, all in RGAE, 365 / 2 / 708 / 36–41, 23–27, 10–14, 15–22; "Soviet Aided Projects: More Autonomy Suggested," TOI, December 11, 1968, 13.

47. Isher Judge Ahluwalia, *Industrial Growth in India: Stagnation since the Mid-Sixties* (New Delhi: Oxford University Press, 1985), 109; N. N. Wanchoo meeting with representatives of Bokaro Steel, December 10, 1968, S. A. Skachkov conversation with K. V. R. Reddi, December 2, 1968, and S. A. Skachkov conversation with Minister of Steel Sethi, December 13, 1968, all in RGAE, 365 / 2 / 708 / 15–22, 41–45, 1–6.

48. V. A. Sergeev to A. I. Alikhanov, July 1970, RGAE, 365 / 9 / 578 / 70–105; I. K. Mineev conversation with Damodaran, October 24, 1972, RGAE, 365 / 9 / 1081 / 37–39. For a broader consideration, see I. I. Egorov, "Ekonomicheskaia effektivnost' gosudarstvennogo sektora v Indii: ee faktory i puti povysheniia," in *Ekonomicheskaia politika i gosudarstvennyi kapitalizm v stranakh vostoka*, ed. A. I. Levkovskii (Moscow: Nauka, 1972), 179–207.

49. "Malaviya's Appointment Defended by Minister," TOI, May 1, 1968, 6; "Malaviya Quits as HEC Chief," TOI, January 14, 1969, 13; Krasnoperov conversation with K. D. Malaviya, December 9, 1968, RGAE, 365 / 2 / 2298 / 161–162.

50. D. R. Gadgil to D. S. Joshi, February 1, 1968 (re conversation with Aleksei Kosygin, January 30, 1968), Haksar Papers III, NMML, subject 128; Indira Gandhi to Fakhruddin Ali Ahmed, n.d. (re letter of April 30, 1968), Haksar Papers III, NMML, subject 131; N. M. Trufanov conversation with O. Mirs, December 11, 1968, S. A. Skachkov conversation with Fakhruddin Ali Ahmed, December 10, 1968, S. A. Skachkov conversation with K. D. Malaviya, November 30, 1968, and S. A. Skachkov conversation with Minister of Commerce Dinesh Singh, November 29, 1968, all in RGAE, 365 / 2 / 708 / 7–9, 10–12, 46–51, 56–59; Robert H. Donaldson, "The Second World, the Third World, and the New International Economic Order," in *The Soviet Union in the Third World: Successes and Failures*, ed. Robert H. Donaldson (Boulder, Colo.: Westview Press, 1981), 377.

51. Moiseenko conversation with Vaidyanathan, March 14, 1961; and Val'kov, "Sovetsko-indiiskie politicheskie, ekonomicheskie, i torgovye otnosheniia," August 30, 1961, both in AVPRF, 090 / 23 / 77 / 20 / 30, 61; P. A. Maletin conversation with K. B. Dall, October 29, 1958, RGAE, 365 / 2 / 1955 / 73–74; briefing for K. E. Voroshilov, F. R. Kozlov, and E. A. Furtseva, December 31, 1959, RGANI, 5 / 30 / 301 / 256. This "clearing basis" (*sbalansirovannaia osnova*) was endorsed, for instance, in G. Velikii to Central Committee, April 8, 1959, RGANI, 5 / 30 / 306 / 220.

52. R. A. Ul'ianovskii, "Agrarnye reformy v stranakh blizhnego i srednogo vostoka, Indii, i iugo-vostochno Azii," *Narody Azii i Afriki* 1961:2 (1961): 15–16. For one element of this international socialist division of labor, see Michael Charles Kaser, *Comecon: Integration Problems of the Planned Economies* (Oxford: Oxford University Press, 1965).

53. Santosh K. Mehrotra and Patrick Clawson, "Soviet Economic Relations with India and Other Third World Countries," EPW, August 1, 1979, 1369; Sumitra Chishti, *India's Trade with East Europe* (New Delhi: Indian Institute of Foreign Trade, 1973); Nita Watts and Asha Datar,

"The Development of India's Trade with the Soviet Union and Eastern Europe," *Bulletin of the Oxford Institute of Economics and Statistics* 30:1 (1968): 13, 19; A. Kodachenko, "An Important Form of Economic Cooperation," *International Affairs (Moscow)* 8:2 (1962): 36–43.

54. See the agreement of December 20, 1968, in RGAE, 413 / 13 / 7564 / 65. "Russian Help to Market Plants," *TOI*, December 20, 1968, 1; "A Helping Hand," *TOI*, December 25, 1968, 10; I. Temirsky, "Moscow and Delhi," *New Times*, February 5, 1969, 10–11; Aleksei Kosygin to T. N. Kaul, May 25, 1970, Haksar Papers III, NMML, subject 276.

55. The information in this paragraph comes from various annual editions of *VTSSSR*.

56. V. Spandar'ian, "Spravka ob uchastii gosudarstvennogo i chastnogo sektora ekonomicheski slaborazvitykh stran Azii i Afriki v torgovle s Sovetskim Soiuzom," June 15, 1961, RGANI, 5 / 30 / 371 / 148.

57. W. L. Allison to A. A. Duff, November 10, 1965, Foreign Office Records, UKNA, FO 181 / 1182; M. Rajan Menon, "The Military and Security Dimensions of Soviet-Indian Relations," in Donaldson, ed., *Soviet Union in the Third World*, 232–250; Indo-Soviet military agreements tracked in L. Bruce Laingen to John F. L. Ghiardi, January 30, 1974, SDR, USNA, RG 59, entry A1-5640, box 21; Matthew van Order to David A. Schneider, May 27, 1970, SDR, USNA, RG 59, entry A1-5640, box 13; U.S. Central Intelligence Agency, *Communist Aid Activities in Non-Communist Less Developed Countries 1978* (Washington, D.C.: Central Intelligence Agency, 1978), table 4. The arms transfer data come from Stockholm International Peace Research Institute, SIPRI Arms Transfer Database, https://www.sipri.org /databases/armstransfers.

58. "Summary Record of Discussions during the Visit of Finance Minister, India to the USSR from the 9th to the 17th November 1965," and TTK conversation with Aleksei Kosygin, November 12, 1965, both in TTK Papers, NMML, subject 43.

59. U.S. Central Intelligence Agency, Directorate of Intelligence, *Third World Debt Service to the USSR,* Intelligence Report 70-2 (February 1970), table 6, DDRS, CK234940299; U.S. Central Intelligence Agency, *Communist Aid Activities in the Non-Communist Less Developed Countries, 1979 and 1954–1979* (Washington, D.C.: Central Intelligence Agency, 1979), tables A1, A5.

60. Frankel, *India's Political Economy,* 315.

9. India's Double Crisis and the Price of Aid

1. Indira Gandhi conversation with William S. Rogers, October 24, 1970, P. N. Haksar Papers III, NMML, subject 255. William S. Rogers conversation with Indira Gandhi, October 24, 1970, in *FRUS 1969–1976,* E-7, no. 88.

2. Lloyd I. Rudolph and Susanne Hoeber Rudolph, *In Pursuit of Lakshmi: The Political Economy of the Indian State* (Chicago: University of Chicago Press, 1987), 223; Vijay Joshi and I. M. D. Little, *India: Macroeconomics and Political Economy, 1964–1991* (Washington, D.C.: World Bank, 1994), 17–24. See especially the statistical annexes in GOI Ministry of Finance, *Economic Survey, 1975–76* (New Delhi: Government of India, 1976).

3. Atul Kohli, *Democracy and Discontent: India's Growing Crisis of Governability* (Cambridge: Cambridge University Press, 1990); Atul Kohli, *State-Directed Development: Political Power and Industrialization in the Global Periphery* (Cambridge: Cambridge University Press, 2004), esp. 121–122; Rudolph and Rudolph, *In Pursuit of Lakshmi*, 224.

4. Francine R. Frankel, *India's Political Economy, 1947–1977: The Gradual Revolution* (Princeton, N.J.: Princeton University Press, 1978), 388; Jagdish N. Bhagwati and Padma Desai, *India, Planning for Industrialization: Industrialization and Trade Policies since 1951* (Oxford: Oxford University Press, 1970), chapter 9.

5. Michael Brecher, *Nehru's Mantle: The Politics of Succession in India* (New York: Praeger, 1966), chapter 2; Ramachandra Guha, *India after Gandhi: The History of the World's Largest Democracy* (New York: Ecco, 2007), 406.

6. New Delhi Embassy to U.S. Department of State, June 2, 1966, NSF—Country Files, LBJL, box 131; Kuldip Nayar, *India: The Critical Years* (Delhi: Vikas, 1971), 92; Guha, *India after Gandhi*, 411; Kuldip Nayar, *Between the Lines* (Bombay: Allied Publishers, 1969), 92–94; "Decline of Indira's Government," *EPW*, September 3, 1966, 109–110; D. P. Mishra, *The Post-Nehru Era: Political Memoirs* (New Delhi: Har-Anand Publications, 1993), 38.

7. H. N. Bahuguna, "Introduction," in *The Great Upheaval, 1969–1972: The Case of the Indian National Congress in Ferment, Based on Documents Emanating from Official Sources,* ed. A. Moin Zaidi (New Delhi: Orientalia, 1972), xxiii; Baldev Raj Nayar, *India's Mixed Economy: The Role of Ideology and Interest in Its Development* (Bombay: Popular Prakashan, 1989), 262. On the Congress system, see especially Rajni Kothari, "India: The Congress System on Trial," *Asian Survey* 72 (1967): 83–96; Rajni Kothari, "Continuity and Change in India's Party System," *Asian Survey* 10:1111 (1970): 937–948; and Rajni Kothari, "The Political Change of 1967," *EPW*, January 1971, annual number, 231–250.

8. AICC Resolution on the Ten-Point Program, June 25, 1967, and speeches by S. Nijalingappa and Indira Gandhi, April 29, 1967, all in Zaidi, *Great Upheaval*, 65–67, 67–73; Frankel, *India's Political Economy.*

9. Nayar, *India*, 67; Guha, *India after Gandhi*, 436–437; Inder Malhotra, *Indira Gandhi: A Personal and Political Biography* (Boston: Northeastern University Press, 1991), 116; Indira Gandhi, notes on economic policy, July 8, 1969, and general July correspondence, all in Zaidi, *Great Upheaval*, 81–84, 92–102. See also Morarji R. Desai, *The Story of My Life* (Oxford: Pergamon Press, 1979), 2:313–318. Similar advice came from Romesh Thapar; see his wife's memoir: Raj Thapar, *All These Years: A Memoir* (New Delhi: Seminar Publications, 1991), 311–312. C. Subramaniam, among others, depicted the intraparty battles in these terms; see Frankel, *India's Political Economy*, 427, 432–433.

10. Extract from Indira Gandhi's speech at the Seventy-Second Session of Congress, April 27, 1969, in Zaidi, *Great Upheaval*, 71–73; "The Politics of Steel," *EPW*, August 8, 1970, 1326–1327; Keshabananda Das, "Politics of Industrial Location: Indian Federalism and Development Decisions," *EPW*, December 20–26, 1997, 3268–3274; Guha, *India after Gandhi*, 438.

11. Nayar, *India's Mixed Economy,* 245. See also Sudipta Kaviraj, "A State of Contradictions: The Post-Colonial State in India," in *The Imaginary Institution of India: Politics and Ideas* (New York: Columbia University Press, 2010), 224–225.

12. For Indian protests see, for instance, Ts. M. Vinogradov conversation with Kewal Singh, August 19, 1967, Ia. A. Malik conversation with Kewal Singh, September 2, 1967, and Andrei Gromyko conversation with Swaran Singh, September 14, 1967, all in AVPRF, 090 / 29 / 104 / 4 / 65, 68–70, 71–81. Arms transfer data in this chapter come from Stockholm International Peace Research Institute, SIPRI Arms Transfer Database, https://www.sipri .org/databases/armstransfers.

13. D. P. Dhar conversation with Andrei Grechko, March 21, 1969, and report on Indo-Soviet Relations and Pakistan, March 21, 1969, both in P. N. Haksar Papers III, NMML, subject 206; R. Bandari to D. P. Dhar after conversation with Ambassador Pegov, March 27, 1969, D. P. Dhar to Kewal Singh, March 31, 1969, and T. N. Kaul note regarding D. P. Dhar conversation with the foreign minister, April 7, 1969, all in P. N. Haksar Papers III, NMML, subject 203; P. N. Haksar to Indira Gandhi, April 7, 1969, P. N. Haksar Papers I–II, NMML, subject 41; P. N. Haksar note, May 5, 1969, and P. N. Haksar note, May 31, 1969, related to D. P. Dhar letter of May 22, 1969, both in P. N. Haksar Papers III, NMML, subject 139; Indira Gandhi conversation with Aleksei Kosygin, May 6, 1969, P. N. Haksar Papers III, NMML, subject 140.

14. P. N. Haksar note, September 10, 1969, P. N. Haksar Papers III, NMML, subject 203; P. N. Haksar note, March 9, 1971, P. N. Haksar Papers III, NMML, subject 164; P. N. Haksar to D. P. Dhar, February 25, 1971, P. N. Haksar Papers III, NMML, subject 167, emphasis in the original. The Soviet ambassador in New Delhi was N. M. Pegov, an industrial specialist turned diplomat.

15. Douglas Heck to Carleton S. Coon Jr., February 28, 1968, Carleton S. Coon Jr. to Douglas Heck, April 25, 1968, and David Linebaugh to Carleton S. Coon Jr., April 29, 1968, all in SDR, USNA, RG 59, entry A1-5640, box 5; Thomas L. Hughes to William S. Rogers, January 24, 1969, CFPF, USNA, RG 59, DEF 1 INDIA.

16. Agreement cited in Indian Embassy in Moscow to GKES, August 9, 1972, RGAE, 365 / 9 / 985 / 148–150; "Bokaro Expansion: Two Protocols with Russia," *TOI,* February 21, 1970, 1; Romesh Bhandari to S. A. Skachkov, January 27, 1970, and K. C. Pant to S. A. Skachkov, February 24, 1970, both in RGAE, 365 / 9 / 578 / 23, 28; "Spravka: Nauchno-tekhnologicheskoe sotrudnichestvo Sovetskogo Soiuza i Indiei," February 12, 1970, RGAE, 9480 / 9 / 928 / 24–25.

17. Asoka Mehta conversation with P. M. Lomako, May 6, 1965, RGAE, 365 / 2 / 2169 / 82; notes regarding Indian delegation to Gosplan, October 4, 1968, P. N. Haksar Papers III, NMML, subject 198. Data derived from various annual issues of *VTSSSR.*

18. Dharm Narain, *Aid through Trade: A Case Study of India* (Geneva: United Nations Conference on Trade and Development, 1968). Chart from Mining and Allied Machinery Corporation, n.d. (1969?), and Mrs. A. Cour to S. A. Skachkov, April 4, 1969, both in RGAE, 365 / 9 / 43 / 75, 28–29; I.V. Arkhipov conversation with T. N. Kaul and Kewal Singh, May 27, 1970, RGAE, 365 / 9 / 578 / 46–48; D. P. Dhar to T. N. Kaul, March 18, 1971, P. N.

Haksar Papers III, NMML, subject 164; S. Than to J. S. Baijal, April 24, 1972, MEA Records, NAI, WI/239(6)/72-EE.

19. *EA 1967–1968*, appendix 3-A; *EA 1968–1970*, appendix 1; Robert H. Donaldson, *The Soviet-Indian Alignment: Quest for Influence* (Denver: University of Denver Graduate School of International Studies, 1979), 11–13.

20. "Background Note on Indo-Soviet Economic Relations," n.d. (1970–1971?), P. N. Haksar Papers III, NMML, subject 276.

21. Trade agreement of December 26, 1970, RGAE, 413/13/7564/74–86. See also R. K. Jain, ed., *Soviet–South Asian Relations, 1947–1978* (Atlantic Highlands, N.J.: Humanities Press, 1979), 1:375–384.

22. Chester Bowles to Robert S. McNamara, November 15, 1968, SDR, USNA, RG 59, entry A1-5640, box 8.

23. Henry Kissinger, *White House Years* (Boston: Little, Brown, 1979), 848; Henry Kissinger conversation with L. K. Jha, November 9, 1970, in *FRUS 1969–1976*, E-7, no. 94; P. K. Banerjee to C. S. Jha, February 23, 1967, and Indira Gandhi conversation with Richard M. Nixon, April 22, 1967, both in MEA Records, NAI, WII/121/23/67; Robert J. McMahon, *The Cold War on the Periphery: The United States, India, and Pakistan* (New York: Columbia University Press, 1994), 170–171; T. N. Kaul, *Diplomacy in Peace and War: Recollections and Reflections* (New Delhi: Vikas, 1979), 209.

24. Richard M. Nixon, "Informal Remarks in Guam with Newsmen," July 25, 1969, in *PPP: Richard M. Nixon 1969*, 544–557; James W. Davies memorandum for NSC Review Group, March 18, 1969, Presidential Directives, DNSA, PR-308; Jussi M. Hanhimäki, *The Flawed Architect: Henry Kissinger and American Foreign Policy* (Oxford: Oxford University Press, 2004), 53–54; Richard M. Nixon, "U.S. Foreign Policy for the 1970s: A New Strategy for Peace," February 18, 1970, in *FRUS 1969–1976*, 1:195–203; Richard M. Nixon, "Special Message to the Congress Proposing Reform of the Foreign Assistance Program," September 15, 1970, in *PPP: Richard M. Nixon 1970*, 754–756. For background on the announcement, see Jeffrey Kimball, "The Nixon Doctrine: A Saga of Misunderstanding," *Presidential Studies Quarterly* 36:1 (2006): 59–74.

25. Chester Bowles to Christopher Van Hollen, March 26, 1969, USAID Records, USNA, RG 286, entry P266, box 52. Bowles's position is characterized in Henry Kissinger to Richard M. Nixon, June 12, 1969, NSF—Country Files, RMNL, box 595.

26. Henry Kissinger to Richard M. Nixon, July 18, 1969, and National Security Council Review Group, "Military Supply Policy toward South Asia in the Context of General U.S. Posture There," November 22, 1969, both in *FRUS 1969–1976*, E-7, nos. 28, 42; "India Talking Points for President Nixon," July 9, 1969, SDR, USNA, RG 59, entry A1-5640, box 11.

27. W. K. Slatcher conversation with Kenneth Keating, August 13, 1970, CRO Records, UKNA, FCO 37/605; Anthony C. E. Quainton to Grant Mouser, September 1, 1971, SDR, USNA, RG 59, entry A1-5640, box 13.

28. K. B. Lall (Ministry of Foreign Trade and Supply) in New Delhi advisers meeting, July 31–August 1, 1969, in *FRUS 1969–1976*, E-7, no. 29.

29. For early indications of the increase in repayment and decline in net aid—along with the small amounts of debt relief, *EA 1978–1979*, tables XV, 7.2, pp. 282–283. For a helpful summary, see G. Guinday report, December 21, 1967, George Woods Papers, CU / WBGA, folder 30178059; William Gilmartin to Peter Cargill re meeting with I. G. Patel, December 19, 1967, Country Files, WBGA, folder 1844847; "India's Debt Servicing Problem," February 1, 1968, and Morarji Desai to George Woods, January 16, 1968, both in Country Files, WBGA, folder 1844848; Indira Gandhi to Morarji Desai, October 7, 1967, P. N. Haksar Papers III, NMML, subject 121; Indira Gandhi to Morarji Desai, n.d. (December 1967), P. N. Haksar Papers III, NMML, subject 124.

30. Bhagwati and Desai, *India, Planning for Industrialization*, 210. John Prior Lewis, *Quiet Crisis in India: Economic Development and American Policy* (Washington, D.C.: Brookings Institution Press, 1962), 324. William S. Rogers to Raymond Vernon, August 25, 1969, CFPF, USNA, RG 59, AID(US) 15 INDIA. For the 1964 figure ($443 million), see Phillips Talbot to Dean Rusk, May 7, 1965, SDR, USNA, RG 59, entry A1-5254, box 4. For a detailed accounting of the amounts at the time of the ultimate rupee agreement in December 1973, see "Agreement on Public Law 480 and Other Funds between the Government of the United States of America and the Government of India," n.d. (February 1974), Daniel Patrick Moynihan Papers, LC, 376:7, annexes 1–2; U.S. Congressional Research Service, Foreign Affairs Division, *The Availability and Use of Local Currencies in U.S. Foreign Aid Programs* (Washington, D.C.: Government Printing Office, 1974), chapter 5.

31. Jawaharlal Nehru, "Increasing American Activities," March 4, 1954; Jawaharlal Nehru, "Exchange Schemes between India and USA," April 14, 1954; Jawaharlal Nehru to V. K. Krishna Menon, March 12, 1954, all in *SWJN2*, 25:489–493.

32. Donald L. M. Blackmer, *The MIT Center for International Studies: The Founding Years, 1951–1969* (Cambridge: MIT Center for International Studies, 2002), chapter 6; see also David C. Engerman, "West Meets East: The Center for International Studies and Indian Economic Development," in *Staging Growth: Modernization, Development and the Global Cold War*, ed. David C. Engerman, Nils Gilman, Mark H. Haefele, and Michael E. Latham (Amherst: University of Massachusetts Press, 2003), 199–223.

33. Statement of Mr. D. G. MacDonald before U.S. House Foreign Affairs Committee, Subcommittee on Near East and South Asia, March 15, 1973, MEA Records, NAI, WII / 230 / 1 / 73; Maury J. Williams to Ambassador Kenneth Keating, August 29, 1969, USAID Records, USNA, RG 286, entry P266, box 69; reports dated February 13, 1964, June 19, 1967, and October 14, 1969, all in CFPF, USNA, RG59, AID(US) 14 INDIA; Rhodri Jeffreys-Jones, *The CIA and American Democracy* (New Haven, Conn.: Yale University Press, 1989), 162; see also, for Indian reaction, Surjit Mansingh, *India's Search for Power: Indira Gandhi's Foreign Policy, 1966–1982* (New Delhi: SAGE Publications, 1984), 90; P. N. Haksar note, February 12, 1970, P. N. Haksar Papers III, NMML, subject 148; Dennis Kux, *Estranged Democracies: India and the United States, 1941–1991* (Thousand Oaks, Calif.: SAGE Publications, 1994), 284–285; William S. Rogers to Dinesh Singh, February 27, 1970, in *FRUS 1969–1976*, E-7, no. 49; "Lok Sabha Uproar over Foreign Cultural Centres," *TOI*, February 27, 1970, 1; "Cultural Centres: Delhi Stand Irks Rogers," *TOI* March 4, 1970, 1;

NOTES TO PAGES 320–323

"Keating and India Are at Odds on Order Closing 5 Libraries," *NYT*, February 25, 1970, 4; "5 U.S. Cultural Centers Close on India's Orders," *NYT*, May 18, 1970, 3; Dean Rusk to Bowles, January 13, 1969, USAID Records, USNA, RG 286, entry P266, box 52. The Haksar quotation was in reference to the Danforth Foundation; see P. N. Haksar note, May 12, 1969, P. N. Haksar Papers III, NMML, subject 139.

34. The economist Saulnier taught at Columbia University at the time of his appointment. Raymond J. Saulnier, "Report on the Problem of Excess U.S. Holdings of Indian Rupees and a Proposal for Its Solution," included in Raymond J. Saulnier to William S. Rogers, November 20, 1970, SDR, USNA, RG 59, entry A1-5640, box 12.

35. Mehta, "Foreign Aid: Stimulus or Soporific?," May 29, 1970, G. L. Mehta Papers I–II, NMML, Speeches by Him 165.

36. Henry Kissinger to USIA Director, March 9, 1970, Henry Kissinger conversation with L. K. Jha, July 22, 1970, U.S. Department of State to New Delhi Embassy, December 19, 1970, and New Delhi Embassy to U.S. Department of State, December 24, 1970, all in NSF—Country Files, RMNL, box 596; William I. Cargo to U. Alexis Johnson, August 24, 1970, CFPF, USNA, RG 59, AID(US). L. K. Jha to T. N. Kaul, July 8, 1970, P. N. Haksar Papers III, NMML, subject 156; Henry Kissinger conversation with L. K. Jha, February 11, 1971, Henry Kissinger Transcripts, DNSA, KT-426; I. G. Patel to P. N. Dhar, February 3, 1972, PMO Records, NAI, 37/171/1972-PMS. Gandhi did, however, acknowledge the impact of American aid on different regions of India; see Indira Gandhi conversation with John Hannah, February 16, 1970, PMO Records, NAI, 37/171/1970-PMS.

37. Swaran Singh conversation with Kenneth Keating, December 22, 1970, T. N. Kaul Papers I–III, NMML, subject 19; David T. Schneider to Joseph Sisco, February 26, 1971, CFPF, USNA, RG 59, AID(US) INDIA (this document is the source of the subsequent quotations/descriptions).

38. Leonard J. Saccio to Kenneth Keating, January 12, 1970; and John Hannah conversations with I. G. Patel (February 13, 1970), T. N. Kaul (February 16, 1970), and Indira Gandhi (February 16, 1970), all in USAID Records, USNA, RG 286, entry P266, box 69.

39. S. Nijalingappa to Indira Gandhi, October 28, 1969, and Manubhai Shah recollection of Congress (O) Working Committee meeting, June 29, 1970, in Zaidi, *Great Upheaval*, 170, xxv; Guha, *India after Gandhi*, 446; V. M. Dandekar and Nilakantha Rath, "Poverty in India—I: Dimensions and Trends," *EPW*, January 2, 1971, 25–48; Devesh Kapur, John Prior Lewis, and Richard Charles Webb, *The World Bank: Its First Half Century* (Washington, D.C.: Brookings Institution Press, 1997), 230–231.

40. Extract from Indian National Congress Election Manifesto, January 1971, in Zaidi, *Great Upheaval*, 422–423.

41. This paragraph draws on the authoritative account of Srinath Raghavan, *1971: A Global History of the Creation of Bangladesh* (Cambridge, Mass.: Harvard University Press, 2013). For a thorough account of American policy in this crisis, see Gary J. Bass, *The Blood Telegram: Nixon, Kissinger, and a Forgotten Genocide* (New York: Alfred A. Knopf, 2013).

42. Notes on conversations that Henry Kissinger held with the Indian foreign minister and foreign secretary, and with the defense minister and defense secretary, on July 7, 1971, both in MEA Records, NAI, AMS / MISC / 72.

43. Kissinger, *White House Years*, 853–854. On this gambit—a crucial step in establishing detente—see, for instance Hanhimäki, *Flawed Architect*, chapter 8.

44. Richard Helms to Henry Kissinger, July 29, 1971 (with reports on Kissinger message to India), Harold Saunders to Henry Kissinger, September 7, 1971, and Kissinger conversation with L. K. Jha, September 11, 1971, all in *FRUS 1969–1976*, 11:291, 391–393, 407–408; Henry Kissinger conversation with L. K. Jha, February 11, 1971, Henry Kissinger Transcripts, DNSA, KT-426; P. N. Haksar to L. K. Jha, July 21, 1971, P. N. Haksar Papers III, NMML, subject 169; Theodore L. Eliot Jr. to Henry Kissinger, July 21, 1971, NSF—Country Files, RMNL, box 596.

45. D. P. Dhar to T. N. Kaul, April 29, 1971, P. N. Haksar Papers III, NMML, subject 232; T. N. Kaul, *Reminiscences, Discreet and Indiscreet* (New Delhi: Lancers Publishers, 1982), 285–286.

46. Notes regarding L. K. Jha consultation with Swaran Singh and P. N. Haksar in May–June 1971, referenced in MEA, Americas Division, "Reactions and Interactions of American, Chinese and Soviet Policies in This Region," June 9, 1972, MEA Records, NAI, 10-JS(AMS) / 72.

47. Swaran Singh conversations with Andrei Gromyko, June 7 and 8, 1971, and Swaran Singh conversation with Aleksei Kosygin, June 8, 1971, all in P. N. Haksar Papers III, NMML, subject 203; D. P. Dhar conversation with Andrei Gromyko, August 3, 1971, and summary of D. P. Dhar luncheon with Andrei Gromyko, August 5, 1971, both in P. N. Haksar Papers I–II, NMML, subject 51; T. N. Kaul to Swaran Singh and Indira Gandhi, August 3, 1971, P. N. Haksar Papers I–II, NMML, subject 49.

48. T. N. Kaul to Swaran Singh and Indira Gandhi, August 3, 1971, P. N. Haksar Papers I–II, NMML, subject 49. See also Eric Gonsalves to K. Rukmini Menon, March 15, 1972, MEA Records, NAI, WII-103 / 17 / 72-II.

49. "Treaty of Peace, Friendship and Cooperation," August 9, 1971, in Jain, ed., *Soviet–South Asian Relations*, 1:113–116.

50. Kenneth Keating conversation with T. N. Kaul, October 10, 1971, CFPF, USNA, RG 59, POL INDIA-US; "Bulwark of Peace: CPI," *TOI*, August 10, 1971, 8; "Non-Alignment Abandoned, Alleges Anthony" and "Pact Stabilising Factor, Swaran Tells Lok Sabha," both in *TOI*, August 10, 1971, 8; C. Rajagopalachari statement, August 9, 1971, C. Rajagopalachari Papers VI–XII, NMML, subject 79. See also the summary in "Yahya Will Take Note, Says C. R.," *TOI*, August 10, 1971, 8.

51. Henry Kissinger conversation with L. K. Jha, August 30, 1971, and Henry Kissinger conversation with L. K. Jha, September 11, 1971, Henry Kissinger Transcripts, DNSA, KT-345, KT-349; Nayar, *India*, 3; HC-New Delhi to FCO, October 28, 1971, FCO Records, UKNA, DO 133 / 218.

52. T. N. Kaul conversation with R. A. Ul'ianovskii and B. N. Ponomarev, September 10, 1972, T. N. Kaul Papers I–III, NMML, subject 19; Hemen Ray, *The Enduring Friendship: Soviet-Indian Relations in Mrs. Gandhi's Days* (New Delhi: Abhinav Publications, 1989), 45–60. One delegation undertook a nine-hour consultation on military strategy and supplies; see

chief of army staff conversation with Soviet general staff, February 24, 1972, P. N. Haksar Papers III, NMML, subject 242.

53. John N. Irwin II to Richard M. Nixon, August 9, 1971, and Moscow Embassy to U.S. Department of State, August 10, 1971, both in CFPF, USNA, RG 59, POL 21 INDIA-USSR; Kissinger, *White House Years*, 866–867; Henry Kissinger conversation with L. K. Jha, August 9, 1971, Henry Kissinger Transcripts, DNSA, KT-323.

54. Theodore L. Eliot Jr. to Henry Kissinger, August 17, 1971, CFPF, USNA, RG 59, POL 1 INDIA-US; Washington Special Action Group, "Economic Assistance Cut-off for India," September 3, 1971, CFPF, USNA, RG 59, AID(US) INDIA.

55. Bass, *Blood Telegram,* catalogs an extraordinary range of such insults. For an explanation of how such characterizations shaped American policies toward India in an earlier period, see Andrew Jon Rotter, *Comrades at Odds: The United States and India, 1947–1964* (Ithaca, N.Y.: Cornell University Press, 2000).

56. Mansingh, *India's Search*, 87; Washington Special Action Group minutes, December 3, 1971, in *FRUS 1969–1976*, 11:596–604; Christopher Van Hollen, "The Tilt Policy Revisited: Nixon-Kissinger Geopolitics and South Asia," *Asian Survey* 20:4 (1980): 339–61. For more on the escalation in South Asia, see Raghavan, *1971,* chapter 9. Journalist Jack Anderson earned a Pulitzer Prize for these reports; see Jack Anderson, *The Anderson Papers* (New York: Random House, 1973). A summary of Anderson's reporting sent to Kissinger, January 6, 1972, can be found in "Notes, Anderson Papers Material," BEBB45, NSA Online, http://nsarchive2.gwu.edu/NSAEBB/NSAEBB79/.

57. Henry Kissinger conversation with John Connally, December 5, 1971, in *FRUS 1969–1976*, E-7, no. 159.

58. Vinay Verma conversation with Sam Hoskinson, January 5, 1972; and M. Rasgotra to K. Rukmini Menon, January 5, 1972, MEA Records, NAI, WII / 130 / 1 / 72; J. R. D. Tata, cited in Roger Blaugh to William S. Rogers, January 14, 1972, CFPF, USNA, RG 59, POL INDIA-US.

59. David T. Schneider to Joseph Sisco, January 5, 1972, CFPF, USNA, RG 59, AID(US) 8 INDIA; New Delhi Embassy to U.S. Department of State, January 16, 1972, in *FRUS 1969–1976*, E-7, no. 205; New Delhi Embassy to U.S. Department of State, February 5, 1972, CFPF, USNA, RG 59, AID(US) INDIA.

60. "Alternative U.S. Assistance Strategies for India," attached to Maurice J. Williams to Senior Review Group, February 10, 1972, NSF—Country Files, RMNL, box 598. Theodore L. Eliot Jr. to Henry Kissinger, February 15, 1972, SDR, USNA, RG 59, entry A1-5640, box 17.

61. Indira Gandhi quoted in American diplomatic reporting; see New Delhi Embassy to U.S. Department of State, March 8, 1972, in *FRUS 1969–1976*, E-7, no. 232. See also T. N. Kaul, "Economic Aspects of India's Foreign Policy" (address to FICCI), March 26, 1972, T. N. Kaul Papers I–III, NMML, subject 19.

62. For a useful summary of these steps, see David Schneider to Joseph Sisco, October 30, 1972, New Delhi Embassy to U.S. Department of State (re conversation between USAID

mission director Howard Houston and S. Krishnaswami), May 8, 1972, and New Delhi Embassy to U.S. Department of State, May 31, 1973, all in *FRUS 1969–1976*, E-7, nos. 308, 260, 264.

63. John A. Hannah to William S. Rogers, May 19, 1972, USAID Records, USNA, RG 286, entry P409, box 39; U.S. Department of State to New Delhi Embassy, May 11, 1972, in *FRUS 1969–1976*, E-7, no. 261.

64. Curtiss Farrar to John Hannah, June 16, 1972, USAID Records, USNA, RG 286, entry P409, box 39. Kux, *Estranged Democracies*, 307–308; David T. Schneider to Joseph Sisco, April 26, 1972, CFPF, USNA, RG 59, AID(US) 14; India Country Program Plan, 1971–1973, Peace Corps Records, USNA, RG 490, entry P16, box 42; John Chromy, "Why the Peace Corps Left India," India Returned Peace Corps Volunteers 1961–1976, http://ganga633.squarespace.com/stories -to-share/2013/1/21/why-the-peace-corps-left-india-by-john-chromy.html. On local hires, see S. Krishnaswami conversations with Howard Houston, June 14, 1972, and June 28, 1972, both in MEA Records, NAI, WII/130/1/72. On the building, see Daniel Patrick Moynihan journal entry, July 17, 1972, in *Daniel Patrick Moynihan: A Portrait in Letters of an American Visionary* (New York: PublicAffairs, 2010), 298–299.

65. USAID, "Development Assistance Program FY 1974: India," August 1972, USAID Development Experience Clearinghouse, PD-ACC-364, esp. part C.

66. Robert S. McNamara conversation with Y. B. Chavan and I. G. Patel, September 21, 1970, Robert S. McNamara Papers, WBGA, folder 1771075; Robert S. McNamara conversation with the Indian delegation, October 27, 1971, Robert S. McNamara Papers, WBGA, folder 1771076; Patel quoted in Howard Houston to Larry Smucker, July 21, 1972, USAID Records (USNA, RG 286, entry P409), box 50. This skepticism emerged after an initial discussion favoring participation in the debt-rescheduling exercise; see Henry Kissinger to Richard M. Nixon, June 12, 1972, in *FRUS 1969–1976*, E-7, no. 266.

67. Indira Gandhi, as reported by Kenneth Keating in New Delhi Embassy to U.S. Department of State, July 24, 1972, and John N. Irwin II conversation with L. K. Jha, August 2, 1972, in *FRUS 1969–1976*, E-7, no. 293, no. 297; Howard Houston to Larry Smucker, July 21, 1972, USAID Records, USNA, RG 286, entry P409, box 50.

68. USAID, "A New Economic Assistance Relationship with India," attached to Maurice J. Williams to John Hannah, November 2, 1972, and U.S. Department of State/Bureau of Near Eastern Affairs, "Comments on the AID Memorandum: A New Economic Assistance Relationship with India," attached to Herb Rees to Maurice Williams, January 3, 1973, both in USAID Records, USNA, RG 286, entry P270, box 11; Harold H. Saunders and Henry R. Appelbaum to Henry Kissinger, July 13, 1973, and New Delhi Embassy to U.S. Department of State, October 18, 1973, both in NSF—Country Files, RMNL, box 599.

69. Henry Kissinger to Richard M. Nixon, March 7, 1973, Joseph Sisco conversation with L. K. Jha, March 16, 1973, and Moynihan conversation with Indira Gandhi, March 17, 1973, all in *FRUS 1969–1976*, E-8, nos. 111, 117, 118.

70. "Aide-Memoire on Development Assistance Given P. N. Dhar July 19," July 19, 1973, SDR, USNA, RG 59, entry A1-5640, box 19. T. N. Kaul conversation with John Hannah, July 31, 1973,

MEA Records, NAI, WII / 230 / 1 / 73; Harold H. Saunders to Charles A. Cooper, February 13, 1974, NSAD—IEAS Records, GRFL, box 1. The plan is recounted in Charles A. Cooper to Henry Kissinger, February 13, 1974, NSF—Country Files, RMNL, box 600.

71. "Aide-Memoire on Development Assistance Given P. N. Dhar July 19," July 19, 1973, SDR, USNA, RG 59, entry A1-5640, box 19; Kewal Singh conversation with Daniel Patrick Moynihan, March 29, 1973, MEA Records, NAI, WII / 230 / 1 / 73; Henry Kissinger conversation with Y. B. Chavan, July 14, 1973, Henry Kissinger Transcripts, DNSA, KT-784. For a helpful overview of the negotiations, see L. J. Kennon to Daniel Patrick Moynihan, September 13, 1974, 13 Moynihan Papers, LC, 376:6.

72. U.S. Information Service press release, December 13, 1973, MEA Records, NAI, WII / 205 / 13 / 73-I; Henry R. Appelbaum to Brent Scowcroft, December 13, 1973, NSF—Country Files, RMNL, box 599; Henry Kissinger to Richard M. Nixon, December 17, 1973, in *FRUS 1969–1976*, E-8, no. 154; Daniel Patrick Moynihan to Guinness Book of World Records, February 25, 1974, in Moynihan, *Daniel Patrick Moynihan*, 325; Ross McWhirter and Norris McWhirter, eds., *Guinness Book of World Records* (New York: Sterling Publishers, 1977), 410. For the text of the December 13, 1973, agreement see Mansingh, *India's Search*, 385–387.

73. Henry Kissinger conversation with T. N. Kaul, July 14, 1973, Henry Kissinger Transcripts, DNSA, KT-773; T. N. Kaul to Kewal Singh, July 14, 1973, Kaul Papers I–III, NMML, subject 1.

74. U.S. Department of State / Bureau of Near Eastern Affairs, "Comments on the AID Memorandum: A New Economic Assistance Relationship with India," attached to Herb Rees to Maurice Williams, January 3, 1973, USAID Records, USNA, RG 286, entry P270, box 11; Harold H. Saunders to Henry Kissinger, March 26, 1973, NSF—Country Files, RMNL, box 599; T. N. Kaul address to Indo-American Chamber of Commerce, May 3, 1973, and T. N. Kaul conversation with Henry Kissinger, June 15, 1973, both in Kaul Papers I–III, NMML, subject 1; Swaran Singh conversation with Henry Kissinger, April 15, 1974, Kaul Papers I–III, NMML, subject 2; Gerald Ford conversation with T. N. Kaul, August 21, 1974, national security adviser memoranda of conversation, GRFL Online, https://www.fordlibrarymuseum .gov/library/guides/findingaid/Memoranda_of_Conversations.asp. Michael F. Martin and K. Alan Kronstadt, *India-U.S. Economic and Trade Relations* (Washington, D.C.: Congressional Research Service, 2007), figure 6-9.

75. Richard M. Nixon, "Fourth Annual Report to the Congress on United States Foreign Policy," May 3, 1973, in *PPP: Richard M. Nixon 1973*, 348–518; Henry Kissinger to Richard M. Nixon, June 4, 1973, Theodore L. Eliot Jr., to Henry Kissinger, July 24, 1973, and L. Bruce Laingen to Joseph Sisco, January 8, 1974, all in NSAD—IEAS Records, GRFL, box 1; "Basis Laid for Mature Ties with India: Kissinger," *TOI*, November 1, 1974, 10; "The United States and India: Toward a Mature Relationship," 2nd ed., October 1973, Daniel Patrick Moynihan Papers, LC, 373:5; Daniel Patrick Moynihan to Henry Kissinger, September 5, 1973, CFPF, USNA, RG 59, POL 1 INDIA-US.

76. Harold H. Saunders and Charles A. Cooper to Henry Kissinger, September 28, 1973, NSF—Country Files, RMNL, box 599; Walter A. Lundy to David T. Schneider, July 23, 1973,

Daniel Patrick Moynihan Papers, LC, 372:4; Daniel Patrick Moynihan to Kissinger, October 1973, Daniel Patrick Moynihan Papers, LC, 377:9.

77. Indian aide-memoire, July 10, 1972, RGAE, 365 / 9 / 985 / 130–131; notes for prime minister's speech, October 3, 1972, P. N. Haksar Papers III, NMML, subject 184; "First Blast Furnace of Bokaro Commissioned," TOI, October 4, 1972, 1.

78. See, for instance S. A. Skachkov conversation with Ali Ahmed, December 10, 1968, RGAE, 365 / 2 / 708 / 10–14. Skachkov's view is described in Nayar, Between the Lines, 126.

79. Indira Gandhi, quoted in Asoka Mehta, "Seminal Role of Public Enterprises," in Towards Commanding Heights, ed. R. C. Dutt and Raj K. Nigam (New Delhi: Standing Conference of Public Enterprises, 1975), 29; "Expert Group to Go into Industrial Policy," TOI, February 11, 1972, 12; "Holding Firm for Steel Industry from November," TOI, July 16, 1972, 1; Frankel, India's Political Economy, 468. "Semantic Slight," EPW, March 3, 1973, 465–466; Ashutosh Varshney, Democracy, Development, and the Countryside: Urban-Rural Struggles in India (Cambridge: Cambridge University Press, 1995), chapter 4. The new minister, S. Mohan Kumaramangalam, made the political and economic cases for nationalization; see S. Mohan Kumaramangalam, Coal Industry in India: Nationalisation and Tasks Ahead (New Delhi: IBH Publishing, 1973), 51; and S. Mohan Kumaramangalam, speech at Avadi, n.d. (late 1971?), reprinted as "New Model for Governmental Administration of Industry," in Dutt and Nigam, eds., Towards Commanding Heights, 1–21.

80. Francine R. Frankel, "Decline of a Social Order," in Dominance and State Power in Modern India: Decline of a Social Order, ed. Francine R. Frankel and M. S. A. Rao (New Delhi: Oxford University Press, 1989), 1:507; Frankel, India's Political Economy, 463; Kaviraj, "State of Contradictions," 244–245; Stanley A. Kochanek, "Mrs. Gandhi's Pyramid: The New Congress," in Indira Gandhi's India: A Political System Reappraised, ed. Henry Cowles Hart (Boulder, Colo.: Westview Press, 1976), 95–96; V. V. Giri, "Foreword," in Dutt and Nigam, eds., Towards Commanding Heights, 11; R. Ul'ianovskii, "Nekotorye voprosy nekapitalisticheskogo razvitiia," Kommunist, 1971:4 (1971): 103–112; Elizabeth Kridl Valkenier, "Soviet Economic Relations with the Developing Nations," in The Soviet Union and the Developing Nations, ed. Roger E. Kanet (Baltimore: Johns Hopkins University Press, 1974), 228. An exchange took place between R. K. Hazari ("smug accounting") and K. N. Raj ("good returns") in a discussion following R. K. Hazari, "The Public Sector in India," in Economic Development in South Asia, ed. E. A. G. Robinson and Michael Kidron (London: St. Martin's Press, 1970), 93, 99.

81. Sukhamoy Chakravarty, Development Planning: The Indian Experience (Oxford: Clarendon Press, 1987), 58; Nayar, India's Mixed Economy, 313–314, 364–370; Nayar, India, 85; D. P. Dhar lecture at the Centre for Development Studies, April 1974, reprinted in D. P. Dhar, Planning and Social Change (New Delhi: Arnold-Heineman Publishers, 1976), 27–28. For political decisions over economic matters, see Kohli, State-Directed Development, 261. For ideology, see Sudipta Kaviraj, "On the Crisis of Political Institutions in India," Contributions to Indian Sociology 18:2 (1984): 236. On command / demand politics, see Rudolph and Rudolph, In Pursuit of Lakshmi, chapter 7.

82. A. I. Levkovskii, *Tretii mir v sovremennom mire* (Moscow: Nauka, 1970); A. I. Levkovskii, "Spetsfika i granitsy kapitalizma v perekhodnom obshchestve 'tret'ego mir,'" *Mirovaia ekonomika i mezhdunarodnye otnosheniia* 1974:1 (1974): 112–119; A. I. Levkovskii, "O spetsifike gosudarstva v mnogoukladnykh stranakh," *Aziia i Afrika segodnia* 1978:2 (1978), 25–28. For helpful analyses, see Jerry F. Hough, *The Struggle for the Third World: Soviet Debates and American Options* (Washington, D.C.: Brookings Institution, 1985), 56–59; Linda Racioppi, *Soviet Policy towards South Asia since 1970* (Cambridge: Cambridge University Press, 1994), 22–37; and Roderic D. M. Pitty, "Recent Soviet Development Debates: The 'Third World' and the USSR" (PhD diss., Australian National University, 1989), 133–145.

83. V. A. Sergeev conversation with M. Sondhi, July 23, 1973, RGAE, 365/9/1335/18–20; M. Suloev (deputy chair, GKES) to N. K. Baibakov (chair, Gosplan), August 31, 1973, RGAE, 365/9/1248/106–107; T. A. Pai (minister of heavy industries) to S. A. Skachkov, August 13, 1974, RGAE, 365/9/1490/34–35; D. P. Dhar to P. N. Haksar, August 23, 1969, P. N. Haksar Papers III, NMML, subject 141; D. P. Dhar conversation with Andrei Gromyko, February 10, 1975, MEA Records, NAI, WI/103/S/75-EE, vol. 1.

84. S. Than to J. S. Bajal, April 24, 1974, and A. P. Venkateswaran to S. Than, April 29, 1974, both in MEA Records, NAI, WI/239(6)72-EE; *VTSSSR 1975*, 266–277; N. K. Baibakov (chair, Gosplan) conversation with D. K. Borua (minister of oil and gas), November 27, 1973, RGAE, 365/9/1249/162–171; New Delhi Embassy to U.S. Department of State, December 21, 1976, NSAD—NSC-MESA, GRFL, box 4.

85. B. Romanov and L. Eiranov conversation with Prasanta Chandra Mahalanobis, November 8, 1959, RGAE, 365/2/1955/70–71; A. I. Mikoian conversation with TTK, November 17, 1965, AVPRF, 090/27/95/16/60–66. Notes on Indian delegation to Gosplan, October 4, 1968, P. N. Haksar Papers III, NMML, subject 198; drafts of April 13, May 4, May 15, and June 19, 1972, and S. A. Skachkov conversation with M. S. Pathak, December 20, 1972, all in RGAE, 365/9/985/31–37, 46–49, 58–59, 82–84, 119–120, 215–217; agenda for first meeting of Indo-Soviet Joint Commission, January 8, 1973, M. Suloev to N. K. Baibakov, July 31, 1973, and D. P. Dhar to S. A. Skachkov, July 16, 1973, all in RGAE, 365/9/1248/1–4, 106–107, 96–98; "Programme of Cooperation between the USSR and India in the Field of Applied Science and Technology for 1973–74," February 17, 1973, RGAE, 9480/9/1971/7–12. "Agreement on Economic and Trade Cooperation between India and the Soviet Union," November 29, 1973, in Jain, ed., *Soviet-South Asian Relations,* 1:408–412; P. K. Sinai to A. I. Alikhanov, August 7, 1974, RGAE, 365/9/1490/164–166; Indian Embassy in Moscow, *Annual Political Report for 1975,* MEA Records, NAI, WI/108/5/75-EE-I.

86. Protocol on Indo-Soviet Cooperation, November 29, 1973, minutes of Joint Commission meeting November 22–28, 1973, V. N. Gordopolov to V. A. Sergeev, August 13, 1973, A. Balasubramaniam to V. Pashkov, July 19, 1973, and V. N. Gordopolov conversation with P. Krishnamurthi (director, Department of Electronics), November 1, 1973, all in RGAE, 365/9/1338/55–72, 74–82, 12–14, 15–16, 39–40. A. I. Alikhanov to V. N. Gordopolov, October 24, 1973, RGAE, 365/9/1249/84; R. A. Longmere to FCO, April 5, 1973, FCO Records, UKNA, DO 37/1285; aide-memoire, May 16, 1973, RGAE, 365/9/1248/32–33; "New Vistas,"

TOI, November 28, 1973, 6; "Soviet-Aided Ventures March Ahead," *TOI*, December 1, 1974, 7; "Indo-Soviet Talks End with Identity of Views," *TOI*, November 29, 1975, 1.

87. Aleksei Kosygin conversation with Ali Ahmed, June 10, 1969, RGAE, 365/9/140/115a–115z; V. A. Sergeev conversation with M. Sondhi, July 23, 1973, RGAE, 365/9/1335/18–20; V. N. Gordopolov to S. A. Skachkov, October 16, 1973, RGAE, 365/9/1249/73–83. See also the detailed list from September 1974 in RGAE, 365/9/1490/79–80.

88. L. Bruce Laingen, "India: What's Next," January 8, 1974, and Henry Kissinger to Daniel Patrick Moynihan, June 18, 1973, both in NSAD—IEAS Records, GRFL, box 1; Daniel Patrick Moynihan to Kenneth Rush, May 25, 1973, in Moynihan, *Daniel Patrick Moynihan*, 290–293.

89. Kissinger conversation with Kaul, August 15, 1973, Henry Kissinger Transcripts, DNSA, KT-794; Harold H. Saunders and Henry R. Appelbaum to Henry Kissinger, March 18, 1974, and March 28, 1974, both in NSF—Country Files, RMNL, box 600; T. N. Kaul conversation with Henry Kissinger, March 19, 1974, T. N. Kaul Papers I–III, NMML, subject 2.

90. Henry Kissinger to Daniel Patrick Moynihan, June 18, 1973, NSAD—IEAS Records, GRFL, box 1; NSC Undersecretaries Committee, January 24, 1975, NSAD—IEAS Records, GRFL, box 8; Henry Kissinger conversation with Qiao Guanhua, October 2, 1974, Henry Kissinger Transcripts, DNSA, KT-1349; New Delhi Embassy to U.S. Department of State, February 27, 1975, PCF-MESA, GRFL, box 12.

91. U.S. Department of State/Bureau of Near Eastern Affairs, "South Asia," October 4, 1974, NSAD—Transition File, GRFL, box 1.

92. B. M., "Heart-Break in Moscow," *EPW*, September 28, 1974, 1641–1642; "Indo-Soviet Talks," *TOI*, August 24, 1974, 1; P. N. Haksar note on relations with Soviet Union, November 19, 1974, P. N. Haksar Papers III, NMML, subject 269.

93. Indo-US Joint Commission proposals, n.d. (October–November 1974), NSAD—IEAS Records, GRFL, box 8; "Indo-U.S. Relations," *EPW*, October 18, 1975, 1631–1632. M. G. Kaul served as secretary for economic affairs at the Ministry of Finance; B. D. Nag-Chaudhuri was a physicist who served as scientific adviser to the Ministry of Defence. See "Nominees on Indo-U.S. Joint Commission," *TOI*, November 28, 1974, 7; this article also mentions G. Parthasarathy, a foreign service officer who worked especially on cultural and educational connections with the West.

94. T. N. Kaul conversation with John Hannah, July 31, 1973, MEA Records, NAI, WII/230/1/73; T. N. Kaul speech to Indo-American Chamber of Commerce, May 3, 1973, T. N. Kaul Papers I–III, NMML, subject 1. See also R. K. Nehru, "The Current International System and the Indian Approach to It," n.d. (1972?), R. K. Nehru Papers, NMML, subject 7.

Conclusion

1. B. K. Nehru to Morarji Desai, May 21, 1958, and Jawaharlal Nehru note, n.d. (late May 1958), both in PMO Records, NAI, 37/437/58-PMS.

2. John P. Lewis, "Betting on India," January 14, 1965, NSF—NSC Histories, LBJL, 25:6.

3. Rajni Kothari, "The Political Change of 1967," *EPW,* January 1971 annual number, 231–250; Atul Kohli, *Democracy and Discontent: India's Growing Crisis of Governability* (Cambridge: Cambridge University Press, 1990); Lloyd I. Rudolph and Susanne Hoeber Rudolph, *In Pursuit of Lakshmi: The Political Economy of the Indian State* (Chicago: University of Chicago Press, 1987), chapter 4; Francine R. Frankel, *India's Political Economy, 1947–1977: The Gradual Revolution* (Princeton, N.J.: Princeton University Press, 1978), 388.

4. S. Mohan Kumaramangalam, "New Model for Governmental Administration of Industry," in *Towards Commanding Heights,* ed. R. C. Dutt and Raj K. Nigam (New Delhi: Standing Conference of Public Enterprises, 1975), 1–21; R. K. Hazari, "The Public Sector in India," in *Economic Development in South Asia,* ed. E. A. G. Robinson and Michael Kidron (London: St. Martin's Press, 1970), 90–101; Anne O. Krueger, "The Political Economy of the Rent-Seeking Society," *American Economic Review* 64:3 (1974): 291–303. Vijay Joshi and I. M. D. Little, *India: Macroeconomics and Political Economy, 1964–1991* (Washington, D.C.: World Bank, 1994), 120–121; Margaret Garritsen de Vries, *The International Monetary Fund, 1972–1978: Cooperation on Trial* (Washington, D.C.: International Monetary Fund, 1985), 1:58–60, 330–332.

5. Ramachandra Guha, *India after Gandhi: The History of the World's Largest Democracy* (New York: Ecco, 2007), chapters 23–24; Kohli, *Democracy and Discontent,* chapter 11; Myron Weiner, "The Political Economy of Industrial Growth in India," *World Politics* 38:4 (1986): 596–610; Vanita Shastri, "The Political Economy of Policy Formation in India: The Case of Industrial Policy, 1948–1994" (PhD diss., Cornell University, 1995), chapter 7.

6. For a sympathetic overview, see the essays in Jeffrey Sachs, Ashutosh Varshney, and Nirupam Bajpai, eds., *India in the Era of Economic Reforms* (New Delhi: Oxford University Press, 1999). For more skeptical accounts, see the essays in Akhil Gupta and K. Sivaramakrishnan, eds., *The State in India after Liberalization: Interdisciplinary Perspectives* (New York: Routledge, 2011).

7. Data derived from USAID, Foreign Aid Explorer Database, http://explorer.usaid.gov.

8. U.S. Task Force on International Development, *U.S. Foreign Assistance in the 1970s: A New Approach* (Washington, D.C.: Government Printing Office, 1970). Richard M. Nixon memorandum, March 5, 1970, in *FRUS 1969–1976,* 4:309–312; U.S. Congressional Research Service, *The New Directions Mandate and the Agency for International Development* (Washington, D.C.: Congressional Research Service, 1981), part 1-B; Ellen Ziskind Berg, "The 1973 Legislative Reorientation of the United States Foreign Assistance Policy: The Content and Context of a Change" (MA thesis, George Washington University, 1976). For helpful comparisons, see U.S. Congressional Research Service, *The Reorganization of U.S. Development Aid: Comparison and Summary Analysis of Some Official and Unofficial Proposals* (Washington, D.C.: Congressional Research Service, 1973); and Robert E. Asher, "Development Assistance in DD II: The Recommendations of Perkins, Pearson, Peterson, Prebisch, and Others," *International Organization* 25:1 (1971): 97–119. For overviews of the changes to American development aid during the Nixon administration, see David Ekbladh, *The Great American Mission: Modernization and the Construction of an American World Order* (Princeton, N.J.: Princeton University Press, 2010), 221–225, 244–246; Michael E. Latham,

The Right Kind of Revolution: Modernization, Development, and U.S. Foreign Policy from the Cold War to the Present (Ithaca, N.Y.: Cornell University Press, 2011), 167–175; and Vernon W. Ruttan, *United States Development Assistance Policy: The Domestic Politics of Foreign Economic Aid* (Baltimore: Johns Hopkins University Press, 1996), chapter 6. Thanks to Joanne Meyerowitz for sharing her analysis of these events.

9. Mark F. McGuire and Vernon W. Ruttan, "Lost Directions: U.S. Foreign Assistance Policy since New Directions," *Journal of Developing Areas* 24:2 (1990): 127–80. Data come from USAID, Foreign Aid Explorer Database, http://www.explorer.usaid.gov. For an insightful examination of one strand of the rising NGO aid movement, see Paul Adler, "Planetary Citizens: U.S. NGOs and the Politics of International Development in the Late Twentieth Century" (PhD diss., Georgetown University, 2014).

10. Patrick Allan Sharma, "Globalizing Development: Robert McNamara at the World Bank" (PhD diss., University of California–Los Angeles, 2010), 120 (data), chapters 3–4; Devesh Kapur, John Prior Lewis, and Richard Charles Webb, *The World Bank: Its First Half Century* (Washington, D.C.: Brookings Institution, 1997), 1:215–268; Martha Finnemore, "Redefining Development at the World Bank," in *International Development and the Social Sciences: Essays on the History and Politics of Knowledge*, ed. Frederick Cooper and Randall M. Packard (Berkeley: University of California Press, 1997), 203–227.

11. K. N. Brutents, *Tridsat' let na Staroi Ploshchadi* (Moscow: Mezhdunarodnye otnosheniia, 1998), 298, 135; Elizabeth Kridl Valkenier, *The Soviet Union and the Third World: An Economic Bind* (New York: Praeger, 1983), 78–80. For the growing Soviet ambivalence toward the public sector in India, see Stephen Clarkson, *The Soviet Theory of Development: India and the Third World in Marxist-Leninist Scholarship* (Toronto: University of Toronto Press, 1978), chapter 4.

12. Swaminathan S. Aiyer, "No Projects in Sight for Using Soviet Loans," *TOI*, June 6, 1977, 1–2; Robert H. Donaldson, *The Soviet-Indian Alignment: Quest for Influence* (Denver: University of Denver Graduate School of International Studies, 1979), 11–12.

13. U.S. Central Intelligence Agency, *Communist Aid to Less Developed Countries of the Free World, 1975* (Washington, D.C.: CIA, 1976), 1, 5; U.S. Central Intelligence Agency, *Communist Aid Activities in Non-Communist Less Developed Countries, 1979 and 1954–79* (Washington, D.C.: CIA, 1979), tables A1, A5. Jeremy Scott Friedman, *Shadow Cold War: The Sino-Soviet Split and the Third World* (Chapel Hill: University of North Carolina Press, 2015), chapter 5. India arms transfer data come from Stockholm International Peace Research Institute, SIPRI Arms Transfer Database, https://www.sipri.org/databases/armstransfers.

14. USSR Ministry of Foreign Trade, *Vneshniaia torgovlia SSSR, 1922–1981: iubeleinyi statisticheskii sbornik* (Moscow: Vneshtorgizdat, 1982), 14–15; Robert H. Donaldson, "The Second World, the Third World, and the New International Economic Order," in *The Soviet Union in the Third World: Successes and Failures*, ed. Robert H. Donaldson (Boulder, Colo.: Westview Press, 1981), 374–375.

15. Johanna Bockman, "Socialist Globalization against Capitalist Neocolonialism: The Economic Ideas behind the New International Economic Order," *Humanity* 6:1 (2015): 109–128;

Elizabeth Kridl Valkenier, "East-West Economic Competition in the Third World," in *East-West Tensions in the Third World*, ed. Marshall D. Shulman (New York: W. W. Norton, 1986), 176. For a more detailed account of the Soviet responses to the NIEO, see especially Valkenier, *Soviet Union*, chapter 4; Richard B. Day, *Cold War Capitalism: The View from Moscow, 1945–1975* (Armonk, N.Y.: M. E. Sharpe, 1995), chapter 10; and Roger E. Kanet, "Soviet Policy toward the Developing World: The Role of Economic Assistance and Trade," in Donaldson, ed., *Soviet Union*, 331–357.

16. David R. Stone, "CMEA's International Investment Bank and the Crisis of Developed Socialism," *Journal of Cold War Studies* 10:3 (2008): 48–77. More generally, and with a focus on oil, see Stephen Kotkin, *Armageddon Averted: The Soviet Collapse, 1970–2000* (Oxford: Oxford University Press, 2001), chapter 1. The data on aid are not strictly comparable, but the changing ratio is indicative—and dramatic; see U.S. Central Intelligence Agency, *Communist Aid Activities*, table A5; and U.S. Agency for International Development, *U.S. Overseas Loans and Grants and Assistance from International Organizations* (Washington, D.C.: USAID, 1981).

17. Jeffry A. Frieden, *Global Capitalism: Its Fall and Rise in the Twentieth Century* (New York: Norton, 2007), chapters 13–14; Oscar Sanchez-Sibony, *Red Globalization: The Political Economy of the Cold War from Stalin to Khrushchev* (Cambridge: Cambridge University Press, 2014), part 3.

18. Among the most widely circulated (and breathless) celebrations of globalization was Thomas L. Friedman, *The Lexus and the Olive Tree* (New York: Farrar, Straus and Giroux, 1999). For more skeptical and serious accounts, see Saskia Sassen, *Losing Control? Sovereignty in an Age of Globalization* (New York: Columbia University Press, 1996), chapter 1; and Stephen D. Krasner, *Sovereignty: Organized Hypocrisy* (Princeton, N.J.: Princeton University Press, 2001). Frederick Cooper, "What Is the Concept of Globalization Good for? An African Historian's Perspective," *African Affairs* 100:399 (April 2001): 189–213 provides an indispensable historical critique. On the 1970s origins, see Niall Ferguson, Charles S. Maier, Erez Manela, and Daniel J. Sargent, eds., *The Shock of the Global: The 1970s in Perspective* (Cambridge, Mass.: Harvard University Press, 2010); and Daniel J. Sargent, *A Superpower Transformed: The Remaking of American Foreign Relations in the 1970s* (Oxford: Oxford University Press, 2015).

19. Gregory Mann, *From Empires to NGOs in the West African Sahel: The Road to Nongovernmentality* (Cambridge: Cambridge University Press, 2015); and Charles S. Maier, *Once within Borders: Territories of Wealth, Power, and Belonging since 1500* (Cambridge, Mass.: Harvard University Press, 2016), chapter 6.

20. Hans Morgenthau, "A Political Theory of Foreign Aid," *American Political Science Review* 56:2 (1962): 301–309; B. Gafurov to Leonid Brezhnev, March 12, 1966, RGANI, 5 / 30 / 489 / 149. On American critics of aid in the 1960s, see Robert David Johnson, *Congress and the Cold War* (Cambridge: Cambridge University Press, 2006), 94–104.

Acknowledgments

Working on *The Price of Aid* has been an adventure, even more than I anticipated when I set out on this project in the autumn of 2008, during my then newborn son Simon's all-too-brief naps and moments of quiet contentment. Along the way I have accrued many debts—professional, financial, and personal. While repaying these debts seems insurmountable, and rescheduling seems unlikely, let me at least acknowledge them here.

The financial debts are easiest to account for. I am grateful for the time to work on the project that came from leaves funded by the American Council on Learned Societies, which allowed me to return for a delightfully productive— and productively delightful—fellowship at the Radcliffe Institute. A Truman / Kauffman Research Fellowship, a Summer Stipend from the National Endowment for the Humanities, and a Guggenheim Fellowship provided time to reflect and write. Travel was funded through Research Contract 828–04 from the National Council for Eurasian and East European Research, a Senior Short-Term Fellowship from the American Institute of Indian Studies, a Short-Term Grant from the Kennan Institute, and travel grants from the Eisenhower Foundation and the Harry S. Truman Library Institute. Closer to home, the Center for German and European Studies and the Norman Faculty Research funds provided material assistance; Brandeis University administrators, especially department chairs Paul Jankowski and Jane Kamensky as well as Dean Susan Birren, helped arrange my Brandeis commitments to provide time for research and writing. While I am very grateful for this support, none of these funders bear any responsibility for the views expressed in this book.

For my first forays of research in India, I am exceptionally grateful to Srinath Raghavan, whose books provide a model of clarity and concision that I can admire but (as the heft of this volume shows) cannot emulate. I am also grateful to the Centre for Policy Research for hosting my early visits, which coincidentally gave me the chance to reconnect with my friend Navroz Dubash. I am grateful to the CPR's then president Pratap Bhanu Mehta and researcher Sandeep Bhardwaj for their help as well. In Kolkata, Nityananda was a gracious and generous host. Andrei Isserov, whose own scholarship (while remote from this topic) is a model of erudition, played a similar role—as did the Institute for World History (Russian Academy of Sciences) led by A. O. Chubar'ian and M. A. Lipkin. I'm also grateful to the Davis Center for Russian and Eurasian Studies at Harvard University for being such hospitable hosts.

This book relied on an embarrassing number of younger scholars whose research in far-flung libraries and archives made this project possible. I'm especially grateful to Ian Crookston, Subir Dey, and Ol'ga Skorokhodova for extended work. For smaller tasks, thanks to Nathaniel Barr, Cassandra Berman, Fiona Dean, Erin Hutchinson, Alexander Ioffreda, Eric Johnson, Raphäelle Khan, Julie Leighton, Matt Linton, Olga Litvin, Frederike Reuter, William Sharman, Osama Siddiqui, Elaine Spencer, Viroopa Volla, and David Wiley.

My own forays into libraries and archives were made possible—and fruitful—by the extraordinary labors of archivists and librarians. I am grateful to archivists at all of the repositories enumerated in the Note on Sources. I'd especially like to thank Irina Grigor'evna Tarakanova at the Archive of the Russian Academy of Sciences; Sergei Pavlovich Pavlov at the Archive of Foreign Policy of the Russian Federation; Krishna Bhattacharya and her staff at the Indian Statistical Institute; Karen Adler Abramson and Steven Plotkin at the John F. Kennedy Presidential Library; Deepa Bhatnagar, Jyotri Luthra and Sanjeev Gautam at the Nehru Memorial Museum and Library; Nadezhda Mikhailovna Kostrikova at the Russian State Economic Archive; and the whole crew at the U.S. National Archives—David Langbart, Tab Lewis, David Pfeiffer, Brian Phelan, and Amy Reytar.

I was honored to have the chance to speak with some of the subjects of this book and those who knew them. Thanks to Jagdish Bhagwati, Appollon Davidson, Padma Desai, Chandrashekar Pant, Amartya Sen, and Thomas Weisskopf for sharing their experiences and insights.

Other scholars and friends shared their views, offered helpful advice, provided generous feedback, pointed me to useful sources, and otherwise helped me puzzle through aspects of the project. More important, they made the too-often solitary work of a historian into part of a collective intellectual enterprise.

I shudder to recount how often I bored or burdened others in presentations of this work, but am thankful to scholarly audiences near and far for their forbearance, their questions, and their suggestions. I appreciate the insights and support of Sugata Bose and Andrea Graziosi, each of whom co-organized with me a workshop on related topics. Many thanks also to Johanna Bockman, David Gilmartin, Manu Goswami, Andreas Hilger, Alessandro Iandolo, Sunil Khilnani, John Krige, Fred Logevall, Joanne Meyerowitz, Chris Miller, Tim Nunan, Jahnavi Phalkey, Jayita Sarkar, Bruce Schulman, Ben Siegel, Hari Vasudevan, Arne Westad, and Jeremiah Wishon. Special thanks to Brooke Blower, Durba Ghosh and Malgorzata Mazurek for their timely and meaningful interventions, and to Frank Costigliola, Bob McMahon, and Andy Rotter for their many years of support.

That this bulky manuscript became a slightly less bulky book owes much to a handful of brave souls who read far longer versions. A manuscript conference in fall 2016 brought together Sunil Amrith, Mark Bradley, Sarah Phillips, and Ethan Pollock for an immensely productive day that improved the manuscript dramatically. My father Stanley Engerman set aside his own work, and his usual pile of other scholars' manuscripts, to read my manuscript in the late stages. Nick Cullather took advantage of a brief lull in his important work for *Diplomatic History* to do the same. Heather Hughes, Sharmila Sen, and their colleagues at Harvard University Press and Westchester Publishing Services took on the challenge of helping this manuscript become a book. Thanks to my agent Sydelle Kramer for making the connection, to graphic designer Isabelle Lewis for the map and charts, and to Nick Kroeger for the index.

Friends and colleagues have provided advice and support over decades. Ethan Pollock's participation in the manuscript conference only formalized the kind of support and advice that he has been offering since we met up in Moscow in 1993—if not since we traded baseball cards in the 1970s. Paul Sabin read multiple drafts of talks, essays, and introductions, and has been a supportive friend for many years; I'm excited about the prospect of sharing more of our professional lives in the future.

Beyond all of these financial and professional debts, my family has faced a special burden, and has been a source of special joy, long before I started working on *The Price of Aid*. I'm very grateful to my parents, Judith and Stanley Engerman, for continuing to support and to teach me, as they always have. My son, Simon, a newborn when I began thinking about this project, will be nearing the big 1–0 by the time this book appears, and has put up with my absences and preoccupations over all of those years. When I started on this book, my daughter, Nina, was about four years old, and a prolific author of crayon-drawn books, almost neatly stapled; having knocked off three such books in a single morning, she wondered why my book was taking so long. I don't have an excuse but can say, to her relief and mine, that it's finally done. The price of *The Price of Aid* was especially steep for my wife, Stephanie. She dealt alternately with my distracted presence and my absence but remained enthusiastic about the adventure even when I did not. She has supported this book, and me, in big ways and small, since we were married and even before. I look forward to paying down these debts, and to writing future chapters of our life together. I dedicate this book to her.

Index